SOCIAL NETWORKS

A Developing Paradigm

ACADEMIC PRESS
RAPID MANUSCRIPT REPRODUCTION

SOCIAL NETWORKS

A Developing Paradigm

EDITED BY

Samuel Leinhardt

School of Urban and Public Affairs
Carnegie-Mellon University
Pittsburgh, Pennsylvania

1977
ACADEMIC PRESS, INC.   New York   San Francisco   London
A Subsidiary of Harcourt Brace Jovanovich, Publishers

ACADEMIC PRESS, INC.
111 Fifth Avenue, New York, New York 10003

United Kingdom Edition published by
ACADEMIC PRESS, INC. (LONDON) LTD.
24/28 Oval Road, London NW1

ISBN 0-12-442450-3

PRINTED IN THE UNITED STATES OF AMERICA

For Gaea and Zoe and our triad

CONTENTS

Contents

PART III: ROLES AND TRANSACTIONS

PART IV: METHODS

PREFACE

My objective in editing this book was to draw together readings from a variety of social science areas that share the basic premise that structure in social relationships can be fruitfully operationalized in terms of networks. I have attempted to bring together classic works that opened new research areas and works that contain important statements of perspective, method, or empirical findings. Several people provided advice and support during the book's preparation and this is gratefully acknowledged. James A. Davis convinced me of the utility of network ideas in social theory and guided me to many of the readings contained in this book. Others whose aid was material include Anthony P. M. Coxon, Mark S. Granovetter, Paul W. Holland, Edward O. Laumann, J. Clyde Mitchell, Stanley S. Wasserman, Harrison C. White, my reserach assistant Christine Visminas-Clark, and my secretary Marjorie Farinelli. A National Science Foundation grant (SOC 73-05489) to Carnegie-Mellon University has supported my own research on social networks and provided me with time to become familiar with the research literature.

In a book of this sort the number of possible selections always exceeds the number that can be accommodated. This is a particularly vexing problem in a volume of interdisciplinary readings and is aggravated here by the rapid expansion and diversification of research employing the network paradigm. One fears that important areas have been missed and that the few articles included give a hopelessly shallow impression of the areas they represent. Suggestions from others made the task of sifting the relevant literature easier. But the final difficult decisions regarding inclusion or exclusion were mine. So, too, are the selection bias, oversights and errors of omission.

SOCIAL NETWORKS: A DEVELOPING PARADIGM

The chapters in this volume were drawn together for two reasons: (*a*) they contain important ideas about the nature and consequences of structure in social behavior and (*b*) they share a particular analytic paradigm in their approach to studying social structure. The ideas they contain are diverse, the diversity deriving in part simply from the wide variety of disciplines represented, and in part from the continued lack of agreement about the definition of social structure. But while the substantive issues addressed in each of the chapters vary, there is a dominant paradigm that guides the selection of the social behavior data that are studied, influences the way these data are organized for analysis, and specifies the kinds of questions addressed. This paradigm, the **social network paradigm**, operationalizes the notion of social structure by representing it in terms of a system of social relations tieing distinct social entities to one another. Within this framework the issue of structure in social relations becomes one of pattern or systematic organization. It also involves the corollary issues of the interdependence of the patterns formed by different relations, the implications the patterns have for the behavior of the individual entities, and the impact that the qualities of the entities have on the patterns.

The data required for network studies are relational; they are data on what relations obtain between pairs of entities. The entities may be people, or organizations or any other defined social entity. The relations may be any kind of socially meaningful tie. What is of interest to the social scientist is how the relations are arranged, how the behavior of individuals depends on their location in this arrangement, and how the qualities of the individuals influence the arrangement.

In most of the chapters of this book, relational data are conceptualized as the realization of a social network, a theoretical construct that is never actually observed. The data are then viewed as a set of points that represent the entities in the networks, and a set of directed arrows that represent ties between points. The arrows may have additional discriminators associated with them (such as type or weight). This representation has great intuitive appeal and has often been applied with a purely metaphorical intention. Recently, however, network concepts have been applied with an increasing precision and analytical purpose, and consequently the scientific utility of the paradigm has been substantially enlarged. To an important degree the growth in social network research is a function of the improved mathematical and methodological training of social scientists. Although simple analogies between networks and social behavior are often illuminating and helpful, it is not possible to build effective explanatory theories using metaphors. The existence of systematic patterning in networks of relations is usually not obvious, and the difficulties encountered in attempting to verify theoretical propositions about social networks inevitably lead to the use of advanced analytical methods.

To some degree the apparent heavy involvement of mathematics in network research is due to the way network data can be arranged. The traditional data structure is due to Jacob L. Moreno (1934). Moreno, a psychologist, first used the network framework in his "sociometric test," a technique he invented for gathering and organizing relational data on the interpersonal attitudes of individuals in small, informal groups. The technique involves asking people in a group which of their fellows they prefer, Moreno recorded the responses as arrows linking dots. This graphical device, the "sociogram," was eventually superseded by a matrix representation, the "sociomatrix." The latter has much greater potential for manipulation and analysis, although it lacks the sociogram's visual impact. The sociometric representation of relational data remains a primary recording form. Regardless of whether the entities are people, nations, organizations, or any other defined social entity, the convention of rows of individuals sending relations to columns of individuals is the hallmark of sociometric data and has become commonplace. Indeed, sociometric data structures are so useful in structural studies that the term **sociometric analysis** has become nearly synonomous with **structural analysis**. Moreno also gave names to various features of sociometric data that have become jargon. "Stars," for example, were what he called highly chosen individuals, and "isolates" were those rarely chosen. The data representation that Moreno introduced has contributed to the popularity of network concepts because it provided a concrete and appealing image of a social system and created a data structure that was amenable to visual as well as quantitative analysis.

But the analytic paradigm of social network research is more than a device for recording and organizing data. By focusing attention on the ties between individuals, rather than on the qualities possessed by the individuals, it forces social scientists to think about constraints on individual behavior, constraints that are inherent in the way social relations are organized. In so doing it leads us to ask whether there exist any fundamental structural rules: principles that govern and facilitate social interaction.

We engage in theory construction when we posit structural rules. The ease with which social networks can be represented mathematically has the potential of improving the precision and specificity of theories of social structure. Obviously, this does not mean that theories about social structure that are based on the network paradigm are necessarily true. What it means is that when network concepts are employed, the precision of mathematical ideas and the power of mathematical operations can often be used to help us think more clearly and more exactly about structure in social relations. Social structure appears to be complex, and, as a result, the mathematics of social networks (and the kinds of data analysis they lead to) may also be complex—particularly when compared with the level of mathematics traditionally employed in the disciplines where social network ideas currently flourish. One should distinguish between the mathematical nature of social network theory and the mathematics involved in determining wether empirical data behave as theory predicts. Data on social networks are extremely complex and sophisticated statistical and data analytic procedures will be essential in the development of empirically verified social network theory.

The chapters in this collection provide a wide sampling of how social network ideas have been used in the past. I have tried to bring together important efforts that fit into research traditions that are still very much alive. Each chapter originally made an innovative contribution to one of these traditions. The level of mathematical sophistication they contain varies from rudimentary to advanced. While those chapters containing highly technical material can be skipped without too much loss, the reader should be aware that the future of social network research almost certainly will involve an increasing use of mathematics.

This introductory chapter is not meant to review the field of network research. Rather, it is designed to provide the reader with a general impression of the concerns addressed in the chapters. In what follows I have attempted to review the contents of each chapter, to point out how each relates to the other, and to direct attention to other relevant literature. The introduction concludes with a discussion of the volume's organization.

Part I

The chapters in this volume contain studies of the nature and impact of social structure on behavior. Part I focuses on the cognitive organization of social relations and the effects of local social structure on individuals. It begins with a classic work by the psychologist Fritz Heider. In this chapter Heider introduces the concept of "cognitive balance," an organizing principle that, he argues, influences an individual's perception of social relations. Heider's theory consists of a set of arrangements of sentiments, and the statement that some of these are stable and some are not. If sentiment is limited to having one of two values, either positive or negative, then the set Heider considers contains all possible arrangements involving three entities. Heider uses these configurations to model and simplify a relatively complex situation. The situation involves a perceiver p, the perceiver's felt sentiment toward another person o, the perceiver's feeling regarding the sentiment existing between o and a third object or individual x. Some arrangements of the p-o-x situation are advanced by Heider as inherently un-

stable or out of balance and, because of this, give rise to tension in the perceiver's mind. The other configurations are balanced, i.e., they are not tension producing and are stable over time.

Heider's use of extremely simple models allows him to be exclusively
concerned with a relatively distinct situation. Of course, this simplification
means that Heider cannot examine the many subtleties of social perception.
Instead, he is able to concentrate on simple patterns free of complications
and distraction. The trade-off is clear and the outcome is worth the cost. He
is able to identify a set of configurations that he believes are likely to occur,
and another set that he believes are rare. If these hypotheses are true,
then even when subtleties and complicating features are brought back into
the picture, they should not violate the elementary principle of balance.

It is tempting to think that the idea for balance derives from Heider's
training as a Gestalt psychologist, since the concepts of organization and
totality are fundamental to this approach. But this would be incorrect. At a
recent symposium on social network research (Holland and Leinhardt, forthcoming), Heider revealed that his ideas were due to his study of Spinoza.
Heider indicated that Spinoza had described many of the situations Heider
labeled "balanced" and "imbalanced" and, in fact, did all but name the
principle "balance theory."

Cartwright and Harary carry Heider's idea one step further. They start
with Heider's balance model, but relax his focus on a single perceiver p.
They then ask the following question: What pattern would the interpersonal
relations of a group of individuals have if they were balanced? This requires
them to extend the notion of a cognitively balanced situation so that it can
be applied to extant interpersonal relations. Their procedure is to take
Heider's classification of cognitive situations and examine them to find a
summary mathematical rule that they all obey. Such a rule would permit the
straightforward examination of social relations between any number of individuals. To facilitate their investigation, they view the group and the
relations among the group's members as a graph, a set of nodes with connecting edges. Using graph theory, they obtain several versions of a rule that
permits them to specify what conditions hold when a group's relational
graph is balanced.

The mathematical rules have behavioral implications. This, in fact, is
one of the most important benefits of their approach—it brings to light
nonobvious features that result when a group's interpersonal relations
possess a certain simple organization. Their "structure theorem" indicates
that when social relations are balanced, according to their definition of
balance, a group can be characterized as either a single homogeneous clique
or two opposing cliques. The empirical implication is this: If interpersonal
preferences or affective relations are categorized as either positive or
negative, one should be able to take a sociogram and put all the individuals
who like one another into one subgroup and place all those who dislike these

individuals into another subgroup. In other words, if Cartwright and Horary's interpretation of balance theory is correct and balance theory is an important structural rule, then the mathematics of graph theory lead us to expect groups to dichotomize into two distinct and opposed factions. Unfortunately, the enormous experience that social scientists have had with sociometric data simply does not confirm this implication.

Theirs was a compelling theoretical result but it simply was not in accord with reality. Davis, in his first of two chapters, draws our attention to this fact. Extant sociometric data demonstrate that individuals in groups do not divide up into two factions. Instead, they seem to arrange themselves into numerous subgroups. After making this observation, Davis gives graph theoretic conditions that summarize the way individuals in groups can be organized into multiple factions—two, three, or any number. "Structural balance," the name with which Cartwright and Harary distinguish their idea from Heider's, becomes in Davis' elaboration a special case of a more general clustering process, one in which the number of factions or clusters happens to equal two. Davis' conditions for clustering seem far removed from Heider's balance theory. However, if we examine the *p-o-x* configuration in which only negative relations occur, we see that it plays a crucial role in distinguishing between balance in Cartwright and Harary's sense and Davis' notion of clustering. If we accept this configuration as balanced, and Heider is ambivalent on this point, then clustering and structural balance become very closely related.

French, whose chapter on power follows Davis' chapter, does not emphasize his intellectual ties to balance theory either, but the connections are there. For French, power in informal groups is manifested in interpersonal influence, which derives from interpersonal affect. French uses the same approach to modeling social relations as Davis and Cartwright and Harary. But he reverses the direction of the affective edges in the graph. If one individual liked another, French reasons, then the liked individual had attractive power over the one doing the liking. In other words, if I like you, then you have power over me because you have control over the source of my attraction. The more asymmetric the relationship of liking between us, the greater your power. French also assumes that the strength of influence varies with this power. If affect can be modeled as a graph theoretic edge, power can be thought of as an edge pointed in the opposite direction. French then raises the question of how group unanimity is achieved when a difference of opinion exits. Thus, he takes the affective network of a group, reverses it to get the influence network, and examines it to determine how the patterns of these interpersonal relations ultimately affect the opinions of the group members.

One of the graph theoretic structures that French discusses is called a "transitive tournament." This structure is a convenient model for a social hierarchy. In French's case, it is used as a model of a group's influence hierarchy. Transitivity is a fundamental mathematical property. It is an ordering property that can be readily observed in many physical aspects of nature. Heights, for example, are orderable; and are transitive. But do social relations obey such properties, such mathematical rules? In this volume, the historical precedent for raising this question goes to Heider. He originally hypothesized that the perception of interpersonal sentiments between a liked individual and another individual would be balanced and not tension producing if the set of relations among the three entities, the perceiver and two other individuals, obeyed the rule of transitivity. Transitivity is, in fact, what Heider calls balance. In this vein, French's contribution rests in his observation that a natural hierarchy of power will also be transitive.

In their chapter, Holland and Leinhardt show that Heider was simply the first of many behavioral scientists to single out transitivity as an important structural feature of affective relations. Using elementary mathematics they show that many of the models that have been advanced to explain the organization of interpersonal relations in small, informal groups assume that these relations are transitive. That includes the balance notion of Heider and the structural models of Cartwright and Harary, Davis, and French. When relations are symmetric, transitivity yields equivalence classes, cliques. When they are asymmetric, transitivity yields a partial ordering, a hierarchy. Consequently, one might consider transitivity to be a first principle and general model of the local structure of social affect. Different models can be obtained by first assuming that a social relation is transitive and then proposing that it also obeys additional constraints. In other words, it appears that, while they do not explicitly state it, many social scientists assume that interpersonal relations, at least those that are similar to or dependent upon positive affect, obey the mathematical rule of transitivity. Thus, the essential question of whether or not social relations are structured at the local or micro level, the level of individuals, becomes, in essence, the question of whether or not social relations exhibit transitivity.

Although transitivity is a simple mathematical idea, its role in social behavior is not trivial. At the first level of social structure, which is the first stage upon which more macro organization is built, the existence or nonexistence of order is subtle. By using graph theoretic ideas, and simplifying the issue of social structure so that it becomes a question concerning the rules governing patterns in social networks, it becomes possible to explore the issue with a new level of precision. Using techniques like those described in their second chapter, Holland and Leinhardt (1975b) have shown that the hypothesis of the transitivity of interpersonal affect can be confirmed empirically although it is better described as a tendency.

With the chapter by Lorraine and White we move away from a strict focus on interpersonal sentiment toward a more general viewpoint. Simultaneously, we move away from an emphasis on describing features of social networks in the concrete and readily appreciated terms of graph theory. Instead, Lorraine and White discuss social networks in terms of systems of binary relations. A binary relation and a graph of the relation are interchangeable, but by using the algebraic theory of categories instead of graph theory Lorraine and White are able to examine systems of multiple relations with increased ease. This is the essence of their approach to social structure. They view social structure as a network of roles with role relations defined as sets of reciprocal expectations. These are identified with the edges or arrows of a graph. By distinguishing between individuals and their roles, Lorraine and White create a model of society as a relatively lasting network of role relations with individuals occupying multiple roles, while tied to other individuals in ways defined by the relations that are inherent in their roles. According to this approach, individuals may change but the nature of the role does not. Thus, roles impose constraints on the behavior of individual actors, and the structural question becomes one of determining how patterns of role relations fit together in a society. Lorraine and White argue that an important feature of their approach to social networks is that new roles, new compounded relations, are produced through the concatenation of existing relations, and that the rules of concatenation can be determined by examining the structure of the network. Thus, balance theory is for them nothing more than a special case of one role, the role of friend, yielding a new relation, a new friendship, through the transitive rule inherent in the binary relation of friendship. This process is called "functorial reduction," and the relation, positive friendship, is called the "generator." They suggest that the dynamics of group structure can then be interpreted in terms of the concatenation of role relational ties over time.

It is important to understand that for Lorraine and White social network data need not be simply affective sociometric data drawn from small, informal groups. Friendship may be the empirical realization of one aspect of a role, but a role has multiple generators, and each generator is paired with a converse generator. This, in a sense, is similar to the reversal of affect that French employs in developing an influence network, but French separates affect from influence in order to study how unanimity of opinions is reached in groups. Lorraine and White have a different objective. They pursue the nature of equivalencing. They argue that each generator fosters a set of expectations in each individual regarding the behavior of others. When two individuals have mutually similar expectations, then, structurally, they are equivalent. In the global social structure these two individuals become indistinguishable.

Since theoreticians propose that social relations obey mathematical properties, and evidence is growing in support of these hypotheses, the question of how people behave in situations that conflict with these rules arises. Heider argues that perceptual arrangements violating the rules are unstable. Much experimental research has demonstrated that people do expect affective situations to be balanced. DeSoto approaches this problem from a slightly different direction. He asks how people respond to social situations that obey the mathematical rules of structure, and how they respond to those that do not. The response he examines is learning. He invented several hypothetical situations involving social relations that exhibit eight mathematical properties. Using paired associates learning experiments in 19 experimental arrangements, he asks which arrangements are easiest to learn. DeSoto's study indicates that people learn most readily, i.e., they make fewest errors in remembering, those social situations where the relations obey the mathematical properties social scientists ascribe to them. For example, DeSoto finds (as French asserted) that a situation containing influence relations is expected to be asymmetric and transitive, the properties of a transitive tournament. The evidence that DeSoto provides is that people expect social relations to obey certain structural rules, and if they do not, people are likely to assume that they do.

Part II

In Part II the authors consider networks of ties in large social agglomerations, and treat a variety of different types of social relationships. The emphasis here is on empirical studies. Specific extant social networks are investigated to test a variety of structural hypotheses.

In the chapter by Coleman, Katz, and Menzel, the level of analysis is the individual but the context is an entire community. The network studied consists of the ties that connect a town's physicians. The question the authors raise is: How do ideas or attitudes spread through a population? More specifically, in their particular research setting, they address the question of how the structural characteristics of the network of physicians influence the rate at which the physicians adopt a new drug. This is a study of "contagion," a process that sweeps across a population and alters the character of some or all of its members. In this case the contagion process is the diffusion of the behavior: use of a drug. Once a physician engages in the action of prescribing a new drug the physician's character becomes permanently altered. The physician becomes an adopter. Just like an epidemic of disease, the adoptive behavior spreads from one physician to the next. As in an epidemic, the characteristics of certain individuals are altered early, while those of others are not altered until much later, and some individuals remain permanently unaffected.

Coleman, Katz, and Menzel wanted to determine whether any quality of a physician's position in the social network could be associated with time of adoption. With data gathered from pharmacies in a midwestern American town, they were able to determine the month in which each of the community's physicians commenced prescribing a new drug. Then, from interviews of a sample of physicians, they gathered sociometric and personality data. They decided that those physicians who were named frequently by other physicians in the sociometric test, the sociometric stars, were more tightly integrated into the physician network and they hypothesized that these physicians would be early adopters. They also distinguished several kinds of networks that they felt were relevant to the diffusion process: the network of advisors; the network of discussants; and the network of friends. They found that, in this order, the different ntworks had separate effects on the rate of diffusion of the innovation among the physicians and position in each network had different implications for adoption behavior.

Using location in a network, rather than the individual personality factors as variables, Coleman, Katz, and Menzel show that sociometric status and integration, summary qualities characterizing an individual in a social network, are important. Erbe's chapter raises a similar issue but in a different context. He defines gregariousness as the range of an individual's social contacts and integration as the range of an individual's membership in informal groups. Then he seeks to determine if these two qualities of network position affect the probability that an individual will be informed on public issues. Thus, Erbe is assuming the validity of earlier research findings, such as those of Coleman, Katz, and Menzel, that the structure of social relationships is important in the diffusion of information, and tries to sharpen our understanding of which locational factors are most important. Using data gathered by the National Opinion Research Center on 3000 graduate students, he concludes that integration, i. e., contacts with different groups, is more important than gregariousness, i.e., contacts with different individuals.

Structural integration is also the topic of Turk's chapter, but, here again, the context shifts. The actors in this study are not individuals but organizations. Turk's objective is to use the concept of social integration to describe the extent of interorganizational activities and network complexity. He views integration in organizational terms as the density of interorganizational connections. Using data from organizations in 130 U.S. cities with 1960 populations in excess of 100,000, he performs a macrosociological study of the social organization of organizations.

Crane's chapter is another example of an empirical study of a large network in which the research issue is the diffusion of information across interpersonal contacts. She studies an invisible college, an informal social network that is thought to tie scientists into closed, exclusive groups. Those individuals involved in such networks experience the advantage of increased interaction and easy communication. This result could increase the efficiency with which information is transferred from one group member to another, and in science, one presumes, the diffusion of new information to interested parties is crucial. There are also, however, several disadvantages: Invisible colleges might be considered antiequalitarian because they are closed; they seem to create barriers to the entrance of other scientists who may not be members, but who are interested in the field; and they probably cut down on a potentially useful information flow into the group from the outside. Thus, invisible colleges may lead to a form of institutionalized science, a situation in which innovative ideas may be less rather than more likely to surface. While a highly interconnected network may increase the rate at which knowledge diffuses within the group, barriers to membership may reduce the diffusion of knowledge into and out of the group.

Crane surveyed scientists who studied the diffusion of agricultural innovations. She sent questionnaires to 172 rural sociologists who had been involved in this research area—147 cooperated by returning her questionnaire. Her findings are highly reminiscent of those of Coleman, Katz, and Menzel. What she observed was that high productivity was a feature of groups of individuals who communicated heavily (i.e., were cliques in the sense of Davis and of Cartwright and Harary) with one another and collaborated or jointly authored reports. Characteristically, highly productive individuals also had high sociometric status and they were important links in the structure; they played contact roles for others. But Crane also found that outsiders or "hangers-on" played important roles, a finding suggesting that the invisible college model with its strong closed-group assumption may not be completely valid.

A different network, one that is latent rather than invisible, is the topic of Travers and Milgram's chapter. They examine features of the acquaintance network that they argue exists within the population of every society. In this network, knowing individuals directly yields indirect links to other individuals, thus connecting any one person to numerous other people. The concept is less complicated than it sounds. Consider a hypothetical situation in which each individual has the same number of friends, e.g., five. An individual in this case would be directly linked to five other people. Also assume that an individual's frinds do not know one another. Since each friend has five direct friends, an individual can be indirectly linked to 25 other individuals in one step. To these 25 an additional 125 are added at the second remove. Within six removes an individual is in indirect contact with nearly 2000 different people; the network of indirect ties grows rapidly. Of course, in reality, many of these ties would be redundant, and the number of acquaintances that different individuals had would not be constant. It is also likely, however, that most people have more than five friends. Consequently, the number of indirect acquaintances one might have is likely to be very, very large.

The question that Travers and Milgram ask is this: What do chains of acquaintance ties look like in the U.S.? If the social networks that are composed of acquaintance ties are very interconnected and overlapping, then we should observe close linkages when people are chosen at random from the entire nation. To test this hypothesis they devised an experiment in which a collaborator living on the east coast agreed to be the target of an experimental task, which was to get a letter from the midwest to the target. They required that the letter reach its target by going from one authentic acquaintance to the next. Thus, if the task was successfully completed often, and with few intermediaries, the conceptual model of society as a highly interconnected system is rendered more believable, at least along the dimension of acquaintance. Such a conclusion might not seem very important. After all, it does not mean that everyone is acquainted with everyone else. But if we accept the implication of the diffusion research that information and interaction flow between pairs of individuals along affective ties, then we can see that extensive interconnections, even if composed of acquaintance ties, could have important consequences (see Granovetter, 1974, or Lee, 1969, for interesting examples).

What did Travers and Milgram find? They asked 296 randomly selected originators to send messages. Sixty-four messages reached the target, about 29%. An average of 5.2 individuals were involved in each success. The individuals who were one remove from the target appear to have been sociometric stars. As amazing as it may seem, the chains of acquaintance initiated by selecting people at random at one end of the country often managed to reach the target by being passed to a relatively few individuals at the other end of the country. This finding is not unlike that of Crane's concerning the role of sociometric stars as individuals who are critical in connecting up a group of scientists.

In Davis' second chapter we return to a more theoretical concern with structure in social networks. Here Davis is interested in developing a system for stating hypotheses about local structural constraints, hypotheses like those tested by the empirical studies in the other chapters. His approach is a novel one. He uses graph theoretic concepts to create a precise language for making structural propositions, and he uses this language to restate 56 structural propositions already advanced by other scientists. As he shows, many apparently different propositions amount to similar mathematical ideas, and with only a few propositions he achieves a synthesis of much research on social structure.

Part III

Part III contains studies that address issues more common among social anthropologists than sociologists or social psychologists. As a consequence the data often derive from field observations.

The opening chapter is the oldest in the volume. It was Radcliffe-Brown's 1940 presidential address to the Royal Anthropological Society. The point of view that he expresses—understanding social networks is the fundamental task of social anthropology—is now receiving increased acceptance throughout the social sciences. According to Radcliffe-Brown, social phenomena should be identified with the extant social relations joining people. He is explicit in stating that social structure is the network or pattern formed by these relations. Although the concept of social network is used here in a metaphorical sense, and is not tied to any analytical framework, Radcliffe-Brown does succeed in focusing our attention on patterns in the interactions and interpersonal relations of individuals. And he declares openly his belief that these repeated patterns have important substantive significance in themselves. This is an important point of view. For Radcliffe-Brown, the societal social structure is built up from individual pairs of interpersonal interactions, while the social structure simultaneously imposes constraints on which interactions can take place. Now the issue is to determine what forms the patterns take and the nature of the behavioral constraints.

Barnes accepts Radcliffe-Brown's point of view and seeks an understanding of social structure through the study of extant social relations. He studies the ties among members of a Norwegian community. The object of Barnes' study is an understanding of the community's class system. But sensitized to the importance of face-to-face social relations as they result from the organization of society, Barnes examines how class features express themselves at the local level, the level of friendship and acquaintance ties. Social class lines are defined by the equivalence relations expressed by individuals in the community who share symmetric pairs of relations, and who accord each other approximately equal status. Barnes introduces the concept of a "social field," a multigraph of kinship, friendship, and neighborhood ties. He observes that each community member occupies a position in this social field, carrying on activities within it, and by virtue of it, in seemingly direct coordination with all other individuals.

Barnes' research is the earliest empirical field study with an explicit network perspective. For him social status is not simply a category such as "middle income" or "lower class." Instead, it is a quality of location, a position in a complex system of relations in which interaction, behavioral options, information, etc., are a function of that location and the structural properties of the system. In this context, social stratification becomes a concrete dimension of the social structure, and class differences in behavior are not simply happenstance. Instead, they derive from the constraints imposed by structural features of the social field, the concatenation of multiple social relations, which provide individuals with expectations for their own behavior and the behavior of others.

Bott's study of 20 London families continues this use of the social network concept as a research paradigm to guide an empirical field study. Again, the roles that individuals perform are studied, but in this instance it is conjugal roles, the roles of husband and wife within the context of the family. Bott proposes to determine what factors explain variation in the segregated or joint performance of these roles. Segregated roles are those in which one spouse carries out tasks without interacting with the other. Joint performance, however, means that husband and wife share tasks, and are likely to engage in tasks traditionally assigned to the other. Bott first approached this question from the classical, social science point of view. She categorized families using variables such as income status and education, but was unable to explain satisfactorily the extent of role integration in families. Then she categorized the families in terms of a quality of their acquaintance networks. She argues that if one uses the degree of network connectiveness as an explanatory variable, then the extent of conjugal role integration can be better understood. Applied to her analysis, when husband's and wife's acquaintance networks do not overlap but each is highly connected, then conjugal roles tend to be segregated. When the acquaintance networks are not connected but are radial and overlapping, conjugal roles tend to be joint. This study and its findings have given rise to a good deal of controversy (see the second edition of Bott's book [1971] for an extended discussion of both the study and its critics). Its significance rests primarily in its pathbreaking use of structural variables in an attempt to explain commonplace social behavior.

Mayer's chapter is an effort to increase the conceptual clarity of some important network ideas and to apply them in an empirical context. He introduces the notion of a "quasi-group," a potential rather than an actual group based on the common interests of its members. This notion further sensitizes us to the existence of latent linkages between individuals. For Mayer, linkages exist between individuals because of their utility in carrying out transactions that further the interests of the parties involved. Within any specific context, an individual's transactional linkages define an "action-set,"an individual-centered network of actual and potential linkages to other individuals that are included only if they depend on contact with the focal individual. In this framework, the quasi-group represents the overlap of the action-sets of many individuals. The specific transactions that Mayer investigates are those of patronage and brokerage in the context of an election in Dewas, India.

Boyd's chapter is a departure from these empirical studies. It is an effort to use mathematics to describe the kinship structure of primitive societies that have marriage classes and to use the mathematical theory to deduce the nonobvious consequences of such classes. Marriage classes partition a society into equivalence classes, the societies associating social properties with membership in each class. The members, in turn, possess behavioral expectations attributable to their class. Boyd shows that an effective description of these systems can be achieved using simple compositional algebras. In effect, the marriage systems can be summarized in the form of a multiplication table or set of permutation rules. These rules determine the role relations between members of the society who are associated with each marriage class. Such ties are especially important in primitive societies, but the process of concatenation of roles in a marriage system is identical to the general process described by Lorraine and White. Indeed, the concept of homomorphism, which enables Boyd to trace the evolution of kinship systems, is also of fundamental importance to Lorraine and White. But for them a homomorphism is only one type of reduction of relations, i.e., only one way in which a concatenation of relations reduces to another relation. A homomorphism does have a special feature. It is a mapping from one system of relations onto another that preserves structure, a quality that makes the identification of homomorphic relations important in structural analyses. The idea of homomorphism is central to all aspects of modern algebra and, when it can be demonstrated to be isomorphic with social rules, yields a great deal of power for describing these rules in mathematical terms.

The chapters of Parts II and III contain studies of large aggregates of individuals: ties between members of organizations, among authors of a scientific community, among physicians in a town, among kin groups in a society. Nonetheless, the ties between pairs of individuals are micro-level phenomena. In several of the studies (for example, Crane's analysis of scientists, Boyd's description of kinship systems, and Barnes' study of a Norwegian community), the ultimate objective is to relate these micro-level interactions to macro-level patterns. Granovetter, in his chapter, argues that the social network paradigm is especially well suited to this task. He sees it as a bridge between micro- and macro-level social phenomena. Granovetter's idea is simply that the everyday, interpersonal networks of acquaintance, friendship, and contact provide the means by which individual behavior is routinized and agglomerates into large-scale patterns, which are the more usual concerns of social scientists. It is important to understand that Granovetter's point of view, much like Radcliffe-Brown's, is a perspective and not a theory. Radcliffe-Brown focuses our attention on a type of data structure, data on existing interactions between individuals in a society. Granovetter focuses our attention on a particular kind of interpersonal tie—latent or weak—as a way of reconciling two otherwise conceptually distinct aspects of social systems.

As an example of the utility of this perspective, Granovetter examines how variations in the strength of interpersonal acquaintance ties can be related to several large-scale social processes, including the diffusion of information, social mobility, and political organization. Granovetter defines strength in terms of density: Weak ties are those that are not redundant, i.e., they are nearly unique paths between any two people. Strong ties are those that are backed up by many others that pass through intermediaries. Thus, in a strong tie situation a dense web of ties, so to speak, binds a pair of entities together. In a weak tie situation no such dense webbing is present. Strong ties are common features of a clique, in the sense of Cartwright and Harary, or clusters, in Davis' terminology. They are also characteristic, as Holland and Leinhardt show, of the equivalence classes of transitive graphs. But these strongly tied subgroupings are not the focus of Granovetter's discussion. Instead, he examines the role of weak ties, ties that are often characterized as erroneous by other researchers, or simply not discussed. He argues that such weak ties may be extremely important bridges in the transmission of information between subgroupings that are internally highly connected. Weak ties provide shorter paths for communications, and connect pairs who are unlikely to be in the same subgrouping, thus facilitating the diffusion of information. As a concrete example he examines the dissemination of job vacancy information (for an interesting formalization of this discussion see Boorman, 1975). For Granovetter, weak ties, because they do not require much effort to maintain, form the framework with which stronger subcomponents of groups are held together to form larger aggregations.

Part IV

The chapters in Part IV, while occasionally containing applications, are primarily methodological. The empirical verification of the models and hypotheses advanced in earlier chapters usually requires the use of complex methods of data analysis. A typical social network data structure, the sociomatrix, can be easily diagramed and manipulated to verify a structural proposition if the population of individuals is small and the effect under study is strong. But the task quickly becomes intractable as the group size rises, and the effect becomes weak or other factors confound its observation. Even though an exact mathematical model may exist, its empirical verification may require the development of new statistical tools. As the data used for verification become complex and inexact, the need for sophisticated and complex methods increases.

But statistics is used in the study of social networks in another way as well. This involves the direct inclusion of stochastic elements in models of networks and network processes. If structural regularities exist and constrain human behavior, then they probably "tend" to operate rather than work in an all-or-nothing fashion, and they probably operate over time through a developmental process. Some networks, such as those of kinship ties, are likely to be less stochastic than others. Affective ties probably possess a large stochastic component, in the sense that empirical situations will exhibit a high variability in the extent to which they are structured. Several questions arise regarding this evident variability: How much of empirically observed organization in social relations is due to the influence of nonstructural variables, how much to the stage of structural development, how much to the stochastic quality of social ties, and how much to the inadequacy of our structural models? Statistical tools can help us sort out these questions by permitting us to build stochastic elements into our models directly and by facilitating the analysis of heavily confounded empirical data (see Holland

and Leinhardt, 1973, for a discussion of how easily the measurement of structure in sociometric data is confounded by the way the data are collected).

Part IV contains chapters that discuss mathematical and statistical ideas for modeling and analyzing social networks. It opens with a review chapter on graph theory by the mathematician, Frank Harary. Graph theory concepts have, as indicated earlier, been particularly prominent in social network research. Indeed, there is an immediate, intuitive acceptability in the identification of the nodes of a graph and its edges with the individuals of a collectivity and their relational ties. Graph theoretical ideas run through nearly all of the chapters in this volume, even in those that rely on algebraic concepts. Harary, who has been a central figure in the development of modern graph theory, reviews the major graph theory concepts that have been applied in the social sciences.

The methods of graph theory are deterministic, or static in time. A graph is either balanced or not; an individual node either satisfies a stated condition or it does not. The observed graph and the structure it represents are presumed to be identical. An alternative point of view is presented in Rapoport's chapter on one kind of stochastic network, random nets. These are theoretical structures in which the probability that a directed linkage exists between an entity and any other is determined by some random allocation process operating at the level of the nodes. In other words, each node has a set number of linkages, and these tie the node to other nodes in a random fashion. To make the model useful for studying social behavior Rapoport adds various biases to the net. For example, his "distance bias" reduces the probability of a connection between nodes as the distance between them increases, a reasonable assumption for acquaintance or affect. His "reciprocity bias" increases the probability of a return linkage if an asymmetric linkage exists between them, a way of incorporating the finding that friendship tends to be mutual. "Sibling bias," in Rapoport's terminology, increases the likelihood of linkages between nodes if both nodes have been linked to a common third. By adding biases, Rapoport is able to introduce modifications to the basic random model, modifications that are in accord with hypothesized structural properties of social relations (which he calls "axons"). By assuming a biased net as a baseline model, Rapoport can compare the actual features of an empirical social network with the features of a theoretical biased net. The biases act so as to alter the features of the theoretical baseline process. Various features of groups, such as their connectivity and clique structure, have been studied using this approach. Unfortunately, the mathematics are formidable, and exact distributions for the most interesting features of biased nets have not been determined. (See Holland and Leinhardt, 1977, for a related approach to structural dynamics.)

In their chapter on statistical methods, Holland and Leinhardt present an approach for constructing probability models on graphs. They follow a procedure common to inferential statistics and construct the exact theoretical probability distribution for a highly conditioned random graph. This statistical conditioning acts as a control on features of the graph that influence its structure. They then determine the first and second moments, the expectation, and the variance of various subgraphs in order to calculate a standardized test statistic. Their approach focuses on specifying subgraphs that can be associated with substantively interesting structural propositions. Since many models of small-scale social structure hinge on transitivity, they examine the first level at which the transitive condition can hold, the level of triples of nodes. It can be shown mathematically that if all the triads of a graph (subgraphs on three nodes) are transitive, the graph will be transitive (see Flament, 1963). In a binary digraph, a directed graph with edges either present or absent, there are only 16 different kinds of triads, and seven of these contain at least one intransitive triple. In a transitive graph, no intransitive triads should occur. To determine whether or not the affective networks of real groups are transitive, Holland and Leinhardt set up an hypothesis testing apparatus that contrasts the actual occurrence of intransitive triads with those expected under a theoretical random distribution. In other words, they ask whether the number of intransitive triads observed empirically are so few that a random model should be rejected as the generating process. This is the classical null hypothesis test procedure of inferential statistics. The null hypothesis is: The triads are generated by a sufficiently conditional random process and are not a consequence of social structure. The procedure increases in strength as the random model used for comparison brings into consideration more features of the graph. In this way, a strictly limited set of random graphs is contrasted with the observed graph. The set includes graphs that possess many of the same features of the observed graph. Size, various nodal properties, and the number and kinds of pairs of relations are all features to be controlled. The particular random model constructed by Holland and Leinhardt conditions on the group size and the number of types of dyads, but not on other nodal properties (see Holland and Leinhardt, 1975a, 1975b, 1977, and Wasserman, 1977, for extensions of this method, and Davis and Leinhardt, 1970, for an earlier version).

While Holland and Leinhardt develop methods for testing structure at the lowest (sociologically relevant) level, Levine attempts to develop techniques for exploring it at much higher levels. Levine is interested in examining the network of interlocks among directors of large corporations. These organizations have boards of directors, and each director can be a member of other boards. Because the corporations considered (industrial organizations and banks) control a major portion of the nation's production, understanding their social ties may yield insight into the flow of information and influence between them. But data on interlocks are peculiar. Most directors are members of only one or a few corporations, and most boards have few members. The data matrix of these ties is quite large and very sparse or nearly empty. To organize and clarify these data, Levine uses a variant of nonmetric multidimensional scaling, a common clustering technique. Distance between two corporations is defined in terms of the number of links they have in common. The greater the number of links the closer the corporations. This analysis leads Levine to construct a conceptual influence map. It is a spherical arrangement in which corporations that are linked in similar ways to a particular bank are placed in one sector. The bank is the focus of the sector, and the stronger the link between bank and industrial corporation (as determined by number of links), the shorter the radii between the industrial corporation and the bank.

In the chapter by Laumann and Pappi traditional sociometric tests and scaling techniques are combined. They develop a procedure for identifying subsets of high-status, elite individuals who have common interests so that they can study how conflict or cleavage patterns are superimposed on the elite structure of a community. Their method has three stages. First, the elite are identified by taking an opinion survey of a sample of the community's population. Then the elite are given a sociometric questionnaire. Finally, these sociometric data are analyzed by subjecting them to a variant of smallest space analysis. In the empirical study reported, three primary dimensions of the clusterings are chosen on the basis of public issues and individual backgrounds. The method is an elaborate clique-finding device that turns sociometric graph information on pairs into rank order distances to permit the application of a clustering algorithm.

Conclusion

The selections in this volume present a diverse and rich set of examples of an important paradigm in the social sciences: the use of network concepts to make concrete the notion of structure or pattern in social relations. This operationalization guides research efforts toward a specification of structural regularities and an examination of the consequences of structure. What are these consequences? If social structure exists, and even the face-to-face, everyday interactions of people fit into demonstrable patterns, then social structure entails external constraints on human behavior, constraints that limit behavioral options. Not all forms of social interaction occur. Not all possible combinations of relationships are observed. Structural rules influence social behavior making some patterns likely, while others become less likely. Identifying these rules and demonstrating their influence on social behavior is the primary objective of most social network research.

The chapters cover a period from 1940 to 1973, a period of rapid growth in the technical sophistication of the social sciences and in the devlopment of the social network paradigm. Research and theoretical efforts build on one another. These studies often exhibit clear ties to one another

and there is a natural continuity of ideas. This is particularly apparent in the studies that treat micro-level features of social networks, but it can also be observed in the macro-level studies, and in the attempts to bridge the two. The important point, of course, is that the two approaches are bridgeable, and that social network concepts seem to provide an illuminating way of accomplishing the bridging task.

Here, we study social behavior by studying social networks. We concentrate on linkages between people and collectivities in attempts to determine whether their organization has properties that can be summarized by a few fundamental rules. And we use structural features as variables to assess their impact on other aspects of behavior. In a symposium on social structure sponsored by the American Sociological Association, William Goode rendered the following advice on what to study when studying social structure: "Pay attention to the network," he said, "the geometry of its arrangement, and not to the characteristics of things that net describes" (in Blau 1975, p. 74). The chapters that follow do this, they focus on features of social networks that transcend individual empirical realizations, and in so doing they contribute to our ability to understand social behavior.

How to Use This Book

The chapters cannot be easily categorized. Nonetheless, an attempt was made to group them according to the nature of the social relations examined, the size of the network treated, and the research or disciplinary tradition into which they fell. The major deviation from this rule occurs in Part IV, which contains chapters that are more purposefully throught of as descriptions of methods or tools for model building and analysis. Mathematical notions are used in some degree in nearly all of the chapters. A number of chapters presume a more than average familiarity with graph theory or algebra. A reader who is not adept in these topics would do well to skip the chapters noted as mathematically advanced in Table 1. The chapters that report empirical studies often make use of elementary data analysis procedures. These should cause no difficulty. However, some presume familiarity with uncommon techniques. A reader who is not familiar with such material might skip the chapters noted as statistically advanced in the table.

The partitions happen to arrange the substantive chapters into groups relatively homogeneous in terms of discipline. Part I contains studies by social psychologists and sociologists interested in small-scale social systems. Part II contains chapters by sociologists interested in large-scale social systems. Part III contains material traditionally the province of social anthropologists. Sampling from each part will provide a survey of the field,

TABLE 1. **Chapters Classified by Technical Sophistication**

Part	Chapter	Minimal technical sophistication	Statistically advanced	Mathematically advanced
Intro	1			
I	2	×		
	3	×		
	4			×
	5			×
	6			×
	7			×
	8	×		
II	9	×		
	10	×		
	11	×		
	12	×		
	13	×		
	14	×		
III	15	×		
	16	×		
	17	×		
	18	×		
	19			×
	20	×		
IV	21	×		
	22		×	
	23		×	
	24		×	
	25		×	

while concentrating on any one part will yield a more discipline-oriented view.

The material chosen for inclusion in this collection portrays the development of a paradigm that has become an important guide for contemporary social research. Social networks are now a common topic. A reader interested in pursuing this area should follow up the references cited at the end of this introductory chapter. A number of academic journals have begun to publish articles in this area, with several important reports appearing in the 1976 volumes of the *AMERICAN JOURNAL OF SOCIOLOGY*, the *AMERICAN SOCIOLOGICAL REVIEW*, and *THE JOURNAL OF MATHEMATICAL SOCIOLOGY*. The entire issue of the *JOURNAL OF MATHEMATICAL SOCIOLOGY*, Volume V, Number 1, is devoted to research on social networks. Two books, one edited by Mitchell (1969), and the other by Boissevain and Mitchell (1973), contain material representative of recent efforts by British anthropologists and sociologists. A number of monographs including Lee (1969), Granovetter (1974), Kapferer (1972), Boissevain (1974), and Laumann (1972) are worth examining. In September, 1975, the Mathematical Social Science Board sponsored a symposium on social networks at Dartmouth College. This symposium brought together many of the scientists represented in this collection and others who have made important contributions to this research area. The symposium's objectives were to summarize the state of the art in social network theory and research, and to specify outstanding topics for future research. The papers presented at the symposium have been edited and will be published as a single volume (Holland and Leinhardt, forthcoming). This symposium volume will contain an extremely useful review of contemporary research on social networks.

References

Blau, M., Ed.
   1975 *Approaches to the Study of Social Structure*. New York: Free Press.
Boissevan, J.
   1974 *Friends of Friends*. New York: St. Martin's Press.
Boissevan, J. and J.C. Mitchell
   1973 *Network Analysis Studies in Human Interaction*. The Hague: Morton.
Boorman, S.A.
   1975 "A combinatorial optimization model for transmission of job information through contact network." *Bell Journal of Economics* 6 (Spring): 216-49.
Bottt, E.
   1971 *Family and Social Networks*, 2nd ed. London: Tavistock Publications.
Davis, J.A. and S. Leinhardt
   1970 "The Structure of positive interpersonal relations in small groups." J. Berger (ed.), *Sociological Theories in Progress*, Vol. 2. Boston: Houghton Mifflin Company.
Flament, C.
   1963 *Applications of Graph Theory to Group Structure*. Englewood Cliffs, N.J.: Prentice-Hall, Inc.
Granovetter, M.
   1974 *Getting a Job*. Cambridge, Mass.: Harvard University Press.
Holland, P. W. and S. Leinhardt
   Forthcoming *Social Networks: Surveys and Advances*. New York: Academic Press.
Holland, P. W. and S. Leinhardt
   1977 "A dynamic model for social networks." *Journal of Mathematical Sociology* V, No. 1.
Holland, P.W. and S. Leinhardt
   1975a "Local structure in social networks." D.R. Heise (ed.), *Sociological Methodology, 1976*. San Francisco: Jossey-Bass.
Holland, P.W. and S. Leinhardt
   1975b "Structural sociometry." Paper presented at the Advanced Research Symposium on Social Networks, Mathematical Social Science Board, Hanover, New Hampshire (September).
Kapferer, B.
   1972 *Strategy and Transaction in an African Factory*. Manchester: Manchester University Press.

Laumann, E.O.
   1972 *Bonds of Pluralism: The Form and Structure of Urban Social Networks.* New York: Wiley Interscience.
Lee, N.H.
   1969 *The Search for an Abortionist.* Chicago: University of Chicago Press.
Mitchell, J.C.
   1969 *Social Networks in Urban Situations.* Manchester: Manchester University Press.
Moreno, J.L.
   1934 *Who Shall Survive? Nervous and Mental Disease.* Washington, D.C.: Publishing Co.
Wasserman, S. S.
   1977 "Random directed graph distributions and the triad census in social networks." *Journal of Mathematical Sociology* V, No. 1.

Part I: Sentiments and Attitudes

ATTITUDES AND COGNITIVE ORGANIZATION*

Department of Psychology, Smith College

FRITZ HEIDER

Attitudes towards persons and causal unit formations influence each other. An attitude towards an event can alter the attitude towards the person who caused the event, and, if the attitudes towards a person and an event are similar, the event is easily ascribed to the person. A balanced configuration exists if the attitudes towards the parts of a causal unit are similar (1).

It is tempting to generalize from this statement and to omit the restriction to causal unit formation. Do units in general interact with attitudes in a similar way?

In trying out this hypothesis we shall understand by attitude the positive or negative relationship of a person p to another person o, or to an impersonal entity x which may be a situation, an event, an idea, or a thing, etc. Examples are: to like, to love, to esteem, to value, and their opposites. A positive relation of this kind will be written L, a negative one $\sim L$. Thus, pLo means p likes, loves, or values o, or, expressed differently, o is positive for p.

The relation "unit" will be written U. Examples are: similarity, proximity, causality, membership, possession, or belonging. pUx can mean, for instance, p owns x, or p made x; $p \sim Ux$ means p does not own x, etc. Other relations which, in many ways, seem to function like units are: p is familiar with, used to, or knows well o or x, and p is in situation x. In lumping together all these relations we are, of course, aware of the dissimilarities between them. Only in a first approximation can they be treated as belonging to one class.

The hypothesis may be stated in greater detail thus: (a) A balanced state exists if an entity has the same dynamic character in all possible respects (e.g., if p admires and at the same time likes o); in other words, if pLo or $p \sim Lo$ is true for all meanings of L. (We may anticipate here that the analogous statement for pUo does not seem to hold in a general way.) (b) A balanced state exists if all parts of a unit have the same dynamic character (i.e., if all are positive, or all are negative), and if entities with different dynamic character are segregated from each other. If no balanced

*Received in the Editorial Office on October 1, 1945, and published immediately at Provincetown, Massachusetts. Copyright by The Journal Press.

3

state exists, then forces towards this state will arise. Either the dynamic characters will change, or the unit relations will be changed through action or through cognitive reorganization. If a change is not possible, the state of imbalance will produce tension.

The first part of the hypothesis refers to influence of dynamic relations or attitudes on each other. Since the different dynamic relations are not included in each other logically ("p likes o" does not imply "p admires o"), the same o or x can be positive in one respect and negative in another. An example in point is the conflict between duty and inclination. A tendency exists to make the different dynamic relations agree with each other by means of cognitive restructuring (excuses or rationalizations). Another example would be the tendency to admire loved persons and to love admired persons.

More numerous are the possibilities to which the second part of the hypothesis refers. They can be grouped according to the entities making up the configurations: (a) person and non-person (p, x); (b) two persons (p, o); (c) two persons and a non-person (p, o, x); (d) three persons (p, o, q). Many of the examples seem to substantiate the hypothesis. Examples which do not fit may eventually lead to greater insight into the nature of the dynamic characters and of the unit relations. All examples refer to p's life space. This is true even of oLp which therefore means: p thinks that o likes or admires p.

(a) p and x. Since the own person (p) is usually positive, a balanced state will exist if p likes what he is united with in any way, or if he dislikes the x he is segregated from. The cases $(pLx) + (pUx)$ and $(p \sim Lx) + (p \sim Ux)$ are balanced. Examples: p likes the things he made; p wants to own the things he likes; p values what he is accustomed to.

(b) p and o. Analogously, the two balanced states for p and o will be: $(pLo) + (pUo)$ and $(p \sim Lo) + (p \sim Uo)$. Examples: p likes his children, people similar to him; p is uneasy if he has to live with people he does not like; p tends to imitate admired persons; p likes to think that loved persons are similar to him.

pUo is a symmetrical relation, i.e., pUo implies oUp. That they belong to a unit is true for p and o in the same way, though their rôles in the unit may be different (for instance, if U is a causal unit). However, pLo is non-symmetrical since it does not imply oLp. It is in line with the general hypothesis to assume that a balanced state exists if pLo and oLp (or $p \sim Lo$ and $o \sim Lp$) are true at the same time. Attraction or repulsion between p and o are then two-way affairs; the relation is in symmetrical·harmony. pLo is a non-symmetrical relation logically, but psychologically it

4

tends to become symmetrical. Examples: p wants to be loved by an admired o; p dislikes people who despise him. oLp is similar to pLo in its relation to pUo. Examples: p likes to meet people who, he is told, admire him.

(c) p, o, and x. The combinations become more numerous with three entities making up the configurations. Only a few possibilities can be mentioned. We shall always give the balanced state in symbols before stating the examples which refer to it.

$(pLo) + (pLx) + (oUx)$. Both o and x are positive and parts of a unit. Examples: p admires clothes of loved o; p wants to benefit his friend o; p likes to think that his friend benefits him. A seeming exception is the case of envy. If o owns x (oUx) and p likes x (pLx), $p \sim Lo$ may often follow. This exception can be derived from the fact that ownership is a one-many relation. A person can own many things but each thing can, ordinarily, be owned only by one person. Therefore "o owns x" excludes "p owns x," or oUx implies $p \sim Ux$. Since pLx may tend toward pUx, conflict is introduced.

Implications between unit relations often lead to conflict. Lewin's three cases of inner conflict rest on implications. Approach to a positive valence may imply withdrawal from another positive valence. Withdrawal from a negative valence may imply approach to another negative valence. Finally, approach to a positive valence may imply approach to a negative valence if both are located in the same region. Analogously, one can talk of three cases of outer conflict between persons. pUx may imply $o \sim Ux$ (for instance, if U means ownership), and if both want x, conflict (competition) will arise. In the same way conflict appears if p and o want to get away from x but only one of them can do so (if $p \sim Ux$ implies oUx, and vice versa). Lastly, it may happen that p likes x and o hates it, but p and o have to move together (pUx implies oUx, e.g., in marriage). They either can both have x, or both not have it.

Trying out variations of the triad $(pLo) + (pLx) + (oUx)$, we find that $(pLo) + (pLx) + (oLx)$ also represents a balanced case. Examples: p likes what his friend o likes; p likes people with same attitudes. This case is not covered by the hypothesis unless we treat L as equivalent to U. Actually, in many cases the effects of L and U in these configurations seem to be the same. Furthermore, this case shows the psychological transitivity of the L relation. A relation R is transitive if aRb and bRc imply aRc. Thus, p tends to like x if pLo and oLx hold. As in the case of the symmetry of the pLo relation, we again have to stress the difference between logical and psychological aspect. Logically, L is not transitive but there exists a psychological tendency to make it transitive when implications between

5

U relations do not interfere with transitivity. The relation U, too, seems to be in this sense psychologically transitive. $(pUo) + (oUx)$ can lead to pUx; p feels responsible for what people belonging to him do.

Taking into account these considerations, we can reformulate the hypothesis: (a) In the case of two entities, a balanced state exists if the relation between them is positive (or negative) in all respects, i.e., in regard to all meanings of L and U. (b) In the case of three entities, a balanced state exists if all three possible relations are positive in all respects.

The question arises whether, with a triad, one can make any generalizations about balanced cases with negative relations. For instance, $(pLo) + (o \sim Ux) + (p \sim Lx)$ is balanced. Examples: p likes o because o got rid of something p dislikes. In this case two entities, p and o, are related positively to each other, while both are related negatively to the third entity x. This holds generally: the triad of relations is in balance, if two relations are negative and one positive. This statement can be derived from the assumption that L and U are, in a balanced configuration, exchangeable, symmetrical, and transitive. L and U can then be treated as formally analogous to an identity relation. The "balanced" cases with three terms are for this relation: $a = b$, $b = c$, $a = c$; $a = b$, $b \neq c$, $a \neq c$; $a \neq b$, $b \neq c$, $a \neq c$. By substituting L or U for the identity sign one obtains the balanced cases for these relations, though the case with three negative relations does not seem to constitute a good psychological balance, since it is too indetermined.

Therefore, the second part of the hypothesis must be stated as follows: (b) In the case of three entities, a balanced state exists if all three relations are positive in all respects, or if two are negative and one positive.

$(pLo) + (oLx) + (pUx)$. Examples: p likes o because o admired p's action; p wants his friend o to like p's productions; p wants to do what his friends admire.

$(pUo) + (pLx) + (oLx)$. Examples: p wants his son to like what he likes; p likes x because his son likes it.

(d) p, o, and q. Among the many possible cases we shall only consider one. $(pLo) + (oLq) + (pLq)$. Examples: p wants his two friends to like each other. This example shows, as the parallel case with x instead of q, the psychological transitivity of the L relation.

However, the transitivity of the L relation is here restricted by implications between unit relations when L represents a one-one love relation. p does not want his girl friend o to fall in love with his boy friend q because oLq in this case implies $o \sim Lp$, which conflicts with pLo. Jealousy, as well as envy and competition, is derived from implications between unit relations.

After this discussion of the different possibilities there are several more points worth mentioning which refer to examples of different groups. One is the problem of self evaluation. High self regard of p can be expressed by pLp, low self regard by $p \sim Lp$ (though the two p's in these expressions are not strictly equivalent). All of the examples so far considered presupposed pLp. However, one also has to take into account the possibility of $p \sim Lp$. As to be expected, it plays a rôle contrary to that of pLp. Examples: if p has low self regard he might reject a positive x as too good for him; if p has guilt feelings he will think he ought to be punished; if his friend admires his product he will think it only politeness. A negative action attributed to himself will produce $p \sim Lp$, etc.

The equivalence of the L and U relations seems to be limited by the fact that often the U relation is weaker than the L relation. One can assume, that pLx brings about pUx (p wants to have a thing he likes) more often than pUx produces pLx (p gets to like a thing which belongs to him). Again $(pLo) + (oLx)$ usually will lead to pLx (transitivity), but $(pUo) + (oUx)$ will not do so if there holds at the same time $p \sim Lo$.

We saw that one can derive forces towards actions, or goals, from the configurations. It can also happen, that the choice of means to a goal is determined by these patterns. If p wants to produce oLx, and he knows that oLp holds, he can do so by demonstrating to o the relation pLx, because $(oLp) + (pLx)$ will lead to oLx. If p wants to bring about oLp, and he knows that oLx holds, he can produce pUx, for instance, he will perform an act o approves of.

An examination of the discussed examples suggests the conclusion that a good deal of inter-personal behavior and social preception is determined—or at least co-determined—by simple cognitive configurations. This fact also throws light on the problem of the understanding of behavior. Students of this problem often mentioned the aspect of rationality which enters into it. Max Weber and others pointed out one kind of rationality in behavior, namely, the rationality of the means-end relation. Choosing the appropriate means to gain an end makes for a "good," a "rational" action, and we can understand it. In Lewin's concept of hodological space this kind of rationality is elaborated. However, understandable human behavior often is not of this sort, but is based on the simple configurations of U and L relations. Since they determine both behavior and perception we can understand social behavior of this kind.

7

REFERENCE

1. HEIDER, F. Social perception and phenomenal causality. *Psychol. Rev.*, 1944, **51**, 358-374.

64 Kensington Avenue
Northampton, Massachusetts

STRUCTURAL BALANCE: A GENERALIZATION OF HEIDER'S THEORY [1]

DORWIN CARTWRIGHT AND FRANK HARARY

Research Center for Group Dynamics, University of Michigan

A persistent problem of psychology has been how to deal conceptually with patterns of interdependent properties. This problem has been central, of course, in the theoretical treatment by Gestalt psychologists of phenomenal or neural *configurations* or *fields* (**12, 13, 15**). It has also been of concern to social psychologists and sociologists who attempt to employ concepts referring to social *systems* (**18**).

Heider (**19**), reflecting the general field-theoretical approach, has considered certain aspects of cognitive fields which contain perceived people and impersonal objects or events. His analysis focuses upon what he calls the *P-O-X* unit of a cognitive field, consisting of *P* (one person), *O* (another person), and *X* (an impersonal entity). Each relation among the parts of the unit is conceived as interdependent with each other relation. Thus, for example, if *P* has a relation of affection for *O* and if *O* is seen as responsible for *X*, then there will be a tendency for *P* to like or approve of *X*. If the nature of *X* is such that it would "normally" be evaluated as bad, the whole *P-O-X* unit is placed in a state of imbalance, and pressures

[1] This paper was prepared as part of a project sponsored in the Research Center for Group Dynamics by the Rockefeller Foundation.

will arise to change it toward a state of balance. These pressures may work to change the relation of affection between *P* and *O*, the relation of responsibility between *O* and *X*, or the relation of evaluation between *P* and *X*.

The purpose of this paper is to present and develop the consequences of a formal definition of balance which is consistent with Heider's conception and which may be employed in a more general treatment of empirical configurations. The definition is stated in terms of the mathematical theory of linear graphs (**8, 14**) and makes use of a distinction between a given relation and its opposite relation. Some of the ramifications of this definition are then examined by means of theorems derivable from the definition and from graph theory.

HEIDER'S CONCEPTION OF BALANCE

In developing his analysis of balanced cognitive units, Heider distinguishes between two major *types* of relations. The first concerns attitudes, or the relation of liking or evaluating. It is represented symbolically as **L** when positive and as ~**L** when negative. Thus, *PLO* means *P* likes, loves, values, or approves *O*, and *P~LO* means *P* dislikes, negatively

9

values, or disapproves O. The second type of relation refers to cognitive unit formation, that is, to such specific relations as similarity, possession, causality, proximity, or belonging. It is written as U or $\sim U$. Thus, according to Heider, PUX means that P owns, made, is close to, or is associated with X, and $P \sim UX$ means that P does not own, did not make, or is not associated with X.

A *balanced state* is then defined in terms of certain combinations of these relations. The definition is stated separately for two and for three entities.

In the case of two entities, a balanced state exists if the relation between them is positive (or negative) in all respects, i.e., in regard to all meanings of L and U . . . . In the case of three entities, a balanced state exists if all three relations are positive in all respects, or if two are negative and one positive (9, p. 110).

These are examples of balanced states: P likes something he made (PUX, PLX); P likes what his friend likes (PLO, OLX, PLX); P dislikes what his friend dislikes (PLO, $O \sim LX$, $P \sim LX$); P likes what his enemy dislikes ($P \sim LO$, $O \sim LX$, PLX); and P's son likes what P likes (PUO, PLX, OLX).

Heider's basic hypothesis asserts that there is a tendency for cognitive units to achieve a balanced state. Pressures toward balance may produce various effects.

If no balanced state exists, then forces towards this state will arise. Either the dynamic characters will change, or the unit relations will be changed through action or through cognitive reorganization. If a change is not possible, the state of imbalance will produce tension (9, pp. 107–109).

The theory, stated here in sketchy outline, has been elaborated by Heider so as to treat a fuller richness of cognitive experience than would be suggested by our brief description. It has been used, too, by a number of others as a point of departure for further theoretical and empirical work. We shall summarize briefly some of the major results of this work.

Horowitz, Lyons, and Perlmutter (**10**) attempted to demonstrate tendencies toward balance in an experiment employing members of a discussion group as subjects. At the end of a discussion period each subject was asked to indicate his evaluation of an event (PLX or $P \sim LX$) which had occurred during the course of the discussion. The event selected for evaluation was one which would be clearly seen as having been produced by a single person (OUX). The liking relation between each P and O (PLO or $P \sim LO$) had been determined by a sociometric questionnaire administered before the meeting. Would P's evaluation of the event be such as to produce a balanced P-O-X unit? If so, P's evaluation of O and X should be of the same sign. The experimental data tend to support the hypothesis that a P-O-X unit tends toward a balanced state.[2]

The social situation of a discussion group can be better analyzed, according to Horowitz, Lyons, and Perlmutter, by considering a somewhat more complex cognitive unit. The evaluation of X made by P, they argue, will be determined not only by P's evaluation of O but also by his perception of the evaluation of X given by others (Qs) in the group. The basic unit of such a social situation, then, consists of the subject, a

[2] One of the attractive features of this study is that it was conducted in a natural "field" setting, thus avoiding the dangers of artificiality. At the same time the setting placed certain restrictions on the possibility of manipulation and control of the variables. The data show a clear tendency for P to place a higher evaluation on Xs produced by more attractive Os. It is not clearly demonstrated that P likes Xs produced by liked Os and dislikes Xs produced by disliked Os.

person who is responsible for the event, and another person who will be seen by the subject as supporting or rejecting the event. This is called a *P-O-Q-X* unit. The additional data needed to describe these relations were obtained from the sociometric questionnaire which indicated *P*'s evaluation of *Q* (*PLQ* or *P*~*LQ*), and from a question designed to reveal *P*'s perception of *Q*'s support or rejection of *X*, treated by the authors as a unit relation (*Q***U***X* or *Q*~**U***X*).[3]

Although these authors indicate the possibility of treating the *P-O-Q-X* unit in terms of balance, they do not develop a formal definition of a balanced configuration consisting of four elements. They seem to imply that the *P-O-Q-X* unit will be balanced if the *P-O-X* and the *P-Q-X* units are both balanced. They do not consider the relation between *Q* and *O*, nor the logically possible components of which it could be a part. Their analysis is concerned primarily with the two triangles (*P-O-X* and *P-Q-X*), which are interdependent, since both contain the relation of *P*'s liking of *X*. We noted above that the data tend to support the hypothesis that the *P-O-X* unit will tend toward balance. The data even more strongly support the hypothesis when applied to the *P-Q-X* unit; *P*'s evaluation of *X* and his perception of *Q*'s attitude toward *X* tend to agree when *P* likes *Q*, and to disagree when *P* dislikes *Q*. It should be noted, however, that there was also a clear tendency for *P* to see *Q*'s evaluation of *X* as agreeing with his own whether or not he likes *Q*.

In a rather different approach to the question of balanced *P-O-X* units,

Jordan (11) presented subjects with 64 different hypothetical situations in which the **L** and **U** relations between each pair of elements was systematically varied. The subject was asked to place himself in each situation by taking the part of *P*, and to indicate on a scale the degree of pleasantness or unpleasantness he experienced. Unpleasantness was assumed to reflect the postulated tension produced by imbalanced units. Jordan's data tend to support Heider's hypothesis that imbalanced units produce a state of tension, but he too found that additional factors need to be considered. He discovered, for example, that negative relations were experienced as unpleasant even when contained in balanced units. This unpleasantness was particularly acute when *P* was a part of the negative relation. Jordan's study permits a detailed analysis of these additional influences, which we shall not consider here.

Newcomb (17), in his recent theory of interpersonal communication, has employed concepts rather similar to those of Heider. He conceives of the simplest communicative act as one in which one person *A* gives information to another person *B* about something *X*. The similarity of this *A-B-X* model to Heider's *P-O-X* unit, together with its applicability to objective interpersonal relations (rather than only to the cognitive structure of a single person), may be seen in the following quotations from Newcomb:

A-B-X is . . . regarded as constituting a system. That is, certain definable relationships between *A* and *B*, between *A* and *X*, and between *B* and *X* are all viewed as interdependent. . . . For some purposes the system may be regarded as a phenomenal one within the life space of *A* or *B*, for other purposes as an "objective" system including all the possible relationships as inferred from observations of *A*'s and *B*'s behavior (17, p. 393).

---

[3] Whether this relation should be treated as **U** or **L** is subject to debate. For testing Heider's theory of balance, however, the issue is irrelevant, since he holds that the two relations are interchangeable in defining balance.

Newcomb then develops the concept of "strain toward symmetry," which appears to be a special instance of Heider's more general notion of "tendency toward balance." "Strain toward symmetry" is reflected in several manifestations of a tendency for A and B to have attitudes of the same sign toward a common X. Communication is the most common and usually the most effective manifestation of this tendency.

By use of this conception Newcomb reinterprets several studies (1, 4, 5, 16, 20) which have investigated the interrelations among interpersonal attraction, tendencies to communicate, pressures to uniformity of opinion among members of a group, and tendencies to reject deviates. The essential hypothesis in this analysis is stated thus:

If A is free either to continue or not to continue his association with B, one or the other of two eventual outcomes is likely: (a) he achieves an equilibrium characterized by relatively great attraction toward B and by relatively high perceived symmetry, and the association is continued; or (b) he achieves an equilibrium characterized by relatively little attraction toward B and by relatively low perceived symmetry, and the association is discontinued (17, p. 402).

Newcomb's outcome a is clearly a balanced state as defined by Heider. Outcome b cannot be unambiguously translated into Heider's terms. If by "relatively little attraction toward B" is meant a negative L relation between A and B, then this outcome would also seem to be balanced. Newcomb's "continuation or discontinuation of the association between A and B" appear to correspond to Heider's U and $\sim U$ relations.

STATEMENT OF THE PROBLEM

This work indicates that the tendency toward balance is a significant determinant of cognitive organization, and that it may also be important in interpersonal relations. The concept of balance, however, has been defined so as to apply to a rather limited range of situations, and it has contained certain ambiguities. We note five specific problems.

1. *Unsymmetric relations.* Should all relations be conceived as symmetric? The answer is clearly that they should not; it is possible for P to like O while O dislikes P. In fact, Tagiuri, Blake, and Bruner (21) have intensively studied dyadic relations to discover conditions producing symmetric relations of actual and perceived liking. Theoretical discussions of balance have sometimes recognized this possibility—Heider, for example, states that unsymmetric liking is unbalanced—but there has been no general definition of balance which covers unsymmetric relations. The empirical studies of balance have assumed that the relations are symmetric.

2. *Units containing more than three entities.* Nearly all theorizing about balance has referred to units of three entities. While Horowitz, Lyons, and Perlmutter studied units with four entities, they did not *define* balance for such cases. It would seem desirable to be able to speak of the balance of even larger units.

3. *Negative relations.* Is the negative relation the *complement* of the relation or its *opposite*? All of the discussions of balance seem to equate these, but they seem to us to be quite different, for the complement of a relation is expressed by adding the word "not" while the opposite is indicated by the prefix "dis" or its equivalent. Thus, the complement of "liking" is "not liking"; the opposite of "liking" is "disliking." In general, it appears that $\sim L$ has been taken to mean "dislike" (the opposite relation) while

12

~U has been used to indicate "not associated with" (the complementary relation). Thus, for example, Jordan says: "Specifically, '+L' symbolizes a positive attitude, '−L' symbolizes a negative attitude, '+U' symbolizes the existence of unit formation, and '−U' symbolizes the lack of unit formation" (11, p. 274).

4. *Relations of different types*. Heider has made a distinction between two types of relations—one based upon liking and one upon unit formation. The various papers following up Heider's work have continued to use this distinction. And it seems reasonable to assume that still other types of relations might be designated. How can a definition of balance take into account relations of different types? Heider has suggested some of the ways in which liking and unit relations may be combined, but a general formulation has yet to be developed.

5. *Cognitive fields and social systems*. Heider's intention is to describe balance of cognitive units in which the entities and relations enter as experienced by a single individual. Newcomb attempts to treat social systems which may be described objectively. In principle, it should be possible also to study the balance of sociometric structures, communication networks, patterns of power, and other aspects of social systems.

We shall attempt to define balance so as to overcome these limitations. Specifically, the definition should (a) encompass unsymmetric relations, (b) hold for units consisting of any finite number of entities, (c) preserve the distinction between the *complement* and the *opposite* of a relation, (d) apply to relations of different types, and (e) serve to characterize cognitive units, social systems, or any configuration where both a relation and its opposite must be specified.

THE CONCEPTS OF GRAPH, DIGRAPH, AND SIGNED GRAPH

Our approach to this problem has two primary antecedents: (a) Lewin's treatment (15) of the concepts of whole, differentiation, and unity, together with Bavelas' extension (2) of this work to group structure; and (b) the mathematical theory of linear graphs.

Many of the graph-theoretic definitions given in this section are contained in the classical reference on graph theory, König (14), as well as in Harary and Norman (8). We shall discuss, however, those concepts which lead up to the theory of balance.

A *linear graph*, or briefly a *graph*, consists of a finite collection of *points* [4] $A, B, C, \cdots$ together with a prescribed subset of the set of all unordered pairs of distinct points. Each of these unordered pairs, AB, is a *line* of the graph. (From the viewpoint of the theory of binary relations,[5] a graph corresponds to an irreflexive [6] symmetric relation on points $A, B, C, \cdots$. Alternatively a graph may be represented as a matrix.[7])

Figure 1 depicts a graph of four points and four lines. The points might represent people, and the lines some relationship such as mutual liking. With this interpretation, Fig. 1 indicates that mutual liking exists between those pairs of people A, B, C, and D joined by lines. Thus D is in the relation with all other persons, while C is in the relation only with D.

[4] Points are often called "vertices" by mathematicians and "nodes" by electrical engineers.
[5] This is the approach used by Heider.
[6] A relation is irreflexive if it contains no ordered pairs of the form (a, a), i.e., if no element is in this relation to itself.
[7] This treatment is discussed in Festinger (3). The logical equivalence of relations, graphs, and matrices is taken up in Harary and Norman (8).

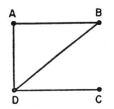

FIG. 1. A linear graph of four points and four lines. The presence of line AB indicates the existence of a specified symmetric relationship between the two entities A and B.

Figure 1 could be used, of course, to represent many other kinds of relationships between many other kinds of entities.

It is apparent from this definition of graph that relations are treated in an all-or-none manner, i.e., either a relation exists between a given pair of points or it does not. Obviously, however, many relationships of interest to psychologists (liking, for example) exist in varying degrees. This fact means that our present use of graph theory can treat only the structural, and not the numerical, aspects of relations. While our treatment is thereby an incomplete representation of the strength of relations, we believe that conceptualization of the structural properties of relations is a necessary first step toward a more adequate treatment of the more complex situations. Such an elaboration, however, goes beyond the scope of this paper.

A *directed graph*, or a *digraph*, consists of a finite collection of points together with a prescribed subset of the set of all ordered pairs of distinct points. Each of these ordered pairs $\vec{AB}$ is called a *line* of the digraph. Note that the only difference between the definitions of graph and digraph is that the lines of a graph are unordered pairs of points while the lines of a digraph are ordered pairs of points. An *ordered pair* of points is

distinguished from an unordered pair by designating one of the points as the first point and the other as the second. Thus, for example, the fact that a message can go *from A to B* is represented by the ordered pair (A, B), or equivalently, by the line $\vec{AB}$, as in Fig. 2. Similarly, the fact that A and D choose each other is represented by the two directed lines $\vec{AD}$ and $\vec{DA}$.

A *signed graph*, or briefly an *s-graph* is obtained from a graph when one regards some of the lines as positive and the remaining lines as negative. Considered as a geometric representation of binary relations, an s-graph serves to depict situations or structures in which both a relation and its opposite may occur, e.g., like and dislike. Figure 3 depicts an s-graph, employing the convention that solid lines are positive and dashed lines negative; thus A and B are represented as liking each other while A and C dislike each other.

Combining the concepts of digraph and s-graph, we obtain that of an s-digraph. A *signed digraph*, or an *s-digraph*, is obtained from a digraph by taking some of its lines as positive and the rest as negative.

A *graph of type 2* (8), introduced to depict structures in which two differ-

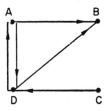

FIG. 2. A directed graph of four points and five directed lines. An $\vec{AB}$ line indicates the existence of a specified ordered relationship involving the two entities A and B. Thus, for example, if A and B are two people, the $\vec{AB}$ line might indicate that a message can go from A to B or that A chooses B.

ent relations defined on the same set of elements occur, is obtained from a graph by regarding its lines as being of two different colors (say), and by permitting the same pair of points to be joined by two lines if these lines have different colors. A *graph of type* τ, $\tau = 1, 2, 3, \cdots$, is defined similarly. In an s-graph or s-digraph of type 2, there may occur lines of two different types in which a line of either color may be positive or negative. An example of an s-graph of type 2 might be one depicting for the same *P-O-X* unit both **U** and **L** relations among the entities, where the sign of these relations is indicated.

A *path* is a collection of lines of a graph of the form $AB, BC, \cdots, DE$, where the points $A, B, C, \cdots, D, E$, are distinct. A *cycle* consists of the above path together with the line EA. The *length* of a cycle (or path) is the number of lines in it; an *n-cycle* is a cycle of length n. Analogously to graphs, a *path of a digraph* consists of directed lines of the form $\overrightarrow{AB}, \overrightarrow{BC}, \cdots, \overrightarrow{DE}$, where the points are distinct. A *cycle* consists of this path together with the line $\overrightarrow{EA}$. In the later discussion of balance of an s-digraph we shall use the concept of a semicycle. A *semicycle* is a collection of lines obtained by taking exactly one from each pair $\overrightarrow{AB}$ or $\overrightarrow{BA}$, $\overrightarrow{BC}$ or $\overrightarrow{CB}$, $\cdots$, $\overrightarrow{DE}$ or $\overrightarrow{ED}$, and $\overrightarrow{EA}$ or $\overrightarrow{AE}$. We illustrate semicycles with the digraph of Fig. 2. There are three semicycles in this digraph: $\overrightarrow{AD}, \overrightarrow{DA}$; $\overrightarrow{AD}, \overrightarrow{DB}$, $\overrightarrow{BA}$; and $\overrightarrow{AD}, \overrightarrow{DB}, \overrightarrow{BA}$. The last two of these semicycles are not cycles. Note that every cycle is a semicycle, and a semicycle of length 2 is necessarily a cycle.

BALANCE

With these concepts of graphs, digraphs, and signed graphs we may

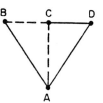

Fig. 3. A signed graph of four points and five lines. Solid lines have a positive sign and dashed lines a negative sign. If the points stand for people and the lines indicate the existence of a liking relationship, this s-graph shows that A and B have a relationship of liking, A and C have one of disliking, and B and D have a relationship of indifference (neither liking or disliking).

now develop a rigorous generalization of Heider's concept of balance.

It should be evident that Heider's terms, *entity*, *relation*, and *sign of a relation* may be coordinated to the graphic terms, *point*, *directed line*, and *sign of a directed line*. Thus, for example, the assertion that P likes O (*PLO*) may be depicted as a directed line of positive sign $\overrightarrow{PO}$. It should also be clear that Heider's two different kinds of relations (**L** and **U**) may be treated as lines of different type. It follows that a graphic representation of a *P-O-X* unit having positive or negative **L** and **U** relations will be an s-digraph of type 2.

For simplicity of discussion we first consider the situation containing only symmetric relations of a single type (i.e., an s-graph of type 1). Figure 4 shows four such s-graphs. It will be noted that each of these s-graphs contains one cycle: AB, BC, CA. We now need to define the sign of a cycle. The *sign of a cycle* is the product of the signs of its lines. For convenience we denote the sign of a line by $+1$ or -1 when it is positive or negative. With this definition we see that the cycle, AB, BC, CA is positive in s-graph a ($+1 \cdot +1 \cdot +1$), positive in s-graph b ($+1 \cdot -1 \cdot -1$), negative

15

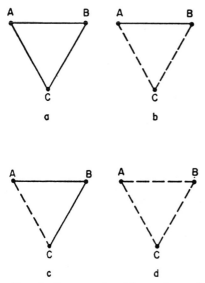

FIG. 4. Four s-graphs of three points and three lines each. Structure *a* and *b* are balanced, but *c* and *d* are not balanced.

in s-graph *c* (+1·+1·−1), and negative in s-graph *d* (−1·−1·−1). To generalize, a *cycle is positive* if it contains an even number of negative lines, and it is *negative* otherwise. Thus, in particular, a cycle containing only positive lines is positive, since the number of negative lines is zero, an even number.

In discussing the concept of balance, Heider states (see **9**, p. 110) that when there are three entities a balanced state exists if all three relations are positive or if two are negative and one positive. According to this definition, s-graphs *a* and *b* are balanced while s-graphs *c* and *d* are not (Fig. 4). We note that in the examples cited Heider's balanced state is depicted as an s-graph of three points whose cycle is positive.

In generalizing Heider's concept of balance, we propose to employ this characteristic of balanced states as a general criterion for balance of structures with any number of entities.

Thus we define an *s-graph* (containing any number of points) as *balanced* if all of its cycles are positive.

Figure 5 illustrates this definition for four s-graphs containing four points. In each of these s-graphs there are seven cycles: *AB, BC, CA; AB, BD, DA; BC, CD, DB; AC, CD, DA; AB, BC, CD, DA; AB, BD, DC, CA;* and *BC, CA, AD, DB*. It will be seen that in s-graphs *a* and *b* all seven cycles are positive, and these s-graphs are therefore balanced. In s-graphs *c* and *d* the cycle, *AB, BC, CA*, is negative (as are several others), and these s-graphs are therefore not balanced. It is obvious that this definition of balance is applicable to structures containing any number of entities.[8]

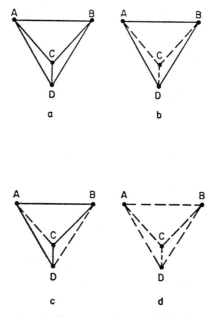

FIG. 5. Four s-graphs containing four points and six lines each. Structures *a* and *b* are balanced, but *c* and *d* are not balanced.

[8] If an s-graph contains no cycles, we say that it is "vacuously" balanced, since all (in this case, none) of its cycles are positive.

The extension of this definition of balance to s-digraphs containing any number of points is straightforward. Employing the same definition of *sign of a semicycle* for an s-digraph as for an ordinary s-graph, we similarly define an s-digraph as balanced if all of its semicycles are positive.

Consider now Heider's *P-O-X* unit, containing two persons *P* and *O* and an impersonal entity *X*, in which we are concerned only with liking relations. Figure 6 shows three of the possible 3-point s-digraphs which may represent such *P-O-X* units. A positive $\overrightarrow{PO}$ line means that *P* likes *O*, a negative $\overrightarrow{PO}$ line means that *P* dislikes *O*. We assume that a person can like or dislike an impersonal entity but that an impersonal entity can neither like nor dislike a person.[9] We also rule out of consideration here "ambivalence," where a person may simultaneously like and dislike another person or impersonal entity.

In each of these s-digraphs there are three semicycles: $\overrightarrow{PO}$, $\overrightarrow{OP}$; $\overrightarrow{PO}$, $\overrightarrow{OX}$, $\overrightarrow{XP}$; and $\overrightarrow{PO}$, $\overrightarrow{OX}$, $\overrightarrow{XP}$. If we confine our discussion to the kind of structures represented in Fig. 6 (i.e., where there is no ambivalence and where all possible positive or negative lines are present), it will be apparent that: when *P* and *O* like each other, the s-digraph is balanced only if both persons either like or dislike *X* (s-digraph *a* is not balanced); when *P* and *O* dislike each other, the s-digraph is balanced only if one person likes *X* and the other person dislikes *X* (s-digraph *b* is balanced); and when one person likes the other but the other

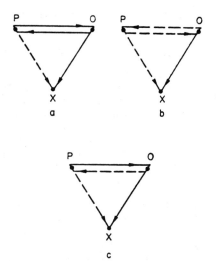

Fig. 6. Three s-digraphs representing Heider's *P-O-X* units. Only structure *b* is balanced.

dislikes him, the s-digraph must be not balanced (s-digraph *c* is not balanced). These conclusions are consistent with Heider's discussion of *P-O-X* units and with Newcomb's treatment of the *A-B-X* model.

The further extension of the notion of balance to s-graphs of type 2 remains to be made. The simplest procedure would be simply to ignore the types of lines involved. Then we would again define an *s-graph of type 2* to be *balanced* if all of its cycles are positive. This definition appears to be consistent with Heider's intention, at least as it applies to a situation containing only two entities. For in speaking of such situations having both **L** and **U** relations, he calls them balanced if both relations between the same pair of entities are of the same sign (see 9, p. 110). There remains some question as to whether this definition will fit empirical findings for cycles of greater length. Until further evidence is available, we advance the above formulation as a tentative definition. Obviously the definition of

[9] In terms of digraph theory we define an *object* as a *point with zero output*. Thus a completely indifferent person is an object. If, psychologically, an impersonal entity is active and likes or dislikes a person or another impersonal entity, then in terms of digraph theory it is not an object.

balance can be given for s-graphs of general type τ in the same way.

SOME THEOREMS ON BALANCE

By definition, an s-graph is balanced if and only if each of its cycles is positive. In a given situation represented by an s-graph, however, it may be impractical to single out each cycle, determine its sign, and then declare that it is balanced only after the positivity of every cycle has been checked. Thus the problem arises of deriving a criterion for determining whether or not a given graph is balanced without having to revert to the definition. This problem is the subject matter of a separate paper (6), in which two necessary and sufficient conditions for an s-graph to be balanced are developed. The first of these is no more useful than the definition in determining by inspection whether an s-graph is balanced, but it does give further insight into the notion of balance. Since the proofs of these theorems may be found in the other paper, we shall not repeat them here.

Theorem. An s-graph is balanced if and only if all paths joining the same pair of points have the same sign.

Thus, we can ascertain that the s-graph of Fig. 7 is balanced either by listing each cycle separately and verifying that it is positive, or, using this

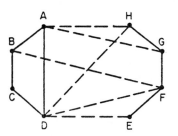

FIG. 7. An s-graph of eight points and thirteen lines which, by aid of the structure theorem, can be readily seen as balanced.

theorem, by considering each pair of possible points and verifying that all possible paths joining them have the same sign. For example, all the paths between points A and E are negative, all paths joining A and C are positive, etc.

The following structure theorem has the advantage that it is useful in determining whether or not a given s-graph is balanced without an exhaustive check of the sign of every cycle, or of the signs of all paths joining every pair of points.

Structure theorem. An s-graph is balanced if and only if its points can be separated into two mutually exclusive subsets such that each positive line joins two points of the same subset and each negative line joins points from different subsets.

Using the structure theorem, one can see at a glance that the s-graph of Fig. 7 is balanced, for A, B, C, D, and E, F, G, H are clearly two disjoint subsets of the set of all points which satisfy the conditions of the structure theorem.

It is not always quite so easy to determine balance of an s-graph by inspection, for it is not always necessarily true that the points of each of the two subsets are connected to each other. Thus the two s-graphs of Fig. 8 are balanced, even though neither of the two disjoint subsets is a connected subgraph. However, the structure theorem still applies to both of the s-graphs of Fig. 8. In the first graph the appropriate subsets of points are A, D, E, H and B, C, F, G; while in the second one we take A_1, B_1, A_3, B_3, A_5, B_5 and A_2, B_2, A_4, B_4.

In addition to providing two necessary and sufficient conditions for balance, these theorems give us further information about the nature of balance. Thus if we regard the s-graph as representing Heider's L-relation in a group, then the structure theorem tells us that the group is necessarily decomposed into two subgroups (cliques) within which the relationships that occur are positive and between which they are negative. The structure theorem, however, does not preclude the possibility that one of the two subsets may be empty—as, for example, when a connected graph contains only positive lines.

The first theorem also leads to some interesting consequences. Suppose it were true, for example, that when two people like each other they can influence each other positively (i.e., produce intended changes in the other), but when two people dislike each other they can only influence each other negatively (i.e., produce changes opposite to those intended). An s-graph depicting the liking relations among a group of people will, then, also depict the potential influence structure of the group. Suppose that Fig. 7 represents such a group. If A attempts to get H to approve of something, H will react by disapproving. If H attempts, in turn, to get G to disapprove of the same thing, he will succeed. Thus A's (indirect) influence upon G is negative. The first theorem tells us that A's influence upon G must be negative, regardless of the path along which the influence passes, since the s-graph is balanced. In general, the sign of the influence exerted by any point upon any other will be the same, no matter what path is followed, since the graph is balanced.

By use of the structure theorem it can be shown that in a balanced group any influence from one point to another within the same clique must be positive, even if it passes through individuals outside of the clique, and the influence must be negative if it goes from a person in one clique to a person in the other. (It should be

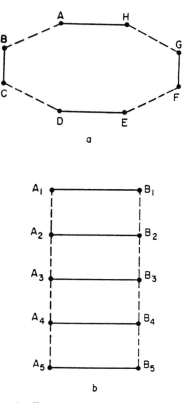

FIG. 8. Two s-graphs whose balance cannot be determined easily by visual inspection.

noted that in this discussion we give the term "clique" a special meaning, as above.) Thus, under the assumed conditions, any exerted influence regarding opinions will tend to produce homogeneity within cliques and opposing opinions between cliques.

Although we have illustrated these theorems by reference to social groups, it should be obvious that they hold for any empirical realizations of s-graphs.

FURTHER CONCEPTS IN THE THEORY OF BALANCE

The concepts of balance as developed up to this point are clearly oversimplifications of the full complexity of situations with which we want to deal. To handle such complex situations more adequately, we need some further concepts.

Thus far we have only considered whether a given s-graph is balanced or not balanced. But it is intuitively clear that some unbalanced s-graphs are "more balanced" than others! This suggests the introduction of some scale of balance, along which the "amount" of balance possessed by an unbalanced s-graph may be measured. Accordingly we define the *degree of balance of an s-graph* as the ratio of the number of positive cycles to the total number of cycles. In symbols, let G be an s-graph,

$c(G)$ = the number of cycles of G,

$c_+(G)$ = the number of positive cycles of G, and

$b(G)$ = the degree of balance of G. Then

$$b(G) = \frac{c_+(G)}{c(G)}.$$

Since the number $c_+(G)$ can range from zero to $c(G)$ inclusive, it is clear that $b(G)$ lies between 0 and 1. Obviously $b(G) = 1$ if and only if G is balanced. We can give the number $b(G)$ the following probabilistic interpretation: the degree of balance of an s-graph is the probability that a randomly chosen cycle is positive.

Does $b(G) = 50\%$ mean that G is exactly one-half balanced? The

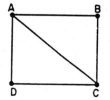

Fig. 9. A graph of four points which can acquire degrees of balance of only .33 and 1.00 regardless of the assignment of positive and negative signs to its five lines.

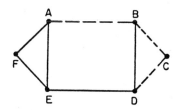

Fig. 10. An s-graph which is 3-balanced but not 4-balanced.

answer to this question depends on the possible values which $b(G)$ may assume. This in turn depends on the structure of the s-graph G. Thus, if G is the complete graph of 3 points and G is not balanced, then the only possible value is $b(G) = 0$, since there is only one cycle. Similarly, if the lines of G are as in Fig. 9, some of which may be negative, and if G is not balanced, then the only possible value is $b(G) = \frac{1}{3}$, and $b(G) = 50\%$ does not even occur for this structure. Thus any interpretation given to the numerical value of $b(G)$ must take into account the distribution curve for $b(G)$, which is determined by the structure of G.

We now consider the corresponding concept of the degree of balance for s-diagrams. Since an s-digraph is balanced if all of its semicycles are positive, the *degree of balance of an s-digraph* is taken as the ratio of the number of positive semicycles to the total number of semicycles.

In a given s-graph which represents the signed structure of some psychological situation, it may happen that only cycles of length 3 and 4 are important for the purpose of determining balance. Thus in an s-graph representing the relation **L** in a complex group, it will not matter at all to the group as a whole whether a cycle of length 100, say, is positive. To handle this situation rigorously, we define an s-graph to be *N-balanced* if all its cycles of length not exceeding

N are positive. Of course the degree of N-balance is definable and computable for any s-graph. Examples can be given of unbalanced s-graphs which are, however, N-balanced for some N. Figure 10 illustrates this phenomenon for $N = 3$, since all of its 3-cycles are positive, but it has a negative 4-cycle.[10]

For certain problems, one may wish to concentrate only on one distinguished point and determine whether an s-graph is balanced there. This can be accomplished by the notion of local balance. We say an s-graph is *locally balanced at point P* if all cycles through P are positive. Thus the s-graph of Fig. 11 is balanced at points A, B, C, and not balanced at D, E, F. If this figure represents a sociometric structure, then the concept of local balance at A is applicable provided A is completely unconcerned about the relations among D, E, F.

Some combinatorial problems suggested by the notions of local balance and N-balance have been investigated by Harary (7). The principal theorem on local balance, which follows, uses the term "articulation point" which we now define. An *articulation point*[11] of a connected graph is one whose removal[12] results in a disconnected graph. Thus the point D is the only articulation point of Fig. 11. We now state the main

theorem on local balance, without proof.

Theorem. If a connected s-graph G is balanced at P, and Q is a point on a cycle passing through P, where Q is not an articulation point, then G is also balanced at Q.

Figure 11 serves to illustrate this theorem, for the s-graph is balanced at A, and is also balanced at B but is not balanced at D, which is an articulation point.

In actual practice, both local balance and N-balance may be employed. This can be handled by introducing the combined concept of local N-balance. Formally we say that an s-graph is *locally N-balanced at P* if all cycles of length not exceeding N and passing through P are positive. Obviously the degree of local N-balance can be defined analogously to the degree of balance.

In summary, the concept of degree of balance removes the limitation of dealing with only balanced or unbalanced structures, and in addition is susceptible to probabilistic and statistical treatment. The definition of local balance enables one to focus at any particular point of the structure. The introduction of N-balance frees us from the necessity of treating all cycles as equally important in determining structural balance. Thus, the extensions of the notion of balance

---

[10] One way of viewing the definition of N-balance is to regard cycles of length N as having weight 1, and all longer cycles as of weight 0. Of course, it is possible to generalize this idea by assigning weights to each length, e.g., weight $1/2^n$ to length N.

[11] A characterization of the articulation points of a graph, or in other words the liaison persons in a group, is given by Ross and Harary (19), using the "structure matrix" of the graph. An exposition of this concept is given in Harary and Norman (8).

[12] By the removal of a point of a graph is meant the deletion of the point and all lines to which it is incident.

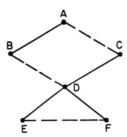

FIG. 11. An s-graph which is locally balanced at points A, B, C but not balanced at points D, E, F.

developed in this section permit a study of more complicated situations than does the original definition of Heider.

ADEQUACY OF THE GENERAL THEORY OF BALANCE

In any empirical science the evaluation of a formal model must be concerned with both its formal properties and its applicability to empirical data. An adequate model should account for known findings in a rigorous fashion and lead to new research. Although it is not our purpose in this article to present new data concerning tendencies toward balance in empirical systems, we may attempt to evaluate the adequacy of the proposed general theory of balance in the light of presently available research.

Our review of Heider's theory of balance and of the research findings related to it has revealed certain ambiguities and limitations concerning (a) the treatment of unsymmetric relations; (b) the generalization to systems containing more than three entities; (c) the distinction between the complement and the opposite of a relation; (d) the simultaneous existence of relationships of different types; and (e) the applicability of the concept of balance to empirical systems other than cognitive ones. We now comment briefly upon the way in which our generalization deals with each of these problems.

Unsymmetric relations. It was noted above that, while theoretical discussions of balance have sometimes allowed for the possibility of unsymmetric relations, no rigorous definition of balance has been developed to encompass situations containing unsymmetric relationships. Furthermore, empirical studies have tended to assume that liking is reciprocated, that each liking relation is symmetric.

By stating the definition of balance in terms of s-digraphs, we are able to include in one conceptual scheme both symmetric and unsymmetric relationships. And it is interesting to observe that, according to this definition, whenever the lines $\overrightarrow{PO}$ and $\overrightarrow{OP}$ are of different signs, the s-digraph containing them is not balanced. Thus, to the extent that tendencies toward balance have been effective in the settings empirically studied, the assumption of symmetry has, in fact, been justified.

Situations containing any finite number of entities. Heider's discussion of balance has been confined to structures containing no more than three entities. The definition of balance advanced here contains no such limitation; it is applicable to structures containing any finite number of entities. Whether or not empirical theories of balance will be confirmed by research dealing with larger structures can only be determined by empirical work. It is clear, however, that our generalization is consistent with the more limited definition of Heider.

A relation, its complement, and its opposite. Using s-graphs and s-digraphs to depict relationships between entities allows us to distinguish among three situations: the presence of a relation (positive line), the presence of the opposite of a relation (negative line), and the absence of both (no line). The empirical utilization of this theory requires the ability to distinguish among these three situations. In our earlier discussion of the literature on balance, we noted, however, a tendency to distinguish only the presence or absence of a relationship. It is not always clear, therefore, in attempting to depict previous research in terms of s-graph theory whether a given empirical relationship should be coordinated to no line or to a negative line.

The experiment of Jordan (11) illustrates this problem quite clearly. He employed three entities and specified certain U and L relations between each pair of entities. The empirical realization of these relations was obtained in the following way: U was made into "has some sort of bond or relationship with"; $\sim U$ into "has no sort of bond or relationship with;" L was made into "like;" and $\sim L$ into "dislike." Viewed in the light of s-graph theory, it would appear that Jordan created s-graphs of type 2 (which may contain positive and negative lines of type U and type L). It would also appear, however, that the $\sim U$ relation should be depicted as the absence of any U-line but that the $\sim L$ relation should be depicted as a negative L-line. If this interpretation is correct, Jordan's classification of his situations as "balanced" and "imbalanced" will have to be revised. Instead of interpreting the $\sim U$ relation as a negative line, we shall have to view it as no U-line, with the result that all of his situations containing $\sim U$ relations are vacuously balanced by our definition since there are no cycles.

It is interesting to examine Jordan's data in the light of this reinterpretation. He presented subjects with 64 hypothetical situations, half of which were "balanced" and half "imbalanced" by his definition. He had subjects rate the degree of pleasantness or unpleasantness experienced in each situation (a high score indicating unpleasantness). For "balanced" situations the mean rating was 46 and for "imbalanced" ones, 57.

If, however, we interpret Jordan's $\sim U$ relation as the absence of a line, his situations must be reclassified. Of his 32 "balanced" situations, 14

have no $\sim U$ relation and thus remain balanced. The mean unpleasantness score for these is 39. The remaining 18 of his "balanced" situations, having at least one $\sim U$ relation, become vacuously balanced since no cycle remains. The mean unpleasantness of these vacuously balanced situations is 51. Of Jordan's 32 "imbalanced" situations, 19 contain at least one $\sim U$ relation, thus also becoming vacuously balanced, and the mean unpleasantness score for these is 51. The remaining 13 situations, by having no $\sim U$ relations, remain imbalanced, and their mean score is 66. Thus it is clear that the difference in pleasantness between situations classed by Jordan as "balanced" and "imbalanced" is greatly increased if the vacuously balanced situations are removed from both classes (balanced, 39; vacuously balanced, 51; not balanced, 66). These findings lend support to our view that the statement "has no sort of bond or relationship with" should be represented as the absence of a line.[13]

Relations of different types. A basic feature of Heider's theory of balance is the designation of two types of relations (L and U). Our generalization of the definition of balance permits the inclusion of any number of types of relations. Heider discusses the combination of types of relations only for the situation involving two entities, and it is clear that our definition is consistent with his within this limitation. It is interesting to note

[13] A strict test of our interpretation of Jordan's data is not possible since he specified for any given pair of entities only either the L or U relation. We can but guess how the subjects filled in the missing relationship. In the light of our discussion of relations of different types, in the next section, it appears that subjects probably assumed a positive unit relation when none was specified, since there is a marked tendency to experience negative liking relations as unpleasant.

that Jordan (11) finds positive liking relations to be experienced as more pleasant than negative ones. This finding may be interpreted as indicating a tendency toward "positivity" over and above the tendency toward balance. It is possible, however, that in the hypothetical situations employed by Jordan the subjects assumed positive unit relations between each pair of entities. If this were in fact true, then a positive liking relation would form a positive cycle of length 2 with the positive unit relation, and a negative liking relation would form a negative cycle of length 2 with the positive unit relation. And, according to the theory of balance, the positive cycle should produce more pleasantness than the negative one. This interpretation can be tested only through further research in which the two relations are independently varied.

Empirical applicability of concept of balance. Heider's discussion of balance refers to a cognitive structure, or the life space of a single person. Newcomb suggests that a similar conception may be applicable to interpersonal systems objectively described. Clearly, our definition of balance may be employed whenever the terms "point" and "signed line" can be meaningfully coordinated to empirical data of any sort. Thus, one should be able to characterize a communication network or a power structure as balanced or not. Perhaps it would be feasible to use the same definition in describing neural networks. It must be noted, however, that it is a matter for empirical determination whether or not a tendency to achieve balance will actually be observed in any particular kind of situation, and what the empirical consequences of not balanced configurations are. Before extensive utilization of these notions can

be accomplished, certain further conceptual problems regarding balance must be solved.

One of the principal unsolved problems is the development of a systematic treatment of relations of varying strength. We believe that it is possible to deal with the strength of relations by the concept of a graph of strength σ, suggested by Harary and Norman (8).

SUMMARY

In this article we have developed a generalization of Heider's theory of balance by use of concepts from the mathematical theory of linear graphs. By defining balance in graph-theoretic terms, we have been able to remove some of the ambiguities found in previous discussions of balance, and to make the concept applicable to a wider range of empirical situations than was previously possible. By introducing the concept *degree of balance*, we have made it possible to treat problems of balance in statistical and probabilistic terms. It should be easier, therefore, to make empirical tests of hypotheses concerning balance.

Although Heider's theory was originally intended to refer only to cognitive structures of an individual person, we propose that the definition of balance may be used generally in describing configurations of many different sorts, such as communication networks, power systems, sociometric structures, systems of orientations, or perhaps neural networks. Only future research can determine whether theories of balance can be established for all of these configurations. The definitions developed here do, in any case, give a rigorous method for describing certain structural aspects of empirical configurations.

REFERENCES

1. BACK, K. The exertion of influence through social communication. *J. abnorm. soc. Psychol.*, 1951, 46, 9–23.
2. BAVELAS, A. A mathematical model for group structures. *Appl. Anthrop.*, 1948, 7, No. 3, 16–30.
3. FESTINGER, L. The analysis of sociograms using matrix algebra. *Hum. Relat.*, 1949, 2, 153–158.
4. FESTINGER, L., SCHACHTER, S., & BACK, K. *Social pressures in informal groups.* New York: Harper, 1950.
5. FESTINGER, L., & THIBAUT, J. Interpersonal communication in small groups. *J. abnorm. soc. Psychol.*, 1951, 46, 92–99.
6. HARARY, F. On the notion of balance of a signed graph. *Mich. math. J.*, 1953–54, 2, 143–146.
7. HARARY, F. On local balance and N-balance in signed graphs. *Mich. math. J.*, 1955–56, 3, 37–41.
8. HARARY, F., & NORMAN, R. Z. *Graph theory as a mathematical model in social science.* Ann Arbor, Mich.: Institute for Social Research, 1953.
9. HEIDER, F. Attitudes and cognitive organization. *J. Psychol.*, 1946, 21, 107–112.
10. HOROWITZ, M. W., LYONS, J., & PERLMUTTER, H. V. Induction of forces in discussion groups. *Hum. Relat.*, 1951, 4, 57–76.
11. JORDAN, N. Behavioral forces that are a function of attitudes and of cognitive organization. *Hum. Relat.*, 1953, 6, 273–287.
12. KOFFKA, K. *Principles of gestalt psychology.* New York: Harcourt, Brace, 1935.
13. KÖHLER, W. *Dynamics in psychology.* New York: Liveright, 1940.
14. KÖNIG, D. *Theorie der endlichen und unendlichen Graphen.* New York: Chelsea, 1950 (originally published in Leipzig, 1936).
15. LEWIN, K. *Field theory in social science.* New York: Harper, 1951.
16. NEWCOMB, T. M. *Personality and social change.* New York: Dryden, 1943.
17. NEWCOMB, T. M. An approach to the study of communicative acts. *Psychol. Rev.*, 1953, 60, 393–404.
18. PARSONS, T. *Essays in sociological theory.* (Rev. Ed.) Glencoe, Ill.: Free Press, 1954.
19. ROSS, I. C., & HARARY, F. Identification of the liaison persons of an organization using the structure matrix. *Mgmt Sci.*, 1955, 1, 251–258.
20. SCHACHTER, S. Deviation, rejection and communication. *J. abnorm. soc. Psychol.*, 1951, 46, 190–207.
21. TAGIURI, R., BLAKE, R. R., & BRUNER, J. S. Some determinants of the perception of positive and negative feelings in others. *J. abnorm. soc. Psychol.*, 1953, 48, 585–592.

(Received January 11, 1956)

From James A. Davis, *Human Relations 20*,
181-187 (1967), by permission.

Clustering and Structural Balance in Graphs

JAMES A. DAVIS[1]

CARTWRIGHT & HARARY (1956) define a signed graph as balanced if all its cycles are 'positive' and state the following theorem:

'An *s*-graph is balanced if and only if its points can be separated into two mutually exclusive subsets such that each positive line joins two points of the same subset and each negative line joins points from different subsets.'

If the theory of structural balance is 'true' when applied to social relationships, it implies a tendency for groups to polarize—to split into exactly two cliques. Thus 'a "balanced" group consists of two highly cohesive cliques which dislike each other' (Harary, 1955-6, p. 144).

Because sociometric studies often suggest that groups may split into three, four, or more cliques, the following question may be asked; What conditions are necessary and sufficient for the points of a graph to be separated into two *or more* subsets such that each positive line joins two points of the same subset and each negative line joins points from different subsets?

We call the multiple clique phenomenon *clustering* to distinguish it from *balance*, although it will be shown that the two are closely related.

STATEMENT AND PROOF OF CLUSTER THEOREMS[2]

In the following discussion terms referring to signed graphs are defined as in Cartwright & Harary (1956). However, a few additional definitions are required. A *clustering* of a signed graph S is a partition of the point set $V(S)$ into subsets P_1, $P_2, \ldots, P_n$ (called *plus-sets*) such that each positive line joins two points in the same subset and each negative line joins two points from different subsets. If S has a unique clustering, its plus-sets are called *clusters*. A *cycle* consists of a path L, joining two points v_i and v_j, together with the line v_iv_j. If L has only positive lines, it is called an *all-positive path*.

THEOREM 1

Let S be any signed graph. Then S has a clustering if and only if S contains no cycle having exactly one negative line.

Proof. We first prove the necessity of this criterion. By hypothesis S has a clustering, and we assume S has a cycle with exactly one negative line, v_iv_j. Now v_i and v_j are

1. The work reported here was supported in part by National Institute of Mental Health Grant K3-MH-25, 412-01. Jack Sawyer and Harrison White provided many helpful comments on a previous version.
2. The statement and proof presented here were kindly provided by Professors Dorwin Cartwright and Frank Harary as a substitute for the author's more lengthy and cumbersome one.

M*

joined by an all-positive path, L. Clearly, all points of L are in the same plus-set since adjacent points of L are all joined by positive lines. But then there is a negative line joining two points in the same plus-set, which is a contradiction.

To prove the sufficiency, we are given that S contains no cycle having exactly one negative line, and we show that S has a partition that is a clustering. We form subsets $A_1, \ldots, A_k, \ldots, A_n$ by the rule that two points are in the same subset if and only if they are joined by an all-positive path. Clearly, the subsets so constructed are maximal and partition $V(S)$. Now every positive line of S joins two points in the same subset A_k. Let v_i and v_j be any two distinct points in A_k. Then v_i and v_j are joined by an all-positive path, and they are not joined by a negative line since S would then have a cycle with exactly one negative line. Hence, all negative lines of S join two points from different subsets, and our partition is a clustering.

FIGURE 1

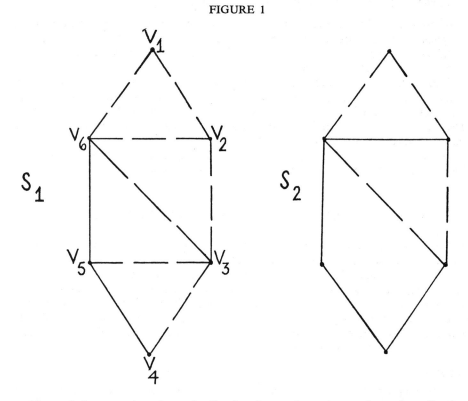

Figure 1 shows a signed graph, S_1, that has a clustering and another, S_2, that does not. The procedure given in the proof of *Theorem 1*, when applied to S_1, yields four plus-sets: $P_1 = \{v_4, v_5, v_6\}$, $P_2 = \{v_1\}$, $P_3 = \{v_2\}$, $P_4 = \{v_3\}$. It should be noted, however, that S_1 has another clustering: $P_1 = \{v_4, v_5, v_6\}$, $P_2 = \{v_1, v_3\}$, $P_3 = \{v_2\}$.

The results of *Theorem 1* are applicable, of course, to any appropriate realization of a signed graph. We might, for example, represent the structure of interpersonal sentiments among a group of people by a signed graph S by letting each point of S correspond to a person. And if two people, v_i and v_j, like each other, we join the corresponding points with a positive line; if they dislike each other, we join them

28

with a negative line. Now let us assume a tendency for these interpersonal sentiments to form a structure whose signed graph has a clustering. In other words, we
assume a tendency for the group to divide into subgroups that correspond to the
plus-sets of a clustering. In this case, all people who like each other are in the same
subgroup and all who dislike each other are in different subgroups. *Theorem 1* gives
a necessary and sufficient condition for the existence of such a structure.

A graph in which every two points are joined by a line is called *complete*. Clearly,
if every two people in a group either like or dislike each other, the corresponding
signed graph is complete. The next theorem gives three criteria for such a structure
to be clusterable. Its statement and proof refer to an *n-cycle*, by which we mean a
cycle of length *n*.

THEOREM 2

The following statements are equivalent for any complete signed graph S.

    (1) S has a clustering.
    (2) S has a unique clustering.
    (3) S has no cycle with exactly one negative line.
    (4) S has no 3-cycle (triangle) with exactly one negative line.

Proof. The equivalence of (1) and (2) is immediate. The equivalence of (1) and (3)
was established by *Theorem 1*. Since (4) follows directly from (3), we need prove
only that (4) implies (3). By hypothesis, S has no 3-cycle with exactly one negative
line. We assume that S has a k-cycle with exactly one negative line, whose points are
labeled $v_1, v_2, \ldots, v_k$, such that the single negative line joins v_1 and v_2. Now the
line $v_1 v_2$ is negative and $v_2 v_3$ is positive. Since S has no 3-cycle with exactly one
negative line, the line $v_1 v_3$ must be negative. Similarly, $v_1 v_4$ must be negative, and in
general, all remaining points must be joined to v_1 by a negative line. In particular,
the line $v_1 v_k$ must be negative. But then the k-cycle has two negative lines, which is
a contradiction.

It is important to note two differences between *Theorem 1 and Theorem 2*, that
is, differences between clustering in a complete graph and in an incomplete graph.

First, in a complete clusterable graph, the plus-sets are unique. There is only
one way to form them. In some incomplete graphs (for example, a large graph with
only a handful of lines 'missing') the plus-sets will be unique. However, in many
incomplete graphs there is more than one acceptable way to form plus-sets. Thus
we distinguish between *clusters*, unique plus-sets, and plus-sets in general.

Putting it another way, a graph may lack clusters for two different reasons:
because it contains internal contradictions in the form of cycles with a single negative line and/or because it is incomplete in such a way as to make the plus-sets
ambiguous.

This notion leads to some thoughts on the dynamics of a social group. Substantive structural theories usually have dynamic implications, hypotheses to the
effect that structures will change toward greater conformity with the model (Flament,
1963, pp. 107–24). One obvious sociological hypothesis is that relationships which
lie on a cycle with a single negative line will tend to change in such a fashion as to
make the graph clusterable. If we think of such a process as 'reducing structural
strain', we can posit an analogous process in incomplete clusterable graphs: 'structural growth'.

Now consider a group of people who are initially all strangers to one another. Let us assume that sentiments will form over time in such a way that the structure always has a clustering. We note in passing that the initial structure satisfies this requirement since a signed graph with no lines has a clustering. Let us assume, further, that sentiments once established remain unchanged. If we know the structure at a given time, can we predict the signs of new sentiments that subsequently develop? In other words, if S is the signed graph of the group at a given time and T is the signed graph of the same group at a later time, can we predict, on the basis of S, the signs of lines that are in T but not in S? The following corollary to *Theorem 1* gives conditions under which definite predictions can be made.

COROLLARY

Let S and T be clusterable signed graphs with the same set of points such that every line of S is in T, and let $v_i v_j$ be a line in T which is not in S.

(1) If v_i and v_j are joined by an all-positive path in S, then $v_i v_j$ is positive.
(2) If v_i and v_j are joined by a path with exactly one negative line, then $v_i v_j$ is negative.
(3) Otherwise, $v_i v_j$ may be either positive or negative.

This corollary follows immediately from *Theorem 1*. The requirement that T have no cycle with exactly one negative line establishes statements (1) and (2). The same requirement for S guarantees that the conditions given in (1) and (2) cannot both hold for the same pair of points. If neither of these holds, all paths joining v_i and v_j in S have at least two negative lines and $v_i v_j$ may be either positive or negative, establishing statement (3).

Consider a sentimental structure S having two people, v_i and v_j, who at a given time neither like nor dislike each other. We may think of them as being in a potential relationship (v_i, v_j). Now if in the future v_i and v_j convert this potential relationship into an actual one, we may be able to predict its sign from the nature of S under the assumption of clustering. If the predicted sign is positive or negative, let us call the relationship (v_i, v_j) *latently positive* or *latently negative*, respectively. Otherwise, (v_i, v_j) is said to be *structurally free*.

The notion may be further expanded by assuming a graph which is neither complete nor perfectly clusterable. Its pair relationships may be classified as follows.

Pairs connected by a positive or negative line are: (1) *strained* if the line lies on a cycle with exactly one negative line; (2) *reinforced* if a reversal in sign would create a cycle with exactly one negative line; or (3) *free* if neither strained nor reinforced. Pairs which are not joined by a line are (4) *latently positive or negative* if their sign can be predicted from the corollary; (5) *latently strained* if either a positive or negative line would create a cycle with a single negative line, or (6) *free* if neither latently positive nor negative nor strained.

This leads to the omnibus hypothesis that compared with free lines of the same original value (positive, negative, or null): (1) reinforced lines will tend to remain the same; (2) latently positive or negative lines tend to shift to the appropriate sign; (3) strained lines will tend to shift in sign or become null; and (4) latently strained lines will tend to remain null.[3]

A second difference between the two theorems must be noted. Statements (3)

3. In sociological terms, (4) is the cross-pressure hypothesis (cf. Davis, 1963, pp. 450-1).

and (4) in the corollary, which are equivalent for complete graphs, are not equivalent for incomplete graphs.

In complete graphs clusterability may be determined by inspection of the 3-cycles, a notion akin to Flament's proof that a complete graph is *balanced* if and only if all its triangles are balanced (Flament, 1963, p. 94) and analogous to the theorem that a tournament is transitive if and only if each triple is transitive (Harary, Norman, & Cartwright, 1965, p. 298). In a 3-cycle each pair is connected by a line and also by a path of length 2. In 3-cycles with a single negative line there is a contradiction between the direct and indirect links for each pair. The pair connected by the negative line are also connected by an all-positive path, a contradiction; while the two pairs connected by direct lines are also connected by paths with a single negative line, also a contradiction. In sociological terms such situations may be interpreted as ones where a pair's direct relationship is inconsistent with that implied by their relationships with a third party.

In incomplete graphs, the absence of triangles with a single negative line is a necessary, but not sufficient condition for clusterability, because even if all triangles meet the criterion there may be longer cycles with a single negative line. Graphs in which all 3-cycles meet the criterion, while some longer cycles do not, may be interpreted as cases of *limited clusterability*, analogous to limited balance (Harary, Norman, & Cartwright, 1965, p. 352). In *Figure 1*, S_2 is an example of limited clusterability.

DISCUSSION

Clustering and balance. A clusterable graph and a balanced graph are related as follows: All balanced graphs are clusterable (a graph with even numbers of negative lines in all its cycles cannot have any cycles with a single negative line); while clusterable graphs may or may not be balanced, depending on the number of disjoint subsets of points.

This asymmetry has a number of substantive implications. First, it enables one to connect the social psychological development of balance theory with sociological hypotheses about subgroup formation. For example, in *The human group*, Homans (1950, p. 113) writes, 'the liking of friends within a group carries with it some dislike of outsiders. The greater the inward solidarity, the greater the outward hostility.' In the present context Homans is postulating tendencies toward clustering, but not necessarily toward balance.

Second, the difference between the two structural principles raises the following question for the theoretician: Because 'consistency' (tendencies toward positive relationships within groups and negative ones between groups) is a necessary but not sufficient condition for polarization, what are the principles which explain why some groups polarize and others divide into multiple cliques? We pose the question and do not pretend to answer it, but the following observations may be relevant.

In the case of symmetrical sentiments (friends and enemies) the Cartwright and Harary balance theorem, as Rapoport (1963, p. 541) and others have noted, generates a number of aphorisms regarding friends and enemies.

(1) A friend of a friend will be a friend, not an enemy.
(2) An enemy of a friend will be an enemy, not a friend.

(3) A friend of an enemy will be an enemy, not a friend.
(4) An enemy of an enemy will be a friend.

It can be shown that the first three propositions will continue to hold under the clustering theorems. The fourth, however, depends on the number of subsets. It holds in the case of two subsets, but not where there are three or more subsets. Putting it another way, group polarization (in a complete graph) is formally identical with clustering plus a tendency for those with a common enemy to become friends, i.e. *coalition formation.*

Third, the clustering theorem gives some perspective on the problem of 'all-negative triangles'. Under the balance theorem, triangles with three negative sides are impossible. Heider himself, however, writes (1958, p. 206), 'If two negative relations are given, balance can be obtained *either* when the third relationship is positive or when it is negative, though there appears to be a preference for the positive alternative.' This is equivalent to two hypotheses: a strong tendency toward clustering and among the clustered states a less strong tendency toward balance.

Clustering and connectedness. A rather different interpretation of clustering is suggested by Bott's well-known study, *Family and social network* (1957, pp. 59–60). She writes:

'Although all the research families belonged to networks . . . there was considerable variation in the "*connectedness*" of their networks. By connectedness I mean the extent to which the people known by a family know and meet one another independently of the family. . . . When many of the people a person knows interact with one another . . . the person's network is close-knit.'

Consider a signed graph S constructed in the following way: We let the points of S represent the families of a community, and we join two points by a positive line if the corresponding families know each other and by a negative line otherwise. Clearly, S is complete. Let us assume that this acquaintance network satisfies the extreme degree of 'connectedness' suggested by Bott—namely, every two families known by a third family know each other. In other words, S contains no 3-cycle with exactly one negative line. By *Theorem 2*, S is clusterable, and the families of the community can be partitioned uniquely into subgroups all of whose members know each other and none of whom know anyone outside the subgroup. Moreover, there will be more than one such subgroup except when everyone in the community knows everyone else. Thus unless one is willing to assume extremely large acquaintance volumes, a social system which is highly 'connected' must be one consisting of a number of relatively small, completely connected subgroups that are isolated from one another; a formulation which appears to fit Bott's description of some of the working class neighbourhoods in her study.

Such a social system is somewhat paradoxical. (1) At the level of the individual, the system is highly connected, for he lies at the center of a dense network of direct and indirect social relationships. (2) At the level of the total system it is highly disconnected, for there are many pairs who have neither direct nor indirect relationships. (3) It is one in which individuals tend to have many ties to a few people and few or no ties to many others.

SUMMARY

Building from the Cartwright and Harary balance theorem, which treats structures that are polarized into two groups, we introduced a new concept, clusterability or division into two or more groups, and a theorem stating the necessary and sufficient condition for it: a signed graph is clusterable if and only if it contains no cycle with exactly one negative line.

When comparing clustering with balance we noted that the idea of clustering helps to build a bridge between social psychological developments in balance theory and sociological theories of subgroup formation. At the same time, it raises a new question: when will a group polarize? A review of aphorisms associated with balance theory suggested that theories of coalition formation may be useful in answer to the question. We also noted that the new theorem may be of use in interpreting Heider's comments on all-negative triangles.

A second theorem was presented showing that a complete graph is clusterable if none of its 3-cycles (triangles) has a single negative line. A comparison of the two theorems led to the notion of *latent, strained, reinforced,* and *free* social relationships. This in turn led to a set of hypotheses about the dynamics of group structures.

Finally, in a different substantive context, we pointed out some formal analogies between clustering and connectedness in a graph. It was shown that a number of the concepts in Bott (1957) can be reinterpreted in terms of clusterability.

REFERENCES

BOTT, E. (1957). *Family and social network*. London: Tavistock Publications.

CARTWRIGHT, D. & HARARY, F. (1956). Structural balance: a generalization of Heider's theory. *Psychol. rev.* **63**, 277–92.

DAVIS, J. (1963). Structural balance, mechanical solidarity, and interpersonal relations. *Amer. J. sociol.* **68**, 444–62.

FLAMENT, C. (1963), *Applications of graph theory to group structure*. Englewood Cliffs, N.J.: Prentice-Hall.

HARARY, F. (1955–6). On the notion of balance of a signed graph. *Mich. math. J.* **2**, 143–6.

HARARY, F., NORMAN, R. & CARTWRIGHT, D. (1965). *Structural models*. New York: Wiley.

HEIDER, F. (1958). *The psychology of interpersonal relations*. New York: Wiley.

HOMANS, G. (1950). *The human group*. New York: Harcourt, Brace.

RAPOPORT, A. (1963). Mathematical models of social interaction. In R. Luce, R. Bush and E. Galanter (Eds.), *Handbook of mathematical psychology*, Vol. II. New York: Wiley, pp. 493–579.

BIOGRAPHICAL NOTE

JAMES A. DAVIS is Associate Professor, Department of Sociology, University of Chicago, and a Senior Study Director, National Opinion Research Center. He received his Ph.D. in sociology in 1955 from Harvard University and has been a visiting professor at the University of Washington, Seattle, and Johns Hopkins University.

From John R. P. French, Jr., *Psychological Review 63*, 181-194 (1956), copyright by the American Psychological Association, reprinted by permission.

A FORMAL THEORY OF SOCIAL POWER

JOHN R. P. FRENCH, JR.

Research Center for Group Dynamics, University of Michigan

This formal theory is a small part of the later stages of a program of empirical research on social influence.[1] It tries to integrate previous findings into a logically consistent theory from which one can derive testable hypotheses to guide future research.[2] The more specific purpose of the theory is to explore the extent to which the influence process in groups can be explained in terms of patterns of interpersonal relations.

In discussing the effects of the majority on conformity by the individual deviate, Asch states, "The effects obtained are not the result of a summation of influences proceeding from each member of the group; it is necessary to conceive the results as being relationally determined" (15, p. 186). Both Heider (18) and Newcomb (29) have treated patterns of opinion and of interpersonal relations as a single system of relations, though they have discussed only two-person groups. The present theory reduces the process of influence in *N*-person groups to a summation of interpersonal influences which takes into account three complex patterns of relations: (*a*) the power relations among members of the group, (*b*) the communication networks or patterns of interaction in the group, and (*c*) the relations among opinions within the group. Thus propositions which have been con-

ceptualized at the group level (e.g., that the strength of group standards increases with increasing cohesiveness of the group) are deduced from concepts at the interpersonal level.

The deductive power and the internal consistency of a mathematical model stem from a set of explicit definitions and postulates stated with enough precision so that one can apply the rules of logic. But the construction of theory by coordinating mathematical definitions and postulates to psychological constructs and assumptions leads to a dilemma: the very precision which gives power to the theory also tends to oversimplify it. For reasons of mathematical convenience one tends to make simple assumptions which so restrict the theory that it may seem unrealistic compared to the complexity observed in social behavior. Game theory, for example, describes certain aspects of how "the rational economic man" ought to behave, but actual economic behavior often departs widely from this simple ideal (20).

The present theory deals with this dilemma partly by utilizing a kind of mathematics, the theory of directed graphs, which does not require the making of precise quantitative assumptions about empirical variables.[3] In addition, the basic concepts and postulates

[1] The work reported in this paper was financed in part by a grant from the Rockefeller Foundation and by a contract with the Group Psychology Branch of the Office of Naval Research.

[2] Similar current attempts to construct mathematical theories of social influence include unpublished papers by Ardie Lubin, by Harold Guetzkow and Herbert Simon, and by Solomon Goldberg.

[3] The theory of directed graphs, which is an extension of graph theory (16), has been studied by Frank Harary and Robert Norman with a view toward utilization by social scientists. A publication of this work is planned for the near future (17). The author is indebted to these mathematicians for specific help in proving the theorems of this theory as well as for their work on the theory of digraphs upon which it is based.

of this theory were chosen to conform to the results of experiments on social influence. Frequently, however, our present knowledge was not adequate for making these choices in precise detail. At these points we attempted to choose postulates which would be essentially correct in their main outlines even though some details would have to be changed as new empirical knowledge accumulates. It is not surprising, therefore, that many of the theorems are quite similar to previous findings about influence on opinions and attitudes, even though no research has been done specifically to test this theory. Nevertheless we have intentionally oversimplified the process of social influence by omitting many important determinants and by making very restrictive assumptions about others. It seemed wise to start by examining the implications of a small number of postulates before proceeding to more complex theories.

The Model

Following the theory of quasi-stationary equilibria of Lewin (23), changes in opinion, attitude, or judgment are conceptualized in terms of forces operating along a unidimensional continuum (5, 12). Social influences are coordinated to force fields induced by person A on person B; and the strength of these forces is assumed to vary with the power of A over B. The potential force field corresponding to this power relation will be actualized only if A communicates to B or interacts with him. When A expresses his opinion or argues for it in a way that influences B, then the force field operating on B has a central position corresponding to A's position along the continuum of opinion. All the forces operating on B are directed toward this central position, so B will tend to change his opinion in a direction which brings him closer to A. Similarly, other members, C, D, E, etc., who communicate

to B may set up force fields on him with central positions corresponding to their own opinions. The actual changes in B's opinion will be in accordance with the resultant force from all these induced forces plus a force corresponding to his own resistance.

In order to derive the exact amount of influence that each member will have on the opinion of every other, let us assume that we are dealing with a unidimensional continuum of opinion which can be measured with a ratio scale. We might think, for example, of the classic experiment on social norms by Sherif (32), where the members of the group were asked to state their opinions about how many inches the light moved as they viewed the autokinetic effect. We shall denote the members of the group by A, B, C, . . . and their initial opinions by a, b, c, . . . respectively, where a is the distance of A's opinion from the zero point on the scale. The abscissa of Fig. 1 shows such a scale of opinion

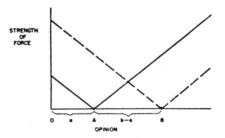

STRENGTH
OF
FORCE

o   a   A   b—a   B
OPINION

Fig. 1. The force fields influencing opinion.

together with the initial opinions of A and B. The ordinate indicates the strength of the forces. The gradient of forces around A represents the forces he can induce on B to agree with his opinion, while the gradient of forces around B represent his tendency to resist changing his opinion. Where these two gradients intersect, a distance of $\frac{1}{2}(a + b)$ from the origin, there is an equilibrium point where the two forces are equal in strength and opposite in direction. At

36

all points to the right of this equilibrium the forces induced by *A* are stronger than *B*'s resistance, so *B* will move toward the point of equilibrium. Conversely, at all points to the left of the equilibrium, *B*'s resistance forces are stronger than *A*'s inductions, so *B* will still move toward the point of equilibrium. Similar calculations of the resultant force and consequent changes of opinion can be made for *A* and for groups with any number of members by placing all members on the same scale and by assuming that the gradient of forces around each member represents both forces he can induce on others and forces he can set up as resistance against others.

The process of influence in a group takes place gradually over a period of time. As one member changes his position and begins to influence others toward his new position, the force fields corresponding to his influence will also shift their central positions. It will be convenient, therefore, to divide the influence process into a sequence of units defined in terms of opinion change rather than in terms of physical time. A *unit* is defined as the time required for all members who are being influenced to shift their opinions to the point of equilibrium of all the forces operating at the beginning of that unit. At the end of the unit, after this shift has taken place, we assume that the members now start to argue for their new opinions. It should be noted that this definition implies that all members respond at the same rate to the forces impinging on them. One possible operational definition of a unit might be a single trial in an experiment such as Sherif's.

This conception of influence as a process over time implies a distinction between direct and indirect influence. In a typical organization the president usually influences indirectly a person at the bottom of the chain of command through orders which are handed down through several subordinates. *Direct influence* is exerted on another person by direct communication which is not channelled through a third person. *Indirect influence* is exerted on another through the medium of one or more other persons. Therefore the direct influence of *A* on *B* always occurs during the same unit, whereas indirect influence requires two or more units. For example, *A* influences *B* directly during the first unit, and *B* influences *C* toward his new opinion during the second unit. Thus *A* has indirectly influenced *C* by transmitting his opinion via *B*. In this model, the power structure and the communication channels of the group are translated into a process of influence over time. In the first unit any member, *A*, influences only those recipients of his communication over whom he has direct power; in the second unit *A*'s influence is also transmitted to all those over whom these intermediaries have power; in the third unit *A*'s influence is transmitted to those who are three steps removed from him in the power structure, etc.

The Postulates

Three main postulates are involved in this model. The first is concerned with interpersonal power. The definition of *power* used in this postulate is the same as that given by Cartwright (6): the power of *A* over *B* (with respect to a given opinion) is equal to the maximum force which *A* can induce on *B* minus the maximum resisting force which *B* can mobilize in the opposite direction.

The *basis* of interpersonal power is defined as the more or less enduring relationship between *A* and *B* which gives rise to the power. French and Raven (in an unpublished manuscript) have discussed five bases: *attraction power* based on *B*'s liking for *A*, *expert power* based on B's perception that A has superior knowledge and information, *reward power* based on A's ability to mediate rewards for B, *coercive power* based on A's ability to mediate punishments for B, and *legitimate power* based on B's belief that A has a right to prescribe his behavior or opinions. Any basis of power can vary in strength: there may be variations in how much B likes A, in how much B respects A's expertness, etc. Postulate 1 is general enough to refer to all bases of social power.

Postulate 1. For any given discrepancy of opinion between A and B, the strength of the resultant force which an inducer A can exert on an inducee B, in the direction of agreeing with A's opinion, is proportional to the strength of the bases of power of A over B.

Attraction as a basis for interpersonal influence has been demonstrated in experiments by Back (2) and by French and Snyder (13), and in field studies by Lippitt, Polansky, and Rosen (25). Expertness as a basis for interpersonal power has been demonstrated in the latter two studies as well as in many others (19, 27, 28). In unpublished experiments French and Raven and French, Levinger, and Morrison have demonstrated that legitimacy and the ability to punish are bases for social power. Heider (18) and Newcomb (29) state their theories in terms of "positive relations," a more general conception which combines several types of power. In most real groups the power relations probably do combine several of the bases discussed here and others too. Postulate 1 refers to all of these bases combined.

Resistance, as a part of the social power discussed in Postulate 1, has not been treated separately nor in detail in this model. In a further development it might be coordinated to such factors as "certainty of own opinion" (13), or as

Kelman (21) and Mausner (26) call it, "prior reinforcement," and to various personality characteristics such as rigidity and authoritarianism (8).

Postulate 2. The strength of the force which an inducer A exerts on an inducee B, in the direction of agreeing with A's opinion, is proportional to the size of the discrepancy between their opinions.

This postulate combines two effects which have been demonstrated in previous research. (*a*) More influence is attempted toward the member who is more discrepant (10, 11, 30). These studies also show, however, that this effect holds only under conditions where the inducee is not rejected. Too great a deviation leads to changes in the attraction power structure of the group and hence to changes in the effects implied by Postulate 1. (*b*) If the amount of influence attempted is held constant, the amount of change in the inducee increases with increasing size of discrepancy. For this latter relation, French and Gyr (12) report correlations of .77, .62, .65, and .83 in different experimental groups. Goldberg (14) also reports a strong tendency for the amount of change to increase with increasing discrepancy, with the inducee moving 30 per cent of the way toward the inducer for discrepancies of all sizes. In a subsequent unpublished theoretical paper,[4] Goldberg also assumes that change in opinion is a direct function of discrepancy until the inducee rejects the credibility (expert power) of the inducer, after which it becomes an inverse function of discrepancy. Again the data support Postulate 2 within the range where the expert power structure of the group is not changed.

Postulate 2 is represented in Fig. 1 by the two increasing gradients of forces

[4] S. C. Goldberg, Some cognitive aspects of social influence: a hypothesis. (Mimeographed.)

around A's opinion and around B's opinion. The two gradients are assumed to be linear, though the evidence cited above would suggest that they are curvilinear. We have made the more convenient assumption because it appears to be true as a first approximation and because it seems to be possible to revise the postulate later, if subsequent empirical data do show curvilinearity, with only minor quantitative changes in the theorems.

Postulate 3. In one unit, each person who is being influenced will change his opinion until he reaches the equilibrium point where the resultant force (of the forces induced by other members at the beginning of the unit and the resisting force corresponding to his own resistance to change) is equal to zero.

Postulate 3 is an application of a basic assumption of Lewin (22) that locomotion or restructuring will take place in the direction of the resultant force whenever that force is greater than zero. Though consistent with a great many empirical studies, this assumption is close to a conceptual definition which cannot be directly tested.

THEOREMS

For lack of space, no attempt will be made to state all the theorems which have been proven nor to give the formal proofs of those presented. Instead we will select some representative theorems and indicate informally the nature of the derivations. In making empirical predictions from these theorems, this theory, like any other, must always assume "other things being equal," including all extrasystem influences and the many factors within the group which are not part of the theory.

The Effects of the Power Structure of the Group

This section presents some theorems concerning the effects of the power structure of the group on the influence process and its outcome. These theorems illustrate how the present theory explains a well known proposition about groups in terms of concepts about interpersonal relations.

This proposition—that the strength of group standards increases with increasing cohesiveness of the group—has been substantiated in several studies (2, 4, 9, 30, 31). A group standard has been defined conceptually as group-induced pressures toward uniformity of behavior or belief, and it may be measured by the degree of conformity of members produced by these pressures. *Cohesiveness* has been defined conceptually as the resultant forces on members to belong to the group, but it has been operationalized in many of these experiments as the attraction of members for one another (7, 24). Festinger, Schachter, and Back (9) have shown that the hypothesized relation is stronger when cohesiveness is operationalized in a way which takes account of the pattern of the sociometric structure instead of a simple summation of choices. But each sociometric choice measuring the attraction of member B toward member A is, according to Postulate 1, a basis for A's power over B. Thus the sociogram of a group can be transformed into the attraction power structure of the group by simply reversing the direction of each arrow. The attraction power structure of the group is a special type of power structure, and hence it is treated in these theorems about power structure and trends toward uniformity of opinion within the group.

The power structure of a group may be represented conceptually in terms of the mathematical theory of directed graphs, called "digraphs." A digraph is a finite set of points A, B, C, . . . and a subset of the directed lines $\overrightarrow{AB}$, $\overrightarrow{BA}$, $\overrightarrow{AC}$, $\overrightarrow{CA}$, $\overrightarrow{BC}$, $\overrightarrow{CB}$, . . . between distinct points. In representing power structures as digraphs, we shall coordinate points to members and directed lines to power relations between members. In this coordination we shall make only relatively crude distinctions in differences of power: if "A has power over B," there is a directed line $\vec{AB}$ in the digraph representing the power structure of the group; if "A does not have power over B," there is no such line.

Various properties of digraphs may be used to characterize power structures of groups. We shall be concerned here primarily with the "degree of connectedness" of power structures. In order to discuss this property we need two definitions: *complete digraph* and *directed path*. A digraph is complete if there exists a directed line from each point to every other point. A power structure would be complete, then, if each member had power over each other member. If we assume that when A chooses B sociometrically B has power over A, then it follows that when every member of a group chooses every other member, the digraph representing the power structure of the group will be complete (e.g., No. 5 in Fig. 2). A *directed path* is a collection of distinct points $A, B, C, \ldots$, together with the lines $\vec{AB}, \vec{BC}, \ldots$ If in the power structure of a group there is a directed path from A to C, it follows that A can exert influence on C even though A may not have direct power over C (there must be a sequence of directed lines originating at A and going to C even though there is no line $\vec{AC}$).

In their work on digraphs Harary and Norman (17) have defined four degrees of connectedness. Their definitions are as follows: (*a*) A digraph is *strongly connected* (or *strong*) if for every pair of distinct points, A and B, there exists a directed path from A to B *and* a directed path from B to A. It follows

that every complete digraph is strong, but not every strong digraph is complete. (*b*) A digraph is *unilaterally connected* (or *unilateral*) if for every pair of points, A and B, there is a directed path from A to B *or* from B to A. (*c*) A digraph is *weakly connected* (or *weak*) if it is impossible to separate the points of the digraph into two classes such that no line of the digraph has one end point in one class and the other end point in the other class. Thus, for every possible separation of all of the points of a weak digraph into two disjoint, nonempty classes, there must be at least one line having one end point in one class and the other end point in the other class. (*d*) A digraph is *disconnected* if it is not weak. Thus a disconnected digraph may be separated into two (or more) disjoint classes of points such that no line goes from one class to the other. From these definitions it is clear that all strong digraphs are unilaterally and weakly connected and that all unilateral digraphs are weakly connected. It is also clear that all weak digraphs are *not* strongly connected. For this reason it is useful to define a digraph as *strictly unilateral* if it is unilateral but not strong, and to define a digraph as *strictly weak* if it is weak but not unilateral. In our discussion here, when we speak of unilateral or weak digraphs we shall mean "strictly unilateral" and "strictly weak."

In groups where each member communicates to all others over whom he has direct power during every unit of the influence process, the amount of uniformity achieved and the speed of achieving it tend to vary with the degrees of connectedness of the power structure, except that no differences were proved for weak vs. disconnected digraphs.

The effect is illustrated in Fig. 2, and generalized later in the first four theo-

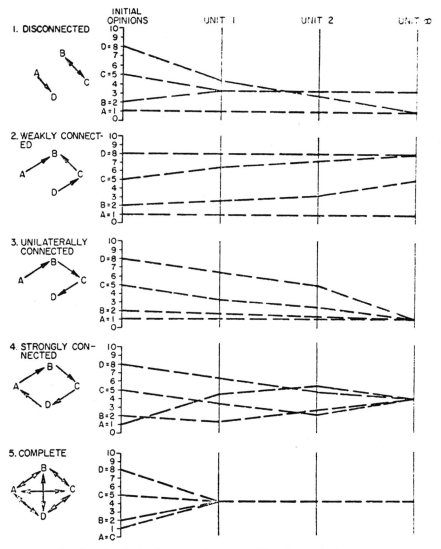

FIG. 2. The effects of connectedness on opinion changes in the group.

rems. In Fig. 2 five different types of structures (complete, strong, unilateral, weak, and disconnected) are illustrated by digraphs of four-person groups. To the right of each structure are curves showing some of the theoretically predicted changes of opinion. The ordinate gives the scale of opinion and, at the left, the initial opinion of members

A, *B*, *C*, and *D*. The line labeled "Unit 1" gives the distribution of opinion after the first unit: the line labeled "Unit 2" gives the distribution of opinion after the second unit; and the line labeled "Unit ∞" gives the equilibrium of opinions reached in an infinite number of units.

The disconnected structure is composed of two cliques, AD and BC. Between these two cliques there are no paths of influence, regardless of direction. Consequently neither clique can influence the other, and each will eventually end up with a different opinion. Within the AD clique, influence is all in one direction, so A will eventually swing D over to his opinion. Since D only moves half-way in each unit, however, he will require an infinite number of units to move all the way. Accordingly the dotted lines show D's opinion converging to A's at infinity while A's opinion remains unchanged. Within the BC clique, influence is mutual, so in the first unit B will influence C to move half-way from 5 to 2 on the opinion scale, and likewise C will influence B to move half-way from 2 to 5. Therefore both B and C will arrive at $3\frac{1}{2}$ on the opinion scale in the first unit and will remain in agreement thereafter.

The weakly connected structure is more highly connected but still does not result in unanimous agreement. In this case there is no directed path, for example, between A and D, so neither can influence the other.

The unilaterally connected structure has a directed path in at least one direction between every possible pair of points. Because it has a higher degree of connectedness, it shows more convergence of opinion.

The strongly connected structure has directed paths in both directions between every possible pair of points. In this example the strongly connected digraph is a cycle, yielding a final common opinion which reflects more equal influence of all members.

The completely connected structure has direct, one-step paths in both directions between the members of every possible pair. It converges in only one unit to a final common opinion.

Theorem 1. For all possible patterns of initial opinion, in a completely con-

nected power structure the opinions of all members will reach a common equilibrium level equal to the arithmetic mean of the initial opinions of all the members, and this final common opinion will be reached in one unit.

Under these conditions where the power and the resistance of all members is equal, we have already illustrated in Fig. 1 that the new opinion of A is equal to $\frac{1}{2}(a + b)$, i.e., the arithmetic mean of the opinions of both members. B's opinion at the end of the first unit b_1 is also equal to $\frac{1}{2}(a + b)$, according to Postulates 2 and 3. Thus this two-person group reaches agreement in one step. The proof of Theorem 1 for an N-person group is a simple extension of this example.

Theorem 2. In an N-person cycle (which is a strongly connected group) the members will reach a final common opinion at the arithmetic mean, $(1/N)(a + b + c + . . .)$, in an infinite number of units.

If A has power over B, then $b_1 = \frac{1}{2}(a + b)$ and b_2, the opinion of B at the end of the second unit, $= \frac{1}{2}(a_1 + b_1)$. In general, B's opinion at the end of any unit will be half-way between his own and A's opinion at the beginning of the unit; so the general difference equation describing B's change of opinion in any unit, n, is: $b_n = \frac{1}{2}(a_{n-1} + b_{n-1})$. Solving these general difference equations for all members constitutes a proof of Theorem 2.

Theorem 3. In a unilaterally connected group the opinions of all members will converge to a final common opinion in an infinite number of steps.

It is an obvious theorem of digraph theory that no strictly unilateral digraph can have more than one point of input zero, i.e., with no directed lines leading to it (because then these two or more points could not have a directed path between them—which violates the definition of a unilateral digraph). It follows that, during every unit, at least one of the two members at the extremes of the range of opinion will be subject to the power of another and will move toward the center, thus restricting the range of opinion still further. Eventually, therefore, all members will arrive at the same opinion. If there is one person in the group with input zero, then all members will eventually agree with his initial opinion, for he will influence the others but no one will influence him.

Theorem 4. In a weakly connected group the members will not reach common agreement except under special conditions in the distribution of initial opinions.

A (strictly) weak digraph contains at least one pair of points with no directed path between them. Thus there are at least two members who cannot influence each other either directly or indirectly.

The disconnected group. When the final equilibrium has been reached, a disconnected group will tend to have at least as many different opinions as there are cliques (i.e., disjoint classes of members), because no clique can influence any other. If all the cliques are themselves either completely connected, strongly connected, or unilaterally connected, it follows from Theorems 1, 2, and 3 that there will be uniformity of final opinions within each clique; but there will be differences among them except under special conditions in the distribution of initial opinion.

Summarizing the theorems illustrated in Fig. 2, we can say that there is a "funnelling effect," a tendency for the opinions of individuals to converge toward one another, and the strength of this tendency increases with increasing connectedness in the power structure of the group. Since the power structure includes the special case of the attraction power of the group, we have a more general group of theorems consistent

with the finding that the strength of group standards is determined by the cohesiveness of the group. Additionally the model predicts the exact level of the group standard as well as the precise degree of conformity at each unit. Thus we have rigorously derived a more differentiated statement of the empirically well-established relation between cohesiveness and group standards.

So far we have considered only all-or-none variations in the power of *A* over *B*; now we will illustrate the effect of continuous variation.

Theorem 5. The greater the bases of power of *A* over *B* (*B*'s attraction to *A*, *B*'s acceptance of *A* as an expert, etc.), the more influence *A* will have on *B* and subsequently on any other person *P* for whom there exists a directed path from *B* to *P*.

According to Postulates 1 and 3, increases in the basis of power of *A* over *B* will increase the strength of the resultant force exerted by *A* on *B* and therefore the amount of change produced in *B*. Similarly in subsequent units this influence will be transmitted, though in a weakened form, from *B* to *P*.

The Effects of Communication Patterns

In the preceding section we have dealt with the restricted case of groups of persons whose power is always utilized in every unit.[5] Earlier we noted that the head of an organization may not communicate to all those over whom he has direct power but will instead follow the established channels of communication. Likewise in a face-to-face group a member may remain silent or may attempt to influence some but not

[5] It is probable that *B* will respond partly to the *relationships* among successive influence attempts by *A*, for example to the consistency among his various arguments or to the simple fact of too much reiteration of the same influence attempt; these factors are omitted from the present model.

others over whom he has power. These patterns of interaction often become stabilized so that they may be treated as more or less consistent channels of communication. It is also clear that the strength of influence attempted can vary continuously, but we shall here treat the communication from A to B as an all-or-none variable so that we can utilize digraph theory.

Now if we reverse the conditions of Theorems 1 through 4 and consider only completely connected power structures with variations in the degree of connectedness of the communication channels, we can apply the same four theorems and proofs. For example:

Theorem 1a. For all possible patterns of initial opinion, in a completely connected communication network, the opinions of all members will converge to a common equilibrium level equal to the arithmetic mean of the initial opinions of all the members; and this final common opinion will be reached in one unit.

Similarly, theorems analogous to 2, 3, and 4 can be stated for strong, unilateral, and weak communication networks, respectively. All possible networks in experiments of the Bavelas type (3) are included in these theorems.

Even where stable communication channels do not exist, this model may be applied provided the interaction pattern is specified for each unit. Consider a strongly connected cycle of three persons. Theorem 2 states that opinions in this group will converge to a final common opinion equal to $\frac{1}{3}(a + b + c)$. In Theorem 6 we assume a particular communication pattern: A exerts influence in the first unit, B and C exert influence in the second unit, A exerts influence in the third unit, B and C in the fourth unit, and so on.

Theorem 6. In a group where the power structure is a three-person cycle in which A has power over B, B has power over C, and C has power over A, and the communication pattern is A, BC, A, BC, . . . , the final common opinion in the group equals $\frac{1}{5}(2a + b + 2c)$.

We note that a change in the interaction pattern changes the outcome considerably. Furthermore B and C no longer have equal influence, even though they have equal interaction patterns and similar positions in the power structure; it is the interaction of these two factors which produces the difference. A has more influence than B because he comes first in the sequence of interaction, but C has more influence than B because he has direct power over A whereas B's power over A is indirect. Intuitively it would appear that the "primacy effect" shown in this theorem can be generalized: the sooner a person speaks the more influence he will have.

The Effects of Patterns of Opinion

In an experiment like Sherif's, each member communicates to every other and the members probably have relatively equal power. In such a completely connected power structure with completely connected communication channels, what happens to the opinion of a single deviate member?

Theorem 7. The amount of change of the deviate toward the opinions of the majority is proportional to the sum of the deviations of all other members from the deviate.

By Theorem 1 the amount of change by the deviate D equals $d_1 - d$ which is equal to $1/N(d + a + b + c + . . .) - d$. Thus the more members in the group the more they will influence the deviate. Also the larger each deviation, the more D will change. Though these predictions are generally congruent with Asch's findings, they probably do not agree in detail (1, 15). However, the conditions of Asch's experiment do not fit the model very well.

44

Leadership

To a large extent leadership consists of a member's ability to influence others both directly and indirectly by virtue of his position in the power structure, including the structure of legitimate authority. Thus leadership may be distributed among many members or concentrated in a few; the pattern of leadership is a distribution which describes the whole group rather than an attribute of single individuals. Figure 2 illustrates the dependence of influence on the total structure of the group.

Compare the influence of member *A* in the weakly connected group with the influence of member *A* in the unilaterally connected group. Both groups start out with the same distribution of opinion, and in both groups *A* has direct influence over only *B*. However, *A*'s influence is markedly different in the two cases; in the weakly connected group the opinions of others diverge more and more from his, whereas in the unilaterally connected group the opinion of all other members converges completely to *A*'s opinion.

The complete distribution of direct plus indirect leadership in a group with any power structure and any communication network may be calculated by matrix multiplication.[6] We may represent the power structure of the group as a matrix where each row shows the power applied to a member and each column shows the power exerted by a member. A *zero* in the cell corresponding to the *a*th row and the *b*th column shows that *B* does not have power over *A*, whereas a *one* in the cell corresponding to the *c*th row and the *d*th column shows that *D* does have power over *C*. Thus the number in a cell represents the number of directed lines from the

[6] See Harary and Norman (16) for a brief review of some related applications of matrix algebra to sociometric data.

person in that column to the person in that row (under the conditions assumed in this paper, always *one* or *zero*). If this matrix *M* is multiplied by itself, then the resulting squared matrix M^2 shows in each cell the number of sequences consisting of two directed lines between the person in the column and the person in the row. The cubed matrix M^3 shows the number of three-line sequences between each pair of persons. By raising the matrix to successively higher powers, we can thus determine the number of directed line sequences, of various lengths, from each member to every other. The matrix *M* gives the directed lines which will result in influence in the first unit; M^2 gives the two-line sequences through which influence will be exerted by the end of the second unit; M^3 gives the three-line sequences through which influence will be exerted by the end of the third unit; etc.

In order to apply this process to Group G in Fig. 3, we construct a matrix of opinion *M* where the columns *a, b, c, d* represent influence exerted by the initial opinions *a, b, c, d* of persons *A, B, C, D*, respectively. The rows represent the influence received by these opinions from all the opinions in the group. Thus the cell entries must show the amount by which an opinion is changed by another opinion during one unit; and these values are given by the coefficients in the right hand side of the general difference equations. For Group G these equations are:

$$a_n = a_{n-1}, \qquad (1)$$
$$b_n = \tfrac{1}{2}(a_{n-1} + b_{n-1}), \qquad (2)$$
$$c_n = \tfrac{1}{2}(a_{n-1} + c_{n-1}), \qquad (3)$$
$$d_n = \tfrac{1}{3}(b_{n-1} + c_{n-1} + d_{n-1}). \qquad (4)$$

The cell *a, a* has an entry of 1, indicating that in any unit *A*'s opinion is completely determined by his previous opinion; accordingly the remaining cells in

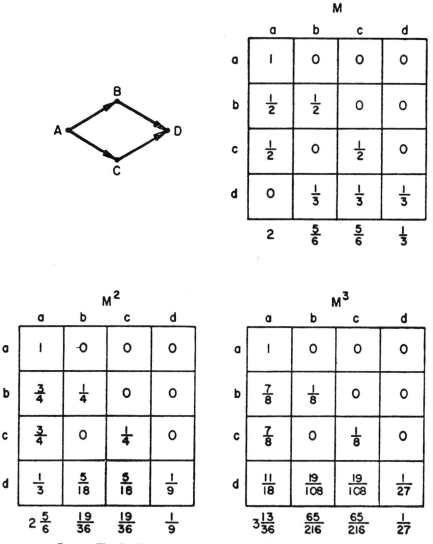

FIG. 3. The distribution of leadership in a weakly connected group.

row a have entries of zero, showing that opinions b, c, d do not influence a, since there are no directed paths from B, C, or D to A. Cells b, a, and b, b have entries of $\frac{1}{2}$ because b_n is a compromise half-way between the previous opinions of A and B, etc.

It will be noted that each row in M (and in M^2 and M^3) sums to 1 because

it represents the total opinion of a member, and the fractions along the row represent the proportion of that opinion determined by each person. The sum of a column in M, on the other hand, represents the total influence of a person's opinion during the first unit on the opinions of all members (including the influence of his initial opinion on his sec-

46

ond opinion—which we have called "resistance").

In M^2 the column sum shows the total influence of a person's initial opinion at the end of the second unit (including the changes produced in both the first and second units). Similarly M^3 shows the cumulative influence at the end of the third unit. The same procedure can obviously be extended to any number of units.

Thus the column totals of the successive powers of M give the distribution of leadership over time, as predicted by this theory. In Group G, we can see that A, the only member with input zero in the power structure, continuously increases his influence at the expense of the other members. B and C, having symmetrical positions in the structure, show the same curves of decreasing influence; but D, who is influenced by all other members, has the least influence.

CONCLUSIONS

This theory illustrates a way by which many complex phenomena about groups can be deduced from a few simple postulates about interpersonal relations. By the application of digraph theory we are able to treat in detail the *patterns of relations* whose importance has long been noted by the field theorists. Even if this treatment does not turn out to be empirically correct, it illustrates the need for some such conceptual and mathematical tools if we are to make progress toward the theoretical integration of psychology and sociology.

REFERENCES

1. ASCH, S. E. *Social psychology.* New York: Prentice-Hall, 1952.
2. BACK, K. W. Influence through social communication. *J. abnorm. soc. Psychol.,* 1951, 46, 9–23.
3. BAVELAS, A. Communication patterns in task-oriented groups. In D. Cartwright & A. Zander (Eds.), *Group dynamics: research and theory.* Evanston: Row, Peterson, 1953.
4. BERKOWITZ, L. Group standards, cohesiveness, and productivity. *Hum. Relat.,* 1955, 7, 509–519.
5. BIDDLE, B. J., FRENCH, J. R. P., JR., & MOORE, J. W. Some aspects of leadership in the small work group. *USAF Tech. Rep.* (Contract 33 [038]—14091), 1953.
6. CARTWRIGHT, D., et al. *Studies in social power.* Ann Arbor: Institute for Social Research, in press.
7. CARTWRIGHT, D., & ZANDER, A. *Group dynamics: research and theory.* Evanston: Row, Peterson, 1953.
8. CRUTCHFIELD, R. S. Conformity and character. *Amer. Psychologist,* 1955, 10, 191–198.
9. FESTINGER, L., SCHACHTER, S., & BACK, K. *Social pressures in informal groups.* New York: Harper, 1950.
10. FESTINGER, L., & THIBAUT, J. Interpersonal communication in small groups. *J. abnorm. soc. Psychol.,* 1951, 46, 92–99.
11. FESTINGER, L., GERARD, H. B., HYMOVITCH, B., KELLEY, H. H., & RAVEN, B. The influence process in the presence of extreme deviates. *Hum. Relat.,* 1952, 5, 327–346.
12. FRENCH, J. R. P., JR., & GYR, J. Influence and role conformity. In D. Cartwright et al., *Studies in social power.* Ann Arbor: Institute for Social Research, in press.
13. FRENCH, J. R. P., JR., & SNYDER, R. Leadership and interpersonal power. In D. Cartwright et al., *Studies in social power.* Ann Arbor: Institute for Social Research, in press.
14. GOLDBERG, S. Three situational determinants of conformity to social norms. *J. abnorm. soc. Psychol.,* 1954, 49, 325–329.
15. GUETZKOW, H. (Ed.) *Groups, leadership and men.* Pittsburgh: Carnegie Press, 1951.
16. HARARY, F., & NORMAN, R. Z. *Graph theory as a mathematical model in the social sciences.* Ann Arbor: Institute for Social Research, 1953.
17. HARARY, F., NORMAN, R. Z., & CARTWRIGHT, D. *Introduction to digraph theory for social scientists.* Ann Arbor: Institute for Social Research, in press.
18. HEIDER, F. Attitudes and cognitive organization. *J. Psychol.,* 1946, 21, 107–112.
19. HOVLAND, C., & WEISS, W. The influence of source credibility on communication

effectiveness. *Publ. Opin. Quart.*, 1952, **15**, 635–650.

20. KATONA, G. Rational behavior and economic behavior. *Psychol. Rev.*, 1953, **60**, 307–318.

21. KELMAN, H. C. Effects of success and failure on "suggestibility" in the autokinetic situation. *J. abnorm. soc. Psychol.*, 1950, **45**, 267–285.

22. LEWIN, K. The conceptual representation and measurement of psychological forces. *Contr. psychol. Theory*, 1938, **1**, 1–247.

23. LEWIN, K. *Field theory in social science.* New York: Harper, 1951.

24. LIBO, L. *The cohesiveness of groups.* Ann Arbor: Institute for Social Research, 1953.

25. LIPPITT, R., POLANSKY, N., & ROSEN, S. The dynamics of power. *Hum. Relat.*, 1952, **5**, 37–64.

26. MAUSNER, B. The effect of prior reinforcement on the interaction of observer pairs. *J. abnorm. soc. Psychol.*, 1954, **49**, 65–68.

27. MAUSNER, B. The effect of one partner's success or failure in a relevant task on the interaction of observer pairs. *J. abnorm. soc. Psychol.*, 1954, **49**, 557–560.

28. MOORE, H. T. The comparative influence of majority and expert opinion. *Amer. J. Psychol.*, 1921, **32**, 16–20.

29. NEWCOMB, T. M. An approach to the study of communicative acts. *Psychol. Rev.*, 1953, **60**, 393–404.

30. SCHACHTER, S. Deviation, rejection, and communication. *J. abnorm. soc. Psychol.*, 1951, **46**, 190–207.

31. SCHACHTER, S., ELLERTSON, N., McBRIDE, DOROTHY, & GREGORY, DORIS. An experimental study of cohesiveness and productivity. *Hum. Relat.*, 1951, **4**, 229–238.

32. SHERIF, M. A study of some social factors in perception. *Arch. Psychol.*, 1935, **27**, No. 187.

(Received March 23, 1955)

TRANSITIVITY IN STRUCTURAL MODELS OF SMALL GROUPS

PAUL W. HOLLAND
Harvard University

SAMUEL LEINHARDT
Carnegie-Mellon University

Our purpose here is to show how various deterministic models for the structure of interpersonal relations in small groups may all be viewed as special cases of a single model: namely, a transitive graph (t-graph). This exercise serves three purposes. First, the unified approach renders much of the mathematical discussion surrounding these various models quite transparent. Many of the arguments boil down to nothing more than defining certain equivalence relations and looking at the resulting equivalence classes. Second, our focus on the general model may stimulate the search for other useful specializations besides those indicated here. We discuss two ways of specializing the model—restrictions on edges and on triads—but other methods can be used. Third, we propose to adopt transitivity as the key structural concept in the

AUTHORS' NOTE: *We wish to acknowledge our indebtedness to Maureen Hallinan and Thomas Pullum for their helpful comments. Also, the continued support of James Davis and Harrison White has been especially beneficial. This research was supported by National Science Foundation Grant GS 2044X, and a Faculty Research Grant from the Social Science Research Council.*

analysis of sociometric data. Other models then become "transitivity plus something else." This provides a framework for the analysis of the fine structure of sociometric data.

Transitivity is not a new idea in the study of interpersonal relations. It is, for example, fundamental to Heider's balance theory. The association between transitivity and "balance" in positive interpersonal sentiment is explicit in several passages of Heider's writing. For example, he remarks that, "In the p-o-x triad, the case of three positive relations may be considered psychologically . . . transitive" (Heider, 1958: 206; compare also: Heider, 1946: 109). The formalization of Heider's theory into the model of "structural balance" by Cartwright and Harary (1956) is, in fact, a very special case of a transitive graph and does not deal with the full generality of Heider's conception as we interpret it here. While Heider was concerned with cognitive balance involving at most three entities, we are interested in the structural consequences of transitive graphs of actual interpersonal relations among many individuals.

Rapoport has used the notion of a "transitivity bias" in the analysis of sociometric data (e.g., Rapoport, 1963). His approach is a probabilistic rather than a deterministic one. Furthermore, for Rapoport, transitivity is only one of a variety of "biases" that affect the structural tendencies in a network; while we are concerned with seeing how far we can go with a deterministic transitive structure.

DESCRIPTION OF A GENERAL TRANSITIVE GRAPH

NOTATION

We adopt the following notation throughout the paper. The set, X, is composed of individuals x, y, z, u, v, w. . . . A binary relation, C, is defined on X. The notation, x C y, indicates that x expresses positive sentiment toward y, or, briefly, that "x chooses y." Equivalently, C defines a directed graph on the elements of X—a directed edge goes *from* x *to* y if and only if x C y. The relational and graph theoretical interpretations of C will be used interchangeably. Three other relations may be defined on X in terms of C. These are:

(1) x M y if and only if x C y *and* y C x.

(2) x A y if and only if x C y *and not* y C x.

(3) x N y if and only if *neither* x C y *nor* y C x.

The relations M, A, and N have simple sociometric interpretations: M denotes mutual choices; A denotes asymmetric or unreciprocated choices; and N denotes null or mutual non-choices. The relations M and A determine C and N so that we may take either (X, C) or (X, M, A) as the basic data and derive the other relations from them. If x M y then we say that x and y are joined by an M-edge. Similarly for A-edges and N-edges. If there are no pairs of *distinct* individuals for which x M y holds then we shall say that M is empty. The same goes for A and N. Finally, we shall have cause to refer to certain subsets of X (such as, M-cliques). These will be denoted by capital letters, U, V, W . . . , and relations defined on these subsets will be denoted by capital letters followed by a superscript asterisk, for example, A*, N*.

MATHEMATICAL DEFINITION OF A TRANSITIVE GRAPH

Definition 1: (X, C) *is a transitive graph (t-graph) if and only if for all* x, y, z *in* X:

(a) x C x

(b) *if* x C y *and* y C z *then* x C z.

For us, the condition (a), reflexivity, is merely a convention to avoid trivial exceptions and no substantive concern is given to it. In the graph theoretic interpretation, condition (a) implies that there are loops at each vertex, but we always ignore these loops. Note that a t-graph is closely related to the notion of a partial order which is a t-graph for which M is empty (i.e., for no distinct elements of X does x M y hold).

THE STRUCTURE OF A TRANSITIVE GRAPH[1]

Theorem 1 summarizes several easily proved properties of M, A, and N when (X, C) is a t-graph. Its proof is omitted.

Theorem 1: If (X, C) *is a t-graph, then for all* x, y, z *in* X:
(a) x M x
(b) x M y *implies that* y M x
(c) x M y *and* y M z *imply that* x M z
(d) x A y *implies that not* y A x
(e) x A y *and* y A z *imply that* x A z
(f) *not* x N x
(g) x N y *implies that* y N x.

Conditions (b), (d), and (g) do not require (X, C) to be a t-graph. Parts (a), (b), and (c) of Theorem 1 assert that when (X, C) is a t-graph, then M is an equivalence relation on X (reflexive, symmetric, and transitive). Thus M partitions X into a system of mutually exclusive and exhaustive subsets with the property that x and y are in the *same* subset if and only if x M y. To indicate that these subsets are defined by M and to give them a name consonant with their social structural interpretation we call them the M-cliques of X and note that an M-clique may be of size one. Each group member who is involved with another in a mutually positive pair relation is in an M-clique with that member and is involved in a mutually positive pair relation with every other member of that M-clique.

The notion of mutuality as identifying subgroup membership is common in the sociometric and social psychological literature. A clear theoretical statement appears in Homans (1950) and it is formally modeled in terms of mutuality in Cartwright and Harary (1956), Davis (1967), and Davis and Leinhardt (1971).

The M-cliques are *compatible* with A and N in a sense that is summarized in the next theorem.

> *Theorem 2: If* (X, C) *is a t-graph and if* u *and* v *are in the same* M-*clique, then for all* x *in* X:
>
> (a) u A x *if and only if* v A x
>
> (b) x A u *if and only if* x A v
>
> (c) u N x *if and only if* v N x.
>
> *Proof:* We shall prove only the "if" part of (a) as the other arguments are similar. Suppose u M v and u A x. Then we certainly have v C u and u C x, so by transitivity we must also have v C x. Could it happen that x C v obtains also? Suppose so. Then x C v and v C u imply that x C u contrary to the assumption that u A x. Therefore v A x holds. *Q.E.D.*

The content of Theorem 2 may be described by saying that in a t-graph all individuals in an M-clique are structurally equivalent in the sense that they all stand in the same relation to any other individual in the group. Thus, if any member of an M-clique chooses an individual outside of that clique, all of his fellow members also choose that individual and if one clique member fails to choose an individual outside the clique then none of his fellow clique members chooses that individual. The main implication of Theorem 2 is that an ordering relation, A*, may be defined on the M-cliques themselves, as follows:

Definition 2: *If* U *and* V *are two distinct M-cliques of* X, *then define* U A* V *if and only if* u A v *for all* u *in* U *and* v *in* V. *Also set* U A* U *for all M-cliques,* U.

The ordering, A*, of the M-cliques is by definition reflexive. From Theorem 1, parts (d) and (e), it follows that

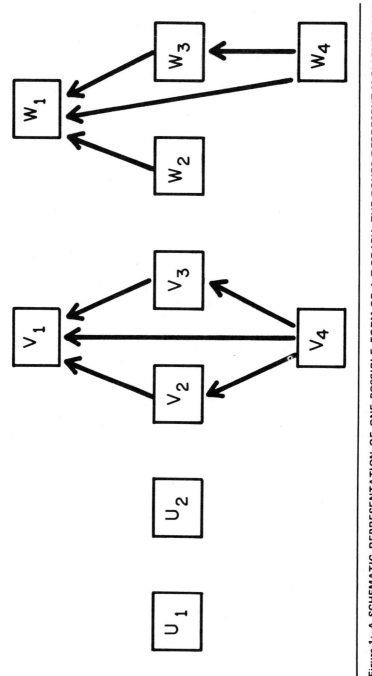

Figure 1: A SCHEMATIC REPRESENTATION OF ONE POSSIBLE FORM OF A T-GRAPH. THE BOXES REPRESENT M-CLIQUES AND THE ARROWS REPRESENT THE RELATION A*.

54

A* is also anti-symmetric and transitive. Therefore, A* is a partial order on the M-cliques of X. The next theorem summarizes the above discussion in terms of the structure of a t-graph. Its proof is evident from the previous discussion and is omitted.

> *Theorem 3: If* (X, C) *is a t-graph then the elements of* X *may be partitioned into M-cliques with the following properties:*
>
> (a) *within each M-clique all pairs of individuals are joined by M-edges;*
>
> (b) *between any two distinct M-cliques all pairs of individuals are either all joined by A-edges with the same direction or all joined by N-edges;*
>
> (c) *the M-cliques when ordered by* A* *form a partial order.*

A rather less intuitive statement of Theorem 3 may be found in Ore (1962: 151). Each part of Theorem 3 has a simple sociometric interpretation. In part (a) the internal structure of each M-clique is characterized by mutual positive sentiment between each pair of clique members. In part (b) the relations between pairs of M-cliques is characterized either by a status ranking of one clique over the other (the case of A-edges) or by no status ranking (the case of N-edges). Finally in part (c) the entire system of M-cliques is characterized as forming a consistent structure in the sense of a partial ordering.

AN EXAMPLE OF A TRANSITIVE GRAPH

The class of distinct t-graphs is very large and there is little hope of accurately describing all of the possibilities in the general case. However, in the following example we try to illustrate the variety that is available with simple structures. Figure 1 illustrates a single group that contains ten M-cliques: U_1, U_2, V_1, V_2, V_3, V_4, W_1, W_2, W_3, W_4. The M-cliques may be of varying sizes, of course, but no group member may belong to more than one. Cliques U_1 and U_2 are unranked relative to any of the other cliques. The cliques V_1, V_2, V_3, and V_4 form a system of "levels" such that everyone on a lower "level" chooses everyone above him. The cliques W_1, W_2, W_3, and W_4 are involved in a ranking system but they do not form such clear-cut "levels" since the individuals in W_4 do not choose those in W_2.

Figure 1 provides an illustration of the variety of organizational patterns which may result after the conditions for a t-graph have been satisfied. It indicates as well how transitivity in positive interpersonal sentiment can result in stratification as well as clustering. This point is particularly important because of the tendency of theorists to view stratification and clustering as two separate dimensions of social structure (see, for example, Homans, 1950; Brown, 1965). While status relationships have previously been identified with asymmetry and clustering with mutuality in positive interpersonal sentiment (Davis and Leinhardt, 1971), the t-graph model indicates that these are simply different expressions of a single social organizational principle. Furthermore, if a t-graph is considered to be a generalization of Heider's balance theory, then the figure illustrates how balance leads to the development of hierarchies as well as cliques.

SPECIAL CASES OF T-GRAPHS OBTAINED BY RESTRICTING THE TYPES OF EDGES AND TRIADS

This section is devoted to examining a variety of special cases of t-graphs. Thus all of the structures mentioned in this section are examples of t-graphs that satisfy further conditions beyond transitivity. We examine only two possible classes of restrictions one might impose on a t-graph. The first concerns restrictions on the types of dyads (or edges) that can appear in the t-graph. The second concerns

56

restrictions on the types of triads that can appear. Other types of t-graphs are mentioned briefly in the section "Other Types of T-Graphs" (p. 121).

If a t-graph has only one type of edge (i.e., all dyads are the same type), then the form of the t-graph is completely determined. "M-edges only" implies that the t-graph consists of a single completely connected M-clique. "A-edges only" implies that the t-graph forms a transitive tournament, that is, a complete linear ordering of all individuals (compare Landau, 1951-1953). "N-edges only" ensures that the t-graph is a totally disconnected set of points.

More interesting possibilities arise when the t-graph is allowed to possess edges of two but not all three types. For example, if only M- and A-edges are allowed, then Theorem 3 implies that the t-graph forms a quasi-series (Hempel, 1952). This type of structure consists of a linearly ordered series of M-cliques as indicated in Figure 2. The possibilities that may arise when only M- and N-edges are allowed are summarized in the following corollary of Theorem 3:

Corollary 1: If (X, C) *is a t-graph and* A *is empty, then* X *may be partitioned into M-cliques such that:*

(a) *within each M-clique, all individuals are joined by M-edges,*

(b) *between any two distinct M-cliques all individuals are joined by N-edges.*

Corollary 1 describes Davis' "clusterable graph" (Davis, 1967). This model as well as the structural balance model of Cartwright and Harary (1956) is usually stated in terms of signed graphs rather than digraphs as done here. However, if positive edges are identified with M, and negative edges identified with N, a signed graph may be considered as a special case of a digraph for which A is empty. This

57

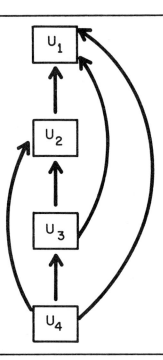

Figure 2: SCHEMATIC REPRESENTATION OF A QUASI-SERIES. BOXES REPRESENT M-CLIQUES AND THE ARROWS DENOTE THE RELATION A*.

interpretation of a signed graph is a purely conceptual device and should not be confused with the practical question of turning sociometric data—which are usually directed graphs—into signed graphs. (In this situation, M-edges are usually scored positive, N-edges are usually negative, but A-edges may be scored either positive or negative depending on one's point of view.)

As indicated in the section "Mathematical Definition of a Transitive Graph" (p. 109), no essential simplification of the structure of a t-graph occurs if no M-edges are allowed. The resulting structure may be a fully general partial order. Table 1 summarizes the result of restricting the edges of a t-graph.

TABLE 1

Edge Types	Resulting Graphs
M only	Completely connected graph
A only	Transitive tournament
N only	Completely disconnected graph
M, A only	Quasi-series
M, N only	Clusterable graph
A, N only	Partial order

Graph types resulting from restricting the edges of a t-graph.

RESTRICTIONS ON THE TRIADS

Figure 3 illustrates the sixteen essentially different (non-isomorphic) triad configurations that may obtain in a directed binary graph. The triads are labeled in the manner used in Holland and Leinhardt (1970). The three numbers refer to the quantity of M, A, and N-edges in the triad, respectively. The letters U, D, T, and C further distinguish the triad types. A few technical points are worth mentioning. First, a *triad* is intransitive if for at least one of the six possible ordered triples of the individuals that make it up, say (x, y, z), it occurs that x C y and y C z but not x C z. Thus a triad may be intransitive from one, two, or all three or the individuals' points of view. Second, a triad may contain up to six transitive ordered triples. Third, if any one of the following three configurations obtains,

x C y and not y C z or

not x C y but y C z or

neither x C y nor y C z,

then the transitivity condition says nothing regarding x C z. These configurations are called vacuously transitive. In Figure 3, the transitive and vacuously transitive triads appear on the left while the intransitive triads appear on the right. The binary relation, C, will be transitive if and only if the graph

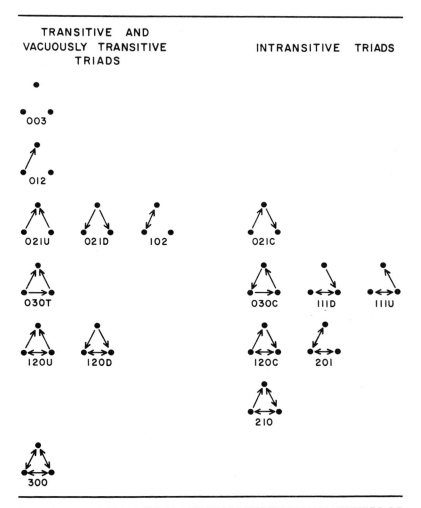

Figure 3: ALL 16 TRIAD TYPES ARRANGED VERTICALLY BY NUMBER OF CHOICES MADE AND DIVIDED HORIZONTALLY INTO THOSE WITH NO INTRANSITIVITIES AND THOSE WITH AT LEAST ONE.

contains no intransitive triads. Thus a t-graph is characterized by possessing only those triad types that fall on the left side of Figure 3. It is evident that restricting the allowable dyads also restricts the allowable triads—for example, when A is empty the only possible triads that any graph (transitive or not) may possess are the types 300, 201, 102, and 003.

The next model considered is structural balance. Davis' characterization of clusterable graphs is that no triad of the 201-type exists in the graph. From our point of view this characterization is equivalent to assuming that C is transitive and A is empty. The structure theorem of Cartwright and Harary (1956) states that a signed graph is balanced (separates into two cliques) if and only if there are no negative 3-cycles. This means no triads of type 201 or 003. From our point of view, structural balance assumes that A is empty and C is transitive plus an added condition that has the effect of restricting the number of possible M-cliques to two at most.

A restriction on the triad types that has the effect of limiting the number of M-cliques seems difficult to justify and this may account for the difficulty of empirically verifying the dichotomization of groups predicted by structural balance. A corresponding restriction can be found for the case when N rather than A is empty. As we have seen when N is empty, the t-graph must be a quasi-series. It will be restricted to a quasi-series with only two levels if the triad type 030T is prohibited.

The final structure we discuss is the model proposed by Davis and Leinhardt (1971). Generalizing a system of completely ranked individuals (transitive tournament) to a system of ranked cliques with one clique per level (quasi-series) suggests the further generalization to ranked *clusters* of cliques—possibly more than one clique per level. This is the model described by Davis and Leinhardt. They called it a partial order but we shall refer to it as a system of ranked clusters. Although the conditions for this model are remarkably close to the definition of transitivity, it does not reach the full generality of a t-graph. Ranked clusters allow M, A, and N all to be non-empty, unlike any of the special cases described so far. M-edges exist between members of an

M-clique as usual; N-edges exist between the M-cliques on a given level, while A-edges exist between M-cliques on different levels. Note that N-edges in the ranked clusters model link cliques of equal status while in the general t-graph cliques linked by such edges are not necessarily comparable. This difference in interpretation of the role N-edges play is crucial. Davis and Leinhardt give a characterization of their model in terms of its triads, and their interpretation of N-edges leads them to exclude a triad included in a general t-graph. In particular, they prove that a directed graph may be arranged into a system of ranked clusters of cliques if and only if it does not contain any of the intransitive triads (the entire right side of Figure 3) or any 012 triads. From our point of view, their theorem may be stated as follows:

> *Theorem 4:* (Davis and Leinhardt, 1971) *A directed graph* (X, C), *is a system of ranked clusters if and only if it is a t-graph and it has no 012 triads.*

The proof of Theorem 4 given by Davis and Leinhardt uses the cluster theorem of Davis (1967). Another line of proof assumes that (X, C) is a t-graph, and examines the implication of no 012 triads for that structure. The following definition and lemma elucidate the essential logic of the argument:

Definition 3: If U *and* V *are two distinct M-cliques of* X, *then define* U N* V *if and only if* u N v *for all* u *in* U *and* v *in* V. *Also set* U N* U *for all M-cliques,* U.

> *Lemma* 1: *Let* (X, C) *be a t-graph and suppose it has no* 012 *triads, then* N* *is an equivalence relation on the M-cliques.*

> *Proof:* By definition N* is reflexive; also Theorem 1 (g) implies that N* is symmetric. It remains to show that N* is transitive. Suppose U N* V and V N* W for three M-cliques. Since U and W and M-cliques by Theorem 3 they either have all A-edges or all N-edges between them. Suppose they have an A-edge; e.g., u A w for some u in U and w in W. Then we have v in V such that u N v, v N w, and u A w. Hence, the triad   u, v, w   is of

type 012 contrary to hypothesis. The same argument applies if w A u holds. Thus U and W have all N-edges between them so that U N* W. *Q.E.D.*

The argument to establish the "if" part of Theorem 4 proceeds by using N* to partition the M-cliques into mutually exclusive and exhaustive *clusters of cliques*. *Within* a cluster of cliques all of the cliques are joined by N-edges and *between* the clusters all of the cliques are joined by A-edges. Theorem 3 ensures that the A-edges from all the cliques in a given cluster go in the same direction so that the clusters are ranked from lowest to highest. The "only if" part of Theorem 4 follows a straightforward enumeration of the possible triads.

From the point of view of a t-graph the Davis-Leinhardt model of ranked clusters consists of an additional assumption that has the effect of drastically reducing the number of possible structures. In particular, a t-graph may contain disconnected components, but a system of ranked clusters cannot. The often noted "sex cleavage" (Gronlund, 1959; Leinhardt, 1968; Moreno, 1953) of children's classroom groups would be an allowable situation under the t-graph model but would disconfirm a model which prohibited the occurrence of 012 triads.

OTHER TYPES OF T-GRAPHS

The restrictions we have discussed so far are all of the form "no subgraphs of size x of the type y." Our attention has been focused on subgraphs of size 2 and 3 (dyads and triads). Many of the important classes of graphs cannot be described in these terms. For example, the condition that a graph be connected cannot be described by saying that it does not possess any subgraphs of a fixed size in particular isomorphism classes. Semilattices, t-graphs proposed by Friedell (1967) as models of organizations, cannot contain disconnected components, but can contain 012 triads unlike the

Davis-Leinhardt model. Semilattices are examples of structures that cannot be characterized by the nonexistence of particular subgraph types.

EMPIRICAL SUPPORT FOR THE T-GRAPH MODEL

Recently, Davis (1970) has carried out an analysis of 742 sociomatrices from diverse small groups. His data provide tentative empirical support for the t-graph model. For each triad type, Davis computes the percent of sociomatrices in his data bank for which the observed number of triads of the given type exceeds the number expected by chance given the distribution of M, A, and N edges in the sociomatrix. (Formulae for these expected values appear in Holland and Leinhardt, 1970.) He then uses these thirteen[2] proportions as the dependent variables to be explained by models of small group structure. The overall results of Davis' analysis appear in Table 2. We have made several modifications including the change to our triad nomenclature and the addition of three new columns:

> (1) the column headed "transitivities" contains the number of ordered triples (or points of view) in each triad type for which the transitivity condition holds and is nonvacuous; (2) the column headed "intransitivities" records the number of times in each triad that a contradiction to transitivity exists; (3) the last column contains the difference between these two quantities.

These columns aid in interpreting Davis' results, for they make it clear that the more intransitive the triad, the less frequently it appears. The columns also indicate an apparent counterbalancing effect resulting from the number of transitivities in a triad. The difference between the number of transitivities and the number of intransitivities predicts very nearly the observed order of infrequency. Those triads with more transitivities are more frequent than chance expectation, and those with more intransitivities are less frequent than chance expectation in proportion to the difference in

TABLE 2
DEFICITS OF TRIADS IN 742 SOCIOMATRICES

Triad Type	Percent Matrices with Triad Infrequent[a]	Transi-tivities	Intransi-tivities	Transitivities minus Intransitivities
030C	90 (441)[b]	0	3	-3
201	90 (651)	0	2	-2
021C	83 (701)	0	1	-1
111U, 111D	78 (716)	0	1	-1
120C	75 (563)	1	2	-1
012	42 (708)	0	0	0
003	41 (649)	0	0	0
210	37 (530)	3	1	2
102	37 (706)	0	0	0
021U, 021D	27 (701)	0	0	0
030T	16 (601)	1	0	1
120U, 120D	7 (567)	2	0	2
300	1 (301)	6	0	6

a. From: Davis, 1970, Table 1, "Total" column: "Percent of Matrices with Triad Frequency Less Than Chance Expectation."

b. Number of matrices with expected value of 1.00 or greater. Triad predictions were not tested when expectation of a triad fell below 1.00 in a matrix.

these two characteristics. The only triad-type that violates this proposition is the 210, but we hasten to point out that our choice of the *difference* between transitivities and intransitivities was arbitrary and that it might be better to give the one intransitivity of the 210 triad more weight than we have.

One substantive interpretation of these results is that there is a tendency in sociometric data away from imbalance (i.e., intransitivity) and that when imbalance does occur it is resolved through transitive closure rather than through the development of vacuous transitivity.

NOTES

1. Transitive graphs are discussed in Harary, Norman, and Cartwright (1965: chs. 10 and 11).

2. Davis has thirteen triad types rather than the sixteen given in Figure 3 because he groups types 111U and 111D together, types 021U and 021D together, and types 120U and 120D together.

REFERENCES

BROWN, R. (1965) Social Psychology. New York: Free Press.

CARTWRIGHT, D. and F. HARARY (1956) "Structural balance: a generalization of Heider's theory." Psych. Rev. 63: 277-293.

DAVIS, J. A. (1970) "Clustering and hierarchy in interpersonal relations: testing two graph theoretical models on 742 sociograms." Amer. Soc. Rev. 35 (October): 843-852.

––– (1967) "Clustering and structural balance in graphs." Human Relations 20, 2: 181-187.

––– and S. LEINHARDT (1971) "The structure of positive interpersonal relations in small groups," in J. Berger (ed.) Sociological Theories in Progress. Boston: Houghton Mifflin.

FRIEDELL, M. (1967) "Organizations as semilattices." Amer. Soc. Rev. 32 (February): 46-54.

GRONLUND, N. E. (1959) Sociometry in the Classroom. New York: Harper.

HARARY, F., R. Z. NORMAN, and D. CARTWRIGHT (1965) Structural Models: An Introduction to the Theory of Directed Graphs. New York: John Wiley.

HEIDER, F. (1958) The Psychology of Interpersonal Relations. New York: John Wiley.

––– (1946) "Attitudes and cognitive organization." J. of Psychology 21: 107-112.

HEMPEL, G. C. (1952) "Fundamentals of concept formation in empirical science," pp. 58-62 in International Encyclopedia of Unified Science II, No. 7. Chicago: Univ. of Chicago Press.

HOLLAND, P. and S. LEINHARDT (1970) "A method for detecting structure in sociometric data." Amer. J. of Sociology (November).

HOMANS, G. C. (1950) The Human Group. New York: Harcourt, Brace & World.

LANDAU, H. G. (1951-1953) "On dominance relations and the structure of animal societies: I. Effect of inherent characteristics. II. Some effects of possible social factors. III. The condition for a score structure." Bull. of Mathematical Biophysics 13 (March): 1-19; (September): 245-262; 15 (June): 143-148.

LEINHARDT, S. (1968) "The development of structure in the interpersonal relations of children." Ph.D. dissertation. University of Chicago.

MORENO, J. L. (1953) Who Shall Survive? New York: Beacon.

NEWCOMB, T. M. (1953) "An approach to the study of communicative acts." Psych. Rev. 60: 393-404.

ORE, O. (1962) "Theory of graphs." Amer. Mathematical Society Colloquium, Vol. 38.

OSGOOD, C. and P. H. TANNENBAUM (1955) "The principle of congruity in the prediction of attitude change." Psych. Rev. 62: 42-55.

RAPOPORT, A. (1963) "Mathematical models of social interaction," in R. D. Luce et al. (eds.) Handbook of Mathematical Psychology. New York: John Wiley.

SCHOPLER, J. (1965) "Social power," pp. 177-218 in L. Berkowitz (ed.) Advances in Experimental Psychology, Vol. 2. New York: Academic.

From Francois Lorrain and Harrison C. White,
Journal of Mathematical Sociology 1,
49-80 (1971), by permission.

STRUCTURAL EQUIVALENCE OF INDIVIDUALS
IN SOCIAL NETWORKS†

FRANÇOIS LORRAIN, HARRISON C. WHITE

Harvard University

The aim of this paper is to understand the interrelations among relations within concrete social groups. Social structure is sought, not ideal types, although the latter are relevant to interrelations among relations. From a detailed social network, patterns of global relations can be extracted, within which classes of equivalently positioned individuals are delineated. The global patterns are derived algebraically through a 'functorial' mapping of the original pattern. Such a mapping (essentially a generalized homomorphism) allows systematically for concatenation of effects through the network. The notion of functorial mapping is of central importance in the 'theory of categories,' a branch of modern algebra with numerous applications to algebra, topology, logic. The paper contains analyses of two social networks, exemplifying this approach.

By interrelations among relations is meant the way in which relations among the members of a social system occur in characteristic bundles and how these bundles of relations interlock and determine one another.‡ By understanding is meant distilling simpler patterns at a higher level of abstraction—simpler not only in having fewer constituents but also in exhibiting interrelations which are more regular or transparent.

Practicable ways of carrying out analyses with data have been developed, in the form of computer programs (Heil 1970). However this approach is not just a novel technique of data reduction; rather, as will presently be explained, it follows from our concern with a set of sociological problems.

Our treatment, which stems from a tradition of algebraic analysis of kinship systems (Weil 1949, White 1963, Courrège 1965, Boyd 1969), differs from other

†This work was supported under grants GS–448 and GS–2689 to H. C. White from the National Science Foundation, which is gratefully acknowledged. Special thanks are due to Scott Boorman, whose unfailing criticism gave us much cause for reflection and led us to numerous revisions. Discussions, in seminars or otherwise, particularly with Daniel Bertaux, Mark Granovetter, and John MacDougall, have also been helpful. However, the undersigned are clearly responsible for any imperfections that may remain. This paper is the product of the synthesis of an unpublished paper by H. C. White ('Notes on Finding Models of Structural Equivalence', 1969) and certain results taken from an unpublished paper by F. Lorrain ('Tools for the Formal Study of Networks, I.', 1968) and from the latter's doctoral dissertation (Lorrain 1970, in press). The determinant stimulus that led us to the ideas set forth in the present paper came from Boyd's 1966 dissertation (the core of which was subsequently published—Boyd 1969), where the decisive step was made, introducing and exemplifying a particular type of reduction of a network. Friedell's (1967) notion of 'office structures' within organizations also pointed in the same direction.

‡For a brilliant formulation of the problem, see Nadel 1957. However he emphasizes mainly cultural interrelations of role sets.

67

approaches to the analysis of networks—such as graph theory, the theory of electric circuits, or production scheduling—in that it handles the points of view of all nodes simultaneously. It also differs from other approaches in the study of social networks in that it consists of concurrent dual treatments of individuals on the one hand and relations on the other. Although the elements of our framework are stable expectations held by persons, it should be possible to deal in this way with macroscopic flows either of material resources or of abstractions—such as information, uncertainty, attitudes—as seen by an observer. Such flows involve aggregates of individuals in equivalent positions within the abstract global structure. Moreover these aggregates will vary according to the particular abstract point of view taken; many such overlapping global patterns can coexist or conflict at the same time.

In order to do justice at least in part to the bewildering complexity of social structure, it is important to take into account the possibly very long and devious chains of effects propagating within concrete social systems through links of various kinds. It is partly owing to these indirect effects, together with the largely extrinsic driving force of membership renewal†, that social structures and processes can so vastly transcend the individual consciousness of actors and investigators. Another consequence is that cultural systems of cognitive orientations, or of values, or of norms, however complex and however crucial, can only constitute a small part of the social phenomenon. Although some global structural aspects may be culturally recognized and be expressed in strong and important social norms, this is not necessarily so for all such aspects. It is exceedingly important to realize that, as soon as an abstract cultural framework is inscribed within a set of concrete persons, coming and going, being born and dying, wholly unanticipated consequences may result. Thus when we speak of the global network structure of a social system, we have in mind the overall objective logic of this system as it exists concretely in a population of so many individuals related in such and such ways. This is why simultaneous treatment of individuals and of relations is essential. One of the deepest misunderstandings in prevailing sociological theories is their failure to distinguish effectively between individuals and social positions.

RELATIONS AND GRAPHS

The total role of an individual in a social system has often been described as consisting of sets of relations of various types linking this person as ego to sets of others (see for example Gross et al. 1958). Let us represent individuals as nodes which are not distinguished by intrinsic attributes such as sex; this restriction will be discussed later. Let us draw an arrow with a label from one person to another to represent a type of role relation. Thus total roles will appear as sets of variously labelled arrows, not as higher order structures. 'Counterpart' role relations directed back to the given person are simply treated as parts of the sets of role relations of the others. In other

---

†White (1970) deals extensively with membership renewal in organizations, particularly emphasizing the duality of individuals and social positions, and showing that objective flows of vacancies through an organization are the crucial phenomenon, not careers.

words, total roles are broken down into directed ties of different kinds occuring within pairs of persons.

An important requirement is that these links correspond to clear expectations among the population considered. Definition of different types of role relation is a question of substantive theory related to the particular purposes of a study (for an example of a systematic analysis see Davis 1969). Deciding which particular ordered pairs of nodes exhibit a given type of tie is an empirical question, but one based on abstraction, since ties of several different types may hold at the same time between a given pair of nodes. The problem of measurement of social relations is a difficult one; unfortunately most existing sociometric tests seem hardly acceptable as tools for the measurement of systematic structure.†

The pattern of occurences of a relation of a given type within a network, i.e. the set of all ordered pairs of nodes exhibiting this type of relation, constitutes a directed graph. Hereafter the term *graph* will mean directed graph and will be used interchangeably with the term *binary relation*, which simply means a set of ordered pairs of nodes. Let us assign to each type of role relation a capital letter as a label. A specific tie in the graph of a relation labelled, say, R will be represented in the usual way as aRb, where a, b are nodes and the direction of the tie is by convention from a to b.

Definition of social relations will be tied to the given population by *one major restriction*: if the graphs for two types of social relation are identical, i.e. if they consist of exactly the same ordered pairs of nodes, the two will be treated as a single type.

Of course it is conceivable that two culturally distinct role relations may happen at some time to have identical graphs in a given population. However it does not seem very probable that they would remain distinct for a long time, if the coincidence of their graphs persists. (Compare this with Gause's ecological axiom, Slobodkin 1961, p. 123.) This is a sociological argument. Roles are not isolated abstract entities: they exist only in so far as they have dynamic reality in a concrete population. A role involves more than just two persons: the concrete patterning of flows along the graph of a relation as well as the ways these flows concretely interlock and overlap with other types of flow are probably more important in shaping the content of a role relation than even the most articulate cultural specifications. The above restriction is not a matter of emphasis on extension rather than on intension of role concepts; the point is rather that, as far as internal flows of a system and aggregates of individuals are concerned, it is not necessary to distinguish in the abstract what is nowhere concretely distinguished. However such a point of view requires an important precaution. The domain of people and relationships considered must be relatively bounded and complete: it makes but little sense, in this perspective, to select an arbitrary subset of a social system and to submit it to the type of analysis we propose, because the structure of global flows could thereby be critically distorted. Naturally this in no way excludes that the given domain be also part of a wider system and interact or even overlap with other systems.

By definition a role relation must imply reciprocal expectations. (See Nadel 1957,

†As clearly shown by P. W. Holland and S. Leinhardt in an unpublished paper, 'Masking: The Structural Implications of Measurement Error in Sociometry,' 1969.

69

Chapter 2, for an unusually clear discussion of role as a concept.) Formally, if a role relation labelled R is recognized then there necessarily exists a *converse* role relation, which can be labelled R^{-1}, such that, for any nodes a, b, aRb if and only if $bR^{-1}a$. Of course, by definition, $(R^{-1})^{-1}$ is precisely the relation R. This *principle of reciprocity* is another manifestation of the reality, of the objectivity sui generis of social phenomena. However this principle may not fully apply to 'relations' corresponding to relatively imprecise 'sociometric choices'; such a case will be presented and analyzed in a later section.

The converse relation R^{-1} must be distinguished from the 'counterpart' roles mentioned earlier, which are simply role relations of the same generic kind as R. Several distinct role relations and their respective converses may simultaneously hold on certain pairs: e.g. aRb, $aS^{-1}b$, aTb, together with $bR^{-1}a$, bSa, $bT^{-1}a$.

Symmetry is a particularly important aspect of social relations. Consider a type of role relation R. Suppose that expectations of one person of a pair in the graph of R toward the other are the same as the other's toward the first, and let this be true for every pair of nodes included in the graph of R. Then not only is each tie symmetric, but the graph as a whole is symmetric, i.e., for any nodes a, b, aRb if and only if bRa. Thus the graph of the converse R^{-1} coincides with the graph of R: $bR^{-1}a$ if and only if bRa. The major restriction just stated then applies: since R and R^{-1} coincide, they are treated as a single inclusive role—call it R still. In this sense, a symmetric role relation has no reciprocal role relation. Receiving and acknowledging the friendly expectations projected to one by a friend, for example, is treated as an intrinsic part of one's own projection of the same friendly expectations to him, so long as all pairs in the population are symmetric in this way.

Merger of R and R^{-1} when R is symmetric can be used as a prototype in arguing again for the one major restriction. The great complexities and subtleties of a role relation, between two particular persons or as viewed in general in a culture, are being excluded as far as possible from this analysis. Our approach is orthogonal to Friedell's (1969), who is concerned with the deep structure of mutual perceptions in social groups. The whole thrust is toward how patterns of role relations fit together in a population. From this point of view, it is not important to distinguish passive from active on one person's side of a role tie unless the two aspects occur separately somewhere in the population.

This argument suggests an ambiguity which must be resolved when defining a role relation. Let F be the graph of role ties found in a population using a definition of the role relation of friend elicited from informants and their culture. In many pairs, no doubt, there will be a symmetric tie with the role relation holding in both directions. Let this subset of pairs and their ties be represented by a subgraph of F called S. A substantive judgment must then be made as to whether the S ties are so different from the others that there are really two distinct role relation types, even though they are not recognized explicitly by the population. Davis and Leinhardt† have adopted this strategy of splitting S from F (see also Davis 1968). A typical example of this type of situation is the distinction between reciprocal use of the second person singular of

†J. A. Davis and S. Leinhardt, 'The Structure of Positive Interpersonal Relations in Small Groups', unpubl. paper, 1968.

verbs in verbal interaction and use of the second person singular reciprocated by use of the second person plural or third person, a distinction of outstanding importance in many languages. Once again the point is that the nature and content of ties is closely related to the pattern of their distribution among individuals, to which close attention must be given in the course of analysis as well as in field-investigation.

COMPOUND RELATIONS IN SOCIAL NETWORKS

Dynamics and structure in a population cannot be captured from the mere count of role relations by type—as proposed by Wolfe and Schenk (1970), for example—any more than from a census of attitudes or attributes of individuals. The problem is how to get at the interweaving of pair relations into the complex tapestry of social structure and process. The theory of electric circuits comes to mind as an analogue, particularly in the elegant formulation of Kron (1939), ably simplified and restated by LeCorbeiller (1950), or in the formulation of Slepian (1968). There are three crucial defects in the analogy, exploration of which can guide further treatment of social ties.

1. Ties in social networks often generate other ties or the elimination of other ties, unlike branches in an electric circuit which are the given skeleton of a network changed only by an outside agency, the designer.

2. The driving forces in an electric network are external to its logic, scattered arbitrarily in branches of it, whereas the activation of the population rests on impulses generated at each of the nodes, whether or not with external stimulation.

3. The nature of a tie, as argued earlier, depends in part on the pattern of all ties of that type among the population in comparison with the patterns of all ties of various other types. More generally, the nature of the ties between a given pair of persons depends on their (and others') perceptions of how these ties fit in with other role relations among the population. Whereas the nature of a branch in an electric network is fixed by design, although of course its operation depends on what flows develop elsewhere (perhaps directly through mutual inductance) and breakdown can occur because of overload.

Composition of Relations and the Algebraic Notion of Category

Everyone recognizes the reality of indirect ties, ties to one's boss' friend, or one's roommate's relative, or one's ally's enemy. Indirect ties are even sometimes themselves institutionalized and part of a role system, as in the case of kinship ties. The relation of such indirect or secondary ties with one another and with the direct or primary ties is an obvious way to capture the interweaving of role relations into a structure on the population.

Denote RS the secondary relation linking a to b, implied by the existence of a node x such that aRx and xSb. RS will be referred to as the *compound* of R and S, and this operation of compounding will be called *composition*. Whenever aRx and xSb then necessarily $a(RS)b$; however the converse of this will often not be true: in general, if $a(RS)b$ then there does not necessarily exist an x such that aRx and xSb: for example, the compound relation RS might happen to be quite strongly institutionalized in its own right, so that if x left the system in one way or another a would keep his RS tie to b. This is important and relates to our argument that a relation involves more than just two persons (or three, for that matter). We shall later encounter a number of examples of compounds of relations having this property.

Let us then extend our conception of composition of ties so that there may be compounds of any order, such as RSS, $RRR^{-1}S$, etc.; refer to this extended operation simply as the *composition operation* of the network considered. By the major restriction stated previously, there can be only a finite number of such compound types of relation—because there is only a finite number of possible binary relations on a finite population. Certain equations then must hold among strings of relation symbols: otherwise there would be as many relation types as there are such strings, that is an infinite number. For example, if the graph of R coincides exactly with the graph of RR then by our major restriction R and RR will be treated as a single type of relation and the following equation will hold: $R = RR$. This particular equation implies that R is transitive: whenever aRb and bRc then always aRc. In addition the social nature of converse relations is such that all equations of the type $(RS)^{-1} = S^{-1}R^{-1}$ must hold in any network.

We shall deal later with the problem of defining a composition operation when initially only primary, *generator* ties are explicitly given. For the moment, let us suppose that we have a full composition operation for a given network.

This operation represents the basic logic of *concatenation*, the basic logic of *interlock* among the relations constituting the network. Of course this operation is meaningful only in so far as the generator relations are clearly defined; otherwise it would make no sense to distinguish, say, RS from RR, or from SRS^{-1}, etc. The composition operation constitutes one of the main differences between our approach and the more usual 'sociometric' treatments of social networks; it stands for quite a different level of structure.

Note that compound relations, as here defined, are independent of the particular intermediary people involved: the nature of such compound relations depends only on the types of tie that are concatenated to form the compound relation in question. This is because all nodes can be active sources of information and motivation (see point 2 above).

Note also that the compound of two relations, say, X and Y is not necessarily defined: if it is never the case that three nodes a, b, c of the given network are such that aXb and bYc, then the relation XY simply does not occur in the network, there is no point in even speaking of it, in so far as this particular network is concerned. Again, even if the compound XY would happen to make sense culturally, if for some length of time X and Y persisted in concatenating nowhere in the network, it is doubtful that the compound XY would retain any effective social reality.

Let us refer to either generator or compound types of relation as *morphisms*. Some compound morphisms will be explicitly recognized, others will not—which in no way implies that they have less real an effect. These morphisms, together with their composition operation and their graphs on the set of nodes constitute a *category*. More precisely:

72

Definition. A *category* C is constituted by a class *CObj*—the elements of which may be called nodes but are usually called *objects*—, together with a class *CMor*—the elements of which are called *morphisms*—, and provided with a structure of the following type.

1. To each ordered pair (a, b) of objects is assigned a subset $(a, b)Mor$ of *CMor*. The elements of $(a, b)Mor$ are referred to as the morphisms *linking a to b*. If M is a morphism linking a to b, this may be indicated by writing aMb. It is understood that every morphism appears as a link for at least one pair of objects.

2. If objects a, b, c and morphisms M, N are such that aMb and bNc then there is amorphism MN linking a to c, called the *compound* of M and N. The compound MN depends only on M and N: it is independent of any particular objects a, b, c that might be involved in their concatenation. If on the other hand there are no objects a, b, c through which M and N concatenate as above, then the compound of the two morphisms is *undefined*, the expression 'MN' has no meaning. This operation of compounding of morphisms is called the *composition operation* of C.

3. If objects a, b, c, d and morphisms M, N, P are such that aMb, bNc, and cPd, then $(MN)P = M(NP)$, so that there is no ambiguity in speaking of the compound of M, N, and P through a, b, c, d: it is a unique morphism—which may as well be denoted simply by MNP, deleting the parentheses—, linking a to d: $a(MNP)d$. This is the property of *associativity* of the composition operation. Of course, by 2, MNP is independent of the particular a, b, c, d involved in the concatenation of the three morphisms.

The concept of category is an important one because it takes a network *as a network*, combining together in a unit the *three* levels of objects, of morphisms, and of concatenation of morphisms. In a category all objects are considered simultaneously, while graph theory considers only particular cycles and paths linking definite nodes; neither does graph theory consider any classification of paths into types according to the types of the links concatenated.†

A final remark. There is no objection to seeing composition of morphisms as developing in time (see point 1 above on electric networks). Generation of a full pattern of indirect effects—even if none of them would be of a conscious nature—can conceivably take some time; in such a case compound morphisms would become meaningful only relative to a long enough period.

---

†This definition of a category differs in some respects from the usual definition of a category in mathematics: according to the present definition a category does not necessarily have identity morphisms and a morphism can apply to more than one ordered pair of objects. (A standard reference on categories is Mitchell 1965). This definition renders possible a richer dialectic between objects and morphisms and is better adapted to psychological and sociological applications. Thus, at the immediate level of a social network represented as a category in the sense just defined, the mathematical theory of categories in its present form has but little relevance, although the spirit is the same. However in the study of whole classes of such categorical networks category theory becomes directly relevant and proves to be quite useful in establishing certain results (see Lorrain 1970). Hereafter the term category will refer exclusively to the notion as defined here. Although the major restriction stated in the section 'Relations and Graphs' in general does not apply to a category, it will be understood to apply to all categories hereafter considered.

Composition When No Explicit Composition Operation Is Given

Frequently, in mathematics, structures consisting of certain elements are considered, where a certain type of combination of these elements would be useful for structural analysis but no explicit rule for such combination is given. Often in such cases rules of combination are defined in a purely abstract, formal manner and are used as a basis for further treatment. We shall follow a similar course for social networks.

Let a social network be given, containing various types of role relations, but where there seems to be no natural composition operation available. First consider as many compound relations as there are 'words' that can be formed by using as letters the labels of the role relations given at the start—call these *generators*—, without any limitation to the length of words or to the order of letters within them. Consider two generators R, S. There is no alternative, in this case where only primary relations are given at the start, but to define the graph of the compound relation RS to be the unique graph such that: for all nodes a, b, $a(RS)b$ if *and only if* there exists a node x such that aRx and xSb. In other words the *graph* of RS here is exactly the composition of the *graph* of R and the *graph* of S. Similarly, define the graph of a tertiary relation RSS to be the composition of the graph of RS and the graph of S, or equivalently as the composition of the graph of R and the graph of SS, composition of graphs being associative. And so on.

Denote by G our (non-empty) set of generator relations. Once again, although an infinite number of words can be formed with elements of G as letters, only a finite number of graphs will be generated by composition of generators, since there is only a finite number of possible binary relations on a finite population. This set of graphs —denote it by S_G—, considered together with the operation of composition of these graphs, constitutes a *semigroup*: the composition of any two elements of S_G is again an element of S_G and composition is furthermore associative. The infinite set of words can be partitioned into a finite number of classes such that any two words in the same class have exactly the same graph. By the major restriction stated above, all the words within a class will be considered to represent a single type of relation, to which will correspond a unique element of S_G. This means that in general the same type of relation can be denoted by more than one word. Such partitions of sets of words are dealt with in the theory of free semigroups and their homomorphic reductions (see for example Clifford and Preston, pp. 40 ff.) and in extensions of this theory to the more general case of categories.

Now define a category C_G as follows. The objects of C_G will be the nodes of our network. With only one possible exception to be discussed below, the morphisms of C_G will be all the types of relation generated from G, which are of course in one-to-one correspondence with their graphs, the elements of S_G. A morphism M will link an object a to an object b if and only if a is tied to b in the graph of M. The composition operation of morphisms will follow exactly the composition operation of the semigroup of graphs S_G. If we add only the slight modification just mentioned and to be presently described, this structure is seen to satisfy all requirements of our definition of a category. Such a category structure captures adequately the network properties in which we are interested here and can form a useful basis for further analysis. A concrete example will be described in detail in a moment and will be analyzed further n this paper.

74

One particular binary relation is important here: the empty or *zero* relation, i.e. the relation consisting of the empty subset of the set of all ordered pairs of nodes. This relation—denote it O—has the property that, for any binary relation R, $RO = OR = O$. Now it may happen that O is one of the elements of S_G, i.e. that there exist certain types of compound relation not exhibited by any pair of nodes in the given network. In such a case O must be excluded from the morphisms of C_G, if C_G is fully to satisfy point 1 of the definition of a category. This is the modification that was just announced. Hence the compound of two morphisms is zero in the unmodified C_G if and only if in the modified C_G this compound is undefined (see point 2 of the definition of a category). Hereafter C_G will denote only the modified C_G. It may seem artificial to exclude O from C_G, but we shall see later that such an exclusion is important; the fact that two types of relation never concatenate in the network is of crucial sociological significance, because it indicates a form of disjunction, break, or decoupling within the structure. Moreover, contrary to the C_G and S_G case, in general it is not sufficient to add a zero to the morphisms of a category to obtain a semigroup; we shall encounter examples of such categories below, pp. 66 and 69.

Another graph is of special importance: the *identity* relation I. This is the apparently trivial graph linking every node to itself: it consists exclusively of 'self-loops'. I has the property that for any binary relation R on the given set of nodes $RI = IR = R$; i.e. I acts as an *identity element* in semigroups of binary relations. Usually I will not be an element of S_G, however; whether or not to add I to S_G—and add it also, as a new *identity morphism*, to C_G—depends on the interpretation of the model to be constructed. Identity morphisms will play a central role in our treatment of social networks as categories.

Note, finally, that, although in C_G composition of morphisms coincides by definition with composition of their graphs, this is not in general true of all categories. This remark was already made at the beginning of the previous subsection and must once again be emphasized. Concrete examples of such categories will be considered later.

An Example

Let us compute the category C_G for a population of five persons and the set of two generators P and P^{-1} illustrated in Figure 1. Exactly twenty-one distinct types of relation are generated from P and P^{-1}: the shortest words representing them are listed in Table 1 and the graphs of a few of them are given in Figure 2. In Table 1

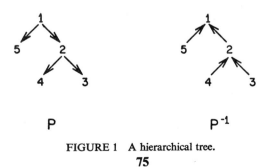

P   P⁻¹

FIGURE 1   A hierarchical tree.

75

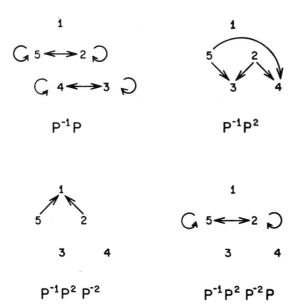

FIGURE 2   Graphs of four of the types of relation in Table 1

and Figure 2, P^2 stands of course for PP, P^{-2} for $P^{-1}P^{-1}$, etc. It is not hard to show that any other 'word' has the same graph as one of these twenty-one words and hence, by our major restriction, is considered to represent the same type of relation. Six equations are sufficient to equate any word to one of the twenty-one types: $PP^{-1}P = P$, $P^2P^{-2}P^2 = P^2$, $P^3 = O = OP = PO$, and the ones equating the converses of these: $P^{-1}PP^{-1} = P^{-1}$, $P^{-2}P^2P^{-2} = P^{-2}$, $P^{-3} = O = P^{-1}O = OP^{-1}$. An example

TABLE 1

List of the twenty-one distinct types of relation generated by
P and P^{-1} of Figure 1.

$\begin{cases} P^{-1}P,\ P^{-2}P^2;\ I\ \text{(the identity, adjoined to } C_G,\ \text{not generated)} \\ PP^{-1},\ PP^{-2}P,\ P^{-1}P^2P^{-1},\ P^{-1}P^2P^{-2}P,\ PP^{-2}P^2P^{-1} \\ P^2P^{-2} \end{cases}$

$\begin{cases} P,\ P^{-1}P^2,\ PP^{-2}P^2 \\ P^2P^{-1},\ P^2P^{-2}P \end{cases}$

$\begin{cases} P^{-1},\ P^{-2}P,\ P^{-2}P^2P^{-1} \\ PP^{-2},\ P^{-1}P^2P^{-2} \end{cases}$

P^2

P^{-2}

O (generated for example as P^3)

Note.—The assignment to separate lines and the further grouping by brackets are used in a later section, together with the adjoined identity I.

76

of a deduction from these equations is: $PP^{-1}P^2P^{-2}P=(PP^{-1}P)(PP^{-2}P)=P(PP^{-2}P)$ $= P^2P^{-2}P$. In such deductions, there is complete freedom in the use of parentheses since composition in S_G—which here is isomorphic to composition of types of relation —is associative. The empty relation O will be excluded from the set of morphisms of C_G and the identity morphism I (linking each object to itself) will be added, so that C_G will have twenty-one morphisms. Table 2 gives the distribution of morphisms among pairs of objects in C_G. In Table 3 is shown a part of the composition table of

TABLE 2

Distribution of morphisms among ordered pairs of objects in the category C_G generated from P and P^{-1} of Figure 1.

$(1,1)Mor = \{I, PP^{-1}, P^2P^{-2}\}$

$(2,2)Mor = \{I, P^{-1}P, PP^{-1}, PP^{-2}P, P^{-1}P^2P^{-2}P, PP^{-2}P^2P^{-1}\}$

$(5,5)Mor = \{I, P^{-1}P, P^{-1}P^2P^{-2}P\}$

$(3,3)Mor = (4,4)Mor = \{I, P^{-1}P, P^{-2}P^2\}$

$(1,2)Mor = \{P, P^2P^{-1}, P^2P^{-2}P\}$

$(1,5)Mor = \{P, P^2P^{-2}P\}$

$(2,3)Mor = (2,4)Mor = \{P, P^{-1}P^2, PP^{-2}P^2\}$

$(5,3)Mor = (5,4)Mor = \{P^{-1}P^2\}$

$(1,3)Mor = (1,4)Mor = \{P^2\}$

$(2,5)Mor = \{P^{-1}P, PP^{-2}P, P^{-1}P^2P^{-2}P\}$

$(3,4)Mor = \{P^{-1}P, P^{-2}P^2\}$

Note.—The morphisms associated to an ordered pair such as (2,1) are the converses of the morphisms of the pair (1,2): $(2,1)Mor = \{P^{-1}, PP^{-2}, P^{-1}P^2P^{-2}\}$.

TABLE 3

Part of the composition table of the category C_G generated from P and P^{-1} of Figure 1.

	P	$P^{-1}P^2$	$PP^{-2}P^2$	$P^{-1}P$	$P^{-2}P^2$
P^{-1}	$P^{-1}P$	$P^{-2}P^2$	$P^{-2}P^2$	$P^{-2}P$	✕
$P^{-2}P$	$P^{-2}P^2$	$P^{-2}P^2$	$P^{-2}P^2$	$P^{-2}P$	✕
P^2	✕	✕	✕	P^2	P^2

the morphisms of C_G: this table is the same as the composition table of S_G, except that where a cross occupies a cell in the former—meaning that composition of the two particular morphisms involved is undefined in C_G—a zero would occur in the table of S_G. More than 43 % of the cells in the composition table of C_G are undefined: there is a large amount of decoupling among morphisms in C_G (compared to 0 % decoupling in a semigroup).

Twenty-one types of relation among five people may seem an unreasonably high number. However this is still orders of magnitude smaller than the total number of possible binary relations on a set of five elements, namely $2^{5 \times 5}$, i.e. more than 33 millions! Moreover, we shall use C_G only as a base from which to extract the simpler global patterns we are looking for. The advantage of using a base such as C_G is that it takes systematic account—albeit in an apparently too refined manner—of the way the generator relations concatenate in the original network. The possibility must be left open that the many compound types of relation generated—more than one of which may occur at the same time within a single pair of nodes—correspond to substantially distinct types of relation, flow, or effect. This relational multiplicity within a single pair might be consciously manipulated, or it might correspond to an objective ambiguity involving conflicts of relation quite independent of the will of individuals, etc.

The number of morphisms of C_G depends critically on the structure of the graphs of the generator relations. If in the previous example the ties of P were not oriented ties but symmetric ties, then only three distinct relation types would be generated, S_G being then the cyclic semigroup of order three and period two (Clifford and Preston, p. 19). The size and structure of C_G can also vary immensely if even only one node is deleted or added: if node 2 was deleted from the previous example, C_G would have only five morphisms: $I, P, P^{-1}, PP^{-1}, P^{-1}P$. This serves as a caution applying to the delimitation of the network to be studied; this is an important caveat, already expressed above.

Endomorphisms
At first sight, self-loops in the graph of a type of relation, such as the loop $1(P^2P^{-2})1$ in the hierarchy example, might not seem relevant. However these loops—or *endomorphisms*—certainly represent real feedback effects (whether individuals be aware of them or not) which form an integral part of the structure and can be of crucial importance in its dynamics. Furthermore, certain endomorphisms are in a sense part of an individual's consciousness of his position in the structure, they are part of his identity; endomorphisms thus acquire a great significance when searching for possible persons in the network with which a given person is most likely to identify or ally. Endomorphisms will be of considerable moment in the following.

AGGREGATION OF RELATIONS AND
STRUCTURAL EQUIVALENCE AMONG INDIVIDUALS: FUNCTORS

Reductions
Our purpose will now be to derive models of aggregation of relations and of individuals, by mapping C_G—or any representation of a social network as a category—onto a smaller, simpler, *reduced* category. This will involve two simultaneous map-

pings: one of objects and the other of morphisms.† Naturally, if the composition operations of the original and the reduced categories are to mean anything, these mappings should also be compatible with these two operations. Such a mapping of a category onto another is a *functorial reduction*, hereafter simply called *reduction*. Reductions are examples of *functors*, a more general kind of mapping between two categories. Reductions and functors will be defined more precisely below.

A reduction of a category constitutes a 'point of view', a 'cross-section', a 'projection' of this category, leaving out certain aspects of its structure and retaining others. Many such reductions, such points of view on a category are possible, more or less refined and overlapping to varying degrees. Virtually nothing can be done with a category such as C_G outside of the context of its reductions and their interrelations; only in this context can its sociological fruitfulness be assessed.

One might expect the social process to operate in such a way that the enormous cognitive and emotional complexities involved in multiple compound relations in a social network C inevitably become structured into the simpler pattern of some reduction of C, where possibly whole classes of nodes become structurally equivalent and hence may be considered as units. Certain reductions of C might perhaps delineate latent macrostructures within C, which could become realized socially under certain circumstances (examples of this will be described later). Some reductions might even happen to be invariant in time, while C could be in a state of incessant change; this would express in a rigorous way the idea of social continuity. An example of such a time-invariant reduction, to which we shall return later, is the structure of clans and clan relationships in societies with certain types of kinship system. More than one time-invariant reduction of C could exist, some of which individuals in C might be quite unaware of, or might be strongly reluctant to acknowledge.

Reduction of Morphisms

Let a category C be given, representing a social network. We shall now examine in more detail what should be meant by a reduction of the morphisms of C, leaving aside reduction of objects until the next section. Interdependence of reduction of objects and reduction of morphisms will appear fully only when sociological criteria for reduction will be discussed in the last part of this paper, where examples of reduction will be considered.

Let D be another category, with the same objects as C but with perhaps different morphisms, i.e. $CObj = DObj$ but possibly $CMor \neq DMor$. Suppose f is a mapping of $CMor$ onto $DMor$ (see Footnote). If f is to represent a meaningful reduction of C to D then at least the following three conditions should be satisfied.

1. Whenever aMb in C then $a(Mf)b$ in D: every link between two objects in C becomes a link in D.

Thus a reduction of C to D maps every occurrence of a morphism (type of relation) M in C to a unique type of relation Mf in D.

---

†A *mapping m* of a set A into a set B is any rule assigning to every element x of A a unique element of B, denoted xm and called the *image* of x. m maps A onto B if every element of B is the image of an element of A; in this case B obviously cannot have more elements than A has, so that in general if m is onto it can be viewed as a *reduction* of A to B.

79

2. Whenever aQb in D then there exists a morphism N of C such that $Q = Nf$ and aNb: every link between two objects in D is the image of a link between these two objects in C.

Conditions 1 and 2 can also be expressed as follows: the graph of a morphism Q of D is exactly the *union* of the graphs of all the morphisms of C of which Q is the image.

Condition 1 implies that whenever the compound of two morphisms M, N of C is defined in C, then the compound of Mf and Nf is necessarily defined in D (see point 2 of the definition of a category). We shall also require a third condition of f:

3. If the compound MN of morphisms M, N of C is defined in C then the composition operations are such that $(MN)f = (Mf)(Nf)$.

This necessitates an important remark. In a semigroup, composition of any two elements is defined. A *homomorphism* of a semigroup S into a semigroup T is a mapping g of S into T such that, for all elements X, Y of S, $(XY)g = (Xg)(Yg)$. However, condition 3 does not imply that a reduction of the category C_G defines at the same time a homomorphism of S_G onto a reduced semigroup; this can be seen as follows. In condition 3 the equation $(MN)f = (Mf)(Nf)$ has no meaning if MN is undefined; now MN is undefined in C_G if and only if $MN = O$ in S_G; thus the equation $(XY)f = (Xf)(Yf)$ can be required of elements X, Y of S_G only in the case where $XY \neq O$. Such a relaxation of the homomorphism requirement for semigroups was made by Boyd (1969), who did not use categories. However this extension of the notion of semigroup homomorphism is still insufficient to cover all cases of reduction of categories: as already remarked, the set of morphisms of a category does not necessarily constitute a semigroup, even if a zero is added, and even if this category is a reduction of C_G: this will be made clear in an example, p. 69. A homomorphism of a semigroup onto another is only a particular case of reduction of morphisms in a category.

Let C be again any category, and suppose that there is a morphism E of C such that, for every morphism M of C, both EM and ME are defined and $EM = ME = M$. In other words, E acts as an identity morphism in C (although its graph can be different from that of the identity relation I and the latter is not necessarily a morphism of C). Then Ef has exactly the same properties in D: this is due to condition 3 together with the fact that f maps *CMor onto DMor*. Thus the image, through a reduction, of an identity morphism is again an identity morphism.

We shall say that two morphisms M, N in *CMor* having the same image in *DMor* —i.e. such that $Mf = Nf$—are *identified*. This will also be denoted by the equation $M \equiv N$. To identify two morphisms means to lump them together, widening their definition so that both become the same morphism in the image. When dealing with social networks, all such identifications of morphisms should occur in dual pairs: i.e. $M \equiv N$ if and only if $M^{-1} \equiv N^{-1}$. Obviously the relation $\equiv$ among the morphisms of C is an equivalence relation; the image morphisms are in one-to-one correspondence with the equivalence classes of $\equiv$. In general every such identification entails other identifications if condition 3 above is to be satisfied; in particular, if the compounds MN and $M'N'$ are defined in C and if $M \equiv M'$ and $N \equiv N'$ then by condition 3 we must also have $MN \equiv M'N'$. Conversely, it is easy to show that any

80

equivalence relation on *CMor* having the latter property defines a possible reduction of *C*.

It is not always necessary or convenient to compute a reduction in detail. Often a few basic identifications are sufficient, from which all other identifications and hence all the properties of the reduction can be deduced; the basic identifications then constitute the axioms of the reduced structure. It is often not easy or even impossible to compute the reduction implied by a set of identifications; an example is the theory of free groups and their reductions (Coxeter and Moser 1965), which is applied in the theory of a type of classificatory kinship system (White 1963). However, when *C* is finite and given in detail, it is easy to compute the reduction entailed by any set of identifications; computations too long to do by hand are done on a computer (Heil 1970). The exact procedure of such a computation will be made clear when dealing with examples later on.

Structural Equivalence of Objects

Objects *a*, *b* of a category *C* are *structurally equivalent* if, for any morphism *M* and any object *x* of *C*, *aMx* if and only if *bMx*, and *xMa* if and only if *xMb*. In other words, *a* is structurally equivalent to *b* if *a* relates to every object *x* of *C* in exactly the same ways as *b* does. From the point of view of the logic of the structure, then, *a* and *b* are absolutely equivalent, they are substitutable.

Indeed in such a case there is no reason not to identify *a* and *b*. Clearly, the relation of structural equivalence among objects of *C* is an equivalence relation, so that *CObj* can be partitioned into classes of structurally equivalent objects. We can then define in an obvious way a reduced category *Csk*, the *skeleton* of *C*, whose objects are those equivalence classes and whose morphisms and their composition operation are exactly the same as in *C*. Here the reduction mapping of morphisms is the trivial identity mapping and the reduction mapping of objects maps an object of *C* to its equivalence class which is an object of *Csk*. If the nodes of *C* are individuals, then the nodes of *Csk* are groups of structurally equivalent individuals, i.e. maximal relationally homogeneous groups. Concrete examples of such reductions will be described later.

In most social networks represented by a category of the type of C_G no two distinct objects are structurally equivalent. Structural equivalence of nodes usually appears only once a reduction of the morphisms of C_G has been accomplished. Here then two mappings, one of morphisms and one of objects, will be combined into a single reduction operation. Such double mappings exemplify the full notion of *functorial reduction*. The formal conditions which such a double mapping must satisfy are the same as conditions 1 to 3 above, except that the mapping of objects must be applied in addition to the mapping of morphisms when passing from *C* to *D*. Condition 2 must here be interpreted in the context of Nadel's argument that relations between groups of individuals in social systems are based on invariant aspects of, ultimately, relations between individuals (Nadel 1957, pp. 13 f.)

A functorial reduction is a particular kind of *functor*, the only difference being that in a functor neither the mapping of objects nor that of morphisms is required to be *onto*. Thus a functor is any double mapping of objects and morphisms leaving invariant both the distribution of morphisms among objects and the composition operation. (On functors see Mitchell 1965.) Functors furnish the only rational basis for a meaningful classification of category-like networks. Higher-order categories, where objects are themselves categories and morphisms are functors, and functors between such higher-order categories play an important role in the theory of the lower-order categories.

As a consequence of such double reductions, structural equivalence of objects will vary according to which particular reduction of morphisms is applied. A wider notion of *homothety* is involved here, that is a notion of similarity of position of individuals in a social network, this similarity being relative to particular abstract 'points of view' (reductions) taken on the structure. For example, homothety could correspond to clustering of individuals into disjunct interest groups, common interest being defined by similarity of position relative to some abstract, analytic perspective on the structure. Many such clusterings into interest groups can cross-cut at the same time. Unanticipated equivalences or solidarities in the overall structure between apparently very remote individuals might become visible as a consequence of a reduction. But of course, in general, structural equivalence does not imply actual or conscious solidarity. Concepts of structural equivalence have been used more or less implicitly in the literature; an instructive case is provided by Rosenthal (1968, p. 258) on the subject of coalitions between political parties.

Care must be taken to distinguish being in the same position in a structure and being in isomorphic positions. For example, in a structure consisting of a simple exchange cycle between social groups, no two groups are in the *same* position (i.e. are structurally equivalent), but on the other hand any two groups are in *isomorphic* positions. This could be described as a distinction between *local* and *global* homogeneity.

One can show that if a category C possesses an identity morphism E, whose graph contains the identity relation I, then two objects a, b of C are structurally equivalent if and only if aEb and bEa. In the case of social networks where each type of relation has a unique converse, all identifications among morphisms occur in dual pairs (e.g. $M \equiv N$ and $M^{-1} \equiv N^{-1}$); thus, if E is an image of I (as it will usually be), we must have $E = E^{-1}$, because $I = I^{-1}$: i.e. here the graph of E is more than just reflexive (it includes I) and transitive ($EE = E$), but it is also symmetric, so that it coincides exactly with the graph of structural equivalence among nodes. We now see the importance of identity morphisms in the computation of reductions. In the language of abstract networks of social positions (Lorrain, in press), an identity morphism corresponds to the theoretical possibility of considering the structure from the point of view of a generic ego, either an individual ego or, if structural equivalence is involved, a collective subgroup ego.

The number of possible reductions of a given C_G can be enormous. Thus far we have merely developed a framework for models of structural equivalence. In the choice of reductions lie the main substantive issues.

APPLICATIONS

Criteria for Reduction
A mixture of two strategies may be used in trying to determine meaningful reductions. They will be described in this section and applied immediately in the following sections.

One strategy we call *cultural*, which looks for possible identifications of morphisms solely on the basis of the cultural content of the morphisms, without regard to their actual graphs. If, in a network of friendship relations, the content of the generic friendship tie F is such that friends of friends are most probably also friends, then the identification $FF \equiv F$ could be made so that in the reduction the F relation would become fully transitive. Or if the generic friendship tie is such that it is symmetric and relatively strong, then the identification $F \equiv I \equiv F^{-1}$ (which also implies $FF \equiv F$ since $II = I$) would be reasonable and in the reduction the classes of structurally equivalent individuals would be cliques of mutual friends. If an 'enemy' relationship N is also given and it is felt that enemies of friends are just as fully enemies as are friends of enemies then the following equations should be imposed: $FN \equiv NF \equiv N$; thus, in particular, composition of F and N would become commutative. It is precisely such a cultural strategy that is used by Lounsbury (1964 a, b) in his analysis of kinship nomenclatures by reduction rules—although there we do not necessarily have a functorial reduction in the strict sense, because the rules are usually ordered according to precedence. One possible starting point for the cultural strategy can be to consider the equations that reduce the infinite set of 'words' to the finite S_G, as done above in deriving S_G for the generators of Figure 1.

The other strategy we call *sociometric*, which considers the actual graphs of the morphisms, identifying those that have many ordered pairs in common, or identifying to I some morphisms that have many self-loops and many symmetric ties in their graph: then in the reduction the nodes linked by these morphisms will become structurally equivalent and hence will be identified. Two morphisms whose graphs have a majority of ordered pairs in common are in similar positions within the composition operation and it is reasonable to identify them in a reduction—the more so as we have already argued that two types of relation with the same graph should be considered a single type.

Note that in a social network represented as a category the graph of a morphism RR^{-1} necessarily consists only of loops and symmetric ties, because $(RR^{-1})^{-1}$ $= (R^{-1})^{-1}R^{-1} = RR^{-1}$. Often such morphisms will be identified to the identity morphism I; we shall do so in an example about to be described. As made clear by Figure 3, $RR^{-1} \equiv I$ implies that any two nodes each related by R to a third node will be structurally equivalent in the reduction and hence identified.

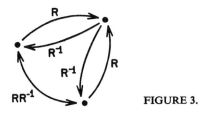

FIGURE 3.

There may be other, better strategies for reduction. Although the two ones just described considerably restrict the number of possible reductions of a network, much remains to be done to relate them more effectively to the actual dynamics of social systems. But, whatever results of this, one thing should by now be obvious:

identification of morphisms and homothety of individuals are necessarily closely interdependent.

Exploration of possible reductions of a given network is feasible only on a computer. We are currently using programs developed by Heil (1970), which compute reductions of morphisms, structural equivalence, and accomplish various other tasks useful for such an exploration.

Reduction of a Hierarchical Tree

Consider the tree of Figure 1. Let us start from the category C_G generated by P and its converse P^{-1}, computed previously. $P^{-1}P$ is the morphism whose graph (see Figure 2) contains the greatest number of loops and of symmetric ties. Applying the sociometric strategy, let us then pose $P^{-1}P \equiv I$. This single identification reduces the number of morphisms of C_G by more than half; more precisely, all the morphisms in a line of Table 1 become identified. Take, for example, line 4: $P^{-1}P \equiv I$ implies that $\quad P^{-1}P^2 = (P^{-1}P)P \equiv IP = P \quad$ and $\quad PP^{-2}P^2 = PP^{-1}(P^{-1}P)P \equiv PP^{-1}IP$ $= PP^{-1}P = P$. The composition operation of the reduced morphisms is given in Table 4; their graphs are given in Figure 4, where structurally equivalent nodes have been lumped together. Individuals at the same *level* in the hierarchy become identified.

Note that the composition of the *graphs* of two morphisms M, N of this reduction is in general not equal to the graph of the compound morphism MN. No more is required than that the former be a subgraph of the latter. For example the composition of the graph of P^{-1} and the graph of P (see Figure 4) consists of two loops (a, a) and (b, b); however the graph of $P^{-1}P = I$ contains in addition the $(1, 1)$ loop.

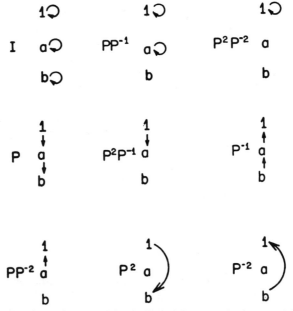

FIGURE 4 Graphs of morphisms in the reduction of the network of Figure 1, implied by the identification $P^{-1}P \equiv I$. a represents the set of nodes 2 and 5, b the set of nodes 3 and 4.

TABLE 4

Composition table of the functional reduction of the network of
Figure 1, implied by the identification $P^{-1}P \equiv I$.

	I	PP^{-1}	P^2P^{-2}	P	P^2P^{-1}	P^{-1}	PP^{-2}	P^2	P^{-2}
I	I	PP^{-1}	P^2P^{-2}	P	P^2P^{-1}	P^{-1}	PP^{-2}	P^2	P^{-2}
PP^{-1}	PP^{-1}	PP^{-1}	P^2P^{-2}	P	P^2P^{-1}	PP^{-2}	PP^{-2}	P^2	✕
P^2P^{-2}	P^2P^{-2}	P^2P^{-2}	P^2P^{-2}	P^2P^{-1}	P^2P^{-1}	✕	✕	P^2	✕
P	P	P^2P^{-1}	✕	P^2	✕	PP^{-1}	P^2P^{-2}	✕	PP^{-2}
P^2P^{-1}	P^2P^{-1}	P^2P^{-1}	✕	P^2	✕	P^2P^{-2}	P^2P^{-2}	✕	✕
P^{-1}	P^{-1}	P^{-1}	PP^{-2}	I	PP^{-1}	P^{-2}	P^{-2}	P	✕
PP^{-2}	PP^{-2}	PP^{-2}	PP^{-2}	PP^{-1}	PP^{-1}	✕	✕	P	✕
P^2	P^2	✕	✕	✕	✕	P^2P^{-1}	✕	✕	P^2P^{-2}
P^{-2}	P^{-2}	P^{-2}	P^{-2}	P^{-1}	P^{-1}	✕	✕	I	✕

Note.—The meaning of the double lines is explained further in the text.

This first reduction of C_G is still somewhat complex for a population of five persons: either they or observers might find the structure difficult t grasp. Now, by definition of a hierarchical tree,† where each person (except the topmost one) has a unique immediate superior, the morphism PP^{-1} occurs exclusively as an endomorphism; from a cultural standpoint, it is then reasonable to pose a further identification: $PP^{-1} \equiv I$. This second reduction, where $PP^{-1} \equiv P^{-1}P \equiv I$, may be considered either as a direct reduction of C_G or as a reduction of the previous reduction where only $P^{-1}P \equiv I$. This is more conveniently accomplished by working with Table 4. In such a table one can verify in the following way if a given partition of the set of morphisms represents a possible reduction.

Consider one such partition, indicated by double lines in Table 4. By extending the double lines of the partition throughout the table supercells are determined. The

†By this we do not mean a transitive relation; in the language of partial orders the tree here is the Hasse diagram of the general authority relation. See Szász 1963, pp. 17 f.

partition will represent a possible reduction—i.e. one satisfying condition 3 above—if and only if, given any supercell, the morphisms appearing in it are all in the same class of the given partition. Such is the case of the partition of Table 4. But if it had not been the case, for example if our partition had involved only the identification $PP^{-1} \equiv I$, then we should have arrived exactly to the partition of Table 4 simply by grouping certain lines together (and also the corresponding columns together) so that the supercells would satisfy the required property; of course only the groupings necessitated by the original identification must be effected and no others. Thus the double lines in Table 4 give exactly the reduction of C_G implied by the equation $PP^{-1} \equiv P^{-1}P \equiv I$; this is the reduction indicated by brackets in Table 1. This reduction could also have been computed by algebraic manipulation of equations, as in the case of the previous reduction.

Table 5 gives the composition operation of this reduction of Table 4. The graphs of morphisms in this further reduction of C_G are given in Figure 5. These are exactly

TABLE 5

Composition table of the functorial reduction of the network of Figure 1, implied by the identifications $PP^{-1} \equiv P^{-1}P \equiv I$.

	I	P	P^{-1}	P^2	P^{-2}
I	I	P	P^{-1}	P^2	P^{-2}
P	P	P^2	I	$\times$	P^{-1}
P^{-1}	P^{-1}	I	P^{-2}	P	$\times$
P^2	P^2	$\times$	P	$\times$	I
P^{-2}	P^{-2}	P^{-1}	$\times$	I	$\times$

the global roles which one would expect, in this case. Later on we shall effect even further reductions of this reduced category.

Similar results are obtained whenever the identifications $PP^{-1} \equiv P^{-1}P \equiv I$ are made in a tree (see Footnote p. 67). All individuals at the same level in the tree (counting levels from the top) become structurally equivalent and are identified: this is because $P^{-1}P \equiv I$ implies that, for all positive integers k, $P^{-k}P^k \equiv I$. If there are $n+1$ levels, then there are exactly $2n+1$ morphisms: $I, P, P^2, \ldots, P^n, P^{-1}, P^{-2}, \ldots, P^{-n}$. The composition operation is simply the following: given integers i, j (positive or negative), $P^i P^j$, if defined, is equal to P^{i+j} (here we pose $P^0 = I$). Composition thus is commutative.

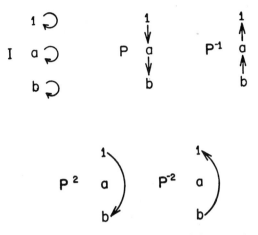

FIGURE 5 Graphs of morphisms in the reduction of the network of Figure 1,
implied by the identifications $PP^{-1} \equiv P^{-1}P \equiv I$. a and b as in Figure 4.

Note that if we added to these morphisms a zero and defined $MN = O$ whenever
the compound MN is undefined, then the result would not be a semigroup, if $n > 0$,
because then composition would not be associative: e.g. $P^n(P^nP^{-n}) = P^nI = P^n$ but
$(P^nP^n)P^{-n} = OP^{-n} = O$. Note also that this does not contradict point 3 of the
definition of a category.

Such a reduction of a tree is very meaningful in organizations such as armed forces,
where every person at a given level is expected to obey the orders of any person at a
higher level. Moreover, in such a case, the reduction constitutes a time-invariant
picture of the hierarchy, which remains the same whatever be the changes in number
of branches, span of control, etc., so long as the number of levels is not changed.

Kinship, Role Trees

Certain kinship systems are based on identifications of the type $RR^{-1} \equiv I$. Denote
by C the father-child relationship and by W the husband-wife relationship. Applying
a cultural argument, we can impose $CC^{-1} \equiv I$. *Classificatory* kinship systems are
those where in addition $C^{-1}C \equiv I$ is required, so that siblings are structurally equivalent and groups of siblings are considered as units in the system; this is Radcliffe-
Brown's principle of the unity of the sibling group (Radcliffe-Brown 1950, pp. 23 ff.).
A refinement of this framework is possible where siblings are distinguished by sex.
If in addition $WW^{-1} \equiv W^{-1}W \equiv I$ is required, then the society is partitioned into
'marriage classes': there is a unique predetermined class from which a woman of a
given class must take her husband, and conversely. This would be a society with strict
prescribed marriage. Such structures—call them *elementary* kinship systems—have
been extensively studied by Lévi-Strauss (1949) and by White (1963); Lévi-Strauss'
definition of an elementary kinship structure is less restrictive, however.

Other identifications occur frequently in elementary kinship systems. One example
is $WC \equiv CW$, corresponding to a rule of matrilateral cross-cousin marriage. Another

example is $C^n \equiv I$, for some positive integer n; this means that successive generations in a given patrilineage will be arranged along a cycle of length n, the $(n+1)$-th generation being in the same kinship class as the first, etc. The case $n = 2$ is particularly frequent and is referred to in the literature as a system with 'alternating generations'.

When such 'cultural' identifications are applied to an infinite abstract role tree containing all possible kinship roles relative to a generic ego, they amount to folding in and rolling up the tree in a systematic way such that in the end a finite structure is obtained. The intuitive verbal analysis of White (1963, Chapter 1) amounts precisely to this and such an operation can be described as a functorial reduction (see Lorrain 1970).

Such a finite elementary kinship structure can also be obtained 'sociometrically' as a functorial reduction of the network of kinship relations in the concrete population, as shown by Boyd (1969) in the language of semigroups and homomorphisms.†
The elementary kinship structure is then seen to represent a time-invariant reduction of the detailed kinship network in the population.

Classificatory Reduction
Reduction of a tree to a linear ordering of levels, considered previously, is a prototype of a more general kind of reduction, *classificatory reduction*, the result of which is a type of category called a *quasi-homogeneous space*, of which elementary kinship structures, componential analyses, and classical affine space are examples. The classificatory reduction of a category that satisfies the 'principle of reciprocity' results from identifying *all* endomorphisms to the identity; this represents an extreme form of the sociometric strategy. It is possible (see Lorrain, in press) to construct, using this notion of classificatory reduction, a theory embracing the core of classificatory kinship nomenclatures, elementary kinship structures, systems of binary oppositions, componential analysis, hierarchies with levels, and balance theory. Such a theory offers multiple points of view on the same structures and can be expressed in dual ways, emphasizing either relations distributed among pairs of individuals or individuals allocated to social positions.

Restrictions on the Composition Operation
Only in kinship networks or in formal hierarchies are very long 'words' known to represent a meaningful type of relation. This suggests limiting the length of words, by considering a long word to be 'undefined' whenever its graph is distinct from the graph of any shorter word. This would give rise to a truncated composition table, in which reduction of morphisms could proceed as usual. A word is perhaps not very significant if it has more letters than there are nodes in a given network; word length should be limited still more drastically if attenuation of indirect structural effects with length of path is considered severe. The model then would focus more on local structure, overlap between successive neighborhoods being the basis of any long range order; in extreme form the model collapses back to a more conventional sociometric

†There is however an error in Boyd's theorem (1969, p. 145), which was not in a previous mimeographed version of that paper: a condition must be added, so that the operators considered in the theorem are everywhere defined.

88

analysis of graphs. For example, step by step transmission of social influences—say diffusion or gossip—is probably adequately captured by looking at generator ties alone, so long as there are no regular patterns of alliance and compartmentalization. But it is exactly such patterns which can be found by the search for models of structural equivalence from the category C_G.

In some situations it might prove necessary to define a new type of binary relation reporting whether an individual knows another well quite aside from the feelings and expectations they have for one another. Then only those generator ties that coincide with knowledge ties would be permitted as first steps in compound ties. Such a principle has been applied in a sociometric study by White (1961). It might even prove necessary, in some cases, to include data on perceptions of ties by third parties to obtain more realistic accounts of which secondary ties exist and are effective.

Reduction of an Actual Social Network

The network considered here is abstracted from data collected by Sampson (in press).† The population consists of the members of a monastery. This group was a residual of a long period of turmoil and conflict between a more progressive tendency —the 'young turks'—and a more conservative one—the 'loyal opposition'. It continued as a group for a relatively short time (approximately two weeks), during which it remained isolated from previous members and after which is disintegrated. However, although there was not time enough for social integration to come to conclusion, the relations measured were considered clear enough to warrant an analysis by categorical-functorial methods. Two generator relations are considered, P and N, whose graphs are given in Figure 6. aPb means that a likes b most, is influenced by him most, or sanctions him positively most frequently; P is thus a general positively oriented relationship. aNb means that a likes b least, esteems him least, or sanctions him negatively most frequently; N is thus a general negatively oriented relationship.

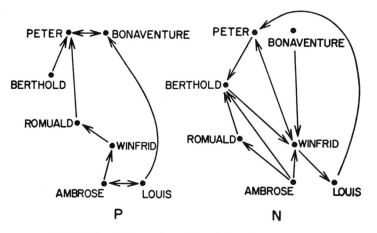

FIGURE 6   Positive and negative relations in a monastery.

†Interpretation of the results was greatly facilitated by the kind help of Dr. Sampson.

89

Other degrees of the relationships were in the data, but they were excluded for the purpose of the present analysis. Moreover, because these two relations do not correspond to a well enough delineated set of social expectations, their converses were not included as generators.

In spite of there being only two generators, the number of morphisms in C_G is enormous, probably at least several hundred. Accordingly, the length of 'words' was limited to between five and six letters, keeping only seventy morphisms. But the reductions that were then operated were so drastic that this limitation did not change the final result to the slightest extent.

Reductions of C_G to categories with four or five morphisms only were first effected, by applying the sociometric strategy. For example, since P and P^3 have eight ties in common as compared to twelve ties in one or the other, P was identified to P^3. This implies $P^2 \equiv P^4$, but these two morphisms have exactly the same graph, so that they are already considered equal in C_G. N^2, N^3, N^4, and N^5 have between 60 and 97% of their ties in common, so that the identification $N^2 \equiv N^3$, which implies $N^3 \equiv N^4 \equiv N^5$, was imposed. And so on. However these reductions with four or five morphisms were still difficult to interpret and further reductions were operated. Only four non-trivial ones were possible, two with three morphisms and two with two morphisms. The latter two are given in Figures 7 and 8, where the same labels P and N are retained for their images. In those reductions structural equivalence does not depend on an identity morphism, none having been included in C_G.

In the reduction of Figure 7, N has become a universal neutral relation linking every node to every other node. This neutrality is obvious in the composition operation

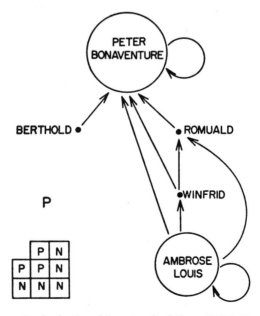

FIGURE 7   A first example of reduction of the network of Figure 6. Only the graph of P is shown; the graph of N is a trivial one linking every node to every other node.

90

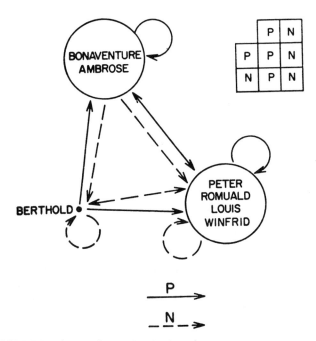

FIGURE 8. A second example of reduction of the network of Figure 6.

of this reduction, where N acts as a zero morphism. P is transitive, so that the structure takes the form of a partial order. It is significant that Peter and Bonaventure become identified: they were clearly the leading, most influential elements of the group at that time, although for very different reasons, Bonaventure being rather above the battle and Peter leading the 'loyal opposition'; note that Peter and Bonaventure are not equivalent in the reduction of Figure 8.

In relation to Figure 7, it is remarkable that Romuald and Winfrid were the first to leave the group. Romuald had come late and was caught between the two tendencies and Winfrid had been very much associated with the 'young turks'. On the other hand Berthold, a member of the 'loyal opposition', was really a special case, close to Peter, but very isolated from the others; Ambrose, although linked positively to one of the 'young turks', was a member of the 'loyal opposition', closely tied (symmetrically) to Louis, who was closest to Bonaventure. As we shall see in the next section, the intermediary nodes in an ordering (such as in Figure 7) are really in quite a particular position: structurally speaking, and however paradoxical this may seem, the two extremes are in fact closer to each other than to the intermediaries and, in so far as the structure is correctly represented, they are more likely to ally, leaving the intermediaries to themselves. Such a situation was certainly the case in the group considered and seems to be reflected in the structure of the reduction of Figure 7. As a matter of information, Peter was the third person to leave, having obviously lost his function as leader of the opposition as soon as Romuald and Winfrid were gone.

The reduction of Figure 8 is quite interesting; in particular the clusters of nodes are totally different from·those in the reduction of Figure 7. Unfortunately our lack of familiarity with the concrete social situation of which these networks are abstractions prevents us from a full interpretation. Nevertheless, it is remarkable that Berthold once again appears as an isolate and that Romuald and Winfrid, those closest to the 'young turk' tendency and who were the first to leave and also Peter, whose departure followed immediately, are grouped together. The case of Louis being also lumped with these three is rather puzzling, however. Note also the 'ambiguous' (*P and N*) relations linking both the two-men node and the one-man node to the four-men node and also linking the latter to itself. Of course P and N must be understood as 'positive' and 'negative' only in a very generalized sense; their reality could hardly be assessed by the more impressionistic methods of observation. Note also that the graphs of P and N in this reduction are isomorphic although one appears rotated relative to the other.

The composition operation in Figure 8 is also interesting, especially if we consider its representation as a graph in Figure 9. This graph represents the 'role' system involved in the social network of Figure 8; roles are themselves related by role relations, because of the interlocks represented by composition: e.g. N links P to N, in Figure 9, because $PN = N$ (see Figure 10 for a more inspiring visual representation of a role relation linking two roles). Figure 9 shows a 'positive' and a 'negative' role: the positive one relates positively to itself and negatively to the negative one, the negative role relates positively to the positive one and negatively to itself. This is a rather familiar type of social situation.

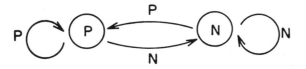

FIGURE 9   Graphic representation of the composition operation in Figure 8.

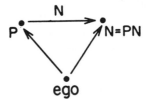

FIGURE 10   Roles related by a role relation.

On the Solidarity and Alliance of Extremes

Consider the linear hierarchy category of Figure 5 and Table 5; denote it by H_0. The sole identification $P^2 \equiv P^{-2}$, without any other identifications, defines a possible reduction of H_0, as is easily verified by glancing at Table 5. One can also see from Table 5 that this reduction—denote it H_1—is the one nearest to H_0, in the sense that any other reduction of H_0 involves more than one identification.

The composition operation of H_1 is given in Table 6. Note that in H_1 the compound of any two morphisms is defined, i.e. any 'role' can interlock with any other 'role'. Moreover, as in H_0, composition in H_1 is commutative. P^{-1} can now also be written as P^3. This composition operation is isomorphic to that of the cyclic group of order four, i.e. to the table of addition of integers modulo four: simply write 0 instead of I, 1 or -3 instead of P, 2 or -2 instead of Q, 3 or -1 instead of P^{-1}. No further structural equivalence of objects appears when passing from H_0 to H_1.

TABLE 6

Composition table resulting from
identification of P^2 to P^{-2} in Table 5.

	I	P	Q	P^{-1}
I	I	P	Q	P^{-1}
P	P	Q	P^{-1}	I
Q	Q	P^{-1}	I	P
P^{-1}	P^{-1}	I	P	Q

Note.—Q is the common image of P^2 and P^{-2}.

A symmetric relation such as Q between the two extremes of a hierarchy is not a rare occurrence in classificatory kinship systems and is referred to as 'intergenerational solidarity'. There is an obvious analogy to the ideology according to which citizens can be called the masters of their top executives, the servant of the people.

Now only one non-trivial reduction of H_1 is possible: it is the one where $I \equiv Q$ and $P \equiv P^{-1}$. Call it H_2. H_2 has two morphisms, I and R, with I and Q of H_1 mapping to I of H_2, P and P^{-1} of H_1 mapping to R of H_2. The composition operation is $II = RR = I$, $IR = RI = R$. This is isomorphic to the composition operation of the cyclic group of order two, i.e. to the addition operation of integers modulo two. In H_2 nodes 1 and b are structurally equivalent so that H_2 takes the form of two symmetrically related moieties (see Figure 11). If R were a 'negative' relation and I a 'positive' one, then this would be a classical situation of 'structural balance', a notion examined in the next section. If H_0 represented a segment of a kinship lineage, H_2 would correspond to a case of 'alternating generations', mentioned earlier.

We now clearly see in what sense we could say, in the last section, that the extreme positions in an ordering are structurally closer and the intermediary ones less 'stable', perhaps more likely to become opposed to both extremes in the case of conflict. Of course this makes sense only in so far as the given structure is correctly described by such a hierarchical arrangement.

93

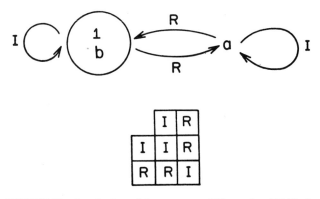

	I	R
I	I	R
R	R	I

FIGURE 11 A reduction of the category of Figure 5 and Table 5.

Balance Theory as a Special Case of Functorial Reduction

At first sight balance theory is a simple variation of graph theory and thus has little connection with the elaborate algebraic structures derived from role graphs. Further inspection shows that balance theory, in the formulation of Abelson and Rosenberg (1958), can be expressed as a special kind of functorial mapping of a category. The image category is required to be just the graph of the cyclic group of order two (see Figure 12)—call it the *two-category*. Only two generator roles are allowed, both symmetric so that each is its own converse. Further, one particular generator role, that thought to represent positive feeling, is mapped to the image identity. The other generator is mapped to the other morphism in the two-category. Compound roles are not defined explicitly, but all ties corresponding to paths with the same structure are mapped to the same image element. The 'addition' of different ties between a given pair corresponds to seeing if they all map to the same image element. The requirement that all closed cycles be 'positive', in Cartwright and Harary's (1956) graph-theoretic formulation, corresponds to an extreme form of the 'sociometric' criterion for a reduction used earlier: this requirement means that all endomorphisms

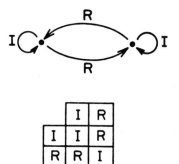

	I	R
I	I	R
R	R	I

FIGURE 12 The two-category: the graph of the cyclic group of order two. This category is isomorphic to the one in Figure 11.

94

are mapped to the identity; this is a case of 'classificatory reduction'. Thus we see how such a functor partitions the set of nodes into two classes, positive relations holding only within the same class and negative relations linking only individuals in distinct classes.

Balance theory shares the weaknesses of the categorical-functorial approach (see discussion in conclusion) but has a number of further weaknesses. If a structure is not 'balanced' resort must be had to measures of the 'amount' of imbalance, and adequate measures of this type remain to be devised (see Boorman 1970). Whereas in the categorical approach one can look for the coarsest possible non-trivial functorial reduction and the resulting model of structural equivalence can just as reasonably be called 'balanced', whatever the number of equivalence sets and image relations.† In the categorical approach there is no need to require any of the generator roles to map to the image identity. For many theoretical purposes it is more fruitful to require not a direct tie but having direct ties to the same person as the criterion for being together in a clique. Little systematic work on extending balance theory to non-symmetric roles has been published, and never more than two generator roles are used.

Nothing is lost by using the categorical approach. Search for a reduction to the two-category will show whether the structure is in fact 'balanced' and, if so, produce the required two cliques. The reduction of Figure 11 is an example; the cliques here are 1, 3, and 4 versus 2 and 5 (see Figure 1). Even in this simple example something is gained by the categorical approach. The cliques and the two image roles are derived from data on role ties that need not be symmetric nor have any positive or negative affective qualities. Instead one can discern on structural grounds a likely line of cleavage which may become realized in explicit social relation only later.

The generalization of balance theory proposed by Davis (1967), which includes the possibility of there being more than two cliques, can also be represented by functors. However, here not all endomorphisms will be mapped to the identity.

CONCLUSION

Networks will probably become as important to sociology as Euclidian space and its generalizations are to physics. Unfortunately the mathematical theory of networks is far from having attained a degree of development even remotely comparable to that of modern topology and analysis. Graph theory (Berge 1967, Ore 1962) has little unity and has little to say on interrelations between relations, dealing essentially with isolated graphs; moreover it does not offer any criteria for reduction and comparison of graphs. Little motivation seems to have developed within the sociometric tradition to study interrelations among relations. However, papers by Davis and Leinhardt (see Footnote p. 52), Holland and Leinhardt (see Footnote p. 51), and Boyle (1969) are stimulating exceptions to this.

The categorical-functorial framework, at least as applied here, has several weaknesses. One is that it seems insensible to distance between nodes in the network of

---

†A manuscript by J. A. Davis entitled 'Boundary Relationships' (1965) develops similar ideas in terms of multiple graphs.

generator ties, although of course the unreduced C_G gives full account of such distance. Certain network properties seem not to be characterizable by the composition operation of morphisms. Friedell (1967) has suggested that semilattices, a type of partial order less restrictive than a tree, may be a plausible representation of the reality of authority structures when individuals have more than one immediate supervisor; however, it is impossible to characterize a semilattice only be the composition operation of its representation as a category (Lorrain 1970).

Strength of ties and intensity of flows should really be handled quantitatively. It should be feasible to treat in a systematic and global manner networks where numbers are associated to ties. Representation of these networks as tensors and the use of tensor fields is one possible formalization.

Although individual attributes such as sex can easily be represented by differentiating ties according to the sex of their endpoints, this makes less sense for more continuous attributes such as age. However around visible attributes such as age, race, or sex there often cristallize crucial ideologies of role differentiation, of inferiorization, or of exploitation. There seems to be no obvious general way to integrate attributes to a network representation. This is a real and difficult problem, even though we have argued that social differentiation is essentially a function of the interweaving of social relationships.

Another important direction for development of functorial reduction ideas would lie in formalization of numerical reduction criteria, e.g. of the idea of the 'simplest' reduction within a certain structural 'distance' of an initial category. A collection of models of structural distance is analyzed in an integrated fashion by Boorman (1970), who shows how simple metrics on sets and partitions naturally generalize to highly interpretable and computable metrics on semigroups and related algebraic objects. At the same time, developments of this approach could provide much needed stability for categorical network theory. Even a single exception to a rule generally valid in a social system represented as a category can totally disrupt its reduction, even making it trivial: it should be possible to approach the problem of 'exceptions', as well as the problem of measurement error, with the help of appropriate measures of structural approximation. These metric concepts could also be used to evaluate relative degrees of structural equivalence among the elements of a structure.

In a sense, our approach requires homogeneity of point of view among the members of a social network. However this really applies only to generators and, even if all individuals agree in their perception of generator ties, competing ideologies differing in their global interpretation of the system are still conceivable. A social network does not form a unitary block. A network in fact *consists* of holes, decouplings, dissociations; ties can reflect conflict as well as solidarity, they reflect interdependence, not necessarily integration. Numerous points of view on a network are possible, latent lines of scission can be drawn. In short, our notion of network is closest to a dialectical notion of totality (see Lefebvre 1955), and as such could provide the foundation for a treatment of social dynamics. As has been shown in the case of language (see Jakobson 1957, p. 10), synchrony does not coincide at all with statics, in systems where there is relative decoupling or autonomy of parts: conceptions of synchronic structure are of crucial importance in the question of dynamics, and conversely.

Nevertheless, in this paper we have not really faced the question of diachrony. To do so it would be particularly important to consider the responses of structures to—and their shaping by—such driving forces as the demographic factors of birth and death, the inputs from concrete everyday social practice, and the absolutely crucial factor of material resources. The dual processes of allocation of individuals to social positions and of social positions to individuals would be a central concern here, special attention being paid to actual numbers—such is the subject, for example, of White's *Chains of Opportunity* (1970). Links should be made explicit between these considerations and mathematical theories of morphogenesis in dynamical systems (Thom 1968, 1969).

The main strength of the categorical-functorial approach is in locating sets of individuals, however large or small be the direct distance between any two in a set, who are placed similarly with respect to all other sets of individuals, to the extent that total relations and flows are captured by the aggregation of detailed relations consonant with those equivalence sets of individuals. The notions of class society and of imperialism are prototypical examples of such global structural representations. Structurally coherent solutions encompassing all individuals at once, rather than successive calculations of connections between more and more remote individuals, are the goal of the analysis.

REFERENCES

Abelson, R. P., and Rosenberg, M. Symbolic psychologic. *Behavioral Science*, 1959, 3, 1–13.
Berge, Cl. *Théorie des graphes et ses applications*. 2nd ed. Paris: Dunod, 1967.
Boorman, S. A. Metric spaces of complex objects. Unpubl. honors thesis, Harvard College, 1970.
Boyd, J. P. The algebra of kinship. Unpubl. doctoral dissertation, University of Michigan, 1966.
Boyd, J. P. The algebra of group kinship. *Journal of Mathematical Psychology*, 1969, 6, 139–167.
Boyle, R. P. Algebraic systems for normal and hierarchical sociograms. *Sociometry*, 1969, 32, 99–119.
Cartwright, D., and Harary, F. Structural balance: a generalization of Heider's theory. *Psychological Review*, 1956, 63, 277–293.
Clifford, A. H., and Preston, G. B. *The algebraic theory of semigroups*. Vol. 1. Providence (R. I.): American Mathematical Society, 1961.
Courrège, Ph. Un modèle mathématique des structures élémentaires de parenté. *L'Homme*, 1965, 5 (3–4), 248–290.
Coxeter, H. S. M., and Moser, W. O. *Generators and their relations for discrete groups*. Berlin: Springer 1965.
Davis, J. A. Clustering and structural balance in graphs. *Human Relations*, 1967, 20, 181–187.
Davis, J. A. Statistical analysis of pair relationships. *Sociometry*, 1968, 31, 102 ff.
Friedell, M. Organizations as semilattices. *American Sociological Review*, 1967, 32, 46–54.
Friedell, M. On the structure of shared awareness. *Behavioral Science*, 1969, 14, 28–39.
Gross, N., Mason, W. S., and McEachern, W. *Explorations in role analysis*. New York: Wiley, 1958.
Heil, G. H. Computer aided study of the algebraic structure of sociograms. Unpubl. honors thesis, Harvard College, 1970.
Jakobson, R. Typological studies and their contribution to historical comparative linguistics. In *Reports for the Eighth International Congress of Linguists*, Oslo: Oslo University Press, 1957, Supplement, pp. 1–11.
Kron, G. *Tensor analysis of networks*. New York: Wiley, 1939.
LeCorbeiller, P. *Matrix analysis of networks*. Cambridge (Mass.): Harvard University Press, 1950.
Lefebvre, H. La notion de totalité dans les sciences sociales. *Cahiers internationaux de sociologie*, 1955, 18 (1), 55–77.

Lévi-Strauss, Cl. *Les structures élémentaires de la parenté.* 1st ed., Paris: Presses universitaires de France, 1949. 2nd ed., Paris, The Hague: Mouton, 1967.

Lorrain, F. The network-organisation of social systems and cultural modes of classification. Unpubl. doctoral dissertation, Harvard University, 1970. (Transl. of Lorrain in press, plus a mathematical appendix.)

Lorrain, F. *Organisation réticulaire des systèmes sociaux et modes culturels de classification.* Paris, The Hague: Mouton, in press.

Lounsbury, F. G. A formal account of the Crow- and Omaha-type kinship terminologies. In *Explorations in cultural anthropology,* ed. by W. H: Goodenough, New York: McGraw-Hill, 1964, 351–393. (a)

Lounsbury, F. G. The structural analysis of kinship semantics. In *Proceedings of the Ninth International Congress of Linguists,* ed. by H. G. Lunt, The Hague: Mouton, 1964, 1073–1093. (b)

Mitchell, B. *Theory of categories.* New York: Academic, 1965.

Nadel, S. F. *The theory of social structure.* London: Cohen & West, 1957.

Ore, O. *Theory of graphs.* Providence (R. I.): American Mathematical Society, 1962.

Radcliffe-Brown, A. R. Introduction to *African systems of kinship and marriage,* ed. by A. R. Radcliffe-Brown and D. Forde, London: Oxford University Press, 1950, 1–85.

Rosenthal, H. Voting and coalition models in election simulations. In *Simulation in the study of politics,* ed. by W. D. Coplin, Chicago: Markham, 1968.

Sampson, S. F. *Crisis in the cloister.* Cambridge (Mass.): Harvard University Press, in press.

Slepian, P. *Foundations of network analysis.* New York: Springer, 1968.

Slobodkin, L. B. *Growth and regulation of animal populations.* New York: Holt, Rinehart and Winston, 1961.

Szász, G. *Introduction to lattice theory.* 3rd ed. New York, London: Academic, 1963.

Thom, R. Topologie et signification. *L'Age de la science,* 1968 (4), 1–24.

Thom, R. Topological models in biology. *Topology,* 1969, **8,** 313–335.

Weil, A. Sur l'étude algébrique de certains types de loi de mariage (système Murngin). In Lévi-Strauss 1949, Chapter 14.

White, H. C. Management conflict and sociometric structure. *American Journal of Sociology,* 1961, **67,** 185–199.

White, H. C. *An anatomy of kinship.* Englewood Cliffs (N.J.): Prentice-Hall, 1963.

White, H. C. *Chains of opportunity.* Cambridge (Mass.): Harvard University Press, 1970.

Wolfe, A. W., and Schenk, F. W. On structural comparison of networks. *Canadian Review of Sociology and Anthropology,* 1970, **7.**

From Clinton B. DeSoto, *Journal of Abnormal and Social Psychology 60*, 417-421 (1960), copyright 1960 by the American Psychological Association, reprinted by permission.

LEARNING A SOCIAL STRUCTURE[1]

CLINTON B. DE SOTO

Johns Hopkins University

FOR some years social psychologists have shown increasing interest in mathematical properties of social structures, ranging from investigations of the extent to which sociometric choices are mutual to experimental manipulations of the centrality of communication networks. This interest has been accompanied, however, by a curious lack of concern with the subjects' (Ss') views of these properties. For example, in the studies of mutuality of sociometric choices, the Ss are not ordinarily asked if *they* expect the choices to be mutual. Only recently, in such work as Tagiuri's (1958) generalization of sociometry, relational analysis, and Heider's (1958) discussion of naive psychology, has there been serious concern with the Ss' perception of such properties.

Apparently psychologists have assumed that Ss cannot or do not appreciate these properties. Yet folklore is full of essentially mathematical statements about interpersonal relations: "The way to get someone to like you is to like him," "You can't serve two masters," "There's always a faster gun somewhere." And recent questionnaire studies (De Soto & Kuethe, 1958, 1959) have demonstrated that Ss ascribe such properties rather freely to interpersonal relations, sometimes accurately, sometimes inaccurately.

Historically social psychologists have repeatedly been compelled to recognize the importance of cognitive processes in man, to the need, for example, for crediting people with role expectations as well as role behaviors. This fact makes it appear unwise to ignore their readiness to assign mathematical properties to interpersonal relations. It makes it important to look for effects of such attributions of properties in activities besides answering questionnaries. There are in the literature many findings which are suggestive of such effects. For example, Kogan and Tagiuri

[1] This work was supported in part by Grant NSF-G4827 from the National Science Foundation. The writer is grateful to Martin N. Narun and Daniel M Glasner for aid in the collection of data.

(1958) found that people expect those they choose to choose one another, thus evidencing, for a special case, their expectation that sociometric choices will be mutual.

One task in which Ss' tendencies to assign properties to interpersonal relations might be expected to have especially prominent effects is that of learning a social structure. Learning a social structure means learning the relations among a set of people. It is a task that usually faces a person when he enters a social group, and it can be quite difficult as indexed by the information he must assimilate. It is a reasonable prediction that his assignments of properties to the relations which form the structure, operating as expectancies or hypotheses, will facilitate or hinder his learning of the structure according to their validity. The present study was designed to verify this general prediction and also to examine in more detail some of the psychological processes involved.

The study was basically a verbal learning experiment in which Ss learned miniature social structures. The dependent variable was the number of trials required. There were two independent variables: the interpersonal relation that formed the structure, and the mathematical properties of the structure. In their questionnaire study of the properties assigned to various interpersonal relations, De Soto and Kuethe (1959) found that the relations fell into two main classes: those regarded as asymmetric, which were also regarded as transitive, and those regarded as symmetric, some of which were also regarded as transitive and some of which were not. For the present study, the relation "influences" was chosen to exemplify the relations people expect to be asymmetric and transitive, "likes" was chosen to exemplify those expected to be symmetric and transitive, and "confides in" was chosen to exemplify those expected to be symmetric but not transitive.

Structures characterized by eight different sets of mathematical properties were used. Four-man structures were used because they were the largest Ss could learn with relative

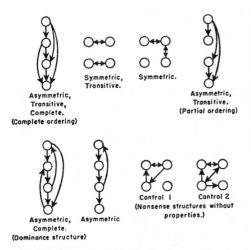

FIG. 1. Structures used in the learning experiment.

ease in pilot studies. The structures are depicted in Fig. 1, with circles representing people and arrows a relation. An arrow going from one circle to another means the first person stands in the given relation to the second; if the relation is "influences," it means the first person influences the second. The requirements for the various properties may be defined informally as follows: For symmetry, the arrows must go in both directions, or not at all, between a pair of individuals. For asymmetry, the arrows must never go in both directions between a pair of individuals. The requirement for transitivity is more complex. If there is an arrow from Individual a to Individual b, and another from Individual b to Individual c, then, for the transitive property to hold, there must be one from a to c. For the complete property to hold, there must be at least one arrow connecting the individuals in all possible pairs. More formal definitions of these and other properties are given by Coombs, Raiffa, and Thrall (1954) and Kershner and Wilcox (1950). The names given to some of the structures in Fig. 1 are based on their properties.

The task given each S in the experiment was to learn one of the structures. He did not see a drawing of the structure, however, nor was the relation represented by abstract arrows. Instead, the arrows were replaced by one of the flesh-and-blood relations, "influences,"

"likes," or "confides in," and he had to learn, by repeated trial and error, whether or not Jim likes Ray, whether or not Ray likes Stan, and so on for the 12 ordered pairs of names which exist in a four-man structure. This arrangement of the task avoided unintended suggestions to the S about properties of the structure and approximated the real-life case where people learn a social structure by observing the pair-wise interactions among its members rather than from devices like organizational charts.

An experimental condition in this study was a combination of one of the abstract structures and one of the interpersonal relations. There were 19 experimental conditions. Each of the first three structures in Fig. 1 was formed from each of the three relations, producing 9 conditions, and the remaining five structures were formed from the relations "influences" and "likes," producing 10 more conditions. The first 9 conditions were the basic experimental ones, since a crucial interaction was predicted for them. On the basis of the conclusion by De Soto and Kuethe (1959) that college students (used as Ss in that study and this) are alert to power based orderings, it was predicted that they would expect the relation "influences" to be asymmetric and transitive and, possibly, complete and would therefore learn a complete ordering based on "influences" more readily than one of the symmetric structures, while for "likes" and "confides in," which Ss expect to be symmetric, the converse would be true. The remaining conditions were included to provide further analytical possibilities.

METHOD

The experimental method resembled that of traditional paired-associates learning experiments. The Ss, male undergraduates at Johns Hopkins University, were assigned randomly, nine to each of the 19 experimental conditions, and were run individually.

Their task is described well by the instructions given them:

This experiment is on the learning of interpersonal relationships. There are four people involved, Bill, Jim, Ray, and Stan, and your job is to learn who likes who among these people.

On the upper side of each of these cards are printed the names of two of the four people. In each case, the first person either does or does not like the second. If he does, it says so on the other side of the

100

card. If he doesn't, nothing is printed on the other side of the card.

When I tell you to begin, look at the names on the top card. If you think the first person likes the second, say so. If you don't think he does, say so. For example, if the first name were Sam and the second were Charlie, you would say either "Sam likes Charlie" or "Sam doesn't like Charlie." Then, turn the card over and see whether or not he does, and place the card on a new pile.

Go through the rest of the cards the same way, and then I will shuffle them and you can go through them again. As we go through the cards again and again, you should learn better and better who likes who.

Take your time. Don't rush.

The above are the instructions given to all Ss who learned a social structure based on "likes." The instructions given to Ss who learned a social structure based on "influences" or "confides in" were identical in form except that the appropriate one of the following definitions was added: "To influence someone means to have some degree of control over what he does"; "To confide in someone means to have complete faith and confidence in him so that you trust him with secrets or rely on him for help."

Each S worked with a deck of 12 cards appropriate for his experimental condition.

RESULTS

The difficulty of learning the various social structures was measured by the mean number of trials required by the Ss to learn them to a criterion of two successive correct trials. These means are shown in Table 1. The standard errors of the means, highly correlated with their values, range from 1.06 to 4.27.

The hypothesized interaction between relations and structures is evident in Table 1. The Ss learned a complete ordering based on "influences" very readily, but had somewhat more difficulty with symmetric structures

TABLE 1
MEAN TRIALS TO CRITERION

Structure	Relation		
	Influences	Likes	Confides in
Asymmetric, transitive, complete (complete ordering)	8.9	14.7	16.2
Symmetric, transitive	12.9	10.9	9.1
Symmetric	11.7	13.0	10.9
Asymmetric, transitive (partial ordering)	12.1	14.7	
Asymmetric, complete (dominance structure)	26.4	23.7	
Asymmetric	16.3	29.1	
Control 1	16.1	20.6	
Control 2	16.7	21.0	

based on "influences." They had difficulty learning a complete ordering based on "likes" or "confides in," but learned symmetric structures based on these relations easily. An analysis of variance performed on the data for these nine conditions yielded an interaction mean square significant at the .01 level.

Examination of the remaining ten means shows that the partial ordering was learned relatively easily, at least when based on "influences," but the other conditions were all difficult, some of them exceedingly so. Particularly striking is the finding that the asymmetric and complete structure based on "influences" took substantially longer to learn than any of the nonsense structures, rather than showing facilitation from the fact that its properties were partly as expected by the Ss.

DISCUSSION

The experimental results clearly support the general hypothesis that people's assignments of mathematical properties to an interpersonal relation influence the ease with which they learn a social structure based on the relation, and they invite analysis of the psychological processes involved.

Perhaps the most remarkable finding is this: although the combination of the asymmetric, transitive, and complete properties (complete ordering) greatly facilitates the learning of a social structure based on "influences," the combination of only the asymmetric and complete properties (dominance structure) seems to make the learning task even more difficult than it is for structures without properties. The Ss failed completely to profit from the latter combination of properties, although in principle it too could be a valuable aid to learning a structure. Why?

It appears an inescapable conclusion that for the Ss these properties were not independent of one another, even though they are independent mathematically, and even though Ss are able to ascribe them separately to relations when questioned (De Soto & Kuethe, 1958, 1959). De Soto and Kuethe noted a tendency for Ss usually to ascribe the transitive property whenever they ascribed the asymmetric property to a relation. Evidently this tendency to couple the properties is so powerful that it prevents people from using the properties in isolation when learning a social structure. People expect mathematical properties in social structures, to be sure, but they expect them in bundles, and incomplete bundles are of no use to them.

It is as if the Ss had a theory about the social structure, a mathematical model for it which was very helpful when its properties corresponded with those of the social structure, but which had to be applied in an all-or-nothing manner in the sense that it was not readily abridged in the face of some lack of correspondence and became instead a hindrance. Such a theory, marked by certain essential properties but doubtlessly skeletal and sketchy in other respects, seems most aptly called a *schema*, roughly following Bartlet (1932) and Woodworth (1938).

The present data, then, might be interpreted to indicate that the Ss possessed an ordering schema which they automatically applied to a social structure based on the relation "influences," although not to one based on "likes" or "confides in." "Influences" might be said to tap or arouse people's ordering schema. This ordering schema, the residue perhaps of countless experiences with social and nonsocial orderings in the world, seems to be marked by the properties of asymmetry, transitivity, and, possibly, completeness. Thus the Ss expected these properties in a social structure based on "influences," but not as independent expectations; rather, as derivatives of the overriding expectation that the structure was an ordering. Perhaps the dominance structure was more difficult than the nonsense structures because it perpetually titillated and tantalized the Ss' ordering schema, preventing the suppression of it that occurred for the nonsense structures.

Evidence that more sophisticated students of social structures also possess and can be victims of an ordering schema is found in many writings about peck rights among birds. Birds establish peck rights on the basis of pair-wise encounters, a process which insures that the eventual social structure is asymmetric and complete, but not that it is transitive. The birds, being simple-minded creatures not possessed of an ordering schema, thus innocently build a social structure that puzzles

and provokes more thoughtful creatures who write about the "pecking out of order," "curious exceptions," "irregularities," "imperfect orderings," "lack of a hierarchy," "polygonal dominance," "cyclic pecking," "triangular pecking," and "complex, triangular hierarchies" (Allee, 1931; Collias, 1944; Murchison, 1935; Murphy, Murphy, & Newcomb, 1937; Schjelderup-Ebbe, 1935). People consider this primitive and simple social structure surprising and complex because they expect an ordering. To turn the thing around, it may be that the expectation of an ordering tends to *produce* an ordering, that human social groups would show fewer orderings and more dominance structures and even property free structures if it were not for the shared expectation of orderings.

The finding that the partial ordering was learned quite readily when based on "influences," with the Ss' ordering schema presumably aroused, suggests that the property of completeness is a less integral part of the ordering schema than the properties of asymmetry and transitivity. However, any partial ordering can be mathematically treated as made up of two or more complete orderings (Coombs & Kao, 1955; Kershner & Wilcox, 1950), and it is possible that the Ss accomplished essentially this analysis of the partial ordering.

The property of symmetry seems to be fairly easy to detect and utilize even when it is not expected, as in the structures based on "influences." The results suggest that for "likes" and "confides in" a symmetric and transitive structure is learned easier than a merely symmetric one, but the differences are not large, and it should be noted that the so-called symmetric and transitive structure of Fig. 1 is only *vacuously* transitive (Kershner & Wilcox, 1950), having too few members to be truly transitive. Thus, it is impossible to say more than that a lack of transitivity is not the severe handicap in learning symmetric structures that it is in learning asymmetric ones. This conclusion is consistent with the view expressed earlier (De Soto & Kuethe, 1959) that the primary property ascribed to these relations is symmetry, and that transitivity is ascribed secondarily, only after long experience which teaches that relations like "likes" are commonly transitive, dividing people into cliques or friendship groups. The grouping schema, as applied to interpersonal relations at least, is a higher development of the symmetry schema.

SUMMARY

By means of a learning experiment it was shown that a social structure is easiest to learn when it possesses the mathematical properties people expect in it. People attribute the properties of asymmetry, transitivity, and completeness (the properties of an ordering) to the relation "influences." If a social structure formed of the relation "influences" has these properties, they learn it readily. If it is symmetric, or if it has no mathematical properties, they have more difficulty; and if it is asymmetric and complete but not transitive (a dominance structure), they have great difficulty. Similarly, structures based on "likes" or "confides in" are learned most readily when they are symmetric, as people expect them to be. The findings were interpreted as reflecting the operation of schemas in the Ss.

REFERENCES

ALLEE, W. C. *Animal aggregations: A study in general sociology.* Chicago: Univer. Chicago Press, 1931.

BARTLETT, F. C. *Remembering.* Cambridge: Cambridge Univer. Press, 1932.

COLLIAS, N. E. Aggressive behavior among vertebrates. *Physiol. Zool.*, 1944, **17**, 83–123.

COOMBS, C. H., & KAO, R. C. Non-metric factor analysis. *Engng. res. Bull.* No. 38. Ann Arbor: Univer. Michigan Press, 1955.

COOMBS, C. H., RAIFFA, H., & THRALL, R. M. Some views on mathematical models and measurement theory. *Psychol. Rev.*, 1954, **61**, 132–144.

DESOTO, C. B., & KUETHE, J. L. Perception of mathematical properties of interpersonal relations. *Percept. mot. Skills*, 1958, **8**, 279–286.

DESOTO, C. B., & KUETHE, J. L. Subjective probabilities of interpersonal relationships. *J. abnorm. soc. Psychol.*, 1959, **59**, 290–294.

HEIDER, F. *The psychology of interpersonal relations.* New York: Wiley, 1958.

KERSHNER, R. B., & WILCOX, L. R. *The anatomy of mathematics.* New York: Ronald, 1950.

KOGAN, N., & TAGIURI, R. Interpersonal preference and cognitive organization. *J. abnorm. soc. Psychol.*, 1958, **56**, 113–116.

MURCHISON, C. The experimental measurement of a social hierarchy in *gallus domesticus:* I. The direct identification and direct measurement of social reflex no. 1 and social reflex no. 2. *J. gen. Psychol.*, 1935, **12**, 3–39.

MURPHY, G., MURPHY, L. B., & NEWCOMB, T. M. *Experimental social psychology.* (rev. ed.) New York: Harper, 1937.

SCHJELDERUP-EBBE, T. Social life of birds. In C. Murchison (Ed.), *Handbook of social psychology.* Worcester, Mass.: Clark Univer. Press, 1935.

TAGIURI, R. Social preference and its perception. In R. Tagiuri & L. Petrullo (Eds.), *Person perception and interpersonal behavior.* Stanford, Cal.: Stanford Univer. Press, 1958.

WOODWORTH, R. S. *Experimental psychology.* New York: Holt, 1938.

(Early publication received October 22, 1959)

Part II: Information, Interaction, and Acquaintance

From James Coleman, Elihu Katz, and Herbert
Menzel, *Sociometry 20*, 253-270 (1957), by
permission. A fuller report can be found
in Coleman, Katz, and Menzel, "Medical
Innovation," Bobbs-Merrill (1966).

The Diffusion of an Innovation among Physicians[1]

JAMES COLEMAN, ELIHU KATZ, *University of Chicago*

HERBERT MENZEL, *Columbia University*

Anthropologists and sociologists have long been concerned with the processes through which customs, practices, attitudes, or messages spread. Traditionally, these processes have been studied by examining the ecological distribution of the trait at successive points in time. In a few cases, the actual transmission of messages from person to person has been traced out (e.g., 1, 3, 4, 5, 10). A still different approach to the study of this problem is reported in this paper. The population is physicians in four cities; the item whose use was spreading was a new drug; and the study focused on the ongoing social processes which finally led to widespread adoption of the drug by these physicians.

Data were collected 15 months after a new drug with wide potential use, here called "gammanym," had been placed on the market. By this time almost all the doctors in relevant specialties in the four cities studied had used the drug, some almost immediately, others only after a considerable interval of time. The research problem, stated most concretely, is this: What were the social processes which intervened between the initial trials of the drug by a few local innovators and its final use by virtually the whole medical community? The results reported below concern the effectiveness of networks of interpersonal relations at each stage of the diffusion process. The study is to be reported in full elsewhere (2); a pilot study has already been reported upon (9). A separate article by one of us describes the cumulative research experiences which led to the decision to focus explicitly upon interpersonal relations, using sociometric techniques (6).

METHODS—I

The method of survey research, involving structured interviews with a sample of physicians, was used. But since the problem as defined

[1] This article may be identified as Publication No. A 239 of the Bureau of Applied Social Research, Columbia University. An earlier version was read at the annual meeting of the American Sociological Society, Detroit, Michigan, September 8, 1956. We are indebted to Helmut Guttenberg for creative assistance throughout the project. Philip Ennis, Marjorie Fiske, Rolf Meyersohn, and Joseph A. Precker participated in the design of this study. The preparation of this paper was facilitated by funds obtained from a grant made to the Bureau of Applied Social Research by the Eda K. Loeb Fund.

concerned the social structure which linked these doctors together, it was necessary to deviate in two important ways from the customary survey design which, in effect, treats individuals as so many independent units of observation. (a) Each doctor interviewed was asked three sociometric questions: To whom did he most often turn for advice and information? With whom did he most often discuss his cases in the course of an ordinary week? Who were the friends, among his colleagues, whom he saw most often socially? In response to each of these questions, the names of three doctors were requested. This made it possible to trace out the links by which each doctor was connected with the rest of the medical community. (b) It was decided to include in the sample, as nearly as possible, *all* the local doctors in whose specialties the new drug was of major potential significance. This assured that the "others" named by each doctor in answer to the sociometric questions were included in the sample, so that it became possible to characterize pairs or chains of socially connected doctors. Accordingly, 125 general practitioners, internists, and pediatricians were interviewed; they constituted 85 per cent of the doctors practicing in these fields in four Midwestern cities, ranging in population from 30,000 to 110,000.[2]

The dependent variable of the analysis which follows is the month during which each doctor first used the drug. This information was *not* obtained in the interviews; it was obtained through a search of the prescription records of the local pharmacies for three-day sampling periods at approximately monthly intervals over the 15 months following the release date of gammanym. In this way, the month during which each doctor first used the drug was ascertained.[3] The research is thus based on three kinds of data: the month of each doctor's first prescription for the new drug, obtained through a search of pharmacists' files; data about the informal social structure of the medical community, derived from doctors' replies to sociometric questions in an interview; and many individual attributes of each doctor, likewise obtained by interview.

[2] In addition, 103 doctors in other specialties were also interviewed, thus making a total sample of 228, or 64 per cent of all doctors in active private practice in these cities. The analysis presented here is based only on the 125 general practitioners, internists, and pediatricians, except that sociometric designations accorded them by the remaining 103 doctors were included when measuring the sociometric status of the 125.

[3] The date so ascertained will tend to be slightly later than the doctor's actual introduction date, due to the sampling of days. The interval between sampling periods was made to alternate between 32 and 25 days, so that each two successive sampling periods included all 6 days of the working week. Records were obtained from 64 of the 84 drug stores in the four cities. Of the remaining 20, only two had any significant pharmaceutical business.

Before presenting the results concerning interpersonal relations, the results concerning other ("individual") determinants will be briefly characterized. As expected, the date on which a doctor first prescribed the new drug was related to a large number of his *individual* attributes, e.g., his age, the number of medical journals he subscribed to, his attachments to medical institutions outside his community, and certain attitudinal characteristics. To illustrate the relationship of drug introduction date to such individual attributes, one of the latter will be singled out: the doctor's relative orientation to his professional colleagues and to patients, inferred from his answer to the following question:

How would you rank the importance of these characteristics in recognizing a good doctor in a town like this?
a. The respect in which he is held by his own patients
b. His general standing in the community
c. The recognition given him by his local colleagues
d. The research and publications he has to his credit

The following rankings were classified as "profession-oriented": cdab, cadb, cbda, cabd; the following rankings were classified as "patient-oriented": abcd, acbd, acdb, bacd. The 14 doctors who gave other rankings were assigned to one group or another by a rank-order scaling procedure which will be described in detail elsewhere (2).

Figure 1 shows the relationship of the resulting classification to the date of introduction of the new drug. The solid curve represents those doctors who were classified as profession-oriented, and shows the cumulative proportion of gammanym users among them for each month. Thus, for example, by the fourth month 40 per cent of these doctors had used gammanym; by the sixth month over 50 per cent. The lower curve similarly represents the doctors who were classified as patient-oriented; by the sixth month only 42 per cent had used the drug. Thus the more profession-oriented doctors in these cities generally used the drug earlier than the less profession-oriented ones.[4] Similar results were obtained for many other individual attributes—i.e., attributes describing individuals without reference to their social relations with one another.

[4] The difference between the mean adoption dates of the two groups in Fig. 1 is 2.8 months, which is significant at the .01 level, using a standard two-tailed test of difference between means of normally distributed variables. It should be pointed out, however, that the argument of this report does not rest on the statistical significance of isolated findings so much as on the consistency of the results of several diverse approaches with one another and with prior theoretical notions. It is doubtful that significance tests in the usual sense are meaningful in situations like the present. For a detailed statement of our position in this matter, see (8, p. 427).

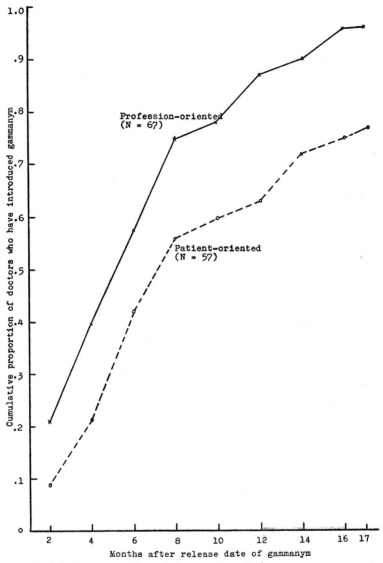

Profession-oriented
(N = 67)

Patient-oriented
(N = 57)

Months after release date of gammanym

Cumulative proportion of doctors who have introduced gammanym

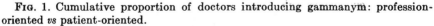

FIG. 1. Cumulative proportion of doctors introducing gammanym: profession-oriented *vs* patient-oriented.

But even stronger relations were found when we turned to *social* attributes—those characterizing a doctor's ties to his local colleagues. Doctors who were mentioned by many of their colleagues in answer to any of the three sociometric questions used the drug, on the average, earlier than those who were named by few or none of their colleagues. More generally

110

speaking, the degree of a doctor's integration among his local colleagues was strongly and positively related to the date of his first use of the new drug. Figure 2 shows, for example, the results with regard to the network of friendships. The "integrated" doctors—those named as "friends" by three or more of their colleagues—were much faster to introduce gammanym

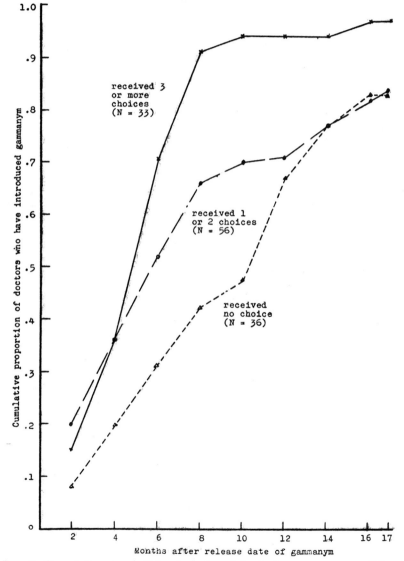

FIG. 2. Cumulative proportion of doctors introducing gammanym: differences in integration on friendship criterion.

into their practices than the rest. The networks of discussion and of advisorship yielded similar findings.

Two important contrasts differentiate Figure 2 from Figure 1, and, more generally, social attributes from individual ones, in their relation to gammanym introduction. First, the relationship in Figure 2 (as measured, for example, by the difference between the mean drug introduction dates of the extreme groups) is greater than that in Figure 1; greater, in fact, than the relationship of the introduction date of gammanym to all but one of the many individual characteristics which were examined. (The single exception is the doctor's total prescription volume for the general class of drugs which includes gammanym: the greater his use of drugs of this type, the earlier did he introduce gammanym.)[5] This emphasizes the importance of social contacts among doctors as a crucial determinant of their early use of the new drug.

But it may reasonably be questioned whether the relationship shown in Figure 2 may not arise merely because the measures of social integration are themselves associated with some personality or other individual differences which predispose a doctor to early introduction. It is in answer to this question that a second contrast between Figures 1 and 2 is relevant.

Notice that the two curves in Figure 1 are roughly parallel, differing from one another only in vertical displacement. This is true as well in most of the remaining charts (not shown) which relate individual characteristics to gammanym introduction. The curves in Figure 2, by contrast, differ from each other in shape as well as location: the curve for the more integrated doctors, although not starting out much higher than the other curves, rises steeply upward with a slight gain in slope at the fourth month, while the curve for the more isolated doctors rises at a moderate and almost constant slope. To put it differently, the integrated doctors were little different from their isolated colleagues at the very beginning; but then their rate accelerated to produce an increasing gap between the curves. In contrast, the profession-oriented doctors in Figure 1 differed from the patient-oriented from the very start almost as much as later on.

The constant difference between the profession-oriented and patient-oriented doctors suggests that they differ individually in their receptivity to new developments in medicine. On the other hand, the accelerating difference between the integrated and isolated doctors suggests a kind of "snowball" or "chain-reaction" process for the integrated: They are

[5] The difference between the mean drug introduction dates of those high and low on integration according to the 3 sociometric questions used is 3.1, 4.1, and 4.3 months. The difference between those with high and low total prescription volume for this general class of drugs is 5.0 months. Only one other individual characteristic (number of journals read) produced a mean difference of as much as 4.0 months.

112

individually little different in receptivity from their more isolated colleagues, but as their fellows come to use the drug, they pick it up from these doctors themselves; and as more of their fellows come to use it, their chances of picking it up are greater.

The difference between the two kinds of relationship to drug introduction is also shown by Table 1, which compares the individual variables and the social variables in their relation to gammanym introduction at two points in time: 1 month and 7 months after the drug was introduced. For each of these dates, the table shows the average difference in per cent of gammanym users (a) between those measuring "high" and "low" on each of twelve individual variables and (b) between those measuring "high" and "low" on three measures of social integration. The latter are based on choices received in response to the three sociometric questions mentioned earlier. The twelve individual variables include all those examined which showed a difference of two or more months in mean date of introduction between the high and the low groups.

The size of these differences measures the size of the relationship at the two times. As is evident, the social integration measures show a slightly *smaller* relationship than do the individual variables after 1 month, but a much *larger* relationship after 7 months. Thus, as exemplified by the comparison between Figures 1 and 2, the socially integrated doctors "pull away" from their isolated colleagues, while the doctors differing in some individual attribute simply maintain their intrinsically different receptivity as time goes on.

Figures 3 and 4 show the difference between two corresponding theoretical "models" of the introduction process. In Figure 3, the upper and lower curves both express a model of "individual innovation"; the difference between the two is simply that the receptivity is greater for the upper. This difference in individual innovation rate or receptivity corresponds, we suggest, to the difference between profession-oriented and patient-oriented doctors (and between doctors who differ in other individual attributes as

TABLE 1

The Average Relation of Twelve "Individual" Variables and of Three Measures of Social Integration to the Rate of Gammanym Introduction at Two Points in Time

	Average Difference in Per Cent of Gammanym Users between High and Low Groups		Ratio of Differences
	After 1 Month	After 7 Months	
Individual variables..........	9.2	27.4	2.98
Social integration............	8.7	40.3	4.64

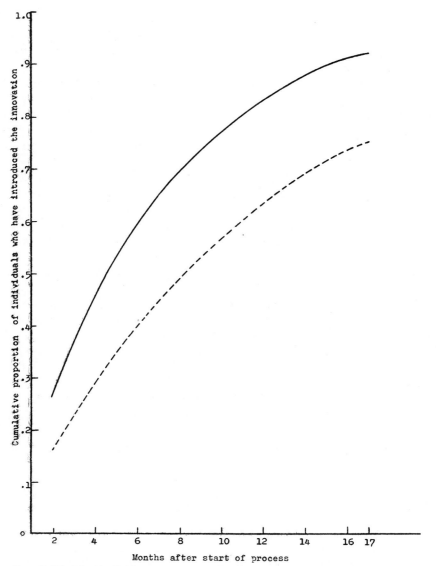

Fɪɢ. 3. Model of individual innovation, showing effects of differences in individual receptivity, k.

$$\frac{dy}{dt} = k(1 - y)$$

114

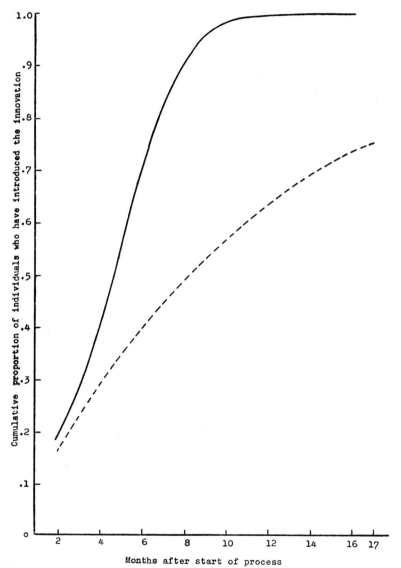

FIG. 4. Comparison of model of "chain-reaction" innovation with model of individual innovation.

$$\frac{dy}{dt} = ky(1 - y)$$

well). In contrast, in Figure 4 the upper curve (which is roughly similar in shape to the curve for the integrated doctors) represents a snowball process in which those who have introduced pass on the innovation to their colleagues. (This curve is described by an equation which has been used to characterize rates of population growth, certain chemical reactions, and other phenomena which obey a chain-reaction process.) The lower curve in Figure 4 is still the individual innovation process. (Technically, the individual and snowball processes are described by equations on the graphs, which can be paraphrased as follows: *Individual process*—the number of doctors introducing the new drug each month would remain a constant percentage of those who have not already adopted the drug. *Snowball process*—the number of doctors introducing the new drug each month would increase in proportion to those who have already been converted.)

In short, these comparisons suggest that the process of introduction for those doctors who were deeply embedded in their professional community was in fact different from the process for those who were relatively isolated from it. The highly integrated doctors seem to have learned from *one another*, while the less integrated ones, it seems, had each to learn afresh from the journals, the detail man (drug salesman), and other media of information.

METHODS—II

This result called for a more detailed investigation into the ways in which the networks of relations among the doctors affected their introduction of the new drug. Such an investigation required a shift of focus from doctors to relationships among doctors or to the networks themselves as the units of analysis. Various methods could have been devised to do this. We chose to record the behavior of *pairs* of doctors who were sociometrically related to one another, reasoning that if the networks of relations were effective, then pairs of doctors who were in contact must have been more *alike* in their behavior than pairs assorted at random. That is, if there was a snowball or chain-reaction process of drug introduction from one doctor to another, then adjacent links in the chain—pairs of socially related doctors— should have introduced the drug about the same time.

In order to test this hypothesis for the discussion network, Figure 5 was constructed. (Similar figures were constructed for the networks of friendship and advisorship.) Each sociometric pair was assigned to a column of this matrix according to the gammanym introduction date of the chooser, and to a row according to the gammanym introduction date of the doctor chosen. (A mutual choice constitutes two pairs in this tabulation, since any chooser and his choice constitute a pair.) Pairs of doctors who introduced the drug during the same month (interval zero) fall

116

Date of first use by chooser (months after release)

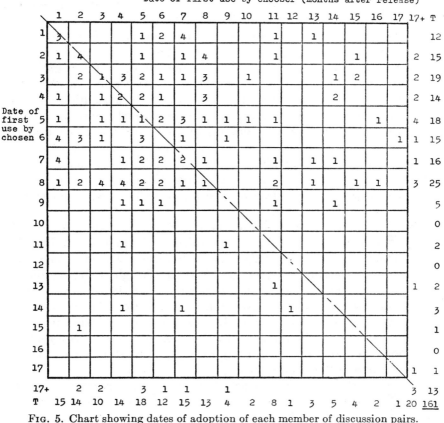

Date of first use by chosen	1	2	3	4	5	6	7	8	9	10	11	12	13	14	15	16	17	17+	T
1	3			1	2	4					1		1						12
2	1	4		1		1	4				1				1			2	15
3		2	1	3	2	1	1	3		1				1	2			2	19
4	1		1	2	2	1		3						2				2	14
5	1		1	1	1	2	3	1	1	1	1					1		4	18
6	4	3	1		3		1		1								1	1	15
7	4			1	2	2	2	1			1		1	1				1	16
8	1	2	4	4	2	2	1	1			2		1		1	1		3	25
9				1	1	1					1			1					5
10																			0
11				1				1											2
12																			0
13													1					1	2
14				1			1						1						3
15		1																	1
16																			0
17																		1	1
17+		2	2		3	1	1		1									3	13
T	15	14	10	14	18	12	15	13	4	2	8	1	3	5	4	2	1	20	161

FIG. 5. Chart showing dates of adoption of each member of discussion pairs.

in the main diagonal; pairs of doctors who differed in introducing the drug by an interval of one month fall into cells adjoining the diagonal; and so on.

The resulting distribution of these intervals for the sociometric pairs was then compared to the corresponding distribution of intervals for a set of "random pairs" which has the following characteristics. If a pair is selected at random: (a) the probability that the chooser-member of the pair introduced gammanym during a particular month is the same as in the actual sample but is independent of the introduction date of the doctor chosen; (b) the probability that the chosen member introduced gammanym during a particular month is the same as in the actual sample but is independent of the introduction date of the doctor making the choice. Thus, for example, among the random pairs, those who introduced gammanym in the first month and those who did so in the seventh gave equal portions of their choices to other first-month introducers. Similarly, those who introduced

117

gammanym in the first month and those who introduced it in the seventh *received* equal portions of their choices from first-month introducers. Operationally, a set of "chance" frequencies satisfying these criteria can easily be obtained by computing for each cell of Figure 5 the product of the associated marginal totals, divided, for convenience, by the grand total.[6]

Contrary to expectations, the proportion of pairs whose members had introduced gammanym during the same month, one month apart, two months apart, and so on, according to the chance model proved to be almost identical to the proportion of actual discussion pairs who had introduced gammanym simultaneously or with varying intervals. The results for pairs of friends and for advisor-advisee pairs were similarly disappointing. This meant the rejection of our original hypothesis that pairs of doctors in contact would introduce the drug more nearly simultaneously than pairs of doctors assorted at random.

There was, on the other hand, the earlier evidence that the doctor's integration was important to his introduction of gammanym. This dictated a more intensive look at the behavior of pairs of doctors. Accordingly, we raised the question whether the networks, though ineffective for the *whole* period studied, may have been effective for the *early* period, immediately after the drug was marketed. An inspection of Figure 5 suggests that this could easily be the case. If only the upper left-hand portion of the matrix, representing the first two, three, or four months, is considered, then there appears to be a tendency for both members of a pair to introduce the drug in the same month.

In order to describe this tendency more precisely, it was decided to eliminate from consideration those associates of each doctor who used the drug only after *he* did. That is to say, the following question was now asked of the data: How closely did the drug introduction of each doctor follow upon the drug introductions of those of his associates who had introduced the drug before him? The answer is: very closely, for early introducers of the drug; not at all closely, for late introducers of the drug.

This result is based on a measure for each month, obtained by dividing up the total matrix of pairs of doctors as shown in Figure 6. The single cell in the upper left-hand corner represents those pairs both of whose members introduced the drug in the first month. The L-shaped section next to it contains the pairs which consist of one doctor who introduced the drug in

[6] A complication arose from the fact that the study was carried on in four different cities, with sociometric choices between cities excluded. This could spuriously raise any measure of pair-wise similarity of behavior, if there are large differences in behavior between the cities. (This fact was called to our attention by Jack Feldman of NORC). In order to avoid such a spurious relation, "chance" frequencies, as above described, were calculated separately from the marginal totals for each city, and only then summed over the cities.

Date of first use by chooser

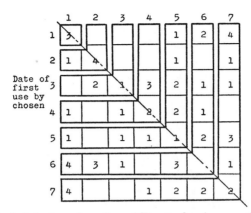

Fig. 6. Exploded view of portion of Fig. 5, showing monthly segments.

the second month and one who introduced it in the first *or* second. The next L-shaped section contains all pairs which consist of one third-month adopter and one third-month-or-earlier adopter, and so on. It was now possible to determine the average interval for the sociometric pairs in each L-shaped section; likewise the average interval for the corresponding random pairs. On this basis, a measure of simultaneity was computed for each section, according to the formula:

Measure of Simultaneity (positive) =

$$\frac{\text{(avge. interval for random pairs)} - \text{(avge. interval for sociometric pairs)}}{\text{avge. interval for random pairs}}.$$

This measure expresses the difference between the random and actual intervals as a fraction of the difference between the random interval and complete simultaneity (i.e., an interval of zero). The measure thus has a maximum of 1, and is zero when pairs are no closer than chance. In those cases where the actual interval exceeded the random interval, a different denominator was used.[7]

[7] Measure of simultaneity (negative) =

$$\frac{\text{(avge. interval for random pairs)} - \text{(avge. interval for sociometric pairs)}}{(s - 1) - \text{(avge. interval for random pairs)}}$$

s being defined as the number of the latest month included in the particular L-shaped section. (E.g., $s = 4$ in the case of pairs consisting of one fourth-month adopter and one fourth-month-or-earlier adopter.) When the index has a negative value, it therefore expresses the difference between the random and actual intervals as a fraction of the difference between the random interval and the maximum interval that is possible.

119

The values of the index are plotted in Figure 7 for the second through the sixth months. Separate curves are plotted for pairs of friends, discussion pairs, and advisor-advisee pairs. The interpretation of these results must be tentative because of the small numbers of cases; on the other hand, the patterns which emerge are rather consistent.

Figure 7 suggests, first of all, that the networks of doctor-to-doctor contacts operated most powerfully during the first 5 months after the release of the new drug: such influence as any doctor's drug introduction had upon his immediate associates evidently occurred soon after the drug became available. (Figure 7 omits the later months during which the index is negative or very small.) Second, the three networks did not behave identically.[8] The discussion network and the advisor network showed most pair-simultaneity at the very beginning and then progressively declined. The friendship network shows initially less pair-simultaneity than the other two, but—with some instability—appears to reach its maximum effectiveness later. Finally, after the fifth or sixth month following the release of the new drug, none of the networks any longer showed pair-simultaneity beyond chance.

These results, however tentative, suggest that there may be successive stages in the diffusion of this innovation through the community of doctors. The first networks to be operative as chains of influence appear to be those which connect the doctors in the professional relationships of advisors and discussion partners. Only then, it seems, does the friendship network become operative—among those doctors who are influenced in their decisions more by the colleagues they meet as friends than by those whom they look to as advisors or engage in discussion during working hours. Finally, for those doctors who have not yet introduced the drug by about 6 months after the drug's release these networks seem completely *inoperative* as chains of influence. The social structure seems to have exhausted its effect; those doctors who have not responded to its influence by this time are apparently unresponsive to it. When they finally use gammanym, they presumably do so in response to influences outside the social network, such as detail men, ads, journal articles, and so on, and not in response to their relations with other doctors.

But one further phase in the social diffusion of gammanym can be discerned by examining separately the sociometrically integrated and the

[8] Many of the sociometric ties reappear in two or three of the networks. The three sociometric questions yielded a total of 958 "pairs" within the sample of 125 doctors; but since some of these pairs were identical in answer to two or all three of the questions, there were only 704 *different* pairs. This overlap is still small enough to allow differences in patterns to emerge, as shown in the text.

relatively isolated doctors. One would expect the networks of doctor-to-doctor contact to show their effectiveness first among the more integrated doctors and only then among those who are less integrated in their medical community. It has already been seen (Fig. 2 and text) that the more isolated doctors, on the average, introduced gammanym considerably later than the socially more integrated doctors. We now propose, however, that when more isolated doctors *did* introduce the drug early, it was not with the help of the social networks. While the networks were operative as channels of influence *early* for the integrated doctors, they were operative

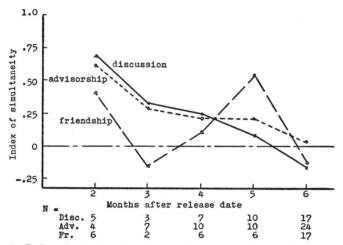

Fig. 7. Index of pair-simultaneity for three networks at different times.

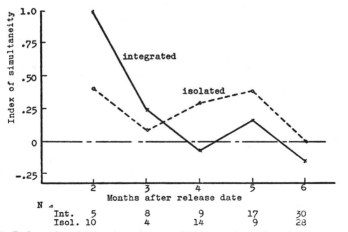

Fig. 8. Index of pair-simultaneity at different times for doctors differing in integration

121

only later for the more isolated ones. This is what seems to have occurred. Figure 8 plots the index of simultaneity separately for more and less integrated doctors. (The graphs show weighted averages for all three networks; separately the numbers of cases would be so small as to produce erratic trends.)

The peak of effectiveness of doctor-to-doctor contacts for the well-integrated doctors appeared in the earliest month for which it can be plotted—the second month—after which effectiveness sharply declined. For the relatively isolated doctors, by contrast, the networks were not so effective at first as were those for the integrated doctors, but they maintained their effectiveness longer. Thus it appears that the networks of relations were effective not only for the more integrated doctors but also for the relatively isolated doctors who introduced the drug during the first 5 months of the drug's availability.

CONCLUSION

The above results, taken together, suggest a process which may be summarized as follows: At first the influence of these social networks operated only among the doctors who were integrated into the community of their colleagues through ties of a professional nature—as advisors or as discussion partners. Then it spread through the friendship network to doctors who were closely tied to the medical community through their friendship relations. By this time, social influence had also become operative in the more "open" parts of the social structure—i.e., among the relatively isolated doctors. Finally, there came a phase during which most of the remaining doctors introduced gammanym but did so in complete independence of the time at which their associates had introduced it: the networks now showed no effect. For the integrated doctors, this phase began about 4 months after the drug's release; for the isolated doctors, it began about 6 months after the drug's release. This picture is of course a tentative one, for the small size of the sample introduces variability, and there may be factors which produce spurious results.

There remains the question: Why should these sociometric ties to colleagues who have used the drug be influential during the first months of the drug's availability, but not later? One possible answer lies in the greater uncertainty about the drug that must have prevailed when it was new. (Data not reported here show that those doctors who introduced gammanym early did so far more tentatively than those who introduced it later.) We know from work in the tradition of Sherif that it is precisely in situations which are objectively unclear that social validation of judgments becomes most important.

More generally, this explanation implies that a doctor will be influenced more by what his colleagues say and do in uncertain situations, whenever and wherever they may occur, than in clear-cut situations. This explanation was confirmed by further data from the study which show that doctors influence each other more in treatments whose effects are unclear than in treatments whose effects are clear-cut. This topic will be dealt with in detail elsewhere (7).

CONCLUDING METHODOLOGICAL NOTE

A word should be added about the significance of research of this kind, aside from the possible interest in its specific substantive findings. It exemplifies a methodological approach which will, we feel, assume a larger role in the social research of the next decade: namely, making social relationships and social structures the units of statistical analysis. To be sure, the analysis of social relations has always been the sociologist's business. Nevertheless, most empirical studies have either treated and described a community, a factory, a hospital ward, or any other large grouping of people as a single unit, or else they have statistically analyzed data collected on hundreds or thousands of single inividuals, as in the typical "survey" study. What has been missing until recently is study designs which would explicitly take into account the structuring of single persons into larger units, and yet allow sophisticated quantitative treatment. The techniques of sociometry can meet this purpose, but have, with some notable exceptions (e.g., 4, 11), been applied chiefly to small closed groups and primarily for descriptive purposes.

The attempt reported here has been to carry out a design and analysis which would effect a marriage between sociometric techniques and survey research, in order to investigate quantitatively problems of the sort which community studies have ordinarily investigated by qualitative means. The attempt, of course, points up many more problems than it even partially solves: e.g., how to integrate an analysis of formal social structures with an analysis of informal ones; how to proceed from pair-analysis to the analysis of longer chains and complex networks; and so on. A set of methodological and substantive problems awaits the researcher. It is suggested that the solution will give sociologists important new tools with which to investigate social dynamics.

REFERENCES

1. Back, K., *et al.*, "A Method of Studying Rumor Transmission," in L. Festinger *et al.*, *Theory and Experiment in Social Communication*, Ann Arbor, Michigan: Research Center for Group Dynamics, University of Michigan, 1950, 307–312.
2. Coleman, J. S., E. Katz, and H. Menzel, "The Diffusion of a Medical Innovation" (tentative title), Glencoe, Illinois: The Free Press (in preparation).
3. Dodd, S. C., "Diffusion is Predictable," *American Sociological Review*, 1955, 20, 392–401.
4. Festinger, L., S. Schachter, and K. Back, *Social Pressures in Informal Groups*, New York: Harper, 1950, Chap. 7.
5. Jennings, H. H., "Leadership and Isolation," in G. E. Swanson, T. M. Newcomb, and E. L. Hartley, eds., *Readings in Social Psychology*, New York: Holt, 1952.
6. Katz, E., "The Two-Step Flow of Communication: An Up-to-Date Report on an Hypothesis," *Public Opinion Quarterly*, 1957, 21, 61–78.
7. Katz, E., J. S. Coleman, and H. Menzel, "Social Influence on Decision-Making in Ambiguous Situations—Some Data from a Survey among Physicians" (unpublished).
8. Lipset, S. M., M. A. Trow, and J. S. Coleman, *Union Democracy*, Glencoe, Illinois: The Free Press, 1956.
9. Menzel, H., and E. Katz, "Social Relations and Innovation in the Medical Profession: The Epidemiology of a New Drug," *Public Opinion Quarterly*, 1956, 19, 337–352.
10. Moreno, J. L., *Who Shall Survive?*, Beacon, New York: Beacon House, 1953, 440–450.
11. Riley, M. W., J. W. Riley, Jr., and J. Toby, *Sociological Studies in Scale Analysis*, New Brunswick, New Jersey: Rutgers University Press. 1954.

124

From William Erbe, *American Journal of Sociology* 67, 502-516 (1962), copyright by the University of Chicago, by permission.

GREGARIOUSNESS, GROUP MEMBERSHIP, AND THE FLOW OF INFORMATION[1]

WILLIAM ERBE

ABSTRACT

The influence of gregariousness (the range of social contacts) and integration in an informal group (indexed by self-defined membership) on the diffusion of information are compared with data from a national sample of graduate students. The information advantage of highly gregarious individuals is found to be explained primarily by the fact that they are more likely to be group members. Information is found to be more diffused in highly cohesive departments (characterized by the presence of many groups), especially among non-integrated students, thus indicating the importance of the relative density of group interaction in the flow of information. The importance of group interaction is attributed to (1) the number and heterogeneity of sources of information available in a group and (2) the continuity of group relations.

Research in the field of mass communications in recent years has paid increasing attention to the importance of interpersonal networks of communication in the diffusion of information. Concepts such as "gregariousness" and "integration" have been used in describing the flow of information and influence; sometimes almost interchangeably, without due consideration to nominal definitions of these terms, and the differing implications that these variables might have for communications research.

Here, we will examine some of the ways in which gregariousness, or the range of social contacts, and integration, or membership in informal groups, influence the probability that the individual will be informed on given issues. In addition, we shall compare the effect of group membership in populations where many groups exist to the effect in populations where there is low group density, to show a contextual

effect in the existence of a relatively large amount of group interaction in a population. Our hypotheses will be tested with data from a large national sample of graduate students.

Gregariousness has been treated as the social variable of reference in one major communication study: *Personal Influence.*[2] This study, motivated by the discovery of opinion leadership in Erie County,[3] was an attempt to specify the influence of ordinary persons to high-status persons, celebrities, party leaders, and the like. Gregariousness, defined as "the extent of social contacts," was found to be related to opinion leadership in the areas of marketing, fashion, and movie-going, and to be a more important predictor of opinion leaderships in the public affairs area than status in the life-cycle or socioeconomic status.[4]

[1] Expanded and revised version of a paper read at the annual meetings of the Pacific Sociological Association, Tucson, Arizona, April 13, 1961. The data are taken from the National Opinion Research Center's Survey 415, which was sponsored jointly by the National Academy of Sciences–National Research Council, The American Council of Learned Societies, and the Social Science Research Council. The study was directed by James A. Davis. The author is indebted to James A. Davis and Charles Wright for critical reading and commentary on this paper.

[2] Elihu Katz and Paul F. Lazarsfeld, *Personal Influence* (Glencoe, Ill.: Free Press, 1955).

[3] Paul F. Lazarsfeld, Bernard Berelson, and Hazel Gaudet, *The People's Choice* (New York: Columbia University Press, 1948).

[4] The index of gregariousness was constructed from the answers to two items in the questionnaire. First, the respondents were asked: "How many people are there with whom you are friendly and talk with often, who are not and never have been your neighbor?" It was thought that this answer gave the analysts a measure of "the magnitude of the individual's sphere of intimate, informal relationships beyond the immediate en-

Most subsequent communication studies which have taken account of social variables have attempted to deal with the intensity as well as the extent of social relationships. The focus of empirical attention has shifted to the spread of innovation or the diffusion of information, thus emphasizing the flow of communication content in addition to, or instead of, influence on individual decision-making. Studies of the spread of the use of new drugs among physicians by Coleman, Katz, and Menzel show a definite relationship between clique integration and adoption of a new drug. The findings suggest that innovation tends to flow along the lines of interpersonal relations, and that physicians adopt a new drug simultaneously with other physicians with whom they are in close personal contact.[5]

A study by DeFleur and Larsen, *The Flow of Information*, has shown the importance of the family as a communication network. Using leaflet material dropped over Western cities as their original communication, they are able to show the operation of the two-step flow of communication, with the family as an important oral link between perception of the original message by a relatively small proportion of the population and its general dissemination to the mass of the community.[6]

Perhaps more directly comparable to the data we shall present here are the findings of Lipset, Trow, and Coleman with respect to formal and informal participation in the social life of printers by members of the International Typographical Union. The authors found that active members of printers' clubs, as opposed to non-active members and non-members, were more likely to be correctly informed about the stand of the two parties contesting for union leadership on the clause of the Taft-Hartley Act which requires the signing of a non-Communist affidavit. Active club members were also more likely to become informed about the issues that separated the two internal parties than non-active members or non-members. In addition to this, individuals who were high on the authors' "index of informal social relations" were more likely to become informed on internal issues that divided the parties. The authors conclude that "regardless of the manifest purposes of those who take part in the formal or informal activities of the occupational community, these activities do play an important role in increasing the knowledge of and involvement in union politics of previously inactive or relatively uninterested printers."[7]

There would seem to be a sufficient accumulation of studies to show that social relationships are important factors in the flow of information, but very little evidence on what kinds of social relationships make what kinds of difference. The fact that gregariousness and group membership have not been treated simultaneously poses our first problem: the comparison of the effect on the distribution of information of hav-

<hr/>

virons of the household." The second question asked about the respondents' membership in voluntary associations. The individuals who possessed both the traits of having more than the median number of friends and of belonging to one or more voluntary associations were classified "high gregarious." Those who neither belonged to a voluntary organization nor had the median number of friends were classified "low gregarious." All others who answered both questions were put in the "medium" category (cf. Katz and Lazarsfeld, *op. cit.*, pp. 227–28).

[5] Herbert Menzel and Elihu Katz, "Social Relations and Innovation in the Medical Prefession: The Epidemiology of a New Drug," in Eleanor E. Maccoby, Theodore M. Newcomb, and Eugene L. Hartley (eds.), *Readings in Social Psychology* (3d ed.; New York: Henry Holt & Co., 1958), pp. 532–45, and James Coleman, Elihu Katz, and Herbert Menzel, "The Diffusion of an Innovation among Physicians," *Sociometry*, XX (1957), 253–70.

[6] Melvin L. DeFleur and Otto N. Larsen, *The Flow of Information* (New York: Harper & Bros., 1958), chap. viii.

[7] Seymour Martin Lipset, Martin A. Trow, and James S. Coleman, *Union Democracy* (Glencoe, Ill.: Free Press, 1956), p. 88.

ing a wide number of speaking acquaintances in a given population with that of being integrated into a day-to-day informal group. We can make an analytical distinction between these two attributes, although, as we shall show, there is a fairly large overlap between these types of persons; there are many individuals who are just "sociable." But we are familiar with persons who are gregarious, but not integrated; we speak of such a person as one who has "many acquaintances but few friends." On the other hand, we refer to individuals who are group members, but who do not know many people, as the "cliquish type."

The design of the Personal Influence study emphasized gregariousness, having a relatively large number of personal contacts "beyond the environs of the household," as an important factor in opinion leadership. It may very well be that gregariousness is highly associated with *leadership*, for informal group studies have shown the leader of a group to have more contacts outside the group than have the rank and file members.[8] The latter studies, of the International Typographical Union and of drug adoption among physicians, have emphasized group membership and the part that it plays in the diffusion of information and innovation. These studies are more in the tradition of the literature on primary groups which emphasizes the importance of the group in molding the view of the world and sanctioning the actions of the individual members.

However, gregariousness and group membership might be differentially related to the possession of information, and we might set up alternative theories about the operation of these social variables. A theory that emphasized the importance of gregariousness would assert that the more people one knows, even on a casual basis, the more one is likely to be exposed to oral communications of all kinds and therefore the more likely to be informed. A theory that stressed integration would hold that only in a group which maintained an interest in certain topics would the likelihood of informed and purposeful communication about those topics be maximized, and thus membership in an interested group is the more likely to provide one with information. Furthermore, integration breaks down what Festinger and his associates have called "restraining forces" against communication.[9] Individuals communicate to other persons with whom they have intimate and continuous contact with less reserve than is used with dealing with more casual acquaintances. Finally, an integration theory would emphasize the importance of social support: in cases where objective evidence is lacking, one is more dependent on the opinions of associates.[10]

The difference in importance of gregariousness and group membership would be shown most quickly by comparing the two extreme types mentioned above. If gregariousness were the most important social determinant of the acquisition of information, the cliquish person would have no advantage over his non-integrated counterpart. On the other hand, if group membership were the crucial social variable in the diffusion of information, we should expect the highly gregarious but non-integrated person, the "gadabout," to have no special advantage.

Festinger and his associates have compared the knowledge of the content of a rumor, in a housing development, of persons who claim a large and unspecified number of friends, persons who present a shorter and more specific number of friends, and persons who claimed no friends at all in the area. The authors found that indi-

[8] William F. Whyte, *Street Corner Society* (Chicago: University of Chicago Press, 1943), chap. vi.

[9] Leon Festinger *et al.*, "A Study of a Rumor: Its Origin and Spread," *Human Relations*, I (1948), 464–86.

[10] Coleman, Katz, and Menzel, *op. cit.*, pp. 268–69.

viduals who have the smaller but more definite number of friends are more likely to know "what is going on" than persons who say they have "a hundred friends" in the village, and that both of these groups are more likely to be "informed" than the self-designated isolates.[11] The rumor study presented the sets of gregarious and integrated individuals as mutually exclusive categories. Assuming the reliability of this type of answer, as we shall be forced to do below, we know that the respondents who claim large numbers of friends are highly gregarious, and the authors make the assumption (because of the absence of specific names from their response) that they are not group members, but we have no positive testimony from the respondents on this question. We assume that the individuals who turned in shorter lists, but who named specific friends, are integrated with those persons, and that those who presented neither names nor numbers are neither gregarious nor integrated. We do not know, from the data, whether the individuals who claim many unnamed friends are including in this group a lesser number of really intimate contacts, nor whether individuals who confined their responses to the list of their most immediate friends have also a large reservoir of more casual contacts. Our data on graduate students indicate that gregariousness and integration are highly associated, and that an event attributable to intensive and limited personal relationships might very well be the result of extensive and more superficial relationships.

The study at hand concerns American graduate students and a subject in which they are most vitally concerned: money. The data are taken from a study of a national sample of graduate students, conducted in autumn, 1958, by the National Opinion Research Center, the central subject of which was the current financial situation of the American graduate student

[11] Festinger *et al.*, "A Study of Rumor," *op. cit.*, pp. 478–79.

and his attitudes toward his financial status. We shall use the sample of graduate students to test our counter-hypotheses about the relative effect of gregariousness with the other graduate students versus integration with an informal group of fellow students, in providing the graduate student with information about financial opportunities.

The National Opinion Research Center's sample of graduate students is a two-stage stratified cluster sample of the enrolment of American graduate schools in autumn, 1958. The sample is confined to students in departments which offer the Ph.D. in the "traditional arts and sciences," which means that strictly professional departments and schools of medicine, law, education, etc., are excluded, along with quasi-professional and applied areas such as art, pharmacy and rural sociology. The first step in the sampling was to draw twenty-five schools from the universe of graduate schools offering the Ph.D. in the traditional arts and sciences. Once the universities had been drawn, a quota was assigned to each school and a sample the size of the quota was drawn by random methods from the total enrolment of students studying for advanced degrees in the traditional arts and sciences in the university. The sample of schools and students was drawn in such a way that every student currently enrolled in a department falling in the sample universe had an equal probability of being drawn. The total sample size was set at 3,000, and questionnaires were collected from 2,842 respondents, for a completion rate of nearly 95 per cent.

Gregariousness with other graduate students was measured in the following way: each respondent was asked to indicate the number of students in his department whom he knew "well enough to stop and chat with on the street for a few minutes." We had obtained information from the respective universities on the total enrolment in the student's department. For each size department, a distribution was generated and quartiled, the student being classified according to the quartile of students known in which he fell, for departments the size of the department in which he was enrolled.[12] Persons in the first quartile of students known, for each size of department, were classified "high gregarious"; those who fell in the fourth quartile were classified "low gregarious." In addition, students who claimed to know no other students in the department were classified "non-gregarious." They are grouped with the low-gregarious individuals in the following tables.

Each student is classified as being integrated or non-integrated on the basis of his yes-or-no answer to the question: "Do you belong to a group of students which

TABLE 1

GREGARIOUSNESS AND INTEGRATION

Gregariousness	Percentage Integrated	No.
High (first quartile)	68	(597)
High medium (second quartile)	58	(688)
Low medium (third quartile)	45	(669)
Low (fourth quartile)	22	(678)

maintains informal contacts outside the classroom?" Group members are self-designated. The size of the sampling interval of a national sample made the gathering of sociometric data impractical.

Table 1 shows the association between gregariousness and integration. We observe that the two variables are highly related. The explanation of this relationship lies beyond the scope of this paper, but two alternative theories might be briefly stated. The first theory holds that gregarious behavior is an expression of a gregarious attitude, the attribute of "sociability" referred to earlier in the paper,

and that sociable people who have a great many dyad contacts are more likely to find persons so congenial to themselves as to motivate them to form more permanent social attachments with them. An alternative theory would explain gregariousness in terms of integration; people who have repeated contacts with certain others are more likely to expand the circle of their acquaintance through meetings with friends of their friends from other social environments. At any rate, we may expect that any information or opinion item that correlates with one of these variables will, in all likelihood, correlate with the other.[13]

The items of information which we will use to compare the effects of integration and gregariousness pertain to graduate finances. The first set of questions concerns the kinds of financial aids available to the students in the respondent's department. The respondents were asked: "What is your impression of the chances for graduate students in your department and in your stage of study getting the following?"

1. Teaching assistantships
2. Research assistantships
3. Scholarships and fellowships for tuition "plus"
4. Scholarships and fellowships for full tuition only
5. Scholarships and fellowships for part tuition
6. Part-time jobs of a non-academic type
7. Part-time teaching in night-school or nearby institutions

The second set of responses we shall consider belongs perhaps more in the domain of opinion than of information, although the testimony of graduate students about what might be going on in their department should be classified as extremely informed opinion. The respondents were asked: "From what you know,

[12] Gregariousness is controlled for departmental size, since the number of other students known in the department varies with the size of enrolment in the department. Since neither individual integration nor departmental cohesiveness is related to department size, neither is controlled.

[13] This finding also raises the possibility that previous findings in communication studies which show the importance of either gregariousness or group membership show also the importance of the other.

to what extent do the following criteria influence the allocation of stipends in your department?"

1. Grades
2. Faculty's personal impressions
3. Financial need

For each one of these items the graduate students were presented with a set of precoded answers, ranging from "good" to "not so good" for the financial-aid questions; from "very important" to "not important" for the allocation criteria items. In each case, one of the precoded answers was "no idea," and it is this latter category which interests us. A person who circles the "no idea" response for any of these items is admitting a complete lack of information, correct or incorrect; he is unable to say whether the chances for getting this kind of financial aid are good or bad, whether these criteria for the allocation of stipends are important or not important.[14]

On the hypothesis that both gregariousness and integration favor the collection of information, we should predict that persons who are highly gregarious and persons who are integrated will be less likely to answer "no idea" to these items than persons who are not so gregarious and not integrated. Table 2 shows the relationship between gregariousness and the possession of information in these matters. In most of the cases the difference between the most and least gregarious students is about 14 per cent; the exceptions are the questions concerning scholarships just equal to tuition and fees and part-time teaching work, where the difference is 9 per cent, and the questions on part-tuition scholarships and part-time non-academic work, where gregariousness has no effect. The table shows little or no difference between the two upper quartiles, with the third level of gregariousness falling about midway between the most and least gregarious.

Table 3 shows the probability of being uninformed about the same items when group integration is controlled. Again, we note the average difference for response which shows the effect to be about 14 per cent, with the exception of full-tuition scholarships, where the difference is reduced to 8 per cent. As was the case with respect to gregariousness, the questions concerning part-tuition scholarships and part-time non-academic work fail to show the social effect. One response appears to be affected by gregariousness, but not by integration; this is the question on the availability of part-time teaching jobs.

Two of the ten items fail to show the effect of either of the interpersonal vari-

[14] Terminology such as "information" or "knowledgeability" is used in connection with these items, although no attempt is made here to verify the correctness of respondents' replies. Indeed, the virtue of using the "no idea" category is that objective verification is made unnecessary. It must be stressed that "no idea" is not "no answer" to the question. The non-respondents have been left out of the percentaging operations in the tables that accompany this work. Thus, the respondents we are working with here admit to being uninformed about these items. In view of the known tendency of survey respondents to express themselves on questions about which they know little or nothing, we do not believe that the number of uninformed is exaggerated by this procedure. Those readers who believe, however, that the status of being "informed" should be accorded only to respondents who give right answers to questions of fact may look upon this as a report of the influence of social variables on "opinion" rather than on "information." We have no objection to this transformation; indeed, the similarity of this research to the Festinger rumor study was suggested above, but we do point out that the dependent variable is cognitive opinion, as opposed to normative opinion. The graduate departments have never been classified as to whether the chances for financial aid in their department are in fact "good" or "bad," and of course there is no way of verifying the criteria for the allocation of stipends in the department. In general, we find that various subgroups among the graduate students who are relatively optimistic about their chances for getting financial aid do in fact possess stipends in higher proportions. The positive and negative responses to the items perhaps reflect the personal chances of the individual with more accuracy than the relative generosity of the department.

ables, and we might speculate on the reasons. In the case of the part-tuition scholarships, it may be that their scarcity makes them unlikely topics of conversation; only 110 respondents (less than 4 per cent of the sample) have such stipends. Scholarships and fellowships which just equal tuition and fees are more common, but not as common as the "tuition plus" stipend, which may also account for the attenuation of the social effect on response concerning the tuition-only scholarship.

On the other hand, more than a thousand of the respondents work some hours on part-time jobs outside the department, so that there is no accounting for the

TABLE 2

INABILITY TO ANSWER TEN INFORMATION AND OPINION QUESTIONS, BY GREGARIOUSNESS*

(Percentage Unable To Estimate)

	GREGARIOUSNESS			
	High	High Medium	Low Medium	Low
Availability of:				
Teaching assistantships	6 (588)	8 (680)	13 (676)	20 (689)
Research assistantships	11 (584)	14 (670)	18 (663)	25 (687)
Scholarships and fellowships for tuition "plus"	12 (586)	14 (677)	20 (673)	27 (690)
Scholarships and fellowships for full tuition only	21 (580)	22 (671)	25 (670)	30 (685)
Scholarships and fellowships for part tuition	27 (574)	25 (660)	27 (659)	31 (677)
Part-time non-academic jobs	25 (585)	27 (676)	28 (667)	29 (681)
Part-time teaching jobs	31 (583)	34 (673)	39 (664)	40 (679)
Importance for allocation of stipends of:				
Grades	14 (590)	17 (684)	19 (677)	26 (692)
Faculty personal impressions	18 (589)	21 (682)	24 (673)	33 (687)
Financial need	24 (587)	33 (678)	31 (670)	39 (683)

* Numbers in parentheses here and in tables that follow represent percentage base; numbers change from item to item because of different rates of non-response.

TABLE 3

INABILITY TO ANSWER TEN INFORMATION AND OPINION
QUESTIONS, BY INTEGRATION

(Percentage Unable To Estimate)

	INTEGRATION	
	Integrated	Non-integrated
Availability of:		
Teaching assistantships	4 (1,294)	18 (1,383)
Research assistantships	9 (1,268)	23 (1,368)
Scholarships and fellowships for tuition "plus"	10 (1,283)	25 (1,387)
Scholarships and fellowships for full tuition only	20 (1,273)	28 (1,375)
Scholarships and fellowships for part tuition	26 (1,254)	28 (1,360)
Part-time non-academic jobs	28 (1,285)	26 (1,375)
Part-time teaching jobs	35 (1,278)	37 (1,373)
Importance for allocation of stipends of:		
Grades	12 (1,296)	24 (1,392)
Faculty personal impressions	16 (1,294)	30 (1,382)
Financial need	25 (1,287)	37 (1,375)

failure of the question on part-time non-academic work to associate with either variable on these grounds. The other non-departmental information item concerning part-time teaching jobs is associated with gregariousness but not with integration. These two responses about non-departmental opportunities will be considered in detail below, in connection with Table 5, where specifications will be made of the relationship between integration and ability to answer these questions.

tion effect remains constant, while the effect of gregariousness virtually disappears among the integrated, and is attenuated among the non-integrated. In seven of the eight comparisons, the likelihood of possessing information is equal to or greater among those who are at the lowest level of gregariousness, but integrated, than for those at the highest level of gregariousness, but not integrated. The sole exception is in the case of the question on part-time teaching, which was not

TABLE 4

GREGARIOUSNESS, INTEGRATION, AND INABILITY TO ANSWER EIGHT
SELECTED INFORMATION AND OPINION QUESTIONS

(Percentage Unable To Estimate)

GREGARIOUSNESS	AVAILABILITY OF:						IMPORTANCE OF:	
	Assistantships		Scholarships		Part-Time Work Teaching	Grades	Faculty Personal Impressions	Financial Need
	Teaching	Research	Tuition "Plus"	Tuition Only				
Integrated:								
High............	3 (398)	7 (394)	8 (395)	19 (390)	30 (393)	12 (399)	14 (399)	21 (397)
High medium...	5 (399)	9 (393)	10 (393)	20 (391)	34 (393)	12 (398)	16 (398)	28 (396)
Low medium....	5 (296)	11 (290)	13 (294)	20 (292)	40 (294)	13 (297)	17 (295)	23 (294)
Low............	7 (149)	10 (149)	9 (148)	20 (147)	41 (145)	15 (149)	22 (149)	33 (148)
Non-integrated:								
High............	14 (185)	18 (185)	20 (186)	24 (185)	34 (185)	17 (186)	28 (185)	30 (185)
High medium...	13 (275)	21 (271)	18 (277)	24 (273)	34 (274)	23 (279)	28 (277)	40 (275)
Low medium....	17 (363)	23 (356)	25 (362)	29 (361)	36 (364)	24 (362)	28 (362)	37 (361)
Low............	23 (506)	28 (503)	31 (507)	31 (503)	39 (501)	27 (509)	34 (505)	40 (501)

We will compare the effect of gregariousness with integration on the probability of being informed about these matters by cross-tabulating the percentage of those uninformed against the two variables simultaneously. If the gregariousness effect tends to disappear, we may say that informal group membership is conducive to the possession of information, but not gregariousness; if the integration effect disappears, we may say the opposite. The effects of the two variables are compared in Table 4, where we have omitted the two responses which are not associated with the variables. Here we see that the integra-

associated with integration at the zero order. Thus, comparing the two extreme analytical types, the information advantage appears to accrue to the cliquish person, as opposed to the "gadabout," thus replicating the finding of Festinger and his associates in the rumor study. The only gregariousness effect retained by this cross-tabulation is a slight and not unexpected tendency for the disparity between the integrated and the unintegrated to be slightly less among the high gregarious than among the low gregarious.

Sociologists generally define a group as "a number of persons in continuous interaction." We suggest that interaction, as such, is not the most important determinant of the strategic position of group members in the flow of information in graduate departments. Interaction is, of course, necessary to the accumulation of information which characterizes group members, but it is not sufficient cause for that accumulation, for persons who engage in extensive interaction with other students in the department are more likely to be "stumped" by questions about conditions in the department than persons who do not have such extensive contacts, but who are members of groups. We submit that the key to the understanding of the advantageous position of group members with respect to the possession of such information lies in the *number* of group members and in the *continuity* of their interaction.

We say their number because, using the imagery of Simmel,[15] every group represents the convergence of a set of social circles: the individual circles of contacts, or role sets, of the members. Every student group is composed of heterogeneous elements: some of the students are integrated with the faculty, other group members have extensive contacts among the student body of the department; some of the members have contacts with faculty and students in other schools, while still other group members may know persons of the administrative staff who have access to special kinds of information. The common knowledge of every member of the group represents a pooling of this information, which is based on resources superior to those of even the most gregarious of individuals.[16] Dyad contacts bring together only two sets of social circles —those of ego and alter. Group participation brings together as many sets of contacts as there are group members. The extent of the difference between the pools of information being tapped is appreciated more if one recalls that each member of a group brings his own set of social contacts to the interaction situation, and that each of these contacts has in turn his own set, so that the difference in size of the resource population tends to grow exponentially as the size of the group is increased. Of course, there may be considerable overlap between the contacts of group members; the more diverse and heterogeneous the contacts of group members, the greater increment in possession of information might be expected. Generally, however, we may expect a group—provided it is larger than a dyad itself—to mobilize a greater informant population than would a casual acquaintanceship.

Although numbers in interaction are the life of a social group, its very special nature lies in the continuity of that interaction, for all populations—even such a sequestered aggregate as a graduate department—are in a state of constant change and realignment. Interruptions and distractions have a tendency to reduce the information levels of integrated and non-integrated alike. We shall

[15] Georg Simmel, *The Web of Group Affiliations,* trans. Reinhard Bendix (Glencoe, Ill.: Free Press, 1955). See translator's note, p. 125. The image is more fully developed in the German text (cf. Simmel, "Die Kreuzung sozialer Kreise," in *Soziologie* [Munich: Duncker & Humblot, 1922], pp. 305–44). The translator's comment that "a literal translation of this phrase, 'the intersection of social circles,' is almost meaningless" is perhaps hasty, in the light of the development of set theory in modern algebra. It seems to this writer that Simmel was groping for (and just about making contact with) a conception of the individual representing an intersection of traits derived from association with a unique union of social sets (groups). This article follows this imagery in that it pictures the combined information resources of individuals in interaction as the union of information potential of all the groups with which they are associated.

[16] In connection with the explanation presented here and in the following paragraph, cf. Marjorie E. Shaw, "A Comparison of Individuals and Small Groups in the Rational Solution of Complex Problems," in Maccoby, Newcomb, and Hartley (eds.), *op. cit.,* pp. 564–75, and Herbert Gurnee, "A Comparison of Collective and Individual Judgments of Fact," *Journal of Experimental Psychology,* XXI (1937), 106–12.

illustrate this point with a cross-tabulation of the effect of integration and seniority, number of years the student has been enrolled in the department (Table 5). In this table, we observe (from the base numbers in the parentheses) that seniority and integration are associated. Not surprisingly, there is a tendency for the proportion integrated to grow from the first through the fourth years of graduate study; however, the proportion integrated drops below 50 per cent among students who have been enrolled in the department more than four years. We also note that seniority does tend to confer an advantage with respect to information, but (1) its effect is not as important as that of integration and (2) the effect tends to disappear among those who have been enrolled in the department more than one year, among both integrated and non-integrated students, and even to reverse slightly in some cases among the students who have been enrolled more than four years.

We attribute this finding to the fact that students who have been enrolled in graduate departments for a long time usually have dropped out somewhere along the way to do something else. The departmental careers of such students contain discontinuities, and they have gotten out of touch with what is happening in the department. The price of keeping in touch is interaction —several hours per week, every week—with other persons in the department, comparing notes, noting the appearance of new opportunities and the closure of old opportunities, correcting erroneous impressions, confirming informed hunches. It is the constant flow of ostensibly petty and trivial details which keeps the integrated student more current on departmental developments.

The response to the two items about nondepartmental financial opportunities does not follow the general pattern of Table 5. In the case of information about part-time non-academic and teaching jobs we observe (1) that the senior students are more likely to be informed (except in the case of non-integrated students with respect to non-academic work), (2) that the group membership effect does not appear (in fact reverses in the case of non-academic jobs) except among the most senior graduate stu-

TABLE 5

YEAR OF GRADUATE STUDY IN DEPARTMENT, INTEGRATION, AND INABILITY TO ANSWER
NINE SELECTED INFORMATION AND OPINION QUESTIONS
(Percentage Unable To Estimate)

YEAR IN DEPARTMENT	ABILITY OF:						IMPORTANCE OF:		
	Assistantships		Scholarships		Part-Time Work		Grades	Faculty Personal Impressions	Financial Need
	Teaching	Research	Tuition "Plus"	Tuition Only	Non-academic	Teaching			
Integrated:									
First..........	7 (447)	14 (444)	12 (446)	18 (444)	31 (446)	41 (442)	17 (447)	23 (445)	31 (445)
Second........	2 (332)	6 (325)	11 (329)	20 (326)	29 (329)	37 (326)	9 (335)	12 (334)	21 (334)
Third–fourth....	3 (342)	6 (337)	9 (340)	21 (339)	28 (341)	30 (340)	9 (342)	11 (342)	21 (337)
Fifth and later..	5 (166)	7 (165)	8 (161)	20 (157)	22 (162)	23 (163)	15 (165)	16 (166)	25 (165)
Non-integrated:									
First..........	20 (559)	28 (557)	28 (559)	30 (553)	26 (553)	41 (553)	27 (564)	37 (559)	43 (557)
Second........	15 (295)	18 (289)	21 (297)	24 (295)	24 (294)	34 (294)	20 (293)	24 (291)	36 (292)
Third–fourth....	15 (300)	17 (295)	20 (300)	24 (298)	25 (299)	32 (296)	19 (303)	24 (302)	32 (298)
Fifth and later..	19 (203)	26 (201)	29 (203)	32 (202)	30 (202)	35 (203)	25 (204)	27 (204)	34 (200)

rolled in the department more than four years. We also note that seniority does tend to confer an advantage with respect to information, but (1) its effect is not as important as that of integration and (2) the effect tends to disappear among those who have been enrolled in the department more than one year, among both integrated and non-integrated students, and even to reverse slightly in some cases among the students who have been enrolled more than four years.

We attribute this finding to the fact that students who have been enrolled in graduate departments for a long time usually dents, at which stage the familiar association does appear. It will be remembered that information about part-time non-academic jobs is associated with neither of the social variables at the zero order, and that information about part-time teaching is associated with gregariousness, but not with group membership.

The reappearance of the integration effect among the students with the longest tenure in the department is probably related to the discontinuities in their graduate careers mentioned above. When a graduate student drops course registration entirely, it is common for him to become either a full-time assistant in some activity of the department or, if such employment be unavailable, to seek employment outside the department. Thus, the older graduate students have more experience with and interest in non-departmental opportunities. They are able to contribute more because of their experience and they are motivated to contribute more because the topic is seen as more relevant to the interests of their fellow group members. The chances for financial help from the department become attenuated after several years of enrolment, also, and this motivates them to seek as well as to pass on information about these opportunities, while the students in later cohorts are still anticipating and getting financial help from within the department.[17] The younger students are thus less involved in the non-departmental financial aid situation, and such communication is less likely to enter the agenda of interaction in their groups.

The foregoing assumptions about relevancy might also explain the slight advantage that first- and second-year non-integrated students appear to have concerning information about part-time non-academic

jobs. Integrated students are more informed about stipends and they are also more likely to have stipends.[18] Stipend-holding is thought to be an important determinant of integration in that (1) assistants are more likely to be exposed to other students in the department in non-classroom contexts; (2) persons who hold scholarships and fellowships are less likely to be forced to take jobs which would interfere with their interaction with other students. Stipend-holding thus facilitates contact with other students in the department, and the attendant exposure raises the probability of becoming a group member, especially in the first year of study in the department, when the graduate student is unknown. The persons who do not hold stipends are more likely to spend their non-classroom hours in outside jobs, and thus less likely to become integrated. Therefore, turning the previous sentence the other way, the non-integrated students in the early years of enrolment are more likely to have experience and involvement in the part-time non-academic job market. The fact that the veteran non-integrated students appear slightly less informed about part-time non-academic jobs than their younger counterparts may be a reflection of the tendency of the older non-integrated students to move into the full-time non-academic job market.[19]

We have observed that information about part-time teaching is associated with gregariousness while information about part-time non-academic work is not. This is perhaps attributable to the fact that teaching is

[17] The importance of the factors of relevancy and involvement in the flow of communication are discussed in Festinger *et al.*, "A Study of Rumor," *op. cit.*, and in Leon Festinger, Stanley Schachter, and Kurt Back, *Social Pressures in Informal Groups* (New York: Harper & Bros., 1950), chap. vii.

[18] Factors in the structure of graduate education which facilitate the integration of the student are discussed in William Erbe, "Student Integration and Departmental Cohesiveness in American Graduate Schools" (unpublished Ph.D. dissertation, University of Chicago, 1961). (Microfilmed.)

[19] The occupational situation of American graduate students is described in the final report of the NORC graduate student survey (see James A. Davis, "Stipends and Spouses—The Consumer Finances of Graduate Study in America" [Chicago: National Opinion Research Center, 1961]). (Mimeographed.)

such a narrowly defined activity, compared to the range of non-academic work. (From the earlier tables we can see that knowledge about part-time teaching is the least distributed of any information about financial aid.) Thus, a student with non-departmental contacts would presumably have about as good a chance as a student with extensive departmental contacts to acquire information about non-academic work, but an individual who knew many other students, including the older cohort of students who are more knowledgeable about part-time

dents; that the conglomeration of knowledge associated with the presence of many groups in the department creates an atmosphere more conducive to the obtaining of information than the atmosphere of a department in which relatively few groups exist. Specifically, we are interested in whether the integrated and non-integrated students in "high-cohesive" departments have an advantage in the gathering of information over their opposite numbers in "low-cohesive" departments.

When our students were asked whether

TABLE 6

INABILITY TO ANSWER TEN INFORMATION AND OPINION QUESTIONS, BY DEPARTMENTAL COHESIVENESS AND INTEGRATION WITH FELLOW STUDENTS

(Percentage Unable To Estimate)

	High-Cohesive Departments		Low-Cohesive Departments	
	Integrated	Non-integrated	Integrated	Non-integrated
Availability of:				
Teaching assistantships	3 (1,116)	11 (792)	16 (103)	30 (449)
Research assistantships	8 (1,094)	18 (785)	20 (101)	35 (440)
Scholarships and fellowships for tuition "plus"	10 (1,108)	19 (792)	15 (102)	37 (451)
Scholarships and fellowships for full tuition only	19 (1,098)	25 (787)	21 (101)	35 (448)
Scholarships and fellowships for part tuition	25 (1,082)	25 (778)	24 (100)	33 (445)
Part-time non-academic jobs	29 (1,108)	26 (789)	24 (102)	27 ((445)
Part-time teaching jobs	35 (1,103)	37 (787)	31 (101)	37 (446)
Importance for allocation of stipends of:				
Grades	11 (1,117)	20 (803)	20 (102)	34 (446)
Faculty personal impressions	15 (1,116)	25 (799)	25 (101)	40 (441)
Financial need	26 (1,110)	34 (793)	24 (101)	46 (440)

academic opportunities, would have a slight advantage in the matter of teaching jobs.

Our final task is to examine the effect of the structure of the department on knowledgeability about these financial matters. The hypothesis advanced here is that there is a contextual effect[20] created by the social organization patterns of the graduate stu-

they belonged to informal groups, they were also asked whether the students in their departments tended, on the whole, to form such groups. Departments in which a majority of the respondents said that the students did tend to form groups were classified as "high cohesive," while departments in which a majority of the respondents said that the students tended not to form groups were classified as "low cohesive."[21] Table

[20] Cf. Patricia L. Kendall and Paul F. Lazarsfeld, "Problems of Survey Analysis," in Robert K. Merton and Paul F. Lazarsfeld (eds.), Continuities in Social Research (Glencoe, Ill.: Free Press, 1950), pp. 195–96; and Peter M. Blau, "Structural Effects," American Sociological Review, XXV (1960), 178–93, esp. 190 ff.

[21] As is the case with integration, the information taken from our respondents is here used at face value. The rationale of using a majority vote on the existence of groups in the department as

136

6 shows the effect of integration on the possession of information when departmental cohesiveness is held constant.

One may make three types of comparisons in Table 6. First of all, comparing the relationship between the likelihood of being informed and integration status, controlled for departmental cohesiveness, we observe that the difference between integrated and non-integrated is preserved in both types of departments except in the cases of part-tuition scholarships and part-time employment. The integration effect (influence of individual groups participation) does not disappear when cohesiveness (influence of the density of group interaction) is held constant. We have already speculated on situational reasons why integration is not associated with information on the three items in which the effect does not appear. Table 6 adds only the following facts: (1) that non-integrated students in low-cohesive departments are less likely to be informed

about all kinds of fellowships (including those for part tuition) than are the integrated students, and (2) that integrated students in low-cohesive departments are slightly more often informed about part-time teaching jobs.

In the second set of comparisons from Table 6, we note the differential information level of the integrated students in high-cohesive departments as opposed to low cohesive departments. Five of the ten comparisons show no advantage for the group members in highly cohesive populations, and the integrated students in the low-cohesive departments may even have a slight advantage with respect to non-departmental opportunities.

Previous speculations about relevancy and involvement in financial-aid markets may be relevant here. We have indicated that stipend-holding is an important predictor of student group membership. We also find, and are not surprised, that aggregate stipend-holding is related to departmental cohesiveness, since the distribution of many stipends makes greater numbers of students available for fraternization.[22] Thus, students in low-cohesive departments are less likely to get stipends of all kinds, more likely to be involved in the market for non-departmental financial aid. They are also more likely to be interested in the less remunerative types of fellowships, and in the possibility of cases of financial hardship providing the basis for the award of a fellowship or assistantship.

The foregoing speculation might also be used to account for the greater probability of information among students in the highly cohesive departments, because these students are more accustomed to basing their financial plans on the expectation of a tuition "plus" scholarship or an assistantship. However, though part-time work and low-value scholarships are more important to the students in low-cohesive departments, the types of financial aid about which the high cohesive students appear to be more

---

an indicator of the cohesiveness of that department takes into account the fact that the "objective" reports given by the respondent-informants will be colored by their own group experience. We reason that asking whether or not groups exist among the student body of a student's department is equivalent to asking him if he has seen or heard of the existence of such groups. The more groups in the department, the more likely the respondent will know of their existence, and the more likely he will report so. The majority vote is here used as a measure of the density of group interaction in the department. The fact that more than half the respondents from a department did not report the existence of groups should not be taken as evidence that there are no groups in the department, but that groups are so few and far between that less than half of the students sampled had observed, directly or indirectly, their existence. We have no other information on the cohesiveness of the department, other than that given by the respondent; however, the classification correlated highly with response to a question which asks the respondents whether they spend a majority of their leisure time with other graduate students in their department, an item from the graduate-student survey which might be considered similar to the sociometric analyst's index of in-group choices, a traditional measure of population cohesiveness.

[22] Erbe, *op. cit.*

137

informed are the most common, in both high and low cohesive departments,[23] so that we observe a real information advantage for students who are group members in populations characterized by the presence of many groups.

A cohesiveness effect suggests the operation of a communications network among the graduate students. The more densely the grapevine grows, the more likely one is to be informed. The existence of a relatively larger number of informal groups in the department facilitates the possession of information. Among the integrated students, the explanation for this advantage would seem to lie in the fact that a department in which there are many groups raises the probability of overlap in the social circles of the individual. The existence of a plurality of groups provides the individual with more chances for multiple group affiliation. Previous studies of patterns of primary group membership have shown that individuals who belong to primary groups at all usually belong to several of them.[24] If the analysis presented above concerning the facilitation of information diffusion by the group is correct, then it would seem that the multiply integrated student brings to the interaction vortex of any one group not only the fruits of heterogeneous dyad contacts but also the accumulation of information provided by heterogeneous group contacts, with all the benefits of number and continuity referred to above. Thus, the groups which exist in high-cohesive departments are made more productive of information when they are part of a larger network of communications.

The contextual effect of high density of group interaction is best illustrated in the third set of comparisons from Table 6, between the non-integrated in high- and low-cohesive departments. Here we observe the association of high cohesiveness with

[23] *Ibid.*

[24] P. H. Fisher, "An Analysis of the Primary Group," *Sociometry*, XVI (1953), 272–76.

knowledgeability in the response to all questions except those on part-time employment. Whatever may be the case with the integrated students, high cohesiveness contributes to the information of the non-integrated. It is with respect to the information of the non-integrated that we observe the function of the "grapevine," and perhaps also an unanticipated function of gregariousness. We know that the integrated students are also the more gregarious students, and we reason that the social contacts of gregarious group members are not confined to other group members. Therefore, the explanation of the information advantage held by non-integrated individuals in high-cohesive departments may be that the accumulation of information within the group is made available to non-group members as a result of outside interaction by group members. The high-cohesive departments are, by definition, the departments in which a relatively large number of groups exist. The more groups the greater the likelihood that non-group members will engage in interaction with group members. Since the group represents a repository of financial information, therefore, the more likely even the non-member to be exposed to informed communication.

In conclusion, our data would seem to support three general assertions about the effect of interpersonal relations on the flow of information:

1. Integration with a peer group is conducive to the possession of information, even on a highly salient subject, compared to non-integration.

2. High gregariousness, the maintenance of extensive acquaintanceships with other individuals in the referent population, is also associated with the possession of information, but this effect seems to be caused mostly by the fact that highly gregarious persons are also more likely to be group members.

3. High density of group interaction in the population of reference is, in and of it-

self, conducive to the possession of information, especially among non-integrated students, although the integrated students within such a population are more likely to be informed than the non-integrated.

The explanation put forth for these findings was that the group, by bringing together persons whose collective resources of information were greater than those of any individual, and by providing a continuously operating market in which information could be exchanged and verified, constituted a node of such information. Departments in which relatively large numbers of these groups exist constitute a network, such that the integrated individual brings a greater quantity of seemingly reliable information to the group, and the unintegrated individual, through dyad contacts with such persons, is more likely to possess information than his counterpart in a department which is not served by such a network.

The significance of social structures as communication networks will continue to be a matter of concern to researchers in this field. Especially wanting are coding and analysis techniques with which to apply quantitative social structural concepts to the findings of survey data on individuals. But along with this quantitative refinement must come the development of such descriptive and analytical conceptual apparatus as will enable the researcher to go beyond the depiction of social structure in communication processes, to develop systematic theory specifying the conditions under which these effects hold or do not hold. When these refinements are added to existing procedures, it will be possible to make more subtle analyses of communication processes.

STATE UNIVERSITY OF IOWA

From Herman Turk, *American Sociological Review 35*, 1-20 (1970), by permission.

INTERORGANIZATIONAL NETWORKS IN URBAN SOCIETY: INITIAL PERSPECTIVES AND COMPARATIVE RESEARCH *

Herman Turk

The University of Southern California

The activity levels and complexity of new interorganizational networks are observable consequents of prior degrees of social integration defined in organizational terms. This proposition was specified and tested in terms of the flow of poverty funds from Federal agencies to and among organizations within the 130 largest American cities.

The city's extralocal integration was measured by the number of national associational headquarters it contained, and integration among its local units by the incidence of communitywide civic associations as well as degree of control by its municipal government. With some exceptions, the extralocal variable predicted the level of interorganizational activity, while local integration predicted complexity within a portion of the interorganizational network. Expedient or normative demand, inferred from poverty rates and other forms of deprivation, only made positive contributions to such prediction where the prior levels of integration were high.

The study provides empirical support of an interorganizational level of analysis; it outlines directions for further research in urbanized social systems; and it demonstrates the need to employ both additive and multiplicative models of social organization.

INTRODUCTION

A NY large and complex social setting, such as a modern society or one of its urban components, may be viewed as an aggregate of organizations (associa-

* Parts of this report were written in collaboration with Robert Jiobu and presented as a paper at the 1969 Annual Meetings of the American Sociological Association in San Francisco. Mr. Jiobu held an assistantship under a Biomedical Sciences Support Grant to the University of Southern California by the National Institute of Mental Health. A Health Sciences Scholar award to the author by the National Institutes of Health and the National Library of Medicine supported his own participation and the processing of source materials. The research is an extension in part of studies he executed for the Department of Labor's Bureau of Work Programs (Turk, 1967a, 1967b). Computing assistance was provided by the University of Southern California's Computer Sciences Laboratory and by the Health Sciences Computing Facility, which is sponsored by the National Institutes of Health under Grant FR-3 to the University of California, Los Angeles. Deepest thanks are extended to Theresa G. Turk for her professional help in many ways.

tions), which appear, disappear, change, merge, and form networks of relations with one another (suggested to varying degrees by Warren, 1956; Greer and Orleans, 1962; Turk and Lefcowitz, 1962; Hauser, 1965; Evan, 1968; Guetzkow, 1966). This patterned aggregate has been called an "interorganizational field" by some (Warren, 1967; Turk, 1969) and, for certain purposes, makes use of an independent level of analysis. On that level, characteristics of the interorganizational situation may be used to predict other characteristics of the same situation over time, without reference to such more conventional and microscopic units of analysis as individuals and role categories, or to the rates that such units may produce (for example, see propositions by Emery and Trist, 1965 and Stinchcombe, 1965).

The following report describes a controlled, longitudinal study at the interorganizational level of analysis, which emphasizes prediction on the basis of broad assumptions about interorganizational phenomena. The preexisting organizational characteristics of the 130 largest American cities were employed to predict relative levels of interorganizational *activity* in the Federal War on Poverty and *complexity* within the interorganizational networks that served it.

ASSUMPTIONS WHICH UNDERLIE THE INTER-
ORGANIZATIONAL LEVEL OF ANALYSIS

Any given level of investigation requires that predictions be made from certain units of analysis (and relations among them) to other units (and their relations) which belong to the same class—this without reference to their respective subunits. The present instance requires a rationale for the analysis of large-scale social settings at the organizational and interorganizational level without reference to populations and status-role categories. Our rationale lies in the assumption that individual behaviors depend upon the presence of organizations that encourage or accept them and that organizations are primary determinants of regularities and uniformities in human potential for such behaviors. Organizations must be assumed to be both the formulators and the means of individual action: organizations are the actors which comprise any large and complex structure.

Populations and subpopulations are seen in terms of their effects upon large-scale social settings through the various organizations which they form or join, which they serve, for which they are source objects, from which they acquire norms or receive status, and which can act on their behalf. Populations are clienteles and electorates, repositories of specialized knowledge and of the capacity for bureaucratic participation, recruitment reservoirs, and diffuse sources of legitimation or ideological denial through collective expression. They may also be viewed as undifferentiated means of disposal and support through such mechanisms as consumption, donation, taxation, and investment. These various behavioral and attitudinal potentials of the population are themselves assumed to be organizationally determined.

Once certain more conventional thought models are put aside, it becomes difficult to identify "community roles" or "revolu-tionary roles" within large urban settings which are not defined by such enacted formal groups as voluntary associations, government agencies, churches, militant groups, commissions, or the public relations departments of large corporations. It proves to be even more difficult to conceive of roles at the societal level outside the context of national and international organizations. Power positions within larger cities and nations appear to rest heavily upon organizational memberships (Rostow, 1953; Mills, 1956; Galbraith, 1958; Babchuk *et al.*, 1960; Freeman *et al.*, 1962; Hawley, 1963); prestige may depend upon organizational memberships (Stinchcombe, 1965); and organizations appear to absorb an ever-increasing number of occupational roles, including craft-like, or professional roles. Even diffuse orientations vis-a-vis the broader setting may be acquired and exercised through contacts with organizations of all kinds, and not only those specializing in the transmission of influence (Parsons, 1956; Eisenstadt, 1965; Stinchcombe, 1965; Turk *et al.*, 1966). Further, settings marked by *cleavages* might also be expected to include a *variety* of organizational proponents for each point of view and a variety of organizational means for its implementation.

If mass responses to the broader setting are both formulated and enacted by organizations, it is reasonable to redefine the setting in terms of such organizations and the relations which exist among them. Recently, sociologists (Levine and White, 1961; Litwak and Hylton, 1962; Levine *et al.*, 1963; Warren, 1967; Turk, 1969) have used such familiar concepts as consensus, conflict, exchange, differentiation, and integration to refer to interorganizational relations within broad settings. These same concepts may be used to describe the setting itself in interorganizational terms.

INTEGRATION AND THE SPECIFIC FRAME
OF REFERENCE

The present study defines social integration in organizational terms and provides a test of its ability to predict new interorganizational activities and the complexity of certain networks within which these activities took place.

Interorganizational Consequences of Integration. The greater the integration of a social setting, the greater is its capacity *either* to support *or* to resist new interorganizational activities and arrangements. This proposition has been suggested by a discussion of the effects of "richness" within a social setting in either providing facilities conducive to the establishment of organizations or constituting means of resisting their encroachment (Stinchcombe, 1965). Solidarity among organizations and interorganizational networks within the setting could provide the resources, predictability, and imperative control for new interorganizational networks. But such solidarity could just as readily provide the basis of a united front against interorganizational emergence or colonization. Thus the direction of the causal connection between prior organizational integration and new networks of organizations will be considered an empirical question until conditions may be specified under which integration leads to either support or resistance.

Local and Extralocal Integration. A polarity between community and large-scale (mass) society has been suggested by Warren (1956), Vidich and Bensman (1958), Stein (1960), Mott (1965: 165–184), Walton (1968), and others. Gains in the integration of the community are at the expense of integration in mass society and vice versa. This is consonant with the more general idea of an inverse relationship between the solidarity of a social system and that of its subsystems (Riecken and Homans, 1954; Gouldner, 1959; Turk and Lefcowitz, 1962; Starbuck, 1965). From this standpoint one would expect the interorganizational patterns which indicate *local integration* within a regional entity to be negative correlates of the external organizational linkages that determine the level of its *extralocal integration.* However, much of the evidence has been anecdotal and phrased in terms of modalities among individual actors. At the interorganizational level one could also consider the reverse; namely, either mode of integration might provide organizational *facilities* which are required by the other mode, the result being a positive correlation between the two integrative levels.

Comparative urban studies have not always drawn the local-extralocal distinction, largely for want of appropriate data. Those which have concerned themselves with nationwide phenomena such as urban renewal (for example, Hawley, 1963 and T. Clark, 1968) restricted themselves mainly to the role of local integration in pursuing goals whose origin is extralocal in part. It may also be observed that some statistical data may indicate either or both types of integration; for example, export activities may refer to a city's solidarity through the division of labor or to its self-sufficiency and adaptive ability vis-a-vis the environment (Duncan and Riess, 1950; Nelson, 1955). They can just as easily refer, however, to its fragmentation and loss of self-determination, since enterprises that operate at the national level may have little or no reason to establish many relations with one another at the local level or with local organizations.

Since the direction of association between local and extralocal integration is not clear at the interorganizational level of analysis, the effects of each form of integration upon new interorganizational phenomena will be described independently.

The Demand for New Interorganizational Phenomena. Although emphasis has been placed upon the effects of organizational integration upon activity levels and complexity within new interorganizational networks, another independent variable merits consideration. Whether expressed directly in some form of mass appeal or—as the present frame of reference would have it—through certain organizational channels, the question of the *demand* for new interorganizational phenomena cannot be avoided. Without at least some demand for them, there will be *no* interorganizational networks either to be facilitated or to be resisted by different levels of local and extralocal integration. Thus the effects of organizational integration will first be described independently of the effects of demand.

RESEARCH OBJECTIVES AND HYPOTHESES

The research sought to assess the utility of an interorganizational level of analysis for macrosociological problems. Defining so fundamental a concept as social integration in organizational terms and using its indicators to predict the characteristics of new interorganizational networks appeared to constitute a significant first step. Organizational measures of both local and extralocal integration were linked to subsequent interorganizational phenomena—first independently, then jointly with the effects of demand for these new phenomena.

The level of a local unit's *extralocal* integration was defined as (1) the number of organizational linkages with the broader society. The level of its *local* integration was defined as (2) the occurrence of community-wide, non-governmental organizations with coordinative potential and (3) the amount of control exercised by its governmental organization. These variables were used to predict (1) the *activity level* of a new kind of relational network composed of local organizations as well as nonlocally based organizations of a broader society and (2) complexity within a portion of this network. The nature of this network required that *demand* be assessed in terms of the availability of potential clients. The following hypotheses were tested with cities as the local units and federal agencies as the organizational units of the broader society.

(1) *The activity level* of a new interorganizational network having both local elements and externally based societal components is a function of (a) the preexisting number of organizational linkages between the local unit and the broader society, (b) prior occurrence of non-governmental organizations which can coordinate the local unit, and (c) the amount of control exercised by local government.

(2) The establishment of a *complex* interorganizational network having both local elements and externally based societal components is a function of (a) the preexisting number of organizational linkages between the local unit and the broader society, (b) prior occurrence of nongovernmental organizations which can coordinate the local unit, and (c) the amount of control exercised by local government.

The *directions* of these hypothesized relationships eluded prediction for reasons already given under the specific frame of reference. Although not formulated as an hypothesis, the direction of whatever effect *demand* might have had was assumed to be

positive. The operational definitions and procedures used appear on the pages that follow.

RESEARCH DESIGN

Investigation centered upon the local and extralocal linkages of the 130 incorporated cities in the United States which had 1960 populations of more than 100,000 inhabitants. Each city constituted a separate unit of analysis. The organizational index of each city's extralocal integration and the two organizational indices of its local integration were measured in late 1960 and early 1961; so were most of the variables included for purposes of control. The two interorganizational network measures described contractual relations among Federal agencies and local organizations in the War on Poverty during mid-1964—mid-1966. Multiple regression permitted controlled prediction over a span of from three to five years. All measures used in the regression analysis appear on Table 1, together with their sources. Table 2 gives their intercorrelations.[1] The details of measurement follow in the sequence shown on the tables.

Extralocal Integration. The national headquarters of voluntary associations provided a 1960 measure of extralocal integration. Using 21 categories, which ranged from business and health associations through religious and patriotic, the *Encyclopedia of Associations* (1961) listed the number of such headquarters in each of the study cities. Face

---

[1] *Statistical Note.* All continuous variables were rank-scored from 0–129 throughout this study, so that they could be used in product-moment computation and complex regression analysis without *ad hoc* adjustments for individual quirks of distribution.

Where dichotomous (dummy) variables were employed, product-moment coefficients (r) and standardized regression coefficients (Beta) will sometimes be expressed as explicit proportions of their absolute values under maximum contingency (Table 2 contains the unadjusted values). It can be shown that the original coefficient is approximated wherever skewness does not affect its value; but the adjusted value communicates the degree of association more faithfully where such an effect occurs. Since none of the probabilities to be reported are based upon the coefficients themselves, this method can only illuminate, not distort.

Unless noted otherwise, all correlation coefficients are based on 130 cases. Their unadjusted two-tailed values at the .05 and .01 levels are .18 and .22, respectively.

validity may be claimed, for the number of networks which converge upon one place is just another way of referring to its societal integration—i.e., the external connections of that place. It should also be observed that most of the listed associations represented the interests of a large number of specific organizations or of major role-categories within them. Thus, such an association often reflected what is nationally held in common along certain specialized lines, and the presence of its headquarters within a given city should also signify the *institutional* integration of that city into the broader sociocultural setting.

The added advantages of this organizational index over others are that it (1) includes all of the institutional sectors of society (economic, religious, patriotic, recreational, etc.); (2) surpasses its alternatives in reflecting societal rather than regional orientation; and (3) is based upon organizations whose location is most likely to depend upon communicative centrality and least likely to be affected by such unique factors as the availability of special resources, facilities, markets, or clienteles. Nevertheless, certain direct and indirect alternatives to this measure could also be employed as criteria for its validation (Table 1 and what follows).

The older and larger cities were expected to be the ones most intimately and elaborately interwoven with the broader society; and the expectation is borne out by correlations of .71 and .69 between the number of national headquarters and size and age respectively. That banking activity may be taken as another indicator of extralocal linkages (i.e. of the city's economic dominance) is borne out by its correlation of .53 with number of headquarters.

Cities were also ranked according to the number of establishments within each business category which might have an export emphasis—i.e., serve nonresident persons and nonlocal organizations.[2] These data were used to construct an index of the diversity of export ties, which varied directly as the degree

of similarity among a city's rankings. That export diversity was associated with the mean of all ranks (r=.44) implies that the more diversified a city, the larger the *absolute number* of export establishments, whatever their type.

As expected, the number of national headquarters proved to be correlated with the diversity of export establishments (r=.49). By way of control and also as expected, a similarly constructed index of diversity among maintenance (i.e., non-export) establishments [3] proved to be weakly correlated (r=.18) with the headquarters measure. Finally, industrialization, a variable which might confound various organizational measures, was virtually unrelated to this extralocal headquarters index (r=.12).

The high correlations of the national headquarters measure with size, age of city, banking activity, centrality ratings, and export diversity were virtually unaltered when they were computed separately for each of the five geographic regions. Thus, both the nature of the national headquarters index as well as its uniform correlations with the criterion variables attest to its validity as a measure of extralocal integration.

Local Integration. Two organizational indices were used to assess local integration: (1) community-wide voluntary associations were taken to signify the presence of mechanisms for concerted action as well as the absence of highly organized cleavages within the city as of early 1961; (2) 1960 municipal revenue was taken as a measure of integration in terms of control exercised by the city's government over the community's affairs.

(1) Community-wide Associations. Williams and Adrian (1959) have provided data which hint at the part played by community organizations—e.g., service clubs, business associations, and a municipal employee union —in mobilizing partisan political activity. If such groups go uncontested in any city or if alternative organizations are lacking, they might very likely constitute the *only* means of concerted action—political or otherwise— even though portions of the population may

---

[2]Manufacturing; lumber, building, and hardware; automotive dealers; apparel and accessory stores; eating and drinking places; merchant wholesale; wholesale trade; hotels, motels, and tourist camps; motion picture theaters; other amusement and recreational establishments; hospitals.

---

[3] General merchandise establishments; food stores; gasoline service stations; drug stores; personal services; auto repairs and services; garages.

TABLE 1. NAMES, DESCRIPTIONS, AND SOURCES OF ALL MEASURES

Variable	Measure	Description (Source Reference)
Extralocal Integration	National Headquarters	Number of national association headquarters, 1960 (Encyclopedia of Associations, 1961)
Local Integration	Community-wide Associations	Knowledgeables' mention of integrative community associations, 1961 (see text)
	Municipal Revenue	Per capita city government revenue, 1960 (U.S. Bureau of the Census, 1962a)
New Interorganizational Activity	Per Capita Poverty Funding	Per capita Federal War on Poverty dollars (see text) as of April 1, 1966 (U.S. Office of Economic Opportunity)
Complex Interorganizational Network	CAA's NYC Sponsorship	Funding by two Federal agencies and Neighborhood Youth Corps (NYC) sponsorship by a local federation—i.e., Community Action Agency—(see text) as of June 6, 1966 (U.S. Office of Economic Opportunity and Department of Labor files)
Control: Elementary Interorganizational Network	Other NYC Sponsorship	Funding by one Federal agency and NYC sponsorship only by individual organizations (see text) as of June 6, 1966 (ibid.)
Control: Demand	Poverty	Percent of families with 1959 incomes under $3,000 (U.S. Bureau of the Census, 1962a)
	Nonwhite	Percent of population nonwhite, 1960 (ibid.)
	Out of School	Percent of youths 14–17 not in school, 1960 (ibid.)
Control: Extralocal Integration	Age of City	Number of censuses since reaching 50,000 population, 1960 (U.S. Bureau of the Census, 1961)
	Size	Population size, 1960 (ibid.)
	Banking Activity	Per capita bank deposits, 1960 (U.S. Bureau of the Census, 1962a)
	Export Diversity	Diversification of export establishments, 1963 (U.S. Bureau of the Census, 1967; see text)
	Region Emphasis	Location within a diversified or financial region, 1950 (Nelson, 1955; T. Clark, 1968)
	Intergovernmental Revenue	Percent of municipal revenue from intergovernmental sources, 1960 (U.S. Bureau of the Census, 1962a)
	Migration	Percent who lived in a different county five years earlier, 1960 (ibid.)
Control: Local Integration	Reform Government	One each added for city manager, nonpartisan elections, and all councilmen elected at-large, 1962 (see text)
	Foreign Stock	Percent native born of foreign or mixed parentage, 1960 (U.S. Bureau of the Census, 1962a)
	Private Schools	Percent of elementary school children in private schools, 1960 (U.S. Bureau of the Census, 1962b)
	Voter Turnout	Percent of adults voting for President, 1960 (U.S. Bureau of the Census, 1962a)
	Density	Persons per square mile, 1960 (ibid.)

146

Control: Ideology	Democratic Vote	Percent Democratic in county two-party Presidential vote, 1960 (*ibid.*)
Control: Experience	Welfare Expenditures	Per capita municipal welfare expenditures, 1960 (*ibid.*)
	Education Expenditures	Per capita municipal education expenditures, 1960 (*ibid.*)
Control: Complex Variables	Education	Median school years completed by ages 25 and over (as a measure of SES), 1960 (*ibid.*)
	Industrialization	Value added by manufacturing, 1958 (*ibid.*)
	Northeast	Connecticut, Massachusetts, New Jersey, New York, Pennsylvania, and Rhode Island
	East Central	Illinois, Indiana, Michigan, Ohio, and Wisconsin
	West	Arizona, California, Colorado, Hawaii, Iowa, Kansas, Minnesota, Missouri, Nebraska, New Mexico, Oregon, Utah, and Washington
	Southwest	Arkansas, Louisiana, Oklahoma, and Texas
	Southeast	Alabama, District of Columbia, Florida, Georgia, Kentucky, Maryland, Mississippi, North Carolina, Tennessee, and Virginia

be unrepresented. Under such circumstances, which can be ascertained, the community-serving organization might also indicate the absence of organized cleavages as well as constitute a facility for specialized nonmember groups who would be linked to it as "clients." Form letters elicited essay answers from knowledgeable informants in 104 of the 130 cities (mayor or city manager, city planner, city editor, school board head, chamber of commerce official, fund drive organizer, urban sociologist, or their respective designates) to broad questions about citizen participation, civic pride, cohesion, conflict, and the distribution of power. Although phrased in terms of "persons," "groups," and "kinds of people," the questions yielded unsolicited but explicit mention in 76 of the cities that one or more voluntary associations either implemented or supplemented their manifest purposes by symbolizing, serving, coordinating, influencing, or acting on behalf of the community itself. Such "community-wide associations," as they will be called in the rest of the report, included broad-based fraternal organizations, booster groups, community chest organizations and other fundraising groups (not just drives), boys' clubs, a labor council, a taxpayers' association, chambers of commerce, and various business-professional clubs. These reports were unaccompanied by any reference to the organized representation of contested and enduring special interests.

It might be argued that the unqualified mention by informed persons of publicly oriented organizations which they, as well as others, found to have integrative significance (Babchuk and Edwards, 1965) and their failure to mention organizational contestants (see Greer and Orleans, 1962) constitute evidence that integration occurred and cleavages were lacking. Nonetheless, there were other means of assessing index validity. First, the split-half agreement in such voluntary mention (or non-mention) of association was 70% by Robinson's method (Robinson, 1957) within cities providing multiple replies (the mean number of respondents was 2.3). Second, letters from 59 of the cities permitted classification of the community elite as monolithic or pluralistic.

Despite unresolved controversy about the meaning and measure of such classification

147

Table 2. Unadjusted Intercorrelations among All Measures *

Measure	1	2	3	4	5	6	7	8	9	10	11	12	13	14	15	16	17	18	19	20	21	22	23	24	25	26	27	28	29	30	31
1. Natl. Headquarters		−06	40	31	18	06	06	19	04	69	71	53	49	29	10	−24	−19	17	28	19	40	12	30	17	−04	12	07	05	09	−14	−11
2. Community-wide Assns.			−08	06	19	−14	11	07	00	03	−09	33	01	13	−05	04	26	−16	−05	−08	−11	04	06	−08	01	−04	−11	−08	12	−09	13
3. Municipal Revenue				48	32	−02	−02	16	09	49	23	33	14	13	28	−37	26	41	36	26	52	34	64	76	−32	34	46	−12	−16	−36	11
4. P. C. Poverty Fund.					44	12	06	13	14	40	22	19	14	−02	15	−32	−24	29	32	27	33	38	32	38	−34	20	33	00	−15	−20	−02
5. CAA's NYC Sponsor.						−37					12	16	15	10	14	−37	−12	14	19	22	27	27	34	34	−39	20	29	−02	−24	−15	11
6. Other NYC Sponsors.							02	55	47	32	14	05	23	10	20	−06	03	−08	13	−27	−23	−01	05	07	−09	−31	−33	−13	−37	04	56
7. Poverty								02	47	08	14	−06	01	−09	07	−06	03	03	02	−02	00	05	01	−13	−08	02	06	05	05	07	09
8. Nonwhite									55	−04	10	05	12	−11	−01	09	12	−47	−40	−52	−16	06	05	07	−39	−31	−09	−33	−37	32	56
9. Out of School										32	28	23	07	06	04	−04	−08	−49	−29	−46	07	05	16	17	−33	01	−21	−04	−33	07	57
10. Age of City											14	10	13	−11	01	−08	12	−07	−23	−14	−22	07	08	27	25	−49	05	14	13	−41	26
11. Size												54	48	33	16	01	−66	−36	38	63	66	60	50	42	46	35	−44	40	42	10	−15
12. Banking Activity													30	16	01	−12	−05	01	08	19	43	23	33	19	02	−04	−05	−13	23	02	01
13. Export Diversity														52	−01	−27	−09	−07	11	13	18	16	15	12	18	−09	20	21	−07	−12	00
14. Region Emphasis															36	32	09	−01	14	12	18	13	08	02	01	24	10	14	−14	−03	−05
15. Intergovt. Revenue																−07	−01	01	63	71	46	35	04	08	04	03	06	10	05	−09	−05
16. Migration																	−22	05	08	09	08	07	28	46	−24	20	06	19	−19	−23	16
17. Reform Govt.																		−18	−49	−66	−50	−54	−41	−34	−28	67	−68	−56	39	29	20
18. Foreign Stock																			50	−25	−30	−34	−23	−22	−11	38	−29	−33	32	11	13
19. Private Schools																				71	66	48	42	24	23	28	32	64	−24	11	−31	−58
20. Voter Turnout																					64	23	33	24	13	−28	−10	43	58	04	−09	−31	−49
21. Density																						46	35	31	34	−10	−38	46	47	25	−09	−31	−51
22. Democratic Vote																							42	48	34	−38	−31	34	52	26	12	−44	−40
23. Welfare Expend.																								42	22	−27	24	34	37	16	−18	−17	−16
24. Educ. Expend.																									56	−31	37	22	50	−01	−10	−14	−40	−08
25. Education																										−40	−46	−38	−12	57	13	−23
26. Industrialization																											33	45	−33	−25	−40	−21	−16
27. Northeast																												−25	−29	−18	−21	−26
28. East Central																													−29	−25	−18	−23
29. West																														−29	−24	−19
30. Southwest																															−24	
31. Southeast																																

* Zero order product-moment coefficients with decimal points omitted. Also see Footnote 1.

148

(Smith and Hood, 1966; Gilbert, 1968), the assumption is reasonable that any correlation it might have with the community's organizational structure would be in the direction of pluralism-cleavage. Thus the inverse relationship observed between pluralism and the mention of community-wide associations $(r/r_{max}=.37, p<.01)$ is accepted as further validation of our index. Incomplete data and their ambiguous nature prevented the power structure index from being used in the multiple regression analysis and therefore from appearing on Tables 1 and 2. Third and last, nonpartisan elections have been said to signify the absence of institutionalized conflict between political parties, the city manager system to reflect lack of dissent about the goals of government, and at-large election of councilmen to diminish the direct representation of special interests (Banfield and Wilson, 1967; Alford and Scoble, 1965; Greer, 1962; Lineberry and Fowler, 1967; Alford and Lee, 1968; Wolfinger and Field, 1968). Each of these events measures the absence of cleavage; and—combined into the single score of "reform government" shown on Table 1 (described by T. Clark, 1968 and yielding an estimated Spearman-Brown reliability of .75 in the present analysis)— these political indicators proved to discriminate between cities in which community-wide associations were mentioned and all of the remaining cities (N=130, $r/r_{max}=.33$, $p<.01$). Moreover, the directions of all the correlational indicators of validity remained undisturbed when they were assessed separately for each of the five regions.

The reform government measure might itself have been used to indicate mechanisms for concerted community action and the absence of cleavages. However, the correlation of this index with Democratic presidential preferences in 1960 was −.23 (see Table 2, $p<.01$), a leaning which had already been observed at the microlevel by Williams and Adrian (1959). The correlation between the associations measure and Democratic voting, on the other hand, was negligible ($r/r_{max}=$ .05). Moreover, the proportion of foreign stock within the population (Table 1), a measure of potential cleavage to be discussed later, yielded negative correlation with the mention of community-wide associations (as it did with the reform index), attaining a value of −.16, which falls just short of significance at the .05 level. Thus the associations measure appeared to resemble the reform index in certain respects, but it is not as exclusively governmental in its manifest content or as likely to be complicated by political partisanship.

Based upon these consistent and persuasive criteria, a dichotomous (dummy) index was constructed which distinguished cities in which one or more community-wide associations were mentioned (by persons other than their functionaries) from all the other cities. Adopted to assure comparability in the cases used from one analysis to the next, this scoring method tends to depress rather than inflate correlation with other variables; for some of the cities scored as having no integrative associations could indeed have had them. But the bias is conservative in its effect and resulted in an understatement of correlation.

(2) Municipal Revenue. Per capita municipal revenue, in part, reflects the city government's ability to tax and, therefore, also reflects its control over resources, as well as any increment which may result from the symbolic connection between taxation and community integration (Angell, 1947; Stinchcombe, 1965). More immediately, however, municipal revenue indicates the degree of control the city's government has over community affairs, for its correlation with the per capita number of city employees was found to be .75.[4]

Measured in a somewhat different way, the degree of control is also indicated by a very high correlation of .94 with per capita expenditures by the city government. That the level of such control tended to remain constant over most sectors of governmental activity was confirmed by positive correlation coefficients between per capita municipal revenue and per capita rates of city expenditures for education (.76), welfare (.64), health and hospitals (.50), police (.50), fire protection (.52), and sanitation (.19). Further analysis suggested that the size of the municipal budget was also associated with

---

[4] The source of this and all other measures used to validate the municipal revenue index is the U.S. Bureau of the Census (1962b), which provided 1960 data.

the city government's share (its autonomy) vis-a-vis county, state, and federal government in the provision of education, welfare, and health services—another measure of its capacity to integrate through control.

None of these correlations were disturbed during the course of a region-by-region analysis (except that none of the Southwestern cities had welfare budgets). Therefore, per capita municipal revenue was adopted as the second index of local integration, one assumed to measure the level of organizational control over the community.

Interorganizational Activity Level. The Economic Opportunity Act (1964) and its amendments inauguarated the interorganizational relations described in the following discussion. It authorized several federal agencies coordinated by the U.S. Office of Economic Opportunity to encourage, negotiate and enter into contractual relations with, and fund the anti-poverty efforts of, local organizations or local federations. Unlike the case of urban renewal (Guttenberg, 1964; Glazer, 1966; Wilson, 1966:489–558), massive public resistance did not appear to be a complicating factor requiring control, at least during the period covered by our data. The data collection period was terminated in 1966, because subsequent requirements of "participation by the poor" might have reduced the program's suitability as a relatively pure instance of interorganizational relations. At least until the cutoff date of April 1, 1966, the *per capita number of poverty dollars* which flowed into a city constituted an excellent index of the activity level of a new network of federal and local organizations within each city.

The generalizability of this index—at least as far as other federal programs are concerned—is suggested by moderate correlation between per capita poverty funding and two programs of the Department of Housing and Urban Development. The 1959 urban renewal status of cities of this study had been classified as inactive, project planning, contract executed, and project completed (U.S. Housing and Home Finance Agency, 1960). Correlation between this four-point ordinal scale based on 1959 data and per capita poverty funding in 1966 is .30. Another variable, whether or not the city was one of 42 in this study that were part of the

first wave of announced Model Cities (Los Angeles Times, November 17, 1967), yielded a correlation of .40 with per capita poverty funding.

Interorganizational Complexity. That part of the poverty program called the Neighborhood Youth Corps (NYC) permitted *controlled* inquiry into the occurrence of certain kinds of complex anti-poverty networks. Local organizations or local federations funded to sponsor such projects undertook to provide training, work experience, counseling, and placement for disadvantaged youth and young adults. In certain cases this meant that the local sponsor had to seek other organizations as loci of work or training. The American values of self-help, education, and the rights of youth, which these projects symbolized, probably made this component of the War on Poverty even less vulnerable to open public resistance than the rest of the program.

More important, however, was the occurrence of simple and complex variants among the interorganizational networks of NYC sponsors and their granting agencies. In one such kind of system, the projects involved the national headquarters and regional offices of both the U.S. Department of Labor, which funded all NYC projects, and the U.S. Office of Economic Opportunity, which funded newly established community organizations called Community Action Agencies. A Community Action Agency was itself an interorganizational system, a federation, since its board consisted of major functionaries from various organized sectors of the community (for example, the mayor or his representative, the school superintendent or a member of his staff, labor union officials, officials of the Catholic Archdiocese, and representatives of various civic groups and associations of businessmen). Sponsorship by a Community Action Agency of one or more of the NYC projects within a given city meant a *complex* interorganizational network. By way of contrast, the *elementary* alternative was sponsorship of NYC projects by one or more autonomous or semiautonomous organizations having far less broadly-based structures than those of the federative Community Action Agency. Requiring funding by only one federal agency (the Department of Labor), and most often already in existence before the War on Poverty, this less complex form of sponsorship included such organizations as non-profit welfare agencies, school systems, church groups, labor unions, and municipal departments.

The 130 cities could thus be classified into those served by *complex interorganizational networks* on June 6, 1966 (29 with at least one NYC project sponsored by a Community Action Agency), those served by *elementary interorganizational networks* (43 with NYC projects, none of which were sponsored by a Community Action Agency), and those *without any interorganizational network* of the kind in question (58 with no Neighborhood Youth Corps projects). This scheme yielded two dichotomous (dummy) measures: (1) whether or not the city was served by a complex network and (2) whether or not it was served by an elementary network. The first of these was used as a major dependent variable, the second only for purposes of providing a control condition which was virtually identical in content but different along the key dimension of network complexity.

Demand for the Interorganizational Network. Demand for these anti-poverty networks was measured by the number of potential clients (rate of *deprivation*) because that number was likely to have effects upon (1) rates of simple petition by the needy, (2) the invocation of War on Poverty norms within the community or by the Federal Government, (3) attempts to avoid depletion of local welfare resources, (4) perception of a ready clientele by initiators of new programs. Poverty rates, proportion of non-white, and proportion of youth out of school were used as indicators of demand.

Other Sources of Variation. The absence of published analyses bearing directly upon questions we have raised required the very careful exercise of control. Allowances were made for unanticipated effects by including indices which might either explain relationships among the several measures we have discussed or serve as their substitutes. The associational measure of extralocal integration was expected to encompass the variables used to validate it; nonetheless, this expectation was assessed by retaining the more trustworthy of those variables in the analysis. Three other indicators of external ties were also included: the Nelson-Clark index of the region's economic emphasis, the level of intergovernmental revenue, and rates of migration into the city. A similar procedure was followed in the case of local integration; reform government and population heterogeneity have already been discussed in this light, but the use made of private schools might also have described cleavages within the population. Population density was included as a crude measure of interaction and interdependence, while voter turnout was taken as a potential measure of *esprit*.

Allowances were also made for the potential effects of variables other than integration upon the networks under study. Demand has already been mentioned. The size of the Democratic presidential vote was taken as a measure of ideological commitment to the program under study—namely, as another form of demand. Moreover, the question of prior experience with related welfare and educational programs had to be taken into account; thus the city's education and welfare expenditures were also included as control variables. Finally, the omnibus nature of geographic regions as controls has already been discussed; to these were added the other complex variables of socioeconomic status (measured by population education) and industrialization.

Table 1 shows the assignment of the control indicators to their several major categories (directions of effect not indicated); clearly, however, several of these measures could have been assigned to other categories as well. Thus intergovernmental revenue, expenditures for welfare and education, proportions of foreign stock, enrollment in private schools, and education could all reflect variations in ideology; migration may be inversely associated with local integration; and the city's size and age, as well as the regional measure of export employment, are sufficiently broad in meaning to be included in the residual category. Though many of the control measures could be interpreted in several ways, their use assured very demanding tests of the hypotheses which have been stated.

Interorganizational Activity. All 28 of the independent and control measures were used in a stepwise analysis that permitted any one of them to enter and remain in the regression equation, provided that its partial correlation with interorganizational activity was significant at the .20 level; the .20 criterion made it unlikely that an eventually important variable would be overlooked. However, only those standardized partial regression coefficients (*betas*) which reached the .10 significance level are reported. Spuriousness was minimized by establishing a second regression equation with *all 28 indices,* in order to make certain that all variables making an appreciable contribution in the shorter equation continued to do

so in the longer one. The first two columns of Table 3 describe the outcome of these analyses.

Two of the three organizational indicators of integration supported the first hypothesis. The city's extralocal linkages, measured by the number of national headquarters within it, proved to be positively and independently associated with the dollar measure of interorganizational activity in the federal poverty program; so was the integrative potential of city government, measured by municipal revenue. Contribution by the 1960 Democratic vote probably signified ideological commitment to the War on Poverty, which became manifest in the level of interorganizational activity. Whether the negative effect of socioeconomic status rested upon ideological grounds or whether it signified

TABLE 3. PREDICTION OF INTERORGANIZATIONAL ACTIVITY IN POVERTY DOLLARS, COMPLEX INTERORGANIZATIONAL NETWORKS WITH CAA SPONSORSHIP OF NYC PROJECTS, AND ELEMENTARY INTERORGANIZATIONAL NETWORKS WITH OTHER SPONSORSHIP OF NYC PROJECTS ON THE BASIS OF INTEGRATION AND CONTROL MEASURES

Predictor	Prediction of Per Capita Poverty Funding (Explained Variance=32%)		Prediction of NYC Sponsorship by CAA (Explained Variance=67%)		Prediction of Other NYC Sponsorship (Explained Variance=24%)	
	r*	beta**	r	beta	r	beta
National Headquarters	.31	.18	.40 [b]	...	.10 [f]	...
Municipal Revenue	.48	.28	.44 [c]	...	−.02 [g]	...
Democratic Vote	.38	.21	.38 [c]	...	.06 [h]	...
Education	−.34	−.18	−.59 [d]	...	−.10 [g]	...
Community-wide Assns.	.07 [a]	...	.42	.36 [b]	−.18	−.27 [i]
Education Expenditures	.38	...	.47	.21 [e]	−.16	−.33 [g]
Nonwhite	.13	...	.36	.40 [c]	.07 [h]	...
Voter Turnout	.27	...	.31	.46 [c]	−.02 [g]	...
P.C. Poverty Funding	...	...	.61	.35 [e]	.15	.25 [h]

* Zero order product-moment coefficient based upon ordinal data. See Footnote 1, also for significance levels.

** Standardized partial regression coefficient, which has not been tabulated where it failed to achieve p<.10. Unless noted otherwise, the *beta* is significant at least at the .05 level.

[a] *Beta* and r were computed as proportions of their .85 maxima.

[b] *Beta* and r were computed as proportions of their .45 maxima.

[c] *Beta* and r were computed as proportions of their .72 maxima. The multiple correlation coefficient, upon whose square the estimate of explained variance in the CAA sponsored network is based, was also adjusted by this value.

[d] *Beta* and r were computed as proportions of their −.72 minima.

[e] p<.10. *Beta* and r were computed as proportions of their .72 maxima.

[f] *Beta* and r were computed as proportions of their .59 maxima.

[g] *Beta* and r were computed as proportions of their −.81 minima.

[h] *Beta* and r were computed as proportions of their .81 maxima. The multiple correlation coefficient, upon whose square the estimate of explained variance in the non-CAA sponsored network is based, was also adjusted by this value.

[i] p<.10. *Beta* and r were computed as proportions of their −.76 minima.

the absence of organizational channels to the poor cannot be resolved with the data at hand; it should be noted, however, that low education, *not deprivation*, predicted activity level within the anti-poverty network.

Occurrence of Complex Networks. Two regression analyses tested the second major hypothesis. Techniques and criteria were identical to those just described, except that the prediction measures included level of interorganizational activity in the overall poverty program and therefore numbered 29. The third and fourth columns of Table 3 show the effects of these measures upon the presence or absence of a complex interorganizational network which included two federal departments and federation sponsorship of an NYC project. That a complex network rather than program content had been predicted was assessed by using these same 30 measures to predict the presence or absence of a more elementary NYC network (see the fifth and sixth columns of Table 3) consisting of one federal department and individual organizations. Thus the second hypothesis should be assessed by comparing the two middle columns on Table 3 with the two on the right.

Only one of the integration measures proved to predict complex networks. Mention of community-wide integrative organizations by knowledgeable informants during early 1961 was positively associated with the presence of a complex network in 1966. Indeed, slightly over three-quarters of the complex networks were established within the 76 communities identified as having these associations. The positive effect of funding upon the occurrence of complex networks, as well as their controls, is to be expected and requires no discussion. That educational activity affected the presence of a complex network may either bespeak the community's experience with related programs or its ideological receptivity to them; but since school systems constituted *alternative* means to sponsorship by the community action agency, the possibility of any regular competition for programs on their part must be denied. *Only one of the deprivation measures,* the most visible one of race, affected the etablishment of a complex network; the reason for this will be discussed later.

Voter turnout, but not partisanship, also helped to predict the complex network. This may suggest turnout as an index of "moral integration" within the local field, to use Angell's term (1947). National and local voting have been found to lie along a common continuum. Bollen (1961:184, 430), and Alford and Lee (1968) suggested that large voter turnout in local elections may reduce the level of alienation from community affairs. Indeed, whether people vote at all (not how they vote) has been viewed as a normative act at the aggregate level (see Campbell *et al.,* 1954:194–199; Lipset *et al.,* 1954:1126–1134; Lane, 1959:42–52; Kornhauser, 1959:64–73; Lipset, 1960:286; Turk *et al.,* 1966). But this line of reasoning is speculative; its implementation awaits further data.

Activity level aside, these forecasters of complex networks are seen to be negative or missing in the case of elementary networks; these appear to have been little more than correlates of funding level—i.e., of inputs to the city. Undue emphasis must not be placed upon the negative signs attached to several of the coefficients, for the complex and elementary dichotomies were constructed so that one is partly the negative of the other. This method allowed the effect of integration upon the creation of complex networks to be measured independently of the network's content or its activity level. Its execution led to unambiguous results. Complex networks proved to be functions of community-wide associations, voter turnout, educational expenditures, and proportion nonwhite. Elementary networks were not. Both kinds of network depended upon poverty funds.

Extralocal and Local Aspects of the Network. Half of the predicted relationships were confirmed. In none of these cases did integration have a negative influence upon the nature of the interorganizational network; thus any inhibitory effect which integration might have had was not in evidence.

The distribution of the observed effects was such, however, to encourage farther examination of the three organizational measures of integration. Multiple regression analysis did not disturb the patterns of association reported earlier between the national headquarters measure of extralocal integration and the criteria used to validate it.

Multiple regression also supported the validity of community-wide associations as a measure of local integration by upholding its previously reported positive association with reform government and provided additional evidence by sharpening the *negative* contribution made by proportion of foreign stock in the population. The latter rate has been taken as a measure of community cleavages (Alford and Scoble, 1965; Alford and Lee, 1968). Assuming the city's age to be an indicator of structural stability permits the positive contribution made by that variable to be taken as further support for the validity of the community association measure. Such support was augmented by the positive effect of a city's location in the West, which may be presumed to indicate a low level of socioeconomic cleavage. Further, *local integration proved to be inversely associated with extralocal integration.* Once the influences of other sources of variation were removed, the number of national headquarters was shown to have a *negative* effect upon the mention of community-wide associations (adjusted $beta = -.34$, $p < .05$). Rather than denying the validity of either index, this event lent strong support to the prevalent theories of mass society we have mentioned.

Prediction of municipal revenue by regression techniques did, however, force a re-evaluation of the meaning of that measure. Two classes of significant and meaningful prediction were observed: (1) *differentiation and interdependence,* attested to by the postive effects of proportion foreign stock, proportion nonwhite, industrialization, and population density, as well as negative effect (the presumably fragmenting influence) of export diversity, and (2) *extra-local orientation,* witnessed by banking activity, municipal revenue from intergovernmental sources, the city's age, and migration rates that were independent of population growth (which also permitted a contribution to be made by the national headquarters index once their effects were removed).

What appears to be clear and unambiguous, once these additional analyses are considered in the light of Table 3, is that interorganizational activity levels—i.e., inputs to

the city from without—depended upon prior extralocal integration (measured by national headquarters), while the existence of complex networks depended upon the city's local integration (measured by community-wide associations). Litwak and Hylton (1962) and Burton Clark (1965) have suggested that interorganizational systems tend to be loosely organized entities. Possibly the rare, closely coordinated version can only exist in a homogeneous *and* highly organized field.

It is equally clear that the municipal revenue measure did not fulfill its intended purpose. Shown to be more than simply an index of government control, its extralocal components might serve to explain the contribution which it made to the prediction of interorganizational activity level. Indeed, it has been suggested that large municipal governments tend to surpass smaller ones in the facilities they have for seeking outside funding (Advisory Commission for Intergovernmental Relations, 1967a:150–153). That it might also signify both cleavages and interdependence among local elements could account for its lack of direct association—either positive or negative—with the occurrence of complex interorganizational networks.

The Role of Demand. Not fully unexpected in the light of previous studies (Advisory Commission on Intergovernmental Relations, 1967b:142–149; Turk, 1967a; Turk, 1967b) was the very minor part played by demand. Poverty, proportion of youth out of school, and proportion nonwhite had no apparent influence upon the interorganizational flow of poverty funds; and only the last of these affected the presence of a complex network.

This immediately suggested the possibility of a multiplicative effect—the model used thus far was additive. So the question was raised whether the degree to which demand affected either interorganizational activity or interorganizational complexity might not have rested upon prior levels of integration. Strong affirmation is provided on Table 4.

All three indicators of demand are shown to be significantly and positively associated with the dollar measure of interorganizational activity at only the highest levels of the two integration measures that had themselves predicted activity. Moreover, in five

154

Integration Measure (n)	Zero Order Correlation between Per Capita Poverty Funding and			Zero Order Correlation* between CAA Sponsorship of NYC Projects and		
	Poverty	Nonwhite	Out of School	Poverty	Nonwhite	Out of School
National Headquarters						
Upper third (44)	.18[a]	.18[a]	.18[a]	...	...	...
Middle third (43)	—.14	.05	.00	...	...	...
Lower third (43)	—.07	—.16	—.07	...	...	...
P.C. Municipal Revenue						
Upper third (44)	.35[c]	.26[b]	.35[c]	...	...	...
Middle third (43)	.09	.00	—.09	...	...	...
Lower third (43)	—.16	—.12	—.22[a]	...	...	...
Community-wide Associations						
Mentioned (76)	...	...	...	.32[c]	.34[c]	.12
Not mentioned (54)	...	...	...	—.14	.06	.27[b]

* Correlation coefficients have not been adjusted, since only relative size and significance level are of interest.

[a] p<.10 (one-tailed).
[b] p<.05 (one-tailed).
[c] p<.025 (one-tailed).

of six instances, the less the integration, the less positive was the association between demand and level of poverty funding.

A similar consequence may be noted on the right hand side of Table 4 for the occurrence of complex networks. The positive contribution which the proportion nonwhite had been observed to make (see Table 3) now proved to be restricted to those cities which had had at least one community-wide association. A similar pattern may be observed in the case of poverty. A reversal in the third instance may have resulted from inadequacies in the out-of-school rate as a measure of deprivation. Further regression analyses showed that industrialization, age of city, Northeastern location, and in-migration contributed positively to this measure—indices which may suggest the rate's correlation with certain forms of *integration*.

The results on Table 4, including the one deviant instance, point sharply to the combination of capability and need which serves to predict so many social processes, but which has been ignored so often—perhaps because of the ubiquitous use of linear models. Neither ability nor incentive can have an effect when the value of the other is too low.

CONCLUSIONS AND NEW DIRECTIONS

Summary and Conclusions. Using the number of national headquarters as its measure, a city's organizational integration into the broader society—its *extralocal integration*—proved capable of predicting the activity level of a new interorganizational network having both local and nonlocal elements. Composed of two federal anti-poverty agencies plus a federation of local organizations at the very least, a complex portion of such a network tended to occur where a high organizational level of *local integration* had been indicated by the preexistence of community-wide associations. *Demand*—i.e., the practical or normative pressures posed by deprivation rates within the population—was important to these interorganizational outcomes only where organizational integration had been high.

One can only speculate as to the detailed processes involved, but it appears very likely that both the interorganizational links that tie the city to its sociocultural environment, as well as those which connect its internal elements, provide latent or active structures which may be used or modified for new purposes, provide points of articulation, or at the very least serve as models for new interorganizational systems. Prior linkages with the broader society can convey the materials and messages necessary for interorganizational activity, while local integration under common organizations can provide the means or models for the central coordination of elaborate networks. Not only the several other forms which can be taken by these two varieties of negative entropy, but also the conditions under which they enable *resistance* to new linkages or flows, demand future study.

The major conclusion to be drawn is this: *Definition of the urban setting in terms of multi- and interorganizational variables has proven fruitful. These variables were capable of predicting one another's values over time, it appears, without the intervention of non-organizational sources of variation.* Transactions involving the federal government but different federal agencies were predictable, one from the other; but it is even more impressive that the two most unambiguous predictors of interorganizational transactions involving the federal government were themselves two major categories of non-governmental organizations. Equally noteworthy in support of the main conclusion is the relative paucity of prediction in terms of population characteristics. Finally, the immediate inverse association which has been claimed between environmental adaptation and local integration—two functional problems of all social systems (Parsons and Smelser, 1956) —could clearly be observed in terms of the kinds of organizations that prevail. The evidence is sufficient to ask whether the organization is not the proper unit in the analysis of modern, large-scale social systems, whether these systems are not interorganizational systems in the main. It is not at all unlikely in macrosociology that such concepts as differentiation and integration refer more readily to relations among organizations than to relations among statuses and roles.

New Directions. This first venture into the large-scale, comparative study of interorganizational systems has demonstrated the feasibility of their controlled prediction. Moreover, it points to new work that is essential if theory in this area is to be extended. The present investigators would like to have had measures of interorganizational fields which could distinguish among fragmentation, conflict, and the division of labor (cf. Turk, 1963). Such measures have yet to be constructed. Equally provocative is the idea of "richness" in the interorganizational field, be it in terms of the sheer numbers of interrelated organizations (Stinchcombe, 1965) or in terms of the occurrence of more comprehensive organizations (Emery and Trist, 1965). Whichever version of the concept is selected, it cannot receive adequate measure until censuses of organizations broaden their scope.

The joint effect of incentive and capacity which has been observed exists at all levels of analysis, from the intrapersonal to the intersocietal. This finding is important because of the generality of its content, but it should also highlight the analytic model upon which it was based. A compelling claim has recently been made that most social phenomena are multiplicative in their effects (Dodd and Christopher, 1966). This is not the place to affirm or to modify such a general claim. It is sufficient to observe that comparative urban studies of interorganizational relations (and comparative urban studies of all kinds) should go more deeply into the *joint* operation of variables, a task which the present sample permitted us only to begin.

REFERENCES

Advisory Commission on Intergovernmental Relations.
1967a Fiscal Balance in the American Federal System: Vol. 1. Washington, D.C.: U.S. Government Printing Office.
1967b Intergovernmental Relations in the Poverty Program. Washington, D.C.: U.S. Government Printing Office.
Alford, Robert R. and Eugene C. Lee.
1968 "Voting turnout in American cities." American Political Science Review 47 (September):796–813.
Alford, Robert R. and Harry Scoble.
1965 "Political and socio-economic characteristics of American cities." Pp. 82–97 in The Municipal Yearbook 1965. Chicago: International City Managers Association.
Angell, Robert C.
1947 "The social integration of American cities of more than 100,000 population." American Sociological Review 12 (June):335–340.
Babchuk, Nicholas and John N. Edwards.
1965 "Voluntary associations and the integration hypothesis." Sociological Inquiry 35 (Spring):149–162.

Babchuk, Nicholas, Ruth Marsey and C. Wayne
Gordon.
 1960 "Men and women in community agencies."
      American Sociological Review 25 (June):
      399–403.
Banfield, Edward C. and James Q. Wilson.
 1967 "Power structure and civic leadership."
      Pp. 417–432 in Jeffrey K. Hadden *et al.*
      (eds.), Metropolis in Crisis. Illinois: F. E.
      Peacock.
Bollens, John C. (ed.).
 1961 Exploring the Metropolitan Community.
      Berkeley: University of California Press.
Campbell, Angus, Gerald Gurin and Warren E.
Miller.
 1954 The Voter Decides. Evanston, Illinois: Row
      Peterson.
Clark, Burton R.
 1965 "Interorganizational patterns in educa-
      tion." Administrative Science Quarterly 10
      (September):224–237.
Clark, Terry N.
 1968 "Community structure, decision-making,
      budget expenditures, and urban renewal in
      51 American communities." American So-
      ciological Review 33 (August):576–593.
Dodd, Stuart C. and Stephen C. Christopher.
 1966 "Products predict interaction where sums
      do not." Sociological Inquiry 36 (Winter):
      48–60.
Duncan, Otis Dudley and Albert J. Reiss, Jr.
 1950 Social Characteristics of Urban and Rural
      Communities. New York: Wiley.
Economic Opportunity Act of 1964, Public Law 88–
452.
 1964 United States Statutes at Large, Volume 78,
      1964. Washington: U.S. Government Print-
      ing Office.
Eisenstadt, S. N.
 1965 "Bureaucracy, bureaucratization, markets
      and power structure." Pp. 177–215 in S. N.
      Eisenstadt, Essays on Comparative Institu-
      tions. New York: Wiley.
Emery, F. E. and E. L. Trist.
 1965 "Causal texture of organizational environ-
      ment." Human Relations 18 (February):
      21–32.
Encyclopedia of Associations, Vol. II.
 1961 Geographic and Executive Index. Detroit:
      Gale.
Evan, William.
 1966 "The organization set: toward a theory of
      interorganizational relations." Pp. 173–191
      in James D. Thompson (ed.), Approaches
      to Organizational Design. Pittsburgh: Uni-
      versity of Pittsburgh Press.
Freeman, Linton C., T. J. Fararo, W. Bloomberg
and M. H. Sunshine.
 1962 Metropolitan Decision-Making. New York:
      Syracuse University Press.
Galbraith, John Kenneth.
 1958 The Affluent Society. Boston: Houghton
      Mifflin.
Gibbs, Jack P. and Walter T. Martin.
 1962 "Urbanization, technology, and the division

of labor: international patterns." American
      Sociological Review 27 (October):667–677.
Gilbert, Claire.
 1968 "The study of community power: a sum-
      mary and a test." Pp. 222–243 in Scott
      Greer, Dennis L. McElrath, David W.
      Minar, and Peter Orleans (eds.), The New
      Urbanization. New York: St. Martin's
      Press.
Glazer, Nathan.
 1966 "The renewal of cities." Pp. 175–192 in
      The Editors of Scientific American, Cities.
      New York: Alfred A. Knopf.
Gouldner, Alvin W.
 1959 "Reciprocity and autonomy in functional
      theory." Pp. 241–270 in Llewellyn Gross
      (ed.), Symposium on Sociological Theory.
      New York: Harper and Row.
Greer, Scott.
 1962 Governing the Metropolis. New York:
      Wiley.
Greer, Scott and Peter Orleans.
 1962 "Mass society and parapolitical structure."
      American Sociological Review 27 (Octo-
      ber):634–646.
Guetzkow, Harold.
 1966 "Relations among organizations." Pp. 13–
      44 in Raymond V. Bowers (ed.), Studies
      on Behavior in Organization: A Research
      Symposium. Athens, Georgia: University
      of Georgia Press.
Guttenberg, Elbert Z.
 1964 "The tactical plan." Pp. 197–215 in Melvin
      M. Webber *et al.,* Explorations in Urban
      Structure. Philadelphia: The University of
      Pennsylvania Press.
Hauser, Philip M.
 1965 "Urbanization: an overview." Pp. 49–52 in
      Philip M. Hauser and Leo Schnore (eds.),
      The Study of Urbanization. New York:
      Wiley.
Hawley, Amos H.
 1963 "Community power and urban renewal
      success." American Journal of Sociology
      68 (January):422–431.
Kornhauser, William.
 1959 The Politics of Mass Society. Glencoe,
      Illinois: Free Press.
Lane, Robert E.
 1959 Political Life. Glencoe, Illinois: Free Press.
Lenski, Gerhard E.
 1954 "Status crystallization: a non-vertical di-
      mension of social status." American Socio-
      logical Review 19 (August):405–413.
Levine, Sol and Paul E. White.
 1961 "Exchange as a conceptual framework for
      the study of interorganizational relation-
      ships." Administrative Science Quarterly
      5 (March):585–601.
Levine, Sol, Paul E. White and Benjamin D. Paul.
 1963 "Community interorganization problems in
      providing medical care and social service."
      American Journal of Public Health 53
      (August):1183–1195.
Lineberry, Robert L. and Edmund P. Fowler.
 1967 "Reforms and public policies in American

cities." American Political Science Review 61 (September):701–716.

Lipset, Seymour Martin.
1960 Political Man: The Social Bases of Politics. Garden City, New York: Doubleday.

Lipset, Seymour Martin, Paul F. Lazarsfeld, Allen H. Barton and Juan Linz.
1954 "The psychology of voting: an analysis of voting behavior." Pp. 1126–1134 in Gardner Lindsey (ed.), Handbook of Social Psychology. Cambridge, Massachusetts: Addison-Wesley.

Litwak, Eugene and Lydia F. Hylton.
1962 "Interorganizational analysis: a hypothesis on coordinating agencies." Administrative Science Quarterly 6 (March):397–420.

Mills, C. Wright.
1956 The Power Elite. New York: Oxford University Press.

Mott, Paul E.
1965 The organization of Society. New York: Prentice-Hall.

Nelson, Howard J.
1955 "A service classification of American cities." Economic Geography 31 (July):189–210.

Nolting, Orin F. and David S. Arnold (ed.).
1963 The Municipal Year Book, 1963. Chicago: The International City Managers' Association.

Parsons, Talcott.
1956 "Suggestions for a sociological approach to the theory of organizations-I." Administrative Science Quarterly 1 (June):5–19.

Parsons, Talcott and Neil J. Smelser.
1956 Economy and Society: A Study in the Integration of Economic and Social Theory. Glencoe, Illinois: The Free Press.

Riecken, Henry W. and George C. Homans.
1954 "Psychological aspects of social structure." Pp. 786–832 in Gardner Lindsey (ed.), Handbook of Social Psychology, Vol. II. Cambridge: Addison-Wesley.

Robinson, W. S.
1957 "The statistical measure of agreement." American Sociological Review 22 (February):17–25.

Rostow, W. W.
1953 The Dynamics of Soviet Society. New York: W. W. Norton and Co.

Sjoberg, Gideon.
1964 "The rural-urban dimension in preindustrial, transitional, and industrial societies." Pp. 127–159 in Robert E. L. Faris (ed.), Handbook of Modern Sociology. Chicago: Rand McNally.

Smith, Joel and Thomas Hood.
1966 "The delineation of community power structures by a reputational approach." Sociological Inquiry 36 (Winter):3–14.

Starbuck, William H.
1965 "Organizational growth and development." Pp. 451–533 in James G. March (ed.), Handbook of Organizations. Chicago: Rand McNally.

Stein, Maurice R.
1960 The Eclipse of Community. New York: Harper and Row.

Stinchcombe, Arthur L.
1965 "Social structure and organizations." Pp. 142–193 in James G. March (ed.), Handbook of Organizations. Chicago: Rand McNally.

Turk, Herman.
1963 "Social cohesion through variant values: evidence from medical role relations." American Sociological Review 28 (February):28–37.
1967a "The establishment of manpower-poverty projects and relations between them in large American cities." Mimeographed. Unpublished report for the U.S. Department of Labor.
1967b A Method of Predicting Certain Federal Program Potentials of Large American Cities. Los Angeles: Laboratory for Organizational Research, University of Southern California.
1969 "Comparative urban studies in interorganizational relations." Sociological Inquiry 38 (Winter):108–110.

Turk, Herman and Myron J. Lefcowitz.
1962 "Toward a theory of representation between groups." Social Forces 40 (May):337–341.

Turk, Herman, Joel Smith and Howard P. Myers.
1966 "Understanding local political behavior: the role of the older citizen." Pp. 254–276 in Ida Harper Simpson and John C. McKinney (eds.), Social Aspects of Aging. Durham: Duke University Press.

U.S. Bureau of the Census.
1961 Census of the Population: 1960 Number of Inhabitants, United States Summary. Washington: U.S. Government Printing Office.
1962a County and City Data Book, 1962. Washington: U.S. Government Printing Office.
1962b Census of the Population: 1960 General Social and Economic Characteristics, United States Summary. Washington: U.S. Government Printing Office.
1967 County and City Data Book, 1967. Washington: U.S. Government Printing Office.

U.S. Housing and Home Finance Agency.
1960 Fourteenth Annual Report. Washington: U.S. Government Printing Office.

U.S. Office of Economic Opportunity.
1966 Poverty Program Information as of 1 April, 1966. Washington: U.S. Office of Economic Opportunity.

Vidich, Arthur J. and Joseph Bensman.
1958 Small Town in Mass Society. New York: Doubleday and Company.

Walton, John.
1968 "Differential patterns of community power structure." Pp. 441–459 in Terry N. Clark (ed.), Community Structure and Decision-

Making: Comparative Analyses. San Francisco: Chandler.

Warren, Roland L.
  1956 "Toward a reformulation of community theory." Human Organization 15 (Summer):8–11.
  1967 "The interorganizational field as a focus for investigation." Administrative Science Quarterly 12 (December):396–419.

Williams, Oliver P. and Charles R. Adrian.
  1959 "The insulation of local politics under the nonpartisan ballot." American Political Science Review 43 (December):1052–1063.

Wilson, James Q.
  1966 Urban Renewal: The Record and the Controversy. Cambridge: The M.I.T. Press.

Wolfinger, Raymond E. and John Osgood Field.
  1968 "Political ethos and the structure of city government." Pp. 159–196 in Terry N. Clark (ed.), Community Structure and Decision-Making: Comparative Analyses. San Francisco: Chandler.

From Diana Crane, *American Sociological Review 34*, 335-352 (1969), by permission.

SOCIAL STRUCTURE IN A GROUP OF SCIENTISTS:
A TEST OF THE "INVISIBLE COLLEGE"
HYPOTHESIS *

DIANA CRANE

Johns Hopkins University

The existence of social organization within a research area may be inferred (a) if scientists who have published in the area have more social ties with one another than with scientists who have not published, and (b) if scientists who have published in the area can be differentiated by degree of social participation within the area. Using a mail questionnaire, sociometric data on different types of scientific relationships were obtained from scientists, all of whom had published in a particular problem area. Respondents chose scientists who had not published in the area as often as they chose scientists within the area. Analysis of direct and indirect ties, using Coleman's method for analysis of sociometric connectedness, revealed that a tie with one or more of the highly productive scientists brought other scientists of less productivity into a large network of influence and communication. Similarities between this type of social organization and that of the "social circle" are discussed.

ONE type of social group which has received relatively little attention from sociologists is the group comprised of scientists who work on similar research problems. This neglect is probably due to the amorphous character of this type of group. Its members are highly individualistic and widely separated geographically. Participation is voluntary. Turnover is very high; the majority of scientists have only one or two publications in any research area (Price, 1963). Even the boundaries of research areas are difficult to define since most scientific work can be classified in numerous ways, and, often, agreement among scientists regarding the categorization of certain work is far from unanimous. It can thus justifiably be asked whether anything resembling social organization exists in a research area.

Studies of informal communication among scientists indicate that scientists working on similar problems are usually aware of each other and in some cases attempt to systematize their contacts by exchanging reprints with one another (Libbey and Zaltman, 1967; Menzel, 1960; Paisley, 1965). Price has stated that some but not all scientists in a particular research area maintain a high level of informal communication and that

information received in this manner is essential for the conduct of effective research (Price, 1963). The amount of material published in some fields is so large that it cannot be monitored effectively by any other means. Kuhn (1962) has argued that groups of scientists develop shared definitions of their work, paradigms which interpret findings and guide new research. In other words, scientists adjust to the problems of dealing with knowledge in their fields by forming social organizations of various kinds, based upon shared communication and shared interpretations of the situation.

However, the existence of "invisible colleges" has been difficult to prove. Scientists have many contacts with other scientists in their own research areas and in other fields, some fleeting, some lasting. If social organization exists in a research area, it is of a highly elusive and relatively unstructured variety. The present research was designed to discover if anything resembling social organization could be observed in a research area. For this purpose, a sociometric analysis of a group of scientists with common research interests was required.[1] The existence of so-

* This research was supported by Grant GN–527 from the National Science Foundation. I am grateful to Derek Price for support and advice and to David Vachon, Edwin Olson and Erik Steiner for developing a computer program for Coleman's method of tracing sociometric connectedness.

[1] Although there have been a number of studies of informal communication among scientists, a sociometric study of communication patterns among scientists who are doing research in the same area had not been attempted before. Nicholas Mullins (1966) did a sociometric analysis of informal communication but did not focus upon a particular field. Several sociometric studies are currently in

cial organization could be inferred (a) if scientists who had published in a particular research area had more social ties with one another than with scientists who had not published in the area, and (b) if scientists who had published in the area could be differentiated in terms of degrees of social participation within the area, suggesting the existence of leadership in the field.

THE MEASUREMENT OF SOCIAL TIES

If social organization exists in a research area, it is likely to be based on a number of different types of social ties. Informal communication regarding research findings, research-in-progress, and research techniques represents one way in which members of a problem area can be linked to one another. In the present study, information about informal communication was obtained only from those currently engaged in research in the field, a subsample of 52 members from a total of 147 respondents.

In addition to informal communication, several other types of ties between scientists exist. Collaboration occurs in several ways. In the case of formal collaboration (as indicated by bylines on research publications), communication between two or more scientists about their research was so important that it received formal recognition in the publication itself. However, collaboration among scientists may occur before research reaches the stage of formal publication. Another form of collaboration takes place when a student writes a thesis under the direction of one or more teachers; other teachers not formally directing the thesis may play a role in the development of the thesis, and this relationship also represents a kind of collaboration.

---

progress, for example, Lingwood (1968), APA Project on Scientific Information Exchange in Psychology (1968), and a dissertation by David Vachon (1969), who was the first to use the Coleman Sociometric Connectedness Program with this type of data. For analysis of problem areas using different techniques, see Fisher, 1966 and 1967, Mullins, 1968 and Russett, 1969. For analyses of scientific literature which relate to this problem, see Cole (1962 and 1963), Kessler (1965), Kessler and Heart (1962), McGrath and Altman (1966), Meadows (1967), Parker et al. (1967), Price and Beaver (1966), Stevens (1953), Stoddart (1967) and Weinstein (undated).

Finally, there are intellectual linkages represented by the influence of one scientist's work upon that of another. Citation references in journal articles are direct indications of such influences, and studies of citations have been made (Garfield, 1964; Kessler, 1965; Weinstein, undated). This type of relationship can also be measured by asking scientists to name others who have influenced them in their selection of problems and techniques. Questions of this sort do not elicit data identical to that obtained using linkages among citations. The latter method is more precise and provides more complete information. In addition, the question used in the present study deliberately restricted the scope of the information requested in order to simplify the task of the respondent. Respondents were asked about influences on the selection of problems and techniques but not about influences upon the course of the research. However, many articles include numerous citations, but the relative importance of each citation may vary considerably from a reference to a scientist whose work has had a very strong influence on the author to a scientist whose work is relevant only in connection with a minor point. The use of a questionnaire to elicit some of this information probably has the advantage of obtaining the most important influences, rather than a complete list of major and minor influences.[2]

---

[2] A copy of the questionnaire which was used to elicit information concerning social ties in the area will be sent upon request. The question requesting names of scientists who had influenced the respondents' selection of research problems was not answered by 41% of the group. A similar question requesting names of scientists who had influenced their selections of research techniques was not answered by 59%. This was partly because these questions were not asked of respondents who had written a thesis in the area and nothing more (34 or 23% of the sample), although six of these respondents answered these questions anyway. Failure to respond to these questions was related to low productivity and lack of commitment to the area. A few scientists indicated that the research topic had been assigned to them. Other respondents claimed that these questions were difficult. The degree of perceived difficulty seemed to depend on whether the respondent thought that he was being asked to list every possible influence or only those which had been especially important (the latter was what was requested). In the lengthy career of a scientist influences on the development of re-

Each of these several different types of ties among scientists produces a somewhat different picture of the relationships within the problem area and between members of the area and outsiders. But the juxtaposition of these various indicators of linkage may provide an approximate picture of the degree of the relationship of each with every other. Combining several indicators into a composite index supplies further information about the group. Some members may be related to other members through influences on the selection of problems or techniques, others through some type of collaboration or through informal communication, but, if social organization does exist in a research area, most members should be related to others in at least one of these ways.[3]

As has been indicated previously, these measures are essentially sociometric, involving ties between one scientist and another. Some can be meaningfully looked at in terms of the degree of reciprocity involved; others cannot. Analysis of this type of data, especially for large groups, has always been somewhat problematical for sociologists. For the purpose of this study, it seemed preferable to rely on three methods. The first was simply an overall quantitative statement of the number of choices of various kinds directed both within and without the problem area.

The second was a method of assessing the extent of direct and indirect[4] relationships between members of the problem area. For example, a scientist who communicates with another scientist may obtain indirectly information which was transmitted to the second scientist by a third. A scientist (A) collaborating with another (B), who has in turn collaborated with others (C and D), may benefit indirectly from the work of C and D. Similarly, students, through the mediating efforts of their thesis director, may be in contact with one another even if they are in different settings.

When scientists in an area are linked by ties based on influences regarding the selection of research problems and techniques, their publications in the field build upon ideas expressed in previous works and are closely related. Price (1965) has argued that this is the case in fields where new knowledge is developing rapidly.

All techniques for assessing indirect relationships in groups other than analysis by manual procedures, which are impractical with large groups, are approximate (Coleman, 1964:447). The technique which was used here was a modification of one which was devised by James Coleman (1964:444–455).[5] The choices of members of a group are arranged in matrix form where one axis represents choices made by a member of the group; the other axis, choices received by a member. Continuous multiplication of the matrix by itself provides a means of locating the indirect relationships between the individuals represented in the matrix.[6] This analysis provides figures indicating the total number of persons to whom a particular scientist's choices directly or indirectly lead and the total number of persons choosing him directly or indirectly. In addition, it is possible to construct a measure of connectivity for a group as a whole. This is done by dividing the number of connections which occur (either from or toward individuals) by the total number of connections which could possibly occur.

---

search can be numerous, but it is quite possible that only a relatively small number of names are very significant in any particular problem area. Some respondents seemed to have difficulty or were unwilling to make the effort to distinguish such influences.

[3] A more difficult problem is that of evaluating the degree of cohesion which occurs. One solution is to define cohesion by means of probability considerations. The probability of each possible structure occurring by chance could be used in assessing the actual outcome, but such probabilities are difficult to construct when the number of choices permitted to each individual is unlimited. An alternative approach is to compare many groups of the same type. If data were available for scientists in many problem areas, one would then be able to evaluate a particular set of data according to such standards. However, in this study, data are presented in which choices within and without the group are compared, and choices by members of different subgroups are also compared.

[4] An indirect relationship is one in which A is linked to C because both are in communication with B.

[5] The program which was used here is a substantial revision and correction of the program which Coleman outlines in his book (Coleman, 1964:466–468).

[6] It is theoretically possible to find all the indirect ties. The algorithm used to solve the problem is not complete. However, it does obtain the vast majority of all the different connections among individuals.

Finally, direct and indirect relationships among members of different subgroups within the problem area were analyzed. For this purpose, members of the problem area were divided into five groups on the basis of productivity in and commitment to the area. The latter was measured in terms of continuity of interest in the area. Using three levels of productivity and two of continuity, it was possible to form six groups, of which five actually occurred in this problem area. Members of three subgroups indicated in response to an item on the questionnaire that they had continued to do research in the area: (1) eight High Producers, each of whom had published more than ten papers in the area; (2) eleven Moderate Producers, who had published four to ten papers in the area; (3) 33 Aspirants, who had published fewer than four papers in the area. Members of two subgroups indicated that they had not continued to do research in the area: (1) nine Defectors, each of whom had published four to ten papers in the area; (2) 86 Transients, each of whom had published fewer than four papers in the area. Every one with more than ten papers continued with his research in the area.

DESIGN OF STUDY

The selection of a suitable group of scientists was complicated by the fact that scientific fields can be defined as broadly as a discipline or as narrowly as a problem area (a cluster of closely related problems) and by the fact that the precise boundaries of research areas are usually difficult to define.

Among the different types of groups to which scientists belong, the problem area appeared to be the most suitable for an exploratory study, both because it is likely to be fairly small and because the bases for the relationships between members of the group (the scientists' immediate research interests) are fairly specific. An intensive case study of a particular problem area was used to develop techniques and hypotheses which could later be applied to a larger sample of problem areas.

Since scientists frequently work in more than one problem area at a time and often shift areas of interest and, in addition, tend to define the relevance of their work in

different ways, it is difficult to locate all the scientists who have worked in a particular problem area. At least four methods of locating members of a problem area are possible: the use of bibliographies, abstracting services, citation networks and sociometric data. Each of these methods has limitations in terms of locating a complete list of members. Lists of abstracts and bibliographies reflect the evaluations of relevance made by the compilers; citations reflect the evaluations of relevance of authors as do sociometric questions. In each case, some references or some names are likely to be omitted.

Although these problems cannot be solved completely, the availability of a bibliography, designed especially for maximum completeness and compiled by a highly productive member of a problem area, provided one means of dealing with the problem outlined above. Use of such a list made it likely that a very high proportion of members of the relevant group would be located.[7]

The problem area selected for this study, the diffusion of agricultural innovations,[8] was part of the research specialty—rural sociology. Since the "invisible college" hypothesis was developed from observations of the be-

[7] Use of such a bibliography entailed accepting the judgment of its compiler regarding the scope of the field and relevant publications. (It is recognized that other authors would supply equally acceptable but somewhat different bibliographies.) The validity of his judgment was borne out by the finding that two-thirds of the respondents placed their publications (on the list) within the area of "diffusion of agricultural innovations" or some variation of this label. Over four-fifths of the more productive members defined the field in this way. The author of the bibliography has stated that "In our continued searchings we now find very few studies that are over one year old. Our confidence is further bolstered when we receive few additional publications or suggestions for inclusion from the leading researchers to whom we send copies of an annual bibliography on diffusion (Rogers and Bettinghaus, 1966)."

[8] The diffusion of innovations has been studied in several academic disciplines (anthropology, economics, geography, psychology), in another research specialty within sociology (medical sociology), and in several applied fields (journalism, communication, consumer behavior, and industrial engineering) (Rogers, 1962; Rogers and Stanfield, 1966). The existence of research on a similar topic in a variety of disciplines is not uncommon. For example, the study of science as an institution and the study of formal organizations exhibit similar patterns.

havior of scientists in fast-moving specialties within physics, the selection of a research area in the social sciences might seem inappropriate. However, an analysis of the 403 papers published in the area between 1941 and mid-1966 revealed that it possessed several of the characteristics which have been found in the literature in the natural sciences (Price, 1961): (1) Growth of the field (number of papers published per year) had progressed through the first three of the four stages which Price has described as being characteristic of scientific literature, (2) the number of new authors entering the field per year showed the same series of stages of growth, (3) A few authors in the area had been highly productive and a majority had produced one or two papers. Although the field contained a larger proportion of single author publications (61%) than would be expected for a research area in the natural sciences, so many factors are believed to influence the amount of collaboration in a research area, and these factors are so imperfectly understood that this characteristic did not seem important enough to disqualify the area for a study of this type.

A second aspect of this problem area which might be considered to limit its usefulness for a case study of this sort is the type of situation in which research in this field has been conducted. For reasons related to the history of rural sociology, research in the diffusion problem area has often been financed and conducted in agricultural experiment stations (Kaufman, 1956). As a result, much of the research has had an applied character. However, this research is not carried out under the conditions of restricted communication which usually characterize applied research in industry. Rural sociologists studying diffusion have been in excellent communication with one another.[9] Thus, the applied character of some of the research does not appear to have inhibited the devel-

opment of informal social organization in the field.

Using the most recent bibliography compiled for the area (Rogers, 1966), questionnaires were sent to 172 of the 221 scientists listed,[10] both junior and senior authors; 147 replies were received. Each respondent was sent a letter which included references to his publications as listed in the bibliography and was requested to respond to the questionnaire with respect to those publications only (rather than with respect to any other publications he might have produced).[11]

The aim of the study was to obtain some information regarding the circumstances surrounding publication in the area from every scientist who had ever published in it. Since publications in the area began to appear in 1941, some respondents were describing events which had taken place many years ago. The majority of the publications in the area have appeared in the last ten years. An alternative plan would have been to focus upon only those scientists who had published within the last five years. This would, however, have reduced the size of an already small sample. In addition, it would not have

---

[9] Rogers describes these activities as follows: "The Rural Sociological Society annually devotes several sessions of papers to diffusion, and many studies are published in the Society's journal, *Rural Sociology*. Semiannual meetings of Midwestern rural sociologists studying diffusion are sponsored by the Farm Foundation, and out of these conferences have grown several summary publications and bibliographies." (Rogers, 1962:38)

[10] Due to an oversight, questionnaires were not sent to 15 junior authors, each of whom had one collaborative publication. The considerable period of time which had elapsed since some of the publications had appeared made it difficult to locate a number of members of the group. Addresses were traced by writing to university alumni offices and by searching relevant biographical directories but were unavailable for 34 members of the group; 79% of the remaining members of the group responded. The overall response rate was 67%. Telephone interviews were conducted with 17 members who did not return the questionnaire. Obtaining responses was complicated by the fact that about a quarter of the sample was residing abroad. Since the investigation was viewed as a case study for developing techniques for studying problems of this kind, the questionnaire was not extensively pretested but was tested principally in interviews with colleagues. In addition, ten pretest versions were sent to members of the problem area of which four were returned.

[11] Publications included theses, papers presented at professional meetings, and agricultural experiment station bulletins and reports, as well as journal articles and two books. Data regarding scientific communication should specify precisely which particular research by each scientist should be the referent for his response. Since scientists are often involved in research in more than one area, failure to specify precisely the relevant research can lead to the collection of many irrelevant names.

TABLE 1. NUMBER OF CHOICES RECEIVED BY
MEMBERS OF PROBLEM AREA AND OUTSIDERS[a]

Number of Choices Received	Affiliation of Scientist Chosen:	
	Problem Area	Outsiders
0	46	....
1	23	63.7
2	9	20.5
3– 5	10	12.5
6–10	5	3.0
11–20	4	0.3
21–50	2	0
Over 50	1	0
Total	100	100
N	(221)	(389)

[a] Choices were made by members of the problem area with respect to informal communication, current collaboration, theses directors, thesis influence and influences on the selection of problems and techniques. A scientist could be chosen more than once by the same respondent with respect of different categories as listed above.

provided an overall picture of the development of the problem area. Even though information about publications written many years ago may not be as precise as information about recent publications, it seemed preferable to have information about both types of publications in order to understand the social organization of the area.

CHOICES WITHIN AND OUTSIDE THE AREA:
THE GROUP AND OUTSIDERS

On every measure examined, respondents were about as likely to choose a scientist who had not published in the area as they

were to choose one who had. Out of a total 1351 choices made by all respondents on all the different types of ties, outsiders were named 684 times (51%) and problem area members 667 times (49%). Does this suggest that a social group within the area did not exist? There are three reasons for arguing that these figures do not imply the absence of social organization within the problem area.

First, the majority of "outsiders" were selected only once; 84% were chosen no more than twice; twelve, or 3%, were named more than five times. Within the problem area, about half the members were never named;[12] 78% were chosen twice or less. Most of these scientists had been relatively unproductive; many had only a brief contact with the problem area. On the other hand, 26, or 12%, were named more than five times. Fifteen, or 7%, were named more than ten times. Thus, the social organization of the problem area appeared to be centered around a small and relatively productive proportion of the total membership.

Since only one outsider was named more than ten times, there did not appear to be a group of outsiders whose influence had similar weight. The twelve outsiders who received

[12] In a sample of high energy physicists who were asked to name the two persons with whom they most frequently exchanged information, the proportion of physicists not named was slightly more than a third (Libbey and Zaltman, 1967:31–32).

TABLE 2. NUMBERS OF CHOICES RECEIVED BY SUBGROUPS OF THE DIFFUSION PROBLEM AREA

Number of Choices Received	Subgroup Affiliation of Scientist Chosen					
	High Producers	Moderate Producers	Defectors	Aspirants	Transients	Total Group
0	0	0	0	24	43	31
1	0	0	11	39	34	29
2– 5	0	73	33	27	16	23
6–10	0	27	22	9	5	8
11–20	38	0	22	0	2	5
21–50	38	0	11	0	0	3
Over 50	25	0	0	0	0	1
Total[a]	101	100	99	99	100	100
N	(8)	(11)	(9)	(33)	(86)	(147)

$\tau_{yx}=.39$ (See Footnote b)

[a] Percentages in this and subsequent tables do not always total 100 due to rounding error.
[b] For computation of tau, the categories of the dependent variable were combined as follows: 0–10, over 10. Goodman and Kruskal's tau indicates the proportion of errors saved in predicting the dependent variable if the independent variable is known (Blalock, 1960:232–234).

more than 5 choices could be characterized in three ways. One was a scientist working in the problem area who had not yet published at the time the questionnaires were mailed but who published during the following year. Two others had published numerous articles in an adjacent problem area, the study of the diffusion of medical innovations. Most of the remaining frequently-chosen outsiders had achieved a high degree of eminence. Seven out of nine had been president of the American Sociological Association or the Rural Sociological Society. Thus these scientists were well known in the discipline as a whole.

There was some indication that the relationships between respondents and members of the problem area were different from their relationships with scientists who had not published in the area. Respondents were asked to indicate if they had any personal acquaintance with the scientists whom they mentioned as having influenced their selection of problems in the area. Of 246 choices of problem area members, 76% were designated as personal acquaintances; of 256 choices of outsiders, 57% were indicated to be personal acquaintances. This outcome suggests that to some extent the influence of outsiders was exerted through publications, while that of insiders was exerted through personal contact.

The problem area which included 221 scientists was able to compete with respect to choices with members of a very much larger population, the former receiving 49% of the total 1351 choices. The outsiders were drawn from several disciplines (unfortunately, this information was not available for many of the outsiders) which altogether include more than twenty thousand scientists.[13] Similar distributions of choices have been found in the analysis of citation references (Swanson, 1966). About half the articles on a particular subject tend to be concentrated in a dozen or so journals; the remainder are widely scattered. Something analogous to the phenomenon of "reference scattering" seems to occur in relation to these measures of scientific relationships.

CHARACTERISTICS OF MEMBERS OF SUBGROUPS IN THE DIFFUSION PROBLEM AREA

Selection of Group Members versus Outsiders.—The five subgroups differentiated on the basis of productivity and commitment to the area were expected to exhibit varying degrees of linkage both with the members of the group and with those who had not published in the area. When all types of ties were considered together, one subgroup of highly productive members appeared to be equally strongly linked to the area and to outsiders.[14] Another subgroup (one which was relatively unproductive) appeared to have a relatively peripheral relationship to the area as well as to outsiders. The other three subgroups ranged between these two in degree of linkage to the area and to outsiders. This suggests that both types of ties are characteristic of productive scientists in a research area.

Direct and Indirect Ties by Subgroups.—When direct and indirect choices of the members of the various subgroups were measured using the Sociometric Connectedness Program, the differences between the subgroups emerged more definitively. Among the subgroups currently doing research in the area, informal communication choices by the High and Moderate Producers linked them to more members of the group than did the choices of the Aspirants. In addition, a high proportion of choices by others led to the High Producers, placing them in the center of a fairly sizeable communication network. (Table 4 shows how frequently a scientist is

[13] Eighty-one percent of the members of the problem area who returned the questionnaire (147 scientists) were sociologists (defined as having received a doctorate in the area or, in the absence of a doctorate, a master's degree). A few of these individuals were also identified with other disciplines as well (i.e. had received degrees in joint programs). Thirteen percent were in anthropology, agricultural economics, economics, agricultural extension, or psychology; 5% were in a number of other fields. Thirty-eight percent of the outsiders were sociologists; 22% were in anthropology, agricultural economics, economics, agricultural extension, or psychology; 7% were in several other fields. No information was available for 32% of the outsiders.

[14] In this table, and the tables which follow, percentages are frequently based on very small figures. However, the percentage differences between High Producers and the other subgroups are in most cases large and are so consistently in the same direction that the data, when considered as a whole, provides substantial evidence for the hypothesis being examined here.

TABLE 3. Percentages of Subgroups in the Problem Area Having at Least One Tie[a] with Other Members of the Area and with Outsiders

Percentages of Subgroup Having	Subgroup					
	High Producers	Moderate Producers	Defectors	Aspirants	Transients	Total[*] Group
One or more ties with members of problem area	100	91	89	88	66	76
One or more ties with outsiders	100	91	78	94	58	72
No ties	0	0	0	6	22	14
N	(8)	(11)	(9)	(33)	(86)	(147)

[a] The following types of ties were included: informal communication, current collaboration, thesis directors, thesis influence, and influences on the selection of problems and techniques. Reciprocal communication and published collaboration were excluded since choices of outsiders were not relevant to those categories.

TABLE 4. Direct and Indirect Choices of Members of Subgroups by Members of Subgroups in the Diffusion Problem Area as Measured by the Coleman Sociometric Connectedness Program

1. Type of Choice: Informal Communication[a]

Number of Times Members of Subgroups Are Chosen Directly or Indirectly	Subgroup Affiliation						
	High Producers	Moderate Producers	Defectors	Aspirants	Transients	Non-respondents	Total Group
0*	0	27	..	68	..	..	50
1–10*	0	27	..	23	..	..	21
11–20	0	0	..	0	..	..	0
Over 20	100	46	..	9	..	..	29
Total	100	100	..	100	..	..	100
N	(8)	(11)	..	(33)	..	..	(52)

$\tau_{yx} = .57$

2. Type of Choice: Most Important Communication[a][•]

Number of Times Members of Subgroups Are Chosen Directly or Indirectly	Subgroup Affiliation						
	High Producers	Moderate Producers	Defectors	Aspirants	Transients	Non-respondents	Total Group
0	0	46	..	79	..	..	62
1–10*	86	45	..	18	..	..	32
Over 10*	14	9	..	3	..	..	6
Total	100	100	..	100	..	..	100
N	(8)	(11)	..	(33)	..	..	(52)

$\tau_{yx} = .38$

3. Type of Choice: Reciprocal Communication[a]

Number of Times Members of Subgroups Are Chosen Directly or Indirectly	Subgroup Affiliation						
	High Producers	Moderate Producers	Defectors	Aspirants	Transients	Non-respondents	Total Group
0	25	64	..	85	..	..	71
1–5*	12	18	..	9	..	..	12
Over 5*	63	18	..	6	..	..	17
Total	100	100	..	100	..	..	100
N	(8)	(11)	..	(33)	..	..	(52)

$\tau_{yx} = .22$

168

Number of Times Members of Subgroups Are Chosen Directly or Indirectly	\multicolumn{7}{c}{4. Type of Choice: Published Collaboration}

4. Type of Choice: Published Collaboration

Number of Times Members of Subgroups Are Chosen Directly or Indirectly	High Producers	Moderate Producers	Defectors	Aspirants	Transients	Non-respondents	Total Group
0*	0	18	0	43	45	27	34
1–10*	12	55	78	45	40	62	50
11–20	25	0	11	3	5	5	5
Over 20	63	27	11	9	10	5	11
Total	100	100	100	100	100	99	100
N	(8)	(11)	(9)	(33)	(86)	(74)	(221)

$\tau_{yx} = .15$

5. Type of Choice: Influences on Problem Selection [d]

Subgroup Affiliation

Number of Times Members of Subgroups Are Chosen Directly or Indirectly	High Producers	Moderate Producers	Defectors	Aspirants	Transients	Non-respondents	Total Group
0*	0	9	11	73	78	..	63
1–10*	12	82	44	24	19	..	26
11–20	0	0	0	0	0	..	0
Over 20	88	9	44	3	3	..	11
Total	100	100	99	100	100	..	100
N	(8)	(11)	(9)	(33)	(86)	..	(147)

$\tau_{yx} = .45$

6. Type of Choice: Thesis Directors [d]

Subgroup Affiliation

Number of Times Members of Subgroups Are Chosen Directly or Indirectly	High Producers	Moderate Producers	Defectors	Aspirants	Transients	Non-respondents	Total Group
0	12	46	45	52	60	..	54
1–10*	38	18	55	39	26	..	31
11–20*	0	0	0	0	0	..	0
Over 20*	50	36	0	9	14	..	16
Total	100	100	100	100	100	..	101
N	(8)	(11)	(9)	(33)	(86)	..	(147)

$\tau_{yx} = .05$

7. Type of Choice: Total Ties [d] [e]

Subgroup Affiliation

Number of Times Members of Subgroups Are Chosen Directly or Indirectly	High Producers	Moderate Producers	Defectors	Aspirants	Transients	Non-respondents	Total Group
0*	0	0	0	21	24	..	19
1–100 [f]*	0	36	0	30	8	..	14
Over 100	100	64	100	49	68	..	67
Total	100	100	100	100	100	..	100
N	(8)	(11)	(9)	(33)	(86)	..	(147)

$\tau_{yx} = .14$

[a] Only choices of those members of the problem area currently engaged in research in the field are included in these computations.

[b] Asterisks indicate that categories were combined for computation of tau.

[c] Respondents were asked to rate from 1 to 5 the importance of each communication tie for their research. Those ties which were rated 4 or 5 were considered as the most important ties.

[d] Only choice of respondents (not non-respondents) were included in these computations.

[e] Total ties included informal communication, current collaboration, published collaboration, thesis directors, thesis influence, influence on the selection of problems and influence on the selection of techniques.

[f] All these scores were between 1 and 5.

linked to others by their choices of him; it does not show his choices of others.)

High Producers were more likely to be linked to others through communication ties which they considered to be very important for their research; moreover, a high proportion of choices of this type by others also led to them. The communication choices of the High Producers were more frequently reciprocated than were those of the other groups, again suggesting their central position in the group.

The High Producers were also linked through published collaboration to a large number of other members of the area, suggesting that much of the collaboration in the area had been conducted in association with High Producers. In addition, the High Producers had played an important role in the area as thesis directors.[15]

The High Producers were not predominantly linked to others in the area through their own choices of influences on the selection of problems; however, they did receive a much higher number of direct and indirect choices with respect to this type of influence. They had apparently played an important role for many members of the area in the selection of research problems. The Defectors were the only other group that had played a significant role in this respect. However, comparisons of direct and indirect choices suggested that their role had been largely indirect. They had influenced the High Producers, who, in turn, had influenced many of the other members of the group. The role of the High Producers as influences on the selection of research techniques was less pronounced, although choices of members of the area were also more likely to lead to them than to members of other subgroups.

When all types of links were examined together, the High Producers, the Moderate Producers and the Defectors were linked to many members of the area through their own choices. The Aspirants were linked to fewer members and the Transients to even fewer. The High Producers and the Defectors also dominated on the receipt of choices. One hundred percent of the High Producers and

of the Defectors had very high scores, much higher than any of the remaining groups. Thus, the High Producers, sometimes in company with the Moderate Producers, sometimes along with the Defectors, provided orientation for the other members of the area.

The group connectivity scores show the extent to which members of each subgroup had activated their potential relationships with each other and with members of other subgroups. This measure can be computed in two ways: (a) the number of choices of members of the entire group made by a subgroup in relation to the total number of possible choices and (b) the number of choices of a particular subgroup made by its members and members of other subgroups in relation to the total number of possible choices. The first measures how often members of a subgroup choose other members; the second measures how often members of a subgroup are chosen by members of the entire group. The High Producers' choices tended to relate them to more members of the area than did the choices of other subgroups. However, with respect to certain ties, they were chosen by members of other subgroups more frequently than they chose members of these subgroups. For example, 21% of the possible links between High Producers and other members of the area currently active in research were realized on the basis of the High Producers' own choices with respect to informal communication. Through the choices of others, 47% of the potential ties with members of the area were realized. With respect to influences on the selection of problems, only 4% of their potential links with other members of the area were filled as a result of their choices. On the basis of the choices by others in the area, 21% of these relationships were filled. A similar type of difference appears when all types of ties were considered simultaneously.

This set of tables suggests that differences between the subgroups within the problem area existed. One subgroup, the most productive one, appeared to have more ties with the entire group than the other subgroups, although on certain measures the Moderate Producers and the Defectors exhibited a similar degree of linkage. Since the High Producers were more frequently linked to the

---

[15] The High Producers also were more likely to be chosen with respect to the influence of teachers (other than thesis directors) upon the thesis.

TABLE 5. PROPORTION OF POSSIBLE TIES ACTIVATED AMONG SUBGROUPS OF THE DIFFUSION PROBLEM AREA AS MEASURED BY COLEMAN'S GROUP CONNECTIVITY SCORES [a]

Proportion of Possible Ties Activated re	Subgroup Affiliation					
	High Producers	Moderate Producers	Aspirants	Defectors	Transients	Total Group [b]
Informal communication						
Choosing [c]	.205	.237	.124	....	....	.161
Chosen	.468	.283	.039	....	....	.161
Most important communication						
Choosing	.154	.089	.025	....	....	.049
Chosen	.122	.069	.011	....	....	.049
Reciprocal communication						
Choosing [b]	.115	.021	.010	....	....	.029
Current collaboration						
Choosing	.032	.014	.004	....	....	.010
Chosen	.026	.014	.005	....	....	.010
Published collaboration						
Choosing [b]	.093	.038	.017	.033	.019	.022
Thesis directors						
Choosing [d]	.079	.056	.017	.012	.026	.028
Influences on problem selection						
Choosing	.039	.080	.041	.039	.021	.032
Chosen	.214	.023	.007	.127	.015	.032
Influences on technique selection						
Choosing	.018	.030	.013	.001	.005	.009
Chosen	.059	.008	.005	.027	.004	.009
Thesis influence						
Choosing	.005	.010	.005	.001	.003	.004
Chosen	.031	.003	.001	.016	.001	.004
Total ties [e]						
Choosing	.664	.673	.590	.664	.474	.536
Chosen	.801	.518	.392	.802	.542	.536

[a] The number of possible ties is obtained by multiplying the number of cases in the group by the number of cases minus one (to eliminate self-choices). The sum of all the individual scores representing the number of direct and indirect relationships with other members gives the number of relationships which actually occur. The group connectivity score represents the proportion of possible ties which actually occur. The number of possible ties for a subgroup is obtained by multiplying the number of cases in the subgroup by the number of cases in the total group minus one. Only respondents currently engaged in research in the area are included in the first four measures. The remaining measures include all respondents (N=147). Published collaboration also includes non-respondents (N=221); the non-respondents' score was .015.

[b] These scores are the same for "Choosing" and "Chosen."

[c] "Choosing" represents a score based on respondents' own choices; "Chosen" represents a score based on choices by others of the respondents.

[d] These scores are the same for "Choosing" and "Chosen" since the relationship between thesis director and student was assumed to be a reciprocal one.

[e] Total ties included informal communication, current collaboration, published collaboration, thesis directors, thesis influence, influence on the selection of problems and influence on the selection of techniques.

group as a whole by the choices of others than by their own choices, it would seem that they had a high degree of visibility in the problem area. Many others looked to them for orientation. Thus the connectivity which developed in this area appeared to be at least partially the result of a large number of choices directed toward a few members. Anyone choosing even one of these individuals was brought into contact with a large network of individuals. This is a reasonable outcome in science where students or collaborators of very productive scientists are brought into contact, directly or indirectly, with many other scientists in the field. However, for some members, this contact had been very brief. Many of the Transients appeared to have had only peripheral contact with the area. In some cases, they seemed to have been drawn almost involuntarily into the activities of the area and to have detached themselves as quickly as possible. Comments on the questionnaires implied that some members of this group were unaware of any "tradition" of research in the area.

CHANGES IN THE NETWORK OF SOCIAL TIES OVER TIME

So far, the group has been described without reference to the fact that members belonged to the group at different times and for different lengths of time. This approach is justified by the fact that, in a research area, scientists who are no longer working in a field continue in a sense to be the colleagues of those who are presently working in the field since their publications provide the basis for future research. However, as was described earlier, the amount of activity in the area steadily increased during the 25-year period examined. During the first ten years of activity in the area, only 5% of the members were active. Between 1948 and 1958, the number of authors entering the area doubled every three years. After 1958, the number of authors entering the field doubled every five years; the increase per year stabilized at approximately 17 authors per year. The trend for the number of publications was similar. Between 1951 and 1960, 49% of the authors entered the field, most of this increase occurring during the latter part of the decade. Another 46% entered between 1961 and 1966.

Since, as we have seen, the High Producers were very influential in the area, tracing the development of their interest in the field would help to explain the growth of the area.

Two High Producers entered the field in the first decade, apparently influenced by the publications of a Defector and a Transient who had been active during that period. In the middle of the second decade, each of these High Producers had a student who also became a High Producer. Another thesis director and his student, both High Producers, entered the field at the same time along with a collaborator who also became a High Producer. By 1957, all of the High Producers had entered the field. Although almost two-thirds of the Aspirants and more than one-third of the Transients entered after 1960, only 11% of the more productive scientists (those with more than three publications in the area) entered the field in that period. Since at that time interest in the field was beginning to diminish relative to its earlier rate of exponential growth, this suggests that productive scientists may be especially sensitive to the potentialities for growth in a field in making their selection of research problems.

The influence of members who had published in the area steadily increased relative to those who had not published. Before 1956, about 25% of the theses written in the field were directed by members of the area. From 1956 to 1966, close to two-thirds of the theses in the area were directed by members of the area. The number of scientists mentioning only outsiders as influences on their selection of research problems in the area decreased from 38% among scientists entering the field before 1951 to 9% among scientists entering after 1956.[16] Examination of the total number of choices by members of the group with respect to influences on the selection of problems in various periods revealed that, among scientists entering the area prior to 1951, 42% of the choices were for members. Between 1951 and 1955, the figure was 38%. Among scientists entering between 1956 and 1960, 57% of the choices were for members. Among scientists entering after 1960, the comparable figure was 48%. The proportion of collaborative publications also increased from 22% before 1951 to 30% in 1951 to 1955, 41% in 1956 to 1960, and

---

[16] The date of a scientist's first publication in the field was used as the date of his entry into the field.

37% after 1960. These last two distributions suggest that the field was somewhat more integrated from 1956 to 1960 (the second half decade of rapid exponential growth) than at other periods. A slight decline in integration parallels the shift from exponential to linear growth.

The influence of the High Producers also increased over time. None of the theses written in the area by scientists entering the field before 1956 were directed by High Producers. After 1956, 38% of the theses in the area were directed by High Producers, a subgroup representing 8 individuals. Twenty-seven percent of the theses were directed by members of the four remaining subgroups representing 139 respondents. Similarly, the proportion of scientists in the group mentioning High Producers as having influenced their selection of research problems increased from 25% among scientists entering prior to 1951 to 39% among scientists entering after that date, more than twice as high as the proportion naming any of the other subgroups. More than 50% of the total number of choices of this type by scientists entering the field after 1950 were for High Producers.

Another development reveals the changes which were taking place in the field. On the basis of collaboration and student-thesis director relationships, members of the area were assigned to distinct subgroups of varying sizes (see Crane, 1968a; Price and Beaver, 1966). A scientist was assigned to a particular group of collaborators if he had a published collaboration with at least one of its members or had been the student or thesis director of at least one of its members. Before 1956, the group consisted of small groups of collaborators and student-teacher pairs and a number of isolates. After 1956, when the group as a whole increased in size, some of these small groups expanded. Two large groups emerged, with 27 and 32 members respectively, as well as several medium-size groups with five to 13 members.[17] A number of new small groups with 2 to 4 members and numerous isolates appeared. Few of the small groups lasted more than a couple of years.[18] Turnover among the isolates was also high. Medium-size groups, especially the relatively larger ones, were more durable. Four had lasted more than ten years. One of the two large groups had lasted more than ten years; the other had lasted eight years.

Six of the eight High Producers were members of the two large groups. The remaining two belonged to the largest of the medium-

_____

[17] These sizes represent the number of members each collaboration group had during the entire period, 1941 to mid–1966.

[18] The duration of a collaboration group was measured inclusively by finding the number of years from the date of the earliest publication by one of its members to the date of the most recent publication by a member.

TABLE 6. FREQUENCY TOTAL AND AVERAGE DURATION FOR GROUPS BY SIZE[a]

Number of Authors in Group	Frequency	Total Number of Authors in Group	Average Duration of Group (in Years)[b]
1	47	47	1.3
2	9	18	1.1
3	5	15	1.6
4	3	12	5.0
5	1	5	1.0
6	4	24	9.0
7	1	7	7.0
9	1	9	22.0
12	1	12	11.0
13	1	13	12.0
27	1	27	8.0
32	1	32	14.0
Total	75	221	Mean 2.9

[a] Includes non-respondents although student-teacher relationships were unknown for them.

[b] Duration of a collaboration group was measured inclusively by finding the number of years from the date of the earliest publication by one of its members to the date of the most recent publication by a member.

173

sized groups. The large groups of collaborators appeared to reflect the way in which the High Producers exerted their influence upon the field, i.e., by surrounding themselves with students and collaborators among whom turnover was frequently high. Thus, these large groups of collaborators, under the direction of High Producers, provided continuity and structure in a situation which would otherwise have been amorphous due to the continual arrivals and departures of less committed scientists.

It seems plausible that these large groups could have exercised control over the direction of research in the area. Since their approach to the field was so visible due to the large number of publications produced by these groups, scientists outside these groups who had other types of approaches might have found it difficult to exert a comparable influence. A content analysis of publications in the area by the compiler of the bibliography which lists them (Rogers, 1966) made it possible to determine (a) the collaboration group affiliation of the first users of all dependent and independent variables appearing in empirical studies in the area, and (b) the number of times each variable was used. Variables appearing for the first time in publications by scientists who were not members of the large groups were not less frequently used than variables appearing for the first time in publications by members of large groups. On the other hand, more than half the variables ever used first appeared in publications by members of large groups and by members of two of the medium-sized groups (Crane, 1968b).

CONCLUSION

As predicted, the social group which was described here was not one which was tightly knit or closed to external influences. "Outsiders" played an important role in influencing the activities of members of the group. That a social group within the problem area existed was principally apparent from the number of choices received by a relatively small number of members of the group. It appeared that members of the area were not so much linked to one another directly but were linked to each other indirectly through these highly influential members. The importance of these scientists was not obvious, except in terms of productivity, unless one examined their many and varied influences on the remaining members of their field, each of whom might be affected in only one or two ways and for short periods of time.

A question which remains to be discussed is how a group of this kind can best be conceptualized theoretically. Price has popularized the term "invisible college" which refers to an elite of mutually interacting and productive scientists within a research area. However, this conceptualization does not comprehend two aspects of the social organization of research areas which have emerged from the analysis presented here: (a) the interaction between the most active and influential members of the area and the "rank and file" and (b) the role of "outsiders" in the organization of the area.

Of the various types of social organization which have been identified by sociologists, the social circle would appear to be the one which best describes the social organization of a research area (Kadushin, 1966). The social circle is not well instituted, compared to the bureaucracy or even to less formalized entities such as the tribe or the family. Members come together on the basis of their interests rather than propinquity or ascribed statuses. Indirect interaction, interaction mediated through intervening parties, is an important aspect of the social circle. It is not necessary to know a particular member of a social circle in order to be influenced by him. Certain characteristics are more common to members of a particular social circle than to non-members, but members do not necessarily share all or even most of these defining characteristics. Each member is usually aware of some but not all other members. The exact boundaries of the social circle are difficult to locate.

While something comparable to a social circle may at times develop in a research area, it seems unlikely that it would exist at all times in all research areas. In some areas, nothing of the sort may develop. In areas in which social circles do develop, their size and importance to their members are likely to change from one period to another. There is some indication that absence of continuity of personnel in a research area is associated with lack of productivity in the area and the

174

failure of knowledge to disseminate and to cumulate (Fisher, 1966, 1967). In some cases the same research problems tend to be treated again and again (Barton and Wilder, 1964). This suggests that the presence of scientists whose productivity is sufficient to make them visible to most of those who enter the field, even briefly, produces a social circle which in turn plays an important role in the normal growth of the research area.

The diffusion problem area studied here is the only problem area devoted to the study of diffusion in which a sizeable number of papers have been published. Each of the other areas has remained quite small (Rogers and Stanfield, 1966:5). It can be argued that an important factor in the growth of this area was that a few individuals developed a high degree of commitment to it and as a result were able both to direct the activities of others in the field and to make it visible as a research area. Since all research areas in a research specialty (and to a lesser extent in science as a whole) are potentially related to one another, one group becomes separated from others only when certain scientists develop a strong interest in the field and assert its independence, even temporarily, from its context.

On the other hand, since ties between members of the area and "outsiders" were numerous, it can also be asked whether it is meaningful to speak of specialties or problem areas at all. Mullins (1966) has argued that it is not. It was suggested above that choices of "outsiders" were analogous to the phenomenon of "reference scattering"; about half the articles on a subject tend to appear in a few "core" journals, the rest being widely scattered. Perhaps the importance of both "core" and "scatter" can best be understood by assuming that each was the exclusive mode of organization of scientific activity. For example, if there was no "scatter," scientists would be divided into small groups, sharing the same interests, speaking only to each other, and reading and citing only each other's work. If this were the case, problem areas would have the characteristics of what sociologists in other contexts refer to as "sects." Religious sects break away from the church and build separate organizations, emphasizing aspects of doctrine or policy which they believe have

been ignored or misinterpreted by the church. The religious sect is a relatively closed system, resisting external influences rather than attempting to adapt to them. Members who deviate from orthodox views on any issue are quickly expelled (see, for example, Coser, 1954; Johnson, 1963; Yinger, 1957:144–155). If scientific problem areas had these characteristics, science would consist of hundreds of disparate groups, none of which would have any communication with or relevance for each other.

Science is actually organized in exactly the opposite fashion. Emotional neutrality is one of the norms of science (Barber, 1962: 125–127); psychological overinvestment in one's scientific ideas is frowned upon. Groups which attempt to advocate particular points of view to the exclusion of others without adequate empirical substantiation are often referred to as "schools" of thought and are considered unscientific. Most problem areas are open to influences from other fields. The desire for originality motivates scientists to maintain contacts with scientists and scientific work in areas different from their own in order to enhance their ability to develop new ideas in their own areas. Scientists in problem areas are usually committed more to the solution of the problem than to the group itself. The problem area can best be understood as a temporary unit which deals with special problems and then dissolves after one or several decades when the problems have either been solved or been determined to be unsolvable.[19]

On the other hand, if there was only "scatter" in science and no "core," scientific knowledge would not cumulate. A high proportion of ideas would be lost. Swanson (1966) claims that an important proportion of the scientific literature is so scattered as to defy the efforts of any individual to bring all of it together. If all the literature on a particular subject was so scattered, it would be impossible for scientists to build on each other's work. Each scientist would be working by himself and with perhaps a few other scientists whom he accidently discovered. The existence of a "core" of journals in the literature, and of scientists in the problem

---

[19] Bennis (1966) has argued that this type of organization is the prototype of an organization designed to produce innovation.

area, provides a kind of repetitiveness in scientific communication, insuring that certain ideas will be repeated sufficiently so that the relevant scientists may be assured of receiving at least some of the currently important findings. There are integrating factors in science as well as disintegrating factors.[20] Both are necessary, the former to permit scientific knowledge to cumulate and grow, the latter to prevent it from becoming a completely subjective, sect-like phenomenon.

Future studies will be needed to perfect the methods for studying groups of this kind.[21] For example, it would be useful to compare the results of different techniques for locating groups of scientists, such as the use of comprehensive bibliographies, abstracting services, citations, and sociometric data with "snowball" samples (Goodman, 1961; Mullins, 1966). In order to obtain a complete picture of activities in a problem area, information regarding scientists who have made very many or very few contributions is needed. While comprehensive bibliographies cannot be expected to be 100% complete, they are likely to provide a high proportion of both types of participants. If an adequate list of authors can be compiled from the scientific literature or other sources, the use of sociometric data obtained from "snowball" samples is probably less appropriate for locating members of a particular area since a high proportion of members in other areas tend to be mentioned. Kessler (1965) has shown that scientific publications form groups on the basis of common citation references but no attempt has yet been made to explore the social ties among authors drawn together in this fashion. Cluster analysis (Bailey, 1969) is being used

to locate groups of scientists with similar interests on the basis of thematic similarities in the contents of research grant applications. This technique which could also be used to analyze the contents of abstracting services will be combined with analysis of social relationships among members of such groups.

Evaluation of different methods for analyzing this type of data is needed. The present study used Coleman's Sociometric Connectedness Program to examine the relationships between members of an entire group. Sociometric techniques for determining non-intersecting cliques are still inadequate (Lingwood, 1968:20). However, if a group is actually a social circle, one would not expect to find distinct cliques based on sociometric ties. A true social circle should consist of a complex and undivided network of relationships. If such a group is to be meaningfully partitioned, it ought to be done on the basis of criteria other than social relationships. In the present paper, productivity and commitment to the area were used. Price and Beaver (1966) have suggested a method of locating cliques which utilizes ties based on published collaborations. Communication and influence ties between units formed on this basis have been examined (Crane, 1968a). Russett (1969) relied upon factor analysis to identify within a problem area subgroups who tended to cite each other's publications.

Finally, the points of intersection between problem areas should be examined. If science actually consists of hundreds of groups of scientists, each of which concentrates upon a cluster of related problems, future studies should trace the movement of communication and influence from one area to another. Here sociometric data obtained from snowball samples would be useful. Starting from lists compiled from the scientific literature and other sources of scientists from several areas in the same discipline, interviews with successive waves of respondents would pinpoint the nature of their relationships to different social circles.

---

[20] Mullins (1966) has argued that the integrating factor in science is a set of orientations toward which research can be directed. For example, research can emphasize chemical or physical aspects of nature, structure or process, control or energy. Such dimensions, however, would appear to incorporate such disparate kinds of work as to be unlikely to play a role comparable to that attributed here to the core members and core journals of the problem area.

[21] For a discussion of methods of studying social circles consisting of political leaders, see Kadushin, 1968.

REFERENCES

Allen, T. J. and S. I. Cohen.
1966   Information flow in an R and D laboratory. Unpublished manuscript.

APA Project on Scientific Information Exchange in Psychology.
1968 "Networks of informal communication among scientifically productive psychologists." Unpublished manuscript.

Bailey, D.
1969 "Cluster analysis of physiological psychology grant requests and descriptors." Unpublished manuscript, University of Colorado.

Barber, B.
1962 Science and the Social Order. New York: Collier Books.

Barton, A. H. and D. E. Wilder.
1964 "Research and practice in the teaching of reading: a progress report," pp. 361–398 in Matthew B. Miles (ed.), Innovation in Education. New York: Bureau of Publications, Teachers College, Columbia University.

Bennis, W. G.
1966 Changing Organizations. New York: McGraw-Hill, Chapter 3.

Blalock, H. M.
1960 Social Statistics. New York: McGraw-Hill, pp. 232–234.

Cole, P. F.
1962 "A new look at reference scattering." Journal of Documentation 18 (June):58–64.
1963 "Journal usage versus age of journal." Journal of Documentation 19 (March):1–11.

Coleman, J. S.
1964 Introduction to Mathematical Sociology. New York: The Free Press of Glencoe: 447–455.

Coser, L.
1954 "Sects and sectarians." Dissent 1:360–369.

Crane, D.
1968a "Communication, collaboration, and influence: a study of formal and informal collaboration among scientists." Unpublished manuscript.
1968b "The diffusion of innovations in science: a case study." Unpublished manuscript.

Fisher, C. S.
1966 "The death of a mathematical theory: a study in the sociology of knowledge." Archives for History of Exact Sciences 111:137–1959.
1967 "The last invariant theorists: a sociological study of the collective biographies of mathematical specialists." European Journal of Sociology VIII:216–244.

Garfield, E.
1964 The Use of Citation Data in Writing the History of Science. Philadelphia: Institute for Scientific Information.

Goodman, L. A.
1961 "Snowball sampling." Annals of Mathematical Statistics 32:148–170.

Johnson, B.
1963 "On church and sect." American Sociological Review 28 (August):539–549.

Kadushin, C.
1966 "The friends and supporters of psychotherapy: on social circles in urban life." American Sociological Review 31 (December):786–802.
1968 "Power, influence and social circles: a new methodology for studying opinion makers." American Sociological Review 33 (October):685–699.

Kaufman, H. F.
1956 "Rural Sociology, 1945–55." pp. 104–105 in Hans L. Zetterberg (ed.), Sociology in the United States of America. Paris: UNESCO.

Kessler, M. M.
1965 "Comparison of the results of bibliographic coupling and analytic subject indexing." American Documentation 16 (July):223–233.

Kessler, M. M. and F. E. Heart.
1962 "Concerning the probability that a given paper will be cited." Unpublished paper.

Kuhn, T. S.
1962 The Structure of Scientific Revolutions. Chicago: University of Chicago Press.

Libbey, M. and G. Zaltman.
1967 The Role and Distribution of Written Informal Communication in Theoretical High Energy Physics. New York: American Institute of Physics.

Lingwood, D. A.
1968 "Interpersonal communication, scientific productivity, and invisible colleges: studies of two behavioral science research areas." Paper read at the colloquium: Improving the Social and Communication Mechanisms of Educational Research, sponsored by American Educational Research Association, Washington, D.C.

McGrath, J. E. and I. A. Altman.
1966 Small Group Research: A Synthesis and Critique of the Field. New York: Holt, Rinehart and Winston.

Meadows, A. J.
1967 "The citation characteristics of astronomical research literature." Journal of Documentation 23 (March):28–33.

Menzel, H.
1960 Review of Studies in the Flow of Information Among Scientists. New York: Columbia University, Bureau of Applied Social Research, 2 Volumes (Mimeo).

Mullins, N. C.
1966 "Social Networks Among Biological Scientists." Unpublished Ph.D. dissertation, Harvard University.
1968 "Social origins of an invisible college: The phage group." Unpublished paper read at the meeting of the American Sociological Association, Boston, 1968.

Paisley, W. J.
1965 The Flow of (Behavioral) Science Information: A Review of the Research Literature. Palo Alto: Institute for Communication Research, Stanford University.

Parker, E. B., W. J. Paisley and R. Garrett.
1967 Bibliographic Citations as Unobtrusive

Measures of Scientific Communication. Palo Alto: Institute for Communication Research, Stanford University.

Price, D. J. de S.
1961 Science Since Babylon. New Haven: Yale University Press, Chapter 5.
1963 Little Science, Big Science. New York: Columbia University Press, Chapter 2.
1965 "Networks of scientific papers," Science 149 (July 30):510–515.

Price, D. J. and D. de B. Beaver.
1966 "Collaboration in an invisible college." American Psychologist 21 (November): 1011–1018.

Rogers, E. M.
1962 Diffusion of Innovations. New York: Free Press.
1966 Bibliography on the Diffusion of Innovations. Diffusion of Innovations Research Report, No. 4. East Lansing: Michigan State University.

Rogers, E. M. and E. P. Bettinghaus.
1966 "Comparison of generalizations from diffusion research on agricultural and family planning innovations." Paper presented at the American Sociological Association, Miami Beach, August 30, 1966.

Rogers, E. M. and J. D. Stanfield.
1966 "Adoption and diffusion of new products: emerging generalizations and hypotheses," unpublished paper presented at the Conference on the Application of Sciences to Marketing Management, Purdue University.

Russett, B. M.
1969 "Methodological and theoretical schools in international relations." Unpublished manuscript, Yale University.

Stevens, R. E.
1953 "Characteristics of subject literatures." ACRL Monographs, No. 6:10–21.

Stoddart, D. R.
1967 "Growth and structure of geography." Transactions and Papers of the Institute of British Geographers, Publication No. 41:1–19.

Swanson, D. R.
1966 "Scientific journals and information services of the future." American Psychologist 21 (November):1008.

Vachon, D.
1969 "Differential Productivity of Colleague Groups at Two Research Frontiers." Unpublished Ph.D. dissertation, Georgetown University.

Weinstein, N.
undated "The development of theoretical cosmology, 1963–1965; or 'Que sçais-je?'" Unpublished manuscript.

Yinger, J. M.
1957 Religion, Society and the Individual. New York: Macmillan.

From Jeffrey Travers and Stanley Milgram,
  Sociometry 32, 425-443 (1969), by permission.

An Experimental Study of the Small World Problem*

JEFFREY TRAVERS

Harvard University

AND

STANLEY MILGRAM

The City University of New York

Arbitrarily selected individuals (N=296) in Nebraska and Boston are asked to generate acquaintance chains to a target person in Massachusetts, employing "the small world method" (Milgram, 1967). Sixty-four chains reach the target person. Within this group the mean number of intermediaries between starters and targets is 5.2. Boston starting chains reach the target person with fewer intermediaries than those starting in Nebraska; subpopulations in the Nebraska group do not differ among themselves. The funneling of chains through sociometric "stars" is noted, with 48 per cent of the chains passing through three persons before reaching the target. Applications of the method to studies of large scale social structure are discussed.

The simplest way of formulating the small world problem is "what is the probability that any two people, selected arbitrarily from a large population, such as that of the United States, will know each other?" A more interesting formulation, however, takes account of the fact that, while persons a and z may not know each other directly, they may share one or more mutual acquaintances; that is, there may exist a set of individuals, B, (consisting of individuals $b_1, b_2 \ldots b_n$) who know both a and z and thus link them to one another. More generally, a and z may be connected not by any single common acquaintance, but by a series of such intermediaries, a-b-c- $\ldots$ -y-z; i.e., a knows b (and no one else in the chain); b knows a and in addition knows c, c in turn knows d, etc.

To elaborate the problem somewhat further, let us represent the popula-

* The study was carried out while both authors were at Harvard University, and was financed by grants from the Milton Fund and from the Harvard Laboratory of Social Relations. Mr. Joseph Gerver provided invaluable assistance in summarizing and criticizing the mathematical work discussed in this paper.

179

tion of the United States by a partially connected set of points. Let each point represent a person, and let a line connecting two points signify that the two individuals know each other. (Knowing is here assumed to be symmetric: if a knows b then b knows a. Substantively, "knowing" is used to denote a mutual relationship; other senses of the verb, e.g. knowing about a famous person, are excluded.) The structure takes the form of a cluster of roughly 200 million points with a complex web of connections among them. The acquaintance chains described above appear as pathways along connected line segments. Unless some portion of the population is totally isolated from the rest, such that no one in that subgroup knows anyone outside it, there must be at least one chain connecting any two people in the population. In general there will be many such pathways, of various lengths, between any two individuals.

In view of such a structure, one way of refining our statement of the small world problem is the following: given two individuals selected randomly from the population, what is the probability that the minimum number of intermediaries required to link them is 0, 1, 2, . . . k? (Alternatively, one might ask not about the minimum chains between pairs of people, but mean chain lengths, median chain lengths, etc.)

Perhaps the most direct way of attacking the small world problem is to trace a number of real acquaintance chains in a large population. This is the technique of the study reported in this paper. The phrase "small world" suggests that social networks are in some sense tightly woven, full of unexpected strands linking individuals seemingly far removed from one another in physical or social space. The principal question of the present investigation was whether such interconnectedness could be demonstrated experimentally.

The only example of mathematical treatment dealing directly with the small world problem is the model provided by Ithiel Pool and Manfred Kochen (unpublished manuscript). Pool and Kochen assume a population of N individuals, each of whom knows, on the average, n others in the population. They attempt to calculate P_k, the probability that two persons chosen randomly from the group can be linked by a chain of k intermediaries. Their basic model takes the form of a "tree" or geometric progression. Using an estimate of average acquaintance volume provided by Gurevitch (1961), they deduce that two intermediaries will be required to link typical pairs of individuals in a population of 200 million. Their model does not take account of social structure. Instead of allowing acquaintance nets to define the boundaries of functioning social groups, Pool and Kochen must, for the purposes of their model, conceive of society as being partitioned into a number of hypothetical groups, each with identical populations. They are then able to devise a way to predict chain lengths within and between such hypothesized groups.

In an empirical study related to the small world problem Rapoport and Horvath (1961) examined sociometric nets in a junior high school of 861 students. The authors asked students to name in order their eight best friends within the school. They then traced the acquaintance chains created by the students' choices. Rapoport was interested in connectivity, i.e. the fraction of the total population that would be contacted by tracing friendship choices from an arbitrary starting population of nine individuals. Rapoport and his associates (Rapoport and Horvath, 1961; Foster et al., 1963; Rapoport, 1953; 1963) have developed a mathematical model to describe this tracing procedure. The model takes as a point of departure random nets constructed in the following manner: a small number of points is chosen from a larger population and a fixed number of "axones" is extended from each of these points to a set of target points chosen at random from the population. The same fixed number of axones is then extended from each of the target points to a set of second generation target points, and the process is repeated indefinitely. A target point is said to be of the tth remove if it is of the tth generation and no lower generation. Rapoport then suggests a formula for calculating the fraction, P_t, of the population points which are targets of the tth remove. He is also able to extend the formula to nonrandom nets, such as those created in the Rapoport and Horvath empirical study, by introducing a number of "biases" into the random net model. Rapoport shows that two parameters, obtainable from the data, are sufficient to produce a close fit between the predictions of the model and the empirical outcome of the trace procedure.[1]

Rapoport's model was designed to describe a trace procedure quite different from the one employed in the present study; however, it has some relation to the small world problem. If we set the number of axones traced from a given individual equal to the total number of acquaintances of an average person, the Rapoport model predicts the total fraction of the population potentially traceable at each remove from the start, serving precisely the aims of the model of Pool and Kochen. (It should, however, be noted that Rapoport's model deals with asymmetric nets, and it would be difficult to modify the model to deal with general symmetric nets, which characterize the small world phenomenon.)

Despite the goodness of fit between Rapoport's model and the data from

---

[1] There is additional empirical evidence (Fararo and Sunshine, 1964) and theoretical support (Abelson, 1967) for the assumption that two parameters are sufficient to describe the Rapoport tracing procedure, i.e. that more complex biases have minimal effects on connectivity in friendship nets.

two large sociograms, there are unsolved problems in the model, as Rapoport himself and others (Fararo and Sunshine, 1964) have pointed out. The Pool-Kochen model involves assumptions difficult for an empirically oriented social scientist to accept, such as the assumption that society may be partitioned into a set of groups alike in size and in internal and external connectedness. In the absence of empirical data, it is difficult to know which simplifying assumptions are likely to be fruitful. On the other hand, with regard to the empirical study of Rapoport and Horvath, the fact that the total population employed was small, well-defined, and homogeneous leaves open many questions about the nature of acquaintance nets in the larger society.[2] An empirical study of American society as a whole may well uncover phenomena of interest both in their own right and as constraints on the nature of any correct mathematical model of the structure of large-scale acquaintanceship nets.

PROCEDURE

This paper follows the procedure for tracing acquaintance chains devised and first tested by Milgram (1967). The present paper introduces an experimental variation in this procedure, by varying "starting populations"; it also constitutes a first technical report on the small world method.

The procedure may be summarized as follows: an arbitrary "target person" and a group of "starting persons" were selected, and an attempt was made to generate an acquaintance chain from each starter to the target. Each starter was provided with a document and asked to begin moving it by mail toward the target The document described the study, named the target, and asked the recipient to become a participant by sending the document on. It was stipulated that the document could be sent only to a first-name acquaintance of the sender. The sender was urged to choose the recipient in such a way as to advance the progress of the document toward the target; several items of information about the target were provided to guide each new sender in his choice of recipient. Thus, each document made its way along an acquaintance chain of indefinite length, a chain which would end only when it reached the target or when someone along the way declined to participate. Certain basic information, such as age, sex and occupation, was collected for each participant.

---

[2] In addition to the Pool-Kochen and Rapoport work, there are numerous other studies of social network phenomena tangentially related to the small-world problem. Two well-known examples are Bailey's *The Mathematical Theory of Epidemics* and Coleman, Katz and Menzel's *Medical Innovation*. Bailey's work deals with diffusion from a structured source, rather than with convergence on a target from a set of scattered sources, as in the present study. The Coleman, Katz and Menzel study deals with an important substantive correlate of acquaintance nets, namely information diffusion.

We were interested in discovering some of the internal structural features of chains and in making comparisons across chains as well. Among the questions we hoped to answer were the following: How many of the starters —if any—would be able to establish contact with the target through a chain of acquaintances? How many intermediaries would be required to link the ends of the chains? What form would the distribution of chain lengths take? What degree of homogeneity in age, sex, occupation, and other characteristics of participants would be observed within chains? How would complete chains differ from incomplete on these and other dimensions?

An additional comparison was set up by using three distinct starting subpopulations. The target person was a Boston stockbroker; two of the starting populations were geographically removed from him, selected from the state of Nebraska. A third population was selected from the Boston area. One of the Nebraska groups consisted of bluechip stockholders, while the second Nebraska group and the Boston group were "randomly" selected and had no special access to the investment business. By comparisons across these groups we hoped to assess the relative effects of geographical distance and of contact with the target's occupational group. Moreover we hoped to establish a strategy for future experimental extensions of the procedure, in which the sociological characteristics of the starting and target populations would be systematically varied in order to expose features of social structure.

The primary research questions, then, involved a test of the feasibility and fruitfulness of the method as well as an attempt to discover some elementary features of real social nets. Several experimental extensions of the procedure are already underway. A more detailed description of the current method is given in the following sections.

PARTICIPANTS. *Starting Population.* The starting population for the study was comprised of 296 volunteers. Of these, 196 were residents of the state of Nebraska, solicited by mail. Within this group, 100 were systematically chosen owners of blue-chip stocks; these will be designated "Nebraska stockholders" throughout this paper. The rest were chosen from the population at large; these will be termed the "Nebraska random" group. In addition to the two Nebraska groups, 100 volunteers were solicited through an advertisement in a Boston newspaper (the "Boston random" group). Each member of the starting population became the first link in a chain of acquaintances directed at the target person.

Intermediaries. The remaining participants in the study, who numbered 453 in all, were in effect solicited by other participants; they were acquaintances selected by previous participants as people likely to extend the chain toward the target. Participation was voluntary. Participants were not paid, nor was money or other reward offered as incentive for completion of chains.

THE DOCUMENT. The 296 initial volunteers were sent a document which was the principal tool of the investigation.[3] The document contained:

a. a description of the study, a request that the recipient become a participant, and a set of rules for participation;
b. the name of the target person and selected information concerning him;
c. a roster, to which each participant was asked to affix his name;
d. a stack of fifteen business reply cards asking information about each participant.

Rules for Participation. The document contained the following specific instructions to participants:

a. Add your name to the roster so that the next person who receives this folder will know whom it came from.
b. Detach one postcard from the bottom of this folder. Fill it out and return it to Harvard University. No stamp is needed. The postcard is very important. It allows us to keep track of the progress of the folder as it moves toward the target person.
c. If you know the target person on a personal basis, mail this folder directly to him (her). Do this only if you have previously met the target person and know each other on a first name basis.
d. If you do not know the target person on a personal basis, do not try to contact him directly. Instead, mail this folder to a personal acquaintance who is more likely than you to know the target person. You may send the booklet on to a friend, relative, or acquaintance, but it must be someone you know personally.

Target Person. The target person was a stockholder who lives in Sharon, Massachusetts, a suburb of Boston, and who works in Boston proper. In addition to his name, address, occupation and place of employment, participants were told his college and year of graduation, his military service dates, and his wife's maiden name and hometown. One question under investigation was the type of information which people would use in reaching the target.

Roster. The primary function of the roster was to prevent "looping," i.e., to prevent people from sending the document to someone who had already received it and sent it on. An additional function of the roster was to motivate people to continue the chains. It was hoped that a list of prior participants, including a personal acquaintance who had sent the document to

[3] A photographic reproduction of this experimental document appears in Milgram, 1969: 110–11.

the recipient, would create willingness on the part of those who received the document to send it on.

Tracer Cards. Each participant was asked to return to us a business reply card giving certain information about himself and about the person to whom he sent the document. The name, address, age sex and occupation of the sender and sender's spouse were requested, as were the name, address, sex and age of the recipient. In addition, the nature of the relationship between sender and recipient—whether they were friends, relatives, business associates, etc.—was asked. Finally, participants were asked why they had selected the particular recipient of the folder.

The business reply cards enabled us to keep running track of the progress of each chain. Moreover, they assured us of getting information even from chains which were not completed, allowing us to make comparisons between complete and incomplete chains.

RESULTS

COMPLETIONS. 217 of the 296 starting persons actually sent the document on to friends. Any one of the documents could reach the target person only if the following conditions were met: 1) recipients were sufficiently motivated to send the document on to the next link in the chain; 2) participants were able to adopt some strategy for moving the documents closer to the target (this condition further required that the given information allow them to select the next recipient in a manner that increased the probability of contacting the target); 3) relatively short paths were in fact required to link starters and target (otherwise few chains would remain active long enough to reach completion). Given these contingencies, there was serious doubt in the mind of the investigators whether any of the documents, particularly those starting in an area remote from the target person, could move through interlocking acquaintance networks and converge on him. The actual outcome was that 64 of the folders, or 29 per cent of those sent out by starting persons, eventually reached the target.

DISTRIBUTION OF CHAIN LENGTHS. *Complete Chains.* Figure 1 shows the frequency distribution of lengths of the completed chains. "Chain length" is here defined as the number of intermediaries required to link starters and target. The mean of the distribution is 5.2 links.

It was unclear on first inspection whether the apparent drop in frequency at the median length of five links was a statistical accident, or whether the distribution was actually bimodal. Further investigation revealed that the summary relation graphed in Figure 1 concealed two underlying distributions: when the completed chains were divided into those which approached the target through his hometown and those which approached him via

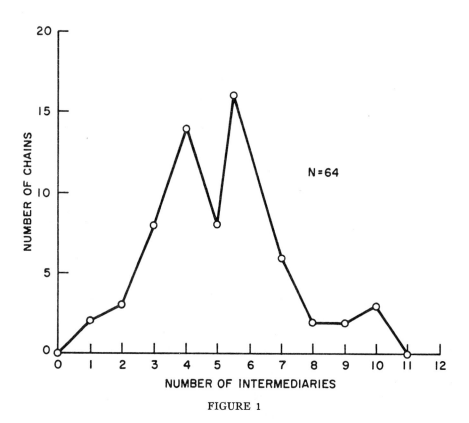

FIGURE 1

Lengths of Completed Chains

Boston business contracts, two distinguishable distributions emerged. The mean of the Sharon distribution is 6.1 links, and that of the Boston distribution is 4.6. The difference is significant at a level better than .0005, as assessed by the distribution-free Mann-Whitney U test. (Note that more powerful statistical tests of the significance of differences between means cannot be applied to these data, since those tests assume normality of underlying distributions. The shape of the true or theoretical distribution of lengths of acquaintance chains is precisely what we do not know.)

Qualitatively, what seems to occur is this. Chains which converge on the target principally by using geographic information reach his hometown or the surrounding areas readily, but once there often circulate before entering the target's circle of acquaintances. There is no available information to narrow the field of potential contacts which an individual might have within the town. Such additional information as a list of local organizations

186

of which the target is a member might have provided a natural funnel, facilitating the progress of the document from town to target person. By contrast, those chains which approach the target through occupational channels can take advantage of just such a funnel, zeroing in on him first through the brokerage business, then through his firm.

Incomplete Chains. Chains terminate either through completion or dropout: each dropout results in an incomplete chain. Figure 2 shows the number of chains which dropped out at each "remove" from the starting population. The "0th remove" represents the starting population itself: the "first remove" designates the set of people who received the document directly from members of the starting population. The "second remove" received the document from the starters via one intermediary, the third through two intermediaries, etc. The length of an incomplete chain may be defined as the number of removes from the start at which dropout occurs, or, equivalently, as the number of transmissions of the folder which precede dropout. By this definition, Figure 2 represents a frequency distribution of the lengths of incomplete chains. The mean of the distribution is 2.6 links.

The proportion of chains which drop out at each remove declines as

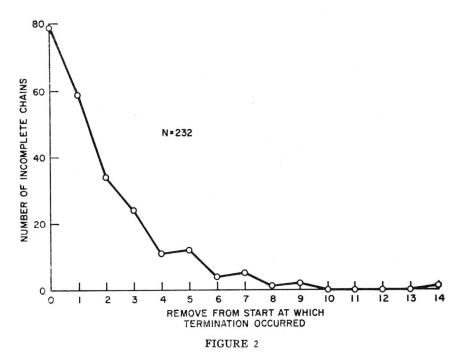

FIGURE 2

Lengths of Incomplete Chains

187

chains grow in length, if that proportion is based on all chains active at each remove (those destined for completion as well as incompletion). About 27 per cent of the 296 folders sent to the starting population are not sent on. Similarly, 27 per cent of the 217 chains actually initiated by the starters die at the first remove. The percentage of dropouts then appears to fall. It also begins to fluctuate, as the total number of chains in circulation grows small, and an increasing proportion of completions further complicates the picture.

It was argued earlier that, in theory, any two people can be linked by at least one acquaintance chain of finite length, barring the existence of totally isolated cliques within the population under study. Yet, incomplete chains are found in our empirical tracing procedure because a certain proportion of those who receive the document do not send it on. It is likely that this occurs for one of two major reasons: 1) individuals are not motivated to participate in the study; 2) they do not know to whom to send the document in order to advance it toward the target.

For purposes of gauging the significance of our numerical results, it would be useful to know whether the dropouts are random or systematic, i.e., whether or not they are related to a chain's prognosis for rapid completion. It seems possible, for example, that dropouts are precisely those people who are least likely to be able to advance the document toward the target. If so, the distribution of actual lengths of completed chains would understate the true social distance between starters and target by an unknown amount. (Even if dropouts are random, the observed distribution understates the true distribution, but by a potentially calculable amount.) We can offer some evidence, however, that this effect is not powerful.

First, it should be clear that, though people may drop out because they see little possibility that any of their acquaintances can advance the folder toward the target, their subjective estimates are irrelevant to the question just raised. Such subjective estimates may account for individual decisions not to participate; they do not tell us whether chains that die in fact would have been longer than others had they gone to completion. People have poor intuitions concerning the lengths of acquaintance chains. Moreover, people can rarely see beyond their own acquaintances; it is hard to guess the circles in which friends of friends—not to mention people even more remotely connected to oneself—may move.

More direct evidence that dropouts may be treated as "random" can be gleaned from the tracer cards. It will be recalled that each participant was asked for information not only about himself but also about the person to whom he sent the document. Thus some data were available even for dropouts, namely age, sex, the nature of their relationship to the people

188

TABLE 1

Activity of Chains at Each Remove

	All Chains					Incomplete Chains Only		
Remove	Chains Reaching this Remove	Completions at this Remove	Dropouts at this Remove	Per cent Dropouts	Remove	Chains Reaching this Remove	Dropouts at this Remove	Per cent Dropouts
0	296	0	79	27	0	232	79	34
1	217	0	59	27	1	153	59	39
2	158	2	34	22	2	94	34	36
3	122	3	24	20	3	60	24	40
4	95	8	11	12	4	36	11	31
5	76	14	12	16	5	25	12	48
6	50	8	4	8	6	13	4	31
7	38	16	5	13	7	9	5	55
8	17	6	1	6	8	4	1	25
9	10	2	2	20	9	3	2	67
10	6	2	0	0	10	1	0	0
11	4	3	0	0	11	1	0	0
12	1	0	0	0	12	1	0	0
13	1	0	0	0	13	1	0	0
14	1	0	1	100	14	1	1	100

preceding them in the chain, and the reason the dropout had been selected to receive the document. These four variables were tabulated for dropouts versus non-dropouts. None of the resulting contingency tables achieved the .05 level of statistical significance by chi-square test; we are therefore led to accept the null hypothesis of no difference between the two groups, at least on this limited set of variables. Of course, a definitive answer to the question of whether dropouts are really random must wait until the determinants of chain length are understood, or until a way is found to force all chains to completion.[4]

SUBPOPULATION COMPARISONS. A possible paradigm for future research using the tracing procedure described here involves systematic variation of the relationship between the starting and target populations. One such study, using Negro and White starting and target groups, has already been completed by Korte and Milgram (in press). In the present study, which involved only a single target person, three starting populations were used (Nebraska random, Nebraska stockholders, and Boston random.) The relevant experimental questions were whether the proportion of completed chains or mean chain lengths would vary as a function of starting population.

Chain Length. Letters from the Nebraska subpopulations had to cover a geographic distance of about 1300 miles in order to reach the target, whereas letters originating in the Boston group almost all started within 25 miles of his home and/or place of work. Since social proximity depends in part on geographic proximity, one might readily predict that complete chains originating in the Boston area would be shorter than those originating in Nebraska. This presumption was confirmed by the data. As Table 2 shows, chains originating with the Boston random group showed a mean length of 4.4 intermediaries between starters and target, as opposed to a mean length of 5.7 intermediaries for the Nebraska random group. ($p \leqq .001$ by

---

[4] Professor Harrison White of Harvard University has developed a technique for adjusting raw chain length data to take account of the dropout problem. His method assumes that dropouts are "random," in the following sense. An intermediary who knows the target sends him the folder, completing the chain, with probability 1. Otherwise, an intermediary throws away the folder with fixed probability $1-a$, or sends it on with probability a. If sent on, there is a probability Q_i (which depends on number of removes from the origin) that the next intermediary knows the target. The data is consistent with a value for a of approximately 0.75, independent of remove from the origin, and hence with a "random" dropout rate of 25 per cent. The limited data further suggest that Q_i grows in a "staircase" pattern from zero (at zero removes from the starting population) to approximately one-third at six removes, remaining constant thereafter. Based on these values, the hypothetical curve of completions with no dropouts resembles the observed curve shifted upward; the median length of completed chains rises from 5 to 7, but no substantial alteration is required in conclusions drawn from the raw data.

TABLE 2

Lengths of Completed Chains

Population	Frequency Distribution — Number of Intermediaries												
	0	1	2	3	4	5	6	7	8	9	10	11	Total
Nebraska Random	0	0	0	1	4	3	6	2	0	1	1	0	18
Nebraska Stock	0	0	0	3	6	4	6	2	1	1	1	0	24
Boston Random	0	2	3	4	4	1	4	2	1	0	1	0	22
All	0	2	3	8	14	8	16	6	2	2	3	0	64

Means	
Starting Population	Mean Chain Length
Nebraska Random	5.7
Nebraska Stockholders	5.4
All Nebraska	5.5
Boston Random	4.4
All	5.2

a one-tailed Mann-Whitney U test.) Chain length thus proved sensitive to one demographic variable—place of residence of starters and target.

The Nebraska stockholder group was presumed to have easy access to contacts in the brokerage business. Because the target person was a stockbroker, chains originating in this group were expected to reach the target more efficiently than chains from the Nebraska random group. The chain-length means for the two groups, 5.7 intermediaries for the random sample and 5.4 for the stockholders, differed in the expected direction, but the difference was not statistically significant by the Mann-Whitney test. The stockholders used the brokerage business as a communication channel more often than did the random group; 60.7 per cent of all the participants in chains originating with the stockholder group reported occupations connected with finance, while 31.8 per cent of participants in chains originating in the Nebraska random group were so classified.

Proportion of Completions. As indicated in Table 3, the proportions of chains completed for the Nebraska random, Nebraska stockholder, and Boston subpopulations were 24 per cent, 31 per cent and 35 per cent, respectively. Although the differences are not statistically significant, there is a weak tendency for higher completion rates to occur in groups where mean length of completed chains is shorter. This result deserves brief discussion.

Let us assume that the dropout rate is constant at each remove from the start. If, for example, the dropout rate were 25 per cent then any chain would have a 75 per cent probability of reaching one link, $(.75)^2$ of reaching two links, etc. Thus, the longer a chain needed to be in order to reach completion, the less likely that the chain would survive long enough to run its full course. In this case, however, chain-length differences among the three groups were not sufficiently large to produce significant differences in completion rate. Moreover, if the dropout rate declines as chains grow long, such a decrease would off-set the effect just discussed and weaken the observed inverse relation between chain length and proportion of completions.

TABLE 3

Proportion of Completions for Three Starting Populations

	Starting Population							
	Nebraska Random		Nebraska Stock.		Boston		Total	
Complete	18	(24%)	24	(31%)	22	(35%)	64	(29%)
Incomplete	58	(76%)	54	(69%)	41	(65%)	153	(71%)
	76	(100%)	78	(100%)	63	(100%)	217	(100%)

$\chi^2=2.17$, df.=2, $p>.3$, N.S.

COMMON CHANNELS. As chains converge on the target, common channels appear—that is, some intermediaries appear in more than one chain. Figure 3 shows the pattern of convergence. The 64 letters which reached the target were sent by a total of 26 people. Sixteen, fully 25 per cent, reached the target through a single neighbor. Another 10 made contact through a single business associate, and 5 through a second business associate. These three "penultimate links" together accounted for 48 per cent of the total completions. Among the three, an interesting division of labor appears. Mr. G,

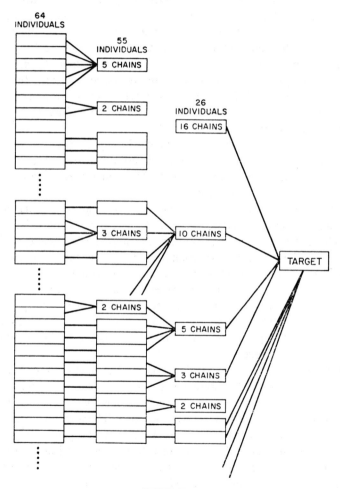

FIGURE 3

Common Paths Appear as Chains Converge on the Target

who accounted for 16 completions, is a clothing merchant in the target's hometown of Sharon; Mr. G funnelled toward the target those chains which were advancing on the basis of the target's place of residence. Twenty-four chains reached the target from his hometown; Mr. G accounted for $\frac{2}{3}$ of those completions. All the letters which reached Mr. G came from residents of Sharon. By contrast, Mr. D and Mr. P, who accounted for 10 and 5 completions, respectively, were contacted by people scattered around the Boston area, and in several cases, by people living in other cities entirely. On the other hand, whereas Mr. G received the folder from Sharon residents in a wide variety of occupations, D and P received it almost always from stockbrokers. A scattering of names appear two or three times on the list of penultimate links; seventeen names appear once each.

Convergence appeared even before the penultimate link. Going one step further back, to people two removes from the target, we find that the 64 chains passed through 55 individuals. One man, Mr. B, appeared 5 times, and on all occasions sent the document to Mr. G. Other individuals appeared two or three times each.

ADDITIONAL CHARACTERISTICS OF CHAINS. Eighty-six per cent of the participants sent the folder to persons they described as friends and acquaintances; 14 per cent sent it to relatives. The same percentages had been observed in an earlier pilot study.

Data on patterns of age, sex and occupation support the plausible hypothesis that participants select recipients from a pool of individuals similar to themselves. The data on age support the hypothesis unequivocally; the data on sex and occupation are complicated by the characteristics of the target and the special requirement of establishing contact with him.

Age was bracketed into ten-year categories and the ages of those who sent the document tabled against the ages of those to whom they sent it. On inspection the table showed a strong tendency to cluster around the diagonal, and a chi-square test showed the association to be significant at better than the .001 level.

Similarly, the sex of each sender was tabled against the sex of the corresponding recipient. Men were ten times more likely to send the document to other men than to women, while women were equally likely to send the folder to males as to females ($p < .001$). These results were affected by the fact that the target was male. In an earlier pilot study using a female target, both men and women were three times as likely to send the document to members of the same sex as to members of the opposite sex. Thus there appear to be three tendencies governing the sex of the recipient: (1) there is a tendency to send the document to someone of one's own sex, but (2) women are more likely to cross sex lines than men, and (3) there is a tendency to send the document to someone of the same sex as the target person.

The occupations reported by participants were rated on two components—one of social status and one of "industry" affiliation, that is, the subsector of the economy with which the individual would be likely to deal. The coding system was *ad hoc,* designed to fit the occupational titles supplied by participants. Tabling the status and "industry" ratings for all senders of the document against those of respective recipients, we observed a strong tendency for people to select recipients similar to themselves on both measures ($p<.001$ for both tables). However, the strength of the relationship for industry seemed to be largely due to a tendency for the folder to stay within the finance field once it arrived there, obviously because the target was affiliated with that field. Moreover, the participants in the study were a heavily middle-class sample, and the target was himself a member of that class. Thus there was no need for the document to leave middle-class circles in progressing from starters to target.

When separate contingency tables were constructed for complete and incomplete chains, the above results were obtained for both tables. Similarly, when separate tables were constructed for chains originating in the 3 starting populations, the findings held up in all 3 tables. Thus, controlling for completion of chains or for starting population did not affect the finding of demographic homogeneity within chains.

CONCLUSIONS

The contribution of the study lies in the use of acquaintance chains to extend an individual's contacts to a geographically and socially remote target, and in the sheer size of the population from which members of the chains were drawn. The study demonstrated the feasibility of the "small world" technique, and took a step toward demonstrating, defining and measuring inter-connectedness in a large society.

The theoretical machinery needed to deal with social networks is still in its infancy. The empirical technique of this research has two major contributions to make to the development of that theory. First, it sets an upper bound on the minimum number of intermediaries required to link widely separated Americans. Since subjects cannot always foresee the most efficient path to a target, our trace procedure must inevitably produce chains longer than those generated by an accurate theoretical model which takes full account of all paths emanating from an individual. The mean number of intermediaries observed in this study was somewhat greater than five;

additional research (by Korte and Milgram) indicates that this value is quite stable, even when racial crossover is introduced. Both the magnitude and stability of the parameter need to be accounted for. Second, the study has uncovered several phenomena which future models should explain. In particular, the convergence of communication chains through common individuals is an important feature of small world nets, and it should be accounted for theoretically.

There are many additional lines of empirical research that may be examined with the small world method. As suggested earlier, one general paradigm for research is to vary the characteristics of the starting person and the target. Further, one might systematically vary the information provided about the target in order to determine, on the psychological side, what strategies people employ in reaching a distant target, and on the sociological side, what specific variables are critical for establishing contact between people of given characteristics.

REFERENCES

Abelson, R. P.
  1967   "Mathematical models in social psychology." Pp. 1–54 in L. Berkowitz (ed.) Advances in Experimental Social Psychology, Vol. III. New York: Academic Press.
Bailey, N. T. J.
  1957   The Mathematical Theory of Epidemics. New York: Hafner.
Coleman, J. S., E. Katz and H. Menzel
  1966   Medical Innovation: A Diffusion Study. Indianapolis: Bobbs-Merrill.
Fararo, T. J. and M. H. Sunshine
  1964   A Study of a Biased Friendship Net. Syracuse: Youth Development Center, Syracuse University.
Foster, C. C., A. Rapoport and C. J. Orwant
  1963   "A study of a large sociogram II. Elimination of free parameters." Behavioral Science 8(January):56–65.
Gurevitch, M.
  1961   The Social Structure of Acquaintanceship Networks. Unpublished doctoral dissertation, Cambridge: M.I.T.
Korte, C. and S. Milgram
           Acquaintance Links Between White and Negro Populations: Application of the Small World Method. Journal of Personality and Social Psychology (in press).
Milgram, S.
  1967   "The small world problem." Psychology Today 1(May):61–67.
  1969   "Interdisciplinary thinking and the small world problem." Pp. 103–120 in Muzafer Sherif and Carolyn W. Sherif (eds.) Interdisciplinary Relationships in the Social Sciences. Chicago: Aldine Publishing Company.

Pool, I. and M. Kochen
    A Non-Mathematical Introduction to a Mathematical Model. Undated mimeo. Cambridge: M.I.T.

Rapoport, A.
    1953   "Spread of information through a population with socio-structural bias." Bulletin of Mathematical Biophysics 15(December):523–543.
    1963   "Mathematical models of social interaction." Pp. 493–579 in R. D. Luce, R. R. Bush and E. Galanter (eds.) Handbook of Mathematical Psychology, Vol. II. New York: John Wiley and Sons.

Rapoport, A. and W. J. Horvath
    1961   "A study of a large sociogram." Behavioral Science 6(October):279–291.

STRUCTURAL BALANCE, MECHANICAL SOLIDARITY, AND INTERPERSONAL RELATIONS

JAMES A. DAVIS

ABSTRACT

Balance theory, a theoretical system developed by Cartwright and Harary to formalize concepts set forth by Heider, is used with slight modifications to restate fifty-six sociological and social-psychological propositions from the writings of Berelson, Lazarsfeld, and McPhee; Coleman; Davis; Durkheim; Festinger; Fiedler; Homans; Katz and Lazarsfeld; Lazarsfeld and Merton; Lipset, Trow, and Coleman; Merton and Kitt; and Stouffer *et al.* The propositions are grouped under (*a*) *Person, Other,* and *X*, (*b*) group structure, (*c*) changes in attitudes and opinions, and (*d*) values.

Almost seventy-five years ago Durkheim wrote: "Social life comes from a double source, the likenesses of consciences and the division of social labor" (5, p. 226). Less than a year ago, George Caspar Homans wrote:

The first and most obvious thing to be said (about conformity) is that if members of a group are to resemble one another in their behavior, some of them must find this similarity valuable or rewarding. Similarity is not always rewarding. . . . The division of labor means differences in labor, and it often pays off. But we are now dealing with the case in which similarities rather than differences are valuable [11, pp. 114–15].

The powerful effects of similarity and difference between people as explanatory principles in analyzing human behavior have not, of course, gone unnoticed in the interim. Of the two, however, similarity has received more attention, and it is the burden of this paper that the point has been reached where it is possible to spell out a theory of similarity (what Durkheim would call mechanical solidarity) that organizes a number of principles and hypotheses in recent research.

In particular, the ideas presented here are culled from five clusters of authors and studies: (*a*) a group of social psychologists mostly influenced by Gestalt thinking in general and Kurt Lewin in particular (2, 6–9); (*b*) George Homans' two theoretical books (10, 11); (*c*) a series of studies by sociologists associated with Columbia University and the Bureau of Applied Social Research (1, 3, 12, 13, 15); (*d*) the theory of relative deprivation (4, 16, 17); and (*e*) Durkheim (5).

In order to avoid the appearance of acute megalomania it must be made clear what this essay is and what it is not. On one hand, the author makes no claim of originality or profundity, his belief being that almost all the conclusions either can be found in the works cited or are familiar principles of human behavior. On the other hand, there is no claim that the proposed theory subsumes, integrates, or codifies any or all of these works. Running through the writings mentioned above are a number of concepts and propositions that can be restated (with some inevitable distortion) in a common language and in terms of a small number of postulates. Some of these concepts and propositions are: structural balance (2, 9), magnitude of dissonance (6), abilities and opinions (7), liking and cognitive unit formation (2, 9), sentiments (10, 11), constraint versus warm friendly relations (10), pressures toward uniformity (6), social comparisons (7), distributive justice (11), subgroup formation (4), relative deprivation (4, 16, 17), choice of reference group (16), assumed similarity (8), cross-pressures (1), polarization of social opinions (3), attachments (10), the effects of shop size on social relations (15), friendship

199

(10, 13), self-selected and involuntary social relations (15), mechanical solidarity (5), "homophily" and "heterophily" (13).

The remainder of this paper is an exposition of the theory organized as follows: (*a*) discussion of the formal language and concepts, (*b*) major postulates, (*c*) derived propositions about interpersonal relations, (*d*) derived propositions about group structure, (*e*) derived propositions about attitudes and values.

This essay should be considered as an attempt at deductive theoretical analysis, not as a review of the literature.

THE THEORY

The theory submitted here consists of three parts: (*a*) a formal apparatus combining graph theory and elementary algebra, (*b*) an interpretation of the formal concepts in terms of social psychological concepts, and (*c*) a set of postulates that provide the basic propositions. With some slight modifications, the theory is that developed by Cartwright and Harary (2).

THE P-O-X EQUATION

The formal apparatus of the theory can be expressed in eight definitions:

Def. 1. A linear graph, or briefly, a *graph*, consists of a finite collection of *points, A, B, C* . . . , together with all unordered pairs of distinct points. Each of these pairs (e.g., *AB*) is called a *line*.
Def. 2. Lines may vary in *type* (or "kind" of relationship) and *sign* (plus or minus) or *numerical value*.
Def. 3. The *net value* of a line of two or more types is the sum of the values for each type.
Def. 4. A *path* is a collection of lines of the form *AB, BC, . . . DE*, where the points *A, B, C, D,* and *E* are distinct.
Def. 5. A *cycle* consists of the above path together with the line *EA*.
Def. 6. The *value of a cycle* is the product of the net values of its lines.
Def. 7. A cycle with a positive value is *balanced*, a cycle with a negative value is *unbalanced*.
Def. 8. The *net value of a graph* at point *P* is

the sum of the values of the cycles in which *P* is a point.

Definitions 1, 2, 4, 5, 6, and 7 are taken almost literally from Cartwright and Harary.[1]

The only important difference in our theory is the addition of definitions 3 and 8, which concern multiple types of lines and/or multiple cycles. The assumption is that each is a sum (not a product) and that net values of lines are to be "calculated" prior to the calculation of the values of the cycle. Thus, different cycles must include different points.

So far, the apparatus presented is devoid of any content, and the definitions given could apply to people, switching circuits, messages, kinship relations, etc. Again following Cartwright and Harary, together with Heider (2, 9), let us provide interpretations for points.

Def. 9. *Person (P)* is the individual whose behavior is predicted by the theory, the point whose net value is being considered.
Def. 10. *Other (O)* is some additional individual.
Def. 11. *X* is some value or social object, sometimes a third individual.

Thus, in the analysis of voting, *P* might be a particular voter, *O* might be Person's best friend, and *X* might be a candidate or political party.

Our interpretations of lines are as follows:

Def 12. *Liking:*
    This refers to a person's evaluation of something, as when Person likes or admires, approves, rejects, or condemns [adapted from 9, p. 200].
Def. 13. *Unit Formation:*
    "In addition, there is a unit relation . . . the parts of such units are perceived as belonging together in a specially close way. But also two (or

[1] The reader who is unfamiliar with the theory will find a very clear exposition in their article, which is reprinted in Dorwin Cartwright and Alvin Zander, *Group Dynamics* (2d ed.; Evanston, Ill.: Row, Peterson & Co., 1960).

more) separate entities can form a unit. The two entities may be related through similarity, causality, ownership, or other unit-forming characteristics" [9, pp. 200–201].[2]

In order to shift from a language to a theory it is necessary to state the fundamental propositions or postulates from which the specific inferences or hypotheses of the theory will be drawn.

POSTULATE I: People prefer positive net values.
    a) If possible, people will act to shift the net value of their cycles from negative to positive or from a positive to a greater positive value.
    b) Low values are associated with feelings of distress, tension, discomfort, etc. The lower the value, the greater the distress (or dissonance).

POSTULATE II: Liking has a positive value; its opposite, disliking, has a negative value; indifference has a value of zero.

POSTULATE III: Unit formation has a positive value; its opposite, the segregation relationship, has a negative value.

Although put in our words, these too are quite close to the basic assumptions in Heider and Cartwright and Harary. The idea also has a partial overlap with Festinger's concept of dissonance (6), although Festinger's concept is more general. We will use "unbalanced" and "dissonant" as synonyms in our exposition, although there is more to dissonance than sheer structural unbalance.

Although the postulates are designed to place some social psychological flesh on the formal bones of the theory, the principles are rather abstract. The following example may serve to illustrate the theory in concrete terms.

One of the better known case studies in

[2] Definitions 12 and 13 are taken directly from Heider (9).

the marriage and family literature involves the structural imbalance incurred by two Veronese adolescents, Juliet Capulet and Romeo Montague. Although their families are bitter enemies, the two fall in love, and in Act II, Scene 2, Juliet muses, "O Romeo, Romeo! wherefore art thou Romeo? . . . 'Tis but thy name that is my enemy" . . . etc.

Although the situation perhaps loses some literary value in translation into balance theory, it will serve to illustrate the definitions and postulates outlined above.

The *points* are: *Person* (Juliet), *Other* (Romeo), and X (the Montague name).

The *lines, types,* and *signs* are: *Person-Other* (liking, positive to say the least);

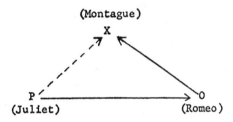

FIG. 1.—The *P-O-X* cycle

Other-X (unit formation, positive . . . i.e., Romeo is strongly associated with his family name); and *Person-X* (liking, negative . . . Juliet hates Montagues).

The *cycle* consists of the three lines connected as shown in Figure 1 (following the convention that positive lines are solid, negative lines dotted).

The *value* of the cycle is *negative* and the cycle is *unbalanced* (a positive times a positive times a negative value gives a negative product).

Juliet is distressed because she would prefer a positive value (Postulate I) and she acts to increase the value of the cycle (Postulate I*a*) by shifting the *O-X* line toward the negative, that is, by dissociating Romeo from his name. If successful this would make the cycle positive (and ruin the play).

201

While graph theory has not been used much by sociological theorists, a case can be made that the ideas of the theory have been widely acepted in sociology in other formulations.

Clearly the Cartwright-Harary-Heider concept of "liking" has an immediate transfer to sociological theories, a number of which say in other words that if P likes O he will tend to prefer or develop relationships with X similar to O's relationship to X.

Homans' concept of "sentiments" in *The Human Group* is practically identical with liking, and we shall see later that his analysis of the relationships among three persons (10, pp. 248–52) is straightforward balance theory, given that "warm friendly relations" are the equivalent of liking, and "constraint" is construed as "disliking."

A number of attitude and opinion theorists associated with Columbia University and the Bureau of Applied Social Research have come at the same idea from the opposite direction—the effect of identical attitudes toward X on P's liking for O.

Coleman writes: "As in an argument between friends, a discussion which begins with disagreement on a point in question often ends with each disliking the other. . . . Conversely, a relationship which begins with two people agreeing in tastes and interests often ends with both liking one another" (3, pp. 10–11).

The authors of *Union Democracy* draw a similar inference: "the less likely he [a worker] is to find people who share his salient values and attitudes . . . the less likely are those relations to develop into close and intimate friendships" (15, p. 157).

One of the most explicit developments of this idea is in Lazarsfeld's and Merton's paper, "Friendship as a Social Process" (13), with its concepts of "homophily" and "heterophily."

While the implicit or explicit acceptance of liking as a factor in PO bonds is almost universal among sociologists, less attention has been given to sociological equivalents of the unit relationship. Heider himself treats it as a very broad category, including any psychological or reality factor that leads to the perception of grouping or segregating certain elements into a figure against the ground of all remaining elements.

When we come to ask what sorts of things should lead P to see himself and *Other* grouped together perceptually, at first glance the possibilities seem endless—membership in the same group, high rates of interaction, identification, etc. While all of these undoubtedly are important, our theory will consider only one factor similarity.

Def. 14. Considering P and one or more *Others*, and a set of social attributes including X, the *similarity* between P and O (symbolized by r_{PO}) is the correlation between P and O over all the attributes other than X.

That is, the similarity between P and O is defined as the correlation between P and O in terms of social attributes other than X.

In more eloquent, but less operational, language this is what Durkheim presumably meant by his concept of envelopment by the collective conscience, which amounts to a correlation between people in terms of social characteristics. The greater the correlation, Durkheim might say, the stronger the collective conscience and the greater the mechanical solidarity. "Solidarity which comes from likeness is at its maximum when the collective conscience completely envelops our whole conscience and coincides at all points with it. But at that moment, our individuality is nil" (5, p. 130).

A more recent, but similar, line of argument for the claim that similarity leads to positive PO bonds comes from writers who have analyzed social comparisons.

Let us begin with the "theory of relative deprivation" (4, 16, 17). The theory originally appeared in the empirical research of *The American Soldier* series, was codified by Merton and Kitt, and has recently been translated into a formal system using the calculus of probabilities (4). The general idea is that men evaluate their own lot by comparison with others. The knotty theoretical question, of course, is "what others?" The authors of *The American Soldier* do not treat the problem directly; in fact, as Merton and Kitt note, they do not even define relative deprivation. Merton and Kitt note three formal possibilities: persons "with whom they were in actual association," persons "of the same status or in the same social category," and persons "who are in some pertinent respect of different status or in a different social category," but they do not opt for one of these to the exclusion of the rest, saying:

This suggests the general hypothesis that some similarity in status attributes between the individual and the reference group must be perceived or imagined, in order for the comparison to occur at all. Once this minimal similarity obtains, other similarities and differences pertinent to the situation will provide the context for shaping evaluations (16, p. 61).

The clearest stand for the similarity hypothesis is taken by Homans in his discussion of "distributive justice" (11). Although in his formal theory the idea is developed from the concept of "investments" and the claim that personal attributes are investments, Homans clearly favors the similarity hypothesis: "the heart of these situations is a comparison. . . . In effect Person asks himself: 'Am I getting as much as other men in some respect like me would get in circumstances in some respect like mine?' " (11, p. 76).

From this we believe it is only a short step to the more general proposition that to the degree that *Person* and *Other* are similar in their general social attributes, *Person* will prefer that their liking or unit relationships regarding a specific attribute be similar (i.e., balanced).

A slightly different position, however, is taken by the writer who has been most explicit on the subject. In Festinger's theory of social comparison processes, he states:

Hypothesis III: The tendency to compare oneself with some other specific person decreases as the difference between his opinion or ability and one's own increases [7, p. 120].

At first glance, it appears that Festinger, too, seems to favor the "similarity hypothesis," but a close reading raises some problems. In our terms, his hypothesis read literally is that P only compares with O if they are relatively or absolutely identical in terms of X. If so, it would be circular to argue that the relationship between P and O affects P's relationship with X if it is also hypothesized that the relationship between P and O is determined by their relationship with X. Logically the outcome—the prediction of a tendency toward balance—could be derived from this hypothesis, but the formulation presents these technical difficulties.

From here on we shall limit our consideration of unit formation to the single factor of objective similarity, although definition 13 is broader than that.

Having reviewed the formal definitions and postulates and having seen that a number of sociological and social psychological writings can be interpreted as accepting these principles, we are now ready to proceed to draw a number of inferences about various forms of social behavior. It should be stressed, however, that we are not proposing a general theory of interpersonal relationships, but rather a number of "other things equal" propositions. In particular, the theory ignores three classes of variables that undoubtedly should be in any general theory.

First, the theory ignores differentiation and the effects of a division of labor—Durkheim's organic solidarity and Homans' exchange process. The benefits that accrue to *Person* from exchange and division of labor are precisely the forces that serve to compensate for or offset tendencies toward balance. We do not believe that the two ideas are contradictory, however. Rather, we believe that it requires some exchange profit to reward *Person* so that he will enter unbalanced situations. Thus, while the essential postulate of balance theory is "Birds of a feather flock together," the essential postulate of exchange theory is "Politics makes strange bedfellows," which are not contradictory if politics is construed as meaning "some mutual benefit."

Second, a general theory of interpersonal relations should include social interaction as a variable. Interaction can be conceived as a third kind of graph variable, and indeed some of Homans' propositions in *The Human Group* can be restated in terms of balance theory assuming that interaction has the status of liking or unit formation. On the other hand, a case can be made that interaction is not a variable at all but a factor intensifying the effects of other variables. This is, in effect, one of the major theoretical shifts in Homans' work between *The Human Group* and *Social Behavior*. Unfortunately, we have not been able to work out a formalization of the role of interaction that does not lead to one or more bizarre theorems and, hence, will ignore variations in interaction.

Third, we shall assume that *P* is unlikely to grossly misperceive *O*'s situation. While there is a large research literature indicating that people can and do maximize balance by distorting or misperceiving others' likes and dislikes, we shall consider only situations of such degree of contact that misperception is, except momentarily, excluded as a solution to the problem of achieving balance. Thus, while it is possible for people to kid themselves about the stands of distant political figures, or transient experimental groups, we shall assume that over the long haul people cannot kid themselves much about their wives, friends, and colleagues.

The inferences are divided into four groups: (*a*) propositions about *Person, Other*, and *X;* (*b*) propositions about group structure; (*c*) propositions about changes in attitudes and opinions; (*d*) propositions about values. Derivations will be numbered and indicated by a capital D (e.g., D1, D2 . . .).

PERSON, OTHER, AND X

D1. The more similar *Person* is to *Other*, the more *Person* will like *Other*.

This proposition, which has been treated perceptually by Fiedler (8) is based on the following reasoning. We have considered *P* and *O* in terms of a set of attributes, one of which is *X*. The selection of *X* being arbitrary, each of the attributes can be an element in a balance cycle involving *P* and *O*. Now the more similar *P* and *O* are in terms of characteristics, the greater the proportion of the cycles with a positive (PX) (OX) product. If, in turn, the (PX) (OX) product is positive, a positive value for (PO) will raise the value of the cycle and thus add to net value. Because liking adds to the positive value of (PO), it follows that similarity leads to liking.

For simplicity, we shall refer to people who are more similar than different, as peers.

Def. 15. *Person* and *Other* are peers if r_{PO} is positive.

D2. The value of *P*'s liking for *O* tends to be the same as the value of *O*'s liking for *P* (i.e., liking tends to be symmetrical).

Because the correlation r_{PO} is symmetrical, its value is the same for *P* and *O*. Hence, if D1 is true for *P* it is true for *O*, and their degrees of liking should be similar. It should be noted that the theory does not state that similarity is a necessary condition for liking, merely a sufficient one. Liking based on "exchange" is not, as noted above, within the purview of the theory.

While it may be elaborating the obvious, we shall have use of the following definition:

Def. 16. If *P* likes *O* and *O* likes *P*, *P* and *O* are friends.
D3. Friends tend to become similar in activities.
D4. Friends tend to become similar in attitudes.

Derivations 3 and 4 are, of course, the obverse of D1, with activities interpreted as unit formation regarding *X* and attitudes as liking regarding *X*. However, some attributes are changeable (habits, tastes, hobbies, etc.) while some (sex, intelligence, age, etc.) are unmodifiable even under pressures to maximize balance. Just as a positive (OX) (PX) value is congruent with liking, liking makes the (PO) bond more positive and is hence congruent with increased similarity in *X*, if *X* is subject to voluntary change.

D5. If *P* and *O* are friends but differ in their degree of liking, the one with the greater degree of liking will imitate the one with the lesser, rather than vice versa.

Although liking tends toward symmetry, it need not be completely so. If there is a discrepancy, the individual with the greater liking has the greater (PO) value, and the greater pressure to seek similarity vis-à-vis *X*, an idea somewhat like Willard Waller's "Principle of Least Interest."

Having stated the basic derivations regarding *P*, *O*, and *X*, we can begin to treat somewhat more complicated situations involving more than two people, first considering the situation where *X* is a person and then the situation where there are two *Others* and a single *X*.

In *The Human Group* Homans develops the proposition, "the relationship between two persons A and B is partly determined by the relationships between A and a third person C, and between B and C" (10, pp. 248–61). If his statements regarding interaction are deleted, the same conclusions can be drawn from balance theory. Thus, rephrasing the proposition on his page 251:

D6. If the relationships between *Person* and *Other* and between *Other* and *X* (where *X* is a third individual) are both marked by dislike, the relationship between *Person* and *X* may be friendly.

By ringing the changes on this formulation, we may add the following:

D7. If *Person* likes *Other* and *Other* dislikes *X*, *Person* will tend to dislike *X*.
D8. If *Person* likes *Other* and *Other* likes *X*, *Person* will tend to like *X*.
D9. If *Person* dislikes *Other* and *Other* likes *X*, *Person* will tend to dislike *X*.

Having considered liking among three people, let us elaborate the situation further by considering three people and *X*.

One of the most famous ideas in communications research is that of "cross-pressures." Like many important ideas in this area it is hard to spell out formally, but a reasonable definition appears in *Voting:*

As we have seen, family and friendship formation and social discussion generally take place among people who are *alike* socially in the politically relevant respects (e.g., class and religion). But not always. When memberships in two strata overlap, small group formations and social discussions spread among people alike in some respects but not in other important ways [1, p. 128].

Berelson *et al.* draw the following conclusions about the consequences of such situations:

An individual who is characterized by any type of cross-pressure is likely to change his mind in the course of the campaign, to make up his mind late, and occasionally, to leave the field and not to vote at all [1, p. 284].

The translation of this into our terms is given by Figure 2, where solid lines indicate positive values and dotted lines, negative values.

To the extent that *Person* has a positive bond to $Other_1$ and also to $Other_2$ (where the *Others* may be social groups) it becomes increasingly difficult for him to adopt a stable attitude toward *X*. If, for instance, he likes *X*, the value of the $(P)(O_1)(X)$

triangle becomes positive, but the value of the $(P)(O_2)(X)$ triangle becomes negative. The general proposition is as follows:

D10. To the extent that *Person* has equal positive ties to two *Others* who have equal and opposite degrees of liking for X, the net value of any attitude toward X approaches zero for *Person*.

In order to avoid reifying groups, a fuller analysis could be developed using individuals. Thus, the lines in Figure 2 may be thought of as the average of the values of the personal relationships between Person and group members, and group members and X.

Working out some of the possibilities in detail gives the following propositions:

D11. The greater the cross-pressuring for *Person* (i.e., the more equal the opposite values), the weaker his attitude (liking) toward X.

D12. If *Person* does adopt a positive or negative attitude toward X it will be the attitude of the *Other* with the strongest degree of liking or disliking toward X, provided that *Person*'s bonds to the two groups are equal.

D13. If *Person* does adopt a positive or negative attitude toward X, it will be that of the *Other* to whom he has the stronger positive tie (liking or similarity) providing that the strengths of the *Others'* attitudes toward X are equal.

D14. If *Person* does adopt an attitude toward X, he will tend to lower his liking for the *Other* with whom he is now in imbalance and increase his liking of the *Other* with whom he is now in balance.

GROUP STRUCTURE

Having stated the basic derivations from the theory in terms of *Person, Other,* and X, we can now proceed to a different level of analysis, the statistical properties of groups. That is, instead of considering a particular $(P)(O)(X)$ triangle, we shall treat the properties of the distributions of triangles in groups which vary in the distribution of particular variables.

In doing so, we shall make two assumptions of statistical and substantive impor-

tance. First, it is assumed that the group is large enough so that the distribution for the entire group approximates the distribution of *Others* for each particular *Person*. In a group of thirty, which is split fifty-fifty in political preference, if *Person* is a Democrat, 52 per cent of the *Others* are Republicans, which is pretty close to 50 per cent. In a group of two, however, split fifty-fifty in political preference, 100 per cent of the *Others* are of the opposite political persuasion.

Second, we shall assume that the communication in the group is such that each member receives an essentially similar and

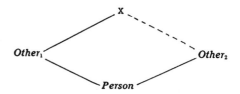

FIG. 2.—The cross-pressure situation

accurate perception of the characteristics of the group as a whole.

It is probably true that these two assumptions are antithetical, the larger the group the less adequate the communication and the smaller the group the more distortion introduced by subtracting *Person* from the distribution of *Others*. Nevertheless, it would appear fair to say that the assumptions, while extremely useful in facilitating the deductions, affect only the degree of precision, not the essentials of the predictions.

It is a persistent observation in field studies of human behavior that in groups of moderate size there is a tendency for subgroups or cliques to form.

Def. 17. A subset of group members whose average liking for each other is greater than their average liking for the other members is a *clique*.

The development of cliques has been analyzed in some detail by Homans (10), Lazarsfeld and Merton (13) and Lipset *et al.* (15). Homans emphasizes the importance of differential rates of interaction in clique formation, a major theme of *The Human Group* being that differentials in social interaction determined by work (the external system) lead to differentials in liking, other sentiments, and activities so that "the activities of a sub-group may become increasingly differentiated from those of other sub-groups up to some limit imposed by the controls of the larger group to which all the sub-groups belong" (10, p. 136). Our impression is that the research literature over a variety of studies tends to support the claim that in day-to-day social life, differences in rates of interaction are the major factor behind subgroup formation. Our theoretical analysis, however, is assuming that interaction rates are uniform within a group, and hence we may proceed to consider other variables. For groups with undifferentiated patterns of interaction, Lazarsfeld and Merton and the authors of *Union Democracy* have stressed the importance of "value homophily" and "similarity." Taking their lead, we may state the following proposition:

D15. For any given X or social characteristic the greater the number of categories into which it is (perceived to be) divided the greater the number of cliques which will form.

Given our proposition that positive bonds follow from similarity, it follows that where there is internal differentiation mutual bonds will tend to develop among subsets, and liking will be greater within cliques than between clique members and the rest of the group. Thus, a group composed of members of one religion cannot form cliques differentiated in religion; a group composed of members of two religions will tend to form two cliques based on religion; a group composed of members of N religions will tend to form N cliques based on religion.

D16. Unless the attitudes or characteristics are totally confounded, or there is no internal variation, the greater the number of characteristics or attitudes, the larger the number of cliques which will form.

Derivation 16 simply says that the addition of another characteristic will add to the possible logical cross-partitions of the group and hence to the number of cliques, unless the characteristic is totally undifferentiated or so confounded that there are no people falling in the logically possible additional classes.

D17. Cliques are more likely to form on the basis of strong attitudes than on the basis of weak ones.

As the absolute value of the liking of X increases, the mean value of bonds in homogeneous cliques increases and the mean value of bonds to non-clique members with opposite attitudes decreases, so that strong attitudes are predicted to produce greater clique differentiation than weak ones.

Considering N attributes, the greater their intercorrelation over individuals:

D18. The larger the size of the clique formed by those who share the attributes;

D19. The greater the differentiation between members of the clique formed by those who share the attributes and other members of the group;

D20. The greater the proportion of the group falling into two hostile cliques, one composed of those sharing all the attributes and one composed of those sharing none of the attributes.

While it may not be obvious, derivations 18, 19, and 20 attempt to restate some key propositions in Coleman's *Community Conflict* (3, pp. 21–23).

The argument can be put in terms of the statistics of association in contingency tables. Consider, for example, three attributes, A v a, B v b, and C v c. There are eight possible combinations, of which we are interested in ABC, abc, and the remaining six which we will call "intermediate." Persons in ABC possess all the attributes, persons in abc possess none of the attributes, and persons in the intermediate category possess some, but not all.

If A, B, and C are independent, the frequency of each type is given by multiplication of the marginal frequencies for the relevant attributes. If, however, there are

207

positive associations, then the groups AB, AC, and BC will contain more than the expected frequencies and (assuming no interactions) ABC will have a higher frequency than under independence. Thus, the greater the associations the greater the size of ABC and the clique formed by those in ABC (D18).

By the same argument, the size of abc must increase if association occurs or increases. Consequently, the size of "intermediate" must decline. Considering the members of ABC, as association increases, the number of "outsiders" who are in abc increases and the number of "outsiders" in intermediate decreases, meaning that a greater proportion of the outsiders have "nothing in common" with the clique members and a smaller proportion have "something in common" with clique members. According to the theory this should lead to increasing the difference between mean liking within the clique and mean liking outside, and hence the differentiation between ABC and the rest of the group (D19). Finally, as increasing association means an increase of the frequency of ABC and abc and a decrease of the frequency of intermediate, it follows that as the intercorrelations increase the percentage of the group falling in the antithetical (and thus, according to the theory, hostile) cliques ABC and abc increases (D20).

These propositions appear to restate Coleman's concept of "interlocking memberships" and the propositions on subgroup formation in "A Formal Interpretation of the Theory of Relative Deprivation" (4).

We can now establish a typology of group structures by combining the inferences from D15, D16, D17, D18, D19, and D20.

The rows in Table 1 stand for differences in the absolute number of dimensions. The columns designate differences in the associations among the dimensions. In the right-hand column is the extreme case where there are strong associations which are consistent in the sense that a reflected matrix would have a high preponderance

of positive signs. In the left-hand column is the opposite situation where the associations are low or associated in such a way that even a reflected matrix contains a large number of negative signs.

Def. 18. The *unity* of a group is the inverse of the variation (variance, standard deviation, etc.) in value of the member-member likings. The opposite of unity will be called *fragmentation*.

Definition 18 says that a unified group is one in which all members tend to like each other to the same degree and a fragmented group is one in which there tend

TABLE 1

TYPES OF GROUP STRUCTURE

No. OF DIMENSIONS	ASSOCIATIONS AMONG DIMENSIONS	
	Low or Inconsistent	High and Consistent
Many.......	"Interlocking"	"Polarized"
Few.........	"Simple"	"Dichotomized"

to be extremes of liking and disliking within the group. Note that this aspect of group structure is not the same as mean liking considered in definition 17. A group in which everybody is faintly hostile to everybody else is considered to be more unified and less fragmented than one in which most everybody dislikes most everybody but a few people like each other very much. The combination of unity and high average liking should, perhaps, be termed "solidarity."

D21. *Group Structure and Unity:*
 a) *Simple:* In such groups there are few dimensions and they are not correlated.

For example, some primitive societies and most American primary schools are differentiated around the independent axes of sex and age, such as "old women" or "fifth-grade boys."

By the inferences from our theory a simple group should tend to form a small number of large cliques around the lines of differentiation.

 b) *Dichotomized:* If, in what would otherwise be a simple group, the characteristics tend to be strongly associ-

208

ated, the number of subgroupings remains constant (unless the associations become "perfect") but more and more people are found in one or the other antithetical subgroup.

For example, one might think of the traditional Southern small town organized around the correlated characteristics of race and status, with two large groups of high status whites and low status Negroes, along with the smaller groups of low status whites and high status Negroes.

In comparison with the simple system a dichotomized group will have less unity because more of its people fall into situations where they have high similarity to a large number and low similarity to a large number of group members.

  c) *Interlocking:* If, in what would otherwise be a simple group, the number of dimensions is larger, the number of subgroupings will increase, but the size of cliques will decrease.

For example, one might contrast the high school with the primary school. In addition to sex and grade, high-school students are differentiated on neighborhood, course of study, and extracurricular activities. The high school thus has more dimensions.

In comparison with a simple system, the interlocking system will be more unified, because for any given person there are fewer others who are socially identical or socially disparate. Along with high unity an interlocking group will tend to contain a large number of small cliques which are, however, not highly differentiated. Thus, the high school has both "more cliques" and "more school spirit" than the grade school.

  d) *Polarized:* If, in what would otherwise be a simple group, the number of dimensions is large and the dimensions are strongly and consistently associated, the number of subgroupings increases and the size of polar social groups increases.

For example, one might think of the traditional New England mill towns which at one time were differentiated in wealth, religion, political preference, and nativity, but in such a way that being rich, Protestant, Republican, and native born tended to go together, as did being poor, Catholic, a Democrat, and foreign born.

Such a community should lie between the dichotomized and interlocking in terms of its unity. The degree of cleavage between the polar groups should be high because each additional characteristic reinforces internal similarity and external contrast. Thus the several generations of common history and Protestant religion shared by whites and Negroes in the traditional Southern town are lacking in the mill town, and religion and nationality differences undoubtedly exacerbated the conflicts. However, social characteristics are seldom perfectly correlated, and even though the polar groups are more strongly differentiated than in a dichotomized group, fewer people fall into the extremes. The existence of some rich Catholics, Protestant Democrats, foreign-born Republicans, and poor native-born persons adds to the number of persons not included unambiguously in the polar groups, and thus adds to the unity of the group when compared with the dichotomized group.

From this point of view the existence of complicated group structures is seen as enhancing the unity of the group. At first glance, it may appear that the theory is much akin to Lévi-Strauss's theory of kinship structures (14). It should be noted, however, that the underlying idea is exactly the opposite, although it does not deny Lévi-Strauss's ideas. His theory is one of "organic solidarity" or exchange, rather than mechanical solidarity or similarity. Our theory says nothing about the exchange of women or other valuables between subgroups but rather says, in effect, that the existence of additional subgroups prevents group fragmentation by making less probable the development of large, cohesive cliques set totally apart from the rest of the group.

Let us now consider a final aspect of group structure—size.

In *Union Democracy* (15, pp. 163–75) there is an intensive analysis of the effects of group size, based on differences between small and large shops of printers. The main line of argument goes as follows:

In the small shops, a nonconformist voter to whom union politics is important cannot find that support in the shop itself; the small shops are usually too small to allow the creation within them of subgroups which stand against the political sentiments of the majority in the shop. . . . In the larger shops there are enough men available of similar preferences for a man to find social support for his nonconformism [15, pp. 170–71].

Translating the argument into the language of the theory:

D22. If a group has cliques, the larger the group the greater the probability there is that a clique of size N or larger exists.
D23. The effect of group size on clique membership is stronger for persons whose attitudes and characteristics are in the minority.

In other words, for groups with the same degree of differentiation, the larger the group the greater the absolute number of persons who possess any particular combination of characteristics. Thus, if it is assumed that there is some absolute size necessary for the formation of a clique, the larger the group the greater the probability that a person with a particular combination of characteristics can find sufficient others to form a clique. Because of their smaller number to begin with, the proposition applies with special force to those whose characteristics are atypical. Thus, the probability of formation of cliques of deviants is affected by group size as well as the structure of the characteristics and attitudes in the group.

In the final section of this essay, we shall consider an additional structural factor, the frequency of occurrence of X.

CHANGES IN ATTITUDES AND OPINIONS

A whole tradition of social psychological research (group dynamics) has placed stress on the role of group relationships in the adoption and change in attitudes. Recently Homans has attempted to restate the principles involved (11, pp. 83–129). In addition, Coleman's analysis of community conflict (3) may be thought of as a similar analysis at the level of a larger group. Although the following propositions do not attempt to synthesize such a vast literature, a number of the key propositions

appear to be similar to those in balance theory. The similarity is no coincidence, Cartwright and Harary being members in eminent standing in the group dynamics fraternity.

We shall consider three situations:

Def. 19. *Innovation* is a situation where initially the members either do not possess or have no degree of liking for a given X, and an attempt is made to introduce X into a group.
Def. 20. *Attitude change* is a situation where initially most or all of the members possess X or hold a given attitude and an attempt is made to reverse the situation.
Def. 21. *Conflict* is a situation where initially the members differ in their liking of X, some liking it, some disliking it.

Innovation.—The proposition that social relationships are a factor in the acceptance of new ideas and attitudes has become a major theme in contemporary communications research following the publication of Katz's and Lazarsfeld's *Personal Influence* (12). The general idea of group effects and opinion leadership can be stated in the language of our theory in terms of a general proposition and a series of subsidiary propositions specifying variations in the process.

D24. *Person* is more likely to adopt an innovation if he has a positive tie of liking or similarity to the innovator.

If *Person* has a positive tie to *Other*, when *Other* "suddenly" likes X, *Person* can increase the net value of his relationship by only liking X (provided, of course, that he has no initial dislike of X, this being part of the definition of innovation).

Putting the same idea in terms of group level variables, we can say:

D25. Innovations tend to diffuse rapidly within cliques but slowly between them.

Because cliques are defined in terms of high rates of positive ties, adoption of a new attitude or activity by a member will be followed by acceptance within the clique. Because, however, members of other subgroups and isolates have less positive or even negative bonds with members of the innovating group, they will tend to resist or be late adopters.

D26. Within a group the rate and degree of the acceptance of an innovation is proportional to the degree of liking of the members for each other.

D27. Within a group the rate and degree of acceptance of an innovation is proportional to the homogeneity of the members in social characteristics.

Because liking and homogeneity produce positive ties, and positive ties affect acceptance, derivations 26 and 27 restate in balance theory the common proposition that acceptance is related to group cohesiveness and homogeneity.

D28. Innovations initiated by highly liked people are more likely to be adopted than those initiated by less liked or disliked people.

D29. Members most typical of the group in terms of attitudes and attributes will be relatively more successful as innovators.

Derivation 28 is the "opinion-leader" hypothesis and is a restatement of D5 in terms of average liking rather than a two-person situation.

D30. Members of multiple cliques tend to be sources of innovation, providing that they are not disliked by or dissimilar to clique members.

Marginal men—those with a tie to more than one group—have long been noted as sources of innovations. In balance-theory terms, such a proposition is justified from the following: As an innovation diffuses through a certain clique, it will be eventually adopted by a "marginal member," although because he is less similar to the other clique members he is probably not an early adopter. Once he has adopted the innovation, however, he will tend to be an "early" adopter in his other clique (because he has more positive ties to the clique that began the process than other members of his alternate group). If he is liked in his "other" clique, he will then serve as an in-

fluential in the second clique and a source of innovation.

As the theory predicts that innovation is affected by clique membership, it follows that for larger groups the process of diffusion will vary with group structure as defined above.

D31. In contrast to simple groups, within dichotomized groups acceptance of an innovation tends to begin rapidly but then to slow down or stop before acceptance is universal.

D32. In contrast to simple groups, within interlocking groups acceptance of an innovation tends to begin slowly but to increase in rate and to become complete.

The arguments are as follows. In dichotomized groups, because of the large size of the two antithetical groups the original adoption is likely to be within one of them. Because of the high positive bonds, acceptance will be rapid within this polar subgroup. However, members of the opposite subgroup will tend to resist adoption because of their negative bonds to the adopting group. Therefore, after an original spurt, the innovation will slow down or cease its rate of acceptance. The opposite is predicted to occur in interlocking groups. Here the initial adopting clique is likely to be small and its mean positive bondness not as high as for the polar group. However, because there are fewer antithetical cliques in the interlocking system the process of diffusion should proceed steadily and by a snowball process eventually include most of the group.

Attitude change.—A classical problem in social psychology is that of the process by which a campaign reverses the attitudes (degree of liking of X) of members of a group. A number of common conclusions about this process may be drawn in terms of balance theory.

D33. It is more difficult to reverse the attitudes of individuals when they are members of a group with high consensus on the attitude.

This derivation may be thought of as the balance-theory hypothesis on "social support for attitudes." The reasoning, of course, is that if a larger number of persons in the group like (or dislike) *X*, and *P* has positive ties of liking or similarity to the group, for *P* to reverse his liking of *X* may lower the net value of his cycles considerably. One of the major lessons of research on propaganda and communication is that all too often a communicator must ask *Person* to pay the price of setting himself against his friends in return for the scant gains of changing an attitude.

As before, certain variations in the process may be set forth:

D34. The greater the degree of liking within a group the greater the resistance of its members to attitude change.

D35. The greater the degree of similarity in characteristics and attitudes other than *X* within a group the greater the resistance of its members to changes in attitude toward *X*.

Derivations 34 and 35, of course, merely restate D26 and D27 in terms of attitude change rather than innovation. The opinion-leader hypotheses come out in a different form, however.

D36. Members who dislike or are indifferent to the others are more likely to change their attitudes.

D37. Members who are atypical of the group in characteristics or attitudes other than *X* are more likely to change their attitudes.

While derivations 28 and 29 said that typical and well-liked members tended to be sources of innovations, derivations 36 and 37 say that atypical and uninvolved members tend to be the beachheads for attitude change. The reason is that their bonds to other members are zero, or negative, and hence adoption of an attitude opposite to their associates does not lower their cycle values. Whether members with mild liking or lesser similarity are easy targets is a moot point. One might argue that since their bonds are lesser they have less to lose by changing their attitudes, but one might also argue that they are in danger of losing what little they have. Probably it depends on the value of their bonds to members in other groups. If the group in question is their only source of social rewards, they probably resist change, but if they have a foothold elsewhere they are free to change (10, p. 118). In more formal terms:

D38. For a person with positive bonds in a clique or peer group, group pressure to resist attitude change is inverse to *Person*'s positive attachments to other groups with opposite degrees of liking for *X*.

For purposes of theoretical analysis we have been assuming that the initial situation was one of 100 per cent liking (or disliking). In reality, of course, deviants always exist, and the theory allows us to derive some consequences of continued deviance, in a proposition often presented in group dynamics literature and treated at length in *Social Behavior* (10, pp. 112–29).

D39. In a group in which most, but not all, members like (or dislike) one or more *X*'s, the degree to which a given member is liked is proportional to his adoption of the majority attitudes.

The proposition says that conformity leads to being liked, deviance leads to being disliked. The argument is that the deviant creates unbalanced cycles for conformers who then lower the amount of their dissonance and sometimes change the cycle to positive by lowering their degree of liking for the deviant. Conversely, high liking of those who conform raises the net values of the cycles for other conformers.

Conflict.—What happens when the initial proportion liking (or disliking) *X* is neither zero nor 100, but some intermediate figure, has long been discussed at the microscopic level as "group pressures toward conformity" and has been analyzed recently at the macroscopic level in Coleman's *Community Conflict* (3). According to balance theory the process and outcome will vary according to the structure of the group. We will consider first what is predicted for a clique and then turn to propositions concerning differentiated groups. In each case we shall consider what happens when a "new X" appears and there is a division among the members into those liking and those disliking X.

D40. In a clique attitudes will tend to converge on unanimity.

D41. The greater the degree of liking of the members for each other the faster the convergence and the nearer unanimity the final outcome.

D42. The greater the degree of similarity of the members in terms of attributes other than X the faster the convergence and the nearer unanimity the outcome.

D43. The stronger the initial attitudes the faster the convergence and the nearer unanimity the outcome.

D44. Pressures toward change in attitudes or toward more vigorous proselytizing will be more common for (a) those on the minority side, (b) those with the strongest initial attitudes, (c) those who like the greatest proportion of the other members, (d) those who are most typical of the group in terms of personal characteristics.

D45. The "side" with the greater proportion of well-liked members will tend to win.

The general form of the proposition is now familiar, but the line of reasoning in this case is as follows: The general proposition of convergence stems from these considerations. If initial bonds are positive (as they are by definition in a clique) the emergence of disagreements will lower the net values of the cycles to each member. By either changing their own opinions or by influencing others, the members will tend to raise the level of agreement, the condition giving the highest net gain being unanimity. Derivations 41–43 state the conditions that produce the greatest average dissonance in the group and hence the greatest pressure to achieve unanimity. Derivation 44 enumerates the particular subgroups in the group who will suffer relatively greater dissonance, and hence the greatest pressure to change or change Others. Finally, derivation 45 is another restatement of D5 on imitation.

In the differentiated group containing more than one clique, the process, as analyzed by Coleman, is somewhat different, essentially because positive bonds are not distributed evenly throughout the population. Rather such a population may be thought of as N cliques, whose degree of hostility to each other is a function of the degree to which the total group is interlocking or dichotomized. The development of an issue then simply serves as an additional dimension. The process predicted is as follows:

D46. When an issue arises cliques tend to move toward internal homogeneity, with consequent increased differentiation between cliques.

D47. If the issue is one where feelings are very strong, there will be a tendency toward polarization.

D48. Polarization will be less likely in groups where there was initially a low degree of association in characteristics and attitudes or a high number of dimensions.

D49. Individuals who belong to multiple groups will develop less strong attitudes.

D50. Subgroups that are representative of the group as a whole will tend to take no stand on the issue.

The theory predicts that the process will go as follows: Once an issue arises the subgroups in the community will move toward homogeneity in opinion according to the derivations stated above for cliques. As they become internally consistent, their differentiation from those groups converging toward the opposite side increases (D46). If, however, the issue is very heated, all the subgroups on one side tend to develop a more positive bondedness, and there is a tendency toward the development of two camps (D47). As Coleman notes, the degree and rapidity of polarization will be less where existing characteristics were loosely associated and attachments were thus distributed widely throughout the group (48). In addition, cross-pressured individuals (D49) will tend to have no opinion at all, and groups that are representative of the community (e.g.,

213

civic organizations), being heavily cross-pressured, will tend to take no stand at all (D50), leaving initiative in the hands of "extremist" groups whose internal dissonance is less, a phenomenon characteristic of desegregation conflicts in the American South.

While the propositions have been developed in terms of Coleman's analysis of unstructured community issues such as fluoridation controversies, the derivations also restate some of the major theoretical generalizations from *Voting* (1) on social processes in electoral campaigns. Thus the authors of *Voting* conclude that, as an electoral campaign continues, groups tend to become homogeneous in political attitude ("The campaign increases homogeneity within and polarization between religious groups and occupational groups" [1, p. 149]), and that cross-pressured individuals and groups tend to have unstable and weak voting intentions.

RELATIVE DEPRIVATION

The final social-psychological concept to be considered is relative deprivation (4, 16, 17), the proposition that people tend to assess rewards and punishments not only in terms of their intrinsic hedonic value but also by comparison with standards based on the experience of others (reference persons and groups).

Because we have to treat unit formation and liking for *Person* and *Other* simultaneously, it will be helpful to shift to a more formal approach. The postulates of the theory can be translated into the following:

$$\text{Value to } P = (L_{PX} + U_{PX})$$
$$\times (L_{ox} + U_{ox}) \quad (1)$$
$$\times (L_{PO} + r_{PO}),$$

where L stands for the degree of liking, U for the degree of unit formation, r_{PO} for the correlation between P and O over attributes other than X. Subscripts are asymmetrical except for r_{PO}.

While the previous section concerned

liking, the issue here is possession, or, in the language of the theory, the unit relationship. In considering attitudes, we assumed in effect that the unit relationship was irrelevant, that is, in equation (1), the terms U_{PX} and U_{ox} were equal to zero.

In analyzing relative deprivation, however, liking and possession have to be considered simultaneously.

Def. 22. X is a value if everyone in the group likes X or if everyone dislikes X.

Valuing is not necessarily the same as possessing. One may like money or promotions or good grades but not possess them. One may dislike poverty, demotions, or bad grades but still possess them. With this in mind let us consider what happens when: (*a*) X is a value, (*b*) there is a positive bond between *Person* and *Other*, (*c*) there is a discrepancy between *Person* and *Other* in terms of the possession or degree of possession of X.

We note that if U_{PX} and U_{ox} are both zero, the net value of the cycle to *Person* will be positive under the stipulations, and also that the value will be positive in any situation in which $U_{PX} = U_{ox}$.

Because the stipulations require L_{PX} to be the same as L_{ox} the subscripts can be dropped and the equation rearranged:

$$\text{Value to } P = [L^2 + L \ (U_{PX} + U_{ox})$$
$$+ U_{PX}U_{ox}] \quad (2)$$
$$\times (L_{PO} + r_{PO}).$$

Put this way it can be seen that the contribution of the two U terms is a function of their sum plus their product. Exactly what will happen will depend on the sign and value of L and the specific values of the two U terms, but for present purposes, the following generalizations will serve: (*a*) if L is positive and U_{ox} is some positive number, the value of the cycle to *Person* is proportional to the value of U_{PX}; (*b*) if L is negative and U_{ox} is negative, the value of the cycle to *Person* is inversely proportional to the value of U_{ox}; (*c*)

214

if L is positive and U_{PX} is positive, the value of the cycle to *Person* is directly proportional to U_{OX}; and (d) if L is negative and U_{PX} is negative, the value of the cycle to *Person* is inversely proportional to U_{OX}. Translating from algebra into the language of the theory:

D51. Under the stipulations above, if *Other* possesses an X that both *Person* and *Other* like, the less X that *Person* possesses the lower the value of the cycle to *Person.*

D52. Under the stipulations above, if *Other* does not possess an X that both *Person* and *Other* dislike, the more X that *Person* possesses the lower the value of the cycle to *Person.*

D53. Under the stipulations above, if *Person* possesses an X that both *Person* and *Other* like, the more X that *Other* possesses the greater the value of the cycle to *Person.*

D54. Under the stipulations above, if *Person* does not possess an X that both *Person* and *Other* dislike, the less X that *Other* possesses the greater the value of the cycle to *Person.*

Let us compare these results with the analysis in "A Formal Interpretation of the Theory of Relative Deprivation." In that paper three psychological states were postulated (4, p. 283):

When a deprived person compares himself with a non-deprived person, the resulting state will be called "relative deprivation. . . ."

When a non-deprived person compares himself with a deprived person, the resulting state will be called "relative gratification. . . ."

A person experiencing *either* relative gratification or relative deprivation will also experience a feeling that his deprivation status is different from that of his peers. We will call this "fairness" in the sense that it indicates a belief that there is differential treatment in the in-group.

It thus appears that lack of "fairness" is the logical equivalent of imbalance and that all the propositions about fairness in "A Formal Interpretation" can be translated into balance theory. Specifically, we can restate the propositions on the distri-

bution of rewards to complete our analysis of group structure, begun previously in the consideration of number of dimensions and associations among dimensions.

D55. Within a clique, as the proportion receiving a given value increases (or the proportion not receiving a given negative value decreases):
   a) Cycle values decrease among those whose situation is less favorable.
   b) Cycle values increase among those whose situation is more favorable.
   c) For the group as a whole, average cycle values decrease as reward levels move from zero to 50 per cent and increase as reward levels move from 50 per cent toward 100 per cent.

D56. Within a group with two cliques, the distribution of rewards (or punishments) will affect group differentiation as follows:
   a) To the extent that reward distribution is correlated with clique membership, it will lead to greater clique differentiation.
   b) To the extent that reward distribution tends toward fifty-fifty within a clique, it will lead to lessened clique differentiation.

While balance theory turns out to be involved in the theory of relative deprivation, the theory of relative deprivation cannot be totally encompassed within it. In particular, the idea of relative gratification goes beyond balance theory in a way which indicates some important limits to the theory.

Although relative gratification is postulated to produce a lowering of (POX) cycle value, and people are postulated to prefer high cycle values, the theory of relative deprivation assumes that relative gratification is satisfying to *Person.* How can these two hypotheses be reconciled? We think the answer comes from the fact that the value of the POX cycle is only one of many sources of gratification for ego. Thus, while surpassing one's peers does indeed lower the rewards from peer relationships, the compensation in terms of intrinsic gratification from the reward or the feeling of competitive success may more than compensate for the loss. Whether the value of a positive (*POX*) cycle outweighs the value of the reward (as it apparently does in the case of restriction of output among work groups) or whether the value of the reward is greater (as it is when student peers compete for grades) is not predictable from balance theory alone.

If these reflections are valid, they suggest that balance theory is of decreased utility in social situations where there is a short supply of a highly valuable *X*.

We can illustrate this limitation from the area of politics. According to the theory, if *Person* meets *Other* and it turns out that they both like a given political candidate, the theory predicts that they will tend to like each other precisely because they share a liking. Consider, however, the two candidates themselves. The fact that Kennedy liked the presidency and Nixon liked the presidency did not imply that Kennedy and Nixon liked each other. Although it must be admitted that sometimes competitors do develop a liking because they have something in common (e.g., trial lawyers or rival athletes), in the case of the presidency, although both candidates "liked it," only one could possess it, and this unavoidable asymmetry means that often candidates are willing to sacrifice their positive peer relations to gain the prize.

This important qualification allows us to set the theory in some perspective. We feel that within a broad and important area of social life, the theory presented manages to integrate a considerable number of ideas and findings. At the same time, it is not presented as a complete theory of human behavior. The theory claims that positive cycles of similarity are attractive to people, but it must admit other sources of motivation. The dissimilarity in exchange between differentiated people and the dissimilarity of triumph in competition also are sources of reward that may outweigh the values of the cycles discussed. What balance theory maintains, however, is that there must be some gain in exchange and high reward from competition to offset the imbalances that occur.

SUMMARY

Balance theory, a social-psychological theory developed by Cartwright and Harary (2) to formalize concepts set forth by Heider (9), has been used to restate in a common language fifty-six propositions from the writings of Berelson *et al.* (1), Coleman (3), Davis (4), Durkheim (5), Festinger (6, 7), Fiedler (8), Homans (10, 11), Katz and Lazarsfeld (12), Lazarsfeld and Merton (13), Lipset *et al.* (15), Merton and Kitt (16), and Stouffer *et al.* (17).

Despite the wide range of topics covered by the theory it is not advanced as a general theory of interpersonal relations but as a theory of one major component. It is suggested that a general theory of interpersonal relations must consider, in addition to balance, the exchange process and the effects of competition for scarce values.

UNIVERSITY OF CHICAGO

REFERENCES

1. BERELSON, BERNARD R., LAZARSFELD, PAUL F., and McPHEE, WILLIAM N. *Voting: A Study of Opinion Formation in a Presidential Campaign.* Chicago: University of Chicago Press, 1954.
2. CARTWRIGHT, DORWIN, and HARARY, FRANK. "Structural Balance: A Generalization of Heider's Theory," *Psychological Review,* LXIII (September, 1956), 277–93.
3. COLEMAN, JAMES S. *Community Conflict.* Glencoe, Ill.: Free Press, 1957.
4. DAVIS, JAMES A. "A Formal Interpretation of the Theory of Relative Deprivation," *Sociometry,* XXII (December, 1959), 280–96.
5. DURKHEIM, ÉMILE. *The Division of Labor in Society.* Translated by GEORGE SIMPSON. Glencoe, Ill.: Free Press, 1947.
6. FESTINGER, LEON. *A Theory of Cognitive Dissonance.* Evanston, Ill.: Row, Peterson & Co., 1957.
7. ———. "A Theory of Social Comparison Processes," *Human Relations,* VII (1954), 117–40.
8. FIEDLER, FRED E. *Leader Attitudes and Group*

216

Effectiveness. Urbana: University of Illinois Press, 1958.

9. HEIDER, FRITZ. *The Psychology of Interpersonal Relations.* New York: John Wiley & Sons, 1958.

10. HOMANS, GEORGE CASPAR. *The Human Group.* New York: Harcourt, Brace & Co., 1950.

11. ———. *Social Behavior: Its Elementary Forms.* New York: Harcourt, Brace & World, Inc., 1961.

12. KATZ, ELIHU, and LAZARSFELD, PAUL F. *Personal Influence: The Part Played by People in the Flow of Mass Communications.* Glencoe, Ill.: Free Press, 1955.

13. LAZARSFELD, PAUL F., and MERTON, ROBERT K. "Friendship as a Social Process: A Substantive and Methodological Analysis," in MORROE BERGER, THEODORE ABEL, and CHARLES H. PAGE (eds.), *Freedom and Control in Modern Society,* pp. 18–66. Princeton, N.J.: D. Van Nostrand & Co., 1954.

14. LÉVI-STRAUSS, CLAUDE. *Les Structures élémentaires de la parenté.* Paris: Presses Universitaires de France, 1949.

15. LIPSET, SEYMOUR MARTIN, TROW, MARTIN A., and COLEMAN, JAMES S. *Union Democracy: The Internal Politics of the International Typographical Union.* Glencoe, Ill.: Free Press, 1956.

16. MERTON, ROBERT E., and KITT, ALICE S. "Contributions to the Theory of Reference Group Behavior," in ROBERT K. MERTON and PAUL F. LAZARSFELD (eds.), *Continuities in Social Research: Studies in the Scope and Method of "The American Soldier."* Glencoe, Ill.: Free Press, 1950.

17. STOUFFER, SAMUEL E., SUCHMAN, EDWARD A., DE VINNEY, LELAND C., STAR, SHIRLEY A., and WILLIAMS, ROBIN M., JR. *The American Soldier: Adjustment during Army Life.* Princeton, N.J.: Princeton University Press, 1949.

217

Part III: Roles and Transactions

From A. R. Radcliffe-Brown, *Journal of the Royal Anthropological Society of Great Britain and Ireland* 70, 1-12 (1940), by permission.

ON SOCIAL STRUCTURE

Presidential Address

By A. R. Radcliffe-Brown, M.A.

It has been suggested to me by some of my friends that I should use this occasion to offer some remarks about my own point of view in social anthropology ; and since in my teaching, beginning at Cambridge and at the London School of Economics thirty years ago, I have consistently emphasised the importance of the study of social structure, the suggestion made to me was that I should say something on that subject.

I hope you will pardon me if I begin with a note of personal explanation. I have been described on more than one occasion as belonging to something called the " Functional School of Social Anthropology " and even as being its leader, or one of its leaders. This Functional School does not really exist ; it is a myth invented by Professor Malinowski. He has explained how, to quote his own words, " the magnificent title of the Functional School of Anthropology has been bestowed by myself, in a way on myself, and to a large extent out of my own sense of irresponsibility." Professor Malinowski's irresponsibility has had unfortunate results, since it has spread over anthropology a dense fog of discussion about " functionalism." Professor Lowie has announced that the leading, though not the only, exponent of functionalism in the nineteenth century was Professor Franz Boas. I do not think that there is any special sense, other than the purely chronological one, in which I can be said to be either the follower of Professor Boas or the predecessor of Professor Malinowski. The statement that I am a " functionalist," or equally the statement that I am not, would seem to me to convey no definite meaning.

There is no place in natural science for " schools " in this sense, and I regard social anthropology as a branch of natural science. Each scientist starts from the work of his predecessors, finds problems which he believes to be significant, and by observation and reasoning endeavours to make some contribution to a growing body of theory. Co-operation amongst scientists results from the fact that they are working on the same or related problems. Such co-operation does not result in the formation of schools, in the sense in which there are schools of philosophy or of painting. There is no place for orthodoxies and heterodoxies in science. Nothing is more pernicious in science than attempts to establish adherence to doctrines. All that a teacher can do is to assist the student in learning to understand and use the scientific method. It is not his business to make disciples.

221

I conceive of social anthropology as the theoretical natural science of human society, that is, the investigation of social phenomena by methods essentially similar to those used in the physical and biological sciences. I am quite willing to call the subject "comparative sociology," if any one so wishes. It is the subject itself, and not the name, that is important. As you know, there are some ethnologists or anthropologists who hold that it is not possible, or at least not profitable, to apply to social phenomena the theoretical methods of natural science. For these persons social anthropology, as I have defined it, is something that does not, and never will, exist. For them, of course, my remarks will have no meaning, or at least not the meaning I intend them to have.

While I have defined social anthropology as the study of human society, there are some who define it as the study of culture. It might perhaps be thought that this difference of definition is of minor importance. Actually it leads to two different kinds of study, between which it is hardly possible to obtain agreement in the formulation of problems.

For a preliminary definition of social phenomena it seems sufficiently clear that what we have to deal with are relations of association between individual organisms. In a hive of bees there are the relations of association of the queen, the workers and the drones. There is the association of animals in a herd, of a mother-cat and her kittens. These are social phenomena; I do not suppose that any one will call them cultural phenomena. In anthropology, of course, we are only concerned with human beings, and in social anthropology, as I define it, what we have to investigate are the forms of association to be found amongst human beings.

Let us consider what are the concrete, observable facts with which the social anthropologist is concerned. If we set out to study, for example, the aboriginal inhabitants of a part of Australia, we find a certain number of individual human beings in a certain natural environment. We can observe the acts of behaviour of these individuals, including, of course, their acts of speech, and the material products of past actions. We do not observe a "culture," since that word denotes, not any concrete reality, but an abstraction, and as it is commonly used a vague abstraction. But direct observation does reveal to us that these human beings are connected by a complex network of social relations. I use the term "social structure" to denote this network of actually existing relations. It is this that I regard it as my business to study if I am working, not as an ethnologist or psychologist, but as a social anthropologist. I do not mean that the study of social structure is the whole of social anthropology, but I do regard it as being in a very important sense the most fundamental part of the science.

My view of natural science is that it is the systematic investigation of the structure of the universe as it is revealed to us through our senses. There are certain important separate branches of science, each of which deals with a certain class or kind of structures, the aim being to discover the characteristics of all structures of that kind. So atomic physics deals with the structure of atoms, chemistry with the structure of molecules, crystallography and colloidal chemistry with the structure of crystals and colloids, and anatomy and physiology with the structures of organisms. There is, therefore, I suggest, place for a branch of natural science which will have for its task the discovery of the general characteristics of those social structures of which the component units are human beings.

222

Social phenomena constitute a distinct class of natural phenomena. They are all, in one way or another, connected with the existence of social structures, either being implied in or resulting from them. Social structures are just as real as are individual organisms. A complex organism is a collection of living cells and interstitial fluids arranged in a certain structure ; and a living cell is similarly a structural arrangement of complex molecules. The physiological and psychological phenomena that we observe in the lives of organisms are not simply the result of the nature of the constituent molecules or atoms of which the organism is built up, but are the result of the structure in which they are united. So also the social phenomena which we observe in any human society are not the immediate result of the nature of individual human beings, but are the result of the social structure by which they are united.

It should be noted that to say we are studying social structures is not exactly the same thing as saying that we study social relations, which is how some sociologists define their subject. A particular social relation between two persons (unless they be Adam and Eve in the Garden of Eden) exists only as part of a wide network of social relations, involving many other persons, and it is this network which I regard as the object of our investigations.

I am aware, of course, that the term " social structure " is used in a number of different senses, some of them very vague. This is unfortunately true of many other terms commonly used by anthropologists. The choice of terms and their definitions is a matter of scientific convenience, but one of the characteristics of a science as soon as it has passed the first formative period is the existence of technical terms which are used in the same precise meaning by all the students of that science. By this test, I regret to say, social anthropology reveals itself as not yet a formed science. One has therefore to select for oneself, for certain terms, definitions which seem to be the most convenient for the purposes of scientific analysis.

There are some anthropologists who use the term social structure to refer only to persistent social groups, such as nations, tribes and clans, which retain their continuity, their identity as individual groups, in spite of changes in their membership. Dr. Evans-Pritchard, in his recent admirable book on the Nuer, prefers to use the term social structure in this sense. Certainly the existence of such persistent social groups is an exceedingly important aspect of structure. But I find it more useful to include under the term social structure a good deal more than this.

In the first place, I regard as a part of the social structure all social relations of person to person. For example, the kinship structure of any society consists of a number of such dyadic relations, as between a father and son, or a mother's brother and his sister's son. In an Australian tribe the whole social structure is based on a network of such relations of person to person, established through genealogical connections.

Secondly, I include under social structure the differentiation of individuals and of classes by their social role. The differential social positions of men and women, of chiefs and commoners, of employers and employees, are just as much determinants of social relations as belonging to different clans or different nations.

In the study of social structure, the concrete reality with which we are concerned is the set of actually existing relations, at a given moment of time, which link together certain human beings. It is on this that we can make direct observations. But it is not this that we attempt to describe in its particularity. Science (as distinguished from history or biography) is not concerned with the particular, the unique, but only with the general, with kinds, with events which recur. The actual relations of Tom, Dick and Harry or the behaviour of Jack and Jill may go down in our field note-books and may provide illustrations for a general description. But what we need for scientific purposes is an account of the form of the structure. For example, if in an Australian tribe I observe in a number of instances the behaviour towards one another of persons who stand in the relation of mother's brother and sister's son, it is in order that I may be able to record as precisely as possible the general or normal form of this relationship, abstracted from the variations of particular instances, though taking account of those variations.

This important distinction, between structure as an actually existing concrete reality, to be directly observed, and structural form, as what the field-worker describes, may be made clearer perhaps by a consideration of the continuity of social structure through time, a continuity which is not static like that of a building, but a dynamic continuity, like that of the organic structure of a living body. Throughout the life of an organism its structure is being constantly renewed ; and similarly the social life constantly renews the social structure. Thus the actual relations of persons and groups of persons change from year to year, or even from day to day. New members come into a community by birth or immigration ; others go out of it by death or emigration. There are marriages and divorces. Friends may become enemies, or enemies may make peace and become friends. But while the actual structure changes in this way, the general structural form may remain relatively constant over a longer or shorter period of time. Thus if I visit a relatively stable community and revisit it after an interval of ten years, I shall find that many of its members have died and others have been born ; the members who still survive are now ten years older and their relations to one another may have changed in many ways. Yet I may find that the kinds of relations that I can observe are very little different from those observed ten years before. The structural form has changed little.

But, on the other hand, the structural form may change, sometimes gradually, sometimes with relative suddenness, as in revolutions and military conquests. But even in the most revolutionary changes some continuity of structure is maintained.

I must say a few words about the spatial aspect of social structure. It is rarely that we find a community that is absolutely isolated, having no outside contact. At the present moment of history, the network of social relations spreads over the whole world, without any absolute solution of continuity anywhere. This gives rise to a difficulty which I do not think that sociologists have really faced, the difficulty of defining what is meant by the term " a society." They do commonly talk of societies as if they were distinguishable, discrete entities, as, for example, when we are told that a society is an organism. Is the British Empire a society, or a collection of societies ? Is a Chinese village a society, or is it merely a fragment of the Republic of China ?

If we say that our subject is the study and comparison of human societies, we ought to be able to say what are the unit entities with which we are concerned.

If we take any convenient locality of a suitable size, we can study the structural system as it appears in and from that region, i.e., the network of relations connecting the inhabitants amongst themselves and with the people of other regions. We can thus observe, describe, and compare the systems of social structure of as many localities as we wish. To illustrate what I mean, I may refer to two recent studies from the University of Chicago, one of a Japanese village, Suye Mura, by Dr. John Embree, and the other of a French Canadian community, St. Denis, by Dr. Horace Miner.

Closely connected with this conception of social structure is the conception of " social personality " as the position occupied by a human being in a social structure, the complex formed by all his social relations with others. Every human being living in society is two things : he is an individual and also a person. As an individual, he is a biological organism, a collection of a vast number of molecules organised in a complex structure, within which, as long as it persists, there occur physiological and psychological actions and reactions, processes and changes. Human beings as individuals are objects of study for physiologists and psychologists. The human being as a person is a complex of social relationships. He is a citizen of England, a husband and a father, a brick-layer, a member of a particular Methodist congregation, a voter in a certain constituency, a member of his trade union, an adherent of the Labour Party, and so on. Note that each of these descriptions refers to a social relationship, or to a place in a social structure. Note also that a social personality is something that changes during the course of the life of the person. As a person, the human being is the object of study for the social anthropologist. We cannot study persons except in terms of social structure, nor can we study social structure except in terms of the persons who are the units of which it is composed.

If you tell me that an individual and a person are after all really the same thing, I would remind you of the Christian creed. God is three persons, but to say that He is three individuals is to be guilty of a heresy for which men have been put to death. Yet the failure to distinguish individual and person is not merely a heresy in religion ; it is worse than that ; it is a source of confusion in science.

I have now sufficiently defined, I hope, the subject matter of what I regard as an extremely important branch of social anthropology. The method to be adopted follows immediately from this definition. It must combine with the intensive study of single societies (i.e., of the structural systems observable in particular communities) the systematic comparison of many societies (or structural systems of different types). The use of comparison is indispensable. The study of a single society may provide materials for comparative study, or it may afford occasion for hypotheses, which then need to be tested by reference to other societies ; it cannot give demonstrated results.

Our first task, of course, is to learn as much as we can about the varieties, or diversities, of structural systems. This requires field research. Many writers of ethnographical descriptions do not attempt to give us any systematic account of the social structure. But a few social

225

anthropologists, here and in America, do recognise the importance of such data and their work is providing us with a steadily growing body of material for our study. Moreover, their researches are no longer confined to what are called " primitive " societies, but extend to communities in such regions as Sicily, Ireland, Japan, Canada and the United States.

If we are to have a real comparative morphology of societies, however, we must aim at building up some sort of classification of types of structural systems. That is a complex and difficult task, to which I have myself devoted attention for thirty years. It is the kind of task that needs the co-operation of a number of students and I think I can number on my fingers those who are actively interested in it at the present time. Nevertheless, I believe some progress is being made. Such work, however, does not produce spectacular results and a book on the subject would certainly not be an anthropological best-seller.

We should remember that chemistry and biology did not become fully formed sciences until considerable progress had been made with the systematic classification of the things they were dealing with, substances in the one instance and plants and animals in the other.

Besides this morphological study, consisting in the definition, comparison and classification of diverse structural systems, there is a physiological study. The problem here is : how do structural systems persist ? What are the mechanisms which maintain a network of social relations in existence, and how do they work ? In using the terms morphology and physiology, I may seem to be returning to the analogy between society and organism which was so popular with mediæval philosophers, was taken over and often misused by nineteenth century sociologists, and is completely rejected by many modern writers. But analogies, properly used, are important aids to scientific thinking and there is a real and significant analogy between organic structure and social structure.

In what I am thus calling social physiology, we are concerned not only with social structure, but with every kind of social phenomenon. Morals, law, etiquette, religion, government, and education are all parts of the complex mechanism by which a social structure exists and persists. If we take up the structural point of view, we study these things, not in abstraction or isolation, but in their direct and indirect relations to social structure, i.e., with reference to the way in which they depend upon, or affect, the social relations between persons and groups of persons. I cannot do more here than offer a few brief illustrations of what this means.

Let us first consider the study of language. A language is a connected set of speech usages observed within a defined speech-community. The existence of speech-communities and their sizes are features of social structure. There is, therefore, a certain very general relation between social structure and language. But if we consider the special characteristics of a particular language—its phonology, its morphology, and even to a great extent its vocabulary—there is no direct connection of either one-sided or mutual determination between these and the special characteristics of the social structure of the community within which the language is spoken. We can easily conceive that two societies might have very similar forms of social structure and very different kinds of language, or vice versa. The coincidence of a particular form of social structure and a particular language in a given community is always the result of historical accident. There may, of course, be certain indirect, remote interactions between social structure and language, but these would seem to be of minor importance. Thus the general comparative study of languages can be profitably carried out as a relatively independent branch of science, in which the language is considered in abstraction from the social structure of the community in which it is spoken.

But, on the other hand, there are certain features of linguistic history which are specifically connected with social structure. As structural phenomena may be instanced the process by which Latin, from being the language of the small region of Latium, became the language of a considerable part of Europe, displacing the other Italic languages, Etruscan, and many Celtic languages ; and the subsequent reverse process by which Latin split up into a number of diverse local forms of speech, which ultimately became the various Romance languages of to-day.

Thus the spread of language, the unification of a number of separate communities into a single speech-community, and the reverse process of subdivision into different speech-communities, are phenomena of social structure. So also are those instances in which, in societies having a class structure, there are differences of speech usage in different classes.

I have considered language first, because linguistics is, I think, the branch of social anthropology which can be most profitably studied without reference to social structure. There is a reason for this. The set of speech usages which constitute a language does form a system and systems of this kind can be compared in order to discover their common general, or abstract, characters, the determination of which can give us laws, which will be specifically laws of linguistics.

Let us consider very briefly certain other branches of social anthropology and their relation to the study of social structure. If we take the social life of a local community over a period, let us say a year, we can observe a certain sum total of activities carried out by the persons who compose it. We can also observe a certain apportionment of these activities, one person doing certain things, another doing others. This apportionment of activities, equivalent to what is sometimes called the social division of labour, is an important feature of the social structure. Now activities are carried out because they provide some sort of " gratification," as I propose to call it, and the characteristic feature of social life is that activities of certain persons provide gratifications for other persons. In a simple instance, when an Australian blackfellow goes hunting, he provides meat, not only for himself, but for his wife and children and also for other relatives to whom it is his duty to give meat when he has it. Thus in any society there is not only an apportionment of activities, but also an apportionment of the gratifications resulting therefrom, and some sort of social machinery, relatively simple or, sometimes, highly complex, by which the system works.

It is this machinery, or certain aspects of it, that constitutes the special subject-matter studied by the economists. They concern themselves with what kinds and quantities of goods are produced, how they are distributed (i.e., their flow from person to person, or region to region) , and the way in which they are disposed of. Thus what are called economic institutions are extensively studied in more or less complete abstraction from the rest of the social system. This method does undoubtedly provide useful results, particularly in the study of complex modern societies. Its weaknesses become apparent as soon as we attempt to apply it to the exchange of goods in what are called primitive societies.

The economic machinery of a society appears in quite a new light if it is studied in relation to the social structure. The exchange of goods and services is dependent upon, is the result of, and at the same time is a means of maintaining a certain structure, a network of relations between persons and collections of persons. For the economists and politicians of Canada the potlatch of the Indians of the north-west of America was simply wasteful foolishness and it was therefore forbidden. For the anthropologist it was the machinery for maintaining a social structure of lineages, clans and moieties, with which was combined an arrangement of rank defined by privileges.

Any full understanding of the economic institutions of human societies requires that they should be studied from two angles. From one of these the economic system is viewed as the mechanism by which goods of various kinds and in various quantities are produced, transported and transferred, and utilised. From the other the economic system is a set of relations between persons and groups which maintains, and is maintained by, this exchange or circulation of goods and services. From the latter point of view, the study of the economic life of societies takes its place as part of the general study of social structure.

Social relations are only observed, and can only be described, by reference to the reciprocal behaviour of the persons related. The form of a social structure has therefore to be described by the patterns of behaviour to which individuals and groups conform in their dealings with one another. These patterns are partially formulated in rules which, in our own society, we distinguish as rules of etiquette, of morals and of law. Rules, of course, only exist in their recognition by the members of the society ; either in their verbal recognition, when they are stated as rules, or in their observance in behaviour. These two modes of recognition, as every field-worker knows, are not the same thing and both have to be taken into account.

If I say that in any society the rules of etiquette, morals and law are part of the mechanism by which a certain set of social relations is maintained in existence, this statement will, I suppose, be greeted as a truism. But it is one of those truisms which many writers on human society verbally accept and yet ignore in theoretical discussions, or in their descriptive analyses. The point is not that rules exist in every society, but that what we need to know for a scientific understanding is just how these things work in general and in particular instances.

Let us consider, for example, the study of law. If you examine the literature on jurisprudence you will find that legal institutions are studied for the most part in more or less complete abstraction from the rest of the social system of which they are a part. This is doubtless the most convenient method for lawyers in their professional studies. But for any scientific investigation of the nature of law it is insufficient. The data with which a scientist must deal are events which occur and can be observed. In the field of iaw, the events which the social scientist can observe and thus take as his data are the proceedings that take place in courts of justice. These are the reality, and for the social anthropologist they are the mechanism or process by which certain definable social relations between persons and groups are restored, maintained or modified. Law is a part of the machinery by which a certain social structure is maintained. The system of laws of a particular society can only be fully understood if it is studied in relation to the social structure, and inversely the understanding of the social structure requires, amongst other things, a systematic study of the legal institutions.

I have talked about social relations, but I have not so far offered you a precise definition. A social relation exists between two or more individual organisms when there is some adjustment of their respective interests, by convergence of interest, or by limitation of conflicts that might arise from divergence of interests. I use the term " interest " here in the widest possible sense, to refer to all behaviour that we regard as purposive. To speak of an interest implies a subject and an object and a relation between them. Whenever we say that a subject has a certain interest in an object we can state the same thing by saying that the object has a certain value for the subject. Interest and value are correlative terms, which refer to the two sides of an asymmetrical relation.

Thus the study of social structure leads immediately to the study of interests or values as the determinants of social relations. A social relation does not result from similarity of interests, but rests either on the mutual interest of persons in one another, or on one or more common interests, or on a combination of both of these. The simplest form of social solidarity is where two persons are both interested in bringing about a certain result and co-operate to that end. When two or more persons have a *common interest* in an object, that object can be said to have a *social value* for the persons thus associated. If, then, practically all the members of a society have an interest in the observance of the laws, we can say that the law has a social value. The study of social values in this sense is therefore a part of the study of social structure.

It was from this point of view that in an early work I approached the study of what can conveniently be called ritual values, i.e., the values expressed in rites and myths. It is perhaps again a truism to say that religion is the cement which holds society together. But for a scientific understanding we need to know just how it does this, and that is a subject for lengthy investigations in many different forms of society.

As a last example let me mention the study of magic and witchcraft, on which there is an extensive anthropological literature. I would point to Dr. Evans-Pritchard's work on the Zande as an illuminating example of what can be done when these things are systematically investigated in terms of the part they play in the social relations of the members of a community.

From the point of view that I have attempted briefly to describe, social institutions, in the sense of standardised modes of behaviour, constitute the machinery by which a social structure, a network of social relations, maintains its existence and its continuity. I hesitate to use the term " function," which in recent years has been so much used and misused in a multitude of meanings, many of them very vague. Instead of being used, as scientific terms ought to be, to assist in making distinctions, it is now used to confuse things that ought to be distinguished. For it is often employed in place of the more ordinary words " use," " purpose " and " meaning." It seems to be more convenient and sensible, as well as more scholarly, to speak of the use or uses of an axe or digging stick, the meaning of a word or symbol, the purpose of an act of legislation, rather than to use the word function for these various things. " Function " has been a very useful technical term in physiology and by analogy with its use in that science it would be a very convenient means of expressing an important concept in social science. As I have been accustomed to use the word, following Durkheim and others, I would define the social function of a socially standardised mode of activity, or mode of thought, as its relation to the social structure to the existence and continuity of which it makes some contribution. Analogously, in a living organism, the physiological function of the beating of the heart, or the secretion of gastric juices, is its relation to the organic structure to the existence or continuity of which it makes its contribution. It is in this sense that I am interested in such things as the social function of the punishment of crime, or the social function of the totemic rites of Australian tribes, or of the funeral rites of the Andaman Islanders. But this is not what either Professor Malinowski or Professor Lowie mean by functional anthropology.

Besides these two divisions of the study of social structure, which I have called social morphology and social physiology, there is a third, the investigation of the processes by which social structures change, of how new forms of structures come into existence. Of this important branch of study I have time for only one illustration, from the field of colonial sociology.

Let us suppose that we wish to study and understand what is happening in a British or French colony or dependency in Africa, at the present time. Formerly the region was inhabited by Africans having their own social structure. Now a new and more complex social structure has been brought into existence. The population now includes a certain number of Europeans— government officials, traders, missionaries and, in some instances, settlers. The new political structure is one in which the Europeans have a large measure of control, and they generally play an important part in the new economic structure. The outstanding characteristic of this kind of social structure is that Europeans and Africans constitute different classes, with different languages, different customs and modes of life, and different sets of values and ideas. It is an extreme example of a society compounded of heterogeneous elements. As such it has a certain instability, due to the lack of adjustment of divergent interests.

In order to understand the social changes that are taking place in a society of this kind, it seems to me essential to study the whole set of relations amongst the persons involved. This kind of study was undertaken by some of us in South Africa twenty years ago and is still being continued, profitably, I think. A few years ago, as a result perhaps of re-defining social anthropology as the study, not of society, but of culture, we were asked to abandon this kind of investigation in favour of what is now called the study of " culture contact." In place of the study of the formation of new composite societies, we are supposed to regard what is happening in Africa as a process in which an entity called African culture comes into contact with an entity called European or Western culture, and a third new entity is produced, or is to be produced, which is to be described as Westernized African culture. To me this seems a fantastic reification of abstractions. European culture is an abstraction and so is the culture of an African tribe. I find it fantastic to imagine these two abstractions coming into contact and by an act of generation producing a third abstraction. There is contact, but it is between human beings, European and African, and it takes place within a definite structural arrangement.

You are aware that in certain anthropological circles the term " evolutionary anthropologist " is almost a term of abuse. It is applied, however, without much discrimination. Thus Lewis Morgan is called an evolutionist, although he rejected the theory of organic evolution and in relation to society believed, not in evolution, but in progress, which he conceived as the steady material and moral improvement of mankind from crude stone implements and sexual promiscuity to the steam engines and monogamous marriage of Rochester, N.Y. But even such anti-evolutionists as Boas believe in progress.

It is convenient, I think, to use the term " progress " for the process by which human beings attain to greater control over the physical environment through the increase of knowledge and improvement of technique by inventions and discoveries. The way in which we are now able to destroy considerable portions of cities from the air is one of the latest striking results of progress. Progress is not the same thing as social evolution, but it is, I believe, very closely connected with it.

Evolution, as I understand the term, refers specifically to a process of emergence of new forms of structure. Organic evolution has two important features : (1) in the course of it a small number of kinds of organisms have given rise to a very much larger number of kinds ; (2) more complex forms of organic structure have come into existence by development out of simpler forms. While I am unable to attach any definite meaning to such phrases as the evolution of culture or the evolution of language, I think that social evolution is a reality which the social anthropologist should recognise and study. Like organic evolution, it can be defined by two features. There has been a process by which, from a small number of forms of social structure, many different forms have arisen in the course of history ; that is, there has been a process of differentiation. Secondly, throughout this process more complex forms of social structures have developed out of, or replaced, simpler forms.

Just how structural systems are to be classified with reference to their greater or less complexity is a problem requiring investigation. But there is evidence of a fairly close correlation between complexity and another feature of structural systems, namely, the extent of the field of social relations. In a structural system with a narrow total social field, an average or typical person is brought into direct and indirect social relations with only a small number of other persons. In systems of this type we may find that the linguistic community—the body of persons who speak one language—numbers from 250 to 500, while the political community is even smaller, and economic relations by the exchange of goods and services extend only over a very narrow range. Apart from the differentiation by sex and age, there is very little differentiation of social role between persons or classes. We can contrast with this the systems of social structure that we observe to-day in England or the United States. Thus the process of human history to which I think the term social evolution may be appropriately applied might be defined as the process by which wide-range systems of social structure have grown out of, or

231

replaced, narrow-range systems. Whether this view is acceptable or not, I suggest that the concept of social evolution is one which requires to be defined in terms of social structure.

There is no time on this occasion to discuss the relation of the study of social structure to the study of culture. For an interesting attempt to bring the two kinds of study together I would refer you to Mr. Gregory Bateson's book *Naven*. I have made no attempt to deal with social anthropology as a whole and with all its various branches and divisions. I have endeavoured only to give you a very general idea of the kind of study to which I have found it scientifically profitable to devote a considerable and steadily increasing proportion of my time and energy. The only reward that I have sought I think I have in some measure found—something of the kind of insight into the nature of the world of which we are part that only the patient pursuit of the method of natural science can afford.

From J. A. Barnes, *Human Relations* 7, 39-58
(1954), by permission.

CLASS AND COMMITTEES IN A
NORWEGIAN ISLAND PARISH [1]

J. A. BARNES

I

When we study the social organization of a simple society, we aim at
comprehending all the various ways in which the members of the society
systematically interact with one another. For purposes of analysis we treat
the political system, the pattern of village life, the system of kinship and
affinity, and other similar areas of interaction as parts of the same universe of
discourse, as though they were of equal analytical status, and we strive to
show how the same external factors, principles of organization, and common
values influence these different divisions of social life. This task, though
always difficult, has been accomplished for a growing number of simple
societies, about which we can feel confident that we have an appreciation
of what the society *as a whole* is like. When we turn to the enormously
complex societies of Western civilization our task becomes much more
difficult. Fieldwork in a Western community can lead directly to knowledge
of only a very small sector in the social life of a large-scale society. This
limited area of detailed knowledge has then to be related, as best we can, to
experience and information derived from other parts of the society.

Recently I had the opportunity of studying a parish in Western Norway
called Bremnes.[2] During my fieldwork I did not try to gain first-hand
knowledge of Norwegian society as a whole. Any such attempt would, I
think, have been entirely unsuccessful. Instead I attempted to isolate for
study certain aspects of social life in which I was interested, which were
relatively unknown, and relatively easy to grapple with. Many writers have

1. The first draft of this paper was read at a meeting of the Association of Social Anthropologists
at Oxford on 3 October 1953. I am very grateful to those who took part in the discussion, and to Professor
Ely Devons, for comments and criticism.

2. I carried out this work during 1952-3 as a Simon Research Fellow of the University of Manchester.
I am much indebted to the University for its generous support, and also to St. John's College, Cambridge,
who elected me to a Fellowship. My work was made possible only by the whole-hearted cooperation
of many men and women in Bremnes, for which I am most grateful.

discussed the political history of Norway, the development of its economic institutions, the personality of its inhabitants, their forms of religious belief, and similar topics. Some sociological fieldwork has been carried out in the country, but as yet very little is known about the operation of the social class system in a land which prides itself on its affirmation of social equality. Therefore I decided to concentrate my attention on those kinds of face-to-face relationships through which a class system, if there were one, might operate. I was also interested in the way in which collective action is organized in a society of this kind, and was therefore led to consider the working of committees. I chose to study an island parish partly dependent on industry since I believed that there the field data I sought would be easier both to obtain and to understand than in a town.

Bremnes has a domiciled population of some 4,600. Of every ten men over fifteen years old, three are engaged mainly in fishing, two in agriculture, another two in industry, and one is a merchant seaman. These occupations account for 84 per cent of the adult male population. Another 6 per cent are gainfully employed in other occupations, and the final 10 per cent are retired. The majority of adult women are housewives. These percentages indicate only the principal occupation, for many men divide their time between different ways of earning a living. All farms are small, very few employ paid labour, and few households can live off their land alone. Therefore most peasants spend at least the time from Christmas to Easter fishing for herring, while others work in the local marine-engine factory. A few men are almost full-time administrators, but the bulk of the work of local government is carried out by part-time officials such as the mayor, the parish treasurer, the tax assessors and collectors, and the chairmen of the various standing committees, most of whom have small-holdings as well as their public work to attend to.

Bremnes is part of Norway, and its inhabitants share much of their culture with their fellow countrymen, as well as belonging with them to a single economic, social, and administrative system. Here it is sufficient to mention that Norway is a democratic monarchy with high taxation and comparatively little extremes of poverty and wealth. Over 95 per cent of Norwegians belong to the Lutheran State church. There is no tradition of feudalism, there are no hereditary titles outside the royal family, and virtually all children attend the official elementary schools. An idea strongly stressed in Norwegian thought is that no man should have more privileges than his fellows.

II

Each person in Bremnes belongs to many social groups. In particular he is a member of a household, of a hamlet, of a ward, and he is a member of the parish of Bremnes. At different times and different places membership of

234

one or other of these groups is definitive for what he does. He goes to the prayer-house with his household, sits at weddings with other members of his hamlet, and pays tax according to his parish. There are other series of groups which to some extent cut across these territorially-based ones, although they may themselves be based on territory. Thus for example a man may belong to a hamlet missionary working-party, or to a bull-owning cooperative based on a ward. In formal terms these various groups fit one inside the other, each in its own series. Thus there are three territorially-defined fishermen's associations in the parish. All three belong to the provincial fishermen's association, and this in its turn forms part of the national association. There may be conflicts because of the duties and rights a person has in the various groups in any one series, and there may be conflicts because of his interests in different series. This is true of all societies.

The territorial arrangement of the Bremnes population is fairly stable. The same fields are cultivated year after year, and new land comes into cultivation only slowly. Houses can be moved from site to site, but this is expensive. Land can be bought and sold, but there are several factors tending to discourage frequent sales of land. Thus for the most part the same people go on living in the same houses and cultivating the same land from year to year. This provides, as it were, a stable environment in which social relations are maintained through the decades, and a frame of reference by which individuals can relate themselves to other people. This territorially-based arrangement of persons is, however, only a part of the social system of Bremnes, for men utilize the sea as well as the land. Herring are not cultivated, they are hunted. They are taken from the sea, where there are no territorially defined rights in property. They are caught by men organized in groups of from five to twenty, whose composition varies from year to year much more than do the household groups who work together on the same holding. The fishing vessel, the temporary home of the fishermen, wears out more quickly than a house or a plot of land, and it can be bought and sold comparatively easily. Even more important, there are no women on board. Wives and children remain behind and stay in one place while the men move from one fishing ground to another, and from one crew to another. Here then we have two distinct kinds of social field, a fluid and a stationary, and we shall presently discuss a third field linking these two. The fluid field is the field of industrial activity, in which men earn money by catching fish; the stable field is the field of domestic, agricultural, and administrative activity ashore, where they, or their wives, spend the money.

The Norwegian fishing industry is efficient; technological change is going on continually, and vessels make use of modern equipment like radio telephones, echo-sounding gear, nylon ropes, radar and asdics. It is a highly competitive industry, each vessel striving against all other vessels. Loyalties to kinsmen, neighbours and friends continue to operate, but only to a limited extent. In their own words, "Herring fishing is war." Any man can try to get himself included in a crew and each owner seeks to engage the crew that will catch most fish. During the herring season, men from Bremnes sail in vessels belonging to other parishes, and vessels registered in Bremnes sometimes have on board fishermen from as much as six hundred miles away. In effect, there is something like a free labour market. Men apply for a place in a particular vessel because of contacts they have made, friends or relatives who have already served on board, or the success of the vessel in previous seasons.

An industry of this kind could scarcely operate were the pattern of social relations as fixed and stable as it is in the round of social and economic activities ashore. The greater portion of the herring catch is exported and in order to sell on the world market at a profit the size of the fishing fleet and the amount of capital invested in it have to respond to economic pressures which vary in intensity and point of application. There is a huge marketing organization and various reserve funds which even out part of the differences in earnings between one vessel and another and from year to year. Even so, the amounts earned by the fleet as a whole vary considerably over the seasons, and in any year some crews do very well while others barely earn any money at all. Most of the tasks in fishing can be carried out by any able-bodied man brought up by the sea, so that men can move fairly easily from fishing into other occupations and back again. From the point of view of the individual fisherman, therefore, the herring-fishing industry is intersected by a social field through which he can move fairly freely along lines of friendship and local knowledge, seeking in the main the achievement of economic goals. Every man is in touch, or can put himself in touch, with a large number of other men, differentiated into shipowners, skippers, net bosses, cooks and others, and into good and bad, and to whom he is linked in a variety of ways. The herring-fishing industry also generates its own social field which is influenced by ecological factors, such as the disappearance of the fish, by economic factors affecting alternative opportunities for employment and investment, and by many others. It is a social field only partly made up of an arrangement of lasting social groups.

Thus in terms of this analysis we can isolate three regions or fields in the social system of Bremnes. Firstly there is the territorially-based social field, with a large number of enduring administrative units, arranged hierarchically, one within another. The administration of the parish is carried on through this system, and the same boundaries are used by the voluntary associations. By reason of their physical proximity the smaller territorial units, the hamlets and wards, provide the basis for enduring social relations between neighbours, which find expression in various activities connected with subsistence agriculture, the care of children, religion, entertainment, and the like. The units of the system endure and membership changes only slowly.

The second social field is that generated by the industrial system. Here we have a large number of interdependent, yet formally autonomous units such as fishing vessels, marketing cooperatives, and herring-oil factories, connected with each other functionally rather than hierarchically, yet each organized internally in a hierarchy of command. These units, which often are true social groupings as well as units of organization, do not necessarily persist through time, nor does their membership remain fixed.

The third social field has no units or boundaries; it has no coordinating organization. It is made up of the ties of friendship and acquaintance which everyone growing up in Bremnes society partly inherits and largely builds up for himself. Some of the ties are between kinsmen. A few of them are between people who are not equals, as between a man and a former employer with whom he has kept in contact. Most of the ties are, however, between persons who accord approximately equal status to one another, and it is these ties which, I think, may be said to constitute the class system of Bremnes. The elements of this social field are not fixed, for new ties are continually being formed and old links are broken or put into indefinite cold storage.

Let us examine more closely the distinctive features of this third social field. As we well know, cognatic kinship does not of itself give rise to enduring social groups. I have my cousins and sometimes we all act together; but they have their own cousins who are not mine and so on indefinitely. Each individual generates his own set of cognatic kin and in general the set he and his siblings generate is not the same as that generated by anyone else. Each person is, as it were, in touch with a number of other people, some of whom are directly in touch with each other and some of whom are not. Similarly each person has a number of friends, and these friends have their own friends; some of any one person's friends know each other, others do not. I find it convenient to talk of a social field of this kind as a *network*.[3] The image I have is of a set of points some of which are joined by lines. The points of the image are people, or sometimes groups, and the lines indicate which people interact with each other. We can of course think of the whole of social life as generating a network of this kind. For our present purposes, however, I want to consider, roughly speaking, that part of the total network that is left behind when we remove the groupings and chains of interaction which belong strictly to the territorial and industrial systems. In Bremnes society, what is left is largely, though not exclusively, a network of ties of kinship, friendship, and neighbourhood. This network runs across the whole of society and does not stop at the parish boundary. It links Bremnes folk with their kinsmen and friends in other parishes as well as knitting them together within the parish. A network of this kind has no external boundary,

---

3. Earlier I used the term *web*, taken from the title of M. Fortes' book, *The web of kinship*. However, it seems that many people think of a web as something like a spider's web, in two dimensions, whereas I am trying to form an image for a multi-dimensional concept. It is merely a generalization of a pictographic convention which genealogists have used for centuries on their pedigree charts. Recent modifications of this convention include the tribal "sequences" in W. E. Armstrong, *Rossel Island* (1928), p. 37; "psychological geography" in J. L. Moreno, *Who shall survive?* (1934), pp. 238–47; and "sets" in E. D. Chapple and C. S. Coon, *Principles of anthropology* (1942), p. 284.

nor has it any clear-cut internal divisions, for each person sees himself at the centre of a collection of friends. Certainly there are clusters of people who are more closely knit together than others, but in general the limits of these clusters are vague. Indeed, one of the ways in which a cluster of people emphasize their exclusiveness is to form a group, to which one definitely either does or does not belong. The social ties linking the members of the group are then no longer merely those of kinship or friendship.

In parenthesis we may note that one of the principal formal differences between simple, primitive, rural or small-scale societies as against modern, civilized, urban or mass societies is that in the former the mesh of the social network is small, in the latter it is large. By mesh I mean simply the distance round a hole in the network. In modern society, I think we may say that in general people do not have as many friends in common as they do in small-scale societies. When two people meet for the first time, it is rare in modern society for them to discover that they have a large number of common friends, and when this does happen it is regarded as something exceptional and memorable. In small-scale societies I think this happens more frequently, and strangers sometimes find that they have kinsmen in common. In terms of our network analogy, in primitive society many of the possible paths leading away from any A lead back again to A after a few links; in modern society a smaller proportion lead back to A. In other words, suppose that A interacts with B and that B interacts with C. Then in a primitive society the chances are high that C interacts with A, in a modern society the chances are small. This fact is of considerable practical importance for the study of societies by the traditional techniques of social anthropology, when we try to become acquainted with a limited number of persons whom we observe interacting one with another in a variety of roles. In a modern society, each individual tends to have a different audience for each of the roles he plays. Bremnes, in these terms, is an intermediate society.

In some societies close kinsmen and affines are not necessarily social equals, and in that case the network of kinship ties may have a steep social gradient. Similarly, in our own society, in a street with property ranging gradually from mansions at one end to tenements at the other, we can speak of a network of ties between neighbours who do not regard themselves as equal in social status. However, in Bremnes, as in many other societies, kinsmen, by and large, are approximate social equals. Furthermore, at the present time, unlike conditions which prevailed in Bremnes until about a hundred years ago, neighbours are approximately equal in social status. In Norwegian thought, the idea of equality is emphasized, so that even between persons of markedly different economic status there is less recognition of social inequality on either side than would, I think, be the case in Britain. Thus the social network in Bremnes is largely a system of ties between pairs of persons who regard each other as approximate social equals.

III

The organization of the population of Norway into social classes, assuming that there is such an organization, may be said to manifest itself in Bremnes in the social network I have described. The term *social class* is widely used in general conversation, and naturally it has a great variety of meanings. I think that much of the confusion that has grown up around the term is due to our failure to distinguish these different usages. Thus Marx had in mind definite groups into which the population was divided, which were mutually exclusive, collectively exhaustive, endured through at least several decades, and which recruited members by reference to their position in the economic system. The study of class through clique membership, on the other hand, is closer to the idea of class as a network. For instance, in *Deep South* [4] a series of overlapping cliques are used to define the boundaries of class. Most other approaches to class treat it as a kind of social category, of people possessing approximately the same size of house, or paid about the same amount, or standing at about the same level on some commonly-held scale of social esteem. Lastly there is class as a category of thought, a unit of division used when members of a society mentally divide up the population into status categories. It is clear that the question "How many classes are there?" is meaningless when applied to class as a social category, for there are as many or as few as we choose; and there is often no consensus within a society about class as a category of thought. There may be disagreement about the number of social classes when class is treated as a social group, in the same way as there are disagreements about how many genera and how many species there are in zoological taxonomy; but that is a problem that can be solved. When, however, we look at social class as a kind of network, the question of how many social classes there are falls away completely.

I should perhaps emphasize that the concept of a network is only one tool for use in the analysis of the phenomenon of social class. The other approaches I have mentioned above are equally valid, and indeed are necessary to any understanding of this complex social fact. As we are well aware, there is a fair measure of congruence between the different approaches. In general, most of a man's friends have approximately the same income as he has, live in the same sort of house, are classified together by other members of the society, and fight on the same side in those political and industrial struggles in which, if at all, social classes may perhaps be said to function as groups. For the purposes of this paper I shall nevertheless look at social class from merely the one point of view: as a network of relations between pairs of persons according each other approximately equal status.

---

4. A. Davis, B. B. Gardner, and M. R. Gardner, *Deep South* (1941). For a critique of the class concept from a logician's standpoint, see Llewellyn Gross, "The use of class concepts in sociological research", *American Journal of Sociology*, liv (1948–9), pp. 409–21.

This choice is not entirely an arbitrary one. It arises from the fact that Bremnes is a fairly small community, with no marked differences of culture and, with a few exceptions, minor differences in standards of dress, housing, and the like. In common parlance, there are few class differences in the parish. There are significant differences in income, but these are partly rendered inoperative by the lack of significant differences in patterns of spending. Under these conditions we do not find the emergence of a division of the population into distinct social classes one above the other.

It should be clear that such a division is not ruled out by the idea of class as a network. It is only pairs of persons who are directly in contact with one another in the class network who regard themselves as approximately of equal status; each person does not necessarily regard everyone else in the network as his equal. Suppose that A has a friend B. A regards B as his social equal, perhaps a little higher or a little lower in social status. As we have remarked earlier, not all B's friends are friends of A. Suppose that D is a friend of B, but not a friend of A. Then, if A knows of D at all, he may or may not regard him as his social equal. If, for instance, A regards B as slightly beneath him in social status, but not so far below as to matter; and if B regards D in the same light; then there is the possibility that A will regard D as too far below him to be treated on a basis of equality. Similarly if A is below B and B is below D, A may think that D is too far above him to be treated as an equal. This process is cumulative with every step taken along the network away from any A we chose to start from. Thus for every individual A the whole of the network, or at least that part of it of which he is aware, is divided into three areas or sets of points. One of these sets consists of all those people to whom A is linked by a longer or shorter path, and whom A regards as his social equals. A is similarly linked to each person in the second set, but this set is composed of all the people that A regards as his social superiors. Similarly the people who in A's estimation are his social inferiors form the third set. These sets are like the sets of cousins we mentioned earlier, in that membership of the sets has to be defined afresh for each new individual A that we choose to consider. Thus in the example given above, D belongs to the superior set with reference to A, but to the socially-equal set with reference to B. I think that in some, at least, of the many instances in which people of widely-varying economic position say that they belong to the middle class in a system of three (or more) social classes, they are merely stating that they are aware of the existence of these three sets of persons. It does not of itself imply that society can be divided into three groups with agreed membership.

I do not wish to digress further with the elaboration of this model of a class system. The idea has been developed sufficiently to deal with the comparatively simple conditions prevailing in Bremnes. In the first place, Bremnes is small, with a great deal of intermarriage. Hence in the network the number of links along the path joining any two members of the parish is small, probably never more than four. Secondly, because Norwegian culture is egalitarian, everyone is ready to treat as an equal others whose income, upbringing, interests, and occupation differ widely from his own. Thirdly, despite the egalitarian dogma, people in Bremnes recognize the existence of differences in social status. They have stereotypes of the upper class who live in big houses in the towns, talk a different language, and have different religious beliefs. Bremnes folk also speak of a lower class, people who wander about unashamed, living on charity and scorning the aspirations of respectable citizens. In between these two classes are "plain ordinary people like ourselves". It is, in fact, the familiar egocentric three-class system, with ego in the middle class. Class is here a category of thought. In Bremnes, conditions are simplified in that, for the most part, everyone appears to think of almost everybody else in the parish as belonging to the same class as himself. Most people in the upper and lower classes, as defined by Bremnes folk, live outside the parish. When they visit the parish, members of these classes are treated by most of the resident population either as social superiors or inferiors, and not as equals.

Within the parish community, the range of variation is just sufficient for a few people, perhaps a dozen or so in number, to be regarded by many others as on the upper fringe of their sets of social equals. Yet others treat these dozen persons as social superiors. Similarly, there are a few people who are, in rather oblique fashion, treated as social inferiors by many in the community. However, this recognition of social inferiority is often masked, since it is impolite for anyone to show openly that he considers himself superior to anyone else.

The range of status variation is likely to increase in the future. In the community, some men are wealthier than others and although they only occasionally use their wealth to buy socially conspicuous goods and services such as cars, large houses, expensive clothes, pleasure yachts, and the like, they do buy more expensive education for their children. Up to the age of fourteen all children receive the same education in the parish schools, but it is the sons and daughters of the wealthier section of the population who, in the main, continue their education for a few years more. For many youngsters, this means leaving the parish and coming into contact with ideas and values different from those they have known at home. They acquire skills which, when they leave school, differentiate them from the majority of the labouring population, and which in a generation or two may well lead to sharper cleavages along class lines, or at least to a recognition of wider differences in social position. Similarly, on evidence from other parts of Norway, I think that the people lowest in the Bremnes social scale, most of whom are itinerant pedlars and beggars, are now more sharply distinguished from the rest of the population they were a hundred years ago, when many penurious cottars and day labourers lived in the parish; but I cannot document this for Bremnes.

241

Although there is this tendency towards greater differentiation in social status, it is slowed down by other social processes. Taxation is high, so that it is difficult for a man to amass a fortune, and since capital is taxed as well as income, it is also difficult for him to retain it. As part of the culturally-supported thesis that all should be treated alike, it is universally held that all children should inherit equally. Only a third of a man's wealth can legally be disposed of by will; the remainder must be distributed according to the laws of inheritance or intestacy. In Bremnes few wills are made and in nearly every case all a man's chattels, after provision has been made for his widow, are divided equally among his children. Thus in a society of large families, fortunes are dispersed at death. Even death duties operate differenti-ally on the principle of "he that already hath more shall receive less". Where land is concerned, one child often takes over the whole of his or her father's farm, but even then he (or she) has to buy the land from the father so that the rights of the landless siblings may be protected. In education, inequalities of opportunity are to some extent offset by bursaries and interest-free loans from official sources, and by the custom of allowing adolescents to work for a year or two so that they can save enough to take themselves through the next stage of their education. All these factors hinder the speedy develop-ment of wide social differences even though the trend seems to be in that direction.

Thus in general terms we can say that in Bremnes society, apart from the territorial and industrial systems, there is a network of social ties between pairs of persons arising from considerations of kinship, friendship and acquaintance. Most, but not all, of these ties are between persons who regard each other as approximate social equals, and these ties of approximate equality we regard as one manifestation of the social class system, and shall call the class network. Although each link in the class network is one of approximate social equality, not everyone in the network regards everyone else as his equal, and there are a few people in the parish who are regarded by many others, but not by all, as belonging to a higher class. The class network is utilized for carrying out social activities, such as mutual help and home entertaining; class ties and also ties between people of recognized unequal status are used by men for a variety of other purposes, for example, to find places for themselves in the fishing industry.

IV

Cooperative activity requires some degree of leadership and consensus, whether carried out by enduring groups or by ephemeral groupings of persons linked by a network of social ties. Let us now consider some of the mechanisms by which leadership and consensus are obtained in Bremnes social life. Characteristically a network has no head and, as I have here used the term, no centre and no boundaries either. It is not a corporate body, but rather a system of social relations through which many individuals carry on certain activities which are only indirectly coordinated with one another. In Bremnes, as we have seen, there is little class distinction, but the social activities which are typically carried on through the system of social class are there carried on in the same way as in a society with a larger range of class variation. People invite their friends to supper, or to a sewing party for the mission, or for a shooting trip, on the same basis of apparent approximate equality of social status, which is, I think, definitive of class behaviour. The network of friendship and acquaintance, when men seek out industrial opportunities, is used rather differently. Fish are actually caught, and a large number of distinct activities are brought into close coordination with one another. While fishing, men are no longer equals; they are organized in chains of command and differentiated according to function. For as long as the technical process demands, they are organized in fixed groups standing in a definite relationship one to another. At sea the skipper is in charge of his vessel, the coxswain in charge of his boat; they give orders and their sub-ordinates obey. In the same way the marine-engine factory is organized hierarchically for purposes of production, with a board of directors, managers, foremen, and workmen. The groups of men who are thrown together on board fishing vessels or in the sections of the factory develop and perpetuate other modes of interaction which modify the configurations of the class network besides affecting the productive tasks themselves. In Homans' terminology, there is a clear-cut hierarchically organized external system, whereas the internal system is the network of friendship and acquaintance.[5]

Once we leave the field of organized industrial enterprise, the need for quick decisions and for a clear division of responsibility decreases. The achievement of consensus is valued more highly than speed of autocratic command. Decisions have to be made involving collective action: whether the teachers shall have salmon or cod at their banquet; whether the electricity supply cooperative shall take action against a member who has tampered with his meter; whether a boatload of fishermen shall go ashore to the cinema or to the prayer-ship. Such decisions are important, but their importance lies more in their consequences for face-to-face relations between members of the society than in their technical merits. Hence it is not surprising that the process of reaching the decision to hold a feast in the prayer-house is more complicated than that by which a command is given to cast a net in the sea. This is true whether the prayer-house is one belonging to a local community or to the hierarchically-organized factory.

Yet, as is usual in the Western world, most of the formal associations in Bremnes concerned with non-industrial activities have what appears on paper to be an hierarchical structure suitable for taking quick decisions in an autocratic way. There is, it is true, no one person in Bremnes who is head of

---

5. G. C. Homans, *The Human Group* (1951), pp. 273 ff.

local society, who might be called the chief of the island, but equally Bremnes is not a leaderless society. It is, as we say, a democracy, and there is a common pattern of organization which occurs in nearly every instance of formal social life. Each association has a committee, with powers to act usually for a year but sometimes for longer, elected by an annual general meeting. The committee, if it is big enough, elects a quarter of its members to an executive council to which most of its powers are delegated. The council and the committee each elect one of their members to be treasurer and secretary. The same man is often chairman of committee and council. There is also a deputy chairman and a number of deputy members who function only in the absence of the principal members. This common pattern is followed with only minor variations by sports clubs, missionary societies, producers' co-operatives, and by the local government itself.

All these bodies employ the same procedure for reaching a decision, by simple majority vote of those present and voting, provided there is a quorum. In practice, whenever possible they avoid taking a vote and the great majority of collective decisions are therefore unanimous. This tendency is most marked at the meetings of missionary societies and least at those of the parish council. Even in the parish council, when there is an irreconcilable division of opinion this is sometimes concealed by first taking a trial vote, to decide which view has greatest support; this is followed by a confirming unanimous vote, which alone is recorded in the minutes. Nevertheless there are in fact continual differences of opinion between members of all these different bodies. Why then is the achievement of formally unanimous decisions considered so important? Here I think we are dealing with a principle of fairly wide application. People living and working together inevitably have conflicting interests but in general they have also a common interest in the maintenance of existing social relations. Individual goals must be attained through socially approved processes, and as far as possible the illusion must be maintained that each individual is acting only in the best interests of the community. As far as possible, that is, the group must appear united, not only vis-à-vis other similar groups, but also to itself. Voting is a method of reaching decisions in which divergence of interest is openly recognized, and in which the multiplicities of divergence are forced into the Procrustean categories of *Yes* and *No*. Significantly, voting is rare in simple societies and in small groups of modern society. Membership in a collectivity implies accepting a share in the collective responsibility for the group's actions as well as a share in the decision to act in a certain way. The local associations in Bremnes are in the main face-to-face groups operating in a conservative environment. Even the producers' cooperatives, which had been responsible for introducing technological changes, are made up of men who have been neighbours for many years, who are related by kinship and marriage, and who are not trying to alter the existing pattern of social relations on the island, even though they may be trying to alter the position of the islanders as against the rest of the region. In these conditions voting is an inappropriate procedure.

Furthermore, in voting, the worth of one man relative to another is fixed, and in most voting systems all men have equal votes. When decisions are reached unanimously after discussion, each man gives his own weight to the views of his fellows. Individuals present their views as though they had first been stated by someone else; they speak tentatively and cautiously; they try to win the support of divergent colleagues by saying that they agree with them all. The complex process by which a final decision is reached without the cleavages in the group becoming irreconcilable is one that I am not competent to analyse fully. The process is in part a corollary of the emphasis on equality that is noticeable in Norwegian culture. What is significant for our purposes is that it is a recognizable process which goes on in some social contexts and not in others.

There is one context in which voting by secret ballot is almost invariably used. When new committee members and officers have to be elected, pieces of paper are handed round, everyone writes down his choices and folds over his paper before handing it in. Thus the only topic that never comes up for open discussion is the relative worth of members of the community. I think there are two reasons for this. The election of committee members is the one occasion at which an immediate decision is absolutely necessary to prevent the structure of the association collapsing. Secondly it is difficult, though not impossible, to discuss the merits and demerits of one's friends in their presence without committing oneself so much that the appearance of general amity is threatened. As it is, most elections to local committees in Norway consist of re-voting into office the outgoing members, and sometimes a special sub-committee is appointed to draw up in private a list of nominations, so that voting becomes a formality. In this way the rivalries that threaten the unity of the community are hindered from coming into the open. In Bremnes there is, however, often free discussion about who should serve on those committees involving more hard work than honour.

The parish council differs from the other associations on the island in that it is required to act and cannot be merely a mutual admiration society. It is the local government in a society that is changing, even though it is changing fairly slowly. The leaky church roof must be repaired, and as the population increases more classrooms must be built. The council is under constant pressure from the provincial administration to collect taxes and to spend the money collected. Unlike the missionary societies and chess club and women's institutes, the parish council obtains a large part of the revenue for its projects from the State, and higher authorities audit its accounts, approve its budget, and bombard it with correspondence. It may try to move slowly, but it is continually forced to come to a decision one way or the other on issues about which the community has not yet made up its mind, that is to say, about which there are differences of opinion that have not yet been resolved.

Hence from time to time a vote must be taken. The usual techniques, or as some would say, tricks, are used by the mayor to gain unanimous approval, such as, for example, making the majority record their vote by remaining seated and the minority by standing up; all those who are in two minds about the issue probably fail to spring to their feet. In the same way, members of council try to avoid having to vote on matters in which they have divided loyalties, claiming that because of ties of kinship and affinity they are likely to be biased and therefore cannot discuss a particular matter fairly. On one occasion I observed, when an unusually controversial matter was up for discussion and three members had, one after the other, spoken briefly to say that they were related to the parties in the case and therefore could not take part in the discussion, the mayor intervened to point out that council members were probably all related in one way or another to the parties concerned, but that nevertheless they must come to a decision. Where associations other than the parish council are concerned, such embarrassing situations can usually be avoided. There is no State administrative machinery behind them to keep them going at all costs, and if serious latent differences are allowed to become apparent, the organizations may split.

Formal associations in Bremnes, despite their hierarchical form of organization, are not authoritarian. The existing structure of social relations in a conservative environment is maintained by seeking for apparent agreement for all decisions. With the parish council, speed of decision is more important and voting is more often employed. In industrial enterprises, both in the marine-engine factory and the fishing industry, where the environment is not conservative and quick decisions are needed, there is an hierarchical structure and this is effective and not merely formal.

V

Although there are many leaders of part of the parish, each of whom operates in certain restricted contexts, there is no overall leadership of the parish valid in a wide range of contexts, such as we are familiar with in the primitive world. We might perhaps call the pattern of public life in Bremnes " government by committee ". In formal terms there are no long chains of command on the island. Instead there is a host of small organized groups with overlapping membership, and the whole population is enmeshed in a close web of kinship and friendship which links together all the people on the island, but which also ties them to kinsmen and affines scattered throughout Western Norway, and indeed throughout the whole world. In this system the people formally in positions of leadership are the elected chairmen of the various associations. They hold office for a fixed term but are very often re-elected unless they decide to resign. There are perhaps fifty voluntary associations of one kind or another, as well as about forty standing committees whose members are appointed or recommended for nomination by the parish council. All these men occupy positions of some public responsibility. Slightly more in the public eye are the mayor, the rector and his curate, and the sheriff. None of these men can be said to represent the parish in its totality to the outside world, and all of them are involved with fractional interests within the parish. The sheriff and the rector are perhaps most removed from internal rivalries, but even they take part in politics, although they are civil servants and directly responsible to higher authorities outside the parish. The holders of both these offices stood as parliamentary candidates in the recent election. They are both elected parish councillors and members of various parish council committees in their own right as well as being ex-officio members of other committees. Even more involved in local politics are the mayor and the chairmen of standing committees.

In fact there are no living symbols of parish unity, or of the relation of the parish to other social groups, in any but a restricted sense. There is no one person in a key position who articulates the parish with a wider social system as happens in many simple societies. The mayor comes nearest to this, for he represents the parish on the provincial council, and is sometimes invited to serve as a director on the boards of public utility companies serving the parish. Yet even so he is not the representative of the parish in ecclesiastical or judicial matters or in the affairs of the missionary societies. This lack of a single leader or symbolic head is perhaps due to the fact that the parish is not a corporate group in the same way that, for instance, a minor lineage is a corporate group among the Tallensi.[6] Bremnes is a parish, a unit of civil and ecclesiastical administration and part of the Kingdom of Norway. Yet even in civil and ecclesiastical affairs the parish looks outward in different directions. Ecclesiastically Bremnes is part of Finnås parish union, which is part of Ytre Sunnhordland archdeaconry, which is part of Bjørgvin diocese; in civil matters Bremnes is an immediate subdivision of Hordaland province; while in judicial affairs it forms part of Finnås sheriff's area, which is part of Sunnhordland magistracy. One hundred and fifty years ago Norway was still virtually a Danish colony governed by what we would now call a system of direct bureaucratic rule. The various sections of the bureaucracy were largely separate and the local areas into which the country was divided for different purposes then coincided even less than they do now. During the nineteenth century, as the local population gained a greater share in public affairs, changes were made to bring the ecclesiastical, administrative, fiscal, and judicial divisions into alignment, but the coincidence is still not complete. Indeed the trend is now in the opposite direction, as new systems of organization cut across existing alignments, as for example the Home Guard and the electricity supply grid. The parish is a unit in some of these different organizations, but it is not an exogamous or endogamous unit; it is not an economic unit, and from most points of view it has no culture of its own. Its nearest

6. M. Fortes, *The Dynamics of Clanship among the Tallensi* (1945), p. 99.

approach to a social centre is the parish church, and it is here that the largest crowds gather, that common beliefs are affirmed, and changes in social life receive public recognition. Yet the church is not as widely supported an institution as it once was and its sphere of influence has considerably diminished. Although the process of social specialization has not gone as far in Bremnes as it has, say, in a London suburb, Bremnes is definitely not a simple society. The systems of organization within which the people carry on their activities are not congruent with one another. Neighbours, kinsfolk, workmates, fellow members of associations, are all becoming different.

In general, the mesh of the social network is growing larger. Nevertheless, the organization of Bremnes society is still largely an arrangement of cross-cutting ties and groupings in which not only friends and enemies, but also leaders and followers, are inextricably mixed. No one line of cleavage ever becomes dominant. The territorial system endures and the industrial system commands; but in this society the relationships that are valued most highly are still to be found in the shifting middle ground of social intercourse between approximate equals.

VI

So far we have looked at Bremnes society as an isolated object of study. In conclusion I want very briefly to consider Bremnes in relation to other similar societies. In reality Bremnes is not an isolated society, and there is the large descriptive and analytical problem of understanding the relationship between Bremnes and neighbouring parishes, and between it and the Norwegian State. These problems I shall not deal with here. The problem I want to glance at is a morphological one, of seeing Bremnes as an example of a particular type of society.

The centuries of development, and of stagnation, that lie behind the Bremnes society described in this paper can be summarized as follows. From A.D. 600 until 1300, during the Viking Age and later, the Norwegian State expanded to include all Norway, Iceland, and part of Sweden, with colonies further afield in Scotland, Ireland, the Isle of Man, and Greenland. From 1300 onwards the State declined under pressure from Denmark, Sweden and the Hanseatic League, and suffered badly in the Black Death. In 1380 Norway was joined to Denmark by a dynastic marriage and gradually sank to the effective status of a Danish colony, with a peasantry living largely in a subsistence economy. The administration was carried on mainly by Danes; the Danish language was used exclusively for writing, and commercial and industrial development lagged behind that of Denmark. During the eighteenth century the bureaucracy in Norway began to concern itself with the development of Norwegian, as distinct from Danish, culture and began to agitate for a Norwegian university. There was a considerable divergence of economic interest between Denmark and Norway, which was increased by the vicissitudes of the Napoleonic Wars; communications with Denmark were cut by the British blockade and a Norwegian government was formed. In 1814 a constitution was drawn up, heavily influenced by the ideas of the American Constitution and the French Revolution. Instead of gaining independence the country was, however, joined in a dual monarchy with Sweden. After nearly a hundred years of political struggle this union was dissolved, without fighting, in 1905.

In Viking times all free men attended local assemblies with judicial and legislative authority and later there were higher assemblies made up of representatives of the various localities. In the twelfth century the assemblies began to lose their power, and control of local affairs passed to nominees of the king. Under Danish rule government became more bureaucratic, and the peasants, who provided the bulk of the army, had only the viceroy to protect them against the demands of the land-owning gentry and the Danish-speaking bureaucrats. In the eighteenth century much land passed back into peasant hands, but the common people remained unenfranchised. The 1814 constitution provided for a wide franchise and some wealthier peasants were elected to Parliament. It was, however, not until 1837 that a system of elective local government was introduced. Many of the first rural mayors were bureaucrats, such as priests, sheriffs and judges, but gradually more farmers and peasants were elected. The bureaucracy, which even in Danish times had theoretically been open to all, now began to have members of peasant origin. At the same time the status of the bureaucrats as leaders of local society declined and new positions of eminence appeared; the school teachers being perhaps the first group of mainly peasant origin to acquire semi-professional status.

In Danish times trade was carried on in the countryside by town burghers, but by the end of the nineteenth century there had been considerable inter-marriage between the peasantry and the children of burghers stationed out in the country, and some peasants had started small trading posts on their own initiative. The comparative paucity of capital for investment in the towns meant that small-scale rural enterprises were often started by wealthier peasants rather than by townsfolk. At the same time the economy of the coastal region in the West, the part of Norway to which Bremnes belongs, underwent a change. Since time immemorial there had been fishing for the home market and for export, and as communications by sea and land improved this trade now expanded. Despite considerable set-backs the size of the catch increased over the years as more capital was invested in fishing vessels and nets. Down to the end of the nineteenth century most householders on this coast were both peasant and fisherman, but with the development of commercial fishing a division began to emerge between those who were mainly fishermen and those who were mainly peasants. A few fish salteries owned by town merchants and a few small boat-building yards were established rurally in the nineteenth century, and barrel-making flourished as a cottage industry, yet it is only recently that large-scale rural industrial enterprises have become important in the economy of the fishing districts. There are now several canning factories scattered along the coast and, as electricity becomes more readily available, further industrial expansion is likely. Bremnes, with its marine-engine factory, is more industrialized and has been industrialized longer than many nearby parishes.

Thus a hundred and fifty years ago there were in each rural parish one or two bureaucrats living at a much higher standard than the rest of the population, speaking a different language, and moving from post to post without developing marked local affiliation. Below them in status were a few traders, usually burghers of a town; they had more local ties and were not so mobile as the bureaucrats. The rest of the population were peasants, with the freeholders occupying the highest stratum and accounting for about half of the peasantry. Next came the leaseholders, usually cultivating land owned by Danish-speaking gentry or by rich burghers. Under them came the cottars, or labour tenants, who worked so many days a year for the freeholders in return for the use of small holdings. Finally at the bottom of society were the landless labourers, the indigent, and vagrants. In this system the peasantry, although forming the great bulk of the rural population, had little say in public affairs, were undifferentiated in terms of occupation and culture, but were divided into ranks based on inherited rights in land. This system ended, and Norway became a quasi-independent State with elective local government largely as a result of international politics and social movements among the bureaucrats and in the towns, that is, as a result of social forces external to rural society. Nevertheless, after a generation or so, peasant leadership began to emerge, the old ranking system among peasants broke down; the status of the rural bureaucrats declined, and the rural economy became more diversified.

This sequence of events was in no sense the inevitable consequence of the ending of colonial rule, but it is clear that the break with Denmark supplied the initial impetus that started this train of events in Norway and even in Bremnes. It seems not improbable that similar events may have taken place in other former colonies. One of the major social movements of the twentieth century has been the partial breaking-up of those world-wide empires established by the Powers of Western Europe during the nineteenth century and earlier, and there are many older empires now long since fallen into decay. Yet the problem of the rural effect of political independence does not always receive the attention it merits. When a country achieves independence interest is at first naturally focused on transformations taking place at the centre and in the towns. When the colonial Power is driven out by armed insurrection or as the result of a long political battle, the struggle for liberation is at the same time the process by which a new *élite* is formed to take over from the old colonial governing class. This is presumably what happened in South America, and perhaps in Indonesia. In a large country the formation of a new *élite* has greater social consequences for the towns and centres of government than it has for the countryside. In general colonial *élites* tend to concentrate in towns and military camps and are thinly spread throughout the rural areas. Hence the removal of the colonial Power may not at first have much effect on rural life. Liberation brings fresh faces in board-rooms and government offices, but the same people continue toiling in the fields. The ending of colonial government must of necessity bring about changes at the centre in the political structure of a new nation, but the effect rurally may be largely the replacement of, say, a White District Officer by a Black one. From the point of view of rural society the change to national political independence is then an event external to the system.

At other times the withdrawal of the colonial Power has been an event external to the social system of the colonial territory as a whole. An example of a withdrawal of this latter kind was the ending of Roman rule in Britain, when the critical conditions causing the withdrawal were to be found outside Britain. Yet, however remote from the rural areas may be the causes of colonial decline, in general the rural system will itself tend to change sooner or later. Occasionally rural change may precede political independence, as for instance in Israel, where for once we are fortunate in having more socio-logical information about rural conditions in transition than we have about changes at the centre. However, I think that we may say that usually the countryside lags behind the towns and the central institutions of a developing ex-colony, and changes in the pattern of rural life and family conditions come later and slower, if they come at all.

Thus, when a country is for one reason or another left to govern itself, the effect on the rural areas may be slight, delayed, or entirely lacking. A full discussion of why Bremnes society developed in the way it did cannot be attempted here. I would merely stress that the achievement of national in-dependence was one factor of significance in that development and that the opportunities we have of studying the consequences of similar events in other rural areas should not be overlooked.

The vacuum caused by the withdrawal of a governing *élite* may initiate one social process, as we have seen in Bremnes with the gradual emergence of part-time peasants in key positions in the structure of government and organized social life. Industrialization is a quite distinct process which has occurred and is still proceeding in countries with widely varying forms of political institutions, some of them colonies, some former colonies, and others that have not experienced colonial status for many centuries. The evidence suggests that in all of these, whatever social system they have had in the past, some form of class society develops as industrialization proceeds; or, as I would rather say, that the emergent societies can at least be described partly in the imprecise vocabulary of social class. The process of industrialization has also begun in Bremnes, and is perhaps largely responsible for such gropings towards a class system as we have noted. Comparative evidence from other societies at an early stage of industrialization, and from those in which new *élites* are being formed, may throw more light on the ways in which these two processes reinforce or neutralize one another.

BIOGRAPHICAL NOTE

J. A. BARNES is Reader in Anthropology in the University of London (London School of Economics). He read mathematics and anthropology at Cambridge, graduating in 1939. He studied at Cape Town and Oxford and did field research in Northern Rhodesia while on the staff of the Rhodes-Livingstone Institute. He joined University College London, in 1949 as Lecturer; was elected a Fellow of St. John's College, Cambridge; and in 1952 went to Norway as a Simon Research Fellow, Manchester University.

From Elizabeth Bott, *Human Relations 8*, 345-
383 (1955), by permission.

URBAN FAMILIES: CONJUGAL ROLES AND SOCIAL NETWORKS[1]

ELIZABETH BOTT

In this paper I should like to report some of the results of an intensive
study of twenty London families.[2] The study was exploratory, the aim being
to develop hypotheses that would further the sociological and psychological
understanding of families rather than to describe facts about a random or
representative sample of families. Ideally, research of this sort might best be
divided into two phases: a first, exploratory phase in which the aim would
be to develop hypotheses by studying the interrelation of various factors
within each family considered as a social system, and a second phase consisting of a more extensive inquiry designed to test the hypotheses on a larger
scale. In view of the time and resources at our disposal, the present research
was restricted to the first phase.

The paper will be confined to one problem: how to interpret the variations that were found to occur in the way husbands and wives performed
their conjugal roles. These variations were considerable. At one extreme was
a family in which the husband and wife carried out as many tasks as possible
separately and independently of each other. There was a strict division of
labour in the household, in which she had her tasks and he had his. He gave
her a set amount of housekeeping money, and she had little idea of how much
he earned or how he spent the money he kept for himself. In their leisure

---

1. A first version of this paper was read at the U.N.E.S.C.O. Seminar "Problems of the Family in
the Changing Social Order" at Cologne in June 1954. Later versions were read at seminars at the London
School of Economics in October 1954, and at Manchester University in November 1954. I am grateful
to members of all three seminars, and most particularly to several friends and colleagues, for their pains-
taking and constructive criticisms. Under the title of "A Study of Ordinary Families", an earlier
version of the paper will be included in a forthcoming book of research papers of the International
Seminar on Family Research, to be issued by the U.N.E.S.C.O. Institute for Social Sciences, Cologne.

2. This research was sponsored jointly by the Family Welfare Association and the Tavistock Institute
of Human Relations; it was financed for three years by the Nuffield Foundation. The core research team
consisted of Dr. A. T. M. Wilson (medical psycho-analyst), Miss I. Menzies (psycho-analyst), Dr. J. H.
Robb (sociologist), and the author (social anthropologist). Dr. Wilson supervised the project and conducted clinical interviews; Miss Menzies assisted Dr. Wilson in the analysis of the psychological material
and supervised many of the home interviews; Dr. Robb and the author carried out the sociological field
work, which consisted of home visits and interviews. Mr. H. Phillipson and Mr. J. Boreham of the
Tavistock Clinic administered and interpreted Thematic Apperception Tests.

time, he went to football matches with his friends, whereas she visited her relatives or went to a cinema with a neighbour. With the exception of festivities with relatives, this husband and wife spent very little of their leisure time together. They did not consider that they were unusual in this respect. On the contrary, they felt that their behaviour was typical of their social circle. At the other extreme was a family in which husband and wife shared as many activities and spent as much time together as possible. They stressed that husband and wife should be equals: all major decisions should be made together, and even in minor household matters they should help one another as much as possible. This norm was carried out in practice. In their division of labour, many tasks were shared or interchangeable. The husband often did the cooking and sometimes the washing and ironing. The wife did the gardening and often the household repairs as well. Much of their leisure time was spent together, and they shared similar interests in politics, music, literature, and in entertaining friends. Like the first couple, this husband and wife felt that their behaviour was typical of their social circle, except that they felt they carried the interchangeability of household tasks a little further than most people.

One may sum up the differences between these two extremes by saying that the first family showed considerable segregation between husband and wife in their role-relationship, whereas in the second family the conjugal role-relationship was as joint as possible. In between these two extremes there were many degrees of variation. These differences in degree of segregation of conjugal roles will form the central theme of this paper.

A *joint conjugal role-relationship* is one in which husband and wife carry out many activities together, with a minimum of task differentiation and separation of interests; in such cases husband and wife not only plan the affairs of the family together, but also exchange many household tasks and spend much of their leisure time together. A *segregated conjugal role-relationship* is one in which husband and wife have a clear differentiation of tasks and a considerable number of separate interests and activities; in such cases, husband and wife have a clearly defined division of labour into male tasks and female tasks; they expect to have different leisure pursuits; the husband has his friends outside the home and the wife has hers. It should be stressed, however, that these are only differences of degree. All families must have some division of labour between husband and wife; all families must have some joint activities.

Early in the research, it seemed likely that these differences in degree of segregation of conjugal roles were related somehow to forces in the social environment of the families. In first attempts to explore these forces, an effort was made to explain such segregation in terms of social class. This attempt was not very successful. The husbands who had the most segregated role-relationships with their wives had manual occupations, and the husbands who had the most joint role-relationships with their wives were professionals, but there were several working-class families that had relatively little segregation and there were several professional families in which segregation was considerable. An attempt was also made to relate degree of segregation to the type of local area in which the family lived, since the data suggested that the families with most segregation lived in homogeneous areas of low population turnover, whereas the families with predominantly joint role-relationships lived in heterogeneous areas of high population turnover. Once again, however, there were several exceptions. But there was a more important difficulty in these attempts to correlate segregation of conjugal roles with class position and type of local area. The research was not designed to produce valid statistical correlations, for which a very different method would have been necessary. Our aim was to make a study of the interrelation of various social and psychological factors within each family considered as a social system. Attempts at rudimentary statistical correlation did not make clear how one factor affected another; it seemed impossible to explain exactly how the criteria for class position or the criteria for different types of local area were actually producing an effect on the internal role structure of the family.

It therefore appeared that attempts to correlate segregation of conjugal roles with factors selected from the generalized social environment of the family would not yield a meaningful interpretation. Leaving social class and neighbourhood composition to one side for the time being, I turned to look more closely at the immediate environment of the families, that is, at their actual external relationships with friends, neighbours, relatives, clubs, shops, places of work, and so forth. This approach proved to be more fruitful.

First, it appeared that the external social relationships of all families assumed the form of a *network* rather than the form of an organized group.[3] In an organized group, the component individuals make up a larger social whole with common aims, interdependent roles, and a distinctive sub-culture. In network formation, on the other hand, only some but not all of the component individuals have social relationships with one another. For example, supposing that a family, X, maintains relationships with friends, neighbours, and relatives who may be designated as A, B, C, D, E, F . . . N, one will find that some but not all of these external persons know one another. They do not form an organized group in the sense defined above. B might know A and C but none of the others; D might know F without knowing A, B, C, or E. Furthermore, all of these persons will have friends, neighbours, and relatives of their own who are not known by family X. In

---

3. In sociological and anthropological literature, the term "group" is commonly used in at least two senses. In the first sense it is a very broad term used to describe any collectivity whose members are alike in some way; this definition would include categories, logical classes, and aggregates as well as more cohesive social units. The second usage is much more restricted; in this sense, the units must have some distinctive interdependent social relationships with one another; categories, logical classes, and aggregates are excluded. To avoid confusion I use the term "organized group" when it becomes necessary to distinguish the second usage from the first.

a network, the component external units do not make up a larger social whole; they are not surrounded by a common boundary.[4]

Secondly, although all the research families belonged to networks rather than to groups, there was considerable variation in the *connectedness* of their networks. By connectedness I mean the extent to which the people known by a family know and meet one another independently of the family. I use the term *dispersed network* to describe a network in which there are few relationships amongst the component units, and the term *highly connected network* to describe a network in which there are many such relationships.[5] The difference is represented very schematically in *Figure 1*. Each family has a network containing five external units, but the network of Family X is more connected than that of Y. There are nine relationships amongst the

FIGURE I   *SCHEMATIC COMPARISON OF THE NETWORKS OF TWO FAMILIES*

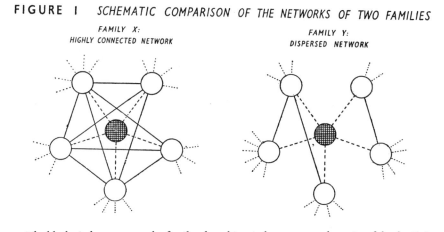

FAMILY X:
HIGHLY CONNECTED NETWORK

FAMILY Y:
DISPERSED NETWORK

The black circles represent the family, the white circles represent the units of the family's network. The broken lines represent the relationships of the family with the external units; the solid lines represent the relationships of the members of the network with one another. The dotted lines leading off from the white circles indicate that each member of a family's network maintains relationships with other people who are not included in the family's network. This representation is of course highly schematic; a real family would have many more than five external units in its network.

---

4. The term "network" is usually employed in a very broad and metaphorical sense, e.g. in Radcliffe-Brown's definition of social structure as "a complex network of social relations" (4). Although he does not define the term, Moreno uses it in roughly the sense employed in the present paper (3). In giving the term a precise and restricted meaning, I follow the recent usage of John Barnes: "Each person is, as it were, in touch with a number of people, some of whom are directly in touch with each other and some of whom are not . . . I find it convenient to talk of a social field of this kind as a *network*. The image I have is of a set of points some of which are joined by lines. The points of the image are people, or sometimes groups, and the lines indicate which people interact with each other" (1, p. 43).

5. Barnes uses the term "mesh" to denote network connectedness. In a network with a small mesh, many of the individuals in X's network know and meet one another independently of X; in a network with a large mesh, few of the individuals in X's network know and meet one another independently of X (1, p. 44).

people of X's network whereas there are only three amongst the people of Y's network. X's network is highly connected, Y's is dispersed.

A detailed examination of the research data reveals that the degree of segregation of conjugal roles is related to the degree of network connectedness. Those families that had a high degree of segregation in the role-relationship of husband and wife had a highly connected network; many of their friends, neighbours, and relatives knew one another. Families that had a relatively joint role-relationship between husband and wife had a dispersed network; few of their relatives, neighbours, and friends knew one another. There were many degrees of variation in between these two extremes. On the basis of our data, I should therefore like to put forward the following hypothesis: *The degree of segregation in the role-relationship of husband and wife varies directly with the connectedness of the family's social network*. The more connected the network, the more segregation between the roles of husband and wife. The more dispersed the network, the less segregation between the roles of husband and wife. This relationship between network connectedness and segregation of conjugal roles will be more fully illustrated and discussed below.

No claim is made here that network connectedness is the only factor affecting segregation of conjugal roles. Among the other variables affecting the way conjugal roles are performed, the personalities of husband and wife are of crucial importance. Most of this paper will be devoted to a discussion of the effect of network connectedness, however, because the importance of this variable has been insufficiently stressed in previous studies of family role structure.

It thus appears that if one is to understand segregation of conjugal roles, one should examine the effect of the family's immediate social environment of friends, neighbours, relatives, and institutions. The question remains, however, as to why some families should have highly connected networks whereas others have dispersed networks. In part, network connectedness depends on the family themselves. One family may choose to introduce their friends, neighbours, and relatives to one another, whereas another may not. One family may move around a great deal so that its network becomes dispersed, whereas another family may stay put. But these choices are limited and shaped by a number of forces over which the family does not have direct control. It is at this point that the total social environment becomes relevant. The economic and occupational system, the structure of formal institutions, the ecology of cities, and many other factors affect the connectedness of networks, and limit and shape the decisions that families make. Among others, factors associated with social class and neighbourhood composition affect segregation of conjugal roles, not solely and not primarily through direct action on the internal structure of the family, but indirectly through their effect on its network. Conceptually, the network stands between the family and the total social environment. The connectedness of a family's network depends on the one hand on certain forces in the total environment and on the other hand on the personalities of the members of the family and on the way they react to these forces.

In this paper a first attempt will be made to carry out an analysis in terms of these concepts. Part I will be devoted to a discussion of conjugal role-segregation in relation to network connectedness. In Part II the relation of networks to the total environment will be discussed.

Whether my central hypothesis, the direct relationship between network connectedness and segregation of conjugal roles, is valid for other families I do not know. At this stage I am not attempting to make generalizations about all families, and I am not concerned with whether or not the families we have studied are typical of others. What I am trying to do is to make a comparative study of the relationship between conjugal role-segregation and network connectedness for each of the twenty families considered as a social system. In so doing I have developed a hypothesis that, with further refinement of definition, preferably in quantifiable terms, might be tested on other families and might facilitate further and more systematic comparisons.

PART I. CONJUGAL ROLE-SEGREGATION AND NETWORK CONNECTEDNESS

A. METHODS OF COLLECTING DATA [6]

Although this paper will be devoted primarily to discussion of the effect of external social relationships on the role-relationship of husband and wife, the research as a whole was designed to investigate families not only sociologically but also psychologically. The research techniques accordingly consisted of a combination of the field-work method of the social anthropologist, in which the group under investigation is studied as a working whole in its natural habitat in so far as this is possible, and the case-study method in which individuals are studied by clinical interviews. No attempt was made to use statistical procedures.

The families studied were "ordinary", in the sense that they did not come to us for help with personal or familial problems, and they were usually able to cope themselves with such difficulties as they had. We sought them out, they did not come to us. In order to simplify the task of comparison, only families with young children were selected; the discussion of conjugal role-segregation and network formation will accordingly be restricted to families in this phase of development. In order further to restrict the number of variables that had to be taken into account, only English families who were Protestant or of mainly Protestant background were selected. All twenty families lived in London or Greater London, but they were scattered all over the area and did not form an organized group. Although the families thus resembled one another in phase of marriage and in national and religious

---

6. For an account of field techniques see J. H. Robb (5).

258

background, they varied considerably in occupation and in socio-economic status; the net incomes of the husbands after tax ranged from £325 to £1,500.

Much difficulty was encountered in contacting suitable families, although the effort to find them taught us a good deal about the way families are related to other social groups. The twenty families were eventually contacted through the officials of various service institutions, such as doctors, hospitals, schools, local political parties, and the like, and through friends of the family. Introductions were most successful when the contact person was well known and trusted by both husband and wife, and the most satisfactory channel of contact was through friends of the family.

After the contact person had told a prospective family about the research and had got their agreement to an explanatory interview by one of the research staff, one of the field workers visited the family at their home to describe what the research was about and what it would involve for the family. The field worker explained the background of the research, the content of the interviews, and the time they would take. He (or she) made it clear that the family could withdraw at any time, that the material would be treated with professional discretion, and that if we wished to publish any confidential material that might reveal the couple's identity, we should consult them beforehand. The research staff also undertook to pay any expenses that the couple might incur as a result of the investigation. Although the provisional and explanatory nature of the first interview was always emphasized, we found that most of the couples who got as far as this interview had usually decided to take part in the research before they met the field worker, chiefly on the basis of what the contact person had told them. We have no systematic information about couples who were consulted but decided not to participate.

After a family had agreed to take part, the field worker paid several visits to them at home in the evening for joint interviews with the husband and wife. He also went at least once during the day at the week-end when he could meet the children and observe the whole family together. There were thirteen home interviews on the average, the range being from eight to nineteen. Each home interview began with half an hour of casual chatting followed by more focused discussions on particular topics during which notes were taken. The topics discussed were: kinship, family background, and personal history until marriage; the first phase of the family from marriage until the birth of the first child; an account of family life at the time of interviewing, including a daily, weekly, and yearly diary, a description of external social relationships with service institutions such as schools, church, clinic doctor, and so forth, with voluntary associations and recreational institutions, and more informal relationships with friends, neighbours, and relatives; an account of the division of labour between husband and wife in overall planning, in the economic support of the family, in domestic tasks, and in child care; and finally, questions were asked about values and ideology concerning family life, social class, money and financial management, and general political, social, and religious questions. These topics were used as a general guide by the field worker; the order of topics and the form of questioning were left to his discretion. Usually he raised a topic, and the couple carried on the discussion themselves with occasional additional questions by the field worker. The discussion frequently wandered away from the assigned topic, but little attempt was made to restrict such digressions, since all the behaviour of husband and wife towards one another and towards the field worker was held to be significant data.

When the home interviews had been completed, the field worker explained the second part of the research, which had been briefly mentioned in the first interview. This consisted of a clinical investigation in which the husband and wife were interviewed at the Tavistock Institute of Human Relations. Fifteen of the twenty families came for clinical interviews. The first such interview consisted of a brief joint meeting of the couple, the field worker, and the psycho-analyst, followed by the individual administration of the Thematic Apperception Tests by two psychologists from the Tavistock Clinic. The husbands and wives then returned separately on future occasions for two or three clinical interviews with the psycho-analyst. The topics covered were health; personal development, and relationships with parents, siblings, and friends; sexual development; the personal relationship between husband and wife, and the effect of the children on the individual and on the family as a whole. Here again the topics were used only as a general guide. The informants were allowed to express their ideas and feelings as freely as possible.

After the clinical interviews were over, the sociological field worker paid a final home visit to bring the investigation to a close. Frequent supplementary visits have been made, however, partly to fill in gaps in the information and partly to work material through with the families prior to publication. All the families know that a book is to be written about them and most of them intend to read it. We plan to publish detailed sociological and psychological accounts of two families; this material has been disguised so that even people who knew the families would have difficulty in recognizing them; in these very detailed, exhaustive accounts, however, it was impossible to work out a disguise so complete that the couple would not recognize themselves, because many of the things that would have had to be altered for such a disguise were essential to the analysis. We have therefore discussed the material with the two families concerned. This process is somewhat upsetting, but the families found it much more acceptable than the prospect of suddenly recognizing themselves laid bare in print without any prior consultation. We took it for granted that the process of digesting an analysis of themselves in sociological and psychological terms would be disturbing, and we accepted the responsibility of helping them with it in so far as they felt the need of assistance. We did not force therapy on them, and we chose families whom we felt could stand the stress with comparative ease. Working the material through with the families was also important for the analysis itself; the reactions of the couples to our interpretations of the facts which they had told us helped us to evaluate and revise our analysis.

In addition to the interviews with the twenty families, discussions about families in general were held with various persons, particularly doctors, who had considerable knowledge of family life. Discussions were also held with various organized groups such as Community Centres and Townswomen's Guilds. These groups had no direct connection with the families we interviewed, and in most cases they were composed of people, usually women, who were considerably older than the research husbands and wives. These discussions were therefore not directly relevant to the analysis of the research families, but they provided useful information on the norms of family life. In a public, group situation, especially one which lasts for only one session, people seem much more willing to talk about norms than to discuss their actual behaviour.

B. DESCRIPTION OF THE DATA

If families are classified according to the extremes of the two dimensions of conjugal role-segregation and network connectedness, four patterns are logically possible: 1. segregated conjugal role-relationship associated with a highly connected network, 2. segregated conjugal role-relationship associated with a dispersed network, 3. joint conjugal role-relationship associated with a highly connected network, and 4. joint conjugal role-relationship associated with a dispersed network. Empirically, two of these patterns, the second and third, did not occur. There were no families in which a highly segregated conjugal role-relationship was associated with a dispersed network; there were no families in which a joint conjugal role-relationship was associated with a highly connected network.

Six of the research families were clustered in the first and fourth patterns. There was one family that conformed to the first pattern, a high degree of conjugal role-segregation being combined with a highly connected network. There were five families that conformed to the fourth pattern, a joint conjugal role-relationship being associated with a dispersed network. These six families represent the extremes of the research set. There were nine families that were intermediate in degree of conjugal role-segregation and similarly intermediate in degree of network connectedness. Finally there were five families that appeared to be in a state of transition both with respect to their network formation and with respect to their conjugal role-relationship.

Among the twenty families, there was thus some clustering at certain points along a possible continuum from a highly segregated to a very joint conjugal role-relationship, and along a second continuum from a highly connected to a dispersed network. The families did not fall into sharply separated types, however, so that divisions are somewhat arbitrary, but for convenience of description, I shall divide the families into four groups: 1. highly segregated conjugal role-relationship associated with highly connected network, 2. joint conjugal role-relationship associated with dispersed network, 3. intermediate degrees of conjugal role-segregation and network connectedness, and 4. transitional families. No claim is made here that these are the only patterns that can occur; further research would probably reveal others. In the following discussion I shall be chiefly concerned not with these divisions, but rather with the fact that the order according to degree of conjugal role-segregation follows the order according to degree of network connectedness, and I shall attempt to show the mechanisms by which this relationship operates.

1. Highly Segregated Conjugal Role-relationship Associated with Highly Connected Network

The research set contained only one family of this type.[7] For convenience I shall call them Mr. and Mrs. N. They had been married four years when the interviewing began and had two small children. In the following discussion, I shall describe their actual behaviour, indicating the points at which they depart from their norms.[8]

External social relationships. Mr. N had a semi-skilled manual job at a factory in an East End area adjacent to the one in which he and Mrs. N lived. He said that many other men in the local area had jobs at the same place, or were doing the same sort of work at similar factories and workshops nearby. Mrs. N did not work, but she felt that she was unusual in this respect. Most of the neighbouring women and many of her female relatives had jobs; she did not think there was anything morally wrong with such work, but she said that she had never liked working and preferred to stay at home with the children. Mr. N said that he thought it was best for her and the children if she stayed at home, and added that he felt it was a bit of a reflection on a man if his wife had to go out to work.

The Ns used the services of a local hospital and a maternity and child welfare clinic. They expected to send their children to the local elementary

---

7. As stated above, I am not primarily concerned in this paper with whether the research families are typical of others, but it is perhaps of some interest that families with highly connected networks and pronounced conjugal role-segregation are by no means rare, and that they appear to occur primarily in long-established working-class areas. Supplementary data about such families was collected in group discussions. See also Michael Young (8, 9) and J. H. Robb (6). In Part II of the present paper I shall discuss some of the factors involved in living in long-established working-class areas, and how these factors affect network connectedness.

8. Problems concerning norms will be taken up in a subsequent paper. I use the term "norm" to mean those items of behaviour which are felt by the members of a family to be prescribed and/or typical in their social circle. Ideal norms are those prescribed rules of behaviour which it is felt that people ought to follow; norms of expectation are those behaviours which are felt to be typical or usual. In my view, norms are partly internalized through experiences with other people and through reading, listening to the radio, and so forth; in part norms are a construction of the members of the family, who re-interpret and re-order the received norms, within limits, in accordance with their own needs. It follows that families vary considerably in their norms, although families with similar social experiences will tend to have broadly similar norms.

school. They were also in touch with the local housing authority because they were trying to find a new flat. These various service institutions were not felt to have any particular relationship to one another, except in the sense that they were all felt to be foreign bodies, not really part of the local life. Mrs. N was a little bit afraid of them, particularly of the hospital and of doctors. On one occasion, while waiting with her baby and the field worker in an otherwise empty hospital room for a doctor to attend to the baby, she said in a whisper, "My husband says that we pay for it [the hospital services, through National Health subscriptions] and we should use it, but I don't like coming here. I don't like hospitals and doctors, do you?"

To the Ns, the local area was definitely a community in the social sense, a place with an identity of its own and a distinctive way of life. They spoke of it with great pride and contrasted it favourably with other areas. "It has a bad name, they say we are rough, but I think it's the best place there is. Everyone is friendly . . . there is no life in the West End compared with the East End. They drink champagne and we drink beer. When things are la-di-da you feel out of place." They took it for granted that the other inhabitants had similar feelings of local pride and loyalty. Both the Ns had grown up in the same area, as had most of their relatives and friends. Trips outside the area were like adventures into a foreign land, especially for Mrs. N, and very few informal social relationships were kept up with people outside the area. Physical distance was felt to be an almost insuperable barrier to social contact.

Physically, the area was far from ideal as a place to live, for the houses were old-fashioned, inconvenient, and crowded. The Ns were faced with a difficult choice of whether to move out of London to a modern flat on a new housing estate, or to stay put in cramped quarters, in the old familiar local area with their friends and relatives. They knew of several other young couples who were faced with a similar dilemma. Group discussions at a local community centre and the research of the Institute of Community Studies indicated that many local residents feel this to be an important social and personal problem (9).

The Ns felt that their neighbours were socially similar to themselves, meaning that they had the same sort of jobs, the same sort of background, the same sort of outlook on life.[9] Because the Ns had grown up in the area, as had many of their relatives and neighbours, they knew a very considerable number of local people, and many of the people they knew were acquainted with one another. In other words, their social network was highly connected. In fact there was considerable overlap of social roles; instead of there being people in three or four separate categories—friend, neighbour, relative, and colleague—the same person frequently filled two or three or ever four of these roles simultaneously.

---

9. Unless otherwise noted, the phrase "socially similar" will be used throughout this paper to describe people who are felt by a husband and wife to belong to the same social class as themselves.

The Ns took it for granted that Mr. N, like other husbands in their social circle, would have some form of recreation that he carried on with men away from home. In his case it was football, although the most common form of recreation was felt to be drinking and visiting in the local pub, where many husbands spent an evening or two a week with their friends; quite frequently some of these men were friends of old standing, men who had belonged to the same childhood gang, and others were colleagues at work. Mr. N had kept in touch with one or two friends of his childhood; he also played football and went to matches with some of his colleagues at work; he mentioned that several of his friends knew one another. Mrs. N knew a bit about these men, but she did not expect to join in their activities with her husband. She had a nodding acquaintance with the wives of two or three of these men, and occasionally talked to them when she was out shopping.

Mrs. N also had her own separate relationships in which her husband did not expect to join. She knew many of her female neighbours, just as they knew one another; she took it for granted that a friendly relationship with a neighbour would be dropped if the woman moved away. Neighbours saw one another on the landings, in the street, in shops, occasionally over a cup of tea inside the flat or house. They talked over their own affairs and those of other neighbours. Neighbours frequently accused one another of something—of betraying a confidence, of taking the wrong side in a children's quarrel, of failing to return borrowed articles, of gossip. One has little privacy in such a situation. But if one wants to reap the rewards of companionship and small acts of mutual aid, one has to conform to local standards, and one has to put up with being included in the gossip. Indeed, being gossiped about is as much a sign that one belongs to the neighbourly network as being gossiped with. If one refuses to have anything to do with one's neighbours one is thought odd, but eventually one will be left alone; no gossip, no companionship.

With the exception of visiting relatives and an occasional Sunday outing with the children, the Ns spent very little of their leisure time in joint recreation with each other; even though they could have got their relatives to mind the children for them, they rarely went out together. In particular, there was no joint entertaining of friends at home. From time to time Mr. N brought a friend home and Mrs. N made tea and talked a bit to the friend; female neighbours often dropped in during the evening to borrow something, but they did not stay long if Mr. N was there. There was no planned joint entertaining in which Mr. and Mrs. N asked another husband and wife to spend an evening with them. Such joint entertaining as existed was carried on with relatives, not with friends. Poverty does not explain the absence of joint entertaining, for the Ns considered themselves to be relatively well off. It did not seem to occur to them that they might spend their surplus money on entertainment of friends; they felt that such money should be spent on furniture, new things for the children, or on large gatherings of relatives at weddings, funerals, and christenings.[10]

There was much visiting and mutual aid between relatives, particularly by the women. The Ns had far more active social relationships with relatives than any other research family, and there was also a great deal of independent contact by their relatives with one another in addition to their contacts with the Ns themselves. In brief, the network of kin was highly connected, more highly connected than those of neighbours or friends. The women were more active than the men in keeping up contacts with relatives, with the result that the networks of wives were more highly connected than the networks of their husbands. Although husbands were recognized to be less active in kinship affairs than their wives, Mr. N paid occasional visits to his mother, both by himself and with Mrs. N. Furthermore, there were some activities for which joint participation by husband and wife was felt to be desirable. At weddings, funerals, and christenings, there were large assemblages of relatives, and on such occasions it was felt to be important that both husband and wife should attend. Recent and prospective weddings, twenty-first birthday parties, and christenings formed an important topic of discussion throughout the interviews with the Ns.

In a group discussion, a man living in the same local area as the Ns and having a similar sort of family life and kinship network summed up the situation by saying, "Men have friends. Women have relatives." Very succinctly he had described the overlapping of roles mentioned above. For Mrs. N, there was no independent category of "friend"; friends were either neighbours or relatives. She had had a succession of girl friends in her adolescence, but she said that she did not see so much of them since they had all got married and had had children. She always described them as "girl friends", not as "friends". Both Mr. and Mrs. N used the term "friend" as if it applied only to men; the term "neighbour"., on the other hand, seemed to refer only to women. Mr. N looked rather shocked when I asked him if he saw much of the neighbours.

Later on in the group discussion, the same man observed, "Women don't have friends. They have Mum." In Mrs. N's case the relationship between herself and her mother was indeed very close. Her mother lived nearby in the same local area, and Mrs. N went to visit her nearly every day, taking

---

10. The absence of the pattern of joint entertainment of friends made our technique of joint interviews with husband and wife somewhat inappropriate for the Ns. Mrs. N was more relaxed and talked much more freely when she and I were alone or when we were together with other women. This was not because of bad relations with her husband; in fact she felt that they had a very successful conjugal relationship and that she was fortunate in having an unusually generous and thoughtful husband. But in spite of this, she felt she could not talk so freely when he was there, and in all probability he had similar feelings. Because of the difficulty in conducting joint interviews, we considered the possibility of interviewing them separately, Mrs. N by the female field worker and Mr. N by the male field worker. But there were two difficulties: first, we wanted to use the same technique with all families so as to simplify the task of comparison, and secondly we felt that separate home as well as clinical interviews would make each partner too suspicious and anxious about what the other was saying.

her children along with her. She and her mother and her mother's sisters also went to visit Mrs. N's maternal grandmother. Together these women and their children formed an important group, helping one another in household tasks and child care, and providing aid for one another in crises. [11] Within the network of relatives, in other words, there was a nucleus composed of the grandmother, her daughters, and her daughters' daughters; the relationships of these women with one another were sufficiently intense and distinctive to warrant the term "organized group" in the sense defined above (p. 347). Mrs. N's female relatives provided some of the domestic help and emotional support that, in other research families, a wife expected to get from her husband. Mrs. N felt tremendously attached to her mother emotionally. She felt that a bad relationship between mother and daughter was unnatural, a complete catastrophe. She would, I feel sure, have been deeply shocked by the seemingly cold and objective terms in which many of the women in the other research families analysed their mothers' characters. The close tie with the mother is not only a source of help, however, but may also be a potential source of friction, for if her husband and her mother do not get along well together, a young wife is likely to feel torn by conflicting loyalties. Mrs. N felt that she was particularly fortunate in that her husband and her mother liked each other.

In brief, there was considerable segregation between Mr. and Mrs. N in their external relationships. In effect, Mrs. N had her network and Mr. N had his. The number of joint external relationships was comparatively small. At the same time, there were many links between their networks: the husbands of some of Mrs. N's neighbours were men who were colleagues of Mr. N, some of Mrs. N's relatives also worked at the same place as Mr. N, and in a general way, his family was known to hers even before Mr. and Mrs. N got married. In other words, the connectedness of the combined networks of Mr. and Mrs. N was high compared to that of the families to be discussed below. But the Ns' total network was sharply divided into the husband's network and the wife's network. Furthermore, her network was more highly connected than his: many of the relatives and neighbours with whom she was in contact saw one another independently of her, whereas there were fewer independent links between Mr. N's colleagues, his football associates, and his friends from childhood.

Conjugal role-segregation. The previous description reveals considerable segregation between Mr. and Mrs. N in their external relationships. There was a similar segregation in the way they carried out their internal domestic tasks. They took it for granted that there should be a clear-cut division of labour between them, and that all husbands and wives in their social circle would organize their households in a similar way. One man said in a group discussion: "A lot of men wouldn't mind helping their wives if the curtains were

---

11. See also Michael Young (8).

266

drawn so people couldn't see." Although the Ns felt that major decisions should be made jointly, in the day-to-day running of the household he had his jobs and she had hers. He had control of the money and gave her a house-keeping allowance of £5 a week. Mrs. N did not know how much money he earned, and it did not seem to occur to her that a wife would want or need to know this. Although the Ns said that £5 was the amount most wives were given for housekeeping, Mrs. N had great difficulty in making it cover all the expenses of food, rent, utilities, and five shillings' saving for Christmas. She told Mr. N whenever she ran short, and he left a pound or two under the clock when he went out the next morning. She said that he was very generous with his money and she felt that she was unusually fortunate in being spared financial quarrels.

Mrs. N was responsible for most of the housework and child care, although Mr. N did household repairs and helped to entertain the children at week-ends. Mrs. N expected that he would do some of the housework if she became ill, but this was usually unnecessary because her mother or her sister or one of her cousins would come to her aid. Indeed, these female relatives helped her a great deal even with the everyday tasks of housework and child care.

Attitudes towards the role-relationship of husband and wife. Mr. and Mrs. N took it for granted that men had male interests and women had female interests and that there were few leisure activities that they would naturally share. In their view, a good husband was one who was generous with the housekeeping allowance, did not waste money on extravagant personal recreation, helped his wife with the housework if she got ill, and took an interest in the children. A good wife was a good manager and an affectionate mother, a woman who kept out of serious rows with neighbours and got along well with her own and her husband's relatives. A good marital relationship was one with a harmonious division of labour, but the Ns placed little stress on the importance of joint activities and shared interests. It is difficult to make any definite statement on the Ns' attitudes towards sexual relations, for they did not come to the Institute for clinical interviews. Judging from Mrs. N's references to such matters when Mr. N was absent, it seems likely that she felt that physical sexuality was an intrusion on a peaceful domestic relation-ship rather than an expression of such a relationship; it was as if sexuality were felt to be basically violent and disruptive. The findings of clinical workers and of other research workers suggest that among families like the Ns, there is little stress on the importance of physical sexuality for a happy marriage (7).

2. *Families Having a Joint Conjugal Role-relationship Associated with a Dispersed Network*

Among the research set there were five families of this type. All the hus-bands had professional or semi-professional occupations. Two of the hus-bands had been upwardly mobile in occupation relative to the occupations of their fathers. All five families, however, had a well-established pattern of external relationships; they might make new relationships, but the basic pattern was likely to remain the same. Similarly, all had worked out a fairly stable division of labour in domestic tasks.

External social relationships. The husbands' occupations had little intrinsic connection with the local areas in which they lived. All five husbands carried on their work at some distance from the area in which their homes were located, although two husbands did some additional work at home. But in no case was there any feeling that the occupation was locally rooted.

Whether or not wives should work was considered to be a very controversial question by these families. Unless they were very well off financially—and none of these five families considered themselves to be so—both husband and wife welcomed the idea of a double income, even though much of the additional money had to be spent on caring for the children. But money was not the only consideration; women also wanted to work for the sake of the work itself. It was felt that if she desired it, a woman should have a career or some sort of special interest and skill comparable in seriousness to her husband's occupation; on the other hand, it was felt that young children needed their mother's care and that ideally she should drop her career at least until the youngest child was old enough to go to school. But most careers cannot easily be dropped and picked up again several years later. Two of the wives had solved the problem by continuing to work; they had made careful (and expensive) provision for the care of their children. One wife worked at home. One planned to take up her special interest again as soon as her youngest child went to nursery school, and the fifth wife was already doing so.

These husbands and wives maintained contact with schools, general practitioners, hospitals, and in some cases local maternity and child welfare clinics. Most of them also used the services of a solicitor, an insurance agent, and other similar professional people as required. Unlike the first type of family, they did not feel that service institutions were strange and alien; it did not bother them when they had to go out of their local area to find such services, and they were usually well informed about service institutions and could exploit them efficiently. They were not afraid of doctors. There was no strict division of labour between husband and wife in dealing with service institutions. The wife usually dealt with those institutions that catered for children, and the husband dealt with the legal and financial ones, but either could take over the other's duties if necessary.

These husbands and wives did not regard the neighbourhood as a source of friends. In most cases husbands and wives had moved around a good deal both before and after marriage, and in no case were they living in the neighbourhood in which they grew up. Four were living in areas of such a kind that only a few of the neighbours were felt to be socially similar to the family themselves. The fifth family was living in a suburb that the husband and wife felt to be composed of people socially similar to one another, but quite different from themselves. In all cases these husbands and wives were polite but somewhat distant to neighbours. In order to have become proper friends, the neighbours would have had to be not only socially similar to the family themselves, but would also have had to share a large number of tastes and interests. Establishing such a relationship takes a long exploratory testing, and the feeling seems to have been that it was dangerous to make the test with neighbours since one ran the risk of being pestered by friendly attentions that one might not want to return. Since many of the neighbours probably had similar feelings, particularly when the neighbourhood was socially heterogeneous, it is not surprising that intimate social relationships were not rapidly established. Since these families had so little social intercourse with their neighbours, they were very much less worried than the first type of family about gossip and conformity to local norms. Indeed, in the circumstances one can hardly say that there were any specifically local norms; certainly there was not the body of shared attitudes and values built up through personal interaction since childhood that was characteristic of the local area inhabited by the Ns.

The children were less discriminating than their parents. Unless restricted by their parents, they played with anyone in the street. This caused some of the parents a certain amount of anxiety, particularly when they felt that the area was very heterogeneous. Other parents adopted the view that mixing with children of other social classes was a good thing. In any case, all parents relied on their own influence and on the education of the children to erase any possibly bad effects of such contact.

It seemed very difficult for these families to find the sort of house and local area in which they wanted to live. They wanted to own a reasonably cheap house with a garden in central London, a house within easy reach of their friends, of plays, concerts, galleries, and so forth. Ideally they wanted a cheap, reliable cleaning-woman-cum-baby-sitter to live nearby, possibly even with the family if they could afford it. Only one family had achieved something approaching this aim. The others were making do with various compromises, impeded by lack of money as well as by the scarcity of suitable houses.

For these families, friends were felt to provide the most important type of external relationship. Not all of each family's friends knew one another; it was not usual for a large number of a family's friends to be in intimate contact with one another independently of their contact with the family. In brief, the network of friends was typically dispersed (unconnected). Husband and wife had usually established friendships over a period of years in many different social contexts—at school, during the course of their professional training, in the Services, at various jobs, very occasionally even because of living in the same neighbourhood. Their friends were scattered all over

London, sometimes even all over Britain. Because the network of friends was so dispersed, their social control over the family was dispersed and fragmented. The husband and wife were very sensitive to what their friends thought of them, but since the friends had so little contact with one another, they were not likely to present a unified body of public opinion. Amongst all the different bits of advice they might receive, husband and wife had to make up their own minds about what they should do. They were less persecuted by gossip than the first type of family, but they were also less sustained by it. Their friends did not form a solid body of helpers.

In marked contrast to the Ns, nearly all of the husband's and wife's friends were joint friends; it was felt to be important that both husband and wife should like a family friend, and if a friend was married, then it was hoped that all four partners to the relationship would like one another. Exceptions were tolerated, especially in the case of very old friends, but both husband and wife were uncomfortable if there was real disagreement between them over a friend. Friendship, like marriage, required shared interests and similar tastes, although there was some specialization of interests among different friends. For example, one couple might be golfing friends whereas others might be pub and drinking friends; still others were all-round friends, and it was these who were felt to be the most intimate.

Joint entertainment of friends was a major form of recreation. Even when poverty made invitations to dinner or parties impracticable, friends were still asked over jointly even if only for coffee or tea in the evening. It was considered provincial for husbands to cluster at one end of the room and wives at the other; everyone should be able to talk to everyone else. These husbands and wives usually had enough shared interests to make this possible. Many of them were highly educated, so that they had a common background of general topics, but even those who lacked such education usually make an attempt to talk about matters of general interest.

After these couples had had children, it had become increasingly difficult for them to visit their friends. Since their friends often lived at a considerable distance, and since most of them were also tied down by young children, mutual visiting had become more and more difficult to arrange. Considerable expense and trouble were taken to make such visiting possible. It was obvious that friends were of primary importance to these families.

There were usually other forms of joint recreation besides visiting friends, such as eating in foreign restaurants, going to plays, the cinema, concerts, and so forth. After children were born, there had been a marked drop in external joint recreation in preference for things that could be done at home. Going out had become a special occasion with all the paraphernalia of a baby-sitter and arrangements made in advance.

These five families had far less contact with their relatives than the Ns. Their relatives were not concentrated in the same local area as themselves, and in most cases they were scattered all over the country, and did not keep in close touch with one another. They formed a dispersed network. It was felt that friendly relations should be kept up with parents, and in several cases the birth of the children had led to a sort of reunion with parents. It seems likely that becoming a parent facilitates a resolution of some of the emotional tensions between adult children and their own parents, particularly between women and their mothers. It is possible that in some cases the arrival of children may exacerbate such tensions, but none of these five families had had such an experience. There are of course some obvious practical advantages in increased contact with parents; they are usually very fond of their grand-children, so that they make affectionate and reliable baby-sitters; if they live close enough to take on this task their services are greatly appreciated.

Among the families with dispersed networks, there was not the tremen-dous stress on the mother-daughter relationship that was described for Mrs. N, although women were usually rather more active than men in keeping up kinship ties. There were also fewer conflicts of loyalty; it was felt that if conflicts arose between one's parents and one's spouse, one owed one's first loyalty to one's spouse. Unless special interests, particularly financial interests, were operating among relatives, there was no very strong obligation towards relatives outside the parental families of husband and wife. Even towards siblings there was often very little feeling of social obligation. These families were very much less subject to social control by their relatives than the Ns, partly because they saw less of them, but also because the network of kin was dispersed so that its various members were less likely to share the same opinions and values.

In brief, the networks of these families were less highly connected than that of the Ns: many of their friends did not know one another, it was unusual for friends to know relatives, only a few relatives kept in touch with one another, and husband and wife had very little contact with neighbours. Furthermore, there was no sharp segregation between the wife's network and the husband's network. With the exception of a few old friends and some colleagues, husband and wife maintained joint external relationships.

Conjugal role-segregation. As described above, these families had as little segregation as possible in their external relationships. There was a similar tendency towards joint organization in their carrying out of domestic tasks and child care. It was felt that efficient management demanded some division of labour, particularly after the children had been born; there had to be a basic differentiation between the husband's role as primary breadwinner and the wife's role as mother of young children. But in other respects such division of labour as existed was felt to be more a matter of convenience than of inherent differences between the sexes. The division of labour was flexible, and there was considerable helping and interchanging of tasks. Husbands were expected to take a very active part in child care. Financial affairs were managed jointly, and joint consultation was expected on all major decisions.

Husbands were expected to provide much of the help that Mrs. N was able to get from her female relatives. The wives of these families with dispersed networks were carrying a tremendous load of housework and child care, but they expected to carry it for a shorter time than Mrs. N. Relatives sometimes helped these wives, but only occasionally; they usually lived at some distance so that it was difficult for them to provide continuous assistance. Cleaning women were employed by four families and a children's nurse by one; all families would have hired more domestic help if they could have afforded it. In spite of their affection for their children, all five couples were looking forward to the time when their children were older and the burden of work would decrease. In so far as they could look so far ahead into the future, they did not expect to provide continuous assistance to their own married children.

It seems likely that in the cases of Mrs. N and other wives with highly connected networks, the burden of housework and child care is more evenly distributed throughout the lifetime of the wife; when she is a girl she helps her mother with the younger children; when she herself has children, her mother and other female relatives help her; when she is a grandmother she helps her daughters.

Attitudes towards the role-relationship of husband and wife. Among the families with dispersed networks, there were frequent discussions of whether there really were any psychological or temperamental differences between the sexes. These differences were not simply taken for granted as they were by the Ns. In some cases, so much stress was placed on shared interests and sexual equality (which was sometimes confused with identity, the notion of equality of complementary opposites being apparently a difficult idea to maintain consistently) that one sometimes felt that the possibility of the existence of social and temperamental differences between the sexes was being denied. In other cases, temperamental differences between the sexes were exaggerated to a point that belied the couple's actual joint activities and the whole pattern of shared interests that they felt to be so fundamental to their way of life. Quite frequently the same couple would minimize differences between the sexes on one occasion and exaggerate them on another. Sometimes these discussions about sexual differences were very serious; sometimes they were witty and facetious; but they were never neutral—they were felt to be an important problem. Such discussions may be interpreted as an attempt to air and to resolve the contradiction between the necessity for joint organization with its ethic of equality on the one hand, and the necessity for differentiation and recognition of sexual differences on the other. "After all," as one husband said, to conclude the discussion, "*vive la différence*, or where would we all be?"

It was felt that, in a good marriage, husband and wife should achieve a high degree of compatibility, based on their own particular combination of shared interests and complementary differences. Their relationship with each other should be more important than any separate relationship with outsiders. The conjugal relationship should be kept private, and revelations to outsiders, or letting down one's spouse in public, were felt to be serious offences. A successful sexual relationship was felt by these couples to be very important for a happy marriage; it was as if successful sexual relations were felt to prove that all was well with the joint relationship, whereas unsatisfactory relations were indicative of a failure in the total relationship. In some cases one almost got the feeling that these husbands and wives felt a moral obligation to enjoy sexual relations, a feeling not expressed or suggested by the Ns.

The wives of these families seemed to feel that their position was rather difficult. They had certainly wanted children, and in all five cases they were getting a great deal of satisfaction from their maternal role. But at the same time, they felt tied down by their children and they did not like the inevitable drudgery associated with child care. Some were more affected than others, but most of them complained of isolation, boredom, and fatigue. "You must excuse me if I sound half-witted. I've been talking to the children all day," was a not uncommon remark. These women wanted a career or some special interest that would make them feel that they were something more than children's nurses and housemaids. They wanted more joint entertainment with their husbands, and more contact with friends. These complaints were not levelled specifically at their husbands—indeed in most cases they felt that their husbands were doing their best to make the situation easier—but against the social situation in which they found themselves and at the difficulty of satisfying contradictory desires at the same time. One wife summed it up by saying, "Society seems to be against married women. I don't know, it's all very difficult."

It may be felt that the problem could be solved if such a family moved to an area that was felt to be homogeneous and composed of people similar to themselves, for then the wife might be able to find friends among her neighbours and would feel less isolated and bored. It is difficult to imagine, however, that these families could feel that any local area, however homogeneous by objective criteria, could be full of potential friends, for their experience of moving about in the past and their varied social contacts make them very discriminating in their choice of friends. Further, their dislike of having their privacy broken into by neighbours is very deeply rooted; it diminishes after the children start playing with children in the neighbourhood, but it never disappears entirely.

3. *Intermediate Degrees of Conjugal Role-segregation and Network Connectedness*

There were nine families of this type in the research set. There was considerable variety of occupation amongst them. Four husbands had professional or semi-professional occupations very similar to the occupations of the second type of family described above. It was in recognition of the fact that

273

these four families were similar in occupation but different in conjugal role-segregation from the second set of families that I concluded that conjugal role-segregation could not be attributed to occupational level alone. Of the five remaining husbands, one was a clerical worker, three had manual occupations similar in general level to that of Mr. N, and one changed from a highly skilled manual job to an office job after the interviewing was completed.

There was considerable variation among these nine families in conjugal role-segregation. Some tended to have a fairly marked degree of segregation, approaching that of the Ns described above, whereas others were closer to the second set of families in having a relatively joint role-relationship. These variations in degree of segregation of conjugal roles within the nine intermediate families did not follow exactly the order according to occupational level. If the occupations of the husbands are arranged in order from the most joint to the most segregated conjugal role-relationship, the order is as follows: manual worker, professional, professional, clerical worker, professional, manual worker, professional, manual worker, manual worker. The variations in degree of segregation follow more closely the variations in degree of network connectedness. The families with the most dispersed networks had the most joint role-relationships, and the families with the most connected networks had the most conjugal role-segregation. The families with the most dispersed networks were those who had moved around a great deal so that they had established relationships with many people who did not know one another.

For brevity of description, I shall treat these nine intermediate families collectively, but it should be remembered that there were variations in degree amongst them, and that both network connectedness and conjugal role-segregation form continua so that it is somewhat arbitrary to divide families into separate types.

External social relationships. The data suggest two possible reasons for the intermediate degree in the connectedness of the networks of these families. First, most of them had been brought up in families whose networks had been less connected than that of the Ns, but more connected than that of the second set of families. Furthermore, with one exception these couples had moved around less than the second type of family both before and after marriage, so that more of their friends knew one another; several of these families had had considerable continuity of relationships since childhood, and they had not developed the pattern of ignoring neighbours and relying chiefly on friends and colleagues that was described as typical of families with very dispersed networks.

Secondly, these families were living in areas where they felt that many of the neighbours were socially similar to themselves. In four cases these were "suburban" areas; in five cases they were mixed working-class areas in which the inhabitants were felt to be similar to one another in general occupational level although they worked at different jobs. Five families were living in or near the area where one or both of the partners had lived since childhood. In two of the remaining four cases, the area was similar to the one in which husband and wife had been brought up. In two cases, the present area differed considerably from the childhood area of one or other partner, but the couple had acclimatized themselves to the new situation.

If the husband and wife were living in the area in which they had been brought up, each was able to keep up some of the relationships that had been formed before their marriage. This was also true of the Ns. The intermediate families differed from the Ns chiefly in that their jobs, and in some cases their education, had led them to make relationships with people who were not neighbours. Many neighbours were friends, but not all friends were neighbours. Even in the case of families in which one or both partners had moved to the area after marriage, each partner was able to form friendly relationships with at least some of the neighbours, who were in most cases felt to be socially similar to the couple themselves. Husband and wife were able to form independent, segregated relationships with neighbours. In particular, many of the wives spent a good deal of their leisure time during the day with neighbouring women. Husband and wife also joined local clubs, most of these clubs being unisexual. (Voluntary associations appear to thrive best in areas where people are similar in social status but do not know one another well; the common activity gives people an opportunity to get to know one another better.)

In local areas inhabited by the intermediate families, many of the neighbours knew one another. There was not the very great familiarity built up over a long period of continuous residence such as was described for the area inhabited by the Ns, but there was not the standoffishness described as typical of the families with very dispersed networks. The intermediate families had networks of neighbours that were midway in degree of connectedness, and the husbands and wives were midway in sensitivity to the opinions of neighbours—more susceptible than the second set of families, but better able to maintain their privacy than the Ns.

Husbands and wives had some segregated relationships with neighbours, but they could also make joint relationships with them if all four partners to the relationship liked one another. Some relationships were usually kept up with friends who had been made outside the area. Couples usually tried to arrange joint visits with these friends. These friends usually did not become intimate with the neighbours, however, so that the network remained fairly dispersed.

Relations with relatives were much like those described above for the second set of families. But if the relatives were living in the same local area as the family, there was considerable visiting and exchange of services, and if the relatives lived close to one another, the kinship network was fairly well connected.

The networks of these families were thus less highly connected than that of the Ns, but more highly connected than that of the second set of families. There was some overlapping of roles. Neighbours were sometimes friends; some relatives were both neighbours and friends. The overlapping was not as complete as it was with the Ns, but there was not the complete division into separate categories—friend, neighbour, relative—that was characteristic of the second set of families. The networks of husband and wife were less segregated than those of the Ns, but more segregated than those of the second set of families.

Conjugal role-segregation. In external relationships, husband and wife thus had some joint relationships, particularly with relatives and with friends, and some segregated relationships, particularly with neighbours and local clubs.

In carrying out household tasks and child care, there was a fairly well-defined division of labour, a little more clearly marked than in the second type of family, more flexible than in the case of the Ns. Husbands helped, but there was a greater expectation of help from neighbours and relatives (if they lived close enough) than among the second set of families.

Attitudes towards the role-relationship of husband and wife. Although there were variations of degree, considerable stress was placed on the importance of shared interests and joint activities for a happy marriage. In general, the greater the stress that was placed on joint organization and shared interests, the greater was the importance attached to sexual relations. Like the families with dispersed networks, the intermediate families stressed the necessity for conjugal privacy and the precedence of the conjugal relationship over all external relationships, but there was a greater tolerance of social and temperamental differences between the sexes, and there was an easier acceptance of segregation in the activities of husband and wife. Wives often wanted some special interest of their own other than housework and children, but they were able to find activities such as attending evening classes or local clubs that could be carried on without interfering with their housework and child care. And because, in most cases, they felt that at least some of the neighbouring women were similar to themselves, they found it relatively easy to make friends among them, and they had people to talk to during the day. They complained less frequently of isolation and boredom than did the wives in families with very dispersed networks.

4. *Transitional Families*

There were five families in varying states of transition from one type of network to another. Two phases of transition can be distinguished among these five families. (a) Families who were in the process of deciding to move from one local area to another, a decision that was requiring considerable restructuring of their networks, and (b) somewhat "de-socialized" families (2), that is, families who had radically changed their pattern of external relationships and had not yet got used to their new situation. There were other families who had gone through the process of transition and had more or less settled down to the pattern typical of families with dispersed or intermediate networks.

(a) *Families in the process of deciding to move.* There were two such families. Both had relatively highly connected networks, and both had been socially mobile and were contemplating moving to suburban areas, which would be more compatible with their new social status. In both cases this meant cutting off old social ties with relatives and neighbours and building up new ones. One couple seemed to feel too bound to the old network to make the break; they also said they did not want to lower their current standard of living by spending a lot of money on a house. The second family moved after the interviewing was completed, and a brief return visit suggested that they would in time build up the intermediate type of network and conjugal role-segregation.

(b) *Somewhat de-socialized families.* There were three families of this type. All three had been brought up in highly connected networks similar to that described for the Ns, and all had moved away from their old areas and the people of their networks. For such a family, any move outside the area is a drastic step. This contrasts with the intermediate families who are not too upset by moving, provided that they move to an area of people who are felt to be socially similar to themselves.

One family had been very mobile occupationally, although they had moved primarily because of the requirements of the husband's occupation rather than to find a neighbourhood compatible with their achieved status. They were living in relative isolation, with very few friends, almost no contacts with neighbours, and very little contact with relatives, most of whom were living at a considerable distance. They seemed to be a bit stunned by the change in their immediate environment. They had some segregated interests, but they felt that joint organization and shared interests were the best basis of a conjugal relationship.

The other two families were working-class and had not been occupationally mobile. These two families were particularly important to the conceptual analysis of conjugal role-segregation, for although they were similar to the Ns in occupational level and in general cultural background, their conjugal role-relationship was more joint. It was their relatively dispersed networks that distinguished them from the Ns.

These two families had moved to a different local area because they could not find suitable accommodation in their old neighbourhoods. They also wanted the amenities of a modern flat, and since their parents had died and many of their relatives had moved away, they felt that their main ties to the old local area were gone. Both these couples seemed to feel that they were strangers in a land full of people who were all strangers to one another, and at first they did not know how to cope with the situation. They did not react to their new situation in exactly the same way. In both cases, husband and wife had turned to one another for help, especially at first, but for various personal reasons, one husband and wife were making a concerted effort to develop joint activities and shared interests, whereas the other couple did not take to the idea of a joint role-relationship with any enthusiasm.

In the first case, husband and wife tried to develop more joint relationships with friends, but this was difficult for them because they had had so little practice; they did not know the culture of a joint role-relationship, and their new acquaintances were in a similar predicament so that they got little external support for their efforts. The husband tried to get his wife to join in his club activities, but the structure of the club was such that her activities remained somewhat segregated from his. The husband helped his wife extensively with household tasks and child care, although he continued to plan the family finances. In the second case, the husband busied himself with his work and friends and spent a great deal of time on various committees with other men; his wife was becoming isolated and withdrawn into the home. They had more joint organization of domestic tasks than they had had before; she urged him to help her because her female relatives lived too far away to be of much assistance.

In both cases, however, nothing could really take the place of the old networks built up from childhood, and both couples felt a good deal of personal dissatisfaction. The husbands were perhaps less drastically affected, since they continued to work at their old jobs and their relationships with colleagues gave them considerable continuity. Both husband and wife often blamed their physical surroundings for their malaise, and they idealized their old local areas. They remembered only the friendliness and forgot the physical inconvenience and the unpleasant part of the gossip. On the whole, although one family had carried the process further than the other, both seemed to be developing a more joint division of labour than that which they had had before, and it seemed likely that they would eventually settle down in some intermediate form of network connectedness and conjugal role-segregation.

The research set did not contain any families who had moved in the other direction, that is, from a dispersed to a more connected network. But personal knowledge of families who had been accustomed to a dispersed network and were having to come to grips with a fairly highly connected one suggests that this type of change is also felt to be somewhat unpleasant. The privacy of husband and wife is encroached upon, and each is expected to take part in segregated activities, a state of affairs that they regard as provincial. These families could have refused to enter into the local network of social relationships, but in most cases they felt that the husband's career required it.

The data having been described, the nature of the relationship between conjugal role-segregation and network connectedness may now be examined in more detail.

Connected networks are most likely to develop when husband and wife, together with their friends, neighbours, and relatives, have all grown up in the same local area and have continued to live there after marriage. Husband and wife come to the marriage each with his own highly connected network. It is very likely that there will be some overlap of their networks; judging by the Ns' account of their genealogy, one of the common ways for husband and wife to meet each other is to be introduced by a person who is simultaneously a friend of one and a relative of the other.

Each partner makes a considerable emotional investment in relationships with the people in his network; each is engaged in reciprocal exchanges of material and emotional support with them; each is very sensitive to their opinions and values, not only because the relationships are intimate, but also because the people in his network know one another and share the same values so that they are able to apply consistent informal sanctions to one another.

The marriage is superimposed on these pre-existing relationships. As long as the couple continue to live in the same area, and as long as their friends, neighbours, and relatives also continue to live within easy reach of the family and of one another, the segregated networks of husband and wife can be carried on after marriage. Some rearrangement is necessary; the husband is likely to stop seeing some of the friends of his youth, particularly those who work at a different place and go to different pubs and clubs; after children are born, the wife is likely to see less of her former girl friends and more of her mother and other female relatives. But apart from these readjustments, husband and wife can carry on their old external relationships, and they continue to be very sensitive to external social controls. In spite of the conjugal segregation in external relationships, the overlapping of the networks of husband and wife tends to ensure that each partner finds out about the other's activities. Although a wife may not know directly what a husband does with his friends away from home, one of the other men is likely to tell his wife or some other female relative who eventually passes the information on, either directly or through other women, to the wife of the man in question. Similarly any defection on the part of the wife is likely to be made known to her husband.

Because old relationships can be continued after marriage, both husband and wife can satisfy some of their personal needs outside the marriage, so that their emotional investment in the conjugal relationship need not be as intense as in other types of family. Both husband and wife, but particularly the wife, can get outside help with domestic tasks and with child care. A rigid division of labour between husband and wife is therefore possible, since each can get outside help. In other words, the segregation in external relationships can be carried over to activities within the family.

Networks become dispersed when people move around from one place to another, or when they make new relationships that have no connection with their old ones. If both husband and wife have moved around a good deal before marriage, each will bring an already dispersed network to the marriage; many of the husband's friends will not know one another; many of the wife's friends will not know one another. After the marriage they will meet new people as well as some of the old ones, and these people will not necessarily know one another. In other words, their external relationships are relatively discontinuous both in space and in time. Such continuity as they possess lies in their relationship with each other rather than in their external relationships. In facing the external world, they draw on each other, for their strongest emotional investment is made where there is continuity. Hence their high standards of conjugal compatibility, their stress on shared interests, on joint organization, on equality between husband and wife. They must get along well together, they must help one another as much as possible in carrying out familial tasks, for there is no sure external source of material and emotional help. Since their friends and relatives are physically scattered and few of them know one another, the husband and wife are not stringently controlled by a solid body of public opinion, but they are also unable to rely on consistent external support. Through their joint external relationships they present a united front to the world and they reaffirm their joint relationship with each other. No external person must seriously menace the conjugal relationship; joint relationships with friends give both husband and wife a source of emotional satisfaction outside the family without threatening their own relationship with each other.

In between these two extremes are the intermediate and transitional families. In the intermediate type, husband and wife have moved around a certain amount so that they seek continuity with each other and make their strongest emotional investment in the conjugal relationship. At the same time, they are able to make some segregated relationships outside the family and they are able to rely on considerable casual help from people outside the family, so that a fairly clearly defined division of labour into male tasks and female tasks can be made.

The transitional families illustrate some of the factors involved in changing from one type of network to another. Husbands and wives who change from a connected to a dispersed network find themselves suddenly thrust into a more joint relationship without the experience or the attitudes appropriate to it. The eventual outcome depends partly on the family and partly on the extent to which their new neighbours build up relationships with one another. An intermediate form of network connectedness seems to be the most likely outcome. Similarly, in the case of families who change from a dispersed to a more highly connected network, their first reaction is one of mild indignation at losing their privacy, but in time it seems likely that they will tend to develop an intermediate degree of network connectedness and conjugal role-segregation.

PART II. NETWORKS IN RELATION TO THE TOTAL ENVIRONMENT

Having discussed the relation of the family to its network, I should like now to consider the factors affecting the form of the network itself. First the general features characteristic of all familial networks in an urban industrialized society will be examined, then I shall turn to consider some of the factors affecting variations from one urban familial network to another.

A. FACTORS AFFECTING THE GENERAL FEATURES OF URBAN FAMILIAL NETWORKS

As described above, all the research families maintained relationships with external people and institutions—with a place of work, with service institutions such as schools, church, doctor, clinic, shops, and so forth, with voluntary associations such as clubs, evening classes, and recreational institutions; they also maintained more informal relationships with colleagues, friends, neighbours, and relatives. It is therefore incorrect to describe urban families as "isolated"; indeed, no urban family could survive without its network of external relationships.

It is correct, however, to say that urban families are not contained within organized groups, for although they have many external relationships, the institutions and persons with which they are related are not linked up with one another to form an organized group. Furthermore, although individual members of a family frequently belong to groups, the family as a whole does not. There are marginal cases, such as the situation arising when all the members of the family belong to the same church or go to the same general practitioner, but in these cases the external institution or person controls only one aspect of the family's life, and can hardly be said to "contain" the family in all its aspects.

In the literature on family sociology, there are frequent references to "the family in the community", with the implication that the community is an organized group within which the family is contained. Our data suggest that the usage is misleading. Of course every family must live in some sort of local area, but very few urban local areas can be called communities in the sense that they form cohesive social groups. The immediate social environment of urban families is best considered not as the local area in which they live, but rather as the network of actual social relationships they maintain, regardless or whether these are confined to the local area or run beyond its boundaries.

Small-scale, more isolated, relatively "closed" local groups provide a marked contrast. This type of community is frequently encountered in primitive societies, as well as in certain rural areas of industrialized societies. A family in such a local group knows no privacy; everyone knows everyone else. The situation of the urban family with a highly connected network is carried one step further in the relatively closed local group. The networks of the component families are so highly connected and the relationships within the local group are so clearly marked off from external relationships that the local population can properly be called an organized group. Families are encapsulated within this group; their activities are known to all, they cannot escape from the informal sanctions of gossip and public opinion, their external affairs are governed by the group to which they belong.

In many small-scale primitive societies, the elementary family is encapsulated not only within a local group, but also within a corporate kin group. In such cases, the conjugal role-segregation between husband and wife becomes even more marked than that described above for urban families with highly connected networks. Marriage becomes a linking of kin groups rather than preponderantly a union between individuals acting on their own initiative.

These differences between the immediate social environment of families in urban industrialized societies and that of families in some small-scale primitive and rural communities exist, ultimately, because of differences in the total economic and social structure. The division of labour in a small-scale society is relatively simple; the division of labour in an industrial society is exceedingly complex. In a small-scale, relatively closed society, most of the services required by a family can be provided by the other families in the local group and in the kin group. In an urban industrialized society, such tasks and services are divided up and assigned to specialized institutions. Whereas a family in a small-scale, relatively closed society belongs to a small number of groups each with many functions, an urban family exists in a network of many separate, unconnected institutions each with a specialized function. In a small-scale, relatively closed society the local group and the kin group mediate between the family and the total society; in an urban industrialized society there is no single encapsulating group or institution that mediates between the family and the total society.

One of the results of this difference in the form of external relationships is that urban families have more freedom to govern their own affairs. In a small-scale, relatively closed society, the encapsulating groups have a great deal of control over the family. In an urban industrialized society, the doctor looks after the health of individual members of the family, the clinic looks after the health of the mother and child, the school educates children, the boss cares about the individual as an employee rather than as a husband, and even friends, neighbours, and relatives may disagree amongst themselves as to how the affairs of the family should be conducted. In brief, social control of the family is split up amongst so many agencies that no one of them has continuous, complete governing power, and within broad limits, a family can make its own decisions and regulate its own affairs.

The situation may be summed up by saying that urban families are *more highly individuated* than families in relatively closed communities. I feel that this term describes the situation of urban families more accurately than the more commonly used term "isolated". By "individuation" I mean that the elementary family is separated off, differentiated out as a distinct, and to some extent autonomous, social group. Of course, in most societies the elementary family is individuated to some extent; one could not say that it existed as a distinct group if it were not. The difference in individuation between an urban family and a family in a relatively closed community is one of degree. It should be remembered, however, that urban families differ among themselves in degree of individuation; families with highly connected networks are less individuated than those with dispersed networks.

The individuation of urban families provides one source of variation in role performance. Because families are not encapsulated within governing and controlling groups, other than the nation as a whole, husband and wife are able, within broad limits, to perform their roles in accordance with their own personal needs. These broad limits are laid down by the ideal norms of the nation as a whole, many of which exist as laws and are enforced by the courts. But informal social control by relatives and neighbours is much less stringent and less consistent than in many small-scale societies, and much variation is possible.

B. FACTORS AFFECTING VARIATION IN URBAN FAMILIES' NETWORKS

Although the immediate social environments of all urban families resemble one another in assuming network form, there are important differences from one urban family's network to another. As has been demonstrated in Part I above, these differences lie in the degree of connectedness of families' networks. Such differences are most clearly marked in the area of informal relationships, that is, in relationships with friends, neighbours, and relatives. These relationships are felt to be of much greater personal and emotional importance than the more specialized and formal relationships that are maintained with doctors, clinics, schools, and so forth, and they are usually maintained with people who are felt to be socially similar to the family themselves.

In the introduction to this paper it was suggested that network connectedness is a function on the one hand of certain forces in the total environment and on the other hand of the family themselves. It now becomes appropriate to discuss this statement in greater detail.

The highly developed division of labour in an industrial society produces not only complexity but also variability. Sometimes conditions are created that favour the development of relatively highly connected networks, sometimes conditions are created that favour relatively dispersed networks. To examine these conditions in detail would take the discussion far away from families and their networks into a study of the ecology of cities and the economic structure of industries and occupations, a task obviously beyond the scope of this paper. I should like, however, to suggest tentatively several factors that appear likely to affect network connectedness.

(1) *Economic Ties among the Members of the Network*

Economic ties operate more forcibly between relatives than between friends and neighbours, but there is a wide range of variation in the operation of such cohesive forces even among relatives. The connectedness of the kinship network is enhanced if relatives hold property rights in common enterprises, or if they expect to inherit property from one another.

The connectedness of kinship networks is also enhanced if relatives can help one another to get jobs. Only certain types of occupation allow such help; in occupations requiring examinations or other objective selection procedures—and most professional and semi-professional occupations fall into this category—relatives cannot give one another much help in this respect, whereas in some less skilled occupations and in certain businesses, particularly family businesses, relatives are able to help one another more directly.

The important point here is that neither the occupational system nor the distribution of property is uniform. Different families are affected in different ways. This means that although families' networks in general and their kinship networks in particular do not play a very large part in the economic and occupational structure, there is a great deal of variation in the way in which economic forces affect families' networks.

(2) *Type of Neighbourhood*

Type of neighbourhood is important not so much in and of itself, but because it is one of the factors affecting the "localization" of networks. If a family's network is localized, that is, if most of the members live in the same local area so that they are accessible to one another, they are more likely to know one another than if they are scattered all over the country.

Since the members of the informal network are usually felt by the family to have the same social status as themselves, localized networks are most likely to develop in areas where the local inhabitants feel that they are socially similar to one another, that they belong to the same social class, whatever their definition of class may be. Such feelings of social similarity appear to be strongest in long-established working-class areas in which there is a dominant local industry or a small number of traditional occupations. As described above, the Ns, the family with the most highly connected network, were living in such an area. It was also an area of low population turnover, at least until the recent war. Formerly people were born, brought up, and died there. Highly connected networks could develop not only because the local area was homogeneous but also because people stayed put. Now, as some of the inhabitants move away, the networks of even those people who remain in the area are becoming more dispersed.

There were no comparable homogeneous neighbourhoods of people belonging to one of the full professions.[12] Neighbourhoods were found, however, in which the inhabitants were relatively homogeneous with regard to income, although they had different occupations. The type and cost of the dwelling was probably an important factor contributing to this type of homogeneity. Such neighbourhoods were found in suburbs; they were also found in certain mixed working-class areas in which there was no dominant local industry. Most of the families with intermediate and transitional networks were living in such areas; one family with a dispersed network was living in such an area, but they ignored their neighbours, whom they felt were socially similar to one nother but not to themselves. Finally, there were some areas that were extremely heterogeneous with regard to occupational level, income, educational background of the inhabitants, and so forth; most of the families with very dispersed networks were living in such areas.

In a very complex way, neighbourhood composition is related to occupation and social class. It is possible to have fairly homogeneous areas of, say, dockworkers or furniture workers, although not all manual occupations are heavily localized, but the structure of the professions is such that it would be most unusual to find a homogeneous area of, say, doctors or lawyers or chartered accountants. On the basis of our data on families, no attempt can be made to analyse the many factors contributing to the formation of local neighbourhoods. The most one can say is that the industrial and occupational system is so complex that it gives rise to many different types of urban neighbourhood. Some are more homogeneous and stable than others. If one were making a detailed study of network connectedness in relation to neighbourhood composition, it would be necessary to work out detailed criteria of homogeneity so that neighbourhoods could be systematically compared; one could then study the relation of different degrees and types of objective homogeneity to the attitudes of local inhabitants towards one another; one could also compare the formation of the networks of families in different types of area. My guess would be that one would not find families with

---

12. University towns are perhaps the closest approximation to a homogeneous area of a single profession. Study of networks and conjugal role-segregation in such areas should be of considerable interest, for certain factors in the situation would be likely to foster a high degree of network connectedness whereas others would discourage it. A homogeneous local area, if perceived as such by the local inhabitants, encourages a high degree of network connectedness. The sexual segregation in the social structure of the colleges may also tend to increase connectedness among men and to reinforce segregation between husband and wife. But most professional men move around during their education and early occupational training, and have professional contacts with people outside their local area, which would discourage network connectedness. As described below, continuity of residence by all members of the network is also an important factor; it seems likely that the population turnover of university towns is relatively high, and that there are few families in which husband and wife are born, brought up, and die in the same university town. Such lack of continuity would tend to prevent a high degree of connectedness.

highly connected networks in heterogeneous areas of high population turn-over, but that one might find both families with highly connected networks and families with dispersed networks in relatively homogeneous, stable areas.

It is most unlikely that one would be able to predict degree of network connectedness from knowledge of the local area alone. Too many other factors are involved—type of occupation, where the husband works, how long the family has lived in the area, perception of the area, and so forth. The family's perception of the people in the area is particularly important. Objective measures of social homogeneity give only a rough indication of how families will feel about their neighbours. Furthermore, it is always necessary to remember that a neighbourhood does not simply impose itself on a family. Within certain limits families can choose where they will live, and even if they feel that their neighbours are similar to themselves they are not compelled to be friendly with them; other criteria besides felt social similarity enter into the selection of friends.

(3) *Opportunities to Make Relationships outside the Local Area*

Networks are more likely to be highly connected if members do not have many opportunities to form new relationships with persons unknown to the other members of the network. Thus, in the case of the family with a highly connected network described above, the husband's work, the relatives of husband and wife, and their friends were all concentrated in the local area. There are no strong sanctions preventing such families from making relationships with outsiders, but there is no unavoidable circumstance that forces them to do so. In the case of the professional families in the research set, their education and professional training had led them to make many relationships with colleagues and friends who did not know one another. Even if such families keep on living in the same area throughout their lives, which is unusual though possible, the husband's pursuit of an occupational career leads him to make relationships with people who do not belong to the family's neighbourhood network, so that the network tends to become dispersed.

In brief, network connectedness does depend, in part, on the husband's occupation. If he practises an occupation in which his colleagues are also his neighbours, his network will tend to be localized and its connectedness will tend to be high. If he practises an occupation in which his colleagues are not his neighbours, his network will tend to become dispersed. One cannot predict this solely from knowledge of occupational level. Most professional occupations require a man to get his training and do his work in different areas from the one he lives in. Some manual occupations require or permit this too; others do not.

(4) *Physical and Social Mobility*

Network connectedness depends on the stability and continuity of the relationships; a family's network will become more dispersed if either the family or the other members of the network move away physically or socially so that contact is decreased and new relationships are established.

Among the research set, there were clear indications that networks became more dispersed when physical mobility had been great. When the number of local areas lived in by both husband and wife before and after marriage is added up, the averages according to network formation are as follows: Families with dispersed networks, 19; families with intermediate networks, 8·2; families with transitional networks, 9·6, and the Ns, the family with the most highly connected network, 2. (In all cases, Service career was counted as one "area".)

Many factors affect physical mobility. Here again the occupational system is a relevant factor. Some occupations permit or encourage social and physical mobility so that networks become dispersed; other occupations encourage stability of residence and social relationships. Social mobility is often accompanied by physical mobility. In the research set, seven families had been occupationally mobile and three had moved or were contemplating moving to an area appropriate to their achieved status. The other four had moved too, but not primarily for status reasons. In general, the networks of socially mobile families tend to become less connected not only because they move physically but also because they are likely to drop old social ties and form new ones. Among the mobile families of the research set, most of the rearranging had been done in adolescence and in the early years of the marriage, and it involved chiefly friends and distant relatives. However mobile the family, husband and wife felt an obligation to maintain contact with their parents; occupational and social achievements were usually felt to be a positive accomplishment for parents as well as for the husband and wife themselves.

Occupation may affect physical mobility even when there is no social mobility. Among the research families many of the professional couples had moved frequently from one local area to another and even from one city to another, and they tended to treat the requirements of the husband's career as the most important factor in deciding whether to move or not; this applied as much to families who were not socially mobile as to those who were. The manual and clerical workers were less likely to give the demands of the husband's career as a chief reason for moving, and only one such family had moved very frequently. The relations between occupation and physical and social mobility are obviously very complex. The important fact is that the occupational system is not uniform; it permits much variation in physical and social mobility and hence much variation in network connectedness.

But decisions to move depend not only on occupational considerations but also on the housing shortage, the type and cost of the house or flat, the family's views on the welfare of their children, relations with relatives, neighbours, and friends in the old area, and on potential relations in the new area, and doubtless many other factors as well. All these considerations must be weighed together when the decision to move is made, although one or other factor may be dominant. Sometimes all considerations point in the same direction; more frequently they have to be balanced against one another. But whatever the reasons, once the move has been made the family's network becomes more dispersed. Even if the family itself does not move, its network will become dispersed if friends and relatives move away.

Network connectedness thus depends on a very complex combination of economic and social forces. Instead of the relatively homogeneous environment of a small-scale, relatively closed society, the total environment of an urban family is exceedingly complex and variable. Many forces affect a family's network, so that there is considerable latitude for the family to choose among several courses of action, and a wide range of variation is possible.

(5) Individual Decision and Choice

The connectedness of a family's network depends not only on external social forces, but also on the family itself. Although the members of a family cannot control the forces of the total environment, they can select from among the various courses of action to which these forces give rise. It is the variability of the total environment that makes choice possible, but it is the family that makes the actual decisions. Decisions are shaped by situational factors but they also depend on the personalities of the members of the family, on the way they react to the situational factors.

Through acts of personal decision and choice husband and wife may affect the connectedness of their network, often without any deliberate intention of doing so; by changing the connectedness of their network they affect in turn their conjugal role-segregation. Thus, if a family with a highly connected network moves out of their old area to a new housing estate, their network will rapidly become more dispersed, and for a time at least they will develop a more joint relationship with each other. If a professional family with a dispersed network moves to a university town because of the husband's career, their network is likely to become slightly more connected even though they may not plan to make it so. If a family with a dispersed network decides to move to a distant suburb because that is the only place where they can find a house that they can afford to buy, they may find themselves extremely isolated—cut off from their friends, unable to make relationships easily with their neighbours, and even more dependent on each other than usual.

Among the research set there were several couples who, for various personal reasons, had almost no informal network at all. Thus two families were living in a state of voluntary isolation or near isolation; they kept up necessary contacts with service institutions and paid a few duty visits to relatives, but that was all. Or again, a husband and wife of the second set of families, for various personal reasons, had almost no friends, although they saw a good deal of their relatives and rather more of their neighbours than the other families of this set. In so far as they had an informal network it was dispersed, but there were far fewer members in it than usual. One of the intermediate families could, if they had wished, have had a network almost as highly connected as that of the Ns, but for various personal reasons they had cut themselves off and had adopted a more home-centred outlook and a more joint role-relationship. Slightly deviant families of this type are aware that their behaviour does not coincide exactly with their own norms, although they usually do not like to discuss their deviance unless they feel that they are above their norm rather than below it.

Personality characteristics may thus affect conjugal role-segregation indirectly because they are a factor in shaping choices that affect the form of the family's network. But personal needs and attitudes, both conscious and unconscious, also affect performance of conjugal roles directly. Two families may have similar networks but slightly different degrees of conjugal role-segregation. Thus the two transitional families discussed above (pp. 369–70) were living in approximately the same social situation, but in one case the husband and wife were trying to develop as joint a conjugal relationship as possible whereas in the second case they were not. Personality factors are of necessity involved in performance of familial roles—and of any role for that matter—but it is only where there is a lack of fit between the personal needs of husband and wife, the social situation in which they find themselves, and the expectations of the members of their networks, that such needs stand out as a separate factor.

Social Class, Network Connectedness, and Segregation of Conjugal Roles

Because of the complexity of the situation it is not surprising that we could not find a simple correlation between class position and segregation of conjugal roles. In my view such segregation is more directly related to network connectedness than to class status as such, although there are probably some aspects of class position that affect conjugal role-segregation directly. For example, if both husband and wife are highly educated, they are likely to have a common background of shared interests and tastes, which makes a joint relationship easy to conduct. Although it is unlikely that teachers deliberately plan to teach children about joint conjugal relationships, higher education is probably a chief means of passing on the ethic appropriate to a joint relationship from one generation to another, and of teaching it to socially mobile individuals whose parents have had a more segregated relationship. It is doubtful, however, whether such education alone could produce joint conjugal relationships; it works in conjunction with other factors.

But for the most part factors associated with class—however one defines that complex construct—affect segregation of conjugal roles indirectly through having an effect on the connectedness of the family's network. To sum up the empirical resultant: Families with highly connected networks are likely to be working-class. But not all working-class families will have highly connected networks.

It is only in the working-class that one is likely to find a combination of factors all working together to produce a high degree of network connectedness: concentration of people of the same or similar occupations in the same local area; jobs and homes in the same local area; low population turnover and continuity of relationships; at least occasional opportunities for relatives and friends to help one another to get jobs; little demand for physical mobility; little opportunity for social mobility.

In contrast, the structure of professions is such that this pattern of forces almost never occurs. Homogeneous local areas of a single profession are very rare; a man's place of work and his home are usually in different local areas; professional training leads him to make relationships with people who do not know his family, school friends, and neighbours; in most cases getting a job depends on skill and training rather than on the influence of friends and relatives; many professional careers require physical mobility. Almost the only factor associated with high-class status that tends to foster network connectedness is ownership of shares in common enterprises by relatives—and this is less likely to occur among professional people than among wealthy industrialists and commercial families.

But because a man has a manual occupation he will not automatically have a highly connected network. He may be living in a relatively heterogeneous area, for not all manual occupations are localized. He may live in one place and work in another. He may move from one area to another. Similarly his friends and relatives may move or make new relationships with people he does not know. A high degree of network connectedness *may* be found in association with manual occupations, but the association is not necessary and inevitable.

In brief, one cannot explain network connectedness as the result of the husband's occupational or class status considered as single determinants. Network connectedness depends on a whole complex of forces—economic ties among members of the network, type of local area, opportunities to make new social contacts, physical and social mobility, etc.—generated by the occupational and economic systems, but these forces do not always work in the same direction and they may affect different families in different ways.

Finally, network connectedness cannot be predicted from a knowledge of situational factors alone. It also depends on the family's personal response to the situations of choice with which they are confronted.

In a situation of such complexity, little is to be gained by trying to explain conjugal role-segregation in terms of single factors. In the approach to this problem, the most useful conceptual model has proved to be that of field theory: "behaviour is a function of a person (in this case a family) in a situation". Performance of conjugal roles is a function of the family in its social network. The form of the social network depends, in turn, partly on the members of the family and partly on a very complex combination of forces in the total social environment.

SUMMARY

1. The conjugal role-relationships of all twenty urban families studied in this research contained both segregated and joint components. There were differences of degree, however. Some couples had considerable *segregation* in their conjugal role-relationship; in such families, husband and wife expected to have a clear differentiation of tasks and a considerable number of separate interests and activities. At the other extreme there were couples who had as much *joint organization* as possible in the role-relationship of husband and wife; in such families husband and wife expected to carry out many activities together with a minimum of task differentiation and separation of interests. There were many degrees of variation between these two extremes.

2. The immediate social environment of an urban family consists of a network rather than an organized group. A *network* is a social configuration in which some, but not all, of the component external units maintain relationships with one another. The external units do not make up a larger social whole. They are not surrounded by a common boundary.

The network formation of the immediate environment of an urban family is brought about by the complexity of the division of labour in the total society. Whereas a family in a relatively closed community belongs to a small number of groups each with many functions, an urban family exists in a network of many separate institutions each with a specialized function. Urban families are not isolated, but they are *more highly individuated* than families in relatively closed communities; urban families are not encapsulated within external governing groups other than the nation as a whole, and they have a relatively large measure of privacy, of autonomy, and of opportunity to regulate their own affairs.

3. The networks of urban families vary in degree of *connectedness*, namely in the extent to which the people with whom the family maintains relationships carry on relationships with one another. These variations in network connectedness are particularly evident in informal relationships between friends, neighbours, and relatives.

These differences in network connectedness are associated with differences in degree of conjugal role-segregation. *The degree of segregation in the role-relationship of husband and wife varies directly with the connectedness of the family's social network.* Four sets of families have been described, and the relationship between the connectedness of their networks and the degree of their conjugal role-segregation has been discussed.

4. Conceptually, the network stands between the family and the total social environment. Variations in network connectedness cannot be explained

in terms of any single factor. Such variations are made possible by the complexity and variability of the economic, occupational, and other institutional systems that create a complex of forces affecting families in different ways and permitting selection and choice by the family. It is suggested that the connectedness of a family's network is a function on the one hand of a complex set of forces in the total environment, and on the other hand of the family themselves and their reaction to these forces. Several situational factors possibly relevant to the connectedness of families' networks have been suggested, including: the extent to which members of the network are bound to one another by economic ties; the type of neighbourhood; opportunities to make new relationships even while continuing to live in the same area; opportunities for physical and social mobility.

REFERENCES

1. BARNES, J. A. "Class and Committees in a Norwegian Island Parish." *Hum. Relat.*, 1954, Vol. VII, No. 1, pp. 39–58.
2. CURLE, ADAM, and TRIST, E. L. "Transitional Communities and Social Reconnection." *Hum. Relat.*, 1947, Vol. I, pp. 42–68, and pp. 240–88.
3. MORENO, J. L. *Who Shall Survive?* Washington: Nervous and Mental Disease Publishing Co., 1934, pp. 256–65.
4. RADCLIFFE-BROWN, A. R. "On Social Structure." *J. roy. anthrop. Inst.*, 1940, Vol. 70, pp. 1–12.
5. ROBB, J. H. "Experiences with Ordinary Families." *Brit. J. med. Psychol.*, 1953, Vol. XXVI, pp. 215–21.
6. ROBB, J. H. *Working-Class Anti-Semite.* London: Tavistock Publications Ltd., 1955.
7. SLATER, E., and WOODSIDE, M. *Patterns of Marriage.* London: Cassell and Co. Ltd., 1951.
8. YOUNG, M. "Kinship and Family in East London." *Man*, 1954, Vol. LIV, Article No. 210, pp. 137–9.
9. YOUNG, M. "The Planners and the Planned—The Family." *J. Tn. Plann. Inst.*, 1954, Vol. XL, No. 6.

BIOGRAPHICAL NOTE

A note on the author of this article appeared in *Human Relations*, Vol. VII, No. 3.

From Adrian C. Meyer, *in* "The Social Anthropology of Complex Societies" (Michael Banton, ed.), Tavistock Publications Ltd., London.

Adrian C. Mayer

The Significance of Quasi-Groups in the Study of Complex Societies

Two concepts of major importance for social anthropologists are those of group and association. Both have been defined in a number of ways. Even in the most inclusive view, however, both bodies are held to consist of a number of members with some form of expected interaction, if not rights and obligations, towards one another. Both the association and the group show an 'even spread' of the membership criteria on which this interaction is based, whether these are highly informal or whether they produce a corporate body. Much fruitful work has been carried out with the aid of these concepts. Nevertheless, they are inadequate for those situations involving another kind of collection of people, which may be termed the 'quasi-group'.

Quasi-groups can be divided into two types. The first can be termed that of the classificatory quasi-group. Here, the classification may be made in terms of the common interests which lie beneath what could also be called a 'potential group'. Ginsberg, for example, defines quasi-groups as entities without a 'recognizable structure, but whose members have certain interests or modes of behaviour in common which may at any time lead them to form themselves into definite groups'.[1] The classification may also be made by an individual in terms of his perceived status *vis-à-vis* others, as Barnes shows in his analysis of class mentioned below. I do not propose to deal with this type of quasi-group. Rather, I shall confine myself to quasi-groups of the second type. These possess a degree of organization, but are nevertheless not groups. They can be called interactive quasi-groups, for they are based on an interacting set of people.

These quasi-groups differ fundamentally from the group and the association. First, they are ego-centred, in the sense of ·depending for their very existence on a specific person as a central organizing focus; this is unlike a group, in which organization may be diffuse. Second, the actions of any member are relevant only in so far as they are interactions between him and ego or ego's intermediary. The membership criteria do not include interaction with other quasi-group members in general.

The interactions of this type of quasi-group occur in an action-set[2] or rather in a series of action-sets. I wish to examine the properties of the action-set by studying it in operation. This I shall do from data gathered in India. But first I must show what is meant by 'set' and how it is related to social network.

Sets are embedded in the matrices of social links contained in social fields, which have also been called networks. Recent use of the terms 'set' and 'network' has been somewhat confusing, and I will therefore try to clarify the distinction between them.

The term network was used by Radcliffe-Brown (1952, p. 190) when he characterized social structure as being a 'network of actually existing social relations' and maintained that this structure should be the object of the anthropologist's investigation. The relations making up the structure were maintained by a convergence of interests, or at least a 'limitation of conflicts that might arise from divergence of interests' (ibid., p. 199). In some cases, the structure could be defined by a single criterion, as for instance in an Australian tribe, where 'the whole social structure is based on a network of such relations of person to person, established through genealogical connections' (ibid., p. 191).

As Firth (1954, p. 4) points out, Radcliffe-Brown used network to express impressionistically 'what he felt by describing metaphorically what he saw' and it was left to Barnes to give the term a more precise definition.

Barnes saw a network as a social field made up of relations between people. These relations were defined by criteria underlying the field – in the case he cites, for instance, these were criteria of neighbourhood and friendship which might in turn subsume kinship and economic connections. The network was 'unbounded' (at least, by the local boundary of the parish studied)[3] and was without leadership or a coordinating organization. Any person had relations with a number of other people, who in turn were linked to further people.[4] The links might cluster in some parts of the network; but if the people concerned formed a group, their group linkages would exist apart from the network, since an extra criterion would have been added to the linkages defining the network.

The definition of network formed the first step in Barnes's analysis. The second was the identification of sets of people on the basis of linkages provided by the network. The set was different in form from the network. For it was centred on a single person (ego), and consisted of the people classified by him according to a certain criterion. These people thus formed only part of the network – that part which ego recognized as being contained in the set. Barnes's purpose was to use the network-set concept to analyse social class. For him, classes consisted of those people whom an ego identified, through his linkages with them, as comprising sets with statuses above, equal to, or below him. The set did not form a group; nor was ego its leader. But it was at that moment a bounded entity. Moreover, the connections which ego had with the various people he identified in the class context were along 'paths' which might consist of more than one link. It should be noted that these sets lacked any purposive content, and can therefore be categorized as classificatory sets. Here, they differ from the interactive set of the type previously discussed by Chapple and Coon (1947, p. 283), with which I shall be concerned in this paper. Nevertheless, both types of set are similar in that they are ego-centred and may contain intermediaries between ego (the originator) and the terminal individuals.

The aspect of Barnes's analysis which has received most attention is his view of the network. Firth admits that the image it presents may be useful and vivid, and Nadel refers to it in his discussion of network. But neither writer considers the part played by the set in Barnes's scheme. For instance, Firth (1954, p. 4) sees Barnes's use of the network as 'a metaphor convenient to describe the personal sets of relationships which characterize the particular structure of a Norwegian fishing community'. I would rather suggest that Barnes conceives of the network as important in so far as it is a *basis* for sets rather than as a means of describing them, and that the two are distinct.

In her study of urban families, Bott uses the term to cover both of Barnes's concepts. On the one hand, a family maintains relationships of friendship, kinship, and neighbourhood with a certain number of other families; these constitute the family's network. On the other hand, each of the other families has its relations with yet other families, many of which are not connected to the initial family at all. Viewed, therefore, from the central family, there is a finite number of relations based on its own interaction, beyond which stretch further links (unbounded from this central family's viewpoint) which have nothing to do with it. Both the bounded and the 'unbounded' entities are included under the rubric network by Bott (1957, p. 58), though it would have been clearer to call the former a set. The articulation between the set of an ego (individual or family) and the network (or social field) which stretches away on all sides is provided by the fact that the 'lateral' links between units other than ego in the set are at the same time elements in other sets centred on these units. Nevertheless, at any given time the component units of a set have a known boundary; it is not one of group membership, as I have pointed out, but of their common connection to the central ego. It is this common link which enables Bott to treat her networks as unit entities which can be analysed and compared.

A reason for Bott's lack of distinction between network and set may well be provided by an ambiguity in Barnes's article itself. On the one hand, Barnes uses the term 'set' in his definition of network, saying

> '. . . I find it convenient to talk of a social field of this kind as a *network*. The image I have is of a *set*[5] of points some of which are joined by lines. The points of the image are people, or sometimes groups, and the lines indicate which people interact with each other. . . . A network of this kind has no external boundary' (Barnes, 1954, p. 43, second italics mine).

Here, set is being used in an indefinite way, to denote the links of a network in the metaphorical way noted by Firth. On the other hand, Barnes uses the term in a different way when he talks of an individual 'generating his set of cognatic kin' and later says '. . . Thus for every individual A the whole of the network, *or at least that part of it of which he is aware*, is divided into three areas or sets of points' (Barnes, 1954, p. 46, my italics). Here, the set is bounded by ego's vision, and is centred on ego. This, I would maintain, is the more significant use of the word as far as analysis is concerned. But the fact that it is used differently in the two passages may have confused the distinction between the bounded and 'unbounded' entities.

Later writers have followed Bott rather than Barnes in their terminology. Thus, Epstein defines network with reference to a particular individual and the linkages he has with others, and goes on to make a distinction between different parts of this network according to the amount of interaction. Here, network is used in Barnes's sense of the set[6]. Again, Lancaster (1961, p. 326) briefly discusses network mainly in Bott's 'unbounded' sense of the word which, she notes, 'tends to interpret "network" in the Barnes manner'. After stressing the unsatisfactory analytical nature of such 'unbounded' entities, she advocates the use of a delimited unit 'such as the total set of Ego's recognized kin' and says that such a unit would be more suited to comparative analysis. This is, in fact, what I believe Barnes to have concluded; but it is not possible to know whether Lancaster was referring to his article here, since Barnes's use of set is not mentioned. Finally, I myself (Mayer, 1962, p. 275) have also referred to networks both as 'unbounded' as well as defined at a particular time (i.e. bounded); the latter I would now call sets.

It should be noted that Nadel also uses the term network, though in a rather different way. For he equates it to system, since he says that it is through 'abstracting from the concrete population and its behaviour the pattern or network (or "system") of relationships' (Nadel, 1957, p. 12) existing between role-playing actors that social structure is arrived at. Nadel notes that Barnes has used the term in a different sense but, though he recognizes the existence of 'open networks', he places his main emphasis on the systematic nature of the linkages between actors which form a network. The analysis of these kinds of linkages is crucial for Nadel in his building up of social structure on a basis of roles. For it is the interlocking of relationships – through the dichotomization of roles – which brings about an expansion of the areas of relationships into networks. These can be of an open-ended kind, similar to the fields envisaged by Barnes; or they can be into bounded sub-groups, whose systematic interrelation makes up the social structure. Nadel stresses that both kinds of network exist in a society, but he is more interested in the latter and therefore devotes little attention to the open-ended network.

To sum up: there has been an attempt by social anthropologists to put forward two concepts for dealing with social situations in which collections of people are found that do not form groups. One is the 'unbounded' network of relationships between pairs of people, making up a field of activity. The other is the finite set of linkages initiated by an ego, which forms part of such a network.[7] Despite some ambiguity over terminology, these two concepts are distinguished by both Barnes and Bott and by others. We can further distinguish between the classificatory set discussed by Barnes, and Bott's set (i.e. the 'network' of her analysis) which is based on interaction around an ego. The latter is made up of people brought into contact in a variety of situations and over a period of time. It is the sum, as it were, of the people involved in a series of purposive action-sets in specific contexts. To find out more about it, therefore, one must first inquire into the characteristics of the action-set. This I will do now, using my own material on political processes in India.

THE DEWAS ELECTORAL SITUATION

My data come from the Dewas District of Madhya Pradesh State in India.[8] The District has a population of 446,901 (1961) and is situated some 75 miles west of the State's capital of Bhopal, and 20 miles north-east of the industrial town of Indore. Part of it is prosperous farming country, in which cotton and wheat are major cash crops. Here is situated Dewas town, the District headquarters and only sizeable urban centre, with a population of 34,577 in 1961.

Until 1948, Dewas town was divided into halves, which were

the capitals of the States of Dewas Senior and Dewas Junior. The town was politically united after the Princely States were merged into the Indian Union in that year, and a single Municipality was constituted. The Municipal Council has a degree of autonomy in civic affairs, and is elected by universal suffrage. There have been three elections, and I wish to focus my attention on the last one, which took place in April 1961.

I have already given a general description of this event elsewhere (Mayer, 1963). There, I considered the types of workers active in the campaign, and the bases on which they and their candidates solicited and attracted votes. The various political parties each had a core of full-time election 'workers' (the English word being used). These primary workers helped with the organization of the campaign – by arranging meetings, etc., and helping to recruit secondary workers. The latter were people who would at least commit themselves to the support of a party (by contrast to a large part of the electorate) and who would perhaps join in canvassing parties and undertake to get the vote out in their localities. There were about 250 primary workers of all parties in the town's 14 wards, and perhaps between two and three times as many secondary workers, out of a total electorate of 16,332.

These workers acted as links between the candidate and the electorate. Sometimes they did this for the advantages they calculated would accrue to them if the candidate were elected; sometimes they were acting because of party loyalty and friendships formed over the years without any thoughts of gain from the election itself; and at yet other times they were discharging specific obligations contracted at earlier times. In the same way, there was an attempt to reach voters on the basis of a past or future benefit. As one shrewd observer told me, 'Every man will bleed; it is a question of knowing which is the vein to open so that he will bleed most.' In consequence, a great deal of the electioneering was carried out by workers, who sought to influence those with whom they had some appropriate relationship. Besides this, the candidate himself canvassed voters, often as a formal duty towards those who wished to have been asked for their vote. Both the general ideological and the local urban policies of the parties, as expressed in public meetings, were also deemed to have played some part in influencing voters. I am less interested in these latter aspects than in the pattern of interpersonal contacts through which votes were said to have been recruited; for it is from these that we can abstract the action-set. To show this I will present the detailed situation in one candidate's campaign.

The ward in which this candidate fought provided one of the key contests of the election. In the previous election, the seat had been won by the Congress party in a triangular contest with the Praja Socialists (PSP) and an Independent. Sixty per cent of the 852 electors had voted, and the Congress (with 210 votes) had just beaten the Independent (205 votes), though the 90 votes gathered by the PSP meant that victory was gained on a minority vote. In the succeeding term of the Municipality, the victor was said to have paid little attention to the repair of his political fences in the ward. He lived in another part of the town, and was a busy professional man. The Independent loser, on the other hand, was a resident of the ward. Over the years, he had built up strong support, partly through people's discontent with the sitting Councillor, and partly through the public and private work which he was sometimes able to do through intercession with officials and so forth.

At the 1961 election, then, the Independent stood again. This time he was an official Jan Sangh candidate. He himself did not appear to be an active party member, but received whatever support the rather sketchy Jan Sangh election organization was able to give him. He was opposed on Congress's behalf by another resident of the ward; this was a man who had recently retired from a senior government post, and who had previously held important appointments in the service of Dewas Senior, to which this part of the town had belonged. The candidate had not been a member of Congress before his retirement, and he too, therefore, was not part of the inner party organization; nevertheless, the support he received from Congress party leaders was considerably greater than that given to the Jan Sangh candidate. By contrast with his opponent, the Congress candidate had not built up any sort of ward support before being nominated, and had to start mobilizing followers there and then. The third candidate, representing the PSP, was a resident of the ward, but had little influence and received minimal support from PSP party leaders. The main contest was therefore between Congress and Jan Sangh.

Physically, economically, and socially, the ward is heterogeneous. Situated at the north-eastern end of the town, a large part of its people live in mud houses built along earthen streets in the same style as in the surrounding villages. Other people live in houses similar to those of wealthier villagers, with inside courtyards formed by house and cattle byres; and yet others reside in urban-style houses surrounded by gardens. Beyond them lie barracks housing a detachment of the State's Special Armed Police, many of whom are eligible to vote. Within the ward, there is no meeting square and few stores exist. People gather mainly within each street, at informal sitting-places under a tree or on the porch of a temple or teashop. This has an obvious effect on the kind of election campaign that can be organized and strengthens the tendency to stress individual contacts, rather than to rely on public meetings.

A survey shows the main occupations of the population to be as set out in *Table 1*.

TABLE 1*

Occupation	%
Manual labour	38·2
Government officials	15·9
Farming and dairying	14·7
Pension	6·5
Construction: artisan and contractor	5·3
Commerce and hotel-keeping	5·3
Services: legal, domestic, medical, etc.	4·7
Other	9·4
Total	100·0

* These figures are compiled from a 20 per cent sample made on the basis of the 1957 voters' list: I doubt whether there have been great changes since then. The information was gathered from knowledgeable residents, rather than from a door-to-door inquiry, but is probably none the less accurate for that. The categories are those of the Dewas Census; where a woman's name appeared on the sample, her husband's occupation was taken.

As might be expected, occupations are to some extent

correlated with the main castes represented in the ward. The same survey shows these to be as set out in *Table 2*.

TABLE 2

Caste	%
Goali	17·1
Bagri	17·1
Lunia	10·0
Balai	9·4
Rajput	8·2
Northern (Rangre) Brahman	8·2
Maratha	6·5
Maharashtrian Brahman	5·9
Other	17·6
Total	100·0

The Brahmans and Marathas are mainly in government service, and many of the Rajputs farm land in the countryside beyond the ward boundaries. In this, they have Goali and Bagri farm labour; there are also a few Bagri policemen and government messengers, and a number of Goali dairymen. For the rest, the men of these castes are manual labourers, as are the Balais and Lunias – the latter specializing in the building trade. Hierarchically, below the Brahmans come Marathas and Rajputs, and Goali, Lunia and Bagri, and Balai follow.

It is clear that a candidate cannot be elected on the support of a single caste, or of a single occupational interest. Hence, pressure has to be brought on various sections of the electorate. This may be in terms of policy, or it may be through linkages stretching from each candidate directly or through inter-mediaries to the voter. The pattern of the Congress candidate's linkages, as they were described to me and as I observed them, is given in the diagram.

I must stress that the diagram shows the links known to me.[9] Further study would possibly have revealed others; but this outline of the situation is, I believe, sufficient to indicate what the full pattern would look like. Moreover, it is probable that, at least where factions are involved, there are several further links before the voter is reached; but I do not know enough about these alignments to be able to show them diagrammatically.

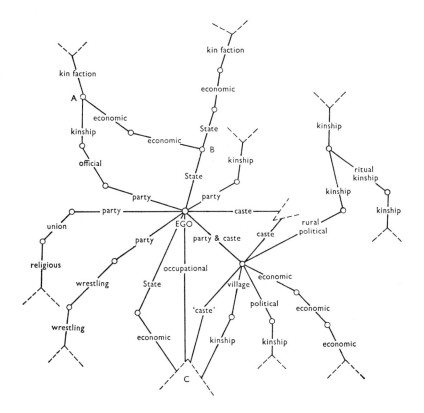

As I have pointed out, these are not the only contacts made by the candidate with the public; nor do they show all the reasons why people supported him. Some, for instance, may have done so because of his party's official policy; others may have voted for him because of the auspiciousness of his party's electoral symbol – the best example in the election of purely ideological support, which in other cases might underlie other reasons (e.g. support of a caste-mate is partly ideological and partly self-interested). But it is these links which are of interest, because I would maintain that they constitute an action-set in the context of this election. What are the characteristics of this action-set, and what is its relation to the underlying network?

One feature of this action-set is that a wide variety of bases for linkage are involved. Included as criteria are kinship, political party, religious sect, and so on. But the crucial point is that, whatever may be these 'outward' bases for the links which together make up the path from candidate to voter, the 'inward' content is always the same – namely political support of the candidate. Thus, action-sets of this kind are formed of links derived from many social fields; but because they are purposive creations by an ego, this purpose gives all the links a common feature, without which the action-set could not be classed under the quasi-group rubric. This results in an action-set whose structure may be similar to the classificatory set described by Barnes, but whose content is different. Rather, it is similar to the set envisaged by Chapple and Coon, at whose centre is an 'originator' of linkages.

A second feature of the action-set is that the links are sometimes, but not always, based on group membership. Many of the candidate's closest links were party-political ones, based on the primary group of active Congress workers which he joined upon his adoption as candidate. Other instances of primary group links are provided by membership of the same wrestling gymnasium, or of a group of religious worshippers.

Examples of links through secondary group membership would be those based on distant kinship relations,[10] and also, perhaps, membership of the same village or trade union – though these latter might be primary group links. Yet further from primary membership were the ties evoked through common caste. A crucial linkage, for example, was made between a Rajput Congress worker and Bagri voters. Bagris, officially a Backward Class, can produce 'historical' evidence which they believe gives them Rajput status. But this is not generally accepted by the Rajputs of Malwa. Hence, when the Congress worker showed that he did not object to eating and drinking with Bagris in their homes, they were greatly attracted to the Congress candidate – particularly since the Rajput supporters of the Jan Sangh were strongly conservative over such matters. More than mere sentiment was involved; for it was said that the Rajput had told the Bagris that they could become members of the newly instituted Dewas branch of the Rajput Parishad, a social organization restricted to Rajputs.[11] I shall return later to this transactional element in linkages.

Some links are not based on group membership at all, of course. Examples would include the economic links of employer-employee, creditor-debtor, storekeeper-customer, etc. Again, people with a history of service to the Maharaja did not form part of any group. The fact that some links are based on group relations does not affect the form of the action-set. For such groups are not contained within the action-set, nor are their aims necessarily relevant to the purpose of the latter. The action-set is a different kind of entity from a group, though it may include group relations in its 'outward' content of links.

A third feature is that (as Barnes shows) the action-set contains paths of linkages, and is thus a combination of relationships linking people directly to ego, and of those linking people to intermediaries who are themselves in direct contact with ego. In this it differs from the units of Bott's analysis, which contained linkages between people who were all directly linked to ego; and one might find it useful to distinguish between simple and complex action-sets on this basis.

Fourth, the action-set is a bounded entity. It is not a group, however. For the basis for membership is specific to each linkage, and there are no rights or obligations relating all those involved; even the common act of voting for ego does not bring members into relation with each other.[12] Moreover, the action-set could not exist without the ego around whom it is formed. Yet, it is different in quality from a category. For members are aware that they form part of a population recruited for a particular common purpose, and they know that there are other linkages similar to theirs – though they may not be able to identify all the other people involved.

Finally, the action-set is not a 'permanent' entity like the group. Although the 'outward' aspects are those of continuing role-relationships – e.g. those of caste, etc. – the 'inward' aspect is that of a linkage based on a specific purposive impulse stemming from ego. This action-set thus exists only at ego's election. Any action-set constructed for a future election might contain a majority of the same people. But many of the linkages would have to be re-made since, as I shall suggest later, they are based on specific transactions. To the extent that the same linkages remain in use in successive contexts of activity, a quasi-group is formed, as I shall discuss later.

THE ACTION-SET IN COMPARATIVE STUDY

A major feature of the action-set is that by contrast with the 'unbounded' network it is limited in its membership and can therefore be used in comparative analysis and in the study of social change. Let me give a few examples from the Dewas electoral situation I have described.

One could compare, for instance, the patterns of linkage in the action-sets of the three candidates in the ward. I did not study in such detail the action-set centred on the Jan Sangh candidate, but it was clear that it differed from that of his Congress opponent. Partly this was because, as I have said, the Jan Sangh candidate had gathered support over the past three years. He therefore had an action-set in which he was generally directly in contact with voters, or at the most stood at one remove from them. By contrast the Congress candidate started to work less than a month before the election. He could therefore make only superficial contacts with most voters, and had to rely on recruiting primary workers, who would then construct their own linkages. There were thus more intermediaries, and longer paths, in the Congress action-set.

This kind of comparison is connected to the analysis of election strategies.[13] I have elsewhere (Mayer, 1963, p. 126) distinguished between 'hard' and 'soft' campaigns in the Dewas elections. In the former, support is lined up at the start, and any attacks on prepared positions are rebuffed by the candidate or his workers, who keep especially close watch on the opposing primary workers. In the latter, a drive at the end of the campaign is calculated to produce enough pressure to win, without the need for elaborate fence-mending among waverers and constant counter-bidding for those who sell their support in some way. In this ward, the Jan Sangh conducted the harder and the Congress the softer campaign. Now, it is possible to argue that an action-set with shorter paths will be more appropriate to a harder campaign. For any damage done by an opponent will be more quickly apparent to the candidate, who can then counteract it. The long-pathed set, on the other hand, would seem to be better for a softer campaign. For it involves a late drive by the largest number of supporters. Hence, whether by design or by their previous connection with the ward, the candidates' strategies and the pattern of their electoral action-sets can be correlated.

Another basis for comparison is the number of lateral links. By lateral link is meant a connection between intermediaries without reference to either ego or the terminal respondents. Lateral links are defined in terms of relevance to the criterion governing the formation of the action-set. In this case, then, only the lateral links connected with ego's election are relevant. This is not to deny, of course, that there are many lateral *network* ties linking people in the action-set, which are not used by ego or his intermediaries to achieve their ends. We must distinguish between the potential material of network links, and those links which are actually used in the action-set's constitution. The lateral linkage in an action-set does not indicate the complete pattern of interaction between members. For instance, in our diagram (p. 107) there is only one lateral linkage (between *A* and *B*) in terms of ego's recruitment of votes; yet, there would have been very many in terms of general interaction, notably those between all the people who were directly linked to the candidate as members of the Congress party. But these latter connections did not appear to recruit voters directly,[14] and so are not relevant to this action-set.

Lateral linkages can be contrasted with what might be called the multipronged linkage. This occurs when a respondent is linked to several intermediaries and possibly directly to ego as well. It differs from the lateral link, which is between intermediaries themselves. An example of a multipronged linkage in the action-set I have described would be the approach by several people to the Bagri voters (marked *C*). In terms of outward content, the lateral linkage brings several pressures to bear on an intermediary to approach the respondent, whereas the multipronged linkage brings several pressures to bear on the terminal respondent himself.

Clearly, the pattern of lateral and multipronged connections will reflect a difference in electoral campaigns. One might speculate, for example, that the part of the electorate at which the greatest number of prongs are pointed is the part which has the critical votes in the election. This would certainly be true as regards the Bagri vote in this ward, for it provided the balance of victory and was notoriously fickle. One might also suggest that the candidate with the action-set having the greatest number of lateral linkages is operating the strongest campaign, since intermediaries who might find a single induce-ment inadequate for their support are fortified by a second incentive coming to them laterally. The matter clearly needs further research; for one could also say that an action set in which no lateral ties exist is one in which loyalties must be firm enough not to require reinforcement. Such an analysis of action-sets could help to examine these and similar hypotheses on the nature of political process.

Another example of the comparative and explanatory value of the action-set comes from an investigation of the content of its linkages. This reveals that linkages exist because they carry transactions furthering in some way the interests of the parties concerned. The interest of the transactor is the same in each case – it is the interest of the ego around whom the action-set has formed (in my example, the interest of his election). The interest of the respondent can vary, ranging from specific aims to be fulfilled immediately after the election (such as help in arranging a marriage), to a generalized interest of potential help of some sort in the future.

This transactional element distinguishes action-set linkage from network linkage. True, persons linked in a network may derive some benefit from their relationships; but this is not because of the very nature of the relationship, and many of these relationships have an only minimally interactional aspect, a fact which prompted Firth's (1954, p. 4) caution when considering their part in defining the network.

In the Dewas example, the transactional element distinguishes the linkages of the action-set from other contacts between candidate and electorate. As I have said, the candidate personally met most of the voters in the ward in the course of his canvassing tours. These meetings were, it is true, transactional in the widest sense of the word; for the candidate would ask for support in return for promises to improve the roads, the water supply, etc. But such appeals to the voter were made publicly, and were made in the same terms to *all* voters. The support given through the linkages in the diagram, on the other hand, were specific to an individual or, at most, a few people. The campaign, therefore, contained activities at two levels: one was a public level, at which promises were given to the general electorate as part of the party's stated programme; the other was the private level, at which the promises given, and obligations encashed, were not necessarily connected with the party's programme for the Municipality. The first could be called diffusely and the second specifically transactional.

These two kinds of contact with electors can be used to distinguish different types of candidate and electoral campaign. In Dewas, for example, there were clear examples of both specifically and diffusely transactional candidates. The latter were mainly concerned with appealing to all sections of the electorate, and therefore phrased their campaign in non-partisan terms, promising to do their best for the ward. The former made no public speeches at all, as far as I could ascertain, and went on few canvassing expeditions in the ward. Instead, they concentrated on recruiting a number of allies who would each bring a few voters with him. The further analysis of why particular candidates operated a particular type of campaign will tell us more about small-town politics and politicians.

A study of action-set linkages in Dewas reveals two types of specific transaction, namely, those of patronage and brokerage. In the first, the transactor has the power to give some benefit which the respondent desires; upon fulfilment of the latter's part the benefit is made available. Examples of this would be the improvement of a road near the respondent's house, or the employment of the respondent (or his relative) in an office over which the transactor has control. The number and extent of such benefits naturally vary with the power of the transactor; but even the most influential is unlikely to be able to please everyone who comes to him, or who needs to be brought into the action-set. He must therefore husband these direct patronage transactions so that they produce linkages with key people who can bring followers with them.

Patronage resources are thus not unlimited; and patronage is an unambiguous transaction, in which the responsibility for any failure to redeem a promise can be clearly put down to the patron. The brokerage transaction differs somewhat in both these respects. A broker is a middle-man, and the transaction is one in which he promises to obtain favours for the respondent from a third person. Thus, brokers are intermediaries for the favours of government officials, or they have influence with powerful townsmen and are said to be able to expedite the business of the respondent. The ultimate responsibility for action rests not on the broker, however, but rather on the person to whom he has access. Clearly, the broker cannot maintain his reputation if too many of his efforts are unsuccessful; but at least some failures can be explained away by putting the blame on his contact. Hence, the broker can enter into more transactions, in relation to his resources of power, than can the patron. Both may make what turn out to be campaign promises at election time; but the broker has greater possibilities of doing so, since the patron will often be inhibited by unfulfilled promises of the past, or the fear of over-extending his activity.

Though these two types of transaction may overlap in practice, and though (as I have said) not all respondents have specific and immediate interests in mind, the distinction helps to explain the linkages of an action-set and their patterning. For instance, the patrons in an action-set may not deal directly with clients, finding it advantageous to shield themselves through intermediary brokers. One may, therefore, expect to find action-sets with longer paths of linkages where there are the more powerful patrons – other things being equal. This may be a reason why the Congress action-set in the diagram had longer paths than did the Jan Sangh action-set in the same ward (as I have noted). For Congress, as the ruling party, held greater powers of patronage in its hands.

ACTION-SET AND QUASI-GROUP

I believe that these examples show the value of the action-set concept in the study of political activities. How is it related to the concept of the quasi-group and what value does this approach have for the study of complex societies?

The action-set exists in a specific context which provides the terms of ego's purpose in forming linkages. When successive action-sets are centred on similar contexts of activity, personnel and linkages may also be similar. By 'superimposing' a series of action-sets, therefore, one may discern a number of people who are more often than not members of the action-sets, and others who are involved from time to time. Taken together, these people form a catchment for ego's action-sets based on this type of context. It is this potential membership which Bott calls a network; for all the people in any family's (or individual's) networks are not recruited on every occasion, but are possible members. Again, Epstein's network is of this sort, and he distinguishes between its effective and extended membership. I have already said why I do not consider network to be a very happy term here. Set is less confusing; it fits into Barnes's terminology and I have talked of classificatory and interactive sets at the start of this paper. But I think it may be well to adopt the word quasi-group, since this best expresses the sociological implications of this type of collection of people and suggests the qualitative difference between the quasi-group and the group.

The quasi-group, then, has the same pattern of linkages as the action-set, and exists through a series of contexts of activity without any formal basis for membership. The people who are more constantly involved in the successive action-sets need not be those closest to ego. It is possible to conceive of a supporter of a candidate in successive elections who is recruited through paths composed of different and transient inter-mediaries. However, when the more constant members *are* at the same time those directly linked to ego, one can characterize them as the 'core' of the quasi-group. This core may later crystallize into a formal group; in the example I have given, this might involve the starting of a ward branch of the Congress party, to which those core members resident in the ward would belong. If it does not become a formal group, it can be seen to be a clique. This is a body of informally linked people, having a high rate of interaction and with that 'even spread' of membership activities which I have said distinguishes the group from the quasi-group. Though possessing leaders, cliques are not ego-centred bodies.[15] Where there is a clique at the centre of the quasi-group, it is possible for different egos, as members of the clique, to evoke the same pattern of linkages in different action-sets having similar contexts, and even in different contexts. Thus, where the core becomes a formal group or a clique, it may be possible to take it, rather than an individual, as the central ego – as Bott takes the whole family, rather than any single member, as her central unit.

It is clear that quasi-groups can be found in many arenas of social activity. In politics, for instance, a succession of action-sets of the kind we have seen to exist in Dewas would add up to form a quasi-group which could be called a faction. For, according to one view,[16] factions are units of conflict activated on specific occasions rather than maintained by a formal organization. They are 'loosely ordered' and with 'structurally diverse' bases of recruitment, and they are made manifest through a linkage of personal authority between leader and follower.[17] They are also based more on transactions than on issues of principle (Mayer, 1961, pp. 135-136), and may have groups or cliques as cores.

One way to study factions is to analyse the action-sets which make them up, focusing on such features as the size of core and periphery, the nature of the outward content of linkages, and the lengths of paths in various situations. From this could be built up a picture of the developmental cycle of factions, since an analysis of the content and pattern of linkages and their correlation with rivalries may reveal to us more about the critical point at which factions split.[18] From such a study would come a greater understanding of political situations involving quasi-groups rather than organized political units.

Quasi-groups also exist in the economic sphere, as an example from Dewas shows. Each of the sub-district towns, and the headquarters of Dewas, is concerned with the purchase of crops and their export from the District. This is done in officially supervised markets, where crop dealers buy from farmers. How do these dealers recruit and maintain their customers? Here, again, we can see action-sets, with the dealer as the central ego. For it is he who recruits a following with an 'inward' linkage based in each case on economic advantage, but with an 'outward' linkage resting on many criteria, including those of locality and common subcaste. We cannot say that all farmers dealing with a particular trader form a group; but since each is aware that many others (some of whom he knows) deal with the same trader they form an action-set at each harvest. Over a succession of harvests, there is some variation in the composition of the action-sets, since there is no compulsion to continue to deal with a particular trader. Nevertheless, there is also a continuity[19] within which a quasi-group is built up – one could call it a clientele. These clienteles can be studied in much the same way as I have suggested for political quasi-groups.

In the field of kinship, too, one can discern quasi-groups. In Central Indian peasant society, for example, a person has a number of kin whom he calls on for help in his affairs. I have called this the kindred of co-operation (Mayer, 1960, p. 4); one might characterize it as a quasi-group formed from a succession of action-sets centred on the individual or his household. Again, in talking of Iban society, Freeman distinguishes between the *de jure* kindred which constitutes a field of cognatic relations, and the *de facto* relationships of moral obligation which a man activates within this field and which form a major basis for recruitment to action-groups containing mainly cognatic kin though also including affines and friends (Freeman, 1961, pp. 202-211).[20] These action-groups sometimes appear to be organized groups (e.g. the travelling groups), but on other occasions seem to correspond to the action-sets I have described, and repeated recruitment might well produce a quasi-group.

The action-sets made up of kin are not mutually exclusive. Kindreds of cooperation form a series of overlapping collections of people and an individual belongs to many at once, as he would not belong to different political factions or clienteles – an exception to this would be where two kinsmen are in opposition and recruit kin as supporters. Again, the outward content of recruitment is always at least partly one of kinship and its entailed moral obligations, whatever other incentives there may be to support ego; hence the content of linkages is less hetero- geneous than it is in other action-sets. Thus we should perhaps see the kin-based quasi-group as a special and more restricted form.

More study is needed of this question, as well as of many others. For instance, what are the circumstances surrounding the emergence of cores and the part they play in the operation of the quasi-group; or what are the influences of space and time on quasi-groups? Again, what are the possibilities of making action-sets more easily comparable? One could, for example, tabulate the content of the first, second, third, etc., links along paths; one could also distinguish paths with different numbers of links, and thereby attempt to present a picture of the action- set without a cumbersome diagram of the kind I have presented. Quantification must, however, adequately express the total configuration, rather than merely categorize the properties of single links and paths; if this can be done, action-sets and consequently quasi-groups can be more easily compared.

CONCLUSION

I have attempted in this paper to see whether certain concepts may not be fruitful for social anthropologists. The identification of the action-set and the quasi-group owes much, of course, to the sociometric approach; it is also connected to analyses of other informal collections of people, such as cliques. Again, the action-set can be seen in terms of status- and role-sets (Merton, 1957, p. 368 et seq.). For a person as an ego has a role-set composed of relations towards intermediaries and terminal respondents; and as an intermediary he has a role-set comprising roles towards ego, respondents and perhaps further inter- mediaries. At a different level, ego and his intermediaries, and the intermediaries and the respondents, are linked by roles chosen from their status-sets. That is, an ego or an intermediary in a Dewas election will choose roles from the role-sets of caste, party, trade union, or from other role-sets in his status-set to attract followers. These two levels are connected with the inward and outward content of action-set linkages respectively.

The title of this paper suggests that I should discuss to what extent these concepts have particular reference to the study of complex societies. But, quite apart from a reluctance to involve myself in an effort to distinguish between complex and simple societies, I suggest that the action-set and the quasi-group are concepts which may apply in *any* situation where no organized groups operate. It is therefore relatively unimportant to assess whether they are more useful in complex than in simple societies. If indeed there are action-sets among, say, the Iban, one clearly cannot restrict the discussion to complex societies. Yet if one defines simple and complex societies as more and less involute (Nadel, 1957, p. 68) systems of role-relations, one might expect social relations in simpler societies to be more likely to be those of common group membership than they are in societies where there is a greater scatter of roles. If this be so, then the organizing of people in a simpler society will be more likely to bring together people with common group membership;[21] thus, in a given context, a sub-group will be more likely to form than an action-set.

Whether or not this be true, I have myself found that an approach of the kind I have outlined presented itself to me in the 'complex situation' of the Dewas election. It may well be that, as social anthropologists become more interested in complex societies and as the simpler societies themselves become more complex, an increasing amount of work will be based on ego-centred entities such as action-sets and quasi-groups, rather than on groups and sub-groups. This paper, therefore, is an attempt to explore and clarify the concepts involved, by applying them to an actual situation.

NOTES

1. Ginsberg (1934, p. 40). Such quasi-groups are noted in field research too (e.g. Sower, 1957, p. 276). See also the use of the term 'collectivity' in this connection (Merton, 1957, p. 299).
2. I am indebted to Dr P. H. Gulliver for this term.
3. One must emphasize that a network is, of course, bounded by the total population which is being examined, or by the discontinuities in social relations produced by its own criteria. Hence, the 'unboundedness' is only relative.
4. Cf. the introduction of the term 'chain' by Moreno (1953, p. 720) as 'an open series of mutual choices on any criterion'.
5. A printer's error makes Bott (1957, p. 59) misquote Barnes as saying 'The image I have is of a net of points . . .'.
6. In saying that Barnes calls it a network when a person 'is in touch with a number of people, some of whom may be in touch with each other, and some of whom may not', Epstein (1961, p. 56) takes only the first part of Barnes's characterization; but this continues, 'each person has a number of friends and these friends have their own friends; some of any one person's friends know each other, others do not' (Barnes, 1954, p. 43). The difference here is between a finite set and an 'unbounded' entity.
7. Cf. the matrix of interrelated pairs constructed by Truman from voting records in the U.S. Congress, within which can be discerned the clusters which he calls blocs (Truman, 1959).
8. Research was conducted in 1960-1961 with the generous aid of the School of Oriental and African Studies, University of London.
9. For simplicity's sake, I have not shown the direct influence people acting as intermediaries may have on voters, but have marked only their links with others in the path itself.
10. I have called all links based on common subcaste 'kin' ties, since the people involved were all more or less distantly related; they are distinct from ties based on the membership of two subcastes in a caste, which I have called 'caste' ties.
11. When asked whether this pledge would be redeemed after the election, another Congress supporter cynically remarked that the issue would never arise. For Bagris would forgo Rajput status if it were pointed out to them that the considerable benefits they now received as a Backward Class would cease forthwith.
12. As Bott (1957, p. 58) says, 'In an organized group, the component individuals make up a larger social whole with common aims, interdependent roles, and a distinctive sub-culture. In network formation on the other hand, only some, not all, of the component individuals have social relationships with one another.'
13. I use this word in its popular, rather than in its game theory, meaning (see Snyder, 1955, p. 79).
14. A large number of links in the diagram are based on statements made by the interested parties to me or to other people in my hearing. Others are the results of my own observations and inferences, and of third-person information. In both cases, there may be other reasons for the actions of people, since it is impossible to know whether motives have been adequately assessed.

15. One must distinguish between those cliques formally recognized by the people themselves (e.g. those dealt with in Whyte, 1955) and those which the observer isolates. Loomis & Beegle (1950, p. 141) provide an example of the latter, in which there is an almost comprehensive series of linkages between clique members and an almost complete discontinuity of relations with the outside.

16. For another approach, see Siegel and Beals (1960).

17. Firth (1957, p. 292), summing up the conclusions of a symposium on factions.

18. For instance, my diagram shows that one of ego's close supporters has almost as many radiating linkages as ego himself. How far can splits be predicted where the linkages of supporters outnumber those of ego?

19. This is due in part to the contracting of debts with the dealer; hence there is less mobility than might be the case were the action-set to rest solely on the price offered by the dealer.

20. Freeman limits the kindred to cognatic kin, excluding affines. I have myself included the latter in my definition (and see Mitchell, 1963, p. 351). The issue here is not a terminological one, however, but one of the constitution of the action-sets and quasi-groups formed from these ties.

21. As Merton (1957, p. 311) puts it, 'in less differentiated societies, group affiliation tends to engage a considerably larger share of each member's personality'.

REFERENCES

BARNES, J. A. 1954. Class and Committees in a Norwegian Island Parish. *Human Relations* 7: 39-58.

BOTT, E. 1957. *Family and Social Network*. London: Tavistock Publications.

CHAPPLE, E. D. & COON, C. S. 1947. *Principles of Anthropology*. London: Cape.

EPSTEIN, A. L. 1961. The Network & Urban Social Organisation. *Rhodes-Livingstone Institute Journal* 29: 29-62.

FIRTH, R. W. 1954. Social Organisation & Social Change. *Journal of the Royal Anthropological Institute* 84: 1-20.

—— 1957. Factions in Indian & Overseas Indian Societies: Introduction. *British Journal of Sociology* 8: 291-295.

FREEMAN, J. D. 1961. On the Concept of the Kindred. *Journal of the Royal Anthropological Institute* 91: 192-200.

GINSBERG, M. 1934. *Sociology*. London: Butterworth.

LANCASTER, L. 1961. Some Theoretical Problems in the Study of Family & Kin Ties in the British Isles. *British Journal of Sociology* 12: 317-333.

LOOMIS, C. P. & BEEGLE, J. A. 1950. *Rural Social Systems*. New York: Prentice-Hall.

MAYER, A. C. 1960. *Caste & Kinship in Central India*. London: Routledge & Kegan Paul.

—— 1961. *Peasants in the Pacific: A Study of Fiji Indian Rural Society*. London: Routledge & Kegan Paul.

—— 1962. System & Network: An Approach to the Study of Political Process in Dewas. In T. N. Madan & G. Sarana (eds.), *Indian Anthropology*. Bombay: Asia.

—— 1963. Municipal Elections: A Central Indian Case Study. In C. H. Philips (ed.), *Politics & Society in India*. London: Allen & Unwin.

MERTON, R. K. 1957. *Social Theory & Social Structure* (Rev. Edn.). Glencoe, Ill.: Free Press.

MITCHELL, W. E. 1963. Theoretical Problems in the Concept of Kindred. *American Anthropologist* **65**: 343-354.

MORENO, J. L. 1953. *Who Shall Survive? Foundations of Sociometry, Group Psychotherapy & Sociodrama*. Beacon: Beacon House.

NADEL, S. F. 1957. *The Theory of Social Structure*. London: Cohen & West.

RADCLIFFE-BROWN, A. R. 1952. *Structure & Function in Primitive Society*. London: Cohen & West.

SIEGEL, B. J. & BEALS, A. R. 1960. Conflict and Factional Dispute. *Journal of the Royal Anthropological Institute* **90**: 107-117.

SNYDER, R. C. 1955. Game Theory & the Analysis of Political Behaviour. In S. K. Bailey *et al.*, *Research Frontiers In Politics & Government*. Washington: Brookings Institution.

SOWER, C. *et al.* 1957. *Community Involvement: The Webs of Formal & Informal Ties That Make for Action*. Glencoe, Ill.: Free Press.

TRUMAN, D. B. 1959. *The Congressional Party: A Case Study*. New York: Wiley.

WHYTE, W. F. 1955. *Street Corner Society*. Chicago: Chicago University Press.

From John Boyd, *Journal of Mathematical
Psychology 6*, 139-167 (1969), by permission.

The Algebra of Group Kinship

JOHN PAUL BOYD

University of California at Irvine, Irvine, California 92650

Group theory and the theory of relations are used to study the kinship of certain
kinds of primitive societies. It will be shown that these societies partition their members
into classes that are permuted by the relations "class X has fathers (mothers) in class
Y" so as to form a regular permutation group. A mathematical characterization of
the conditions under which groups become relevant for the study of kinship is given
and is related to the theory of structural balance. It is argued that the concept of group
extension and its specialization to direct and semidirect products determine the
evolutionary sequences and the coding of these kinship systems. These predictions
are found to be consistent with certain observed changes, geographical distribution,
and habits of usage of the kinship systems under consideration. Generalizations to
aspects of behavior outside of kinship are briefly discussed.

INTRODUCTION

In recent years, many formal descriptive techniques have been developed for
naturally occuring human behavior. See Hammel's (1966) special issue of the *American
Anthropologist* on "Formal Semantic Analysis." The three descriptive techniques
which are discussed in this paper include grammars that recursively generate kinship
systems, the use of abstract group theory to describe a subclass of kinship systems
called marriage class systems, and the "componential analysis" of kinship systems.

As is the case with most innovations, there has been much criticism of these new
techniques. From the mathematical point of view, criticism is easiest to make on the
most formal of these new areas, the use of abstract groups to model marriage class
systems. This line of work was fathered by Lévi-Strauss (1949) and continues through
Kemeny, Snell, and Thompson (1957) to White (1963). This work has restricted
itself largely to definitions and the verification that given societies satisfy these definitions. Little use has been made of the mathematical theory of groups. Particularly
conspicuous by its absence is the concept of homomorphism, which relates different
groups to each other. It will be argued that if a group G_1 evolves into a group G_2, then
G_1 will be a homomorphic image of G_2, but that the remnants of G_1 will be revealed
in the coding of G_2 in its everyday use. Another question which arises is why groups
are relevant instead of some of the other closely related mathematical systems such

319

as groupoids, semigroups, monoids, loops and so on. The group partition theorem gives a partial answer to this problem and also relates the marriage class system to Cartwright and Harary's (1956) theory of structural balance.

The kinship grammars of Lounsbury (1964) are inspired by the formal grammars of Chomsky (1963). There are differences, however, between the syntactic structure of a language and the structure of a kinship system. These differences appear to be understood informally, but are not as explicitly stated as they could be. A fuller treatment of kinship grammars is given in Boyd (1966).

Componential analysis as studied by Goodenough (1956) and others seems to be a valuable tool in the study of meaning. The idea is to represent a relatively large set of discrete concepts as a subset of a Cartesian product of smaller sets. For example, English kinship terms might be represented as elements of the Cartesian product of the sets "generation" = $\{+2, +1, 0, -1, -2\}$, "sex" = $\{male, female\}$, "linearity" = $\{lineal, nonlineal\}$, etc. Thus, the term "mother" would be represented by the list $(+1, female, linear,...)$. Burling (1964) pointed out, however, that there is little objective justification for choosing one representation rather than, say, a random permutation of this representation. This paper attempts to explain why some representations allow colorful names like "sex" to be assigned to the components and why others defy such verbal descriptions.

Perhaps the strongest criticism of these three areas is that they are viewed as distinct. If this criticism is valid, it is partly due to a lack of rigor in their formulations. The value of the abstract mathematical approach to problems is that it can transform superficially different problems into special cases of a general theory. This article succeeds in doing something less than this in that it restricts its attention to marriage class systems. What is attempted is to relate the theory of group structure to the concepts of kinship grammar and componential analysis. The formalisms have been carefully constructed, however, so as to generalize easily to general kinship systems and other semantic structures. An outline of this generalization is given in the conclusions of this article. It was felt, however, to be useful to present a complete article illustrating these concepts in the relatively simple and familiar context of finite groups.

GROUPS, MARRIAGE CLASSES AND STRUCTURAL BALANCE

This section will attempt to characterize societies which have what anthropologists have sometimes called "marriage classes." The classic example of such a society is the Arunta tribe of central Australia as described, for example, by Elkin (1964). The set of basic Yankee kinship terms f, m, b, z, s, d, h, w is often not sufficient for "primitive" kinship systems, which may make more distinctions. In particular, the Arunta distinguish between older and younger siblings. In addition, the sex of the speaker makes a difference in the kinship term that the Arunta use.

The set $\mathcal{A}$ of one-word Arunta kinship terms are: "a man's father," "a man's mother," "a woman's father," "a woman's mother," "elder brother," "elder sister," "younger brother," "younger sister," "a man's child," "a man's son." "a man's daughter," "a woman's son," "a woman's daughter," "wife," and "husband." Other relatives are described by compound expressions from this basic set.

Before continuing it is necessary to summarize the concepts and notation of binary relations that will be used here to describe kinship relations. For further details consult Clifford and Preston (1961). The *Cartesian product* of two sets E and F is denoted by $E_1 \times E_2$ and is defined to be the set of all ordered pairs (x_1, x_2), where $x_1 \in E_1$ and $x_2 \in E_2$. A (*binary*) *relation on* a set E is is a subset of $E \times E$. If A is a relation on E, then xAy means $(x, y) \in A$. The symbols $xA = \{y : xAy\}$. Thus xA is the set of all element that are A-related to x. Conversely, $Ay = \{x : xAy\}$ is that subset of E to whom y is A-related. For example, if $<$ is the usual ordering of the integers, then $0<$ and <0 denote the set of positive and negative integers, respectively. If $X \subseteq E$ then $XA = \bigcup \{xA : x \in X\}$ and $AX = \bigcup \{Ax : x \in X\}$.

The *composition* of two relations A, B on E is denoted by AB and is that relation on E defined by $xABy$ iff there is a $u \in E$ such that xAu and uAy hold. That is, $AB = \{(x, y) : xA \cap By \neq \varnothing\}$. Since $(AB)C = A(BC)$ for all relations A, B, C on E, composition is associative and the set $\mathcal{B}(E)$ of all relations on E forms a semigroup under the operation of composition. In fact, $\mathcal{B}(E)$ is a *monoid* (semigroup with identity) since the *identity* (or *equality*) relation 1_E defined by $x1_Ey$ iff $x = y$ and $x \in E$ satisfies the definition of an identity element : $1_EA = A1_E = A$. $A^n = AA \cdots A$ (n occurrences of A). Composition is expressed in everyday English by the possessive constructions as in "mother's brother" or "brother of the mother."

The *converse* A^{-1} of a relation A is formed by reversing all the ordered pairs in A so that xAy iff $yA^{-1}x$. The converse of "less than" is "greater than," and ("mother")$^{-1}$ = "a woman's son."

Since relations are sets, the set theoretic notions of inclusion, union, and intersection are already defined. Thus, we can make the following definition.

A relation ρ on E is an *equivalence* relation on E iff (i) $1_E \subseteq \rho$ (reflexity); (ii) $\rho \subseteq \rho^{-1}$ (symmetry); and (iii) $\rho^2 \subseteq \rho$ (transitivity) hold.

A *partition* π on a set E is a collection of nonempty subsets of E such that each element of E is an element of exactly one element of π. If π is a partition on E, then the set $\{C \times C : C \in \pi\}$ is an equivalence relation on E and is called the *equivalence relation naturally associated with* π. Conversely, if ρ is an equivalence relation, the collection $\{x\rho : x \in E\}$ is a partition and is denoted by E/ρ.

A relation φ from E into F, (i.e., a subset of $E \times F$) is a *function* iff $1_E \subseteq \rho\rho^{-1}$ and $\rho^{-1}\rho \subseteq 1_F$ (i.e., iff $x\varphi$ is a singleton for all $x \in E$). A function φ is said to be *one-to-one* iff the first inclusion is an equality and *onto* iff the second is an equality. If φ is a one-to-one function from E onto itself then φ is a *permutation*.

The practice of writing the name of the function φ after the argument as in $x\varphi$ is

321

called "suffix" notation as opposed to the more common "prefix" notation, $\varphi(x)$ or φx. Suffix notation is used here since it agrees with the order in which English-speaking anthropologists write kinship terms. That is, "a man's mother's brother" is usually written δ MoBr instead of BrMo (δ). If φ is a function, we shall usually write $x\varphi = y$ instead of $x\varphi y$.

The Arunta kinship system can be succinctly described in this terminology. Let E be the set of people belonging to the Arunta tribe. The E is partitioned into eight marriage classes. Let I be the equivalence relation associated with this partition and denote the partition by E/I. The Arunta culture has some very definite cultural norms with respect to these classes. Specifically, all the fathers of children in a given class come from the same class. Conversely, all the children of men in a given class belong to the same class. Thus, the fatherhood relation on E induces a permutation F on E/I in a natural way: $XF = Y$ iff there is a father of an X in Y. Similarly, the relation "mother of" induces a permutation M on E/I. From these two permutations, others can be derived by composition and taking converses. For example, let us express in terms of F and M the two permutations that White (1963) uses, C and W. C is the permutation defined by $XC = Y$ iff there is a man in X whose child is in Y, and W is defined by $XW = Y$ iff there is a man in X married to a woman in Y. Each pair of permutations can be expressed in terms of the other. Thus, $F = C^{-1}$ and $M = C^{-1}W$ hold on the one hand, and on the other hand we have $C = F^{-1}$ and $W = F^{-1}M$. The use of F and M will result in slightly more elegant formulas, but is otherwise equivalent to the C, W representations.

It is easy to verify that the composition of two permutations is again a permutation. Thus, the set of all possible (finite) compositions of the permutations F and M form a set of G of permutations and is called the permutation group *generated* by F and M. Recall that a *group* is a set G together with a function $*$ from $G \times G$ into G such that (i) (Associativity) $a*(b*c) = (a*b)* c$ for all a, b, $c \in G$; (ii) (Identity) There is an element $1 \in G$ such that $1*a = a*1 = a$ for all $a \in G$; and (iii) (Inverses) For every $a \in G$ there is an $a^{-1} \in G$ such that $a*a^{-1} = a^{-1}*a = 1$.

We shall write ab instead of $a*b$. Note that the inverse of a permutation is its converse.

The Arunta permutation group G generated by F and M has the additional property that for any X, $Y \in E/I$ there is exactly one permutation $P \in G$ such that $XP = Y$. Such a permutation group is called (*right*) *regular* and has the property that every element $P \in G$ can be written uniquely in the form XP for some fixed $X \in E/I$. This means that a new binary operation $\cdot$ can be defined on E/I by $(XP_1) \cdot (XP_2) = X(P_1P_2)$. The group E/I, $\cdot$ is isomorphic to G under the correspondence $XP \leftrightarrow P$.

This results in a curious property when we "graph" a regular permutation group. The Arunta marriage class system is graphed in Fig. 1. The dots represent the elements of E/I. Thus, each dot corresponds to a class of people in E. An arrow is drawn from point X to point Y with its head at Y and labeled with F (or M) iff $XF = Y$

(or $XM = Y$). Since $F = F^{-1}$ for the Arunta, the arrow is given two heads, to suggest the symmetry. By convention M-arrows will be solid; and F-arrows dotted since paternity is conjectural.

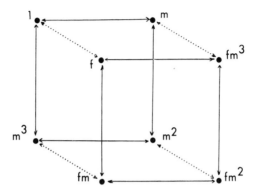

FIG. 1.   The graph of the Arunta marriage class system. M-arrows are solid; and F-arrows, dotted.

Since G is regular, we can choose an arbitrary point and label it 1. Then the other points can be labeled with their unique representations $P \in G$. This has also been done in Fig. 1. Table 1 is the "Cayley multiplication table" for the group G of the Arunta tribe.

TABLE 1

THE ARUNTA MULTIPLICATION TABLE[a]

	1	M	M^2	M^3	F	FM	FM^2	FM^3
1	1	M	M^2	M^3	F	FM	FM^2	FM^3
M	M	M^2	M^3	1	FM^3	F	FM	FM^2
M^2	M^2	M^3	1	M	FM^2	FM^3	F	FM
M^3	M^3	1	M	M^2	FM	FM^2	FM^3	F
F	F	FM	FM^2	FM^3	1	M	M^2	M^3
FM	FM	FM^2	FM^3	F	M^3	1	M	M^2
FM^2	FM^2	FM^3	F	FM	M^2	M^3	1	M
FM^3	FM^3	F	FM	FM^2	M	M^2	M^3	1

[a] Row elements are multiplied on the right by column elements. That is, $z = xy$ is the entry of row x, column y.

Since only two of the set $\mathcal{A}$ of basic Arunta kinship terms have been used thus far, we must now investigate how the entire network of relations on E relates to G. Recall that the set $\mathcal{B}(E)$ of relations on E forms a monoid under the operation of composition since composition is associative and the identity relation 1_E is the identity element. A *submonoid* $\mathcal{A}$ of a monoid $\mathcal{B}$ is a subset $\mathcal{B}$ such that $\mathcal{A}$ contains the identity and is closed under composition. That is, $A, B \in \mathcal{A}$ imply that $AB \in \mathcal{A}$. If $\mathcal{A}$ is just a subset of a monoid $\mathcal{B}$, then the intersection of all submonoids of $\mathcal{B}$ containing $\mathcal{A}$ is the smallest submonoid $\mathcal{A}^*$ containing $\mathcal{A}$ and is called the *submonoid generated by $\mathcal{A}$*. $\mathcal{A}^*$ may be constructed by taking all possible compositions of elements in $\mathcal{A}$ and adding in the identity. Note that if G is a *finite* group and $S \subseteq G$, then S^* is also a group and is called the *subgroup generated by S*. Let $\mathcal{A}^* - \varnothing$ be the submonoid of $\mathcal{B}(E)$ generated by $\mathcal{A}$ but excepting the empty relation $\varnothing$. Suppose φ is a function from $\mathcal{A}^* - \varnothing$ onto G. It is reasonable to require that the structure of G should "approximate" the structure in $\mathcal{A}^*$. That is, if A, B, and AB are members of $\mathcal{A}^* - \varnothing$, then $(A\varphi)(B\varphi) = (AB)\,\varphi$. If φ satisfies this requirement for all $A, B \in \mathcal{A}^* - \varnothing$, then φ is said to be a *homomorphism*. This is a slight generalization of the standard concept of monoid homomorphisms which, however, do not exist in any nontrivial form between $\mathcal{A}^*$ and G if $\varnothing \in \mathcal{A}^*$.

TABLE 2

A TABLE OF THE HOMOMORPHISM φ MAPPING $\mathcal{A}^* - \varnothing$ ONTO THE ARUNTA GROUP G

$A \in \mathcal{A}^* - \varnothing$	$A\varphi \in G$
"elder brother" "elder sister" "younger brother" "younger sister"	$= 1$, the group identity
"a man's father" "a woman's father" "a man's child" "a man's son" "a man's daughter"	$= F = F^{-1}$
"a man's mother" "a woman's mother"	$= M$
"a woman's son" "a woman's daughter"	$= M^{-1}$
"wife" "husband"	$= F^{-1}M = M^{-1}F = FM$

Assume that φ is a homomorphism from $\mathcal{A}^* - \varnothing$ onto G and that "a man's father" φ = "a woman's father" $\varphi = F$ and that "a man's mother" $\varphi = $ "a woman's mother" φ = M. It will be shown that under certain conditions if A, B are relations and if

$A \subseteq B$, then $A\alpha = B\alpha$ and $A^{-1}\alpha = (A\alpha)^{-1}$, where A^{-1} denotes the converse of the relation A, defined by $xA^{-1}y$ iff yAx. Assuming these conditions to hold for the moment, we have Table 2 which shows to what element in G each element of the list of basic relatives given above corresponds.

It should be noted that the set of relations $\mathcal{A}^*$ changes from generation to generation as new members are added to the population E and as the distant dead are forgotten. The only thing that remains constant is the abstract group G.

The question now arises as to how vital is it that G be a group rather than, say, a monoid. It is conceivable that social structures of the form $\varphi : \mathcal{A}^* - \varnothing \to G$ can exist, where G is a monoid and φ is a homomorphism. The "group partition theorem" to be proven below shows under what conditions G must be a group. Recall that a set $\mathcal{A}$ of relations on E is said to be *strongly connected* on E iff $\bigcup \mathcal{A}^* = E \times E$.

GROUP PARTITION THEOREM. *Let $\mathcal{A}$ be a set of relations on a finite set E that is strongly connected. Let φ be a homomorphism from $\mathcal{A}^* - \varnothing$ onto a monoid G. Then the following statements are equivalent*:

(i) *For any $A \in \mathcal{A}^*$, if xAx for some x in E, then $A\varphi = 1$, the identity element of the monoid G.*

(ii) *The relation $\bigcup 1\varphi^{-1}$, which we shall denote by I, is an equivalence relation on E, and $\mathcal{A}^* - \varnothing /\varphi\varphi^{-1}$ is a regular permutation group on the I-classes with the definition $(Ix)(A\varphi\varphi^{-1}) = I(x(\bigcup A\varphi\varphi^{-1}))$.*

(iii) *For all $A, B \in \mathcal{A}^*$, if xAy and xBy for some $x, y \in E$, then $A\varphi = B\varphi$.*

Proof. We first show that (i) implies (ii). To show that $\mathcal{A}^* - \varnothing /\varphi\varphi^{-1}$ is a group, it is necessary to prove that G is a group. That is, we must show that for any element in G, which we can assume to be of the form $A\varphi$ for some $A \in \mathcal{A}^*$, an element $A' \in \mathcal{A}^*$ called a φ-*inverse* of A exists such that $A\varphi A'\varphi = 1$. To show this, suppose that xAy holds for some x, y in E. By strong connectivity, there is an $A' \in \mathcal{A}^*$ such that $yA'x$. Thus, $xAA'x$ holds and by (i), $(AA')\varphi = 1$. But $(AA')\varphi = A\varphi A'\varphi$, so that $A'\varphi$ is the inverse of $A\varphi$. Thus, A' is a φ-inverse of A iff $A'\varphi = (A\varphi)^{-1}$. Note that the converse A^{-1} is always a φ-inverse for A.

To show that I is an equivalence relation, we must prove that I is reflexive, symmetric, and transitive. Since E is strongly connected, there is an $A \in \mathcal{A}^*$ for every $x \in E$ such that xAx holds. By hypothesis (i), $A\varphi = 1$ so that xIx, proving I to be reflexive. Now suppose xIy, so that xAy holds for some A such that $A\varphi = 1$. By strong connectivity, there is a B such that yBx. Therefore, we have $xABx$ and by (i), $(AB)\varphi = 1$. But $(AB)\varphi = A\varphi B\varphi = 1B\varphi = B\varphi = 1$, and hence yIx holds, showing the symmetry of I. If xIy and yIz, then there are $A, B \in \mathcal{A}^*$ such that xAy and yBz hold and $A\varphi = B\varphi = 1$. Therefore, we have $xABz$. But $(AB)\varphi = A\varphi B\varphi = 11 = 1$, showing transitivity and completing the proof that I is an equivalence relation.

Let us denote each equivalence class of relations $A\varphi\varphi^{-1}$ with the symbol $[A]$. To show that each class $[A]$ is a permutation on the I-classes, we will show that each $[A]$ is a one-to-one relation on the I-classes. Suppose that $Ix[A]\ Iy$ and $Ix[A]\ Iz$, where $Ix[A]\ Iy$ means, of course, that there are relations I_1 ; A_1 , $I_2 \in \mathcal{A}^*$ such that $x(I_1A_1I_2)\ y$ hold, $I_1\varphi = I_2\varphi = 1$, and $A_1\varphi = A\varphi$. By strong connectedness, there is a $B \in \mathcal{A}^*$ such that yBz, and hence $(Ix)\ [A][B][A'](Ix)$. But by (i), $1 = ([A][B][A'])\varphi = A\varphi B\varphi A'\varphi$ where A' is a φ-inverse of A from which we can conclude that $B\varphi = 1$ so that yIz holds. This shows that whenever $[A]$ is defined, it is many-to-one. By a similar argument on $[A']$, we can show that $[A]$ is one-to-many. Thus, $[A]$ is one-to-one when defined.

To show that $[A]$ is everywhere defined, let us choose a minimal set of generators S for G that includes $A\varphi$. That is, every element in G can be expressed as a product of elements of S, and if any element is removed from S, this is no longer true. We claim that E is not strongly connected under the set $\mathcal{A}_1 = (S - A\varphi)^* \ \varphi^{-1} \subseteq \mathcal{A}^*$ that map into the subgroup of G generated by $S - A\varphi$. This is true since xAy holds for some x, y in E, and if E were connected under $\mathcal{A}_1$, then there would be a $B \in \mathcal{A}_1$ such that yBx. But then $(Ix)[A][B](Ix)$ would hold, so that by the uniqueness of group inverses $A\varphi = (B\varphi)^{-1}$, contradicting the assumption that G was a minimal generating set. Now if x_1 is an arbitrary point in E, then for any $x_i \in E$, there is by strong connectivity a relation $B_i \in \mathcal{A}^*$ such that $x_1(B_i)\ x_i$ holds. There must exist a k such that $[A] = [B_k]$ for otherwise E would be connected under $\mathcal{A}_1$. More explicitly, for any x_i , $x_j \in E$, we would have $x_i(B_i'B_j)\ x_j$ where B_i' is a φ-inverse of B_i .

Therefore, we have shown that $\mathcal{A}^* - \varnothing /\varphi\varphi^{-1}$ is a permutation group on I-classes. This permutation group is obviously regular since if Ix and Iy are any elements of E/I, there is by strong connectivity an $A \in \mathcal{A}^*$ such that xAy which implies $(Ix)[A] = (Iy)$. We have already seen above that xAy and xBy imply that $A\varphi = B\varphi$, so that this permutation group is regular.

(ii) implies (iii). Suppose xAy and xBy hold for some x, y in E and $A, B \in \mathcal{A}^*$. Then $(Ix)[A] = (Iy)$ and $(Ix)[B] = (Iy)$, and by regularity $[A] = [B]$.

(iii) implies (i). Because φ is onto G, there is an $A \in \mathcal{A}^*$ such that $A\varphi = 1$. Therefore, $1 = A\varphi = (A1_E)\ \varphi = (A\varphi)(1_E\varphi) = 1_E\varphi$, so that $1_E\varphi = 1$. Since $x1_Ex$ holds for all x in E, if $A \in \mathcal{A}^*$ and xAx for some $x \in E$, then by (iii) $A\varphi = 1_E\varphi = 1$. Thus, (iii) implies (i), and the proof of the theorem is complete.

One of the purposes of a theorem of the form, "the following are equivalent," in a science is to improve one's intuition about some of the conditions. For instance, condition (ii) in the Group Partition Theorem may be regarded as the basic or most direct formalization of what anthropologists mean by a marriage class system. For the theorem to be useful, the other conditions should have definite, and perhaps surprising, sociological interpretations. For example, the general assumption that E is strongly connected can be interpreted as meaning that the society is closely knit and homogeneous. That is, everybody is related to everybody else. This assumption would not be met in societies with "endogamous" classes of people, which do not intermarry.

Statement (i) can be interpreted in two stages. First, it requires that for any $x \in E$, there be some relation A such that xAx (this follows from strong connectivity) and A is mapped onto the identity element 1 of G. This can be interpreted by noting that the identity relation 1_E is mapped onto the identity of G. Therefore, any relation A which is mapped onto 1 can be considered to be an extension of, or an approximation to, the equality relation 1_E since A is also represented by 1. The second half of the interpretation is that since *all* A such that xAx must be mapped onto the same element 1, the individual must have, in a sense, a consistent self-image. Lest this sound too fanciful, it should be noted that for a society with a marriage class system, it is empirically true that a mapping of a relation onto G implies an entire set of very definite social obligations, forms of etiquette, and attitudes, as well as describing marriage possibilities. With this in mind, the social interpretation of (iii) becomes clear: the relations between any two individuals must be consistent. That is, though there may be many paths (elements of $\mathcal{A}^*$) relating x and y, they are all mapped onto the same element in G and hence equivalent modulo $\varphi\varphi^{-1}$. This condition is obviously unlikely to be met in a large complicated society with many different kinds of roles.

Various examples of societies that satisfy all the hypotheses of the group partition theorem will be fully discussed later. Perhaps at this point it would be useful to introduce examples that fail to satisfy the hypotheses in various interesting ways.

Example 1: American society is traditionally partitioned into three socioeconomic classes by sociologists. Let A be the relation defined by xAy iff x can legally marry into y's class. Since there is no formal restriction on interclass marriages, A is the universal relation, $E \times E$. Let 1 be the identity relation on social classes. The relation A is everywhere defined, and φ is one to one onto the monoid given by the following multiplication table:

	1	1
1	1	A
A	A	A

All the general hypotheses are satisfied, but (i), (ii), and (iii) all fail to hold.

Example 2: Consider an imaginary society consisting of three persons. Let $\mathcal{A}$ consist of all possible one-to-one functions between the three people. $\mathcal{A}^* = \mathcal{A}$ and is isomorphic to the so-called symmetric permutation group S_3 on three objects. S_3 has six elements in it. Again, all the general hypotheses are satisfied, but the three conditions fail together as they should.

Example 3: Many societies partition their members into classes called "clans" or "sibs" with the rule that individuals can marry anyone not in their own clan but that children belong to their father's clan. Any such system with three or more clans and with the appropriate choices for $\mathcal{A}$ forms a monoid that is not a group since the universal relation $E \times E$ is quickly generated in $\mathcal{A}^*$.

It should be noted that when G is a group of two elements, the graph of $\mathcal{A}$ is what

Cartwright and Harary (1956) call a *balanced graph*, where a line is called *positive* if it is mapped onto the identity 1. In this case the Group Partition Theorem can be rephrased in terms of balance theory if we specialize our terminology to the case $G = \{1, a\}$. Let $\mathcal{A} = \{N, P\}$ be the set of "negative" and "positive" lines, respectively, where $N\varphi = a$ and $P\varphi = 1$. A *walk* from x to y is a relation $A \in \{N, P\}^*$ such that xAy. A *closed walk* at x is a walk from x to x. A walk A is *positive* if $A\varphi = 1$ and *negative* if $A\varphi = a$. Note that, since we have not required G to be a group, it is possible that "positives" and "negatives" multiply as follows: $aa = a$. Of course, since 1 is an identity, the equations $1a = a1 = a$ and $11 = 1$ are forced to hold. In these more restricted terms, the Group Partition Theorem takes the following form:

THEOREM. *If E is strongly connected and if $\varphi : \{N, P\}^* - \varnothing \to G$ is a homomorphism onto $G = \{1, a\}$, then the following are equivalent:*

(i) *Every closed walk is positive.*

(ii) *Pluses and minuses multiply as usual; and the society can be partitioned into two non-empty subsets such that negative relations hold only between persons of different subsets, and positive relations hold only between persons of the same subset.*

(iii) *Any two walks between points x and y have the same sign.*

The best example of balanced graphs in kinship systems is the "moiety" system. Societies which possess a moiety system are partitioned into two halves, or moieties. Marriage is restricted to couples belonging to different moieties. If a child belongs to the same moiety as his father, then the system is called *patrilineal*; if he belongs to the same moiety as his mother, *matrilineal*. Since in both kinds of moiety systems marriage takes place between individuals of different moieties, this relation must be interpreted as the "negative" relation. In a patrilineal moiety system, the relation between father and child is "positive"; and the relation between mother and child, "negative." In a matrilineal moiety system the signs of the relation between parents and children is reversed. If one is distracted by the informal meanings of the words, "positive" and "negative," then it would be better to use the paraphrases, "group identity" and "nonidentity group element." Of course, there are a whole set of beliefs and behaviors associated with the "positive" and "negative" relations in any given moiety system culture, but they will in general have little to do with the English words, "positive" and "negative." See Flament (1963) for an elementary discussion of balance theory as applied to kinship. We now leave the study of $\mathcal{A}$, relations on the set E of people, and direct our attention to the study of the group G.

THE EVOLUTION OF GROUP SYSTEMS

The eight-class Arunta system is quite complicated and certainly is well-structured. While it is not inconceivable that once in operation, the people could maintain the system from generation to generation, it is difficult to understand the origin of the Arunta system. If the system could be broken down into different parts which act independently, or almost independently, of each other, then it would be possible to imagine that these parts, or components, evolved piece by piece in relatively small steps. The problem of specifying the components of a system and the interrelationships among such components may be called the "inside problem." A solution to the inside problem should tell us how an individual or culture has coded the system in question. Such a solution should give predictions about the kind of mistakes that are likely to occur and about the probable direction of change. The approach to the inside problem used here will be to specify a "componential analysis" which represents the system as a Cartesian product. Although our solution will not in general be unique, the class of componential analyses that satisfies the *a priori* criteria to be presented below will be in some cases very much smaller than the class of all possible componential analyses.

Another kind of problem is how to specify the system itself and how to distinguish a given system from all the other systems in a given category. This might be called the "outside problem" for such systems. The solution suggested here for the outside problem is closely related to the inside solution. A system will be specified by a "grammar," which will be a system of defining relations that uniquely specify the system. This outside problem has been more extensively studied than the inside problem. For example, a "grammar of a language" as defined by Chomsky (1963) is similar to an outside grammar in our terms. White (1963) deals with the defining relations of group societies. In addition, Lounsbury (1964) and others have described "kindship grammars," which specify the kindship system in question. Note that for finite systems, like the group societies, the outside problem can be solved by simply enumerating all the elements and their interactions in a "multiplication table" as in Table 1. However, such an enumeration is uninteresting and does not generalize to the infinite case.

Before we can discuss defining relations, however, we have to introduce the concept of a "free monoid on a set S." Usually, S will consist of the letters F and M. The free monoid on S denoted by FM(S), consists of all "words," $(a_1 ,..., a_n)$ using the "letters" $a_i \in S$. If $(a_1 ,..., a_m)$ and $(b_1 ,..., b_n)$ are elements of FM(S), then we define their product by "juxtaposition":

$$(a_1 ,..., a_m)(b_1 ,..., b_n) = (a_1 ,..., a_m , b_1 ,..., b_n).$$

The FM(S) with the operation of juxtaposition is called the *free monoid* on $\mathcal{A}$, where the identity element 1 is interpreted to be the *empty word*.

Suppose $S = \{F, M\}$ and that we wish to impose some "generating relations" on some of the elements of FM(S) such as

$$F^2 = 1, \qquad M^4 = 1, \qquad MF = FM^3,$$

which will uniquely define the Arunta group system. In general, we may wish to impose the generating relations $x_i = y_i$ for i in an index set I and where x_i, $y_i \in \text{FM}(S)$. Let $\beta = \{(x_i, y_i) : i \in I\}$. We wish to associate the largest possible monoid with β which has S as a set of generators and yet where all the relations in β actually hold. In order to efficiently describe this monoid generated by β, we need some more terminology and notation.

If G is a monoid $a \in G$ and $B \subseteq G$, then $aB = \{ab : b \text{ in } B\}$ and $Ba = \{ba : b \text{ in } B\}$, where the product of a and b is written ab. If A and B are subsets of G,

$$AB = \bigcup\{Ab : b \text{ in } B\} = \bigcup\{aB : a \text{ in } A\}.$$

Thus, if $A \subseteq G$, A is a *submonoid* iff $AA \subseteq A$ and $1 \in A$.

A *homomorphism* of a monoid G is a function φ mapping G into another monoid H such that $(ab)\, \varphi = (a\varphi)(b\varphi)$ for all a, $b \in G$. Intuitively, a homomorphism is a "structure preserving" map, and the image $G\varphi$ of a homomorphism φ is an "approximation" of G. A one-to-one onto homomorphism is called an *isomorphism.* $\varphi\varphi^{-1}$ is an equivalence relation on G of a special kind because it has the "substitution property." The following statements about an equivalence relation ρ on a monoid G are equivalent definitions of the *substitution property*:

(i) $a\rho b$ implies $(xa)\, \rho(xb)$ and $(ax)\, \rho(bx)$ for all a, b, $x \in G$

(ii) the product of any two ρ-classes is a subset of some other ρ-class; i.e., $(a\rho)(b\rho) \subseteq (ab)\, \rho$ for all a, $b \in G$

(iii) and $a_1\rho b_1$ and $a_2\rho b_2$ implies $(a_1 a_2)\, \rho(b_1 b_2)$ for a_1, a_2, b_1, $b_2 \in G$.

Equivalence relations with the substitution property are also called *congruence* relations. For reasons of style, both terminologies will be used. If ρ is a congruence on G, then a new binary operation $*$ can be defined on G/ρ by $(a\rho)* (b\rho) = (ab)\, \rho$. G/ρ together with $*$ is called the *quotient monoid* mod ρ. Thus, an equivalence relation with the substitution property may be thought of as a "structure preserving" equivalence in the same sense that a homomorphism is a structure preserving function. If ρ is a congruence relation, instead of $a\rho b$ we often write $a \equiv b \pmod{\rho}$, or perhaps we say, "a equals b modulo ρ." For groups a congruence ρ is completely determined by its *kernel*, the ρ-class containing the identity. This result will be used in the next section to simplify the componential analysis (i.e., coordinate representation) of group societies.

Returning to the congruence $\varphi\varphi^{-1}$ induced by a homomorphism φ, if φ is onto H (i.e., if $G\varphi = H$), then the quotient monoid $G/\varphi\varphi^{-1}$ is isomorphic to H under the "natural" mapping which sends each class $a\varphi\varphi^{-1}$ onto the element $a\varphi$ in H. This mapping is "natural" since $a\varphi\varphi^{-1}\varphi = \{a\varphi\}$.

Returning now to the set β of generating relations on S, let β^* be the intersection of all congruence relations on $\text{FM}(S)$ that contain β. In symbols,

$$\beta^* = \bigcap\{\rho : \rho \text{ is a congruence on } \text{FM}(S) \text{ and } \rho \supseteq \beta\}.$$

This definition makes sense because (i) there always exists at least one congruence, the *universal relation* ω = FM(S) $\times$ FM(S), which contains the relation β, and (ii) the intersection of any number of congruence relations is again a congruence relation. FM(S)/β^* is called the *monoid generated by S subject to the generating relation* β.

Suppose $S = \{x_i : i \in I\}$. Let $S^{-1} = \{x_i^{-1} : i \in I\}$ be a set disjoint from S. The *free group* on S, denoted by FG(S), is the monoid generated on FM($S \cup S^{-1}$) by the relation γ:

$$x_i x_i^{-1} = 1 \qquad \text{for all} \quad i \in I.$$

The free group is a formalization of White's (1963) "kinship role trees," and the formation of β^* from the relation β corresponds to his concept of "closing trees."

If $S = \{F, M\}$, then a *group kinship system*, or simply, a *group system*, is a congruence on FG(S). Note that this definition of group society correctly distinguishes some systems whose groups are isomorphic. For instance, the "matrilineal moiety system" is generated by the relations

$$F^2 = 1, \qquad M = 1,$$

and is distinguished from the "patrilineal moiety system" generated by the relations

$$F = 1, \qquad M^2 = 1,$$

even though the corresponding quotient groups are isomorphic, as are all groups of order two.

Since a congruence relation is also an equivalence relation, β^* is fully specified if we can enumerate all the elements in the equivalence class containing an arbitrary element $x \in$ FM(S). Since $\beta \subseteq \beta^*$, $s\beta t$ or $t\beta s$ implies $s\beta^* t$. By the definition of a congruence relation, $s\beta^* t$ implies $(usv) \beta^*(utv)$, where u and v may be empty words. This property is the origin of the term "substitution property," because it suggests that if $s\beta t$ or $t\beta s$, one can "substitute t for s" in any word $x = usv$ and obtain an equivalent word. Thus, the equivalence class containing x is the set of all elements that can be obtained from x by a finite sequence of β-substitutions.

The defining relations for a large class of group systems are discussed in White (1963). These relations sometimes can be very useful for gaining insights. For example, suppose one of the relations is

$$FM = MF.$$

To the mathematician this means the quotient group will be commutative, but to the anthropologist it means "matrilateral marriage" (if $F^{-1}M \neq M^{-1}F$). Lévi-Strauss (1949) has discussed at length the implications of matrilateral marriage to the social and economic structure. Generating relations can also be used to classify kinship systems,

331

Usually, it is very easy to find a set of defining relations for a given monoid. For a finite monoid $FM(S)/\rho$ one can employ the following algorithm to obtain a finite relation ρ_0 such that $\rho_0^* = \rho$. The *length* $\lg(x)$ of a word $x \in FM(S)$ is the number of letters in it different from 1. That is, $\lg(1) = 0$, and $\lg(xa) = \lg(x) + 1$, where $x \in FM(S)$ and $a \in S$. Let $x_1, ..., x_n$ be a set of representatives from the ρ-classes of minimal length. That is, for each class $x\rho$ there is exactly one $x_i \in x\rho$, and $y \in x\rho$ implies $\lg(x_i) \leqslant \lg(y)$. Let ρ_0 be defined by

$$(x_i a)\, \rho_0 x_j \quad \text{iff} \quad (x_i a)\, \rho x_j$$

for all $a \in S$ and $i = 1, ..., n$. It is easy to show that $\rho_0^* = \rho$.

The construction described above is very inefficient. Usually, a much smaller generating relation can be found by inspection. For example, the Kariera group system, which is of order four, can be defined by the equations

$$F^2 = M^2 = 1, \qquad FM = MF.$$

We now consider the problem of evolutionary sequences. The problem is to determine from the group system of a given society what group systems were likely to have preceded it, and what are the systems into which it may evolve in the near future. Intuitively, one would expect that a group system would change into systems not very different from itself. That is, one would expect evolution to take place in small steps. The difficulty is the word "small." How do we tell a "small" step from a "big" one?

This question is of fundamental importance for the study of algebraic or combinatoric models of behavior. The similarity structure on such systems has far reaching implications as to how the systems are evolved, learned, coded, and processed. To many social scientists, however, the concepts of similarity and nearness suggest a metric space or perhaps even Euclidean n-space. This does not seem to be the proper approach when the phenomena do not have natural and nontrivial metrics. On the other hand, note that in a metric space, two points are identical if and only if their distance is zero, whereas in an algebraic category two structures are considered "identical" if and only if they are isomorphic. By analogy, two algebraic structures are "similar" if and only if one is a homomorphic image of the other. Since the concept of a homomorphism is not symmetric, a word better than "similar" is the more asymmetric "approximates."

In our category of congruences on $FG(S)$ the admissible homomorphisms are just those induced by inclusion. That is, if $\rho_1 \subseteq \rho_2$, then $\varphi : \rho_1 \rightarrow \rho_2$ is defined by $(x\rho_1)\, \varphi = x\rho_2$. We say that the group structure ρ_2 "approximates" ρ_1 iff $\rho_2 \supseteq \rho_1$. ρ_2 is said to be a "closer" approximation than ρ_3 if $\rho_3 \supset \rho_2 \supset \rho_1$, where "$\supset$" denotes proper inclusion. In order to understand the interpretation $\rho_1 \subseteq \rho_2$, note that $\rho_1 \subseteq \rho_2$ is true if and only if every ρ_1-class is contained in some ρ_2-class. Either of these two conditions imply that the quotient group defined on $FG(S)/\rho_1$ can be homomorphically mapped onto $FG(S)/\rho_2$. The *index* of an equivalence relation ρ_2 with respect to another equivalence ρ_1, where $\rho_2 \supseteq \rho_1$, is the average number of ρ_1-classes contained in each ρ_2-class. For finite groups the index is always defined and equal to an integer. The *order* of an equivalence ρ is equal to the index of ρ relative to the universal relation ω. That is, the order of ρ is the number of ρ-classes. Obviously, a smaller index indicates a better approximation.

A congruence σ is said to *cover* a congruence ρ iff $\sigma \supset \rho$ and there is no other congruence π "between" σ and ρ. That is, there is no π such that $\sigma \supset \pi \supset \rho$.

To generate a congruence ρ_2 from a congruence ρ_1, where ρ_2 covers ρ_1, we need only adjoin one ordered pair (x, y) to ρ_1, where $x\rho_1 y$ holds, but $x\rho_2 y$ does not. Because $\rho_1 \subset (\rho_1 \cup (x, y)) \subseteq \rho_2$, we have $\rho_1 \subset (\rho_1 \cup (x, y))^* \subseteq \rho_2$. Since ρ_2 covers ρ_1, we must have equality in the last expression so that $\rho_2 = (\rho_1 \cup (x, y))^*$. In the next section it will be shown that covers are intimately connected with group extensions and componential analysis. Figures 2 and 3 list the one class society ω plus those congruences

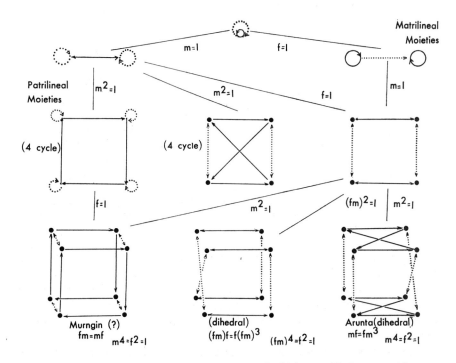

FIG. 2. These are the group systems of orders $\leqslant 8$ which are of index two with respect to their covers and which $F^2 = M^4 = 1$. Also, it is required that $F \neq M$ except for the 1-class system. A line joining two systems indicates the higher system covers the lower. The equations on the lines generate the higher from the lower system. The equations below the lowest systems generate those systems. The data are taken from Lane (1960).

ρ on $FG(S)$ with the following properties: (i) ρ has order $\leqslant 8$ (i.e., ρ has $\leqslant 8$ equivalence classes); (ii) ρ has a cover of index $\leqslant 3$; (iii) $F^2 \equiv 1$ (mod ρ) and either M^4 or $M^3 \equiv 1$ (mod ρ); and (iv) $F \not\equiv M$ (mod ρ).

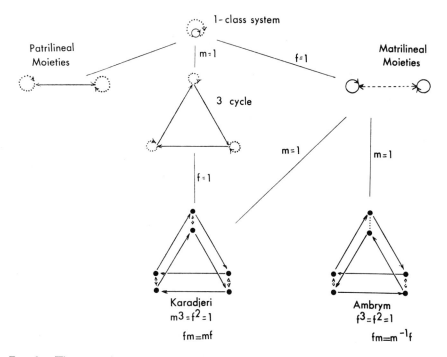

FIG. 3. These are the group structures of order $\leqslant 6$ which are of index $\leqslant 3$ with respect to their covers. Also, we require that $F^2 = 1 = M^3$ and $F \neq M$ except for the 1-class system. The data are taken from Lane (1960).

Restrictions (i) and (iii) are purely arbitrary and are made solely for the purpose of reducing the number of group systems to be drawn. When (iii) holds, but where $F^2 \not\equiv 1$ (mod ρ), the society is said to "equate alternating generations." The only justification for (i) and (iii) is that no group societies were found which violated them. On the other hand, the group systems in Fig. 2 labeled "4-cycle" and "dihedral" do not exist to my knowledge.

Restriction (ii) is more interesting theoretically because the number 3 is small relative to the number 8 found in (i). This means that all existing group systems of order 6 or greater have nontrivial homomorphic images. Thus, certain evolutionary sequences are suggested, which will be examined later. Thus, a five-class system is excluded because it has no nontrivial homomorphic image. This contradicts the intuitively plausible argument that it is a simple matter to insert an extra clan into a cycle as in Fig. 4. Restriction (iv) implies that husbands and their wives are in different classes. This is almost part of the meaning of a "marriage class system."

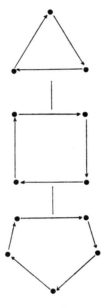

FIG. 4.   This plausible evolutionary sequence is not evolvable under the present restrictions.

It would be evidence against the point of view presented here if group systems existed of large order that were covered only by the universal relation ω. Groups covered only by ω are called *simple*, and our theory would offer no explanation as to how they could evolve by stages. An elementary result of group theory shows that all groups of prime order are simple, so that all group systems of prime order greater than 3 are not evolvable from ω under restriction (ii).

Returning to Fig. 3, notice that the Ambrym system can only evolve from matrilineal moieties. This is a strong prediction which could be tested if we had definite evidence on histrorical sequences in the New Hebrides where the island of Ambrym is found. The best that can be done, however, is to look at the social structure of closely related cultures. Lane and Lane (1958) observed that the areas in Ambrym and nearby South Pentecost that have the six-class system are precisely those areas in contact with the matrilineal areas to the north. Furthermore, the names given to the matrilineal moieties in the six-class system are the same names used in these northern areas. Some areas in Ambrym are patrilineal, however, so that the Ambrym case gives encouragement instead of proof. In fact, Barbara Lane uses this same evidence to support evolutionary sequences that disagree with our theory. For example, she suggests that this six-class Ambrym system evolved from the six-class Karadjeri system. From our point of view, however, the change from Karadjeri system to the Ambrym system is a big jump that includes several steps. Fig. 3 shows that this change requires first losing the split or distinction between 1 and M^2. This leaves the society at the matrilineal moiety system. Next, the society must create a distinction between FM and MF so as to arrive at the Ambrym system. Another even more implausible route would be to go to the 18-class society which is the intersection of the Karadjeri and Ambrym societies and then to erase the appropriate distinctions to arrive at the Ambrym system. In short, it is argued that it is more plausible that the Ambrym came from matrilineal moieties since this only involves making distinctions, whereas the shortest jump from the Kariera system includes making these same distinctions after breaking some others. It seems reasonable, then, to suppose that the matrilineal moiety system is a necessary intermediate step in any slow evolution between the Karadjeri and Ambrym systems.

On the other hand, when a society is the homomorphic image of its successor, there is no dislocation since the earlier society is an approximation of the later structure. Therefore, the change can take place gradually over many generations. Kroeber (1952) reports instances of four-class systems of the Kariera type which seemed almost to have an eight-class system of the Arunta type, except that the new distinction or "component" had not been given a name. One would suspect that violations of the four-class rule would be taken less seriously than a marriage which was incestuous under the four-class (and hence necessarily a violation of the eight-class rule), even with relatives equally distant from ego. Eventually, one would also expect that the eight classes would be given names. The point is that it is not critical when the names are given. Sentiment for this system can evolve slowly and can be codified when convenient. For instance, this could be done when there are no living married couples whose marriages would be defined as incestuous under the new eight-class system. One would suspect that such a situation would arise more easily where there are fewer total marriages. This may correspond to the negative correlation found by Service (1960) between the number of classes and population density in Australia.

Note that in Fig. 2 there are two different ways to evolve the four-class Kariera system. This reflects the various arguments in the literature as to the origins of this system. Our theory has nothing to say on choosing between these allowable sequences.

COMPONENTIAL ANALYSES AND GROUP EXTENSIONS

In its simplest form, the current anthropological technique of "componential analysis" attempts to represent the meaning of a word or concept as a point in a Cartesian product. A slightly more general method requires that meanings be coded as short "words," possibly of variable length, in an "alphabet" of distinctive feature. For example, the Yankee kinship term "mother" can be said to denote a relative that is female rather than male, blood rather than by marriage, lineal rather than collateral, and of the first ascending generation. There are, however, many other less satisfactory ways of distinguishing all the Yankee kinship terms. Thus, a description of the word "mother" as a relative whose spelling begins with the letter "*m*," followed by the letters "*o*,""*t*,""*h*,""*e*,""*r*" would be correct but trivial. We will introduce some formal criteria to distinguish "meaningful" Cartesian representations from "silly" ones.

In order to estimate the magnitude of the problem, let us restrict ourselves to binary representations, where each dimension of the Cartesian product has only two values. We wish to distinguish k objects by means of n binary dimensions. The values on these dimensions might be interpreted as the presence or absence of n attributes. Obviously, k must be smaller than 2^n since a coding of the k objects is some mapping from the 2^n points onto the k objects. However, let us grant that n is as small as possible so that $k = 2^n$. Then there are $(2^n)! = k!$ possible codings. If k is only 8, for example, the number of binary codings of these 8 objects is $8! = 8 \cdot 7 \cdot 6 \cdot 5 \cdot 4 \cdot 3 \cdot 2 \cdot 1 = 40,320$. This is a large number, even though some of the codings are "essentially" the same. That is, many of these codings are "equivalent" in the sense that they can be obtained from each other by exchanging 0's and 1's at every point for a fixed set of components. For instance, if we are given any code, we can obtain a new code by using the old code on all components except the first where we use a one where the old code had a zero and a zero where the old had a one. Thus, given an n-dimensional binary code, there are two possible isomorphisms on the first component (including the identity mapping). Given the mapping on the first component, we can choose independently whether or not to interchange zeros and ones on the second component. In addition, any of the $n!$ permutations on the components yield equivalent codes. Thus, there are $n!2^n$ codes isomorphic to any given code. So the total number of nonequivalent codes is $(2^n)! \, 2^{-n}/n! = (k-1)!/n!$ In the case considered above where $k = 8$, and $n = 3$, the number of nonisomorphic codings is 840, which is still a large number of codings to choose among.

This discussion motivates the following definition of equivalence between codes. A *coding* of G is a one-to-one function α from a Cartesian product $A_1 \times \cdots \times A_n$ onto G. A coding α of G induces a set of n equivalence relations on G called *projections* defined by rule that for any $i = 1,...,n$ and $g, g' \in G$, $g \equiv g'$ (mod i) iff $(g\alpha^{-1})\,i = (g'\alpha^{-1})\,i$. That is, two elements of G are equivalent mod i iff they agree on their ith component. Two codings α and β of G are said to be *equivalent* iff they have the same set of projections.

The problem of coding groups is made sharper by the requirement that not only the set, but the group operation must be coded. That is to say, a given group G must not only be represented as the Cartesian product $G_1 \times G_2$ of *sets*, but in addition at

337

least one of the sets G_1 and G_2 must possess a group operation that somehow is related to the operation in G. In order to make these ideas precise, more terminology has to be introduced from elementary group theory as in MacLane and Birkhoff (1967).

Recall that the *kernel* K of a group homomorphism $\varphi : G \to H$ is the set $1\varphi^{-1}$ of elements mapped onto the identity. The kernel is a subgroup of G since it is closed under products and inverses. For if $x, y \in K$, then (i) $(xy)\,\varphi = (x\varphi)(y\varphi) = 1 \cdot 1 = 1$. which shows $xy \in K$, and (ii) $1\varphi = (xx^{-1})\,\varphi = (x\varphi)(x^{-1}\varphi) = 1(x^{-1}\varphi) = x^{-1}\varphi$ which shows $x^{-1} \in K$. Note also that any element $g \in G$ "commutes" with the kernel in the sense that $Kg = gK$. To show $Kg = gK$ is equivalent to proving that $g^{-1}Kg \subseteq K$. The latter condition holds because if $k \in K$, then

$$(g^{-1}kg)\,\varphi = (g^{-1}\varphi)(k\varphi)(g\varphi) = (g\varphi)^{-1}\,1(g\varphi) = 1$$

so that $g^{-1}kg \in K$. Thus, $g^{-1}Kg \subseteq K$.

Any subgroup N of G such that $Ng = gN$ for all $g \in G$ is called a *normal* subgroup of G. It can easily be seen that the relation ρ on G defined by $x\rho y$ iff $Nx = Ny$ is a congruence. Furthermore, the quotient group G/ρ has N as the kernel of the "inclusion" homomorphism that assigns each $x \in G$ its ρ-class. Since N determines ρ, G/ρ is usually denoted by G/N. The ρ-classes are all of the form Ng for some $g \in G$ and are usually called *cosets* of N.

In group theory the "coding" problem referred to previously is known as the "extension problem," where a group G is described in terms of smaller groups. More precisely, a group G is said to be an *extension* of N by K iff N is a normal subgroup of G and G/N is isomorphic to K.

If N is a minimal normal subgroup of G generated by the element g, then the congruence corresponding to G/N covers the congruence of G and is generated from G by the equation $1 = g$ (see Figs. 2 and 3).

For each $x \in G/N$ choose exactly one $\bar{x} \in G$ such that $\bar{x} \in x$. The set $\{\bar{x} : x \in G/N\}$ is called a *system of representatives* for G/N. For a given system of representations, any $y \in G$ can be represented uniquely as the product $\bar{x}n$ where $\bar{x} \equiv y \pmod{N}$ and where $n \in N$. That is, y can be expressed as the product of a representative equivalent to y and an element of the normal subgroup N.

The relationship of a group extension with our first statement of componential analysis as the representation of an element as a point in a Cartesian product is that there is a one-to-one mapping from the Cartesian product $(G/N) \times N$ onto G given by $(x, n) \leftrightarrow \bar{x}n$. Let us see how this representation behaves with respect to the group operation.

Note that by the substitution property in G/N, $\bar{x} \in x$ and $\bar{y} \in y$ imply $\overline{xy} \in xy$, and hence $\bar{x}\bar{y} \equiv \overline{xy} \pmod{N}$. This means there is for each $x, y \in G/N$ a unique $n_{x,y} \in N$ such that $\bar{x}\bar{y} = \overline{xy}n_{x,y}$. Thus, we can write $(\bar{x}a)(\bar{y}b) = \bar{x}\bar{y}\bar{y}^{-1}a\bar{y}b = \overline{xy}(n_{x,y}\bar{y}^{-1}a\bar{y}b)$. The product $\bar{y}^{-1}a\bar{y}$ is an element of N because N is normal. Therefore, the whole

338

expression $n_{x,y}\bar{y}^{-1}a\bar{y}b$ is also an element of N, so that the right-hand side of the equation above is again of the form $\bar{z}c$ where $z \in G/N$ and $c \in N$. The set of $n_{x,y} \in N$ is called the *factor set*.

Arabic notation is an example of group extension. Let Z be the group of integers under addition, and let Z_k, where $k \in Z$, denote the quotient group with respect to the subgroup generated by k. Then Z_{100} can be represented as an extension of Z_{10} by Z_{10}. Let the normal subgroup N of Z_{100} be $\{0,10,\ldots, 90\}$ and let the system of representatives $R = \{0, 1, 2,\ldots, 9\}$. Then for $x, y \in R$.

$$n_{x,y} = \begin{cases} 0, & \text{if } x + y \leqslant 9 \\ 10, & \text{if } x + y > 9. \end{cases}$$

So, for example,

$$(9 + 10) + (8 + 20) = 7 + (10 + 10 + 20) = 7 + 40.$$

Thus, $n_{x,y}$ plays the role of determining the "carry digit" into N. Note that our notation has the information flowing from left to right, which corresponds to English word order, but which contrasts with Arabic notation and word order. Also, notice that since addition is commutative, every subgroup of the integers is normal.

A group extension of N by G/N is called a *direct product* when a system of representatives N' can be found that is also a normal subgroup. In this case, elements $n_{x,y} = 1$ for all $x, y \in G/N$ and $\bar{x}a = a\bar{x}$ for all $a \in N$ and $\bar{x} \in N'$. The group operation can then be computed, independently for each component:

$$(\bar{x}a)(\bar{y}b) = (\bar{x}\bar{y})(ab)$$

for all $\bar{x}, \bar{y} \in N'$ and $a, b \in N$. The roles of N and N' are symmetric in the sense that G is also an extension of N'. Furthermore, G/N is isomorphic to N' and G/N' is isomorphic to N. If G is the direct product of N by N', we write $G = N \times N' = N' \times N$. MacLane and Birkhoff (1967) give the following necessary and sufficient conditions for a group G to be a direct product of subgroups N and N' : (i) $N \cap N' = 1$; (ii) $NN' = G$; and (iii) $nn' = n'n$ for all $n \in N$ and $n' \in N'$. Note that in this useful characterization of direct products, it is not necessary to check for the normalcy of N or N'. Another way of characterizing direct product codes is the condition that all projections be congruences.

In the Kariera group of Fig. 5, there are three subgroups $\{1, F\}, \{1, M\}$, and $\{1, MF\}$, any two of which satisfy the conditions for direct products. This gives rise to exactly three distinct representations, or codings, of the Kariera group system. These three representations are shown in Fig. 5. The representation using $\{1, F\}$ and $\{1, M\}$ is the combination of patrilineal and matrilineal moieties because of the natural projections onto these moiety systems. In fact, a Cartesian product of a group G, considered as

339

a set, is a direct product extension if and only if the projection mappings $(x, y) \rightarrow x$ and $(x, y) \rightarrow y$ are both homomorphisms.

Unfortunately, there is no formal criterion for choosing among the three direct product representations. Empirically, however, the generational system is not found in Australia so the generators $\{F, M\}$ were chosen so as to make it look bad in the sense of requiring a longer word to generate the subgroup $\{1, FM\}$. On the other hand, White's (1963) choice of generators, $C = F^{-1}$ and $W = F^{-1}M$, favors the patrilineal-

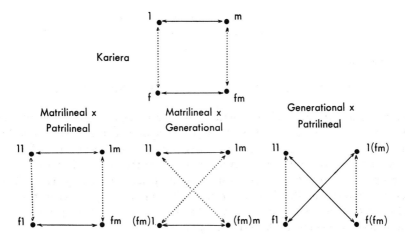

FIG. 5.   The Kariera group system and its three direct product representations.

generational representation. The most discouraging aspect of our analysis of the Kariera is that group theory has not at all reduced the number of possible codings since the number of arbitrary codings is $4!/(2!\,2!\,2!) = 3$, all of which are allowable direct product extensions.

The concept of direct product extension works like a charm, however, for the six-class Karadjeri system. There is only one pair of normal subgroups, $\{1, F\}$ and $\{1, M, M^2\}$, which satisfy the conditions for the direct product. This coding is shown in Fig. 6. Thus, we have chosen one out of the $6!/(2!\,3!\,2!) = 30$ possible codings of six items as the Cartesian product of a two- and a three-element set.

Next, we turn our attention to the Ambrym system shown in Fig. 7. A quick check, however, shows that there does not exist a pair of subgroups satisfying the conditions for a direct product. But there is exactly one normal subgroup $N = \{1, M, M^2\}$ and a system of representatives $\{1, F\}$ that has the property of being a subgroup S. Such an extension is called the *semidirect product* of N by S. Any element of the Ambrym group G can be uniquely represented as the product $\bar{x}n$ where $n \in N$ and $\bar{x} \in S$, but since the system of representatives $\{\bar{x} \mid x \in G/N\}$ form a subgroup S, $\bar{x}\bar{y} = \overline{xy}$ so that the elements of the factor set $n_{x,y} = 1$ for all $x, y \in G/N$. Thus, the product of two elements, $\bar{x}a$ and $\bar{y}b$ in a semidirect product can be written in the relatively simple form

$$(\bar{x}a)(\bar{y}b) = (\bar{x}\bar{y})(\bar{y}^{-1}a\bar{y}b).$$

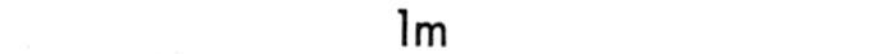

FIG. 6.   The Karadjeri as the direct product of matrilineal moieties and the cycle $(1, M, M^2)$.

This representation for the Ambrym is shown on the right in Fig. 7. The elements of G can also be represented in the form $n\bar{x}$ with the elements $n \in N$ on the left instead of on the right. Since the Ambrym group is noncommutative, a somewhat different representation is obtained and is shown on the left in Fig. 7.

Therefore, group theory has accomplished something for the Ambrym. It has selected two out of the 30 different codings of the six classes in the Ambrym system. The two remaining codings are formed from the same subgroups with either a lefthand or a righthand bias. To be precise, for the right-hand coding of elements in the form $\bar{x}a$, the equivalence relation ρ defined by

$$\bar{x}a \equiv \bar{y}b(\mathrm{mod}\ \rho)\ \text{iff}\ a = b$$

is a *right congruence* in the sense that multiplication on the right preserves ρ-equivalence. That is,

$$u \equiv v(\mathrm{mod}\ \rho)\ \text{implies}\ uw \equiv vw(\mathrm{mod}\ \rho)$$

for all u, v, $w \in G$. To show ρ is a right congruence, suppose that $u = \bar{x}a$, $v = \bar{y}a$ and $w = \bar{z}b$ for $\bar{x}$, $\bar{y}$, $\bar{z} \in S$ and a, $b \in N$. Then $uw = (\bar{x}a)(\bar{z}b) = (\bar{x}\bar{z})(\bar{z}^{-1}a\bar{z}b)$ and $vw = (\bar{y}a)(\bar{z}b) = (\bar{y}\bar{z})(\bar{z}^{-1}a\bar{z}b)$ which shows by the definition of ρ that $uw \equiv vw(\mathrm{mod}\ \rho)$. On the other hand, the equivalence relation λ defined by

$$\bar{a}x \equiv b\bar{y}(\mathrm{mod}\ \lambda) \text{ iff } a = b$$

is a *left congruence* in the opposite sense. Which coding is superior depends upon the handedness of the problem. Thus, if an Ambrym native were asked to what class the mothers or fathers of members of a given class belonged, he would want to use the

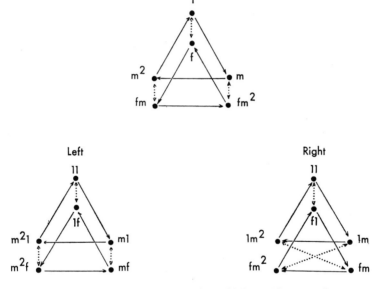

FIG. 7. The Ambrym group system and its right and left semidirect product representations.

right-hand coding, since the computations could be carried out independently on both components. He would want to use for similar reasons the left-hand coding for the question of to what class belong his mother or father's relative of a given type.

Another way of looking at the left and right codes is to consider the problem of finding the appropriate representative for a word in the free monoid $FM(\{F, M\})$. That is, for the right-hand code, one must reduce a string of F's and M's to the form $F^i M^j$ for $i = 0, 1$ and $j = 0, 1, 2$. For a right-hand code, the most efficient procedure is to start decoding at the left and proceed by multiplying on the right. For example, if the word $x = x_1 x_2 \cdots x_n$ where $x_i = F$ or M, first put x_1 into the proper form and then multiply the right by x_2. In general, after $x_1 x_2 \cdots x_i$, $i < n$ has been coded,

342

multiply on the right by x_{i+1}. In this process, it is useful to have a right code since the components can be computed independently of each other. This independence has two consequences. First, it simplifies the computation by making the ith component of xF or xM a function only of F or M and the ith component of x. In an actual performance of this calculation, this would reduce the probability of error at any stage. The second consequence of this independence is that an error on one component does not propagate to other components. Thus, even with an error early in the process, the final answer will still be "close" under any reasonable metric that puts items "close" to each other that agree on "many" components.

Although careful empirical work is needed, we can nevertheless entertain the hypothesis on the basis of the *a priori* arguments presented above that the Ambrym use *both* the right and left semidirect product codes, depending on whether they want to work from left to right or vice versa. This directional bias may be related to Yngve's (1961) "depth hypothesis" concerning right- and left-branching sentence constructions for speakers and hearers. This raises the speculation that one Ambrym code is used for the speaker and the other for the listener. See Chomsky and Miller (1963), however, for a criticism of the depth hypothesis. Finally, it should be noted that although the right code in Fig. 7 appears to be more natural in the sense that it is easier to check out that ρ is a right congruence. This is only because the drawings are *right* regular representations of the groups.

Turning now to the Arunta system, we see that the coding is already half done because of our previous arguments showing that the Arunta arose from the Kariera system. The only normal subgroup N such that the Arunta system G is an extension of N by the Kariera system is $N = \{1, M^2\}$. There is no system of representatives K for G/N such that K is a subgroup. Therefore, G is not the direct or even the semidirect product of N by G/N. If, however, we take as representatives the best coding $K = \{1, F, M, FM\}$ of the Kariera system, then we obtain an extension whose factor set contains a minimal number of nonidentity elements as shown in Table 3. Thus, we obtain a code of the form $F^i M^j M^{2k}$ for $i, j, k = 0, 1$. As with the Ambrym code, if we commute all the elements of the code, we obtain a different handed code. Both such codes for the Arunta are shown in Fig. 8. Note that the equivalence relation ρ defined by

$$1M^j M^k \equiv FM^j M^k (\text{mod } \rho)$$

is a right congruence and the reversed code is a left congruence. Thus, similar remarks apply concerning the use of both codes according to the situation. For the Arunta, then, use of group theory has done a significant job in reducing the number of codes to two out of the total of $8!/(3! \, 2^3) = 840$ equivalence classes of binary codes.

The Arunta codes were constructed with the idea that the Arunta system developed from one of the Kariera type by merely adding on the third component to the Kariera system. Elkin (1964) has actually observed this process taking place. He has seen

TABLE 3

Tables of the Factor Sets $\{n_{x,y}\}$ in the Right and Left Representations of the Arunta Group System as the Extension of $\{1, M^2\}$ by the Kariera Group System with the Two Systems of Representatives $\{1, M, F, FM\}$ and $\{1, M, F, MF\}$

Right

$n_{x,y}$	1	M	F	FM
1	1	1	1	1
M	1	M^2	M^2	1
F	1	1	1	1
FM	1	M^2	M^2	1

x labels the rows; y labels the columns.

Left

$n_{x,y}$	1	M	F	MF
1	1	1	1	1
M	1	M^2	1	M^2
F	1	M^2	1	M^2
MF	1	1	1	1

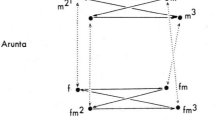

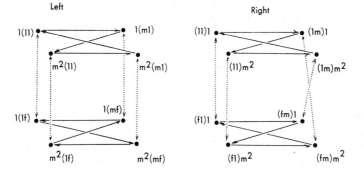

Fig. 8. The Arunta group system and its right and left extensions of 1, M^2 by the Kariera system (represented in parentheses as the direct product of matrilineal and patrilineal moieties).

344

tribes with the four-class Kariera system change over to the eight-class Arunta system. Obviously, this only shows that the transition can take place, not that it must occur in this particular manner. However, the regional distribution of the class systems suggests that these systems are in fact historically related. See Service (1960).

SUMMARY AND CONCLUSIONS

The Group Partition Theorem is a generalization of the theory of structural balance, where the labels of the arrows are elements of an arbitrary group instead of just pluses and minuses under the usual multiplication. The homomorphism that connects the set of nonempty relations generated under composition and the group means that the group gives an approximation of these relations which is invariant under the creation of new relations by marriage and birth and the forgetting of old relations among the dead.

The group system of the Arunta of central Australia has been coded with three binary digits such that when the third component which depends on the other two for its computations is eliminated, the resulting quotient group is isomorphic to the Kariera group system. The Kariera group societies geographically surround the Arunta system. In addition, the transition from the Kariera system to the Arunta system has been observed by anthropologists. The Kariera systems are adjacent to matrilineal and patrilineal systems which extended in pre-European times to the coast. This may correspond to the fact that the two digits of the Kariera direct product code are independent and can be dropped in either order. Thus, in Australia there is historical and geographical evidence consistent with the interpretation of the mathematical statement "N is an extension of G by K" as the empirical hypothesis "G evolves from K by adding on N."

The other geographical area studied is the group of islands around Ambrym in the New Hebrides. Here the Ambrym group system is coded so that when the cycle $\{1, M, M^2\}$ is dropped, there remains a matrilineal system on which the three-cycle subgroup depends for its calculations. Here, again, matrilineal moiety systems are found nearby with the same names for the moieties as the Ambrym have for their moiety components. Here is evidence for the relation between coding in everyday use and the evolutionary sequences based on perturbations of that code.

The approach taken here is a result of the heuristic that a structural description of a behavioral phenomena should also account for the dynamics of its use and its changes through time. This principle has the dual virtue of forcing one to explain more and also of making the original structural description more unique since descriptions incompatible with the operations and the evolution (or learning) of the system can be eliminated.

It is hoped that this paper will be considered as a behavioral science application of abstract algebra in its broadest sense as opposed to group theory. It is believed that the use of groups as models of behavior will continue to be extremely limited. On the other hand, groups are present in any model in the sense that the automorphisms of any structure (i.e., isomorphisms of a structure onto itself) form a group. These automorphism groups can be very useful in a variety of ways. For example, the mappings between "equivalent" codes, as defined in this paper, form an automorphism group for each code.

The essential idea for the coding of systems is the existence of homomorphisms between systems of the same type. Thus, if E is a set with some structure and φ is a structure-preserving function, E may be identified with a subset of $(E/\varphi\varphi^{-1}) \times F$, where F is some set of cardinality equal to the largest class in $\varphi\varphi^{-1}$. These ideas are particularly well worked out for a finite automata. See for example Hartmanis and Sterns (1965), who discuss the "information flow" between components of finite automata. In short, the mathematical tools are already available for the coding of many interesting classes of social science models.

REFERENCES

BIRKHOFF, G. *Lattice theory.* (3rd ed.) Providence: American Mathematical Society, 1966.

BOYD, J. *The algebra of kinship.* Unpublished doctoral dissertation, University of Michigan, 1966.

BURLING, R. Cognition and componential analysis: God's truth or hocus-pocus? *American Anthropologist,* 1964, **66**, 20–28.

CARTWRIGHT, D., AND HARARY, F. Structural balance: A generalization of Heider's theory. *Psychological Review,* 1956, **63**, 277–293.

CHOMSKY, N. Formal properties of grammars. *In* R. D. Luce, R. R. Bush, and E. Galanter (Eds.), *Handbook of mathematical psychology,* Vol. 2, New York: Wiley, 1963. Pp. 323–418.

CHOMSKY, N., AND MILLER, G. Finitary models of language users. *In* R. D. Luce, R. R. Bush and E. Galanter (Eds.), *Handbook of mathematical psychology,* Vol. 2. New York: Wiley, 1963. Pp. 419–492.

CLIFFORD, A., AND PRESTON, G. *The algebraic theory of semigroups.* Providence: American Mathematical Society, 1961.

COHN, P. M. *Universal algebra.* New York: Harper, 1965.

ELKIN, A. P. *The Australian aborigines.* New York: Doubleday, 1964.

FLAMENT, C. *Applications of graph theory to group structure.* Translated by M. Pinard, R. Breton, and F. Fontaine. Englewood Cliffs, New Jersey: Prentice-Hall, 1963.

GOODENOUGH, W. H. Componential analysis and the study of meaning. *Language,* 1956, **32**, 193–216.

HALL, M. *The theory of groups.* New York: Macmillan, 1959.

HAMMEL, E. A. Formal semantic analysis. *American Anthropologist,* 1966, **67**.

HARTMANIS, J., AND STERNS, R. E. *Algebraic structure theory of sequential machines.* Englewood Cliffs, New Jersey: Prentice-Hall, 1965.

KEMENY, J., SNELL, J. L., AND THOMPSON, F. L. *Introduction to finite mathematics.* Englewood Cliffs, New Jersey: Prentice-Hall, 1957.

KROEBER, A. L. *The nature of culture.* Chicago: Univer, of Chicago Press, 1952.

From Mark S. Granovetter, *American Journal of Sociology 78*, 1360-1380 (1973), copyright by the University of Chicago, by permission.

The Strength of Weak Ties[1]

Mark S. Granovetter
Johns Hopkins University

Analysis of social networks is suggested as a tool for linking micro and macro levels of sociological theory. The procedure is illustrated by elaboration of the macro implications of one aspect of small-scale interaction: the strength of dyadic ties. It is argued that the degree of overlap of two individuals' friendship networks varies directly with the strength of their tie to one another. The impact of this principle on diffusion of influence and information, mobility opportunity, and community organization is explored. Stress is laid on the cohesive power of weak ties. Most network models deal, implicitly, with strong ties, thus confining their applicability to small, well-defined groups. Emphasis on weak ties lends itself to discussion of relations *between* groups and to analysis of segments of social structure not easily defined in terms of primary groups.

A fundamental weakness of current sociological theory is that it does not relate micro-level interactions to macro-level patterns in any convincing way. Large-scale statistical, as well as qualitative, studies offer a good deal of insight into such macro phenomena as social mobility, community organization, and political structure. At the micro level, a large and increasing body of data and theory offers useful and illuminating ideas about what transpires within the confines of the small group. But how interaction in small groups aggregates to form large-scale patterns eludes us in most cases.

I will argue, in this paper, that the analysis of processes in interpersonal networks provides the most fruitful micro-macro bridge. In one way or another, it is through these networks that small-scale interaction becomes translated into large-scale patterns, and that these, in turn, feed back into small groups.

Sociometry, the precursor of network analysis, has always been curiously peripheral—invisible, really—in sociological theory. This is partly because it has usually been studied and applied only as a branch of social psychology; it is also because of the inherent complexities of precise network analysis. We have had neither the theory nor the measurement and sampling techniques to move sociometry from the usual small-group level to that of larger structures. While a number of stimulating and suggestive

[1] This paper originated in discussions with Harrison White, to whom I am indebted for many suggestions and ideas. Earlier drafts were read by Ivan Chase, James Davis, William Michelson, Nancy Lee, Peter Rossi, Charles Tilly, and an anonymous referee; their criticisms resulted in significant improvements.

studies have recently moved in this direction (Bott 1957; Mayer 1961; Milgram 1967; Boissevain 1968; Mitchell 1969), they do not treat structural issues in much theoretical detail. Studies which do so usually involve a level of technical complexity appropriate to such forbidding sources as the *Bulletin of Mathematical Biophysics,* where the original motivation for the study of networks was that of developing a theory of neural, rather than social, interaction (see the useful review of this literature by Coleman [1960]; also Rapoport [1963]).

The strategy of the present paper is to choose a rather limited aspect of small-scale interaction—the strength of interpersonal ties—and to show, in some detail, how the use of network analysis can relate this aspect to such varied macro phenomena as diffusion, social mobility, political organization, and social cohesion in general. While the analysis is essentially qualitative, a mathematically inclined reader will recognize the potential for models; mathematical arguments, leads, and references are suggested mostly in footnotes.

THE STRENGTH OF TIES

Most intuitive notions of the "strength" of an interpersonal tie should be satisfied by the following definition: the strength of a tie is a (probably linear) combination of the amount of time, the emotional intensity, the intimacy (mutual confiding), and the reciprocal services which characterize the tie.[2] Each of these is somewhat independent of the other, though the set is obviously highly intracorrelated. Discussion of operational measures of and weights attaching to each of the four elements is postponed to future empirical studies.[3] It is sufficient for the present purpose if most of us can agree, on a rough intuitive basis, whether a given tie is strong, weak, or absent.[4]

[2] Ties discussed in this paper are assumed to be positive and symmetric; a comprehensive theory might require discussion of negative and/or asymmetric ties, but this would add unnecessary complexity to the present, exploratory comments.

[3] Some anthropologists suggest "multiplexity," that is, multiple contents in a relationship, as indicating a strong tie (Kapferer 1969, p. 213). While this may be accurate in some circumstances, ties with only one content or with diffuse content may be strong as well (Simmel 1950, pp. 317–29). The present definition would show most multiplex ties to be strong but also allow for other possibilities.

[4] Included in "absent" are both the lack of any relationship and ties without substantial significance, such as a "nodding" relationship between people living on the same street, or the "tie" to the vendor from whom one customarily buys a morning newspaper. That two people "know" each other by name need not move their relation out of this category if their interaction is negligible. In some contexts, however (disasters, for example), such "negligible" ties might usefully be distinguished from the absence of one. This is an ambiguity caused by substitution, for convenience of exposition, of discrete values for an underlying continuous variable.

Consider, now, any two arbitrarily selected individuals—call them A and B—and the set, $S = C, D, E, \ldots$, of all persons with ties to either *or* both of them.[5] The hypothesis which enables us to relate dyadic ties to larger structures is: the stronger the tie between A and B, the larger the proportion of individuals in S to whom they will *both* be tied, that is, connected by a weak or strong tie. This overlap in their friendship circles is predicted to be least when their tie is absent, most when it is strong, and intermediate when it is weak.

The proposed relationship results, first, from the tendency (by definition) of stronger ties to involve larger time commitments. If A-B and A-C ties exist, then the amount of time C spends with B depends (in part) on the amount A spends with B and C, respectively. (If the events "A is with B" and "A is with C" were independent, then the event "C is with A and B" would have probability equal to the product of their probabilities. For example, if A and B are together 60% of the time, and A and C 40%, then C, A, and B would be together 24% of the time. Such independence would be less likely after than before B and C became acquainted.) If C and B have no relationship, common strong ties to A will probably bring them into interaction and generate one. Implicit here is Homans's idea that "the more frequently persons interact with one another, the stronger their sentiments of friendship for one another are apt to be" (1950, p. 133).

The hypothesis is made plausible also by empirical evidence that the stronger the tie connecting two individuals, the more similar they are, in various ways (Berscheid and Walster 1969, pp. 69–91; Bramel 1969, pp. 9–16; Brown 1965, pp. 71–90; Laumann 1968; Newcomb 1961, chap. 5; Precker 1952). Thus, if strong ties connect A to B and A to C, both C and B, being similar to A, are probably similar to one another, increasing the likelihood of a friendship once they have met. Applied in reverse, these two factors—time and similarity—indicate why weaker A-B and A-C ties make a C-B tie less likely than strong ones: C and B are less likely to interact and less likely to be compatible if they do.

The theory of cognitive balance, as formulated by Heider (1958) and especially by Newcomb (1961, pp. 4–23), also predicts this result. If strong ties A-B and A-C exist, and if B and C are aware of one another, anything short of a positive tie would introduce a "psychological strain" into the situation since C will want his own feelings to be congruent with those of his good friend, A, and similarly, for B and *his* friend, A. Where the ties are weak, however, such consistency is psychologically less crucial. (On this point see also Homans [1950, p. 255] and Davis [1963, p. 448].)

Some direct evidence for the basic hypothesis exists (Kapferer 1969, p. 229 n.; Laumann and Schuman 1967; Rapoport and Horvath 1961;

[5] In Barnes's terminology, the union of their respective primary stars (1969, p. 58).

349

Rapoport 1963).[6] This evidence is less comprehensive than one might hope. In addition, however, certain inferences from the hypothesis have received empirical support. Description of these inferences will suggest some of the substantive implications of the above argument.

WEAK TIES IN DIFFUSION PROCESSES

To derive implications for large networks of relations, it is necessary to frame the basic hypothesis more precisely. This can be done by investigating the possible triads consisting of strong, weak, or absent ties among A, B, and any arbitrarily chosen friend of either or both (i.e., some member of the set S, described above). A thorough mathematical model would do this in some detail, suggesting probabilities for various types. This analysis becomes rather involved, however, and it is sufficient for my purpose in this paper to say that the triad which is most *unlikely* to occur, under the hypothesis stated above, is that in which A and B are strongly linked, A has a strong tie to some friend C, but the tie between C and B is absent. This triad is shown in figure 1. To see the consequences of this assertion,

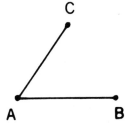

FIG. 1.—Forbidden triad

I will exaggerate it in what follows by supposing that the triad shown *never* occurs—that is, that the *B-C* tie is always present (whether weak or strong), given the other two strong ties. Whatever results are inferred from this supposition should tend to occur in the degree that the triad in question tends to be absent.

[6] The models and experiments of Rapoport and his associates have been a major stimulus to this paper. In 1954 he commented on the "well-known fact that the likely contacts of two individuals who are closely acquainted tend to be more overlapping than those of two arbitrarily selected individuals" (p. 75). His and Horvath's 1961 hypothesis is even closer to mine: "one would expect the friendship relations, and therefore the overlap bias of the acquaintance circles, to become less tight with increasing numerical rank-order" (p. 290). (I.e., best friend, second-best friend, third-best, etc.) Their development of this hypothesis, however, is quite different, substantively and mathematically, from mine (Rapoport 1953a, 1953b, 1954, 1963; Rapoport and Horvath 1961).

Some evidence exists for this absence. Analyzing 651 sociograms, Davis (1970, p. 845) found that in 90% of them triads consisting of two mutual choices and one nonchoice occurred less than the expected random number of times. If we assume that mutual choice indicates a strong tie, this is strong evidence in the direction of my argument.[7] Newcomb (1961, pp. 160–65) reports that in triads consisting of dyads expressing mutual "high attraction," the configuration of three strong ties became increasingly frequent as people knew one another longer and better; the frequency of the triad pictured in figure 1 is not analyzed, but it is implied that processes of cognitive balance tended to eliminate it.

The significance of this triad's absence can be shown by using the concept of a "bridge"; this is a line in a network which provides the *only* path between two points (Harary, Norman, and Cartwright 1965, p. 198). Since, in general, each person has a great many contacts, a bridge between A and B provides the only route along which information or influence can flow from any contact of A to any contact of B, and, consequently, from anyone connected *indirectly* to A to anyone connected indirectly to B. Thus, in the study of diffusion, we can expect bridges to assume an important role.

Now, if the stipulated triad is absent, it follows that, except under unlikely conditions, *no strong tie is a bridge.* Consider the strong tie A-B: if A has another strong tie to C, then forbidding the triad of figure 1 implies that a tie exists between C and B, so that the path A-C-B exists between A and B; hence, A-B is not a bridge. A strong tie can be a bridge, therefore, *only if* neither party to it has any *other* strong ties, unlikely in a social network of any size (though possible in a small group). Weak ties suffer no such restriction, though they are certainly not automatically bridges. What is important, rather, is that all bridges are weak ties.

In large networks it probably happens only rarely, in practice, that a specific tie provides the *only* path between two points. The bridging function may nevertheless be served *locally.* In figure 2a, for example, the tie A-B is not strictly a bridge, since one can construct the path A-E-I-B (and others). Yet, A-B *is* the shortest route to B for F, D, and C. This function is clearer in figure 2b. Here, A-B is, for C, D, and others, not only a local bridge to B, but, in most real instances of diffusion, a much more likely and efficient path. Harary et al. point out that "there may be a distance [length of path] beyond which it is not feasible for u to communicate with

---

[7] This assumption is suggested by one of Davis's models (1970, p. 846) and made explicitly by Mazur (1971). It is not obvious, however. In a free-choice sociometric test or a fixed-choice one with a large number of choices, most strong ties would probably result in mutual choice, but some weak ones might as well. With a small, fixed number of choices, most mutual choices should be strong ties, but some strong ties might show up as asymmetric. For a general discussion of the biases introduced by sociometric procedures, see Holland and Leinhardt (1971b).

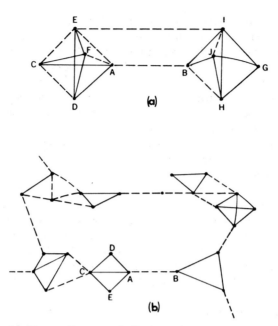

Fig. 2.—Local bridges. *a*, Degree 3; *b*, Degree 13. ———— = strong tie; ———— = weak tie.

v because of costs or distortions entailed in each act of transmission. If v does not lie within this critical distance, then he will not receive messages originating with u" (1965, p. 159). I will refer to a tie as a "local bridge of degree n" if n represents the shortest path between its two points (other than itself), and $n > 2$. In figure 2*a*, *A-B* is a local bridge of degree 3, in 2*b*, of degree 13. As with bridges in a highway system, a local bridge in a social network will be more significant as a connection between two sectors to the extent that it is the only alternative for many people—that is, as its degree increases. A bridge in the absolute sense is a local one of infinite degree. By the same logic used above, only weak ties may be local bridges.

Suppose, now, that we adopt Davis's suggestion that "in interpersonal flows of most any sort the probability that 'whatever it is' will flow from person i to person j is (*a*) directly proportional to the number of all-positive (friendship) paths connecting i and j; and (*b*) inversely proportional to the length of such paths" (1969, p. 549).[8] The significance of weak ties, then, would be that those which are local bridges create more, and shorter, paths. Any given tie may, hypothetically, be removed from a network; the number of paths broken and the changes in average path length resulting

[8] Though this assumption seems plausible, it is by no means self-evident. Surprisingly little empirical evidence exists to support or refute it.

352

between arbitrary pairs of points (with some limitation on length of path considered) can then be computed. The contention here is that removal of the average weak tie would do more "damage" to transmission probabilities than would that of the average strong one.[9]

Intuitively speaking, this means that whatever is to be diffused can reach a larger number of people, and traverse greater social distance (i.e., path length),[10] when passed through weak ties rather than strong. If one tells a rumor to all his close friends, and they do likewise, many will hear the rumor a second and third time, since those linked by strong ties tend to share friends. If the motivation to spread the rumor is dampened a bit on each wave of retelling, then the rumor moving through strong ties is much more likely to be limited to a few cliques than that going via weak ones; bridges will not be crossed.[11]

Since sociologists and anthropologists have carried out many hundreds of diffusion studies—Rogers's 1962 review dealt with 506—one might suppose that the above claims could easily be put to test. But this is not so, for several reasons. To begin with, though most diffusion studies find that personal contacts are crucial, many undertake no sociometric investigation. (Rogers [1962] discusses this point.) When sociometric techniques *are* used, they tend to discourage the naming of those weakly tied to the respondent by sharply limiting the numbers of choices allowed. Hence, the proposed importance of weak ties in diffusion is not measured. Even when more sociometric information is collected there is almost never an attempt to directly retrace the exact interpersonal paths traversed by an (idea, rumor, or) innovation. More commonly, the time when each individual adopted the innovation is recorded, as is the number of sociometric choices he received from others in the study. Those receiving many choices are characterized as "central," those with few as "marginal"; this variable is then correlated with time of adoption and inferences made about what paths were probably followed by the innovation.

[9] In a more comprehensive treatment it would be useful to consider to what extent a *set* of weak ties may be considered to have bridging functions. This generalization requires a long, complex discussion and is not attempted here (see Harary et al. 1965, pp. 211–16).

[10] We may define the "social distance" between two individuals in a network as the number of lines in the shortest path from one to another. This is the same as the definition of "distance" between points in graph theory (Harary et al. 1965, pp. 32–33, 138–41). The exact role of this quantity in diffusion and epidemic theory is discussed by Solomonoff and Rapoport (1951).

[11] If a damping effect is not specified, the whole population would hear the rumor after a sufficiently large number of retellings, since few real networks include totally self-contained cliques. The effective difference between using weak and strong ties, then, is one of people reached per unit of (ordinal) time. This could be called "velocity" of transmission. I am indebted to Scott Feld for this point.

One point of controversy in diffusion studies can be related to my argument. Some have indicated that early innovators are marginal, that they "underconform to norms to such a degree that they are perceived as highly deviant" (Rogers 1962, p. 197). Others (e.g., Coleman, Katz, and Menzel [1966] on the adoption of a new drug by doctors) find that those named more frequently adopt an innovation substantially earlier. Becker (1970) tries to resolve the question of whether early innovators are "central" or "marginal" by referring to the "perceived risks of adoption of a given innovation." His study of public health innovations shows that when a new program is thought relatively safe and uncontroversial (as with the drug of Coleman et al.), central figures lead in its adoption; otherwise, marginal ones do (p. 273). He explains the difference in terms of a greater desire of "central" figures to protect their professional reputation.

Kerckhoff, Back, and Miller (1965) reach a similar conclusion in a different type of study. A Southern textile plant had been swept by "hysterical contagion": a few, then more and more workers, claiming bites from a mysterious "insect," became nauseous, numb, and weak, leading to a plant shutdown. When the affected workers were asked to name their three best friends, many named one another, but the very *earliest* to be stricken were social isolates, receiving almost no choices. An explanation, compatible with Becker's, is offered: since the symptoms might be thought odd, early "adopters" were likely to be found among the marginal, those less subject to social pressures. Later, "it is increasingly likely that some persons who are socially integrated will be affected. . . . The contagion enters social networks and is disseminated with increasing rapidity" (p. 13). This is consistent with Rogers's comment that while the *first* adopters of innovations are marginal, the next group, "early adopters," "are a more integrated part of the local social system than the innovators" (1962, p. 183).

"Central" and "marginal" individuals may well be motivated as claimed; but if the marginal are genuinely so, it is difficult to see how they can ever spread innovations successfully. We may surmise that since the resistance to a risky or deviant activity is greater than to a safe or normal one, a larger number of people will have to be exposed to it and adopt it, in the early stages, before it will spread in a chain reaction. Individuals with many weak ties are, by my arguments, best placed to diffuse such a difficult innovation, since some of those ties will be local bridges.[12] An initially un-

---

[12] These individuals are what is often called, in organizational analysis, "liaison persons," though their role here is different from the one usually discussed. (Cf. the concept in graph theory of a "cut point"—one which, if removed from a graph, disconnects one part from another [Harary 1965].) In general, a bridge has one liaison person on each side, but the existence of a liaison person does not imply that of a bridge. For local

popular innovation spread by those with *few* weak ties is more likely to be confined to a few cliques, thus being stillborn and never finding its way into a diffusion study.

That the "marginal" innovators of diffusion studies might actually be rich in *weak* ties is possible, given the usual sociometric technique, but in most cases this is purely speculative. Kerckhoff and Back, however, in a later more detailed analysis of the hysteria incident, indicate that besides asking about one's "three best friends," they also asked with whom workers ate, worked, shared car pools, etc. They report that five of the six workers earliest affected "are social isolates when friendship choices are used as the basis of analysis. Only 1 of the 6 is mentioned as a friend by *anyone* in our sample. This is made even more striking when we note that these 6 women are mentioned with considerable frequency when other bases for choice are used. In fact, they are chosen more frequently on a 'non-friendship' basis than are the women in any of the other categories" (1968, p. 112).

This finding lends credence to the weak-tie argument, but is inconclusive. A somewhat different kind of diffusion study offers more direct support: the "small-world" investigations of Milgram and his associates. The name of these studies stems from the typical comment of newly introduced individuals who discover some common acquaintance; this situation is generalized in an attempt to measure, for arbitrarily chosen pairs of individuals in the United States, how long a path of personal contacts would be needed to connect them. A booklet is given to randomly designated senders who are asked to forward it toward some named target person, via someone the sender knows personally who would be more likely than himself to know the target. The new recipient then advances the booklet similarly; eventually it reaches the target or someone fails to send it on. The proportion of such chains completed has ranged from 12% to 33% in different studies, and the number of links in completed chains has ranged from two to 10, averaging between five and eight (Milgram 1967; Travers and Milgram 1969; Korte and Milgram 1970).

Each time someone forwards a booklet he also sends a postcard to the researchers, indicating, among other things, the relationship between himself and the next receiver. Two of the categories which can be chosen are "friend" and "acquaintance." I will assume that this corresponds to "strong" and "weak" ties. In one of the studies, white senders were asked to forward the booklet to a target who was Negro. In such chains, a crucial point was the *first* sending of the booklet from a white to a Negro. In 50%

---

bridges, the concept of local liaisons could be developed. In a more microscopically oriented discussion I would devote more time to the liaison role. For now, I only point out that, under the present assumptions, one can be a liaison between two network sectors *only* if all his ties into one or both are weak.

of the instances where the white described this Negro as an "acquaintance," the chain was ultimately completed; completion rate fell to 26%, however, when the white sent the booklet to a Negro "friend." (My computation, based on unpublished data kindly supplied by Charles Korte. See Korte [1967] and Korte and Milgram [1970].) Thus, weaker interracial ties can be seen to be more effective in bridging social distance.

Another relevant study, by Rapoport and Horvath (1961), is not exactly one of diffusion but is closely related in that it traces out paths along which diffusion *could* take place. They asked each individual in a Michigan junior high school ($N = 851$) to list his eight best friends in order of preference. Then, taking a number of random samples from the group (sample size, an arbitrary number, was nine), they traced out, for each sample, and averaged over all the samples, the total number of people reached by following along the network of first and second choices. That is, the first and second choices of each sample member were tabulated, then the first and second choices of *these* people were added in, etc., counting, at each remove, *only* names not previously chosen, and continuing until no new people were reached. The same procedure was followed using second and third choices, third and fourth, etc., up to seventh and eighth. (The theoretical connection of this tracing procedure to diffusion is discussed by Rapoport [1953*a*, 1953*b*, and especially 1954].)

The smallest total number of people were reached through the networks generated by first and second choices—presumably the strongest ties—and the largest number through seventh and eighth choices. This corresponds to my assertion that more people can be reached through weak ties. A parameter in their mathematical model of the sociogram, designed to measure, approximately, the overlap of acquaintance circles, declined monotonically with increasing rank order of friends.[13]

WEAK TIES IN EGOCENTRIC NETWORKS

In this section and the next, I want to discuss the general significance of the above findings and arguments at two levels: first that of individuals, then that of communities. These discussions make no pretense of being comprehensive; they are meant only to illustrate possible applications.

In recent years, a great deal of literature has appeared analyzing the impact on the behavior of individuals of the social networks in which they are imbedded. Some of the studies have emphasized the ways in which

---

[13] This parameter, θ, measures such overlap in the following sense: it is zero in a random net—one in which individuals choose others at random—and is one in a net made up entirely of cliques disconnected each from every other. Intermediate values of θ, however, do not have a good intuitive interpretation in terms of individuals, but only with reference to the particular mathematical model defining the parameter; thus it does not correspond precisely to my arguments about friendship overlap.

behavior is shaped and constrained by one's network (Bott 1957; Mayer 1961; Frankenberg 1965), others the ways in which individuals can manipulate these networks to achieve specific goals (Mayer 1966; Boissevain 1968; Kapferer 1969). Both facets are generally supposed to be affected by the structure of one's network. Bott argued that the crucial variable is that of whether one's friends tend to know one another ("close-knit" network) or not ("loose-knit" network). Barnes makes this dichotomy into a continuous variable by counting the number of ties observed in the network formed by ego and his friends and dividing it by the ratio of possible ones; this then corresponds to what is often called network "density" (Barnes 1969; Tilly 1969).[14]

Epstein (1969) points out, however, that different *parts* of ego's network may have different density. He calls those with whom one "interacts most intensely and most regularly, and who are therefore also likely to come to know one another," the "effective network"; the "remainder constitute the *extended* network" (pp. 110–11). This is close to saying, in my terms, that one's strong ties form a dense network, one's weak ties a less dense one. I would add that one's weak ties which are not local bridges might as well be counted with the strong ties, to maximize separation of the dense from the less dense network sectors.

One point on which there is no general agreement is whether ego's network should be treated as composed only of those to whom he is tied directly, or should include the contacts of his contacts, and/or others. Analyses stressing encapsulation of an individual by his network tend to take the former position, those stressing manipulation of networks, the latter, since information or favors available through direct contacts may depend on who *their* contacts are. I would argue that by dividing ego's network into that part made up of strong and nonbridging weak ties on the one hand, and that of bridging weak ties on the other, both orientations can be dealt with. Ties in the former part should tend to be to people who not only know one another, but who also have few contacts not tied to ego as well. In the "weak" sector, however, not only will ego's contacts not be tied to one another, but they *will* be tied to individuals not tied to ego. Indirect contacts are thus typically reached through ties in this sector; such ties are then of importance not only in ego's manipulation of networks, but also in that they are the channels through which ideas, influences, or

---

[14] But if the crucial question is really whether ego's *friends* know each other, this measure should probably be computed after ego and his ties have been subtracted from the network; distortions caused by failure to do so will be especially great in small networks. It is important to note, also, that in *non*egocentric networks, there is no simple correspondence between density and any "average" measure of the extent to which the various egos have friends who know one another. "Density," as used here, should not be confused with the "axone density" of Rapoport's models—the number of choices issuing from each node of a network.

information socially distant from ego may reach him. The fewer indirect contacts one has the more encapsulated he will be in terms of knowledge of the world beyond his own friendship circle; thus, bridging weak ties (and the consequent indirect contacts) are important in both ways.

I will develop this point empirically by citing some results from a labor-market study I have recently completed. Labor economists have long been aware that American blue-collar workers find out about new jobs more through personal contacts than by any other method. (Many studies are reviewed by Parnes 1954, chap. 5.) Recent studies suggest that this is also true for those in professional, technical, and managerial positions (Shapero, Howell, and Tombaugh 1965; Brown 1967; Granovetter 1970). My study of this question laid special emphasis on the nature of the *tie* between the job changer and the contact person who provided the necessary information.

In a random sample of recent professional, technical, and managerial job changers living in a Boston suburb, I asked those who found a new job through contacts how often they *saw* the contact around the time that he passed on job information to them. I will use this as a measure of tie strength.[15] A natural a priori idea is that those with whom one has strong ties are more motivated to help with job information. Opposed to this greater motivation are the structural arguments I have been making: those to whom we are weakly tied are more likely to move in circles different from our own and will thus have access to information different from that which we receive.

I have used the following categories for frequency of contact: often = at least twice a week; occasionally = more than once a year but less than twice a week; rarely = once a year or less. Of those finding a job through contacts, 16.7% reported that they saw their contact often at the time, 55.6% said occasionally, and 27.8% rarely ($N = 54$).[16] The skew is clearly to the weak end of the continuum, suggesting the primacy of structure over motivation.

In many cases, the contact was someone only marginally included in the current network of contacts, such as an old college friend or a former work-mate or employer, with whom sporadic contact had been maintained

---

[15] Although this corresponds only to the first of the four dimensions in my definition, supplementary anecdotal evidence from interviews makes it likely that, in this case, the entire definition is satisfied by this measure. At the time of research, it had not occurred to me that tie strength would be a useful variable.

[16] The numbers reported are small because they represent a random subsample of 100, who were interviewed personally, of the total sample of 282. The personal interview allowed more detailed questioning. Comparisons between the mail sample and the interview sample on the large number of items which were put to both show almost no significant differences; this suggests that results observed in the smaller sample on those items put to it alone would not be much different in the mail sample.

(Granovetter 1970, pp. 76–80). Usually such ties had not even been very strong when first forged. For work-related ties, respondents almost invariably said that they never saw the person in a nonwork context.[17] Chance meetings or mutual friends operated to reactivate such ties. It is remarkable that people receive crucial information from individuals whose very existence they have forgotten.[18]

I also asked respondents where their contacts *got* the information they transmitted. In most cases, I traced the information to its initial source. I had expected that, as in the diffusion of rumors or diseases, long paths would be involved. But in 39.1% of the cases information came directly from the prospective employer, whom the respondent already knew; 45.3% said that there was one intermediary between himself and the employer; 12.5% reported two; and 3.1% more than two ($N = 64$). This suggests that for some important purposes it may be sufficient to discuss, as I have, the egocentric network made up of ego, his contacts, and *their* contacts. Had long information paths been involved, large numbers might have found out about any given job, and no particular tie would have been crucial. Such a model of job-information flow actually does correspond to the economists' model of a "perfect" labor market. But those few who did acquire information through paths with more than one intermediary tended to be young and under the threat of unemployment; influence was much less likely to have been exerted by their contact on their behalf. These respondents were, in fact, more similar to those using *formal* intermediaries (agencies, advertisements) than to those hearing through short paths: both of the former are badly placed and dissatisfied in the labor market, and both receive information without influence. Just as reading about a job in the newspaper affords one no recommendation in applying for it, neither does it to have heard about it fifth hand.

The usual dichotomy between "formal" or mass procedures and diffusion through personal contacts may thus be invalid in some cases where, instead, the former may be seen as a limiting case of long diffusion chains. This is

[17] Often when I asked respondents whether a friend had told them about their current job, they said, "Not a friend, an acquaintance." It was the frequency of this comment which suggested this section of the paper to me.

[18] Donald Light has suggested to me an alternative reason to expect predominance of weak ties in transfer of job information. He reasons that most of any given person's ties are weak, so that we should expect, on a "random" model, that most ties through which job information flows should be weak. Since baseline data on acquaintance networks are lacking, this objection remains inconclusive. Even if the premise were correct, however, one might still expect that greater motivation of close friends would overcome their being outnumbered. Different assumptions yield different "random" models; it is not clear which one should be accepted as a starting point. One plausible such model would expect information to flow through ties in proportion to the time expended in interaction; this model would predict much more information via strong ties than one which merely counted all ties equally.

especially likely where information of instrumental significance is involved. Such information is most valuable when earmarked for one person.

From the individual's point of view, then, weak ties are an important resource in making possible mobility opportunity. Seen from a more macroscopic vantage, weak ties play a role in effecting social cohesion. When a man changes jobs, he is not only moving from one network of ties to another, but also establishing a link between these. Such a link is often of the same kind which facilitated his own movement. Especially within professional and technical specialties which are well defined and limited in size, this mobility sets up elaborate structures of bridging weak ties between the more coherent clusters that constitute operative networks in particular locations. Information and ideas thus flow more easily through the specialty, giving it some "sense of community," activated at meetings and conventions. Maintenance of weak ties may well be the most important consequence of such meetings.

WEAK TIES AND COMMUNITY ORGANIZATION

These comments about sense of community may remind us that in many cases it is desirable to deal with a unit of analysis larger than a single individual. I would like to develop my argument further by analyzing, in this section, why some communities organize for common goals easily and effectively whereas others seem unable to mobilize resources, even against dire threats. The Italian community of Boston's West End, for example, was unable to even *form* an organization to fight against the "urban renewal" which ultimately destroyed it. This seems especially anomalous in view of Gans's description of West End social structure as cohesive (1962).

Variations in culture and personality are often cited to explain such anomalies. Gans contrasts "lower"-, "working"-, and "middle"-class subcultures, concluding that only the last provides sufficient trust in leaders and practice in working toward common goals to enable formation of an effective organization. Thus, the working-class West End could not resist urban renewal (pp. 229–304). Yet, numerous well-documented cases show that *some* working-class communities have mobilized quite successfully against comparable or lesser threats (Dahl 1961, pp. 192–99; Keyes 1969; Davies 1966, chap. 4).[19] I would suggest, as a sharper analytical tool, examination of the network of ties comprising a community to see whether aspects of its structure might facilitate or block organization.

Imagine, to begin with, a community completely partitioned into cliques, such that each person is tied to every other in his clique and to none outside. Community organization would be severely inhibited. Leafletting, radio announcements, or other methods could insure that everyone was *aware* of

---

[19] This point was brought to my attention by Richard Wolfe.

some nascent organization; but studies of diffusion and mass communication have shown that people rarely *act* on mass-media information unless it is also transmitted through personal ties (Katz and Lazarsfeld 1955; Rogers 1962); otherwise one has no particular reason to think that an advertised product or an organization should be taken seriously. Enthusiasm for an organization in one clique, then, would not spread to others but would have to develop independently in *each one* to insure success.

The problem of trust is closely related. I would propose that whether a person trusts a given leader depends heavily on whether there exist intermediary personal contacts who can, from their own knowledge, assure him that the leader is trustworthy, and who can, if necessary, intercede with the leader or his lieutenants on his behalf. Trust in leaders is integrally related to the *capacity to predict and affect their behavior*. Leaders, for their part, have little motivation to be responsive or even trustworthy toward those to whom they have no direct or indirect connection. Thus, network fragmentation, by reducing drastically the number of paths from any leader to his potential followers, would inhibit trust in such leaders. This inhibition, furthermore, would not be entirely irrational.

Could the West End's social structure really have been of this kind? Note first that while the structure hypothesized is, by definition, extremely fragmented, this is evident only at a macroscopic level—from an "aerial view" of the network. The local phenomenon is cohesion. (Davis [1967] also noted this paradox, in a related context.) An analyst studying such a group by participant observation might never see the extent of fragmentation, especially if the cliques were not earmarked by ethnic, cultural, or other visible differences. In the nature of participant observation, one is likely to get caught up in a fairly restricted circle; a few useful contacts are acquired and relied on for introduction to others. The "problem of entry into West End society was particularly vexing," Gans writes. But eventually, he and his wife "were welcomed by one of our neighbors and became friends with them. As a result they invited us to many of their evening gatherings and introduced us to other neighbors, relatives and friends. . . . As time went on . . . other West Enders . . . introduced me to relatives and friends, although *most* of the social gatherings at which I participated were those of our *first* contact and their circle" (1962, pp. 340–41; emphasis supplied). Thus, his account of cohesive groups is not *inconsistent* with overall fragmentation.

Now, suppose that all ties in the West End were either strong or absent, and that the triad of figure 1 did not occur. Then, for any ego, all his friends were friends of one another, and all their friends were ego's friends as well. Unless each person was strongly tied to *all* others in the community, network structure did indeed break down into the isolated cliques posited above. (In terms of Davis's mathematical treatment, the overall network was "clusterable," with unique clusters [1967, p. 186].) Since it is unlikely that anyone could sustain more than a few dozen strong ties, this would, in fact, have been the result.

Did strong ties take up enough of the West Enders' social time to make this analysis even approximately applicable? Gans reported that "sociability is a routinized gathering of a relatively unchanging peer group of family members and friends that takes place several times a week." Some "participate in informal cliques and in clubs made up of unrelated people. . . . In number, and in the amount of time devoted to them, however, these groups are much less important than the family circle" (1962, pp. 74, 80). Moreover, two common sources of weak ties, formal organizations and work settings, did not provide them for the West End; organization membership was almost nil (pp. 104–7) and few worked within the area itself, so that ties formed at work were not relevant to the community (p. 122).

Nevertheless, in a community marked by geographic immobility and lifelong friendships (p. 19) it strains credulity to suppose that each person would not have known a great many others, so that there would have been *some* weak ties. The question is whether such ties were bridges.[20] If *none* were, then the community would be fragmented in exactly the same way as described above, except that the cliques would then contain weak as well as strong ties. (This follows, again, from Davis's analysis of "clusterability," with strong and weak ties called "positive" and absent ones "negative" [1967].) Such a pattern is made plausible by the lack of ways in the West End to *develop* weak ties other than by meeting friends of friends (where "friend" includes relatives)—in which case the new tie is automatically not a bridge. It is suggested, then, that for a community to have many weak ties which bridge, there must be several distinct ways or contexts in which people may form them. The case of Charlestown, a working-class community which successfully organized against the urban renewal plan of the same city (Boston) against which the West End was powerless, is instructive in this respect: unlike the West End, it had a rich organizational life, and most male residents worked within the area (Keyes 1969, chap. 4).

In the absence of actual network data, all this is speculation. The hard information needed to show either that the West End was fragmented or that communities which organized successfully were not, and that both patterns were due to the strategic role of weak ties, is not at hand and would not have been simple to collect. Nor has comparable information been collected in *any* context. But a theoretical framework has, at least, been suggested, with which one could not only carry out analyses post hoc, but also *predict* differential capacity of communities to act toward common

[20] See Jane Jacobs's excellent, intuitive, discussion of bridging ties ("hop-skip links") in community organization (1961, chap. 6.)

goals. A rough principle with which to begin such an investigation might be: the more local bridges (per person?) in a community and the greater their degree, the more cohesive the community and the more capable of acting in concert. Study of the origins and nature (strength and content, for example) of such bridging ties would then offer unusual insight into the social dynamics of the community.

MICRO AND MACRO NETWORK MODELS

Unlike most models of interpersonal networks, the one presented here is not meant primarily for application to small, face-to-face groups or to groups in confined institutional or organizational settings. Rather, it is meant for linkage of such small-scale levels with one another and with larger, more amorphous ones. This is why emphasis here has been placed more on weak ties than on strong. Weak ties are more likely to link members of *different* small groups than are strong ones, which tend to be concentrated within particular groups.

For this reason, my discussion does not lend itself to elucidation of the internal structure of small groups. This point can be made more clearly by contrasting the model of this paper to one with which it shares many similarities, that of James Davis, Paul Holland, and Samuel Leinhardt (hereafter, the DHL model) (Davis 1970; Davis and Leinhardt 1971; Holland and Leinhardt 1970, 1971a, 1971b; Davis, Holland, and Leinhardt 1971; Leinhardt 1972). The authors, inspired by certain propositions in George Homans's *The Human Group* (1950), argue that "the central proposition in structural sociometry is this: *Interpersonal choices tend to be transitive—if P chooses O and O chooses X, then P is likely to choose X*" (Davis et al. 1971, p. 309). When this is true without exception, a sociogram can be divided into cliques in which every individual chooses every other; any asymmetric choices or nonchoices are *between* such cliques, and asymmetry, if present, runs only in one direction. A partial ordering of cliques may thus be inferred. If mutual choice implies equal, and assymmetric choice unequal, status, then this ordering reflects the stratification structure of the group (Holland and Leinhardt 1971a, pp. 107–14).

One immediate difference between this model and mine is that it is cast in terms of "choices" rather than ties. Most sociometric tests ask people whom they *like* best or would *prefer* to do something with, rather than with whom they actually spend time. If transitivity is built more into our cognitive than our social structure, this method might overstate its prevalence. But since the DHL model could recast in terms of ties, this is not a conclusive difference.

More significant is the difference in the application of my argument to transitivity. Let *P* choose *O* and *O* choose *X* (or equivalently, let *X* choose

O and O choose P): then I assert that transitivity—P choosing X (or X, P)—is most likely when both ties—P-O and O-X—are strong, least likely when both are weak, and of intermediate probability if one is strong and one weak. Transitivity, then, is claimed to be a function of the strength of ties, rather than a general feature of social structure.

The justification of this assertion is, in part, identical with that offered earlier for the triad designated A-B-C. In addition, it is important to point out here that the DHL model was designed for small groups, and with increasing size of the group considered the rationale for transitivity weakens. If P chooses O and O chooses X, P should choose X out of consistency; but if P does not *know* or barely knows X, nonchoice implies no inconsistency. For the logic of transitivity to apply, a group must be small enough so that any person knows enough about every other person to be able to decide whether to "choose" him, and encounters him often enough that he feels the need for such a decision. Including weak ties in my model, then, lessens the expectation of transitivity and permits analysis of intergroup relationships and also of amorphous chunks of social structure which an analyst may ferret out as being of interest, but which are not easily defined in terms of face-to-face groups. Anthropologists have recently referred to such chunks as "quasi-groups" (Mayer 1966; Boissevain 1968).

Since, as I have argued above, weak ties are poorly represented in sociograms, there is little in the DHL empirical studies—which apply statistical tests to sociometric data—to confirm or disconfirm my argument on transitivity. One finding does lend itself to speculation, however. Leinhardt (1972) shows that the sociograms of schoolchildren conform more and more closely to the transitive model as they become older, sixth graders being the oldest tested. He interprets this as reflecting cognitive development—increasing capacity to make use of transitive logic. If my assertion is correct, an alternative possibility would be that children develop stronger ties with increasing age. This is consistent with some theories of child development (see especially Sullivan 1953, chap. 16) and would imply, on my argument, greater transitivity of structure. Some support for this explanation comes from Leinhardt's finding that proportion of choices which were mutual was positively correlated with both grade level and degree of transitivity. In these sociograms, with an average of only about four choices per child, it seems likely that most mutual choices reflected strong ties (see n. 7, above).

CONCLUSION

The major implication intended by this paper is that the personal experience of individuals is closely bound up with larger-scale aspects of social structure, well beyond the purview or control of particular individuals.

Linkage of micro and macro levels is thus no luxury but of central importance to the development of sociological theory. Such linkage generates paradoxes: weak ties, often denounced as generative of alienation (Wirth 1938) are here seen as indispensable to individuals' opportunities and to their integration into communities; strong ties, breeding local cohesion, lead to overall fragmentation. Paradoxes are a welcome antidote to theories which explain everything all too neatly.

The model offered here is a very limited step in the linking of levels; it is a fragment of a theory. Treating only the *strength* of ties ignores, for instance, all the important issues involving their content. What is the relation between strength and degree of specialization of ties, or between strength and hierarchical structure? How can "negative" ties be handled? Should tie strength be developed as a continuous variable? What is the developmental sequence of network structure over time?

As such questions are resolved, others will arise. Demography, coalition structure, and mobility are just a few of the variables which would be of special importance in developing micro-macro linkage with the help of network analysis; how these are related to the present discussion needs specification. My contribution here is mainly, then, exploratory and programmatic, its primary purpose being to generate interest in the proposed program of theory and research.

REFERENCES

Barnes, J. A. 1969. "Networks and Political Process." In *Social Networks in Urban Situations,* edited by J. C. Mitchell. Manchester: Manchester University Press.

Becker, Marshall. 1970. "Sociometric Location and Innovativeness." *American Sociological Review* 35 (April): 267–82.

Berscheid, E., and E. Walster. 1969. *Interpersonal Attraction.* Reading, Mass.: Addison-Wesley.

Boissevain, J. 1968. "The Place of Non-Groups in the Social Sciences." *Man* 3 (December): 542–56.

Bott, Elizabeth. 1957. *Family and Social Network.* London: Tavistock.

Bramel, D. 1969. "Interpersonal Attraction, Hostility and Perception." In *Experimental Social Psychology,* edited by Judson Mills. New York: Macmillan.

Brown, David. 1967. *The Mobile Professors.* Washington, D.C.: American Council on Education.

Brown, Roger. 1965. *Social Psychology.* New York: Free Press.

Coleman, J. S. 1960. "The Mathematical Study of Small Groups." In *Mathematical Thinking in the Measurement of Behavior,* edited by H. Solomon. Glencoe: Free Press.

Coleman, J. S., E. Katz, and H. Menzel. 1966. *Medical Innovation: A Diffusion Study.* Indianapolis: Bobbs-Merrill.

Dahl, Robert. 1961. *Who Governs?* New Haven, Conn.: Yale University Press.

Davies, J. C. 1966. *Neighborhood Groups and Urban Renewal.* New York: Columbia University Press.

Davis, James A. 1963. "Structural Balance, Mechanical Solidarity and Interpersonal Relations." *American Journal of Sociology* 68 (January): 444–62.

———. 1967. "Clustering and Structural Balance in Graphs." *Human Relations* 20 (May): 181–87.

————. 1969. "Social Structures and Cognitive Structures." In R. P. Abelson et al., *Theories of Cognitive Consistency*. Chicago: Rand McNally.

————. 1970. "Clustering and Hierarchy in Interpersonal Relations." *American Sociological Review* 35 (October): 843–52.

Davis, James A., P. Holland, and S. Leinhardt. 1971. "Comment." *American Sociological Review* 36 (April): 309–11.

Davis, James A., and S. Leinhardt. 1971. "The Structure of Positive Interpersonal Relations in Small Groups." In *Sociological Theories in Progress*. Vol. 2, edited by J. Berger, M. Zelditch, and B. Anderson. Boston: Houghton-Mifflin.

Epstein, A. 1969. "The Network and Urban Social Organization." In *Social Networks in Urban Situations,* edited by J. C. Mitchell. Manchester: Manchester University Press.

Frankenberg, R. 1965. *Communities in Britain*. Baltimore: Penguin.

Gans, Herbert. 1962. *The Urban Villagers*. New York: Free Press.

Granovetter, M. S. 1970. "Changing Jobs: Channels of Mobility Information in a Suburban Community." Doctoral dissertation, Harvard University.

Harary, F. 1965. "Graph Theory and Group Structure." In *Readings in Mathematical Psychology*. Vol. 2, edited by R. Luce, R. Bush, and E. Galanter. New York: Wiley.

Harary, F., R. Norman, and D. Cartwright. 1965. *Structural Models*. New York: Wiley.

Heider, F. 1958. *The Psychology of Interpersonal Relations*. New York: Wiley.

Holland, Paul, and S. Leinhardt. 1970. "Detecting Structure in Sociometric Data." *American Journal of Sociology* 76 (November): 492–513.

————. 1971a. "Transitivity in Structural Models of Small Groups." *Comparative Group Studies* 2:107–24.

————. 1971b. "Masking: The Structural Implications of Measurement Error in Sociometry." Mimeographed. Pittsburgh: Carnegie-Mellon University.

Homans, George. 1950. *The Human Group*. New York: Harcourt, Brace & World.

Jacobs, Jane. 1961. *The Death and Life of Great American Cities*. New York: Random House.

Kapferer, B. 1969. "Norms and the Manipulation of Relationships in a Work Context." In *Social Networks in Urban Situations,* edited by J. C. Mitchell. Manchester: Manchester University Press.

Katz, E., and P. Lazarsfeld. 1955. *Personal Influence*. New York: Free Press.

Kerckhoff, A., and K. Back. 1968. *The June Bug: A Study of Hysterical Contagion*. New York: Appleton-Century-Crofts.

Kerckhoff, A., K. Back, and N. Miller. 1965. "Sociometric Patterns in Hysterical Contagion." *Sociometry* 28 (March): 2–15.

Keyes, L. C. 1969. *The Rehabilitation Planning Game*. Cambridge, Mass.: M.I.T. Press.

Korte, Charles. 1967. "Small-World Study (Los Angeles): Data Analysis." Mimeographed. Poughkeepsie, N.Y.: Vassar College.

Korte, Charles, and Stanley Milgram. 1970. "Acquaintance Networks between Racial Groups." *Journal of Personality and Social Psychology* 15 (June): 101–8.

Laumann, Edward. 1968. "Interlocking and Radial Friendship Networks: A Cross-sectional Analysis." Mimeographed. Ann Arbor: University of Michigan.

Laumann, Edward, and H. Schuman. 1967. "Open and Closed Structures." Paper prepared for the 1967 ASA meeting. Mimeographed.

Leinhardt, Samuel. 1972. "Developmental Change in the Sentiment Structure of Childrens' Groups." *American Sociological Review* 37 (April): 202–12.

Mayer, Adrian. 1966. "The Significance of Quasi-Groups in the Study of Complex Societies." In *The Social Anthropology of Complex Societies,* edited by M. Banton. New York: Praeger.

Mayer, Phillip. 1961. *Townsmen or Tribesmen?* Capetown: Oxford.

Mazur, B. 1971. "Comment." *American Sociological Review* 36 (April): 308–9.

Milgram, Stanley. 1967. "The Small-World Problem." *Psychology Today* 1 (May): 62–67.

Mitchell, J. Clyde. 1969. *Social Networks in Urban Situations*. Manchester: Manchester University Press.

Newcomb, T. M. 1961. *The Acquaintance Process*. New York: Holt, Rinehart & Winston.

Parnes, Herbert. 1954. *Research on Labor Mobility*. New York: Social Science Research Council.

Precker, Joseph. 1952. "Similarity of Valuings as a Factor in Selection of Peers and Near-Authority Figures." *Journal of Abnormal and Social Psychology* 47, suppl. (April): 406–14.

Rapoport, Anatol. 1953a. "Spread of Information through a Population with Socio-Structural Bias. I. Assumption of Transitivity." *Bulletin of Mathematical Biophysics* 15 (December): 523–33.

———. 1953b. "Spread of Information through a Population with Socio-Structural Bias. II. Various Models with Partial Transitivity." *Bulletin of Mathematical Biophysics* 15 (December): 535–46.

———. 1954. "Spread of Information through a Population with Socio-Structural Bias. III. Suggested Experimental Procedures." *Bulletin of Mathematical Biophysics* 16 (March): 75–81.

———. 1963. "Mathematical Models of Social Interaction." In *Handbook of Mathematical Psychology*. Vol. 2, edited by R. Luce, R. Bush, and E. Galanter. New York: Wiley.

Rapoport, A., and W. Horvath. 1961. "A Study of a Large Sociogram." *Behavioral Science* 6:279–91.

Rogers, Everett. 1962. *Diffusion of Innovations*. New York: Free Press.

Shapero, Albert, Richard Howell, and James Tombaugh. 1965. *The Structure and Dynamics of the Defense R & D Industry*. Menlo Park, Calif.: Stanford Research Institute.

Simmel, Georg. 1950. *The Sociology of Georg Simmel*. New York: Free Press.

Solomonoff, Ray, and A. Rapoport. 1951. "Connectivity of Random Nets." *Bulletin of Mathematical Biophysics* 13 (June): 107–17.

Sullivan, Harry Stack. 1953. *The Interpersonal Theory of Psychiatry*. New York: Norton.

Tilly, Charles. 1969. "Community:City:Urbanization." Mimeographed. Ann Arbor: University of Michigan.

Travers, Jeffrey, and S. Milgram. 1969. "An Experimental Study of the 'Small-World' Problem." *Sociometry* 32 (December): 425–43.

Wirth, Louis. 1938. "Urbanism as a Way of Life." *American Journal of Sociology* 44 (July): 1–24.

Part IV: Methods

From Frank Harary, *Management Science 5*,
387-403 (1959), by permission.

GRAPH THEORETIC METHODS IN THE MANAGEMENT SCIENCES*[1]

FRANK HARARY[2]

Princeton University and The Institute for Advanced Study

1. Introduction

The purpose of this paper is to illustrate the potential utility of graph theoretical methods for the management sciences. In a series of joint papers (16, 17, 18, 19, 20) with I. C. Ross, we have combined a graph theoretical approach with matrix theory and set theory to handle problems concerning redundancies, liaison persons, cliques, and strengthening and weakening members of a group. The correspondence between these organizational concepts and ideas from graph theory (to be explained below) is as follows. A redundancy is analogous to a directed path which passes through the same point more than once. A liaison person in an organization has the role of a cut point of a connected graph. A clique is taken as a maximal complete subgraph. A strengthening member of a group is one whose presence causes the graph of a group to be more highly connected that the graph obtained when he is absent.

We also mention graphical treatments of status and contrastatus, the attainment of unanimity in a power structure, tournaments and production schedules, and structural balance. The ideas developed in our paper (11) on status and contrastatus were inspired by "Parkinson's Law," the first essay in Parkinson's delightful book (26); contrastatus is defined in terms of the amount of status weighing down on a person in an organization. The development in (12) of a criterion for unanimity in a theory of social power (6) involves the concept of a "power subgroup" which is of independent interest. Tournaments and production schedules pertain to situations in which there is a collection of tasks and a preferred ordering between every pair of tasks. In articles (2, 3, 8, 9, 10) either written jointly with D. Cartwright or motivated by problems suggested by him, we have studied questions involving structural balance in a group in which both positive and negative relationships may occur.

Expository treatments of certain aspects of graph theory are presented for an audience of social scientists in the monographs (14, 15) and in the paper (2). These treat the theory of graphs, directed graphs, and signed graphs, respectively. The work of some other authors in applying either graphical or matrix methods to sociometric or structural data is given in the papers (1, 4, 5, 21, 23, 24, 25, 27). The method of the paper (13), although expressed in different terms, can be

* Received November 1958.

[1] An invited address at the Annual Meeting of TIMS in Philadelphia on October 16, 1958. The preparation of this paper was supported by a grant from the Office of Naval Research.

[2] The author is on leave of absence from the Department of Mathematics and the Research Center for Group Dynamics of the University of Michigan.

utilized to identify certain closely connected subgroups using clustering about the diagonal of the group matrix. The paper (7) studies the problems of enumerating the structurally distinct graphs of various kinds. Finally, the book (22) by König is the most comprehensive available collection of purely graph theoretical results.

The next section discusses the mutual expressibility of graphs and matrices in terms of each other, on which most of this article is based. The main section, which then follows, discusses eight of the areas in which graph theoretic methods related to the management sciences have been developed. We conclude with some brief remarks on the kinds of open problems remaining.

2. Graphs and matrices

Consider a finite collection of *points* a_1, a_2, $\cdots$, a_n and the set of all *lines* joining pairs of these points. A *graph* consists of these points together with a subset of this set of lines. If all the lines are present, the graph is called *complete*. For example, the complete graph of four points may be pictured as G in Figure 1, while H is a graph of four points and five lines which is not complete.

Two points a and b of a graph G are *adjacent* if the line ab is one of the lines of G. Two graphs G_1 and G_2 are *isomorphic* if there exists a one-to-one correspondence between their sets of points which preserves adjacency. For other fundamental concepts in the theory of graphs, with many illustrations, we refer the interested reader to the monograph (14).

A *directed graph* (or *digraph*), consists of n points together with some collection of *directed lines* joining them. We use the notation $\overrightarrow{ab}$ to indicate the directed line *from* point a *to* point b. A comprehensive though elementary introduction to the theory of digraphs intended primarily for social scientists will be given in the monograph (15).

The expressibility of graphs and matrices in terms of each other is well known. Each of these two mathematical models has certain operational advantages. For example, operations corresponding to matrix multiplication and inversion are not as conveniently performed on graphs. An advantage of graphs is the easy pictorial identification of some of the structural properties, especially for small graphs.

Graphs may be regarded as the special case of (symmetric) directed graphs for which whenever the (directed) line $\overrightarrow{ab}$ occurs, so does the line $\overrightarrow{ba}$. In this case these two directed lines taken together correspond to the single line ab of the

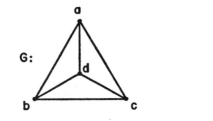
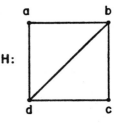

Fig. 1

372

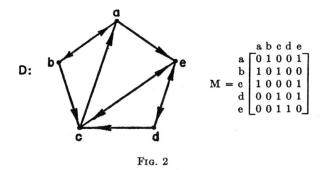

$$M = \begin{array}{c} \\ a \\ b \\ c \\ d \\ e \end{array} \begin{array}{c} a\ b\ c\ d\ e \\ \left[\begin{array}{ccccc} 0 & 1 & 0 & 0 & 1 \\ 1 & 0 & 1 & 0 & 0 \\ 1 & 0 & 0 & 0 & 1 \\ 0 & 0 & 1 & 0 & 1 \\ 0 & 0 & 1 & 1 & 0 \end{array} \right] \end{array}$$

FIG. 2

analogous *ordinary* or undirected graph. We illustrate the one-to-one correspondence between digraphs and matrices. The following contrived example can be regarded as the sociometric data of a five-person group, in which each person makes two choices within the group. Let the five members of the group be a, b, c, d, e. We draw a directed line from one point to another in Figure 2 to indicate the choice by the member corresponding to the initial point of the member indicated by the terminal point. We note that in Figure 2 the arrows on the line joining a and b mean that both the members a and b choose each other, while the single arrow on the line joining b and c indicated that b chooses c but c does not choose b. Here, M is the corresponding (sociometric) matrix in which the rows denote choices made and the columns choices received.

3. Graphical approach to some structural problems in the management sciences

In this section we present an exposition from a unified viewpoint of the following eight topics which are treated elsewhere in the literature:

3.1 Liaison persons
3.2 Cliques
3.3 Strengthening and weakening group members
3.4 Redundancies
3.5 Status and contrastatus
3.6 Tournaments and production schedules
3.7 A theory of social power
3.8 Structural balance

Of course, we shall not be able to take up all of these topics in detail. We shall try, however, to present enough of the conceptual development of each so that an intuitive feeling for the subject matter is acquired. None of the proofs of theorems will be included here.

3.1 Liaison persons. A liaison person in an organization is one who performs the role of sending all messages from one subgroup to another subgroup, and vice versa. (If he is disliked, he is usually regarded as a bottleneck rather than an expediter.) Familiar examples are provided by interpreters or telephone operators. Of course it is not necessary to use the relation of communication, since there can be liaison persons with respect to any interpersonal relation.

We now make this notion more precise and describe a method of locating the liaison persons in a given group.

A *path* between a and e is a sequence of lines $ab, bc, \cdots, de$ in which the points $a, b, c, \cdots, d, e$ are distinct; a *cycle* is a closed path. A graph is *connected* if there is a path joining every pair of points. By the *removal* of a point of a graph, we mean the deletion of this point and also of all the lines of the graph on which this point lies. An *articulation point* or a *cut point* of a connected graph is one whose removal results in a disconnected graph. A *liaison person* in an organization or a group has been described (21, 27) as one whose role corresponds precisely to that of a cut point in the corresponding graph. This fact was utilized in (18) to derive a combined graphical and matrix method for the determination of all the liaison persons in a group whose matrix is given. The method makes use of several known characterizations of cut points (22) and also involves some additional observations. An essential tool is the *matrix of distances* of a graph, i.e., the matrix in which the i, j element is the distance from a_i to a_j, where the *distance* between two points of a graph is the length of any shortest path joining them. The *associated number* of a point of a connected graph is the greatest distance between this point and all other points. A *peripheral point* (compare Bavelas (1)) is a point whose associated number is maximal. A point c is *relatively peripheral* from point b if the distance between b and c is equal to the associated number of b. We are now able to state two sufficient conditions, one of which assures us that a point is not a cut point and the other that it is.

Theorem: All relatively peripheral points are not cut points.

Since every peripheral point is *a fortiori* relatively peripheral, it follows at once that these are also not cut points.

Theorem: If b is a point of a connected graph and c is the only point at a certain distance from b less than the associated number of b, then c is a cut point.

In addition to these two sufficient conditions, which are useful but not comprehensive, the paper (18) has a general method (not included here) which combines matrix calculations with elementary set theoretic reasoning, and determines for each point of a digraph whether or not it is a cut point.

We now refer to Figure 3 to illustrate the above considerations. The accompanying matrix of distances, M_d, enables one to read off both the peripheral points and the relatively peripheral points immediately. Since they are the only

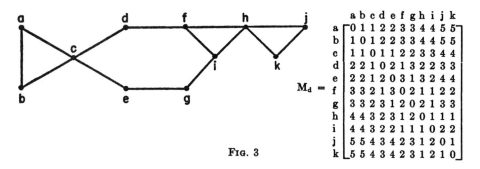

$$M_d = \begin{array}{c|ccccccccccc} & a & b & c & d & e & f & g & h & i & j & k \\ \hline a & 0 & 1 & 1 & 2 & 2 & 3 & 3 & 4 & 4 & 5 & 5 \\ b & 1 & 0 & 1 & 2 & 2 & 3 & 3 & 4 & 4 & 5 & 5 \\ c & 1 & 1 & 0 & 1 & 1 & 2 & 2 & 3 & 3 & 4 & 4 \\ d & 2 & 2 & 1 & 0 & 2 & 1 & 3 & 2 & 2 & 3 & 3 \\ e & 2 & 2 & 1 & 2 & 0 & 3 & 1 & 3 & 2 & 4 & 4 \\ f & 3 & 3 & 2 & 1 & 3 & 0 & 2 & 1 & 1 & 2 & 2 \\ g & 3 & 3 & 2 & 3 & 1 & 2 & 0 & 2 & 1 & 3 & 3 \\ h & 4 & 4 & 3 & 2 & 3 & 1 & 2 & 0 & 1 & 1 & 1 \\ i & 4 & 4 & 3 & 2 & 2 & 1 & 1 & 1 & 0 & 2 & 2 \\ j & 5 & 5 & 4 & 3 & 4 & 2 & 3 & 1 & 2 & 0 & 1 \\ k & 5 & 5 & 4 & 3 & 4 & 2 & 3 & 1 & 2 & 1 & 0 \end{array}$$

Fig. 3

374

points of associated number 5, we see that a, b, j, and k are peripheral points and hence not cut points. Clearly, the points g, e, and d are relatively peripheral from d, f, and g, respectively. Hence g, e, and d are also not cut points by the first theorem.

The associated number of the point i is 4. But c is the only point at distance 3 from i, and $3 < 4$. Therefore c is a cut point by the second theorem. The only points still left are f, h and i. Appealing to the general algorithm (Theorem 3 of (18)), it follows that h is a cut point and that f and i are not cut points. This example is worked out in (18) in all detail. Although the cut points c and h can be picked out of Figure 3 by inspection, the procedure in (18) is universal and works even when the organization is so big that the conversion from its matrix to its graph followed by visual observation of the graph is not practicable.

3.2 Cliques. It is possible to assign several different meanings to the word "clique." In order to determine the cliques in a group, it is very important to know which meaning one has in mind. Among other possibilities there are the following kinds of interpretation of the meaning of a clique (each of which we regard as a maximal subgroup having the stated properties):

1. A collection of people, every pair in the relation to the other.
2. A set of people, "almost all" in the relation to each other.
3. A subgroup in which there is a directed path from each member to each other member.
4. A subgroup in which there is a member with the property that paths from him can reach the rest of the subgroup. Various authors have used these different descriptions, always using the same word "clique" for the subgroup. For example, Festinger (4) uses the first definition of clique, but only discusses groups with exactly one clique. In the paper (19), we have extended this to a general procedure for finding all the cliques in any group.

Forsyth and Katz (5), using a matrix approach, take a stand in favor of re-arranging the rows and columns of a matrix of a group in such a way that as many 1's as possible will be as close to the diagonal as possible. The approach of Weiss (27) is analogous, but he provides a usable approximate algorithm for clustering the 1's near the diagonal. On the other hand, Luce (24) gives a detailed characterization of various different kinds of "almost" completely connected subgroups of a given group, and investigates some of their properties.

In our paper (20) the third kind of clique mentioned above is studied under the name of a "strong component," while in (13) we go one step further and show how the strong components may be clustered in the group matrix. Finally in the monograph (15), the fourth possibility mentioned above is called a "unilateral component" of a digraph.

We now turn to a description of some of these results. Throughout the rest of this discussion we will consistently refer to a *clique* as a maximal subgroup of at least three members, in which each member is in the relation to every other member. Festinger's principal result (4) was the observation that each of the elements in the diagonal of M^3, the cube of the group matrix of a clique with n members, is the number $(n - 1)(n - 2)$.

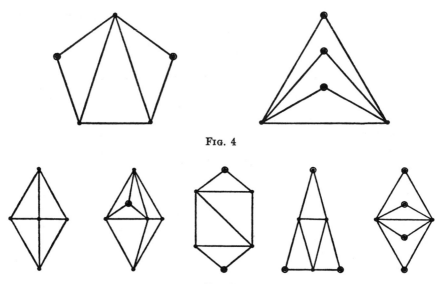

FIG. 4

FIG. 5

Let M be the matrix of a group with respect to a relation. A member of this group is *noncliqual* if he does not belong to any clique. The first thing we want to do is remove all noncliqual members, so that each member that is left will belong to at least one clique. To do this, we find the matrix S described in subsection 3.4, and form the elementwise[3] product $S^2 \times S$. It is easily seen that a member is noncliqual if and only if the corresponding row in the matrix $S^2 \times S$ consists entirely of zeros. Let G be the group obtained after removing all these noncliqual members, and let A be the corresponding submatrix of $S^2 \times S$ after this deletion.

A member of G is *unicliqual* if he belongs to exactly one clique. Two members are *cocliqual* if they belong to at least one clique in common. The general method for finding all the cliques in a group makes effective use of the concept of a unicliqual member.

Theorem: 1. If G has exactly one clique, then every member of G is unicliqual.

2. If G has exactly two cliques, then each clique has a unicliqual member.

3. If G has exactly three cliques, then at least two of these cliques have unicliqual members.

4. If G has n cliques where $n \geq 4$, then there are no restrictions on the number of cliques which may have unicliqual members.

The third part of this theorem is illustrated in Figure 4 which shows two groups with 3 cliques each. The first has two cliques with unicliqual members (circled points) while the second has three. The different possibilities for the fourth part of the theorem are illustrated for $n = 4$ in Figure 5.

---

[3] The *elementwise product* $A \times B$ of two matrices $A = (a_{ij})$ and $B = (b_{ij})$ is the matrix whose i, j element is the product $a_{ij}b_{ij}$.

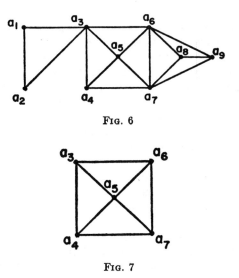

FIG. 6

FIG. 7

The general method for clique detection involves the determination of all cliques having unicliqual members, and iteration of this process after deletion of these members. When there are no unicliqual members in the resulting group, it is split into two subgroups each having fewer cliques such that every clique lies entirely in one subgroup. In view of the above theorem asserting the existence of unicliqual members in groups with a sufficiently small number of cliques (3 or less), we are sure to reduce the group at hand to subgroups which do have unicliqual members.

We illustrate with Figure 6. Here the members a_1, a_2, a_8, and a_9 are unicliqual. The cliques in which they lie are:

$$C_1 = \{a_1, a_2, a_3\} \quad \text{and} \quad C_2 = \{a_6, a_7, a_8, a_9\}.$$

After deleting these unicliqual members we are left with the group of Figure 7 which has no unicliqual members. We may split this into the following subgroups:

$$\{a_3, a_4, a_5, a_6\} \quad \text{and} \quad \{a_4, a_5, a_6, a_7\}.$$

From the first one, we find the cliques

$$C_3 = \{a_3, a_4, a_5\} \quad \text{and} \quad C_4 = \{a_3, a_5, a_6\};$$

while from the second we obtain

$$C_5 = \{a_4, a_5, a_7\} \quad \text{and} \quad C_6 = \{a_5, a_6, a_7\}.$$

3.3 Strengthening and weakening members of a group. Our object is to develop a procedure for deciding whether a given member causes the group to be stronger or weaker by his presence. We shall refer to such group members as "strengthening" and "weakening" respectively. For this purpose we must necessarily use some precise criterion, and we select connectedness for convenience and appropriateness. The main ideas are presented in (20) and (15).

We first illustrate with ordinary graphs; an ordinary graph is either connected or disconnected. There are exactly four mutually exclusive possibilities for each point. If G is connected while G-b is disconnected, then by definition b is a cut point of G. Thus we regard b as a strengthening point since G is stronger than G-b (with regard to connectedness). On the other hand if b is an isolated point and G-b is connected, then b is a weakening point of G. The remaining two cases involve a point whose removal does not affect the connectedness or disconnectedness of G. For want of better terminology, we call such a point a "neutral point."

We now turn to the more general situation for directed graphs. Here we find that if a digraph D is not disconnected, it may be connected in any of three different ways. These kinds of connectedness have been mentioned in the papers (6, 7, 12, 15, 20).

Let b and c be any two points of a digraph D. We say that D is *strongly connected* or *strong* if there exists a (directed) path from b to c *and* one from c to b. The digraph D is *unilaterally connected* or *unilateral* if there is a path from b to c *or* one from c to b. A digraph is *weakly connected* or *weak* if on ignoring the directions on each of its lines, the result is a connected ordinary graph. Finally, D is *disconnected* if it is not even weak.

Obviously every strong digraph is unilateral and every unilateral digraph is weak. In order to divide all digraphs into mutually exclusive connectedness categories, let U_3 be the collection of all strong digraphs, U_2 consist of all unilateral digraphs which are not strong, U_1 contain all weak digraphs which are not unilateral, and U_0 be the set of all disconnected digraphs. In Figure 8, the four digraphs shown are in U_3, U_2, U_1, and U_0 respectively.

We are now ready to give a precise definition of strengthening and weakening members of a group using these disjoint connectedness categories. Let b be any point of a digraph D. If D is in U_i while D-b is in U_j, then the point b is said to be of the *type* $P_{i,j}$. In Figure 9, we write i, j next to a point whenever it is of type $P_{i,j}$. If b is of type $P_{i,j}$, then b is a *strengthening* point if $i > j$; a *weakening* point if $i < j$. Note that there are no points of Figure 9 which are marked 1,3. This is not an oversight; it is a theorem!

Theorem: If D is any digraph in U_1, then there is no point of D whose removal results in a strong digraph. In other words, there are no points in any digraph of type $P_{1,3}$. However, there do exist points of all other types $P_{i,j}$.

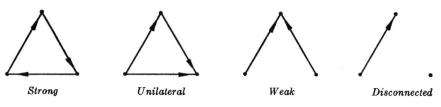

| Strong | Unilateral | Weak | Disconnected |

FIG. 8

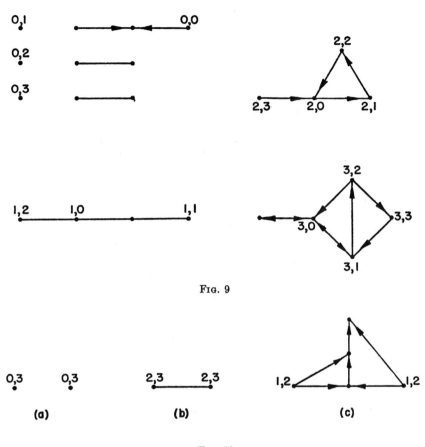

Fig. 9

Fig. 10

The validity of the last sentence of this theorem is seen at once from Figure 9. The following is probably the most startling result in this entire paper.

Theorem: In any group whatsoever, there are at most two weakening members!

In Figure 10, we show three digraphs each of which has exactly two weakening points. Curiously, it follows from these considerations that a digraph with two weakening points either has only two points or is in U_1, i.e., is strictly weak (an observation of Prof. D. Cartwright).

3.4 Redundancies. We begin with an illustration. Consider the digraph D of Figure 2 as a communication network this time. The two directed lines $\overrightarrow{ab}$ and $\overrightarrow{bc}$ form a directed path of length 2 from a to c; while the lines $\overrightarrow{ae}$, $\overrightarrow{ed}$ and $\overrightarrow{dc}$ form a directed path from a to c of length 3. However the lines $\overrightarrow{ba}$, $\overrightarrow{ae}$, $\overrightarrow{ed}$, $\overrightarrow{dc}$, $\overrightarrow{ca}$, and $\overrightarrow{ae}$ are a sequence of lines from b to e which pass through certain points more than once. We call such a line sequence a *redundancy* or a *redundant sequence.* Motivated by the study of the process of the spread of a rumor in a group of people,

Festinger (4) proposed the problem of determining for a given group structure (as represented by a digraph) the number of non-redundant line sequences from each member to each other member.

It is both obvious and well-known that the i, j entry in M^n, the n'th power of the matrix M of a digraph D is the number of line sequences from a_i, the i'th point of D, to a_j, including both the redundant and non-redundant ones. If one can find the matrix, R_n, whose entries give the number of redundant sequences of length n, then this can be subtracted from M^n to obtain a matrix in which the i, j entry is precisely the number of directed paths or non-redundant sequences from a_i to a_j. Luce and Perry (25) obtained such a formula for the 3rd power of the matrix and L. Katz (unpublished) extended this to the 4th power. In the paper (16), we derive an algorithm for determining the number of redundant sequences of any given length, and exploit this to obtain specific formulas which include those for sequences of length 3 and 4 mentioned above and also handle redundancies of length 5 and 6. However a closed formula for finding the matrix of non-redundant paths of arbitrary length in a convenient form still stands as an unsolved problem.

We state the formulas for the cases of redundancies of lengths 3 and 4. Let M be the matrix of a given digraph D, and let M^2, M^3, $\cdots$ be the 2nd, 3rd, $\cdots$ powers of the matrix M, using ordinary matrix multiplication. If A is any square matrix then by the *diagonal matrix of* A, denoted $d(A)$, we mean the matrix obtained from A by leaving the principal diagonal unchanged and having zero everywhere else. The *transpose* of matrix A, denoted by A', is obtained by interchanging the rows and columns of A. If A and B are two square matrices of the same size, then we denote by AB their ordinary matrix product, but we denote by $A \times B$ the matrix[3] whose i, j element is the product of the i, j elements of A and B. Then the matrix $S = M \times M'$ contains only the symmetric part of the matrix M. With this notation, we are now able to write the formulas for R_n for $n = 3$ and 4:

(1) $$R_3 = [Md(M^2) + d(M^2)M] - S$$

(2) $$R_4 = [Md(M^3) + d(M^3)M] + [M^2d(M^2) + d(M^2)M^2] +$$
$$Md(M^2)M - M \times (M^2)' - 2S \times M^2 - [MS + SM].$$

We illustrate the first of these formulas for the digraph D and the matrix M of Figure 2. Since

$$S = \begin{bmatrix} 0 & 1 & 0 & 0 & 0 \\ 1 & 0 & 0 & 0 & 0 \\ 0 & 0 & 0 & 0 & 1 \\ 0 & 0 & 0 & 0 & 1 \\ 0 & 0 & 1 & 1 & 0 \end{bmatrix} \quad \text{and} \quad M^2 = \begin{bmatrix} 1 & 0 & 2 & 1 & 0 \\ 1 & 1 & 0 & 0 & 2 \\ 0 & 1 & 1 & 1 & 1 \\ 1 & 0 & 1 & 1 & 1 \\ 1 & 0 & 1 & 0 & 2 \end{bmatrix},$$

we find at once that:

$$R_3 = Md(M^2) + d(M^2)M - S = \begin{bmatrix} 0 & 1 & 0 & 0 & 3 \\ 1 & 0 & 2 & 0 & 0 \\ 2 & 0 & 0 & 0 & 2 \\ 0 & 0 & 2 & 0 & 2 \\ 0 & 0 & 2 & 2 & 0 \end{bmatrix}$$

To illustrate the 1, 5 entry of this last matrix, we observe that in **Figure 2**, the three redundant sequences from a to e are: $\overrightarrow{abae}$, $\overrightarrow{aece}$, and $\overrightarrow{aede}$. Let P_3 be the matrix of non-redundant paths of length 3; then $P_3 = M^3 - d(M^3) - R_3$, hence

$$P_3 = \begin{bmatrix} 0 & 0 & 1 & 0 & 1 \\ 0 & 0 & 1 & 2 & 1 \\ 0 & 0 & 0 & 1 & 0 \\ 1 & 1 & 0 & 0 & 1 \\ 1 & 1 & 0 & 0 & 0 \end{bmatrix}$$

Referring to the 1, 5 element of P_3, we see from Figure 2 that there is exactly one non-redundant path from a to e; namely $\overrightarrow{abce}$.

3.5 Status and contrastatus. We restrict ourselves to an extremely brief review of some of the ideas in the paper (11). This treatment of structural or positional status is based on the approach that if two individuals have the same number of subordinates in an organization, the one whose subordinates are as far under him as possible will have the greater status. More precisely, we regard the group or organization as in the form of a digraph with respect to whatever relation is under consideration, which for organization theory is usually "delegated authority." Then the *status* of b, written $s(b)$, is defined as the number of immediate subordinates of b plus twice the number of subordinates of b at distance 2 plus three times the number of subordinates of b at distance 3, etc. An immediate corollary of this definition of status is that $s(b)$ is the sum of the distances from b to all other points of the digraph.

Thus referring to the matrix of distances illustrated in Figure 3, we see that the status of a person is equal to the sum of the elements of the corresponding row in the matrix. There is a simple recurrence: the status of a person is equal to the sum of the status numbers of each of his immediate subordinates plus the total number of his subordinates in the organization.

Perhaps the most important concept developed in this regard is that of the contrastatus of a person. This is defined as the status he has in the organization obtained from the original one by reversing the direction in every line. Intuitively the contrastatus of an individual may be regarded as the amount of status weighing down on him from above. In view of this definition, there is a theorem for

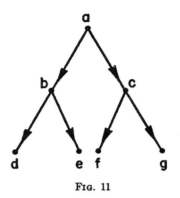

FIG. 11

contrastatus corresponding to each one for status. In Figure 11, $s(a) = 10$ while the contrastatus of a, $s'(a) = 0$. On the other hand $s(d) = 0$ while $s'(d) = 3$. Between these, $s(b) = 2$ and $s'(b) = 1$. This is the figure described verbally by Parkinson (26) in his description of how to get seven employees: $\{a, b, c, d, e, f, g\}$ to do the work of one: $\{a\}$.

If a person is given n subordinates and is told to arrange them in such a way as to maximize his status, then this can be accomplished by arranging them in a directed path. On the other hand his status will be minimized in the digraph in which there is a directed line from him to each of his subordinates, i.e., all his subordinates are immediate. If we are interested in maximizing the *gross status* of an organization with a given number of members, i.e., the sum of the status numbers of all the members, then this is done by arranging the members in the form of a directed cycle containing all of them.

We also describe various other familiar phenomena in organizations in terms of status, including the consultant, structural democracy, autocracy, and laissez-faire, as well as peer groups.

3.6 Tournaments and production schedules. Consider a tournament in which there are n players, every pair of players play each other once, and none of the games ends in a draw. For brevity let us call the resulting digraph D itself a *tournament*; in the mathematical literature D is a *complete oriented graph*.

Another interpretation of complete oriented graphs, in addition to that provided by tournaments, occurs in the consideration of production schedules. If there are n tasks to be done, and if between every pair of tasks there is a preferred ordering which is either more efficient or more economical, then the resulting digraph is also a tournament. There is a rich body of theory with regard to tournaments, much of which is still in the process of publication. Similar questions are studied in statistics as "paired comparisons;" pecking orders in a collection of hens furnish still another example of a tournament. A *complete path* in a digraph D is a directed path which contains all the points of D. A *complete cycle* is a (directed) cycle through all the points of D. The following theorem and its corollary are due to Redei, as reported in König (22).

Theorem: Every tournament has a complete path.

382

Corollary: In any tournament, the number of complete paths is odd.

Theorem: In any tournament there is a point b such that the distance from b to any other point does not exceed 2.

According to a rule of duality for digraphs, one immediately gets the following dual result: In any tournament there is a point c such that the distance from any other point to c does not exceed 2. The following theorem was independently discovered by J. Foulkes and L. Moser (in process of publication).

Theorem: In any strong tournament there is a complete cycle.

Moser provides the following interesting example as a special case of another theorem.

Example: If D is a tournament with nine players and each player wins and loses at least two matches then D is strong.

3.7 A theory of social power. The purpose of the article (12) is to contribute to the interesting theoretical investigation by French by providing a necessary and sufficient condition for the attainment of ultimate unanimity of opinions in a power structure (subject to his axiom system (6)). In addition we demonstrate the isomorphism between his theory and the theory of higher transition probabilities in Markov chains. We are able to exploit this isomorphism by translating known theorems on Markov chains into their corresponding theorems on social power. One of the results obtained in this manner is that every power structure regardless of initial opinion distribution necessarily converges to a stable distribution of ultimate opinions.

In the process of deriving this criterion for unanimity, we employ several concepts which are of independent interest. These include an "automorphic group" and a "power subgroup." For the sake of completeness, we restate the setting in the form of the following three axioms:

Axiom 1: At time $t = 0$, each of the n members holds an initial opinion given by a real number.

Axiom 2: Power (or influence) is exerted only at discrete time units.

Axiom 3: If one member exerts influence on another, then the opinion of the other member after one time unit is the arithmetic mean of the initial opinions of the two members. Similarly, if two members simultaneously act to influence a third member, then his opinion after one time unit is the arithmetic mean of their three initial opinions, etc.

We restrict the rest of this discussion to the statements of the main results in the paper (12), together with enough definitions to make them meaningful. As in Figure 2, let M denote the matrix of a digraph D which represents the power structure of a given group. Let A be the matrix obtained from M by the following process. First replace each 0 in the main diagonal of M by a 1. Then if r is the number of 1's in a given row of this last matrix, replace each 1 in this row by the fraction $1/r$; the result will be called matrix A.

A *stochastic matrix* is a square matrix with non-negative elements in which each row sum is one. A matrix is *doubly stochastic* if not only the row sums, but also the column sums, are unity.

Theorem: A strong group attains unanimity at the arithmetic mean of the initial opinions if and only if its matrix A is doubly stochastic.

In order to obtain results for groups which are not necessarily strong, we require the concept of a power subgroup. A *point basis* (see (15) or (22)) of a digraph is a minimal collection of points from which all points are reachable by a directed path. A *strong component* of a digraph is a maximal strong subgraph. It is well-known that if b is in a point basis S of a digraph and c is any point in the same strong component with b, then the set of points T obtained by removing b from S and adding c is again a point basis. We may now define a *power subgroup* as a subgroup which forms a strong component and has one of its members in a point basis. By the first theorem in this subsection, the final opinions of all members of the same power subgroup of a group are equal. We call this the final opinion of the power subgroup.

Theorem: A group attains unanimity if and only if all its power subgroups have equal final opinions.

3.8 Structural balance. Signed graphs were introduced in the papers (2, 3, 8, 9, 10) for the purpose of studying groups in which there may occur both positive and negative relationships. A *signed graph* is obtained from a graph when some of the lines are designated as *positive* and the remaining lines as *negative*. The *sign of a cycle* is the product of the signs of its lines. A signed graph is *balanced* if all its cycles are positive. Including the definition, it is possible to give : ·· equivalent conditions for balance. We require these concepts for the final section on open problems.

A signed graph is *locally balanced* at a point b if all cycles containing b are positive. A signed graph is *N-balanced* if all cycles of length $\leq N$ are positive. The *degree of balance* of a signed graph is the ratio of the number of positive cycles to the total number of cycles. The *line index* of a signed graph is the smallest number of lines whose removal results in balance. It can be shown that the line index is also equal to the smallest number of lines whose negation (changing sign) results in balance.

A *cycle basis* of graph is a maximal collection of independent cycles (see König (22)). A *positive cycle basis* of a signed graph is a cycle basis in which all cycles are positive. The *bundle* at a point in a graph is the set of all lines incident to that point. The *symmetric difference* of two sets is that set consisting of all those elements which lie in exactly one of these two sets.

Let G be a graph with p points and q lines. Then the *incidence matrix* of G (with respect to an ordering of both the points and the lines) is the p by q matrix in which the i, j entry is 1 if the i'th point a_i is on the j'th line α_j and is 0 otherwise. Thus an incidence matrix of a graph has exactly two 1's in each column. If G is a signed graph, then we define the matrix $J(G)$ as follows. First write the incidence matrix considering G as an ordinary unsigned graph. Then leave those columns corresponding to negative lines unchanged, and in each column belonging to a positive line replace exactly 1 by a -1. A matrix has the *unimodular property* if every minor determinant equals 0, $+1$, or -1.

Theorem:[4] The following statements are equivalent:

---

[4] The equivalence of conditions (1) through (5) is definitional while that of (1) with (6), (7), (8), and (9) is essentially shown in König (22). The equivalence of conditions (1) and

(1) G is a balanced signed graph.

(2) G is locally balanced at each point.

(3) G is N-balanced for all values of N.

(4) The degree of balance of G is 1.

(5) The line index of G is 0.

(6) G has a positive cycle basis.

(7) All paths between the same pair of points of G have the same sign.

(8) The set of all points of G can be partitioned into two disjoint subsets such that each negative line joins two points from different subsets.

(9) The set of all negative lines of G is the symmetric difference of a collection of bundles of G.

(10) The matrix $J(G)$ has the unimodular property.

A discussion of the relevance of structural balance to psychological theory is presented in the paper (2).

Section 4. Open Problems

We state here four important considerations which remain to be handled on both a theoretical and an empirical basis. These include variations in the strength of the relationships between different individuals, relations among more than two individuals at a time, situations involving both positive and negative relationships, and the mixture of different relations on the same group.

4.1 Relations of different strength. It is well-known that there may be different strengths of the same relation, either occuring among different pairs of individuals or among the same two persons at different times. Such variations are exemplified by: liking vs. loving, moderate power vs. complete power, occasional communication vs. frequent communication, etc. The greatest promise for such studies appears to lie in the utility for this purpose of the theory of Markov chains. This well-defined branch of probability theory has implicit in it a directed graph in which the points represent events and the directed lines (each with an assigned positive probability not exceeding 1) represent the possibility of direct passage from one event to another. The analogy between Markov chains and group relations with different strength lies in regarding the strength of a relation as a probability value.

4.2 Triadic relations. All of the structural problems which we have been considering involve relations whose building blocks are made up of relationships on pairs of individuals. These are usually called *binary* or *dyadic* relations. The first possible extension to relations on more than two individuals occurs for three individuals at a time. Such a relation is called *triadic*. As a possible example we have the ordered triple (a,b,c) to stand for "a influences b to talk to c." A fruitful mathematical theory of n-adic relations for $n > 2$ seems to be virtually completely lacking. This is probably due to the fact that binary relations correspond

---

(10) is shown in the papers: K. Heller and C. B. Tompkins, An extension of a theorem of Dantzig, Paper 14, pp. 247–252 in H. W. Kuhn and A. W. Tucker, eds., Linear inequalities and related systems, Annals of Math. Studies, No. 38. Princeton, 1956 and A. J. Hoffman and D. Gale, Appendix to the preceding reference, pp. 252–254.

to matrices, and matrix multiplication is well defined. However, triadic relations are equivalent to three-dimensional matrices, and no one has as yet provided a universally satisfactory definition of multiplication of three-dimensional matrices; it is not certain that this is possible. Attempts along these lines have recently been made in which different authors agree on how reflexivity and symmetry should be defined for triadic, or more generally, for n-adic relations. But there is no agreement on what should be taken as a reasonable definition of transitivity, not even for triadic relations. It is possible that a well-defined empirical approach to this problem might provide a clue to the development of an interesting mathematical theory of n-adic relations.

4.3 Situations involving both positive and negative relationships. While we have made a beginning in the theoretical study of such situations, this does not seem to have been studied empirically for large organizations. As an interesting illustration of a negative relationship, one may say that b has "negative power" over c if when b tries to exert power on c, c not only does not do what b wants him to do, but does something which is as far opposite as possible. Such behavior is often seen in small children. In an interview of a Japanese wife by an American reporter, she showed convincingly that because she had absolute negative power over her husband, she was able to get anything she wanted by distorting her desires. This is also reminiscent of "B'rer Rabbit in the briar patch."

4.4 Mixture of relations. An actual group of people generally has more than one relation simultaneously operating. For example, we may have social choice and communication, liking and power, liking and mutual identification, formal and informal power, etc. The study of the influence of various relations on each other is, at least empirically, in its infancy. However, this appears to be an extremely important field of endeavor.

References

1. BAVELAS, A. A mathematical model for group structures. *Applied Anthropology.* 1948, 7, 16–30.
2. CARTWRIGHT, D. AND HARARY, F. Structural balance: a generalization of Heider's theory. *Psychological Review.* 1956, 63, 277–293.
3. ——. A logical approach to the structure of interpersonal relations. Unpublished manuscript.
4. FESTINGER, L. The analysis of sociograms using matrix algebra. *Human Relations.* 1949, 2, 153–158.
5. FORSYTH, E. AND KATZ, L. A matrix approach to the analysis of sociometric data. *Sociometry.* 1946, 9, 340–347.
6. FRENCH, J. R. P., JR. A formal theory of social power. *Psychological Review.* 1956, 63, 181–194.
7. HARARY, F. The number of linear, directed, rooted, and connected graphs. *Transactions of the American Mathematical Society.* 1955, 78, 445–463.
8. ——. On the notion of balance of a signed graph. *Michigan Mathematical Journal.* 1953–54, 2, 143–146.
9. ——. On local balance and N-balance in signed graphs. *Michigan Mathematical Journal.* 1955–56, 3, 37–41.
10. ——. Structural duality. *Behavioral Science.* 1957, 2, 255–265.
11. ——. Status and contrastatus. *Sociometry,* 1959, 22, 23–43.

12. ——. A criterion for unanimity in French's theory of social power. Chapter 10 in *Studies in Social Power* (D. Cartwright, ed.), Ann Arbor: Institute for Social Research, 1959.
13. ——. A graph theoretic method for the complete reduction of a matrix, with a view toward finding its eigenvalues. To appear in *Journal of Mathematics and Physics*, 1959.
14. HARARY, F. AND NORMAN, R. Z. *Graph theory as a mathematical model in social science.* Ann Arbor: Institute for Social Research, 1953.
15. HARARY, F., NORMAN, R. Z. AND CARTWRIGHT, D. *Introduction to digraph theory for social scientists.* Ann Arbor: Institute for Social Research. To appear in 1960.
16. HARARY, F. AND ROSS, I. C. (Or Ross, I. C. and Harary, F.) On the determination of redundancies in sociometric chains. *Psychometrika.* 1952, 17, 195–208.
17. ——. The number of complete cycles in a communication network. *Journal of Social Psychology.* 1954, 40, 329–332.
18. ——. Identification of the liaison persons of an organization using the structure matrix. *Management Science.* 1955, 1, 251–258.
19. ——. A procedure for clique detection using the group matrix. *Sociometry.* 1957, 20, 205–215.
20. ——. A description of strengthening and weakening group members. *Sociometry*, 1959, 22, 139–147.
21. JACOBSON, E. AND SEASHORE, S. Communication practices in complex organizations. *Journal of Social Issues.* 1951, 7, 28–40.
22. KÖNIG, D. *Theorie der endlichen und unendlichen Graphen.* Leipzig, 1936, (reprinted New York: Chelsea Publishing Company, 1950).
23. LEAVITT, H. J. Some effects of certain communication patterns on group performance. *Journal of Abnormal and Social Psychology.* 1951, 46, 38–50.
24. LUCE, R. D. Connectivity and generalized cliques in sociometric group structure. *Psychometrika.* 1950, 15, 169–190.
25. LUCE, R. D. AND PERRY, A. D. A method of matrix analysis of group structure. *Psychometrika.* 1949, 14, 95–116.
26. PARKINSON, C. N. *Parkinson's Law.* New York: Houghton, Mifflin Co., 1957.
27. WEISS, R. S. *Process of organization.* Ann Arbor: Institute for Social Research, 1956.

From Anatol Rapoport, *Bulletin of Mathematical Biology 19*, 257-277 (1957), by
permission.

CONTRIBUTION TO THE THEORY OF RANDOM
AND BIASED NETS

ANATOL RAPOPORT
MENTAL HEALTH RESEARCH INSTITUTE
UNIVERSITY OF MICHIGAN

The probabilistic theory of random and biased nets is further developed
by the "tracing" method treated previously. A number of biases expected
to be operating in nets, particularly in sociograms, is described. Distribution of closed chain lengths is derived for random nets and for nets
with a simple "reflexive" bias. The "island model" bias is treated for
the case of two islands and a single axon tracing, resulting in a pair of
linear difference equations with two indices. The reflexive bias is extended to multiple-axon tracing by an approximate method resulting in a
modification of the random net recursion formula. Results previously obtained are compared with empirical findings and attempts are made to account for observed discrepancies.

There is increasing interest in the theory of linear graphs which
is felt to be a promising mathematical framework for certain types
of biological and sociological theories, in particular those dealing
with structure. Indeed a graph is primarily a representation of
structure in its most essential sense: the points or nodes are the
elements devoid of all content; the lines connecting them represent
relations which in the simplest case can be characterized by either
presence or absence between each pair of elements. On the simplest
level there is an isomorphism between a linear graph and a matrix.
Also the operation of matrix multiplication is applicable to the deduction of certain theorems about graphs. This mathematical apparatus has been utilized to some degree by several authors (Landahl,
1947; Landahl and Runge, 1946; Luce, 1950; Luce and Perry,
1949; Shimbel, 1948).

Topological properties of linear graphs have found application
to problems of general biology dealing with the "flow chart" organization of physiological function in the work of N. Rashevsky

389

(1954, 1955a,b, 1956) and E. Trucco (1956). Applications to social psychology have also been proposed (Harary and Norman, 1953; Cartwright and Harary, 1956).

In all of this work, the theory of linear graphs appears as an "exact" theory in the sense that each graph is supposed to describe the complete structure of some entity at least in its relevant aspects. In dealing with structures of aggregates involving very large numbers of elements, it seems advisable to develop statistical, probabilistic, or stochastic theories. Some beginnings in this direction have been made (Solomonoff and Rapoport, 1951; Rapoport, 1951a,b, 1953a,b; Katz and Powell, 1954; Allanson, 1956).

However, even a probabilistic theory can be either "exact" or approximate. In an "exact" probabilistic theory it is necessary to define rigorously a "sample space," i.e., the set of all elementary events with their *a priori* assigned probabilities, of which the events of interest (where probabilities are to be calculated) are compounded. Such an approach is taken, for example, by L. Katz and J. H. Powell (*loc. cit.*). The fundamental event is the existence or non-existence of a relation between each ordered pair of elements in a set of N elements. Since there are $N(N-1)$ such pairs from which set $2^{N(N-1)}$ subsets can be selected, it follows that Katz's sample space is the set of $2^{N(N-1)}$ linear graphs. If the probability for the existence of the relation between each pair of the set of N elements is fixed, a set of probabilities is induced on each set of points of the sample space, from which the statistical parameters of such linear graphs can be calculated. Restrictions, such as fixing the total number of existing relations, lead to the consideration of a subspace of the total sample space, which is in fact considered by Katz and Powell.

We could also begin with another assumption, for example, that exactly a directed line segments ("axons" in our terminology) issue from each of N elements. Since there are $\binom{N}{a}$ ways of selecting the targets of each set of a axons, it follows that $\binom{N}{a}^{N}$ graphs of this sort are constructible, indeed all equiprobable if every element is an equiprobable target of every axon. In both of these examples, it is tacitly assumed that all elements are distinguishable. If they are not, the probability distributions on the sample spaces must be modified accordingly. This straightforward "exact" approach depends on combinatorial analysis for its mathematical machinery and soon leads to formidable difficulties.

Another approach is to start not with the sample space of all possible graphs but with the probabilities of the events in the construction of a graph. Starting with an arbitrary element, there will be a certain probability distribution for all possible targets of its axons and so on for each target thus reached. If we consider this "tracing" of the graph as a stochastic branching process, we are still within the realm of an "exact" probabilistic theory. It is possible, however, to abandon rigor in the interest of a more manageable model by dealing only with the expected events at each step of the tracing instead of with the entire distribution of all possible events. This was the method adopted by the author in previous papers on random and biased nets (Rapoport, 1951, 1953a,b). The relation of this method to the "exact" stochastic process was discussed by H. G. Landau (1952). In the special case where only a single axon issues from each element, the "exact" theory can be easily handled. In previous papers (e.g., Rapoport, 1948; Shimbel, *loc. cit.*) the distribution of cycles of all lengths in a random net have been calculated.

We begin our present investigation by calculating the distribution of the lengths of "closed chains" in single axon random nets.

Closed chains in single axon random nets. The construction of such a net begins with the arbitrary selection of an element and the tracing of its axon to its target, say, by a random device in which all elements are equiprobably represented. The tracing then continues to the next target and so on until a previously contacted element is contacted for the second time. When this happens the tracing ends and the chain is closed. Required is to find the probability distribution of closed chain lengths.

Let $p(n)$ = the probability that the tracing is not yet ended on the nth step, i.e., that $n + 1$ distinct sites have been occupied. Then if the total number of sites is N, we have

$$p(n) = \frac{N_n}{N^n}, \tag{1}$$

where $N_n \equiv N(N - 1)\ldots(N - n + 1)$. Then the probability of a chain of length exactly n must be

$$P(n) = p(n) - p(n + 1) = \frac{N_n}{N^n} - \frac{N_{n+1}}{N^{n+1}} = \frac{N_n}{N^n}\left(1 - \frac{N - n}{N}\right) = \frac{nN_n}{N^{n+1}}. \tag{2}$$

391

Remark. It should be noted that while this result can be expected to reflect the distribution of chain lengths in a large population of *nets* constructed in this manner, it cannot be expected to reflect the distribution of chain lengths in a *single net,* because of the overlap of chains. Thus the existence of a closed chain of n steps implies the existence of a closed chain of $n - 1$ steps (namely, the one which starts with the second step of the first chain), etc. In particular, if the entire population happened to fall apart into a number of such separate chains of equal length, the distribution of chain lengths in that population would be an equiprobable one ("square") and not given by (2). This inapplicability of the distribution of chain lengths to a *particular* population in which an axon issues from each site is important to keep in mind when we try to apply such theories to actual biological or sociological nets.

Consider now a sociogram in which every member of a population names one "best friend." The result is a single axon graph of the sort described. However, even if the "best friends" are named entirely at random, the chain lengths in any particular population cannot be expected to be given by (2), because of the dependencies mentioned. Equation (2) describes the distribution of chain lengths where one chain is arbitrarily selected from one population in a large set of populations.

The independent structures in a single random net of this kind are the "cliques." Consider a net in which exactly one axon issues from each site. Therefore each axon has a unique target. However, more than one axon may reach the same target. Some sites may not be targets of any axon. Thus if we trace the chain "forward," that is, to successive targets, we get no branching and the chain ends when a site is repeated. If we trace "backwards," that is, to the origins of the axons, we may get branchings but no repeated sites. Each branch will end when an "isolate" is reached, i.e., a site which is not a target. Thus if we perform both a forward and a backward tracing, we reach a certain subset of the population with which no connections exist from other subsets either via forward or via backward tracings. We call such subsets "cliques." Figure 1 shows such a clique for a single axon net.

Thus cycles, closed chains, and cliques are structures characteristic of single axon nets. A cycle is completely described by its length (except for the identification of the sites involved). A chain consists of a cycle and a tail and is completely described

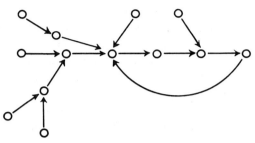

F IGURE 1.

by its total length and the length of its cycle. The problem of describing a clique is more complicated and bears an obvious relation to similar structures in organic chemistry (cf. Pólya, 1936).

Once cliques are classified in some way, the problem arises concerning the distribution of the various types of cliques in a single axon random net. These distributions *should* reflect the actual frequencies of occurrence (provided the number of cliques is not too small) since the cliques are independent of each other.

In multiple axon nets the substructures become increasingly complex, and we are forced to concentrate on simpler characteristics of such nets. One approach taken by the author (Rapoport, 1951a) was to calculate the recursion formula for the *expected* number of new sites contacted on each step of a tracing, that is, the expected number for each step is calculated on the assumption that the expected number was actually contacted on the previous step. In another paper the actual probability distribution for the number of sites was calculated for a given step, given that the total number of sites previously contacted was known (Rapoport, 1951b). Elsewhere the expected total number of sites contacted during the whole tracing, expressed as a fraction of an infinite population, was derived as a function of the "axon density" (number of axons issuing from each site) (Solomonoff and Rapoport, *loc. cit.*).

All these results were obtained for random nets where the underlying assumption is the equiprobability of targets for each axon.

In a situation where we may hope to apply the theory (e.g. structure of neural nets, sociometry, epidemiology, chain reactions) we should expect the operation of substantial biases: the targets of axons are not equiprobable. The introduction of bias leads to formidable difficulties because the abandonment of the assumption

393

of equiprobability destroys the independence of certain fundamental events. In particular the steps of the tracing cease to be independent. Nor can they in general be reduced to a Markoff process except under special assumptions, for now the whole history of a tracing has a bearing on the probability distribution of the events associated with each step.

However, besides the difficulties of calculation, there are other difficulties involved of a more fundamental nature, namely, of stating precisely in mathematical terms what bias is operating. We wish naturally to investigate biases which can be reasonably expected to reflect some situation of interest, but then we find that it is difficult to translate intuitively conceived biases into formal postulates.

To take an example, it is a commonplace observation that the relation of acquaintance is *to a certain degree* transitive in the sense that acquaintances of acquaintances have a greater probability of being acquaintances than arbitrarily selected individuals. However, this "bias," although seemingly clear, is not at all easy to express in terms of biases imposed on the events associated with the tracing procedure. Therefore, it is advisable to introduce biases formally as affecting the events associated with the tracing procedure, so that they can enter the calculations, instead of trying to derive them from the actual situation envisaged. We hope that some of such formally introduced biases may be approximately equivalent in their effects upon the derived statistical parameters to the biases actually operating.

We submit a tentative list of such formal biases.

1. *Geographical distance bias*. The elements are supposed to be immersed in a metric space, and the probability that an axon issuing from one element "synapses" on another is some function of the distance between the two elements. Aside from the difficulties concomitant to this bias in the calculation of conditional probabilities, this model poses the problem of choosing a suitable "space" for a given situation. Clearly, if the net is a sociogram, we are dealing with "social space." Distance in such spaces could be appropriately defined, but nothing whatsoever is known about the dimensionality or metrics of spaces which are appropriate models of social space. In principle we could pose the problem of inferring the character of such a space from the observed statistical parameters, but a theoretical framework for this approach is still

lacking. Where ordinary geometric space can be taken, the latter difficulty is obviated, but the former one remains, as is seen in some formulations of mathematical genetics of populations.

2. *The "island model."* We may suppose that the elements are divided into a number of mutually exclusive subsets within which the connection probabilities are random but where a finite probability exists of crossing from one such subset to another. This is the "island" or "cellulated" model which has been treated in some detail in mathematical genetics (cf., e.g., Wright, 1932). It seems a reasonable model for some types of sociograms.

3. *Overlapping acquaintance circles.* Here an element is generally a member of more than one set, so that even if no crossing of set boundaries occurs, that is, no two elements are connected unless they belong to the same set, nevertheless the entire population can be connected. This model underlies some of the author's previous results on biased nets (Rapoport 1953a,b) in which very crude approximations were used. The following problem illustrates this type of model in a simple but interesting case.

Let the elements be arranged in a linear array and each axon have equal probabilities of connection to each of its $2k$ neighbors (k on each side). It is required to compute the distribution of the lengths of closed chains and cycles. Put in another way, consider a random walk in which 1 to k steps may be taken in either direction and which terminates once a site previously occupied is occupied again. Compute the distribution of the lengths of walks. For $k = 1$, the problem is trivial, because the walk ends if and only if the direction is reversed. For $k = 2$, the problem is considerably more involved. The solution for this case was obtained by C. Foster and the author (in press).

The solution is obtained in iterated form as a sequence of "convolutions." Define

$$F_0(x) = \sum_{i=0}^{i=[x/3]} (1/2)^{x+3i} \frac{(x-2i)!}{(x-3i)!\, i!}.$$

(3)

Then if

$$F_{k+1}(x) = \sum_{i=2}^{x} F_k(x-i)\, (1/4)^i + F_k(x),$$

(4)

395

then the probability of a path of at least n steps is given by

$$p(n) = 2 F_2(n), \tag{5}$$

and the probability of a path of exactly n steps by

$$P(n) = 2 [F_2(n - 1) - F_2(n)]. \tag{6}$$

Generalization is indicated to $k > 2$ and to grids of several dimensions. If solutions for any k and any number of dimensions were available, we could compare such distributions with actual ones (say, in sociograms where the "step" is the naming of the best friend). The best fitting model, where k and the number of dimensions would be the parameters, could then be taken as an "overlapping acquaintance circle" model of social space, an acquaintance circle being a neighborhood of a certain size in a space of a certain number of dimensions.

4. *Reflexive bias.* This is a bias of connection from a target back to the origin of an axon. This model also seems appropriate in the tracing of a sociogram. More generally, the reflexive bias operates with respect to all elements already reached in a tracing, the magnitude of the bias being a function of the number of steps to the element in question.

5. *Force field bias.* Here certain elements are endowed with a "drawing power," so that connection to those elements are more probable. In a special case we may suppose that the population consists of two classes, the "popular" and the "unpopular," the popular elements having a greater probability of being targets. In a neural net these elements would constitute some "center" to which most connections go.

In this paper, we consider the following models related to the probabilistic characteristics of biased nets.

a) Distribution of chain lengths in single axon tracings with mutually exclusive sets with a finite probability of crossing over for the case of two sets.

b) Distribution of chain lengths in a single axon tracing with reflexive bias.

c) An approximate recursion formula for the number of elements reached in successive steps of a multiple axon tracing with reflexive bias.

d) A recursion formula for the case of a force field bias for the special case of two classes.

Data from a sociogram will be compared with the theoretical results previously obtained and discussed in the light of the theoretical results obtained in c and d.

Single axon tracing in a two-set population. Let the two equal sub-populations be called A and B. Let the population of each be M. Let $p(n, k)$ be the probability of tracing a chain of at least $n - 1$ steps, i.e., one in which n sites are occupied, of which $k \leqq n$ are in A, hence $n - k$ are in B. Let the probability of crossing from A to B or vice versa be x. At the completion of the $(n - 1)$st step, the last site occupied is either in A or in B. Let the corresponding probabilities be $p_A(n, k)$ and $p_B(n, k)$ so that

$$p_A(n, k) + p_B(n, k) = p(n, k). \tag{7}$$

Clearly, then, the probability of getting a chain of at least $n - 1$ steps will be given by

$$p(n) = \sum_{k=0}^{n} p(n, k), \tag{8}$$

and it remains to calculate the $p(n, k)$ which in turn will be obtained if $p_A(n, k)$ and $p_B(n, k)$ can be determined. These latter pair of functions of two discrete variables satisfy the following pair of difference equations

$$p_A(n + 1, k) = p_A(n, k - 1)(1 - x) \frac{M - (k - 1)}{M} + p_B(n, k - 1)\, x \frac{M - (k - 1)}{M};$$

$$\tag{9}$$

$$p_B(n + 1, k) = p_A(n, k)\, x\, \frac{M - (n - k)}{M} + p_B(n, k)(1 - x) \frac{M - (n - k)}{M}.$$

We will justify the first of these. The left side is the probability that $(n + 1)$st site to be occupied is in A, there being k occupied sites in A. This can happen if the nth site was also in A, in which case there were $k - 1$ occupied sites in A on the preceding step. The probability of this happening is compounded of $p_A(n, k - 1)$, $(1 - x)$ which is the probability of non-crossing, and

$[M - (k - 1)]/M$ which is the probability of not terminating the chain. Hence the first term on the right. Otherwise, the nth site was in B, in which case the path crossed from B to A; hence the second term on the right. The second equation is justified by a similar argument. Adjoining to the system (9), we have the initial conditions

$$p_A (1, 1) = 1/2; \quad p_A (1, 0) = 0;$$
$$p_B (1, 1) = 0; \quad p_B (1, 0) = 1/2 . \tag{10}$$

Equations (9) and (10) determine the functions $p_A (n, k)$ and $p_B (n, k)$, hence $p(n, k)$, hence $p(n)$, which for the special case $x = 1 - x = 1/2$ reduces to the case of the random single-axon net treated previously (Rapoport, 1948). The case $x = 1$ is equivalent to that treated by Shimbel (*loc. cit.*). The latter is a model for the case where choices are arbitrary but always, say, of the opposite sex. Generalization to an arbitrary number of sets leads to a much more complicated system in which the single parameter k must be replaced by a set of integers representing a decomposition of n. The solutions of the system are then functions of n and $m - 1$ additional parameters where m is the number of sets. To obtain $p(n)$, these functions must be summed over all the decompositions of n.

Single axon tracing with reflexive bias. In a random net the probability that one of the n sites already occupied is a target of the axon issuing from the last site occupied is

$$\frac{n}{N} = \frac{1}{N} + \frac{1}{N} + \ldots \frac{1}{N} \quad (n \text{ terms}). \tag{11}$$

The equality of the terms on the right constitutes the randomness condition. If we weight these probabilities with factors $\beta_{n-i} > 0$ ($i = 1, 2, \ldots, n$), we have reflective bias. We must, of course, have

$$\sum_{i=1}^{N} \beta_{N-i} = N , \tag{12}$$

and it is most natural to suppose that β_{n-i} is independent of n and is a monotone decreasing function of $(n - i)$. Call it $\beta(i)$. A straightforward generalization of (1) then gives

$$p(n) = \frac{[N - \beta(1)][N - \beta(1) - \beta(2)] \ldots \left[N - \sum_{i=1}^{n} \beta(i)\right]}{N^n} =$$

$$\prod_{k=1}^{n} \left[1 - \frac{\sum_{i=1}^{k} \beta(i)}{N}\right] \qquad (13)$$

For large N, we may suppose that N is infinite but that $\beta(i)/N = b(i)$ is finite so that

$$\sum_{i=1}^{\infty} b(i) = 1. \qquad (14)$$

Then

$$\log p(n) = \sum_{k=1}^{n} \log \left[1 - \sum_{i=1}^{k} b(i)\right], \qquad (15)$$

or, passing to approximations by integrals,

$$\log p(n) = \int_0^n \log \left[1 - \int_0^k b(x)\,dx\right] dk. \qquad (16)$$

Suppose now $b(i)$ is a decaying exponential, so that by our normalization condition (14), we must have

$$b(x) = ae^{-ax}. \qquad (17)$$

Equation (16) becomes

$$\log p(n) = \int_0^n \log \left[1 - \int_0^k ae^{-ax}\,dx\right] dk = \int_0^n \log e^{-ak}\,dk$$

$$= -\int_0^n ak\,dk = -an^2/2, \qquad (18)$$

so that

$$p(n) = e^{-an^2/2}. \qquad (19)$$

In other words, in the special case where the reflexive bias is an exponential function of the "distance traversed," the probability of having a chain of length at least n falls off with n as the positive half of the gaussian curve, whose variance is the reciprocal of the decay constant of the distance function.

Reflexive bias in multiple axon tracings. Formally, the result just obtained can be applied to a multiple axon tracing, but its interpretation in that case is far from clear. In the single axon tracing each axon has a unique origin; thus in a chain traced forward each site reached after the first has a unique antecedent. In a multiple axon tracing the sites reached on the nth step are clearly antecedents to those reached on the $(n + 1)$st. But it is not at all clear which are antecedent to which. This information is lost where the tracing is described only in terms of the numbers of sites (or fractions in an infinite population) reached at each step. Nevertheless we will extend the results of the previous section to multiple tracings. We recall the recursion formula derived for a random net (Rapoport, 1951a),

$$P(t + 1) = \left[1 - \sum_{j=0}^{t} P(j) \right] [1 - e^{-aP(t)}], \tag{20}$$

where $P(t)$ is the fraction of sites *newly* contacted on the tth step, and a is the number of axons issuing from each site. In applying this formula, we can solve for a, which appears formally as a function of t, thus

$$\alpha(t) = \frac{1}{P(t)} \log \frac{1 - \sum_{j=0}^{t} P(j)}{1 - \sum_{j=0}^{t+1} P(j)}. \tag{21}$$

To the extent that this function of t appears to be a *constant*, the randomness hypothesis for a given net which yields the values $P(j)$ in a tracing is corroborated. It was further shown (Rapoport 1952a) that the bias of overlapping acquaintance circles is expected to yield

$$\alpha(0) = a,$$
$$\alpha(t) \cong a' < a \, (t > 0). \tag{22}$$

400

That is, $\alpha(t)$ drops from a to a lower value for $t = 1$ as calculated from $P(1)$ and $P(2)$ and remains approximately at that level for the successive steps. Certain data from an information spread experiment (Rapoport, 1953a,b) indicated that $\alpha(1)$ is indeed drastically less than $\alpha(0)$ in all cases but that subsequently $\alpha(t)$ tends to increase with t. This increase was attributed to the conditions of the experiment and was expected to disappear in a sociogram tracing if the overlapping set model is valid. We now examine the behavior of $\alpha(t)$ in the reflexive bias model.

In a random net the probability that a given axon finds a target in any subset is proportional to the size of the subset. In particular the probability that this target is in P_i, the fraction newly contacted on the ith step, is P_i. Let now a bias be imposed so that the probability of finding a contact in P_i is $P_i (1 + \beta_{t-i})$, where β_{t-i} depends on the number of steps between the tth step (the step in question) and the ith step. Then a bias γ is imposed on the remaining targets, i.e., those sites not yet contacted. The normalization condition demands that

$$\sum_{i=0}^{t} P_i(1 + \beta_{t-i}) + \left(1 - \sum_{i=0}^{t} P_i\right)\gamma = 1. \qquad (23)$$

Solving for γ, we have

$$\gamma = \frac{1 - \displaystyle\sum_{i=0}^{t} P_i(1 + \beta_{t-i})}{1 - \displaystyle\sum_{i=0}^{t} P_i}. \qquad (24)$$

We note that for $\beta_{t-i} = 0$, γ reduces to unity, as should be the case. Recall now that equation (20) is an exponential approximation to

$$P(t+1) = \left(1 - \sum_{j=0}^{t} P_i\right)\left\{1 - \left[1 - N\left(1 - \sum_{i=0}^{t} P_i\right)^{-1}\right]^{NaP_t\left(1 - \sum_{i=0}^{t} P_i\right)}\right\}. \qquad (25)$$

Here the second term in the brace is the probability of *not* being a target of any of the axons going to unoccupied sites. When the bias γ is imposed on these axons, the exponent of the bracket acquires γ as an additional factor. Passing again to the exponential approximation, we have for this case

$$P(t + 1) = \left(1 - \sum_{j=0}^{t} P_i\right)(1 - e^{-aP_t \gamma}).$$ (26)

Remembering that $\alpha(t)$ is the coefficient of P_t in the exponent, and substituting (24) into (26), we obtain

$$\alpha(t) = a\left(1 - \frac{\displaystyle\sum_{i=0}^{t} P_i \beta_{t-i}}{1 - \displaystyle\sum_{i=0}^{t} P_i}\right)$$ (27)

The denominator in parentheses always decreases. The numerator, on the other hand, may increase or decrease depending on the behavior of P_i and on the bias parameters β_{t-i} chosen. It is clear however that, for $\beta_{t-i} > 0$, $t > 0$, $\alpha(t) < a$, as is corroborated by all data examined so far. We may ask under what conditions will $\alpha(t)$ be constant for $t > 0$, so that both the overlapping set model developed previously (Rapoport 1953b) and the present reflexive bias model are indistinguishable. This condition is obviously

$$\sum_{i=0}^{t} P_i \beta_{t-i} = A\left(1 - \sum_{i=0}^{t} P_i\right),$$ (28)

where A is a constant, a system of linear equations which may be solved for β_{t-i}. We would expect β_{t-i} to be a monotone decreasing function of i and it would be interesting to verify this result in these cases where $\alpha(t)$ is approximately constant for $t > 0$.

The "force field bias." This case is actually a generalization of the "mutually exclusive set" case where now each set or "island" is characterized by a different probability of being crossed into. In a still more general case, we have a set of directed crossing probabilities between each ordered pair of sets. The simplest case is where a "center" exists, such that all axons find targets in the center. That is to say, the probability of crossing into the center is unity; the probability of crossing out of it is zero; and all targets are equiprobable within the center. Except for the arbitrarily selected set P_0, all the P_i will be in the center; and from the first step of the tracing on, the model is equivalent to a random net. However when dealing with actual data the existence of the center is not known. It may be detected by observing the behavior of $\alpha(t)$ which is deducible directly from the P_i. This "apparent" $\alpha(t)$ will no longer be constant. Another function will be constant, which we now compute.

Let f be the fraction of elements in the "center." Then, since P_0 is chosen arbitrarily, fP_0 of these are expected to be in the center. All the subsequent P_i are also in the center. Equation (20) now has the form

$$P(t + 1) = \left[f - fP_0 - \sum_{j=1}^{t} P(j) \right] [1 - e^{-aP(t)}] . \qquad (29)$$

Solving for the coefficient of P_t in the exponent as before, we have

$$\alpha_1(t) = \frac{1}{P_t} \log \frac{f_1 - \sum_{i=0}^{t} P_i}{f_1 - \sum_{i=0}^{t+1} P_i} , \qquad (30)$$

where now

$$f_1 = f + P_0 (1 - f) . \qquad (31)$$

We see that $f_1 < 1$ so long as $f < 1$. To compute theoretically the behavior of the "apparent" $\alpha(t)$ given by (21), the P_i must be determined from the recursion formula (29), a laborious task since no closed form is known for $P(j)$. However, the effect of the "center" can be estimated in any given set of data in which the $P(j)$ are known.

Applications of the foregoing to some experimental data. A sociogram of an elementary school of some 250 children was obtained in the following way. Each pupil was asked to name ten friends, who were also pupils in the school, in the order of intimacy. In this way there was obtained a card for each child on which ten names were listed, the first of which was supposedly the "best friend" and so on. Single axon and multiple axon tracings could then be made from these cards. We could, for example, make several single axon tracings through the "best friend" in which the target of each axon was always the first name on the card, or through the kth friend, where the target was always the kth name.

So far the only multiple tracings were made with $a = 2$. In particular it had been conjectured on the basis of the overlapping set model that the behavior of $\alpha(t)$ should be given by equation (22). Moreover, it was argued that tracings through the names high on the list should result in a greater departure of $\alpha(t)$ from a for $t > 0$ than tracings through names low on the list. Accordingly 10 tracings each were made through the first two names, the middle two names, and the last two names on the list. The $P(t)$ averaged over the ten tracings and the computed $\alpha(t)$ are given in Tables I, II, and III.

TABLE I

t	0	1	2	3	4	5	6
$P(t)$ ×2500	50	96	122	133	121	104	98
$\alpha(t)$	2.0	1.40	1.25	1.11	1.20	1.32	1.12

Tracing through the first two names on each card.

TABLE II

t	0	1	2	3	4	5	6	7	8	9
$P(t)$ ×2500	50	95	147	195	198	196	183	166	139	102
$\alpha(t)$	2.0	1.70	1.58	1.33	1.46	1.48	1.68	1.74	1.69	2.09

Tracing through the middle two names on each card.

TABLE III

t	0	1	2	3	4	5	6	7	8	9
$P(t)$ ×2500	50	95	157	197	196	151	147	131	111	82
$\alpha(t)$	2.0	1.81	1.50	1.31	1.10	1.52	1.55	1.60	1.51	1.60

Tracing through the last two names on each card.

We note the following characteristics of the data:

1. $\alpha(0) = 2$ in all cases, agreeing exactly with the fixed value of the parameter a, which should be the case since $P(0)$ are se-

lected at random. This is reflected in the near-equality of $P(1)$ in all three cases.

2. $\alpha(1) < 2$ in all cases; moreover the drop is most pronounced in the tracing through the first two names, less pronounced in the tracing through the middle two names, and least pronounced in the tracing through the last two names on the list in qualitative agreement with the theory.

3. Instead of the steady rise in $\alpha(t)$ for $t > 1$ which was observed in the information spread experiment (cf. Rapoport 1953b), $\alpha(t)$ declines in the first half of the process and rises in the last half. (Except for the last value in Table I.)

4. We note that $P(t)$ increases in the first part of the process and decreases in the second. The quantity $\log \left[\left(1 - \sum^{t} P(j)\right/ \left(1 - \sum^{t+1} P(j)\right)\right]$, whose calculation is not shown in the tables, behaves similarly. By our theory, the ratio of these two quantities, that is, $\alpha(t)$, should remain approximately constant for $t > 1$. Their similar behavior facilitates this result, but apparently the variation of $P(t)$ more than compensates for the variation of the other.

If the concave upward curve for $\alpha(t)$ is real and not an artifact of random fluctuation, then the overlapping set model is not corroborated by these data, and we have the choice of either seeking another model or of trying to modify the existing one by some additional considerations. Two attempts were made in this direction, one involving a reflexive bias to the immediately preceeding step only and one involving the postulate of a "center." Both modifications accounted for the successive drops in $\alpha(t)$ for $t = 1, 2, 3, 4$ but resulted in further drops for the remainder of the process thus failing to explain the subsequent rise.

Needless to say additional modifications of the model become increasingly *ad hoc* and eventually lose theoretical significance. Modifications are worth while only if on their basis additional effects can be predicted which are then verified.

It is possible to account qualitatively for the initial fall and subsequent rise of $\alpha(t)$ on the basis of an "island" model and to derive an additional prediction to be tested. Suppose the population is divided into several mutually exclusive sets, and suppose $P(0)$ is sufficiently small so that not all sets are represented in that sample. While no new sets are represented in the $P(t)$, the tracing is equivalent to one in a random net but with a *smaller* population. As a result, the apparent $\alpha(t)$ will be declining. This has not been shown theoretically although it is intuitively evident and can be demonstrated on our set of data. When, however, at some stage of the process a new set is "seeded," the initial rate of increase of $P(t)$ in that set is great, as it always is in the beginning of the tracing and so the over-all rate of increase of $P(t)$ gets a "boost" (or its rate of fall declines) with the result that the apparent $\alpha(t)$ again increases. This should occur every time a new set is crossed into while old ones become saturated. If this is so, then the fluctuations in $\alpha(t)$ should be the more pronounced the smaller the initial fraction $P(0)$.

To test this hypothesis, tracings were done through the first two names, with $P(0) = .04$ instead of .02 as in the other tracings. The results averaged over five tracings as shown in Table IV.

TABLE IV

t	0	1	2	3	4	5	6
$P(t)$ $\times 2500$	100	193	216	207	170	140	112
$\alpha(t)$	2.0	1.33	1.27	1.21	1.26	1.41	1.19

Tracing through the first two names with a larger initial sample.

The "dip" in the middle is still present though seemingly less pronounced. The last value is again lower than the preceding one as in Table I, with which Table IV is in fairly good agreement.

The question of the "dip," then, remains open. Without a thorough statistical analysis it is impossible to say whether the effect is real or a fortuitous result of fluctuations. Thorough statistical analysis cannot be undertaken without a fairly rigorous mathematical model of the process, which, in turn, has to be a genuine stochastic model rather than a recursion equation for the most likely values of $P(t)$.

Discussion. It is evident that questions relating to the statistical structure of nets are exceedingly involved both in their formulation and in the computations they entail. In particular all the multiple axon tracing models so far considered are devoid of mathematical rigor even in their simplest formulation and become increasingly more crude as they are modified by imposed biases, so that it is impossible to tell at which point a mathematical theory gives way to a weakly rationalized, "guessed" equation which might as well have been obtained empirically.

On the positive side, a large number of statistical parameters can be observed in any real net. Given a certain stability of these parameters with respect to several nets of the same type, we could hope to pass from an empirical observation of their behavior to the building of mathematical models from which the statistical parameters could be derived.

As an example, consider once more a single axon sociogram. If it is a random net, then the distribution of sites having respectively none, one, two, etc., axons terminating on them ought to be a Poisson distribution with unity as mean, i.e.,

$$p_1(n) = e^{-1}/n!, \qquad (32)$$

where $p_1(n)$ is the probability of a site receiving n axons. Similarly in a tracing with a axons per site, the distribution ought to be

$$p_a(n) = a^n e^{-a}/n!. \qquad (33)$$

We have examined several single axon tracings in our school sociogram. The single axon tracing through the "best friend" gave a very good fit to the Poisson distribution. However all other tracings (through "second best friend," etc.) gave departures from the Poisson distribution, all in the same direction—the number of "normals" (those receiving a single choice in a single axon tracing) was reduced in each case. The ten-axon tracing involving all the friends named gave a definitely bimodal distribution with a depression at the expected peak. Here may be evidence of a bias roughly described by the force–field model: the population can be divided into the popular and the unpopular. It should be noted incidentally that the Poisson distribution characteristic of a random net is sensitive to some biases but not to others. It would not, for example, be sensitive to the bias of the "island model" provided the populations of the islands were sufficiently large. On the other hand a departure from the Poisson distribution should become apparent in a "force field" bias model.

Another striking result of the single axon tracings has to do with the number of resulting cliques and the sizes of their cycles.

The "best friend" tracing resulted in our population of 250 falling apart into 43 cliques, 12 of them couples, all cycles but one being 2-cycles. Tracing through the "second friend" gave only 27 cliques; tracing through the last friend named only 12 cliques, cycles of various sizes being well represented. Theoretical explanation of this decrease of the number of cliques with the "social distance" associated with the axon which is traced awaits the creation of an appropriate mathematical model.

A method is thus indicated for describing nets of relations in terms of their departures from random nets. Different statistical parameters show different "sensitivities" to departures resulting from different kinds of bias. It seems desirable to have an extensive theory of these dependencies so that a whole *battery* of measurements can be applied to a given net to determine what sort of bias predicts the greatest number of relations among its statistical parameters, expecially since a great number of such statistical parameters can now be empirically obtained by proper use of computing machinery.

LITERATURE

Allanson, J. T. 1956. "Some Properties of a Randomly Connected Neural Network." *Information Theory*. New York: Academic Press; London: Butterworth Scientific Publications.

Cartwright D. and F. Harary. 1956. "Structural Balance: A Generalization of Heider's Theory." *Psychol. Rev.*, **63**, 277–93.

Foster, C. and A. Rapoport. 1957. "The Case of the Forgetful Burglar." *The Mathematical Monthly* (in press).

Harary, F. and R. Z. Norman. 1953. *Graph Theory as a Mathematical Model in Social Science*. Ann Arbor: Institute for Social Research.

Katz, L. and J. H. Powell. 1954. "The Number of Locally Restricted Directed Graphs." *Proc. Amer. Math. Soc.*, **5**, 621–26.

Landahl, H. D. 1947. "Outline of a Matrix Calculus for Neural Nets." *Bull. Math. Biophysics*, **9**, 99–108.

———— and R. Runge. 1946. "Outline of a Matrix Algebra for Neural Nets." *Ibid.*, **8**, 75–81.

Landau, H. G. 1952. "On Some Problems of Random Nets." *Ibid.*, **14**, 203–12.

Luce, R. D. 1950. "Connectivity and Generalized Cliques in Sociometric Group Structure." *Psychometrika*, **15**, 169–90.

———— and A. D. Perry. 1949. "A Method of Matrix Analysis of Group Structure." *Psychometrika*, **14**, 95–116.

Polya, G. 1936. "Sur le nombre des isoméres de certains composés chimiques." *Comptes Rendus Acad. Sci. Paris*, **202**, 1554–6.

Rapoport, A. 1948. "Cycle Distribution in Random Nets," *Bull. Math. Biophysics*, **10**, 145—57.

————. 1951a. "Nets with Distance Bias," *Ibid.*, **13**, 85–91.

————. 1951b. "The Probability Distribution of Distinct Hits on Closely Packed Targets," *Ibid.*, 13, 133–37.

————. 1953a. "Spread of Information Through a Population with Socio-Structural Bias: I. Assumption of Transitivity," *Ibid.*, 15, 523–33.

————. 1953b. "Spread of Information Through a Population with Socio-structural Bias: II. Various Models with Partial Transitivity," *Ibid.*, 15, 535–43.

Rashevsky, N. 1954. "Topology and Life: In Search of General Mathematical Principles in Biology and Sociology," *Bull. Math. Biophysics*, 16, 317–48.

————. 1955a. "Some Theorems in Topology and a Possible Biological Application," *Ibid.*, 17, 111–29.

————. 1955b. "Some Remarks on Topological Biology," *Ibid.*, 17, 207–18.

————. 1956. "The Geometrization of Biology," *Ibid.*, 18, 31–56.

Shimbel, A. 1948. "An Analysis of Theoretical Systems of Differentiating Nervous Tissue," *Bull. Math. Biophysics*, 10, 131–43.

Solomonoff, R. and A. Rapoport. 1951. "Connectivity of Random Nets," *Bull. Math. Biophysics*, 13, 107–17.

Trucco, E. 1956. "On The Information Content of Graphs: Compound Symbols; Different States for Each Point," *Bull. Math. Biophysics*, 18, 237–53.

Wright, S. 1932. "The Roles of Mutation, Inbreeding, Crossbreeding, and Selection in Evolution," *Proc. Sixth Int. Congress Genetics*, 1, 356–66.

A Method for Detecting Structure in Sociometric Data

Paul W. Holland[1]
Harvard University

Samuel Leinhardt[2]
Carnegie-Mellon University

The authors focus on developing standardized measures for models of structure in interpersonal relations. A theorem is presented which yields expectations and variances for measures based on triads. Random models for these measures are discussed and the procedure is carried out for a model of a partial order. This model contains as special cases a number of previously suggested models, including the structural balance model of Cartwright and Harary, Davis's clustering model, and the ranked-clusters model of Davis and Leinhardt. In an illustrative example, eight sociograms are analyzed and the general model is compared with the special case of ranked clusters.

1. INTRODUCTION

A variety of models have been proposed which relate group structure to interdependences among interpersonal relations. Graph theory, because it is concerned with the characteristics of sets of points connected by relations, has been a natural language in which to express these models of small-scale social structure. In their classic paper, Cartwright and Harary (1956) used graph theory to restate Heider's (1946) balance theory and proposed a theorem which, by showing that balance implied the dichotomization of groups along lines of interpersonal sentiment, provided an important insight into the nature of the social structure of groups. Davis (1967) recognized that the decomposition of groups into only two cliques was simply not empirically demonstrable; he expanded upon structural balance by indicating what conditions were necessary for clustering, the development of one or more cliques. Balance, thus, was made a special case of a more general graph theoretic model which seemed more adequately to describe the structure of interpersonal sentiment. Following this work, Davis and Leinhardt (1970) combined two common social structural components, status and clusters, by showing how directed sentiment relations could generate a structure incorporating a system of hierarchically arranged cliques. In a recent report (Holland and Leinhardt 1970), we have shown that even this ranked-clusters

[1] Research supported by National Science Foundation grants GP-8774 and GS-2044X1.

[2] Research supported by a Social Science Research Council postdoctoral fellowship.

model is a special case of a more generally applicable structural model, that of a partial order, and, incidentally, with this model we have re-established the connection to Heider's theory by proposing that transitivity is an important structural property of positive interpersonal sentiment (Heider 1958).

The most general import of these mathematical models is that they demonstrate how complex networks can be the result of interdependencies among interpersonal sentiment relations. Nonetheless, while meaningful theoretical insights can result from expressing social theory mathematically, these are not sufficient in themselves to argue for the the acceptance of theory. It still remains for empirical verification to help us distinguish formal theory from formal nonsense; in this effort graph theory, because of its deterministic quality, has limited use. For example, a statement which implies that a group cannot be balanced if a line between two points serves to link two otherwise disconnected components may follow logically from the axioms of graph theory; it does not make much sense in the logic of empirical sociology. The problem is no less severe in models which purport to be closer representations of reality. A group may similarly fail to be partially ordered or possess a ranked clustering because of one contradictory line. The added complication in these cases is that the offending relation is not readily observed.

If these problems are to be avoided and these models are to be of scientific use, they must be expressed probabilistically and measures which gauge the fit of empirical data to them must be developed. However, when deterministic graph theoretic statements are replaced by propositions of tendency, the acceptance or rejection of a hypothesis becomes complicated, and techniques are necessary which permit the statistical significance of a measured tendency to be judged. While some effort has been made to develop measures of tendency, strength, and fit for the various structural models, there has been only limited discussion of randomness in this context and only meager information exists on the distributions of these structural indices (Harary, Norman, and Cartwright 1965, pp. 339–62; Davis and Leinhardt 1970). Thus, it is extremely difficult (if not impossible) to know the significance of some measured tendency or to gauge, in general, the closeness with which the graph theoretic models of structure describe social behavior.

It is our aim in this paper to present techniques which can assist in solving this problem by developing an index of transitivity for a general model, a partial order, noting that the procedure is applicable to all special cases. We then present a theorem which we use to generate expectations and variances for our structural model. This is followed by a discussion of the appropriateness of several random models for sociometric data, and an explanation of why we have chosen one which constrains pairs. This random distribution is then employed in generating tables of probabilities for our standardized transitivity measure. The approximate normality of this measure is substantiated through the analysis of a simulation study. To demonstrate the use of these techniques, eight sociograms are analyzed and the results obtained are compared with those for the ranked clusterers model of Davis and Leinhardt.

2. A STRUCTURAL MODEL

Sociometric data are often in the form of a set of individuals, X, together with a binary "choice relation," C, defined on X by xCy, if and only if person x chooses person y in the sociometric test. (To avoid trivial exceptions, we make the convention that xCx for all x, even though there is no implication that x actually chooses himself in the sociometric test.) In this paper, sociometric data—that is, (X,C)—will be said to exhibit *structure* if the choice relation C is *transitive*. In technical terms, this means that for any x,y,z in X, if xCy and yCz, then xCz. Briefly, our structural model is that (X,C) is a *partially ordered set* (not necessarily antisymmetric), and the central aim of this paper is to present a method for detecting tendencies in the direction of this type of structure which can be applied to sociometric data. For our present purposes, transitivity is a convenient ideal structural model against which we may compare actual sociograms.

The assumption that C is transitive is general and contains as special cases several earlier models: for example, balance (Cartwright and Harary 1956), clustering (Davis 1968, pp. 544–51), ranked clustering (Davis and Leinhardt 1970), transitive tournaments (Landau 1951a, 1951b, 1953), and quasi-series (Hempel 1952, pp. 58–62). We discuss the substantive basis and implications of this model and relate it to previous ones elsewhere (Holland and Leinhardt 1970), consequently we will only consider these important topics briefly in the next section of this report.

3. TRANSITIVITY AND TRIADS

In a given sociogram, to verify whether or not C is transitive, every ordered triple of distinct individuals (x,y,z) must be examined. If xCy and yCz, then for C to be transitive xCz must also hold. If for some triple x,y,z it occurs that xCy and yCz but x does not choose z, then C is *intransitive*. On the other hand, if xCy but y does not choose z, or if yCz but x does not choose y, or if neither xCy nor yCz, then the question of transitivity is not relevant because the hypothesis of the transitivity condition—that is, the "if" component, is not satisfied—x may or may not choose z without contradicting the transitivity of C. When the hypothesis of the transitivity condition is not satisfied for a particular triple x,y,z, their relationship to each other is *vacuously* transitive.

Figure 1 shows all of the sixteen possible relationships that can obtain between any three people in a sociogram. A single arrow $x \rightarrow y$ means that xCy but y did not choose x (an asymmetric pair). A double arrow $x \leftrightarrow y$ means that xCy and yCx (a mutual pair). No arrow means that neither x nor y chose the other (a null pair).

The triads are labeled according to the number of mutual, asymmetric, and null pairs (in that order) which they contain. Thus, a 201 triad contains two mutual, no asymmetric, and one null pair. Nonisomorphic triad types with equal numbers of pair types are further differentiated by letters (e.g., 021U, 021D, and 021C).

On the left side of figure 1 are the nine triad types that exhibit no intransitivities (the transitive and vacuously transitive triads); on the right side are the seven triad types that exhibit at least one intransitivity (the intransitive triads). By an intransitivity, we mean that for some orientation of three individuals, say x,y,z, we have xCy and yCz but x does not choose z.

To say that C is a transitive relation on X is equivalent to saying that none of the seven intransitive triads appear in the sociogram. To discover whether or not C is transitive for a given sociogram, it is sufficient to examine every unordered triple of distinct individuals to see if the triad they form falls on the left or the right side of figure 1. If they all fall on the left, C is transitive; otherwise, it is not.

By considering the triads of figure 1, we may see how the several structural models we have mentioned can be considered to be special cases of a partial order. Were we unable to find in our examination of a graph's triples either intransitive or 012 triads, then we would have a ranked clustering. Additional absences of 003, 021U, 021D, and 102 triads would mean that a quasi-order existed. If only 003 and 102 triads appeared, the structure would be a clustering. If no 003 triads occurred and only 102 triads were found, balance would be indicated. Finally, 030T triads as the sole arrangements of triples would mean that the graph was a transitive tournament.

Returning to our own model, for a "live" sociogram, C will almost certainly not be transitive. Therefore, the number of intransitive triads possessed by the sociogram is a measure of how transitive C is. If there are only a few intransitive triads in the sociogram, then C is tending toward transitivity. On the other hand, if there are about as many intransitive triads as would be expected by chance, then there is little evidence that C has a tendency to be transitive. Let T be the number of intransitive triads in a given sociogram and μ_T and σ_T be the mean and standard deviation of T under the null hypothesis that the sociogram

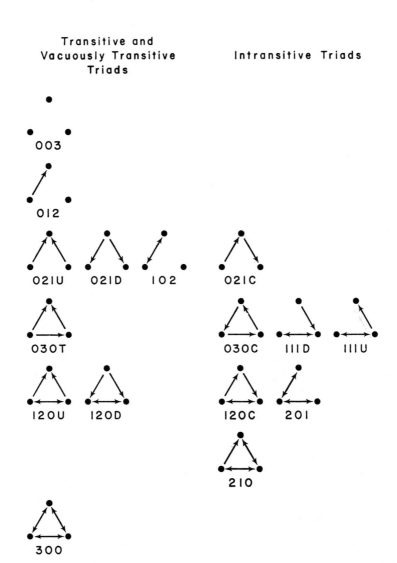

FIG. 1.—All sixteen triad types arranged vertically by number of choices made and divided horizontally into those with no intransitivities and those with at least one.

is "random" (precisely what this means will be discussed in detail in the next section). Define the index τ by:

$$\tau = \frac{T - \mu_T}{\sigma_T}. \tag{1}$$

The measure τ is our proposed transitivity index. It is a minimum when C is transitive and has mean zero and variance one under the assumption that the sociogram is "random."

This type of structural index is similar to that proposed in the paper of Davis and Leinhardt (1970). Their structural model is also defined in terms of triads, but their "non-permissible" triads include one which our model considers to be permissible (i.e., transitive). Their structural index is

$$\delta = \frac{D - \mu_D}{\mu_D}, \tag{2}$$

where D is the number of nonpermissible triads (in their sense) and μ_D is its expected value under the chance hypothesis. The index δ has a minimum of -1.00 and may be expressed in terms of the percentage of fewer nonpermissible triads than expected. When their paper was written, the variance of δ was not known and thus significance levels could not be given for it. There are various theoretical reasons why τ and δ should both have approximate normal distributions under the chance hypothesis; in section 5 we shall indicate the results of a simulation study that support this conjecture. Because τ is in standardized form, approximate significance levels for an observed value of τ may be obtained by referring it to a table of the percentage points of the normal distribution. The appropriate test is one-sided, and rejection of randomness in favor of the transitivity model is indicated by sufficiently large negative values of τ.

The actual computations of T from a sociogram, and of μ_T and σ_T from the formulas given in section 5 are very tedious. Consequently, in practice the value of τ must be found with the aid of a computer. One of us (Leinhardt) has written a FORTRAN IV program that does sociometric analyses, including the computation of τ and δ.[3]

It should also be pointed out that τ and δ may be viewed as generalizations of the index of intransitivity given by Kendall and Smith (1939) for paired comparison data. In that case, there are no mutual or null choices; therefore only two possible triads can occur, and one of these falls on the right side of figure 1. Their measure counted all the examples of intransitive triads in the graph.

[3] This program has been used on the Harvard Computer Center's IBM 360-65, and Carnegie-Mellon University's IBM 360-67. Copies may be obtained from Samuel Leinhardt, Carnegie-Mellon University, School of Urban and Public Affairs, Pittsburgh, Pennsylvania 15213.

4. RANDOM DISTRIBUTIONS IN SOCIOMETRY

The use of "random" distributions to evaluate the statistical significance of observed features in sociograms is a standard practice. Moreno (1953) simulated "random groups" by hand before the theoretical analyses were available. We feel that there are certain subtleties that arise in the choice of random distributions which have not received proper attention. Consequently, this section is devoted to developing a guideline for choosing random distributions for sociometric analyses.

It is convenient to discuss random models in sociometry in the context of sociomatrices rather than sociograms. Let $X_{ij} = 1$ if person i chooses person j, and $X_{ij} = 0$ otherwise. Let $X_{ii} = 0$ by convention; (X_{ij}) is the $g \times g$ sociomatrix. The row total $X_{i+} = X_{i1} + X_{i2} + \ldots + X_{ig}$ is the number of choices made by person i. The column total $X_{+j} = X_{1j} + X_{2j} + \ldots + X_{gj}$ is the number of choices received by person j. The number of mutual choices in the sociogram is

$$M = \sum_{i,j} X_{ij} X_{ji} .$$

An early finding was that sociometric status—the distribution of the X_{+j}—is not in accord with what would be expected by chance. In this case "chance" means that each person i distributed his X_{i+} choices at random to the $g - 1$ other group members. More technically, this means that the "chance" distribution of the X_{+j} was computed under the assumption that all sociomatrices, (X_{ij}), with the given values of the row totals $X_{1+}, \ldots, X_{g+}$ are equally likely. In other words, the chance distribution of choices received was computed *conditionally* on the given values of the choices made. In many applications all subjects make the same number of choices and this simplifies the theoretical calculations.

Another finding was that the number of mutual choices M was larger than expected by chance. As before, "chance" means that the distribution of M was computed under the assumption that all sociomatrices (X_{ij}) with the given row totals were equally likely. However, it seems to us that once the first finding has been observed—differential popularity—it is inappropriate to use the *same* random distribution to evaluate the extent of mutuality. In particular, people receiving many choices are quite likely to be involved in mutual choices, while those receiving none can not be involved in any. This suggests that, once differential popularity is detected, the appropriate chance model for evaluating tendencies toward mutual choices should assume that all sociomatrices (X_{ij}) with the given values of the column totals $X_{+1}, \ldots, X_{+g}$ as well as the row totals $X_{1+}, \ldots, X_{g+}$ are equally likely. In other words, inferences about mutuality should be conditional on *both* the row and

417

column totals of the sociomatrix. Katz, Tagiuri, and Wilson (1958) indicated the difference between the two approaches toward mutuality. Results of Katz and Powell (1954) are basic to further progress in this direction, but as yet these have not been successfully applied to this problem. This practical issue notwithstanding, let us pursue the idea further.

The structural measure τ proposed in section 3 is concerned with the chance distribution of triads. This is a step further into the structure of the sociogram beyond choices received and mutual choices. Accordingly, the appropriate chance distribution for T should fix (1) choices made X_{i+}, (2) choices received X_{+j}, and (3) mutual choices M, and assume that all sociomatrices (X_{ij}) with the given values of these quantities are equally likely. Unfortunately, the mathematical results needed to implement this analysis are not available. Until they are, a reasonable attitude is to ask how can these three conditions be relaxed in order to produce a feasible and yet reasonable chance distribution for T? One promising direction would be to fix choices made *and* the number of mutual pairs. Even this is not available at present. Weakening this criterion one further step leaves us with two possibilities: (1) fix choices made only, or (2) fix the number of mutual, asymmetric, and null pair relations. Since the first alternative is what we are trying to avoid, we have adopted the second. This random distribution was also used by Davis and Leinhardt (1970). Its advantage is that it allows us to eliminate the effect of the number of mutual, asymmetric, and null pairs in the group. Its disadvantage is that it does not allow for the fact that everyone in the group may have made the same number of choices, nor does it allow for the effect of a "star" who receives significantly more choices than the others and the "isolate" who receives significantly fewer choices. Both of these additional constraints eventually should be brought into the analysis.

In detail, the random model we shall use to compute μ_T and σ_T is as follows. Let m, a, and n denote the actual number of mutual, asymmetric, and null pairs, respectively, in a given sociogram. Then $m + a + n = g(g - 1)/2$, the total number of pairs. Randomly and without replacement, these m (mutual), a (asymmetric), and n (null) pairs are distributed to the pairs of group members so that all arrangements are equally likely. In practice this might be done as follows. Assume the individuals are numbered from 1 to g. Put $g(g - 1)/2$ balls, numbered consecutively from 1 to $g(g - 1)/2$, into an urn. Let ball 1 refer to the pair (1,2), ball 2 to pair (1,3), etc.; ball $g - 1$ to pair (1,g), ball g to pair (2,3), ball $g + 1$ to pair (2,4) etc.; and finally ball $g(g - 1)/2$ refer to pair ($g - 1,g$). This is a triangular enumeration of the unordered pairs. The balls are then drawn out of the urn, one at a time without replacement. To the pairs corresponding to the numbers on the first m balls that are drawn, assign mutual pairs. For the next a balls that are drawn, assign asymmetric pairs to the corresponding pairs of individuals. The directions of these asymmetric choices are then decided by a tosses of a fair coin. The remaining n pairs of individuals corresponding to the n undrawn balls are assigned null pair relations. If $m = 0$ and $n = 0$, this is the usual random distribution used in the analysis of paired comparisons.

5. THE DISTRIBUTION OF T

In this section, the mean and variance of T—the number of intransitive triads in a randomly constructed sociogram—is derived. We also discuss the results of a simulation study that bears on the question of the approximate normality of the chance distribution of the standardized variable τ.

Some notation is necessary. Let the intransitive triad types 021C, 030C, 111D, 111U, 120C, 201, and 210 be called type 1, type 2, . . . , type 7, respectively. Let T_i be the number of triads of type i that appear in a given sociogram. Then T, the total number of intransitive triads is

$$T = T_1 + T_2 + \ldots + T_7 . \tag{3}$$

From equation (3) and standard formulas for the mean and variance of a sum of random variables we have the relations

$$\mu_T = \sum_i E(T_i) \tag{4}$$

and

$$\sigma_T^2 = \sum_i \text{Var } (T_i) + 2 \sum_{i < j} \text{Cov } (T_i, T_j) . \tag{5}$$

Hence, in order to calculate μ_T and σ_T^2 it is sufficient to compute $E(T_i)$, $\text{Var}(T_i)$, and $\text{Cov}(T_i, T_j)$. Theorem 1, below, expresses these quantities in terms of certain probabilities which may be computed from the random model. In defining these probabilities it is convenient to let (1,2,3) denote the triad formed by the persons labeled 1, 2, and 3. The "type" of a triad will refer to the seven distinct types of intransitive triads listed above. The probabilities that appear in theorem 1 are defined as follows.

$p(j) = $ Probability that triad (1,2,3) is of type j.

$p_2(i,j) = $ Probability that triad (1,2,3) is of type i and triad (2,3,4) is of type j.

$p_1(i,j) = $ Probability that triad (1,2,3) is of type i and triad (3,4,5) is of type j.

$p_0(i,j) = $ Probability that triad (1,2,3) is of type i and triad (4,5,6) is of type j.

Note that the subscript k on $p_k(i,j)$ refers to the number of nodes that are common to the two triads in question.

Theorem 1: *If* T_i *is the number of triads of type* i *in a random graph on* g *points then,*

(a) $E(T_i) = \binom{g}{3} p(i)$,

(b) $\text{Var}\,(T_i) = \binom{g}{3} p(i)[1 - p(i)] + 3(g - 3) \binom{g}{3} [p_2(i, i) - p_0(i, i)]$

$$+ 3\binom{g-3}{2}\binom{g}{3} [p_1(i, i) - p_0(i, i)]$$

$$+ \binom{g}{3}^{(2)} [p_0(i, i) - p^2(i)] ,$$

(c) $\text{Cov}\,(T_i, T_j) = -\binom{g}{3} p(i)p(j) + 3(g - 3) \binom{g}{3} [p_2(i, j) - p_0(i, j)]$

$$+ 3\binom{g-3}{2}\binom{g}{3} [p_1(i, j) - p_0(i, j)]$$

$$+ \binom{g}{3}^{(2)} [p_0(i, j) - p(i)p(j)] .$$

The quantities $\binom{g}{3}$ and $\binom{g-3}{2}$ that appear in theorem 1 are the binomial coefficients and the expression $\binom{g}{3}^{(2)}$ is the descending factorial $\binom{g}{3}\left[\binom{g}{3} - 1\right]$.

The main value of this theorem is that it indicates what probabilities must be computed from the model and how they are combined to obtain the means, variances, and covariances of the T_i. The proof of theorem 1 is straightforward but tedious and we omit it. A similar theorem is proved by Moran (1947) for the paired comparison case mentioned above, and the technique used there generalizes to prove theorem 1 as well.

Finally, we mention that theorem 1 does not depend on the particular random model we have adopted for its validity. As it is stated—that is, without giving specific values to $p(i)$, $p_2(i,j)$, etc.—theorem 1 is true for any random method of constructing graphs that does not depend on the labels of the points.

In the case of the random distribution we have adopted, there is some simplification in theorem 1. This is due to the fact that $p_1(i,j) = p_0(i,j)$, and hence the third terms in the expressions for $\text{Var}(T_i)$ and $\text{Cov}(T_i, T_j)$ vanish.

In order to use theorem 1 in conjunction with equations (4) and (5) to compute μ_T and σ_T^2, the values of $p(i)$ and $p_k(i,j)$ must be computed. These are given in tables 1, 2, and 3. Throughout these three tables, the descending factorial notation is used, that is,

$$x^{(k)} = x(x-1) \ldots (x-k+1) .\tag{6}$$

The denominators of these probabilities D_1, D_2, D_3 are given by

$$D_1 = \binom{g}{2}^{(3)}\tag{7}$$

$$D_2 = \binom{g}{2}^{(6)}\tag{8}$$

$$D_3 = \binom{g}{2}^{(5)} .\tag{9}$$

To illustrate how these probabilities are calculated we shall consider three examples: $p(1)$, $p_0(1,1)$, and $p_2(1,3)$.

TABLE 1

$D_1 p(i)$ AS FUNCTION OF m, a, n

			TRIAD			
021C	030C	111D	111U	120C	201	210
$\frac{3}{2}a^{(2)}n$	$\frac{1}{4}a^{(3)}$	$3man$	$3man$	$\frac{3}{2}ma^{(2)}$	$3m^{(2)}n$	$3m^{(2)}a$

To compute $p(1)$, note from figure 1 that the triad labeled 021C has two asymmetric pairs and one null pair. The probability of getting these three pairs is

$$\frac{a(a-1)n}{\binom{g}{2}\left[\binom{g}{2}-1\right]\left[\binom{g}{2}-2\right]} \frac{1}{2^2} .\tag{10}$$

The terminal factor of $1/2^2$ comes from the necessity to orient the direction of the two asymmetric choices. But there are three possible positions for the null pair, that is, (1,2), (1,3), or (2,3). Furthermore, once the position of the null pair has been specified there are two ways the two asymmetric pairs can be oriented with respect to each other to produce a triad of type 1. Hence the value of $p(1)$ is $3 \cdot 2 = 6$ times the expression in equation (10) or

$$p(1) = \frac{3}{2} \frac{a^{(2)}n}{\binom{g}{2}^{(3)}} .\tag{11}$$

To compute $p_0(1,1)$ it is useful to remember that, except for the fact that the m, a, and n pairs are distributed without replacement, any two

TABLE 2

$D_2 p_0(i,j)$ AS FUNCTIONS OF m, a, n

TRIAD i	TRIAD j						
	021C	030C	111D	111U	120C	201	210
021C	$\frac{9}{4}a^{(4)}n^{(2)}+a^{(3)}n^{(2)}$	$\frac{3}{8}a^{(5)}n$	$\frac{9}{2}ma^{(3)}n^{(2)}$	$\frac{9}{2}ma^{(3)}n^{(2)}$	$\frac{9}{2}ma^{(4)}n$	$\frac{9}{2}m^{(2)}a^{(2)}n^{(2)}$	$\frac{9}{2}m^{(2)}a^{(3)}n$
030C		$\frac{1}{16}a^{(6)}$	$\frac{2}{3}ma^{(4)}n$	$\frac{2}{3}ma^{(4)}n$	$\frac{4}{3}ma^{(5)}$	$\frac{2}{3}m^{(2)}a^{(3)}n$	$\frac{4}{3}m^{(2)}a^{(4)}$
111D		$\cdots$	$9m^{(2)}a^{(2)}n^{(2)}$	$9m^{(2)}a^{(2)}n^{(2)}$	$9m^{(2)}a^{(3)}n$	$9m^{(3)}an^{(2)}$	$9m^{(3)}a^{(2)}n$
111U		$\cdots$	$\cdots$	$9m^{(2)}a^{(2)}n^{(2)}$	$\frac{9}{2}m^{(2)}a^{(3)}n$	$9m^{(3)}an^{(2)}$	$9m^{(3)}a^{(2)}n$
120C		$\cdots$	$\cdots$	$\cdots$	$\frac{9}{4}m^{(2)}a^{(4)}$	$\frac{9}{2}m^{(3)}a^{(2)}n$	$\frac{9}{2}m^{(3)}a^{(3)}$
201		$\cdots$	$\cdots$	$\cdots$	$\cdots$	$9m^{(4)}n^{(2)}$	$9m^{(4)}an$
210		$\cdots$	$\cdots$	$\cdots$	$\cdots$	$\cdots$	$9m^{(4)}a^{(2)}$

TABLE 3

$D_3 p_2(i,j)$ AS FUNCTIONS OF m, a, n

TRIAD i	TRIAD j						
	021C	030C	111D	111U	120C	201	210
021C	$\frac{1}{4}a^{(4)}n+a^{(3)}n^{(2)}$	$\frac{1}{4}a^{(4)}n$	$\frac{1}{2}ma^{(3)}n+ma^{(2)}n^{(2)}$	$\frac{1}{2}ma^{(2)}n^{(2)}+ma^{(3)}n$	$ma^{(3)}n$	$\frac{1}{2}m^{(2)}a^{(4)}n$	$m^{(2)}a^{(2)}n$
030C	$\cdots$	$\frac{1}{16}a^{(5)}$	$\frac{1}{4}ma^{(3)}n$	$\frac{1}{4}ma^{(3)}n$	$\frac{1}{4}ma^{(4)}$	0	$\frac{1}{4}m^{(2)}a^{(3)}$
111D	$\cdots$	$\cdots$	$ma^{(2)}n^{(2)}+m^{(2)}an^{(2)}+m^{(2)}a^{(2)}n$	$ma^{(2)}n^{(2)}+m^{(2)}an^{(2)}+m^{(2)}a^{(2)}n$	$\frac{1}{2}ma^{(3)}n+m^{(2)}a^{(2)}n$	$m^{(3)}an+2m^{(2)}an^{(2)}$	$m^{(3)}an+2m^{(2)}a^{(2)}n$
111U	$\cdots$	$\cdots$	$\cdots$	$ma^{(2)}n^{(2)}+m^{(2)}an^{(2)}+m^{(2)}a^{(2)}n$	$\frac{1}{2}ma^{(3)}n+m^{(2)}a^{(2)}n$	$m^{(3)}an+2m^{(2)}an^{(2)}$	$m^{(3)}an+2m^{(2)}a^{(2)}n$
120C	$\cdots$	$\cdots$	$\cdots$	$\cdots$	$\frac{1}{4}ma^{(4)}+m^{(2)}a^{(3)}$	$m^{(2)}a^{(4)}n$	$m^{(3)}a^{(2)}+m^{(2)}a^{(3)}$
201	$\cdots$	$\cdots$	$\cdots$	$\cdots$	$\cdots$	$m^{(4)}n+4m^{(3)}n^{(2)}$	$4m^{(3)}an$
210	$\cdots$	$\cdots$	$\cdots$	$\cdots$	$\cdots$	$\cdots$	$m^{(4)}a+4m^{(3)}a^{(2)}$

triads with no common edges are statistically independent. Hence $p_0(1,1)$ is essentially the "square" of $p(1)$, except that descending factorials are used rather than powers. Thus

$$p_0(1, 1) = \frac{3}{2} \frac{a^{(2)}n}{\binom{g}{2}^{(3)}} \cdot \frac{3}{2} \frac{(a-2)^{(2)}(n-1)}{\left[\binom{g}{2} - 3\right]^{(3)}} = \frac{9}{4} \frac{a^{(4)}n^{(2)}}{\binom{g}{2}^{(6)}} . \tag{12}$$

The numerator of this expression appears in the (1,1) position of table 2.

To compute probabilities like $p_2(1,3)$, it is necessary to recognize that there are two possibilities for the common edge between the two triads (1,2,3) and (2,3,4). If triad (1,2,3) is to be of type 1 and triad (2,3,4) is to be of type 3, their common edge (2,3) can be either an asymmetric or a null pair. These give two essentially different cases which are depicted in figure 2. First consider figure 2(a). There are four versions of this case—two possible orientations of the two asymmetric choices in triad (1,2,3) times the two positions for the mutual choice in triad (2,3,4). (The orientation of the asymmetric choice in a triad of type 3 is determined once the position of the mutual choice has been specified.) Each of the four versions of figure 2(a) has probability

$$\frac{ma^{(3)}n}{\binom{g}{2}^{(5)}} \frac{1}{2^3} . \tag{13}$$

Thus the contribution to $p_2(1,3)$ from the cases like figure 2(a) is four times this or

$$\frac{1}{2} \frac{ma^{(3)}n}{\binom{g}{2}^{(5)}} . \tag{14}$$

There are four versions of figure 2(b)—two possible orientations for the asymmetric choice between (2,3) times two possible positions for the other asymmetric in (1,2,3). Each of these four versions of figure 2(b) has probability

$$\frac{ma^{(2)}n^{(2)}}{\binom{g}{2}^{(5)}} \frac{1}{2^2} , \tag{15}$$

hence the contribution to $p_2(1,3)$ from the cases like figure 2(b) is four times this or

$$\frac{ma^{(2)}n^{(2)}}{\binom{g}{2}^{(5)}} . \tag{16}$$

Adding (14) and (16) together gives the value of $p_2(1,3)$, that is:

$$p_2(1,3) = \frac{(1/2)ma^{(3)}n + ma^{(2)}n^{(2)}}{\binom{g}{2}^{(5)}} . \tag{17}$$

The numerator of equation (17) appears in the (1,3) position of table 3.

In order to check our calculations of the mean and variance of T, and to ascertain how well the standard normal distribution approximates the distribution of τ (for the purpose of computing significance levels), we performed a simulation study. Twenty-seven sets of 100 random groups each were generated by a computer program. In each set of 100 random groups, the values of g, m, a, and n were fixed at designated values and random sociograms were generated using an algorithm much like the one described at the end of section 4. For each random socio-gram generated, τ was computed. For each set of 100 simulations, the mean and variance of the 100 values of τ were found, and we recorded the number of times in the set of 100 simulations that τ was less than -1.282, -1.645, and -2.326 (the one-sided negative 10 percent, 5 per-cent, and 1 percent points for the standard normal distribution, respec-tively). The agreement between the theoretical and observed means

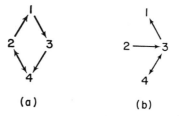

(a)   (b)

FIG. 2.—Two essentially different ways that (1,2,3) can be of type 1 (021C) while (2,3,4) is of type 3 (111D).

and variances of τ for each of the twenty-seven sets of 100 simulation is excellent. This implies that our formulas for computing the mean and variance of T are correct and, more importantly, that our computer program for performing these calculations is correct. It also argues for the adequacy of the pseudorandom number generator used to perform the simulations.

Table 4 summarizes the results of the simulation study that bear on the question of the adequacy of the approximation of the standard nor-mal distribution to the distribution of τ. The overall agreement, across all the values of g, m, a, and n, is very good. Of the total of 2,700 simu-lations, 10.2 percent of the time τ was less than the negative 10-percent point of the normal distribution. The corresponding figures for the 5 per-cent and 1 percent points are 4.7 percent and 1.1 percent, respectively. The actual distribution of τ is discrete, of course, and one expects the normal approximation to be best when the total number of possible values of τ is large. This number is a function of g, the size of the group, but also of the number of mutual (m) and asymmetric choices (a).

Examination of the individual values of τ that result for small groups—size 5, 6, and 7—reveals that the number of possible values of τ is small (sometimes as few as four or five), especially when m and a are also small. In table 4 the twenty-seven different values of g, m, a, and n used are grouped into six classes by the size of g. The number of times τ was

TABLE 4

RESULTS OF SIMULATION STUDY*

g	m	a	n	10 %	5 %	1 %
34	28	70	463	15	6	1
35	119	179	279	8	3	2
34	56	112	393	11	7	1
35	119	119	357	9	7	1
Average %	...	...	...	10.75	5.75	1.25
26	16	41	268	15	4	0
25	60	90	150	9	5	3
25	30	60	210	9	7	2
25	60	60	180	9	4	0
Average %	...	...	...	10.50	5.00	1.25
20	9	24	157	8	5	1
20	38	57	95	12	3	1
20	19	38	133	13	7	1
20	38	38	114	4	4	0
Average %	...	...	...	9.25	4.75	.75
16	6	15	99	11	8	1
16	24	36	60	5	5	3
16	12	24	84	7	3	2
15	21	21	63	7	1	0
Average %	...	...	...	7.50	4.25	1.50
13	4	10	64	16	7	1
12	13	20	33	15	6	3
12	7	13	46	17	5	0
11	11	11	33	18	3	3
10	9	9	27	11	8	1
9	7	11	18	9	6	2
Average %	...	...	...	14.33	5.83	1.67
7	1	3	17	1	1	0
7	2	4	15	14	5	1
6	3	3	9	12	4	1
5	2	3	5	4	4	0
5	1	2	7	7	7	0
Average %	...	...	...	7.60	4.20	0.40
Overall average %	...	...	...	10.2	4.7	1.1

* Number of times τ exceeded the 10 percent, 5 percent, and 1 percent cutoff points for the normal distribution for selected values of g, m, a, and n; 100 simulations for each choice of g, m, a, and n.

significant at the 10, 5, and 1 percent levels for the corresponding 100 simulations are given in the same row. The average of the number of times τ was significant for each of the six classes is also given. These averages range from 7.50 to 14.33 at the 10 percent level, 4.20 to 5.83 at the 5 percent level, and 0.40 to 1.67 at the 1 percent level. Although there is some evidence that the discreteness of the distribution causes trouble in a few cases—$g = 7$, $m = 1$, $a = 3$; $g = 5$, $m = 2$, $a = 3$; $g = 5$, $m = 1$, $a = 2$; and perhaps even $g = 20$, $m = 38$, $a = 38$—the approximation seems to work very well for most of the situations simulated. There is some evidence that for groups of size 11 to 13, the 10 percent point is really about a 15 percent point, but this effect is not carried over to the smaller significance levels. The simple practical conclusion is that if τ is referred to tables of the percentage points of the standard normal distribution and found to be significant at the 5 percent level or less, this is not due to the inadequacy of the normal approximation.

6. A COMPARISON OF τ AND δ

In this section we compare the values of τ and δ in eight sociograms drawn arbitrarily from the sociometry literature. The models upon which these two measures are based differ solely in the acceptability of 012 triads. This triad is vacuously transitive, but nonpermissible for the model of ranked clusters. This difference is an important one, both empirically and theoretically. In the analyses which follow we shall see that some groups possess far more 012 triads than the random model predicts. While these surpluses do not bear directly on the transitivity hypothesis, they are fatal to the ranked-clusters model. Indeed, Davis and Leinhardt (1970) reported that in analyses of sixty groups their hypotheses were strongly contradicted only in the case of the 012 triad. To understand the substantive significance of these findings, it will be necessary to review the structures the two models describe, so that we may see what role 012 triads play in each.

Briefly, Davis and Leinhardt predict that group structure will tend to be arranged into a system of hierarchically arranged levels, each of which may contain one or more cliques of one or more group members. This structure is a product of tendencies in pair relations. People in the same clique, they suggest, will tend to choose and be chosen by each other, while members of different cliques will tend to refrain from choosing one another. A hierarchy is introduced because lower-status group members tend also to choose higher-status members who fail to reciprocate these choices. Postulating that an arrangement of group members which contradicted these tendencies would be "inconsistent" or "uncomfortable" and that group members would tend to avoid them, Davis and Leinhardt singled out triads which presented such inconsistencies, proved that their model was implied when these triads were absent, and showed that there was some empirical justification for their theory. Their example of such a structure appears in figure 3. Since this model of ranked clusters assumes only one hierarchical system, Davis and Leinhardt concluded that the 012 triad was inconsistent: "The two N relations imply that (the group members) are all on the same level, although in different cliques; but the A relation . . . implies that (one group member) is in a higher level" a contradiction (Davis and Leinhardt 1970).

For our model, however, the structural proposition is the association of the transitive property with the interpersonal relation. Since the hypothesis of this condition is not met in the 012 triad, we consider it to be vacuously transitive. Now, if we examine this triad in light of

Levels, Cliques and Relations

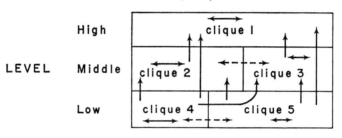

FIG. 3.—An example of ranked clusters from Davis and Leinhardt (1970)

Davis and Leinhardt's conceptualization of the structural role of pairs, we can place the two members linked by an asymmetric pair into a status hierarchy which is unrelated to the third member. This structure is a perfectly legitimate partial ordering. The prevalence of 012 triads, then, might be considered as evidence for the existence within a group of at least two components each of which may contain orderings. Multiple orderings with more than one connected component are common forms of group structure. An excellent example occurs in the often noted "sex cleavage" of children's groups. Figure 4 presents an illustration of an idealized dichotomized children's group in which the boys' and girls' subgroups are separate systems of ranked clusterings. This structure would be a perfect example of the transitivity model, while the prevalence of 012 triads in the group as a whole would contradict the hypothesis of the ranked clustering model.

In table 5, we have listed the results of analyses of eight groups. The last four columns of the table give values for δ, δ_{STD} (a version of δ standardized to have mean zero and variance one), τ, and a standardized measure for 012 triads (012_{STD}). The two new standardized values are computed in a manner analogous to that for τ. Theorem 1 is used to generate variance and covariance terms. While all necessary probabilities are not presented in our tables, their computation is straightforward and the measures are calculated in our computer program. An argument similar to that put forth for the approximate normality of τ supports referring these standardized variables to the normal distribution.

The Davis-Leinhardt model of ranked clusterings predicts that δ will be negative. On the basis of a small simulation study, Davis and Leinhardt suggest that a value of δ that is less than $-.05$ ought to be considered statistically significant. To check this, we compare δ with δ_{STD} (whose statistical significance may be ascertained by reference to normal tables) for the eight groups listed in table 5. Two facts emerge from this comparison. First, δ_{STD} is not monotonically related to δ (e.g., for

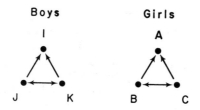

Fig. 4.—A possible group with a two-component system of ranked clusters (N pairs are not connected).

group 1, $\delta = -.152$, while $\delta_{STD} = -3.63$; and for group 2, $\delta = -.091$, while $\delta_{STD} = -4.88$). Second, if we use -1.645 as the 5 percent cutoff point for δ_{STD}, the value of $-.05$ for δ suggested by Davis and Leinhardt is fairly well supported by these eight groups. For only one group (group 4), δ is not significant, while δ_{STD} is—δ is greater than $-.05$, while δ_{STD} is less than -1.645. These two findings suggest to us that the $-.05$ cutoff point for δ is roughly right, but the strength of the significance is not correctly given by the size of δ.

The measures τ and δ_{STD} may be used to compare the transitivity model with Davis and Leinhardt's model of ranked clusterings; τ is significant in all but one case (group 5), while δ_{STD} is significant in all but two cases (groups 5 and 8). Overall, the significant values of τ are more negative than the significant values of δ_{STD}, although not always so (e.g., in group 1 $\delta_{STD} = -3.63$, while $\tau = -2.401$).

The last column of table 5 contains a standardized measure of the number of 012 triads in the group. Since the 012 triad distinguishes the transitivity model from the model of ranked clusterings, it is of interest to see how often this triad occurs in a sociogram. If we use a two-sided

TABLE 5

ANALYSIS OF STRUCTURE IN EIGHT GROUPS

Investigator	Group Characteristics	Criteria and Number of Choices	Group Size	δ	δSTD	τ	012STD
1. Hayes and Conklin (1953)	Tenth-grade girls' biology class	Unlimited "friendship"	13	−.152	−3.63	−2.401	−1.882
2. Hayes and Conklin (1953)	Tenth-grade social studies class, boys and girls	Unlimited "friendship"	24	−.091	−4.88	−5.687	−0.536
3. Horace Mann-Lincoln Institute (1947)	Sixth-grade class, boys	3 best friends	12	−0.69	−1.90	−2.722	+0.563
4. Taba et al. (1951)	Eighth-grade class, boys and girls	3 seating companions	25	−0.46	−2.61	−7.642	+2.764
5. Moreno (1953)	Cottage girls (C13)	5 housemates	29	−.008	−0.52	0.947	−1.173
6. Zeleny (1950)	Graduate and undergraduate students	6 exam-mates	32	−.064	−5.54	−7.729	−0.364
7. Zeleny (1947)	College students	Unlimited work partner	23	−.115	−7.01	−7.836	+0.380
8. Taba and Elkins (1950)	Eighth-grade literature class, boys and girls	3 prefer to sit near	33	.007	0.62	−5.364	+3.454

5 percent test that the 012 triads occur at random, there are only two groups (groups 4 and 8) with significant values of 012_{STD} (i.e., that exceed 1.96 in absolute value). In both of these groups, the value of 012_{STD} indicates that the number of 012 triads is larger than expected by chance. We offer the following tentative explanation of this finding. Leinhardt (1968) found that when classroom groups were divided into sexually homogeneous subgroups and the subgroups analyzed separately, the number of 012 triads became fewer than expected, whereas when the groups were not divided there were more 012 triads than expected by chance. As indicated in figure 4, this finding is consonant with a model that incorporates sex cleavage as well as ranking and cliquing. Sex cleavage of classroom groups has been observed to become stronger through the elementary grades and then weaker during the college years. Returning to the last column of table 5, we note that the two groups with significantly more 012 triads than expected were both eighth-grade classes consisting of boys and girls. The other groups are either older or sexually homogeneous. Our explanation is, therefore, that sex cleavage has created the excess of 012 triads observed in groups 4 and 8.

7. DISCUSSION

Sociologists, with growing frequency and sophistication, are turning to mathematics as a language in which to model social behavior. Two assumptions underlie this trend. One holds mathematics to be a clearer, better way of expressing relationships between variables. The other suggests that mathematical expressions, because they are easily manipulated, will render new, non-obvious relationships apparent (Beauchamp 1970). Clearly, these assumptions have been implicit in the work on graph theoretic models of structure in interpersonal relations and both have been corroborated. The models have produced new understanding of the interdependent relations which link group members, and have suggested a sociological rather than psychological interpretation for consistency or balance theories (Davis 1968). Nonetheless, the test of sociological theory, be it mathematical or verbal, must be empirical. With this in mind we have developed procedures which permit testing of tendencies in sociometric data toward a variety of graph theoretic models of structure. We have presented a theorem which specifies the probabilities needed for standardized measures based on triad frequencies, and have provided formulas for a general model, a partial order. While these formulas are dependent upon the random model chosen, the procedures used to generate them are not, and we discussed why we thought more research was needed on random models for sociometric data. Since our interest in this report was principally methodological, we refrained from data analysis save an illustrative example in which the partial order model was compared with a special case, the ranked-clusters model of Davis and Leinhardt (1970).

REFERENCES

Beauchamp, Murry A. 1970. *Elements of Mathematical Sociology*. New York: Random House.
Cartwright, Dorwin, and Frank Harary. 1956. "Structural Balance: A Generalization of Heider's Theory." *Psychological Review* 63:277–93.
Davis, James A. 1967. "Clustering and Structural Balance in Graphs." *Human Relations* 20:181–87.
———. 1968. "Social Structures and Cognitive Structures." In *Theories of Cognitive Consistency: A Sourcebook*, edited by R. P. Abelson, E. Aronson, W. J. McGuire, T. M. Newcomb, M. J. Rosenberg, and P. H. Tannenbaum. Chicago: Rand McNally.
Davis, James A., and Samuel Leinhardt. 1970. "The Structure of Positive Interpersonal Relations in Small Groups." In *Sociological Theories in Progress*, edited by Joseph Berger, Morris Zelditch, Jr., and Bo Anderson. Vol. 2. Boston: Houghton Mifflin (in press).
Harary, Frank, Robert Z. Norman, and Dorwin Cartwright. 1965. *Structural Models*. New York: Wiley.
Hayes, M. L., and M. E. Conklin. 1953. "Intergroup Attitudes and Experimental Change." *Journal of Experimental Education* 22:19–36.
Heider, Fritz. 1946. "Attitudes and Cognitive Organization." *Journal of Psychology* 21:107–12.
———. 1958. *The Psychology of Interpersonal Relations*. New York: Wiley.
Hempel, Carl G. 1952. *Fundamentals of Concept Formation in Empirical Science*. In *Encyclopedia of Unified Science*. Vol. 2, no. 7. Chicago: University of Chicago Press.
Holland, Paul W., and Samuel Leinhardt. 1970. "A Unified Treatment of Some Structural Models for Sociometric Data." Technical Report, Carnegie-Mellon University, January 1970.
Horace Mann-Lincoln Institute of School Experimentation. 1947. *How to Construct a Sociogram*. New York: Bureau of Publications, Teachers College, Columbia University.
Katz, L., and J. H. Powell. 1954. "The Number of Locally Restricted Directed Graphs." *Proceedings of the American Mathematical Association* 5:621–26.
Katz, L., R. Tagiuri, and T. Wilson. 1958. "A Note on Estimating the Statistical Significance of Mutuality." *Journal of General Psychology* 58:97–103.
Kendall, M. G., and B. B. Smith. 1939. "On the Method of Paired Comparisons." *Biometrika* 31:324–345.
Landau, H. G. 1951a. "On Dominance Relations and the Structure of Animal Societies. I. Effect of Inherent Characteristics." *Bulletin of Mathematical Biophysics* 13:1–19.
———. 1951b. "On Dominance Relations and the Structure of Animal Societies. II. Some Effects of Possible Social Factors." *Bulletin of Mathematical Biophysics* 13:245–62.
———. 1953. "On Dominance Relations and the Structure of Animal Societies. III. The Condition for a Score Structure." *Bulletin of Mathematical Biophysics* 15:143–48.
Leinhardt, Samuel. 1968. "The Development of Structure in the Interpersonal Relations of Children." Ph.D. dissertation, University of Chicago.
Moran, P. A. P. 1947. "On the Method of Paired Comparisons." *Biometrika* 34:363–65.

431

Moreno, J. L. 1953. *Who Shall Survive?* New York: Beacon House.
Taba, H. E., E. Brady, J. Robinson, and W. Vickery. 1951. *Diagnosing Human Relations Needs.* Washington: American Council on Education.
Taba, H. E., and D. Elkins. 1950. *With Focus on Human Relations.* Washington, D.C.: American Council on Education.
Zeleny, L. D. 1947. "Selection of the Unprejudiced." *Sociometry* 10:396–401.
———. 1950. "Adaptation of Research Findings in Social Leadership to College Classroom Procedures." *Sociometry* 13:314–28.

From Joel H. Levine, *American Sociological Review 37*, 14-27 (1972), by permission.

THE SPHERE OF INFLUENCE *

Joel H. Levine

American Sociological Review 1972, Vol. 37 (February):14–27

University of Michigan, Dartmouth College

This is a study of network representation: The data represent a set of interlocked directorates —specifically, the network in which the boards of major banks are interlocked with the boards of major industrials. The problem is to represent this network so as to organize it and describe its major outlines. Using an unfolding variant of smallest space analysis, the problem is solved by a spherical map: the "Sphere of Influence." The sectors of the sphere represent similarly-linked corporations, and the relations among the sectors represent the relations among bank-industrial communities.

THIS is a study of a network of inter-locked directorates—specifically, a study of the network in which we find the boards of major banks, e.g., Chase Manhattan or Morgan Guarantee Trust interlocked with the boards of major industrials such as General Motors or Ford. As a sociologist I approach this network as a problem in sociometry. My problem is to "understand" a large network in the crude, almost a-theoretical sense of being able to represent it, to discern its major outlines, and to distinguish important links from those which are not.

This paper will explore techniques to facilitate this understanding. And it will describe two results, one anticipated and one wholly unanticipated. The anticipated result is a "map" that represents proximities in the network. The unanticipated result is the *configuration* revealed in the map, which— partly for whimsy but mainly because of the data—I will call the "Sphere of Influence."

* This work has been greatly facilitated by public documents of the House Subcommittee on Domestic Finance; I am indebted to Representative Wright Patman and his staff. I am indebted to James C. Lingoes for considerable aid during the preliminary work of this analysis, to Roger Shepard for seminars that introduced me to the concepts of smallest space analysis, and to Stephen Waite who has also given generously of his time. I am indebted to colleagues of the FASR-structural studies seminar at Harvard, and—for causing me to attempt this analysis—I would like to thank Leslie Howard and his students, Phillip Bonacich (Bonacich, 1971a, 1971b), Stephen Berkowitz (Berkowitz, 1971), James Haney, Edward O. Laumann, William D. Phelan, Jr., William Taylor, and Harrison C. White (Lorrain and White, 1971).

This particular network (a subset of data published by Rep. Patman's House Subcommittee on Banking, 1966) is a web of 84 nodes and 150 links. Its size makes it important methodologically; moreover its content makes it a network of putatively immense social importance. These twin forces, the size and the importance of the network, create problems.

First, the size creates problems that are present, but readily solved for smaller networks. In particular, how does one represent a network? A simple network: A is the "friend of" B, B "friend of" C, C . . . D, D . . . E, can be represented as a single straight line from A to B to C . . . to E. This representation is so natural that we barely note it as an object in its own right, distinct from both the data and from the analysis. Yet the representation organizes the data, it enables one to "see" relations, it codes the pattern in a way that can be remembered and thought about, and it suggests attributes such as centrality and distance. All these properties are beyond the data but below the level of formal hypotheses: The value (or deceptiveness) of a representation lies in what it suggests, in its ability to stimulate thought.

For a complex network, one needs the same advantages, but for a complex network this particular kind of line-drawing representation degenerates. For example, suppose I begin to represent my network by drawing the largest industrial (by sales), G.M., as a point and then drawing lines to the banks it connects. Among the fourteen banks used here (the sampling criterion is de-

433

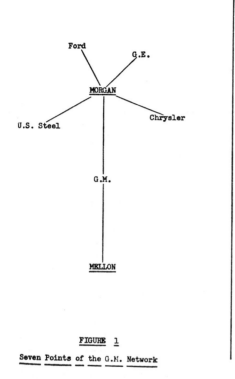

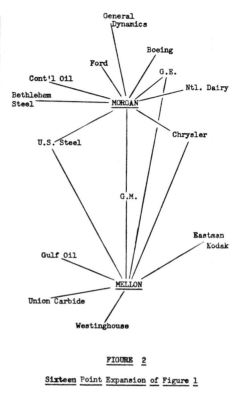

FIGURE 1

Seven Points of the G.M. Network

FIGURE 2

Sixteen Point Expansion of Figure 1

scribed below), G.M. reaches Morgan Guarantee Trust (three links) and Mellon National Bank (one link). Now, Morgan itself connects to U. S. Steel, Ford, G.E., and Chrysler, Figure 1, which is still a tractable picture (seven points). But Morgan is also linked to sixteen more corporations in this sample and Mellon to fourteen, Figure 2, some of which are the same as those for Morgan. This brings in thirty-two points and begins to be an unmanageable thicket of information. Yet it is only a fraction of the full network. Should I continue, I might succeed in making a spectacular picture, but probably not in making one that is useful. What I need is a representation that helps to order and clarify the large network, as a line-drawing representation helps with a small one. The representation should prepare me for theory and higher matters, but the immediate problem is to make this thicket minimally intelligible. The larger the network, the more difficult the problem and, for that very reason, the greater the need.

The representation problem is introduced

by the size of the network. The importance of this particular network makes the problem more intense. Subjectively important data, data that are ideologically potent, demand the utmost objectivity. Their representation (much less their analysis) must be derived by clearly reproducible methods. Too much is "known" about these nodes, new information is broadcast each week in publications from *Barrons* to *Ramparts* and in scholarly journals as well. This familiarity, combined with the complexity, creates the temptation to simplify by using hunches: X is important, let us record its connections. Or, X is powerful, let us document its dominion. Without commenting on the politics of such methods, they are helpful because they help one parse a mass of data. Faced with the knowledge that you are unable to handle the whole, prior "knowledge" helps one select. But such procedures are scientifically treacherous. Such hunches provide no overview, no knowledge of the context within which the "selected" facts exist. One must ask: Would I have reached the same

434

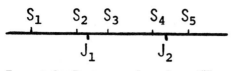

FIGURE 3. ONE-DIMENSIONAL JOINT SPACE ("TRUE
SCALE" ORDER: 1, 2, 3, 4, 5)

overview had I not "known" the participants' names?

Multidimensional Scaling of Networks

This paper addresses both the representation problem and the problem of objectivity
by the use of nonmetric multidimensional
scaling. In particular I am using a nonmetric
unfolding analysis (see Shepherd 1962,
Coombs 1964) implemented for smallest
space analysis by Guttman and Lingoes
(1970).[1] What is a "nonmetric unfolding
analysis" and how does it apply to networks? In the classical application by psychologists, the technique is applied to a set
of "judges" and a set of "stimuli." Let us
assume some attribute, e.g., political liberal-
ism/conservatism on which both the judges
and the stimuli are located as in Figure 3.
The real scale defines a "joint space" in
which both judges and stimuli are scored.
The purpose of the unfolding analysis is to
recover this joint space from the judges'
preference orderings. Judge 1 would prefer

[1] Sociological use of similar smallest-space technique will be found in Laumann and Guttman
(1966) and Laumann (1969), although these applications do not use disjoint sets of points, as the
banks are disjoint from the industrials.

S_2 over S_3, S_1, S_4, S_5—in order of their proximity to his own position, Figure 4a. Judge 2
would prefer S_4, S_5, S_3, S_2, S_1, Figure 4b.
In actual use, of course, the joint space is
unknown, except as it is found by "unfolding" the preferences.

We transfer the unfolding paradigm to
networks by identifying banks as "judges"
and industrial corporations as "stimuli." And
we interpret number of interlocked directors
as "preferences": Mellon National Bank being closer to Gulf Oil (four links) than it is
to ALCOA (three links), or Westinghouse
(two links), or G.M. (one link), or Standard
Oil of New Jersey (zero links). (We could
just as well identify industrial corporations
as judges and banks as stimuli. As long as
the identification is consistent, it makes no
formal difference). What we ask of the unfolding analysis is that it assemble the "preferences" of many different banks into one
joint space, describing the whole network in
one picture.

Overview of the Data

For many years Representative Wright
Patman's committees have been assembling
an impressive collection of data on U. S.
industrial and financial organization. (See
brief selections in Zeitlin, 1970.) One volume, *Commercial Banks and Their Trust
Activities* (1968), records several kinds of
links (directorate interlocks, fund management, and stockholding) between major
U. S. industrial corporations and a selection
of forty-nine banks. The network analyzed

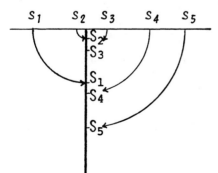

FIG. 4A. Folded Scale of Preferences Reported by Judge 1 (Order: 2, 3,
1, 4, 5)

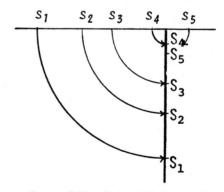

FIG. 4B. Folded Scale of Preferences Reported by Judge 1 (Order: 4, 5,
3, 2, 1)

FIGURE 4. TWO FOLDED SCALES DERIVED FROM THE SAME JOINT SPACE.

in this paper is a subset of Patman's data: using seventy industrials, fourteen banks and one kind of link, shared directors. I chose a subset in order to simplify the problem: If the method were tested on too complex a problem, one could not evaluate the result. Thus, I restricted the sample to three cities: New York, Pittsburgh, and Chicago.[2] At a minimum, the joint space should recover this regionalism (see Warner, Unwalla, and Trimm, circa p. 140).

The seventy industrials and fourteen banks are a completely connected network, Figure 5; (that is, each corporation leads directly or indirectly to all the others). The network is not only connected (which was guaranteed by the selection procedure) but tightly connected (which was *not* guaranteed), making for a redundancy of direct and indirect ties. For example, one can gain an upper bound on a Milgram-style small world analysis (Milgram, 1967) by noting the number of steps from bank to bank: For eight banks, (1, 2, 3, 4, 5, 6, 9, 10) each is connected to any other through exactly one intermediary, e.g., *Chase*-G.E.-*Morgan*, *Chase*-International Paper-*Bankers Trust*, *Chase*-S.O.N.J.-*First Natl. City*. The next shortest path detectable in these data (bank to bank) is bank-industrial-bank-industrial-bank. All the remaining bank—bank links are of this length. As we shall see, this kind

---

[2] These three cities were chosen according to the size of their largest banks. The largest bank (by Patman's ranking on trust assets) in the sample is in New York City. The largest non-NYC bank in the sample is in Pittsburgh. And the largest non-NYC, non-Pittsburgh bank in the sample is in Chicago. Having chosen these three cities, I have used the fourteen banks in these cities (among Patman's original forty nine). Thus I am excluding several large banks in Boston, Cleveland, Detroit, and Philadelphia while including smaller banks in the three cities—e.g., including American National Bank and Trust (trust assets, 1967, 603 million) because it is in Chicago, but excluding Old Colony Trust of Boston (assets 4.2 billion dollars). (Patman's sample itself excludes important banks, e.g., U.S. Trust, and is limited to Eastern banks (Chicago-East) excluding South, Southwestern and Western banks.)

Having chosen the fourteen banks, I selected industrials both interlocked with one or more of the banks and included in *Fortune*'s top one hundred. Thus I am reduced to fourteen banks and seventy industrials. In addition, three industrials have not been mapped due to irremediable errors in the data processing.

of network redundancy is methodologically useful. It makes representation for complex networks in some ways easier than for simple ones.

What I require is a joint space for these eighty-four banks and industrials. All network similarities among banks will be inferred *indirectly* from their links to the industrials; and all network similarities among industrials will be inferred *indirectly* from their links to the banks.

First Result: A Map of the Network

Figure 6 is the three-dimensional joint space (two dimensions are shown, a third dimension separates the banks from the industrials).[3] First, note that this three-dimensional representation does satisfy the minimal requirement: It recovers the regional groupings. That is, based on the pattern of interlocks, one finds regional clusters. Region *per se* is not recorded in Figure 5— region is a variable that I withheld from my "computer" so that I would have a minimal criterion for checking the sense of my results. One finds First National Bank of Chicago at the lower right (and forward among the banks) and nearby, Northern Trust, Harris Trust, American National, and Continental Illinois. Region *per se* is only a geographical fact. The map of directorates shows that the fact is also social. Near these banks (but to the back—among the industrials) are, for example, Standard Oil of Indiana, Armour, Inland Steel, and International Harvester—a Chicago cluster as a *network* (not a geographical) fact. Between the center and the right of the three-dimensional picture, there is a band of Pittsburgh banks and industrials. Finally, occupying half the space at the left and bottom, we find the New York banks.[4]

So we have a reasonable picture. The technique was bound to give us some "picture," i.e., something had to come out of the computer. The regionalism gives me some assur-

---

[3] See the discussion of dimensionality below and the discussion of the "picture" obtained in higher dimensions.

[4] My emphasis here is methodological. But substantively related work can be found in the social ecology (and social cartography) work in Duncan (1960), Duncan and Lieberson (1970) and Lieberson (1971).

	MORGAN GUARANTY TRUST, NYC	CHASE MANHATTAN, NYC	BANKERS TRUST, NYC	FIRST NATIONAL CITY, NYC	MELLON NT'L. B&T, PITT.	MANUFACTURERS HANOVER, NYC	FIRST NATIONAL BANK, CHIC.	CONTINENTAL ILLINOIS, CHIC.	CHEMICAL BANK, NYC	NORTHERN TRUST CO., CHIC.	HARRIS TRUST & SAVINGS, CHIC.	PITT. NT'L BANK, PITT.	UNION NT'L BANK, PITT.	AMERICAN NT'L B&T, CHIC.
1. General Motors	3			1										
2. Ford	2			1										
3. S.O.N.J.		2		1										
4. G.E.	3	1		1	1					1				
5. Chrysler	1	1		1		4	1							
6. Mobil Oil			1	2										
7. Texaco								2					1	
8. U.S.Steel	2			1	1			2						
9. I.B.M.			2	1										
10. Gulf Oil						4								
11. Western Elec.			2			1		1			1			
12. DuPont, E.I. DeNemours								1						
13. Swift Co.							1	2		1	1			
14. Shell Oil							1							
15. Stnd. Oil, Indiana	1						2	1			1			1
17. Beth. Steel	2							2	2					
18. Int. Harvester							1	5		3	3			
19. Westinghouse				1	2						1	1	1	
21. Goodyear T&R	1							1		1	1			
23. Boeing	1			1										
24. Armour							2							2
25. Nt'l. Dairy	1	2				2								
26. Procter & Gamble	1			1										
27. Union Carbide		1		1		3				1				
28. I.T.&T.		1		1										
32. General Dynamics	1							1						
33. Cont'l. Oil	2	2					1							
34. Eastman Kodak				1										
36. United Aircraft	1			2										
37. Monsanto Co.				2										

FIGURE 5   Bank-Industrial Interlocked Directorates

(The number in cell i,j is the number of directors common to the board of industrial i and bank j. The number of interlocks is in every case less than or equal to five.) Source: Commercial Banks and Their Trust Activities; Emerging Influence on the American Economy, Staff Report for the Subcommittee on Domestic Finance, Committee on Banking and Currency, July 8, 1968, U.S. Government Printing Office.

38. General Foods	1 2	2	1 1		
39. Borden			2		
40. Caterpillar Tractor			2		
41. International Paper	1 2			1	
42. Sinclair Oil		2			
43. ALCOA		3			
44. Burlington Ind.	1				
45. American Can	2	2			
46. Union Oil, Calif.			1	1	
48. Continental Can	1				
49. Uniroyal			3		
51. Cities Service	1		1		
53. Grace, W.R., Co.		3 1			
54. Allied Chem.		1			
55. Anaconda	2	2			
56. Armco Steel		1			
63. Reynolds, R.J.Tobacco	1				
64. Atlantic Richfield	1				
65. Deere			1		
67. Gruman Aircraft Engrg.	1				
68. Inland Steel			2 1		1
70. National Steel			1	3	
71. Singer	1 1				
72. Corn Products			1		
75. Goodrich, B.F.	1 1	1			
77. Celanese	1 1				
78. Jones & Laughlin Steel		2		1	
79. FMC Corp.			1		
81. Wilson Co. Inc.	1				
82. Coca Cola	1				
83. American Cyanamid	1				
84. Pitt. Plate Glass		3			
85. Colgate Palmolive	1	1	1 1		
87. Honeywell				1	
88. Borg Warner		1	3		
89. American Home Prod.		2			
90. Owens Illinois		1			
91. Nat'l Cash Reg.		3 1			
93. TRW Inc.		1			
96. Reynolds Metals		1			

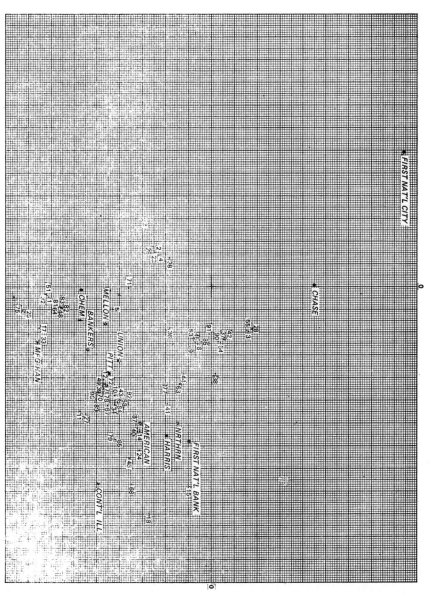

FIGURE 6. BANK–INDUSTRIAL JOINT SPACE

ance that the picture is also useful. But there is also something much stronger in the picture, an unanticipated result which I call the Sphere of Influence.

The Structure of Structure

First, let us examine the map for problems

rather than for reassurance. Note, for example, in the second and third dimensional view, Figure 6, that #10, Gulf Oil, is slightly to the right of the Pittsburgh cluster though strongly linked to Mellon and only Mellon among these fourteen banks. Note #7, Texaco, and #12, DuPont, are close

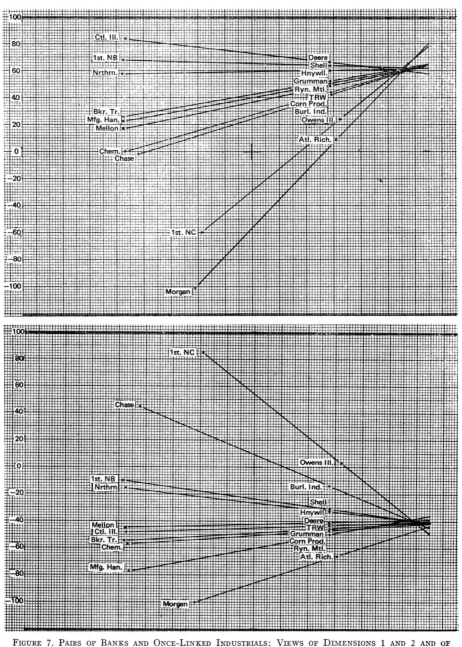

FIGURE 7. PAIRS OF BANKS AND ONCE-LINKED INDUSTRIALS: VIEWS OF DIMENSIONS 1 AND 2 AND OF
DIMENSIONS 1 AND 3

to Gulf though both are linked to Chemical
Bank N.Y., off to their left, and neither
is linked to Pittsburgh. Note that #48,
Continental Can, and #64, Atlantic Rich-

field, linked only to Morgan, appear at the
right, far from Morgan. Note also that #44,
Burlington Industries, appears near the center; whereas Chase is to the upper left. These

440

"discrepancies" in the second and third dimensional map show that a bank's "cluster" does not have the same second and third dimensional coordinates as the bank.

But the location of these "clusters" has a pattern. In Figure 7a an arrow connects Morgan to Atlantic Richfield, showing where to "read" Morgan bank's industrial "cluster." A similar arrow connects Chase to Burlington, Mellon to TRW, etc. Each of these ten industrials is linked once to the bank at the end of the arrow and to no other bank. (There are no exclusive industrials for the other four banks.) The curious thing about the ten arrows is where they point. Figure 7 shows the first- and second; and the first- and third-dimensional views of Figure 6. The ten arrows converge to (approximately) one point: The joint space has a center; the industrials and the banks lie on concentric shells of a sphere.[5]

The Sphere of Influence

Who is at the center? No one: no bank, no industrial. The center is empty. It is where an industrial would be were it linked to no one (and such unlinked industrials were eliminated from the data). From this unlinked center one diverges in the direction of Morgan (if one is Atlantic Richfield), *or* in the direction of Chase (if one is Burlington Industries), or one splits the angle if he is linked to both, e.g., Singer. The separate clusters are organized around one center. Viewed spherically, there is a Morgan *sector,* a Chase *sector,* a Mellon *sector.* Radii indicate the strength of the link, angles indicate direction.

This is a strong result. Eighty-four corporations with 150 links, and 730 non-links, have obligingly arranged themselves in a sphere.[6] And phrases like "sphere of in-fluence" or "sector" which no one takes literally have been reified. The data are telling us what our metaphors should have suggested. Suppose bank B_1 is at the center of its "sphere of influence." For example, Morgan: Morgan is three-linked to G.M. and G.E. so that—*if* more links imply less distance—G.M. and G.E. are near to the center of the Morgan "sphere." Ford, U.S. Steel, Bethlehem Steel, and Continental Oil are a little "farther" away, being twice linked. Chrysler, Boeing, Natl. Dairy, Procter and Gamble, etc. are still farther being once-linked, and Standard Oil of N.J., Mobil Oil, Texaco, IBM, Gulf Oil, etc. are far away from Morgan, by being unlinked to Morgan. But these unlinked corporations do have a distance because, if not directly, then indirectly they are linked. If we draw the Morgan sphere, they are far from its center —we do not know *where* to draw them, but we know they are at some (mean) distance R from the center: They are somewhere on a sphere (or circle, in 2 space) of radius R around Morgan. Now suppose Chase Manhattan is also at the center of its sphere and that those on the periphery of its realm are far away. And suppose that "far away" is approximately R, as in the previous case. Where is the industrial that is far from *both* B_1 and B_2?[7] It is limited. If it is simultaneously on *both* peripheries—R-away from B_1 *and* approximately R-away from B_2—then, in two-space, there are at most two points where it can be located (See Figure 8, points C_1 and C_2).

Suppose an industrial is R-away from Morgan and Chase and R-away from every bank. Then, by definition, the industrial that is far away from every center is itself the center of a sphere of radius R, around which the other centers are arrayed.[8] A sphere is

---

[5] Recall the banks and industrials—the separate shells—were separated at the outset, since I used data on links *between* banks and industrials.

[6] The smallest space computations herein were executed with the Guttman/Lingoes smallest space programs (updated June, 1970) implemented on the IBM 360 at the University of Michigan. Several runs with these data, using different starting points for the three-dimensional solution and different numbers of dimensions, have pointed to the same converging configuration. The results remain exploratory. Much more work is needed to examine their stability: The input is roughly one thousand items (Figure 5) while the output is approximately 250 items (three coordinates for each of the eighty four points). Particularly for a smallest space program (which only "knows" that an input "three" is greater than an input "two"—not how much greater), this is a low ratio of input to output.

[7] Differences in R should tend to diffuse the "center" of Figure 9.

[8] The truly unlinked industrial (not linked directly or indirectly) may be the better meaning for the center. In this case we would have an unresolved anomaly: It would be in the center because of its symmetrical position with respect to all of the banks. But, being in the center, there would be a limit to its distance from all the other points—a

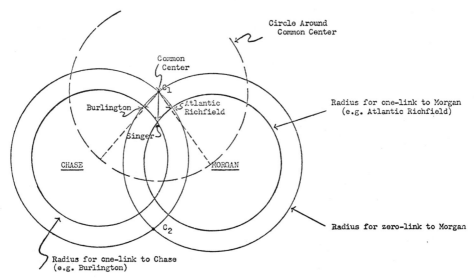

FIGURE 8. SCHEMATIC DRAWING OF THE RELATION AMONG THREE INDUSTRIALS, TWO BANKS, AND THE COMMON CENTER

the locus of points (banks) that are R-distant from one point (the simultaneously distant industrial). Considered separately, we may examine the Morgan-centered network, Chase-centered network, etc. But considered simultaneously the natural and simple view is to subsume them all into one sphere in which each group is a sector. Thus Burlington is at a distance from the common center, diverging from the common center on a radius to Chase. And because Singer is approximately as close to Chase as Burlington is, (1) each is one-linked to Chase (1) and as close to Morgan as is Atlantic Richfield, Singer is on a radius *between* the Chase and Morgan sectors. And although Singer is as close to Chase as is Burlington, Singer is farther from the common center, Figure 8. Thus, in the larger Sphere, the angle establishes the pattern of connection, i.e., the sector to which one belongs. (The length of the radius corresponds to the degree of connection; e.g., an industrial linked once to Chase and once to Morgan should appear approximately in the same sector as an industrial linked twice to each, but should be closer to the common center.[9])

What we have here is a primitive analogue to a Copernican change of reference. If one switches from reference to Morgan, or Chase, or some one corporation ("geo"-centric view) to a view where each is arrayed around a common center ("helio"-centric) the data do not change, but the overview changes and becomes simpler.[10]

Social Cartography: Gnomonic Map

The apparent discrepancies in Figure 6 were not so much true errors as errors of three-dimensional parallax, using rectangular coordinates when spherical coordinates were more appropriate. Figure 6 is the view of the configuration from infinity. It is a parallel projection of a sphere into a plane—which is a poor way of viewing a spherical object,

---

condition which is anomalous because it would be in no way linked to them.

[9] Assuming that the one-distance from Chase is to the two-distance from Chase as the one-distance from Morgan is to the two-distance from Morgan.

[10] Actually there may be two spheres: One is the sphere described in the text. The second may be a sphere whose center is the bank that is linked to no industrial. In this second sphere the banks diverge toward one or more industrials. As there are few banks in this sample as weakly linked as some of the industrials, the second sphere is either absent or suppressed by the fit criterion—in favor of the first sphere. The "stress" between these two possible configurations (logically incompatible for finite-radius Euclidean spheres) should affect the result. One line that may be explored is a change to the so-called "taxicab" metric wherein a single surface *can* lie on two spheres drawn from two different centers.

442

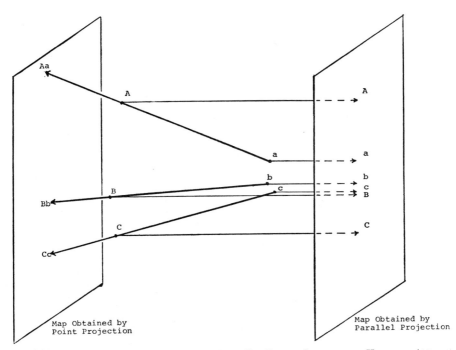

FIGURE 9. TWO ALTERNATIVE PROJECTIONS OF THE SAME SIX POINTS—ILLUSTRATING HOW THE *Apparent* CONFIGURATION IS AFFECTED BY THE PROJECTION. TO THE RIGHT IS A PARALLEL PROJECTION ONTO A PLANE (PRODUCING ONE PLANAR MAP WITH THE ORDER A,A,B,C,B,C). TO THE RIGHT IS A POINT PROJECTION ONTO A PLANE (PRODUCING A PLANAR MAP THAT IS SERIOUSLY ALTERED AND REORGANIZED COMPARED TO THE PARALLEL PROJECTION).

and the cause of the apparent discrepancies. The parallel projection has two flaws. First it distorts angular distance terribly. For example in Figure 9 a parallel projection onto a map separates a from A, and c from C, and puts c closer to B (much as DuPont was separated from Chemical Bank and appeared close to Mellon). Second, the parallel projection in Figure 6 is an unpredictable combination of sector effects and number of links. Thus two points in separate sectors could appear close together because both are close to the center. Or, two points in the same sector could appear far apart because their radii were different.

To the extent that it can be done, geographers are the men who can map a sphere onto a printed page. Thus let us engage in a little "social cartography," remapping Figure 6. To emphasize angular separation, we need a projection from the center point, rather than parallel projection. Thus, borrowed from the physical cartographers, Figure 10 is a "gnomonic projection" of the Sphere of Influence.[11]

Any two-dimensional view of a truly three-dimensional object has both distortions and advantages. The gnomonic projection has the advantage that all points on the same radius are mapped into one point. Thus DuPont is properly represented near Chemical Bank. And Gulf Oil, Jones and Laughlin Steel, and Pittsburgh Plate Glass are properly in the Pittsburgh group. The Morgan sector is near Morgan, etc. Thus, by mapping each radius into a single point, it corrects the major representational flaws of Figure 6. The gnomonic projection has the second advantage that it maps great circle routes into straight lines. Thus Ford, which is linked

---

[11] The graph-paper-grid represents the point of tangency (plane to sphere) at the center of the graph. The grid of circles represents sines of the angles: point-of-tangency to center-of-sphere to point-being-projected. The circular grid only facilitates plotting *in the plane,* and does not directly represent the sphere itself.

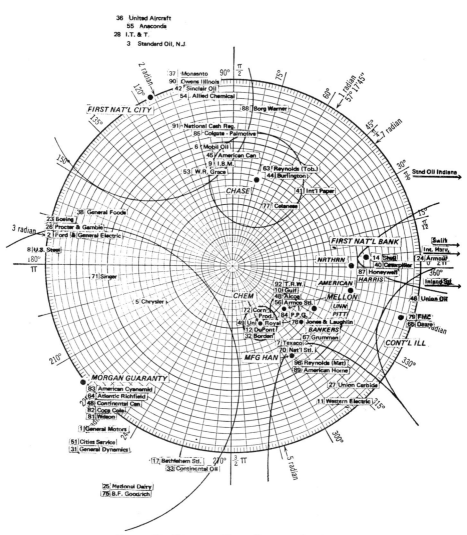

FIGURE 10. GNOMONIC MAP OF SPHERE OF INFLUENCE

to Morgan and First National City, appears near (but not on) the straight line between Morgan and Mellon (magnitudes of the angles are distorted). Singer is near (but not on) the straight line (great circle route) between Morgan and Chase. Thus the spherical map gives a quick approximate overview of the relations in the network.

Data Versus Representation of Data

The gnomonic map is a large sociogram whose sectors indicate relatively well-linked

bank-industrial ties. But the representation is not the *same as* the ties, and it is important to emphasize the difference between the network *data* and the two-dimensional, or three-dimensional or however-many-dimensional representation. The network itself is fourteen dimensional and no fewer number of dimensions will describe it fully; yet I have used three dimensions. The choice of the "correct" number of dimensions is—for this network analysis—a somewhat different problem from the choice of the "correct" number in a typical factor analysis. When one uses fewer dimensions than necessary to describe the data, one always destroys some facts. Typically one chooses enough dimensions to describe the facts that are real: Eliminating some of the dimensions destroys detail, but the detail it destroys is presumed to have been the result of randomness and error. Thus, in a typical factor analysis the economy of dimensions sacrifices detail, but probably increases accuracy. But in the present analysis, six dimensions or three, or one-anything short of fourteen dimensions would suppress some of the *real* links. And suppression is exactly what I want—in order to "see the forest." Which facts will the technique suppress? It will suppress links that are not backed up by a network of redundant linkages: The technique *must* misrepresent something, but it tries to minimize errors. Therefore, if the technique misrepresents the isolated fact, then the error cost is small. But if a bank is close to an industrial through a full network of direct and many indirect links as well, then the technique will place them close together, since not to do so would be to misreport many links. By minimizing error, the technique represents the major, the most redundant outlines, which are exactly what we set out to find. Thus Ford, which is close to Morgan (two links) and First National City (one link) is close to General Electric, General Foods, and U.S. Steel which, while linked to Morgan and First National City, are linked to other banks as well. The representation "suggests" that the Morgan, First National City pair predominates: These industrials, e.g., Ford and G.E., differ in detail; but in gross, low-dimensional outline the representation suggests they are similar in effect. Detail is suppressed—we do not want all the detail, not yet.[12] To begin the analysis, really pre-analysis of a social network, we must, as scientists, be willfully simple-minded. That is the kind of assistance which we required of a system of representation.

Conclusion

We have examined a sociogram of banks and industrials looking for a method that provides for a large network the kind of overview that point-line sociograms provide for small ones. The method used was multidimensional unfolded scaling which is able to compress into two, three, or four dimensions much of the information in the original fourteen dimensional data. Before we venture—or venture with *confidence*—into more substantive analysis, we will need to continue to examine the technique itself. For example: How stable is the configuration? How much leeway should one allow; that is, how well-determined are the angles in Figure 7? I would make a rough allowance of 5 to 10 degrees. But 5 to 10 degrees is a guess subject to much exploration of rounding errors,[13] of algorithms, of "initial configurations," and even subject to exploration of alternate geometries.[14]

For the present, the (Guttman/Lingoes/Coombs) unfolding analysis has been applied to a set of fourteen banks whose boards or directors are interlocked with the boards of seventy large U.S. industrials. The banks and industrials have been mapped into a joint space in which distance corresponds to interlock: the industrials most strongly linked to a bank are near it in the space. While the technique attends to these details of each bank and industrial, it also creates an overall pattern de-emphasizing the neighborhood of any one node. The overall picture is a sphere: the center is empty, one shell of the sphere is filled with industrials and the outer sphere is filled with banks. In the overview, each bank or industrial occupies a "sector" of the overall network, each industrial falling into the appropriate combination of sectors. Reducing the number of dimensions enables one to visualize the major grouping while suppressing non-essential features of the network.

Further analysis will examine both lower and higher dimensions. Here, in three dimensions, Figure 10 is a roughly triangular array with "vertices" Morgan, First National City, and Continental Illinois (New York-Morgan, New York-First Natl. City/Chase, and Chicago-Continental Illinois). In four dimensions the detail is richer, with Mellon emerg-

---

[12] In four dimensions the cluster begins to break-up; General Foods drifts toward Chicago and Chemical Bank, General Electric toward Mellon. (in four-dimensional detail these "drifts" are separate directions. See comments in the text in the discussion of "proper" dimensionality.)

[13] Some rather large matrices have had to be inverted.

[14] See footnotes 8 and 10.

ing as a vertex in its own right—clarifying a region which is crowded and confused in the three-dimensional figure. (Preliminary analysis shows that the two, four, and six dimensional maps are also spherical.) Further analysis will examine a larger universe of data, more cities, more banks, and more industrials. Further analysis will consider the robustness of the "picture"; i.e., how much of the shape and detail of this picture would be affected by missing data—can we reconstruct unreported interlocks? We will examine trends: these 1967 data surely differ in detail from new data for 1972. But how, if at all, would the 1972 representation differ from 1967? Do the dozens of new details outline slow-moving, progressing trends? The "sphere" is designed to complement sociometric technique and answer these questions.

REFERENCES

Berkowitz, Stephen
　1971　The Dynamics of Elite Structure, Ph.D. Dissertation, Brandeis University.
Bonacich, Phillip
　1971a "Factoring and weighting approaches to status scores and clique identification." Journal of Mathematical Sociology, in press.
　1971b "A technique for analyzing overlapping memberships." ms. UCLA.
Coombs, C. H.
　1964　A Theory of Data. New York: Wiley.
Duncan, Beverly and Stanley Lieberson
　1970　Metropolis and Region in Transition. Beverly Hills: Sage Publications.
Duncan, Otis Dudley
　1960　Metropolis and Region. Baltimore: Johns Hopkins Press.
Guttman, L. and J. C. Lingoes
　1970 "Revised Guttman-Lingoes programs." Documented program series, 5/15/70, University of Michigan.
Laumann, Edward O. and L. Guttman
　1966 "The relative associational contiguity of

occupations in an urban setting." American Sociological Review 31:169.
Laumann, Edward O.
　1969 "The social structure of religious and ethnoreligious groups in a metropolitan community." American Sociological Review 34:182.
Lieberson, Stanley
　1971 "An empirical study of military industrial linkages." American Journal of Sociology 76:562–584.
Lingoes, J. C.
　1965 "An IBM–7090 program for Guttman-Lingoes smallest space analysis—I." Behavioral Science 10:183–184.
　1966 "New computer developments in pattern analysis and nonmetric techniques." Uses of Computers in Psychological Research. Paris: Gauthier-Villars, 1–22.
　1968 "The multivariate analysis of qualitative data." Multivariate Behavorial Research 3:61–94.
Lingoes, J. C. and E. Roskam
　1970 "An empirical study of two multidimensional scaling algorithms." Multivariate Behavioral Research 4.
Lorrain, F. and H. C. White
　1971 "Structural equivalence of individuals in social networks." Journal of Mathematical Sociology 1:49–80.
Milgram, S.
　1967 "The small world problem." Psychology Today 22:61–67.
Patman, W.
　1968　Commercial Banks and Their Trust Activities: Emerging Influence on the American Economy. Staff report for the Subcommittee on Domestic Finance, Committee on Banking and Currency. U. S. Government Printing Office.
Shepard, R. N.
　1962 "The analysis of proximities: multidimensional scaling with an unknown distance function, Pts. I and II." Psychometrika 27:125–140, 219–246.
Warner, W. L., D. B. Unwalla and J. H. Trimm
　1967　The Emergent American Society, Volume I: Large Scale Organizations. New Haven: Yale University Press.
Zeitlin, M.
　1970　American Society, Inc., Chicago: Markham.

From Edward O. Laumann and Franz Urban
Pappi, *American Sociological Review 38*,
212-230 (1973), by permission.

NEW DIRECTIONS IN THE STUDY OF COMMUNITY ELITES *

EDWARD O. LAUMANN

University of Chicago

FRANZ URBAN PAPPI

Universität zu Köln

American Sociological Review 1973, Vol. 38 (April):212-230

Recent work in the study of community decision-making appears to be converging on a number of common theoretical and methodological strategies and assumptions. There still remain, however, important weaknesses in the overall theoretical framework and its implied methodology in directing research efforts. Attention is directed to a structural analysis of the community influence system that derives in part from Parsons. Several critical questions are raised concerning the identification of the relevant set of community influentials and the systematic description of their attributes as influentials and the ties that bind them into coalitions depending on the functional issue confronted. Recent advances in graph theory and smallest space analysis are used to examine the consensus-cleavage structure of the community influence system of Altneustadt, a small city in West Germany. Finally, a theoretical strategy and an empirical procedure are proposed for identifying community issues and tracing their impact on the formation of opposing factions and coalitions.

EVEN a cursory review of recent literature on community decision-making systems (cf. Clark, 1968a; Aiken and Mott, 1970; Bonjean et al., 1971) impresses the reader with the number of promising developments in the field. After years of rancorous conflict on methodological issues concerning the *best* way to study the subject (cf. Walton, 1966a, 1966b) and on the relative merits of ruling elite and pluralist

* A version of this paper was originally read at the 67th Annual Meetings of the American Sociological Association, New Orleans, Louisiana, August 28–31, 1972.

We wish to acknowledge with deepest appreciation the advice, encouragement, and help of the following people: Professor Erwin K. Scheuch and Dr. Hans-Dieter Klingemann of the University of Cologne, our research assistant in Germany, Dipl. Soz. Regina Perner, who contributed much to the successful design and implementation of our data-collection procedures, and our American assistants, Richard Senter, John Blair, William Roy, Lois Verbrugge, and Daniel Ayres, of the University of Michigan, who have provided invaluable assistance in the data-analysis phase of the project. We are especially appreciative of the facilities provided by the Zentralarchiv für empirische Sozialforschung under Professor Scheuch's direction as well as the Center for Research on Social Organization at the University of Michigan. Financial support from the following organizations is gratefully acknowledged: Landesamt für Forschung im Ministerium für Wissenschaft und Forschung des Landes Nordrhein-Westfalen, Ford Foundation Behavioral Science Postdoctoral Fellowship (held by the senior author in 1970–71), and the National Science Foundation (GS-32002).

447

models, investigators have begun to assess alternative strategies in designing new studies. The emphasis of the 1950s and early '60s on qualitative case studies, usually of one community at one point in time, following the classic leads of Hunter (1953) and Dahl (1961), has shifted to comparative and quantitative foci in which the objective is to study as many communities as possible, using a wide range of quantitative data.

The contemporary emphasis tends at times to be excessively empirical and pays insufficient attention to theoretical issues. Nevertheless, a fairly explicit theoretical model underlies current efforts—namely, an open-ended system, input-throughput-output model, of community decision-making (cf. Clark, 1968b, 1968c, 1968d). Figure 1 reflects reasonably well the accounting scheme employed in a number of recent and ongoing studies (see, e.g., Clark, 1968b:18; Downes, 1968). This open-ended model posits that certain features of communities, such as population size, regional location, age, industrial and economic base, population stability, and economic and ethnoreligious heterogeneity (i.e., "inputs"), together with attributes of their political institutions, are associated with or determine certain features of their decision-making apparatus, such as the degree of centralization or diffusion of decision-making (i.e., "throughput"). These, in turn, determine which issues will be brought to decision and the decision outcome (i.e., "outputs"). Since "hard" data on inputs and outputs are more readily available and less ambiguous than information regarding the nature of the decision-making ap-

paratus itself, the tendency has been to treat the throughput or "elite decision-making core"—the central object in earlier case studies—as a relatively unobservable "black box" about which only inferences or approximations can be made.

Since the contents of this black box will be the central concern of this paper, we must be especially careful in conceptualizing and measuring social structure—in this instance, the influence structure on the elite level of a community social system. Structure and related descriptive terms such as hierarchy, dominance, differentiation, structural change, and power or class structure, are among the most popular concepts in the sociological lexicon. Despite differences in nuance associated with "structure," the root meaning refers to a persisting order or pattern of relationships among units of sociological analysis, be they individual actors, classes of actors, or behavioral patterns (cf. Nadel, 1957:1–19; Mayhew, 1971; Laumann, 1973). This apparent consensus masks the lack of agreement on the concepts and methodology in terms of which given "social structures" are to be measured, or more modestly, described. Without this agreement, researchers can hardly turn to the more challenging problems of describing structural change.

A TOPICAL OVERVIEW

Our approach thus may appear to be a step backwards inasmuch as we want to describe the theoretical and research strategies of an intensive case study of one small city, Altneustadt (a pseudonym) in West Ger-

Figure 1. An input-throughput-output model for the analysis of community decision making systems.

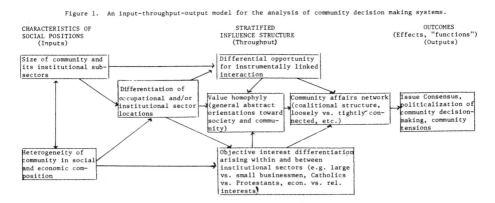

CHARACTERISTICS OF SOCIAL POSITIONS (Inputs)

STRATIFIED INFLUENCE STRUCTURE (Throughput)

OUTCOMES (Effects, "functions") (Outputs)

many. By redirecting attention to the black box, we hope to elucidate the mechanisms whereby inputs are converted into outputs. Although we shall present some substantive results, we wish to stress the more general implications of our theoretical and methodological approach for community elite research. Consequently, we may sometimes be overly brief about the detailed empirical procedures used.

The discussion will proceed in two parts. First, we shall sketch a frame of reference for delineating community influence systems. The community elite is viewed as a set of incumbents of theoretically identified categories of social positions. Description of the structure which results when these positions are linked in a pattern of specified relationships will be a central concern. Two features of individual elite members will be noted: (1) their primary and secondary locations in functionally defined institutional sectors, and (2) their relative influence statuses. Systematic propositions about their respective distributions in the influence structure will be advanced. A methodology will be described that is designed to generate a theoretically relevant description of this influence structure. Second, we shall discuss the structure of conflict in community influence systems. It is difficult to imagine a community comprised of a socially and economically heterogeneous population that lacks disagreements regarding the allocation of scarce community resources. More formally, being good Parsonsians, a central premise of our analysis is that conflict is an endemic, necessary feature of *any* community decision-making apparatus, posing the fundamental functional problem of integration for such structures, that is, the problem of establishing binding priorities among competing goals. Consequently, using a theoretically grounded strategy for identifying community issues and tracing their impact on the formation of opposing factions and coalitions, we shall study how conflict or cleavage patterns are superimposed on the elite structure. We shall first briefly describe the community context which provides the empirical basis for our discussion.

The Community Context: Altneustadt

Altneustadt is a town of 20,000 inhabitants which is not dominated by a nearby larger city. The town is in rich farming country and serves the needs of a large agricultural hinterland. It is the district (county) headquarters for a range of governmental agencies with a correspondingly large number of public officials and bureaucrats. It also has a number of small and intermediate light manufacturing plants owned by local businessmen. Thus, the town has long had a fairly diversified, mainly "middle class" occupational composition. About fifteen years ago, the state government decided to build one of Germany's largest natural science research centers in Altneustadt. This center is now the largest and most important employer in the community.

The Research Center brought a major migration of people to Altneustadt. Approximately one third of the inhabitants are *Neubürger* with status characteristics greatly different from those of the *Altbürger*. Being for the most part university-educated and highly salaried workers, often of urban origin, the *Neubürger* have strong cosmopolitan values and perspectives. In addition, they tend to be Protestants while the *Altbürger* are predominantly Catholics. These basic differences in world views and life styles have led to many conflicts and tensions related to accommodating (if not assimilating) the newcomers. These conflicts have resulted in clearly delineated and perceived coalitions and interest structures which provide the setting for a study of "status" as opposed to "class" politics (cf. Lipset, 1963), since most major groups share "middle-class" socioeconomic status positions but differ fundamentally in their conceptions of appropriate status behavior and styles of life. This, in fact, is the basis of our expectation that the central axis of structural cleavage in Altneustadt will be in the pattern-maintenance rather than the economic or adaptive sector.

Of particular interest is the fact that the SPD (German Social Democratic Party), a party historically rooted in a working-class and predominantly Marxist world view, has been co-opted by the *Neubürger* as the vehicle for expressing their urban, secular, middle-class demands for social change in Altneustadt. Natural scientists and engineers have not been traditional recruits for the SPD. The Christian Democratic Union (CDU) has proved to be a reliable vehicle of control for the *Altbürger*, who maintain a dominant, but increasingly insecure political coalition.

SOCIAL POSITIONS AND INCUMBENTS

A. *Identifying Community Influentials and Their Respective Institutional Sectors*

For our purposes, the unit of structural analysis will be the individual actor (or set of actors) in a particular kind of social position (cf. Parsons, 1951). We thus come to the first crucial question: how are we to identify the domain of relevant social positions for the community influence system? Objections to the reputational and issue approches to identifying elite personnel are well known. Adherents of the reputational technique argue that the issue approach is conservative insofar as it is impossible to detect the impact of nondecisions on the *status quo*. Adherents of the issue approach retort that the reputationalists measure reputations rather than power. Both groups, however, are asking the same question: who governs? The structuralist, or positional approach asks instead, "which positions possess authority or generalized influence in that their incumbents can make binding decisions in their respective institutional sectors or will be consequential in the resolution of community-level issues?" Generally, following Parsons' view of the community as a territorially grounded social system embracing all aspects of social life (cf. Davis, 1948:312; Parsons, 1960:250–79), we first identified prospective community influentials as incumbents of the highest positions of authority in organized collectivities whose primary responsibilities are in one of the four functionally specialized institutional subsectors at the community level of analysis (see Clark, 1968c, for a recent exposition of the AGIL paradigm applied to community institutions; also D'Antonio et al., 1961, for a less theoretically grounded, more "commonsensical" listing of types of community leadership personnel).[1] Parsons (1960:59–

69) argues that there are three levels in the hierarchical structure of organizations: the technical, the managerial, and the institutional. The last is concerned with the articulation of the organization with its larger institutional environment, both by securing its legitimacy in the community and making its claims on scarce community resources, often at the expense of other organizations' claims. On precisely these grounds we can analytically treat the community influence structure as the focus of the integrative subsystem of the community.

Not all community subsystems are likely to be organized into a structure of fully institutionalized and functionally specialized organizations with a full complement of explicitly identified leaders. This is especially true in the integrative and pattern-maintenance sectors of the community which tend to have more fluid organization. We attempted to compensate for this bias of the positional approach by supplementing our list of prospective influentials with nominations by well-informed community members of community influentials not in formally recognized positions.

The distinction we maintain between a social position and the particular actor who occupies that position is crucial. In general, incumbents of "influential" positions spend most of their time devoted to the tasks associated with these positions. But empirical analysis is complicated by the fact that a

---

[1] Parsons' AGIL paradigm was used as the analytic framework for classifying organizations according to their primary functions in the community social system. Given the abstract character of his original formulations, there are some operational difficulties in coding organizations as belonging primarily to one of the four sectors. We coded business firms and banks as economic oranizations

with *adaptive* primacy; top governmental administrative positions, judges, and legislative decision-making bodies as having *goal-attainment* primacy because they make binding decisions for the community as a whole; voluntary associations including unions and political parties as having *integrative* primacy as foci of interest group demands on the polity; and positions in educational, health, religious and cultural organizations as having *pattern-maintenance* primacy. *Notars* in Germany are a specialty in the legal profession concerned with economically relevant activities, such as the preparation of contracts and property transfers, and, consequently, were treated as in the adaptive sector. Although the Natural Science Research Center is the largest employer in Altneustadt, having many important economic consequences, we decided to code it as a pattern-maintenance collectivity, both because its goal objectives are themselves distinctively cultural in their focus and consequences and because, from the community's viewpoint, it poses the problem of the assimilation of its personnel with their distinctive cultural characteristics into a more inclusive pattern of community life.

given actor may simultaneously occupy several "influential" positions in community decision-making—that is, he may wear several hats. We propose to deal with multiple role occupancy operationally by distinguishing an individual's *primary* institutional location or position from his *secondary* position(s) on the basis of the amount of time he spends performing the duties of each.[2]

B. The Rank Order of Influence

Guided by these principles we obtained a list of fifty-one community influentials in Altneustadt, of whom forty-six were successfully interviewed. We then asked: what is the relative influence status of these influentials? That is, can they be differentiated into a hierarchy of influence? This has been a classic concern, especially among those using the reputational approach. Procedurally, we simply asked our influentials to indicate those on the list whom they considered "now in general very influential in Altneustadt" and rank-ordered the number of votes received by each person on the list.[3] There is remarkable consensus among the forty-six respondents concerning the top seven influentials, the top three of whom re-

---

[2] People who spent most of their time· in nonauthority positions were coded separately, and thereby distinguished from individuals whose primary positions of authority were in economic, political, voluntary association, science center, religious or educational/cultural organizations.

[3] Two different questions were asked to measure general influence rank. First, as already discussed, the respondents were asked to name all persons they would say "are now in general very influential in Altneustadt." Second, they were asked to indicate the top three persons from those they had identified in order of their community influence. The rank-order correlation between influence status on the basis of the simple number of mentions and on the basis of a weighted sum of nominations for the top three influentials is .84 (N=31). Given the high correlation between the two procedures and the fact that the "simple mentions" method provided an order for the entire population while the "top three" method covered only the top thirty-one persons, we decided to use the simpler measure as our measure of influence status.

Each respondent was also asked to name other people he felt should be included in our list of community influentials. While a number of suggested additions were made, all but one were mentioned only once. The exception received five nominations and was, consequently, added to our list and interviewed.

ceived forty-six and thirty-seven votes respectively. When we asked Herr K., who was unanimously regarded as "very influential," to name the most influential person in the community, he replied, *"Das bin ich."*

In an effort to validate this influence rank-order at least indirectly, we considered the following evidence. At the beginning of the interview before any mention of our list of influentials, respondents were asked to name persons and groups perceived to be on the supporting and opposing sides of five major community issues. Most people mentioned frequently were on our influentials list. Thirty-eight persons mentioned were not included on that list. However, all were seldom mentioned and only for one issue. We simply multiplied the number of times each person was mentioned as being on one or the other side of an issue by his influence rank (assigning a rank-order of 55 to persons not included in the original list), summed the resulting numbers for each side, and divided by the total number of mentions on the respective side. This number can be regarded as the average influence status of proponents or opponents—the lower the number, the higher the average influence status. (See Table 1.) We were able to predict correctly the winning side for all five issues (p = .03) by picking the side with the higher average influence status.[4]

SOCIAL RELATIONSHIPS

A. The Theoretical Rationale for Describing Community Influence Structures

When we consider how individual influentials interact with one another, we become interested in describing the structure of their interrelationships. It is to this structural analysis that we now turn.

Social structure will be defined as a persisting pattern of social relationships among social positions (cf. Laumann, 1966; especially 1973 for an extended theoretical rationale). A *social relationship* is any link

---

[4] By looking at means and standard deviations of the influence ranks attached to each side of an issue, we can also assess the degree to which a given issue tended to be confined to the higher reaches of the set of influentials (i.e., an internal elite disagreement) or was a broader-based community issue which involved the mobilization of personnel outside the top influential group.

Table 1.   The Average Influence Status of Proponents and Opponents on Five
Community Issues, with Standard Deviations and the Winning Sides
Indicated by Asterisks

Issue	Proponents		Opponents	
	Average Influence Status	Standard Deviation	Average Influence Status	Standard Deviation
Adaptive issue primacy: Industrial resettlement	13.7*	18.2	18.9	13.2
Goal-attainment issue primacy: Construction of new city hall	7.4*	14.8	22.5	14.9
Integrative issue primacy: Community annexation	10.6*	15.2	50.5	14.6
Pattern-maintenance issue primacy: Secular vs. confessional school	26.6*	17.8	28.3	23.3
Permission to hold Pop-festival	29.2	21.0	15.8*	18.1

between incumbents of two social positions that involves mutual but not necessarily symmetric orientations and activities (cf. Homans, 1951; Parsons, 1951; Blau, 1964). If *social differentiation* is defined as the differing allocation of tasks and responsibilities among positions in a social system, then a *differentiated social structure* is one whose actors tend to confine their consensual relationships with others performing similar tasks. In other words, similar positions will tend to cluster, that is, be in closer proximity in the structure, as a function of the higher density of their social ties relative to those with more dissimilar positions.

An important implication of these definitions is that models of social structure will differ to the extent that different social relationships are used as the linking mechanisms for the set of social positions, e.g., informal social contacts as compared to professional or business contacts. We wish, therefore, to devise a methodology that reveals how the pattern of given types of social relationships is structurally differentiated along specifiable dimensions or facets (cf. Guttman, 1959).

In order to interpret the underlying dimensionality of a structure, we must accept a crucial postulate or assumption:

> Similarities in social positions, interests, attitudes, beliefs, and behavior facilitate the formation of consensual relationships among incumbents of social positions.

The corollary is that the more dissimilar two

positions are in status, attitudes, beliefs and behavior of their incumbents, the less likely the formation of consensual relationships and, consequently, the "farther away" they are from one another in the structure. This postulate asserts the *distance-generating mechanism* among social positions and incumbents. There is ample theoretical and empirical justification for accepting such a postulate as a reasonable starting point for analysis (cf. Homans, 1951; Newcomb, 1961; Fararo and Sunshine, 1964; Laumann, 1966, 1973).

B. The Methodology of Structural Analysis: Graph Theory and Smallest Space Analysis

We shall focus on three social relationships among our influentials that provide critical vantage points for viewing a community's influence structure.[5] First, from an instrumental point of view, we shall describe the pattern of *business-professional relationships*, since these are seen in both the functionalist and Marxist literature on community decision-making as important sources of common

---

[5] Three questions are the source of information on these relationships:
   Q33. Would you please indicate the three persons from the list with whom you most frequently meet socially (informally)?
   Q37. Could you now indicate the three persons out of our list with whom you have the closest business or professional contact?
   Q38. Could you please indicate the three persons with whom you most frequently discuss community affairs?

452

interests and claims on the polity and should, therefore, help determine the lines of coalition and cleavage in the community. Respondents were asked to report the three other persons on the list of influentials with whom they were most often in contact in pursuing their primary institutional responsibilities. These are the task-linked, or instrumental, relationships that tie various organizations and collectivities together. Second, we shall describe the pattern of "social" or expressive relationships as it reflects the common interests arising from the influentials' instrumental activities in their primary institutional areas and the shared values, attitudes and concerns arising from their participation in other spheres of community life. These latter derive from such secondary characteristics of the influentials as their religious and educational backgrounds and residence status (*Alt* vs. *Neüburger*). Finally, we shall describe the pattern of *"community affairs" relationships* which are coalitional links among persons with regard to community affairs and may be hypothesized to result from the business-professional and social relations structures and the distinctive political arrangements of the community (cf. Rossi, 1960).

A major objective of recent sociometric efforts (e.g., Alba and Kadushin, 1970, undated; Bonacich, 1972a, 1972b; Coleman and McRae, Jr., 1960; Gleason, 1969; Hubbell, 1965; Levine, 1972; Rosen and Abrams, 1970; Rapoport and Horvath, 1961) has been to develop theoretically grounded, routine procedures to identify cliques, defined according to varying criteria of interrelatedness or "choice" patterns, in a large set of persons. A corollary objective has been to develop graphic techniques for describing how these cliques and persons who belong to no cliques are in turn interrelated.

The "sociogram" whereby individuals are represented by points and choice relations among individuals by (directed) lines was an early effort at graphic representation of the structure of interpersonal relationships (cf. Hunter, 1953; Moreno, 1953; Loomis and Beegle, 1951). But once the set of persons and number of choices (i.e., relationships) exceeded a rather small number, it was discovered that the resulting diagrams become far too complex to be readily interpreted. Indeed, two different investigators could come up with quite different but "equally justifiable" graphic representations of the same matrix of choices that might suggest different interpretations of the same structure. The advent of the computer and the development of several mathematical and statistical techniques that require the computer's large computational resources for their successful application have spurred several strategies for analyzing large sociometric matrices (e.g., Bonacich, 1972a, 1972b; Gleason, 1969; Alba and Kadushin, 1970).

We have combined two recent developments, graph theory and smallest space analysis, to describe our three "relational" structures. Systematic introductions to these developments and discussion of their merits are found in Harary et al. (1965) and McFarland and Brown (1973).

The mathematical theory of digraphs is concerned with postulates and theorems relating to "abstract configurations called digraphs, which consist of 'points' and 'directed lines'" (Harary et al., 1965:v). A graph consists of a set of points and connecting lines in which the direction of the lines is disregarded. Three graph theoretic ideas are of special interest to us: an adjacency matrix (from which all our subsequent analysis proceeds), reachability, and path distance. Consider the following sociometric (adjacency) matrix in which the rows and columns represent three persons, v_1, v_2, and v_3, and the entries in the cells are either "1" or "0" to indicate whether or not v_i (in rows) chooses (is in a relation with) v_j (in columns).

MATRIX 1. AN ADJACENCY MATRIX

		Chosen		
		v_1	v_2	l_3
	v_1	0	1	0
Chooser	v_2	0	0	1
	v_3	0	0	0

This matrix may be diagrammed, as in Figure 2, where points represent persons and directed lines (arcs) between two points represent a relationship. A point v_j is *reachable* from point v_i if there is a path from v_i to v_j, that is, if there is a set of directed lines from v_i to v_j. In our illustration, v_1 can reach v_2 in a

FIGURE 2. GRAPHIC REPRESENTATION OF MATRIX 1

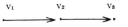

453

path of length "1" and v_3 in a path of length "2", and v_2 can reach v_3 in a path of length "1", but v_2 and v_3 cannot reach v_1. The reachable set R (v) of a point v is the collection of points reachable from v. The *path distance* between two points in a digraph is the *minimum* number of directed lines that must be traversed in order to reach the second point from the first. (The path distance between two points in a graph is the *minimum* number of lines disregarding direction (i.e., the adjacency matrix is symmetric) that must be traversed in order to reach the second point from the first.) Gleason (1969) has devised a computer program that computes the reachability and path distance matrices from adjacency matrices containing up to eighty points. Since we are interested in the presence of a particular relation between two persons, whether or not it is reported by both persons as a mutual choice, we decided to disregard the direction of choices by the simple expedient of symmetrizing the adjacency matrices.

An inspection of the reachability matrix (consisting of "1" if v_j is reachable from v_i in some number of steps and "0" if v_j is not reachable from v_i) immediately tells us which persons were disconnected from which others in the total set of influentials—that is, their pattern of choosing and being chosen were such that they could not reach particular others in the structure. In our data, all respondents were reachable from all other respondents in the social and community affairs graphs in some finite number of steps, while five respondents in the business/professional structure were not reachable by some others. The maximum number of steps along a shortest path from one influential to any other was five both in the business/profession and in the social relations graphs and six in the community affairs graph. One individual, Herr K., who ranks as the most influential man in town, could reach in two or fewer steps 91 percent of the others in the community affairs structure and 73 percent of the others in the social relations structure and in the business/professional structure, respectively. Thus, from one point of view, we might conclude that our influence structure is highly integrated since nearly every leading influential can reach and be reached in each of the three networks by every other

influential in the community. Many disconnected individuals or sets of individuals would indicate a less integrated influence structure, with presumably greater difficulties in coordinating community affairs or resolving issues.

C. Graphic Representations of Influence Structures

By submitting each path distance matrix to a symmetric smallest space analysis (cf. Roskam and Lingoes, 1970; Guttman, 1968), we obtain an acceptable Euclidean two-dimensional representation of each matrix. The program takes account of the rank-order of the path distances (and not their absolute size); it attempts to preserve this rank-order while arranging the points in a space of few dimensions. In each representation the derived Euclidean distances among the points (persons) are a monotonic function of the original path distances among the points. We propose to interpret these pictures according to the theoretical principles suggested in the discussions of characteristics of individual influentials and differentiated social structures. Figures 3, 4, and 5 are the graphic representations of the smallest space solutions. Each person has been uniquely identified with a code providing information regarding his influence status, institutional sector responsibilities, party membership and religious preference. (See the legend for Figure 3 for the complete explanation of the abbreviated code.)

In general, we shall employ two basic principles for interpreting the spaces: the principle of integrative centrality and the principle of sector differentiation. The *principle of integrative centrality* holds that persons playing key integrative or coordinating roles in a given structure will tend to be located in the "central region" of their space—this will, on the average, minimize their distances from (access to) any other person in the space—while persons located increasingly in the periphery should be of declining importance in performing integrative activities for that structure and possibly of increasing importance in representing narrowly defined or interest-specific demands in that structure. This principle of interpreting the spatial solutions implies the identification of a coordinating central re-

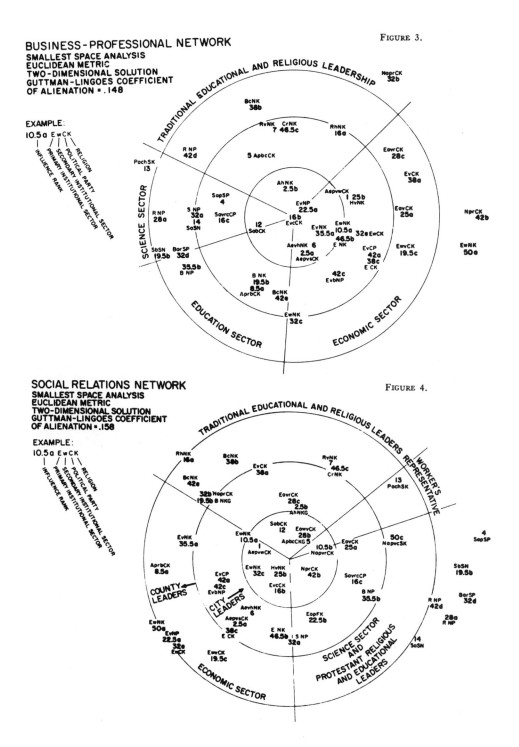

BUSINESS-PROFESSIONAL NETWORK
SMALLEST SPACE ANALYSIS
EUCLIDEAN METRIC
TWO-DIMENSIONAL SOLUTION
GUTTMAN-LINGOES COEFFICIENT
OF ALIENATION = .148

FIGURE 3.

EXAMPLE:
10.5a EwCK
RELIGION
POLITICAL PARTY
SECONDARY INSTITUTIONAL SECTOR
PRIMARY INSTITUTIONAL SECTOR
INFLUENCE RANK

TRADITIONAL EDUCATIONAL AND RELIGIOUS LEADERSHIP

NaprCK
32b

BcNK
38b

RvNK CrNK
7 46.5c

RhNK
16a

R NP
42d

5 ApbcCK

EowrCK
28c

PachSK
13

EvCK
38a

SCIENCE SECTOR

AhNK
2.5b

AepvwCK
I 25b
HvNK

SopSP
4

EvNP
22.5a
16b

EovCK
25a

R NP
28a

5 NP
32a
14
SoSN

SovrcCP
16c

12
SobCK

EvCCK

EvNK EwNK
35.5a 10.5a
46.5b

32e EwCK
E NK

NprCK
42b

SbSN
19.5b

BorSP
32d

AevhNK 6
2.5a
AepvsCK

EvCP
42a
38c
E CK

EwvCK
19.5c

EwNK
50a

35.5b
B NP

B NK
19.5b
8.5a
AprbCK

42c
EvbNP

BcNK
42e

EwNK
32c

EDUCATION SECTOR

ECONOMIC SECTOR

SOCIAL RELATIONS NETWORK
SMALLEST SPACE ANALYSIS
EUCLIDEAN METRIC
TWO-DIMENSIONAL SOLUTION
GUTTMAN-LINGOES COEFFICIENT
OF ALIENATION = .158

FIGURE 4.

EXAMPLE:
10.5a EwCK
RELIGION
POLITICAL PARTY
SECONDARY INSTITUTIONAL SECTOR
PRIMARY INSTITUTIONAL SECTOR
INFLUENCE RANK

TRADITIONAL EDUCATIONAL AND RELIGIOUS LEADERS

WORKER'S REPRESENTATIVE

RhNK
16a

BcNK
38b

EvCK
38a

RvNK
7
46.5c
CrNK

13
PachSK

BcNK
42e

32b NaprCK
19.5b B NKG

EowrCK
28c
2.5b
AhNKG

EwNK
35.5a

SobCK
12

EowvCK
28c

50c
NapvcSK

4
SopSP

EwNK
10.5a
1
AepvwCK

ApbcCKG 5

10.5b
NaprvCK

EovCK
25a

SbSN
19.5b

AprbCK
8.5a

COUNTY
LEADERS

EvCP
42a
42c
EvbNP

CITY
LEADERS

EwNK
32c

HvNK
25b

NprCK
42b

SavrcCP
16c

B NP
35.5b

R NP
42d

BorSP
32d

EvCCK
16b

AevhNK
6

AepvsCK
2.5a
38c
E CK

E NK
46.5b I SNP
32a

EopFK
22.5b

28a
R NP

14
SoSN

EwNK
50a
EwNP
22.5a
32e
EopCK

EwvCK
19.5c

SCIENCE SECTOR
AND
PROTESTANT RELIGIOUS
AND EDUCATIONAL
LEADERS

ECONOMIC SECTOR

455

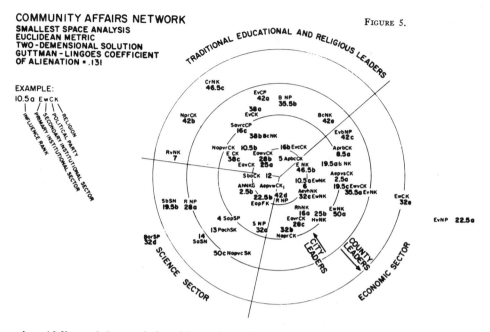

gion (delineated by a circle with a short radius whose center is the centroid) [6] whose membership varies from one structure to another, depending on the nature of the relationship on which it is constructed, and a series of increasingly large concentric rings reflecting, heuristically speaking, "zones" of declining integrative importance.

The *principle of sector differentiation* divides the space into relatively homogeneous regions radiating from the center and including personnel who typically occupy key positions in the same institutional sector and who, therefore, are likely to share common concerns. These sectors represent potential, if not actual, "natural" coalition zones for community issues. Persons in a given functional (institutional) subsystem may at times appear on opposite sides of the central region. When they do, they are likely to be in opposition to each other on some common functional issues. The less localized or regionalized a scatter of points (persons) sharing a common institutional locus, the more likely they will divide on issues of common institutional concern. The more localized a cluster of persons in a common institutional sector, the more homogeneous they will be in attitudes and values and the more they will function as a coordinated proactive or reactive claimant group (coalition) on community issues.

By combining these two principles, we can offer two additional speculations about the structure of the integrative center. First, we hypothesize that a position's location toward the center of the space but in a particular sector may be seen to reflect its potential integrative role as a representative for that sector's interest since, on the one hand, its position close to the center makes it relatively more influential, and, on the other, its location in an institutional sector ties it to other positions in that sector. Second, integrative centers may be seen to be highly biased in composition, over-representing certain sectors while under-representing or completely excluding others. To the extent that certain sectors are excluded from central zone locations (i.e., all their personnel are located in the periphery), we may infer that their impact on decision-

---

[6] The centroid is the center of the smallest space solution. A physical analogy gives an intuitive sense of its meaning: if all points in a two-dimensional smallest space solution were a set of equal weights resting on a weightless plane, the centroid would be that point on which the plane would balance. For a technical discussion, see Roskam and Lingoes (1971).

EXAMPLE

INFLUENCE RANK

```
10.5a E w C K
      | | | | |
      | | | | RELIGION
      | | | POLITICAL PARTY
      | | SECONDARY INSTITUTIONAL SECTOR
      | PRIMARY INSTITUTIONAL SECTOR
INFLUENCE RANK
```

Respondent's influence rank
in the entire elite of 51 persons.
Based on question 25, a measure of
influence depending on other respondents' votes. Subscripts
serve to distinguish respondents
who were tied, i. e., received the
same number of votes.

PRIMARY SECTOR, SECONDARY SECTOR

E - Economy   (A - Sector)

A - Authority position in (G - Sector)
    political system

P - Political Party
W - Economic Association (I - Sector)
V - Social Clubs, Sports

B - Education
R - Religion
C - Culture   (L - Sector)
H - Health and Charity
S - Science

N - Respondent could not be coded into
    any primary sector
(Primary Sector is capitalized; secondary sector or sectors are in lower-
case letters)

PARTY - Political Party of Which
        Respondent is a Member

S = S.P.D. = Social Democratic Party

C = C.D.U. = Christian Democratic
             Union

F = F.D.P. = Free Democratic Party

N = Not a Party Member

RELIGION

K = Catholic
P = Protestant
N = None

making outcomes will be minimized. In other words, the decision-making structure, while performing Almond's function of aggregating interests, has an aggregative bias in favor of some interests and against others (cf. Gamson, 1968:534).

Looking at the three spaces (Figures 3, 4, and 5), we readily see that they do differ among themselves in important ways. The central core of the *business/professional space* includes only the top-ranked community influentials who occupy positions of authority at the city and county administrative levels and personnel who control the largest economic and financial interests in the general area (and who, incidentally, do not in general enjoy as high a reputed influence status as the government leaders). These two groups presumably have much common intercourse concerning the coordi-

nation of government decisions that have bearing on economic matters (such as zoning, housing policy, etc.), and vice versa. Small businessmen, religious, educational, and Research Center personnel are relegated to the peripheral zones but in clearly demarcated sectors at some considerable distance from one another.

The central core of the *social relations space* is composed of a rather different set of personnel, almost all of whom are long resident, Catholic members of the dominant CDU coalition in the city that has run the community for many years. It is noteworthy that high reputed influence is not concentrated in the central region. The differentiation of the economic sector is almost the precise reverse of the business/professional space as it moves from the center, which includes small downtown businessmen and merchants, to the periphery, which includes managers and owners of large manufacturing, financial, and agricultural enterprises located outside the city limits. The research personnel are located by themselves at some considerable distance from the center and from the other sectors, reflecting their highly segregated existence in the "social life" of the community. The traditional religious and educational elite are located opposite them in the space. Herr N., 12 SabCK, is the only Research Center person who has been fully assimilated in the sense of being located in the central zone of the social space; but he differs from his colleagues at the Research Center on nearly every key count—he is a Catholic rather than a Protestant, a social scientist rather than a natural scientist, and a convert from the SPD to the CDU since his arrival in Altneustadt.

Finally, the central core of the *community affairs space* includes a higher density of personnel than the other spaces whose members are recruited from much more heterogeneous institutional sectors and political and religious backgrounds. As one should expect, center personnel are more homogeneous on their reputed influence status in that they tend to be seen as belonging in the upper reaches of the influence hierarchy. The sector divisions, especially toward the periphery, are very similar in character to those of the other two spaces.

If we correlate reputed status as a community influential with distance from the centroid of each of three spaces, we find significant correlations for the business/ professional structure (.40) and the community affairs structure (.30) but an insignificant correlation of .17 for the social relations structure. If we are prepared to regard reputed influence status as a crude indicator of relative "integrative" status in the community social system, then we can take these correlations as at least consistent with but by no means dramatic confirmation of our principle of integrative centrality. We might speculate further that integrative status may mean rather different things in these three relational contexts. Reputed status as a community influential is clearly more relevant to the business/profession and the community affairs structures but is not especially relevant for the social integration of the community elite. If we had assessed reputed "social prominence and esteem" in the sense of Robert Dahl's (1961) "social notables" for all the influentials, we might well have found that this ranking was a more appropriate indicator of integrative status in the social relations structure and was significantly associated with centrality in that structure.

We can make two general statements summarizing our findings regarding the sector structural differentiation of Altneustadt. First, pattern-maintenance personnel are divided into two clearly identifiable regions or clusters at roughly opposite ends of an axis running through the center, with Research Center personnel located at a relatively greater distance from the center (reflecting their weaker influence on community decision-making) and traditional religious and educational leaders at the other end of the axis, some of whom enjoy closer proximity to or inclusion in the integrative cores of the three spaces. It is this axis of differentiation among pattern-maintenance personnel that reflects the principal axis of recurrent, intense cleavage on community issues. Secondly, there is somewhat less differentiation of the adaptive sector since economic personnel tend to cluster in the central region and an immediately adjacent peripheral zone rather than to fall into sharply separated clusters on opposite sides of the central region. The portrayal of the social relations space in Figure 4 reflects most clearly the somewhat weaker potential for an oppositional axis of adaptive personnel where Herr S., 13 PachSK, the only workers' representative in the SPD and the only union member found in the elite, is located diametrically opposite the largest factory owner, Herr F., 22.5a EvNP, and a number of other large businessmen. As expected for this predominantly middle-class community, economic interest differentiation is not so extensively developed and seems to involve primarily differentiation of small business, mercantile interests located in the city from the larger manufacturing and agricultural interests located outside the city limits, rather than labor-management differentiation.

A. Community Issues

Readers concerned with analyzing community conflict over issues may well ask how our structural analysis deals with such matters. Our emphasis on describing the structure of community integration from a Parsonian standpoint seems to confirm the often repeated charge that the framework is simply too static and cannot handle conflict and change adequately (cf. Dahrendorf, 1961:77–82; Gouldner, 1970:353–5). Although we cannot answer all these objections satisfactorily, we would like to consider these questions.

It is useful to distinguish between two broad types of issues and their related outcomes. On the one hand, *instrumental issues* are concerned with controversies over the differing allocation of scarce resources, such as land, jobs, and money, and find their particular locus in the adaptive and integrative sectors of community concern. Lipset (1963) and others have spoken somewhat more narrowly of "class politics" when discussing such issues. For such issues there usually is a fairly obvious calculus of costs and benefits to various interested parties. Conflict over such issues tends to be moderate, often characterized by bargaining and compromise among the contending parties. The specific outcome is the direct result of their relative power or influence. Some political scientists have even thought it possible to devise means for the "rational" or "optimal" resolution of such controversies.

Consummatory or *expressive issues,* on the other hand, are concerned with controversies regarding the maintenance or change in the organization of basic values, commitments, and orientations that shall guide or control community affairs. Such controversies, sometimes termed "status politics" (cf. Lipset, 1963), are usually highly charged with emotional affect and have an "all or none" nature that usually precludes or makes very difficult negotiated settlements among the contending parties. Thus, the nature of the outcome and the level of community tensions often directly depends on how a given issue comes to be defined as one or the other type of issue.

One of the most unsatisfactory aspects of the literature on community decision-making has been the basically atheoretical, ad hoc selection of community issues for analysis such that comparative study of community decision-making is difficult if not impossible. One can identify two favored strategies for identifying and selecting community issues. In the first strategy, the investigator identifies a set of recent issues in a community from newspaper accounts and community informants and selects those for intensive study that meet some criterion of "importance to the community," such as the level of public controversy and mobilization (cf. Dahl, 1961; Polsby, 1963; Freeman *et al.*, 1968). In the second strategy, the investigator selects an issue in which he already has some interest, perhaps because of his interest in a preferred outcome, such as fluoridation of the water supply (cf. Gamson, 1966; Rosenthal and Crain, 1966) or urban renewal (Hawley, 1963; Clark, 1968d), and which has come up for resolution in a number of communities. He wants to ascertain what factors determine a particular outcome. While both strategies enjoy the obvious advantage of relatively clear, unambiguous operational procedures, they both suffer from being heavily tied to all the historical particularities of the specific issues studied and pose serious problems, especially in the first strategy, for comparative analysis.

As Polsby (1963:96; also see Wolfinger, 1971:1078) pointed out some years ago, "there seem to be no satisfactory criteria which would identify a universe of all decisions (issues) in the community." The problem of defining the universe of content from which to sample issues is especially important when one wants to identify "non-issues" or check whether the actual issues are a biased sample (cf. Bachrach and Boratz, 1962, 1963). We think that it is impossible to define a universe of content without an adequate frame of reference for studying community power. At present only two frames of reference seem to be available: the interest group approach and the functional approach. The interest group approach looks for possible partisan groups in a community and identifies possible issues according to some notion of the objective interests of these groups. Since we used the functional approach for analyzing the decision-making structure, it follows that we should use the same approach to define the universe of content of possible issues.[7]

A theoretical scheme for defining and classifying community issues is needed that permits: (1) a definition of the universe of content of possible community issues; (2) a means of defining the biases in the set of issues that actually arise in a community during a given period (that is, communities confront issues sequentially and, therefore, in any period of time may not face issues from the full range of the issue space); (3) a translation of the historical individuality of a given issue into a more theoretically meaningful category that permits comparative analysis; and (4) the generation of hypotheses linking the type of issue to structural characteristics of the community decision-making system. We hope that a step toward constructing such a scheme was taken by our decision to classify community issues according to their functional primacy in the AGIL paradigm of functions confronting any social system (cf. Parsons, 1951; Parsons et al., 1961; Clark, 1968c; Mayhew, 1971).

Obviously issues will often have implications for several functional sectors of the community social system. Much in the same way that we proposed to distinguish between primary and secondary functional foci for our influentials, issues may be seen to have primary and secondary impacts in different institutional sectors. Which of the possible functional definitions of an issue becomes focal or primary will depend on a series of considerations about its emergence in a particular community at a particular time with particular sponsors and opponents.[8]

With our preceding analysis of the structure of community influence, we should be able to predict how given issues will be resolved by determining the functionally specialized sectors likely to be activated by a given functional issue. We can also assess the likelihood of a sector being divided on an issue by examining the relative spread or clustering of personnel in a particular institutional sector in the spatial solutions and their locations with respect to the central integrative core. If there is significant sectoral or integrative differentiation, we can predict the winning coalition as the one favorably located relative to the integrative core and including a higher average level of reputed community influence.

With these general considerations in mind, five issues were selected for intensive study according to two criteria. First, each issue must have had a major impact on community affairs within the past three or four years or might realistically be argued to have such an impact if it became a matter for decision in the near future. Second, the issues as a whole had to be distributed across the four functional problem areas identified in the AGIL paradigm. The issues meeting these two criteria were the following:

(a) re-location of a large industrial firm to Altneustadt (economic or adaptive primacy);
(b) construction of a city hall (political or collective goal-attainment primacy);
(c) incorporation of outlying communities into an expanded city administrative unit (integrative primacy);
(d) establishment of a secular primary school as opposed to the existing confessional school (latent pattern-mainte-

---

[7] We are inclined to agree with such commentators as Ossowski (1963), Lenski (1966), and Stinchcombe (1968) that Marxian and functionally oriented perspectives are by no means as radically incompatible as has sometimes been assumed. They have, of course, obvious differences of emphasis and concern. Marxian oriented analysts tend to see instrumental issues as the substrate of actual or potential community controversy; while functionalists tend to stress expressive issues, seeing group disagreements over fundamental values to arise from considerations in addition to their different relations to the economic structure.

[8] Coding an issue into its appropriate functional

sector is not a simple matter of identifying the institutional sector of the collectivities most likely to be affected. For example, a school bond issue is obviously concerned with the educational system, which is usually treated as functionally specialized with regard to pattern maintenance. But the issue may develop in two quite different directions. It may be regarded as a purely instrumental issue whether the community can afford to pay for another school, given its current obligations. Its functional locus is, therefore, integrative as it concerns establishing its claim of priority in the budget. But the issue may become expressive by focusing not on costs and alternatives foregone but on what type of school program is to be implemented in the new building. In this case, prospective changes in the organization of pattern-maintenance activities are at issue.

nance primacy: education and religion);
and

(e) permission to hold a Pop Festival in Altneustadt (latent pattern-maintenance primacy: public morality, status of youth as a "minority" group with low access to the center of power, intergenerational conflict).[9]

The underlying notion here of sampling issues from various institutional sectors was to provide an opportunity to determine if the elite tended to be correspondingly differentiated into coalitions functionally specialized for "control" in specific sectors or if there was a functionally and structurally undifferentiated unitary elite core (domi-

nant coalition) that made the crucial decisions for all institutional areas (perhaps with specialized "lower-level" personnel to implement these decisions). (See Table 1 for the average influence status of opponents and proponents on each issue.)

B. Graphic Representation of the Cleavage Structure

Figure 6 is identical to the spatial representation of the community affairs structure in Figure 5, but now we have drawn in "fault lines" for each of the five issues that divide the space into proponents and opponents on each issue. Before discussing this consensus-cleavage structure in greater detail we should discuss the operational independence of our various procedures. First, each respondent was asked at the beginning of the interview a series of questions about each issue probing such matters as the individuals and groups he perceived to be most strongly in favor or opposed to the issue, his own position on the issue and degree of actual or likely participation in the decision-process on the issue, as well as his estimate of the level of conflict over the issue and

---

[9] Altneustadt actually confronted issues b, c, and d in the past several years. But because it had not confronted issues having special relevance to the economic subsystem in the recent past and because we saw the city as having especially acute pattern-maintenance problems due to the rapid in-migration of distinctive newcomers, we decided to develop two *hypothetical* issues (a and e) for these two sectors. (See Perrucci and Pilisuk, 1970, for another recent study using hypothetical issues.) Both issues were quite realistic in that they could easily become matters of public or elite debate in the forseeable future and, in fact, generated considerable disagreement among our respondents.

COMMUNITY AFFAIRS NETWORK

FIGURE 6.

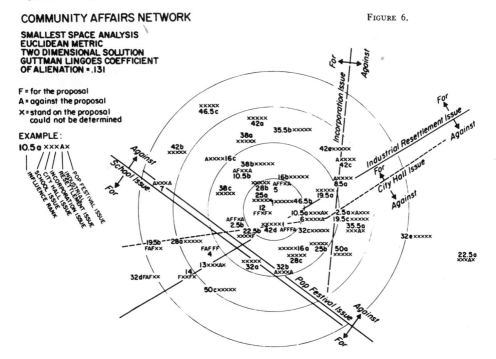

SMALLEST SPACE ANALYSIS
EUCLIDEAN METRIC
TWO DIMENSIONAL SOLUTION
GUTTMAN LINGOES COEFFICIENT
OF ALIENATION = .131

F = for the proposal
A = against the proposal
X = stand on the proposal
    could not be determined

EXAMPLE:

10.5 a xxxAx

461

whether the conflict would be public or confined to the "inner circle" of community influentials. The names of the active participants, pro and con, were spontaneously generated by the respondents—the list of influentials we had identified was not presented until much later in the interview. Second, in order for us to designate an influential as an active proponent or opponent on an issue, at least two respondents had to have spontaneously mentioned him in one or the other capacity. (In most cases attributed and self-reported position and involvement in the issue were the same, but in a number of important cases they were not. Persons on the losing side tended to report themselves on the winning side.) [10]

---

[10] Since this stringent coding rule tended to identify only the most publicly prominent leaders on the opposing sides many of the elite had to be coded as "indeterminate" for any given issue on the basis of the perceptions of others. Did this mean that the fault lines, based on codings of only some elite members, were completely arbitrary? To check this possibility at least indirectly, the following procedure was adopted. All elite members were coded "for" or "against" an issue depending on which side of a fault line they were located. These new codings were then cross-tabulated against the elite members' self-reported positions on the corresponding issues.
Agreement was best for the incorporation issue where 79 percent were placed on the side of the issue in the figure corresponding to their self-reported stands. Agreement was not quite as high for the pop festival and the industrial resettlement issues (69 and 64 percent, respectively), partly because, we suspect, there were hypothetical issues on which elite members could only guess which side of an issue other elite members would take. It declined further for the city hall issue where only 56 percent were correctly placed, but note again that this issue was regarded as the least controversial of all issues posed, and few elite members reported special interest or involvement in it. Only the fit for the school issue was poor (24 percent agreement), but this lack of agreement is more apparent than real. More than ninety percent of the elite members claimed to be for the secular school (the side that won), many more than could actually have favored it given the controversial, divisive and extended character of the public debate. Many persons reporting themselves on the winning side were in fact perceived by other elite members as having been active on the losing side. In general, we detected a definite tendency for people to report themselves on the winning sides of all issues even though their knowledgeable peers saw them to have been on the losing side. Apparently here as elsewhere no one likes to be regarded a loser. We are, therefore, inclined to place much more

It is readily apparent from an inspection of Figure 6 that the fault lines of the oppositional structures and the personnel active on each of the issues do change from one functional issue to another and that some persons, most notably those in the central integrative zones, are likely to be active in more than one issue. In fact, only one person, the most influential man in town denoted by a "1," was perceived to be involved in all five issues.

The fault lines are almost identical on the two pattern-maintenance issues, the school and the Pop Festival, with the newcomers at the Research Center and their allies opposed to nearly everyone else. Although these issues differ considerably in their substantive content, they generated the most public controversy and mobilization of the issues considered. The integrative issue (community incorporation), on the other hand, united all city factions against the county political leadership; while the polity issue of building a new city hall was an inner-elite controversy (there was low public controversy about this issue), arraigning the "city hall crowd" located in the central zone against the periphery who, of course, lost. Finally, the industrial resettlement issue split the economic sector, with the large employers who might be fearful of such a large competitor for a limited labor supply and of their possible unfavorable dislocation in the influence structure opposed to the small retail tradesmen and business people who would probably welcome the expanded business opportunities arising from the population growth likely to be generated by the new employer. (An inspection of the fault lines drawn for the business/professional and social relations spaces, in two figures not reproduced here, leads us to similar conclusions.)

Thus, for even this relatively small community, we see that structural differentiation is extensive enough to generate relatively stable coalitions that are activated differentially depending on the functional issue. Much more could be said about the internal structure of the various coalitions, their influence resources, value orientations, and preferred leadership strategies, which support

---

confidence on perceived positions than self-reported positions.

some of the interpretations we have been making. Hopefully the limited evidence presented has sufficiently indicated the ways our procedures greatly facilitate the systematic description of structural cleavage and consensus (e.g., by identifying who would be "impossible" coalition partners). In addition, this evidence seems to be reasonably consistent with the explicit structural-functional model we have been developing. Consensus-cleavage structures do, of course, change over time. We believe that these techniques could also be used to generate meaningful snapshots at different points in time which in turn could be juxtaposed to describe stability and change in community influence structures over time.

SUMMARY

Recent work in the study of community decision-making appears to be converging on a number of common theoretical and methodological strategies and assumptions. There still remain, however, important weaknesses in the overall theoretical framework and its implied methodology in directing research efforts. Attention is directed to a structural analysis of the community influence system that derives in part from Parsons. Several critical questions are raised concerning the identification of the relevant set of community influentials and the systematic description of their attributes as influentials and the ties that bind them into coalitions depending on the functional issue confronted. Recent advances in graph theory and smallest space analysis are used to examine the consensus-cleavage structure of the community influence system of Altneustadt, a small city in West Germany. Finally, a theoretical strategy and an empirical procedure are proposed for identifying community issues and tracing their impact on the formation of opposing factions and coalitions.

REFERENCES

Aiken, Michael, and Paul Mott (eds.)
1970 The Structure of Community Power. New York: Random House.
Alba, Richard D. and Charles Kadushin
1970 The Construction of Sociograms by Computer Methods. Mimeo. New York: Bureau of Applied Social Research, Columbia University.
Undated "A note on the application of multidimensional scaling to the problem of sociometric clique identification." Unpublished manuscript. Columbia University.
Bachrach, Peter and Morton S. Baratz
1962 "Two faces of power." American Political Science Review 56 (December):947-52.
1963 "Decisions and non-decisions: an analytical framework." American Political Science Review 57 (September):632-42.
Blau, Peter M.
1964 Exchange and Power in Social Life. New York: Wiley.
Bonacich, Phillip
1972a "Technique for analyzing overlapping memberships." Pp. 176-85 in Herbert L. Costner (ed.), Sociological Methodology 1972. San Francisco: Jossey-Bass.
1972b "Factoring and weighting approaches to status scores and clique identification." Journal of Mathematical Sociology 2 (January):113-20.
Bonjean, Charles M., Terry N. Clark, and Robert L. Lineberry (eds.)
1971 Community Politics: A Behaviorial Approach. New York: Free Press.
Clark, Terry N.
1968a Community Structure and Decision-Making: Comparative Analyses. San Francisco: Chandler Publishing Company.
1968b "Who governs, where, when, and with what effects?" Pp. 15-23 in Terry N. Clark (ed.), Community Structure and Decision-Making: Comparative Analyses. San Francisco: Chandler Publishing Company.
1968c "Community structure and decision-making." Pp. 91-126 in Terry N. Clark (ed.), Community Structure and Decision-Making: Comparative Analyses. San Francisco: Chandler Publishing Company.
1968d "Community structure, decision-making, budget expenditures, and urban renewal in 51 American communities." American Sociological Review 33 (August):576-93.
Coleman, James S. and Duncan McRae, Jr.
1960 "Electronic processing of sociometric data for groups up to 1,000 in size." American Sociological Review 25 (October):722-7.
Dahl, Robert A.
1961 Who Governs? New Haven: Yale University Press.
Dahrendorf, Ralf
1961 "Struktur und Funktion. Talcott Parsons und die Entwicklung der soziologischen Theorie." Pp. 49-84 in Ralf Dahrendorf, Gesellschaft und Freiheit. Zur soziologischen Analyse der Gegenwart. Munich: R. Piper Verlag.
D'Antonio, William V., William H. Form, Charles P. Loomis and Eugene C. Erickson
1961 "Institutional and occupational representations in eleven community systems." American Sociological Review 26 (June): 440-6.

Davis, Kingsley
1948 Human Society. New York: Macmillan Company.
Downes, Bryan T.
1968 "Suburban differentiation and municipal policy choices: A comparative analysis of suburban political systems." Pp. 243–67 in Terry N. Clark (ed.), Community Structure and Decision-Making: Comparative Analyses. San Francisco: Chandler Publishing Company.
Fararo, T. J. and Morris H. Sunshine
1964 A Study of a Biased Friendship Net. Syracuse University, Youth Development Center.
Freeman, Linton C.
1968 Patterns of Local Community Leadership. Indianapolis: Bobbs-Merrill
Gamson, William A.
1966 "Rancorous conflict in community politics." American Sociological Review 31 (February):71–81.
1968 Power and Discontent. Homewood, Ill.: Dorsey Press.
Gleason, Terry C.
1969 D.I.P.: A Directed Graph Processor. Mimeo. Ann Arbor, Michigan: Institute Social Research, University of Michigan.
Gouldner, Alvin W.
1970 The Coming Crisis of Western Sociology. New York: Basic Books.
Guttman, Louis
1959 "Introduction to facet design and analysis." Pp. 130–2 in Proceedings of the 15th International Congress of Psychology. Brussels.
1968 "A general nonmetric technique for finding the smallest coordinate space for a configuration of points." Psychometrika 33 (December):469–506.
Harary, Frank, R. Z. Norman and Dorwin Cartwright
1965 Structural Models: An Introduction to the Theory of Directed Graphs. New York: Wiley.
Hawley, Amos H.
1963 "Community power and urban renewal success." American Journal of Sociology 68 (January):422–31.
Homans, George C.
1951 The Human Group. New York: Harcourt, Brace, and World.
Hubbell, Charles H.
1965 "An input-output approach to clique identification." Sociometry 28 (December):377–99.
Hunter, Floyd
1953 Community Power Structure. Durham, North Carolina: University of North Carolina Press.
Laumann, Edward O.
1966 Prestige and Association in an Urban Community. Indianapolis: Bobbs-Merrill.
1973 Bonds of Pluralism. The Form and Substance of Urban Social Networks. New York: Wiley Interscience.

Lenski, Gerhard
1966 Power and Privilege: A Theory of Social Stratification. New York: McGraw-Hill.
Levine, Joel
1972 "The sphere of influence." American Sociological Review 37 (February):14–27.
Lipset, Seymour M.
1963 "The sources of the 'radical right,'" "Three decades of the radical right: Coughlinites, McCarthyites, and Birchers." Pp. 259–377 in Daniel Bell (ed.), The Radical Right. Garden City, New York: Doubleday.
Loomis, Charles P. and J. Allen Beegle
1950 Rural Social Systems. New York: Prentice-Hall, Inc.
MacFarland, David and Daniel Brown
1973 "Social distance as a metric: a systematic introduction to smallest space analysis." Pp. 213–53 in Edward O. Laumann, Bonds of Pluralism. The Form and Substance of Urban Social Networks. New York: Wiley Interscience.
Mayhew, Leon
1971 Society: Institutions and Activity. Glenview, Illinois: Scott, Foresman and Company.
Moreno, Jacob L.
1953 Who shall Survive? Foundations of Sociometry, Group Psychotherapy and Sociodrama. New York: Beacon.
Nadel, S. F.
1957 The Theory of Social Structure. London: Cohen and West
Newcomb, Theodore
1961 The Acquaintance Process. New York: Holt, Rhinehart, and Winston.
Ossowski, Stanislaw
1963 Class Structure in the Social Consciousness. London: Routledge and Kegan Paul.
Parsons, Talcott
1951 The Social System. Glencoe, Illinois: Free Press.
1960 Structure and Process in Modern Societies. New York: Free Press.
Parsons, Talcott, Edward Shils, Kaspar D. Naegele and Jesse R. Pitts (eds.)
1961 Theories of Society: Foundations of Modern Sociological Theory. New York: Free Press, especially pp. 30–79.
Perrucci, Robert and Marc Pilisuk
1970 "Leaders and ruling elites: the interorganizational bases of community power." American Sociological Review 35 (December):1040–57.
Polsby, Nelson W.
1963 Community Power and Political Theory. New Haven: Yale University Press.
Rapoport, Anatol and William Horvath
1961 "A study of a large sociogram." Behavioral Science 6 (October):279–91.
Rosen, Richard and Peter Abrams
1970 "CHAIN: A sociometric linkage program." Mimeo. New York: Bureau of Applied Social Research, Columbia University.
Rosenthal, Donald B. and Robert L. Crain
1966 "Structure and values in local political

systems: the case of fluoridation decisions."
Journal of Politics 28 (February):169–96.

Roskam, E. and James C. Lingoes
1970 "MINISSA-I: A FORTRAN IV (G) program for the smallest space analysis of square symmetric matrices." Behavioral Science 15 (March):204–20.
1971 "A mathematical and empirical study of two multidimensional scaling algorithms." Michigan Mathematical Psychology Program 1:1–169.

Rossi, Peter H.
1960 "Power and community structure." Midwest Journal of Political Science 4 (November):390–401.

Stinchcombe, Arthur L.
1968 Constructing Social Theories. New York: Harcourt, Brace and World.

Walton, John
1966a "Substance and artifact: the current status on research of community power structure." American Journal of Sociology 71 (January):430–8.
1966b "Discipline, method, and community power: a note on the sociology of knowledge." American Sociological Review 31 (October):684–9.

Wolfinger, Raymond E.
1971 "Nondecisions and the study of local politics." American Political Science Review 65 (December):1063–80.

A   B   7
C   8
D   9
E   0
F   1
G   2
H   3
I   4
J   5